International Capital Flows

A National Bureau
of Economic Research
Conference Report

International Capital Flows

Edited by   Martin Feldstein

The University of Chicago Press

Chicago and London

MARTIN FELDSTEIN is the George F. Baker Professor of Economics at Harvard University and president of the National Bureau of Economic Research.

The University of Chicago Press, Chicago 60637
The University of Chicago Press, Ltd., London
© 1999 by the National Bureau of Economic Research
All rights reserved. Published 1999
08 07 06 05 04 03 02 01 00 99   1 2 3 4 5
ISBN: 0-226-24103-3 (cloth)
ISBN: 0-226-24104-1 (paper)

Library of Congress Cataloging-in-Publication Data

International capital flows / edited by Martin Feldstein.
    p.   cm.—(A National Bureau of Economic Research conference report)
    Proceedings of a conference held in Woodstock, Vt., on Oct. 17–18, 1997.
    Includes bibliographical references and indexes.
    ISBN 0-226-24103-3 (cloth : alk. paper). — ISBN 0-226-24104-1 (pbk. : alk. paper)
    1. Capital movements.   I. Feldstein, Martin S.   II. Series: Conference report (National Bureau of Economic Research)
HG3891.I558   1999
332'.042—dc21   99-28727
                                                                    CIP

♾ The paper used in this publication meets the minimum requirements of the American National Standard for Information Sciences—Permanence of Paper for Printed Library Materials, ANSI Z39.48-1992.

Contents

Preface

Although much has been written about international capital flows, this volume may be unique in the scope of its analysis and in the range of the individuals who have contributed to its content. The different parts of the volume look at the main channels of international capital flows (through banks, equity markets, and direct investment), the major new destinations of such capital flows (eastern Europe and the former Soviet Union, Latin America, and Asia), and the benefits and risks associated with such international capital flows. The thirteen background papers written by distinguished economists provide a rich empirical and analytic picture of these different aspects of international capital flows. These background papers are complemented by seventeen personal essays by individuals who have been or currently are actively involved in the various aspects of international capital flows, including Federal Reserve officials, senior corporate executives, and officials from foreign countries and international organizations.

The authors of the background papers and the personal essays met to discuss these issues in Woodstock, Vermont. Summaries of the discussion at the conference appear in the volume.

The conference was held on 17–18 October 1997, a few months after the Asian financial crisis began. The experience in Thailand and Indonesia was reflected in some of the discussion at the conference. But the background research papers were generally written before the crisis began, and the meeting occurred before the full magnitude of the crisis became clear. The focus of the papers was therefore not on the recent events in Asia but on the more fundamental aspects of international capital flows.

This volume is part of a broader recently completed NBER project on international capital flows that includes three specific academic subprojects: Capital Flows and the Emerging Economies, organized by Sebastian Edwards; Currency Crises, organized by Paul Krugman; and International Taxation, organized by James R. Hines, Jr. Separate NBER volumes will be published reporting the research in each of these three subprojects.

Support for this entire project was provided by the Ford Foundation, the Starr Foundation, and the Center for International Political Economy. I am grateful to them for making this work possible.

I am grateful also to the authors of the background papers for their extensive and valuable analyses and to the officials and executives who took time from very busy schedules to share their insights and experience on the process of international capital flows. I also want to thank several members of the NBER staff for their assistance in the planning and execution of the project reported in this volume and the associated conference and preconference meetings, in particular Kirsten Foss Davis and the other members of the NBER Conference Department, Helena Fitz-Patrick, Gerri Johnson, and Norma MacKenzie. I am also grateful to Mihir Desai for preparing the excellent summaries of the discussion.

This project came at a particularly important time because of the problems that have developed in Asia and Latin America and because of the relation between those problems and international capital flows. The NBER will now extend the work in this project with a new study of International Financial Crises that will explore the reasons for the international financial crises that have occurred in Asia and Latin America, the effects of the postcrisis programs that these countries have adopted, and the policies that industrial countries might adopt to reduce the likelihood and severity of such crises in the future.

Martin Feldstein

International Capital Flows: Introduction

Martin Feldstein

Changes in world politics and in technology have led to an explosive growth of international capital flows in recent years, particularly to the emerging market countries and to the nations of eastern and central Europe and the former Soviet Union. The private market in debt finance, in equity capital, and in direct foreign investment has become overwhelmingly larger than current and past official capital flows. These capital flows bring the recipient countries substantial gains by augmenting local saving and by improving both technology and incentives. But as the experience in Latin America in the early 1980s and in Asia in the late 1990s has shown, capital flows can also bring serious problems.

The political changes that contributed to the surge in capital flows deserve emphasis here because they have been largely ignored by economists and are not discussed elsewhere in this volume. The end of the cold war and the collapse of the Soviet Union opened opportunities for investment in a large group of countries that needed capital, management, and technology. The shifting political climate in China also made investment in that country more attractive.

Political change also accounts for the rise in investment in many of the developing countries of Latin America and Asia. Country after country abandoned Marxist ideology and no longer treated capitalist countries as political or ideological enemies. In this environment, they welcomed foreign direct investment from the industrial countries as well as minority equity investments. They privatized state-owned industries and allowed foreigners to invest in these companies. The change in the political climate in these countries also made them more attractive to foreign investors who felt more secure about lending, making equity investments, and locating operating businesses.

Modern technology has changed the management of financial transactions in ways that have expanded international capital flows. Developments in computing and communication capability have made it possible to create precisely defined international index funds at very low cost. Even individual investors can expand their portfolios to include representative equities or bonds from a variety of countries or regions without having to choose particular companies or even particular countries. Through mutual funds that sell such index funds, investors can invest abroad in relatively small amounts.

The relevant technological advances involve more than just computing and communication. It is also financial technology that has encouraged and increased the international flow of investment. Derivative markets allow investors to separate cross-border equity or interest rate risk from cross-border currency risk by hedging the currencies associated with equity or bond positions. This hedging may help to explain an important but still inadequately understood feature of the international capital market: the contrast between the very large volume of gross flows and the very small volume of net flows. Despite the trillions of dollars of gross flows, most national saving remains in the country where it originates.[1]

The most obvious contribution of international capital flows to host countries is to augment the supply of domestic saving in countries with unusually rich investment opportunities. The high marginal product of capital means that capital-importing countries can benefit even when the interest rates and the equity yields to the foreign providers of capital are high.

Despite this contribution, it is important to note that the magnitude of the capital inflows is still small relative to the volume of domestic saving. Most of the investment in plant and equipment and in real estate in every country is financed by domestic saving. This reflects the limited size of current account deficits and associated capital inflows that the international capital market will support. For example, a country in which business investment and housing construction is equal to 20 percent of GDP will have to finance 85 percent of that investment with local saving if its current account deficit is not to exceed 3 percent of GDP.

Direct foreign investment means much more than additions to the stock of capital. It brings with it better technology, modern management, and expanded access to global markets. Portfolio equity investments also help in a different way by exposing local companies to the scrutiny of the international capital markets, requiring greater accounting transparency and more effective corporate governance.

International capital flows also bring advantages to the investors. The companies that bring direct foreign investment acquire market access, lower cost inputs, and opportunities for profitable introduction of more efficient production methods. Portfolio investors typically enjoy higher yields than they would in the industrial countries from which the capital comes as well as an opportunity for risk diversification that can lower the overall risk of the investors' portfolios. The potential benefits of international diversification appear to be so

---

1. This point was first emphasized in Feldstein and Horioka (1980). See also the discussion in Feldstein (1994).

large that financial economists are puzzled by the limited extent to which individual and institutional investors have availed themselves of this opportunity. One explanation for this puzzle may be that investors do not accept the historical risk experience as a good guide to future risk. Concern about the political risks of debt defaults or of tax changes that expropriate equity investments may drive investors to seek the comfort of the low-diversification herd instead of the opportunity of an optimal investment strategy. The recent experience in several Asian countries has involved changes in currency and equity values that greatly exceed the historical experience described by the variances of currency values and equity prices that are used in optimal portfolio models. When historical estimates of risk are adjusted to reflect this recent experience, investors may well be vindicated in their refusal to accept the implications of portfolio theory based on previous historical measures of risk.

The experience of the past two decades has shown that with international capital flows can come substantial risks to both the providers and the recipients of those funds. During the 1970s, the banks of the United States and other industrial countries recycled OPEC surpluses and their own national savings to eager borrowers abroad, particularly in Latin America. Low real interest rates and high commodity prices encouraged borrowers to accept more credit and expand their activities. But when the U.S. Federal Reserve finally acted decisively to reduce spiraling double-digit inflation, real dollar interest rates rose sharply, reducing economic activity and lowering commodity prices and demand. The debtor countries of Latin America, led by Mexico in the summer of 1982, found they could not get the increased credit they needed to pay the high interest rates and to offset the shortfall of export earnings. The result was a debt moratorium that engulfed nearly all of the Latin American countries.

During the rest of the decade, the borrower countries went through a painful transition as they lowered domestic consumption in order to reduce their dependence on imported capital, to pay the high interest rates on their growing debts, and to compensate for the decline in exports. The creditor banks that had lent to the Latin American countries were also hard hit during this period as the loan write-downs impaired bank capital, causing bank regulators to require dividend suspensions and other changes in the banks' activity. Further defaults by the borrower countries could have made major commercial banks technically insolvent and led to their being closed by the regulators.

The Asian problems that began in Thailand in the summer of 1997 are still unfolding. Although a full analysis of the factors that precipitated the widespread series of currency crises remains to be done, it is clear that its fixed exchange rate regime and chronic current account deficit increased the likelihood of a crisis in Thailand. Other local factors that may have contributed to these currency crises include weak financial sectors, rapid increases in real estate prices, and inadequate quantities of foreign reserves. The devaluation of the Chinese yuan and the sharp fall in the yen-dollar exchange rate added to the risks since Thailand and others in the region compete with Chinese producers and had pegged their currency values to the dollar when the yen is a more relevant currency because of local trade patterns. The spread of the crisis from Thailand to Indonesia, Malaysia, South Korea, and other countries reflected a mix of fundamental factors (e.g., devaluation by one country increased the potential trade deficits of the others) and psychological contagion among investors who preferred to abandon the region during a period of stress and uncertainty.

The events in Asia have raised a number of important questions that deserve careful attention. How can emerging market countries act to reduce the risk of future currency and financial crises? When such crises occur, how can they be managed to reduce the adverse effects on the domestic economies? And how can industrial countries revise their own policies to reduce the risk of future crises in international capital markets?

These are questions to which the NBER will return in a future research project. I hope that the current volume is both interesting in itself and useful as a background for that future research.

References

Feldstein, M. 1994. Tax policy and international capital flows. *Weltwirtschaftsliches Archiv* 4:675–97.
Feldstein, M., and C. Horioka. 1980. Domestic saving and international capital flows. *Economic Journal* 90 (358): 314–29.

1 Capital Flows to Latin America

1. Sebastian Edwards
2. Francisco Gil Diaz
3. Arminio Fraga

1. Sebastian Edwards

Capital Inflows into Latin America: A Stop-Go Story?

1.1.1 Introduction

During the late 1980s and early 1990s the vast majority of the Latin American countries embarked on ambitious reforms aimed at modernizing their economies. Country after country turned away from decades of protectionism and government controls and began to experiment with market-oriented policies. Colombia provides a vivid illustration of this regional trend. During the early months of 1990 candidate César Gaviria promised that, if elected president, he would launch a major transformation of Colombia's economic system. In every speech he argued that the development path followed by Colombia since the 1940s had become obsolete and that, in order to achieve rapid growth and improve social conditions for the majority of the population, significant reforms had to be undertaken; he called for a major shake-up of the Colombian economy. On 7 August 1990 César Gaviria was inaugurated as Colombia's constitutional president. During the next four years a set of policies aimed at drastically changing the nature of Colombia's economic structure were put into effect: exchange controls were abolished; imports were liberalized; labor legislation was reformed; controls over direct foreign investment were relaxed; the financial sector was deregulated; legislation governing port operations was modified; the insurance industry was liberalized; and the tax system was mod-

The author is indebted to Alejandro Jara and Kyongchul Kim for assistance.

ernized. This phenomenon was not unique to Colombia, however. Close to Colombia, the administrations of Presidents Fujimori in Peru, Perez in Venezuela, and Sanchez de Losada in Bolivia also embarked on major reform efforts. In other countries a similar trend was followed: Presidents Menem in Argentina, Cardoso in Brazil, and Arzu in Guatemala, among others, also launched important modernization programs during the 1990s. It is not an exaggeration to say that during the first half of this decade most countries in Latin America followed the steps of the two early reformers: Chile and Mexico.[1]

And when the world was about to believe that Latin America had finally changed, the Mexican currency crisis erupted in December 1994. This turn of events generated considerable anxiety among policy analysts, financial operators, and international civil servants. Some asked whether Latin America was indeed ready to adopt market-oriented policies, while others questioned the appropriateness of specific policies, including the use of a rigid nominal exchange rate as a way to reduce inflation. The role played by large capital inflows—which at their peak surpassed 9 percent of Mexico's GDP—has been at the center of almost every postmortem of the Mexican crisis. Some analysts have argued that these massive flows allowed Mexico to increase consumption in spite of weak fundamentals. According to others, the predominantly "speculative" nature of these flows signaled, from early on, that the Mexican experience was bound to run into a serious external crisis. Yet others argued that Mexico's mistake was to have lifted capital controls too early, allowing these speculative flows to disturb the country's macroeconomic foundations. According to these analysts a more appropriate policy stance in Mexico would have been to maintain some form of capital controls, as a number of emerging economies—including Chile, Colombia, and Israel—have done for some time. The proponents of this view argue that capital controls isolate these young economies from volatile short-run capital flows, helping them to reduce their overall degree of vulnerability to external shocks, including speculative attacks.[2]

In the early 1990s it became fashionable to compare Latin America's somewhat traumatic experience with capital inflows with East Asia's supposedly successful capital flow management. The recent currency crises in a number of East Asian countries—including Thailand, Malaysia, the Philippines, Indonesia, and South Korea—have raised, once again, analysts' interest in issues related to the management of capital flows. Questions related to capital account sustainability and the feasibility of fixed nominal exchange rates in a world of capital mobility, among others, have moved to the fore of policy discussions. It may be tempting to argue that Latin America and East Asia are not so different after all. Perhaps it was a matter of timing, with the Mexican crisis leading the way to the more recent developments in East Asia. Moreover, the volatility

---

1. On the Latin American reforms see, e.g., Edwards (1995b).
2. On the Mexican crisis see, e.g., Dornbusch and Werner (1994), Dornbusch, Goldfajn, and Valdes (1995), Bruno (1995), and Calvo and Mendoza (1996). On the benefits and costs of capital controls see, e.g., the essays collected in Edwards (1995a).

experienced by financial markets during the fall of 1997 has raised the question of "contagion." Analysts have wondered whether in an era of capital mobility rumors and changes in expectations in a particular country can spread to other nations with healthy fundamentals.

This paper deals with Latin America's experience with capital flows during the past decade and a half. It concentrates on a number of issues of increasing interest among academics and international observers, including the effect of capital inflows on domestic savings, the effect of capital mobility on the ability to engage in independent monetary policy, and the effectiveness of capital controls. Latin America's experience with capital mobility should be illuminating to scholars interested in other regions of the world. Indeed, as will be seen in this paper, during the past few years the Latin American countries have been a laboratory of sorts, where almost every possible approach to capital mobility has been tried. The paper is organized as follows: section 1.1.1 is the introduction and provides the motivation. Section 1.1.2 reviews the behavior of capital flows to Latin America during the past twenty years. It is shown that during this period the region has gone through wild cycles. In the mid- to late 1970s the countries of Latin America were on the receiving end of petrodollar recycling and were flooded with private capital. All of this came to an end with the eruption of the Mexican debt crisis in 1982. During the next eight years the international capital market dried up for every country in the region, and net private capital inflows became significantly negative. Things changed in 1991, when once again private capital began to pour into the region. In this section I also discuss the most important causes of the surge of capital flows into the area experienced during 1996–97.

In section 1.1.3 I discuss the extent to which capital mobility has been truly restricted in Latin America. I argue that in most developing countries there are significant differences between the degrees of legal capital mobility and of "true" capital mobility, and I provide some estimates of the latter. Section 1.1.4 concentrates on the effects of capital mobility on real exchange rates and international competitiveness. In this section I also address the important question of capital flow sustainability and the dynamics of adjustment, and I briefly discuss issues related to the sequencing of economic reform. Section 1.1.5 concentrates on the effectiveness of monetary policy when there is (some) capital mobility. In particular, I discuss Latin America's experiences with policies aimed at sterilizing capital flows. In this section I also address the role of capital controls as a device for isolating emerging economies from the volatility of international capital markets. I review the experiences of Chile and Colombia, and I argue that, by and large, the effectiveness of capital controls has been limited in these two countries. In section 1.1.6 I deal with the role of the banking sector in intermediating capital flows in Latin American countries. Finally, in section 1.1.7 I present some concluding remarks.

It is important to stress at the outset that Latin America is an extremely diverse region with sophisticated as well as backward economies, with large and very small countries, with stable and volatile economic systems. This variation means that broad generalizations are bound to be misleading and to provide oversimplified views of the region. For this reason, then, in this paper I make an effort to make distinctions among countries, as well as to discuss broad regional trends.

1.1.2   Capital Flows to Latin America: Historical Background and Recent Trends

From Petrodollar Recycling to the Mexican Debt Crisis of 1982

During the 1960s and early 1970s Latin America was basically cut off from private international financial markets. With the exception of limited amounts of direct foreign investment (DFI), very little private capital moved into the region. During most of this period Latin America relied on official capital flows—largely from the World Bank, the Inter American Development Bank (IDB), and the International Monetary Fund (IMF). In a way the region was a captive customer of the multilateral institutions. In the mid- and late 1970s, however, things began to change as international private liquidity increased significantly, and Latin America became a major recipient of recycled "petrodollars." In 1981 alone the region received (net) private capital inflows in excess of 21 percent of exports. Individual country cases, however, differed significantly during this period. While in Brazil, Mexico, and Venezuela a majority of these flows were captured by the government and were used to finance large (and increasing) fiscal deficits, in Argentina and Chile—two nations embarked at the time on early market-oriented reforms—they were largely channeled to the private sector.[3]

By 1981 casual observers of the Latin American scene were surprised by how smoothly things were going. In spite of major commodity price shocks, most countries in the region continued to grow at healthy if not spectacular rates, and a handful in the Southern Cone were even experimenting with market-oriented reforms. What most observers missed at the time—as they would again a dozen years later in Mexico—were four worrisome developments: (1) real exchange rates had appreciated significantly, seriously hurting export competitiveness; (2) domestic saving remained flat, at rates inconsistent with sustainable rapid growth; (3) a large proportion of the capital inflows were being used to finance consumption or investment projects of doubtful quality; and (4) most capital inflows were intermediated by banks that were subject to little supervision, and that lack of oversight quickly became the Achilles' heel of these economies.[4]

---

3. On the behavior of the Latin American economies during this period see, e.g., Dornbusch (1988) and Edwards (1988b).

4. Naturally, since funds are fungible it is very difficult to know exactly how the capital inflows were finally used. The above description, however, gives an accurate picture of the economic developments in the region at that time.

And to make things even worse, during that period productivity growth was extremely low in most of the region.

In August 1982 Mexico informed a stunned international community that it was not able to meet its financial obligations and that it was seeking IMF support and the postponement of its debt payments. The financial community reacted badly to this news, and with traditional herd instinct decided to pull out of Latin America as a region. In late 1982 and early 1983, country after country saw its access to international financial capital markets disappear. Even Chile and Colombia, two countries that obeyed the rules of the game and did not attempt to reschedule their debts, experienced a drying-up of private international financing. They were subject to what Ocampo (1989) has called the Latin "neighborhood effect."

From Muddling Through to the Brady Plan

Between 1982 and 1989 most of the Latin American nations muddled through, while they tried to negotiate debt reduction deals with their private creditors. The initial reaction by the creditor countries was that the debt crisis represented a temporary liquidity problem that could be solved with a combination of macroeconomic adjustment, debt-rescheduling agreements, and some structural reforms. This approach was pushed by the U.S. government and, in practice, was coordinated by the IMF and the World Bank. The official approach called for "new monies" (up to US\$20 billion) to be lent to those countries that indeed engaged in structural reforms. Not surprisingly, the banking community endorsed this view, although it argued for shifting the burden of new financing to multilateral and official institutions: "Realism demands an increased share of new money to be furnished by official sources during the next several years" (Morgan Guaranty 1987, 2). Debt-restructuring operations—IMF-sponsored programs and World Bank structural adjustment loans—were the most important elements of the early official strategy.

The 1984 issues of the IMF's *World Economic Outlook* and the World Bank's *World Development Report* included optimistic projections, predicting a steady decline of the debt-export ratio in the Latin American countries until 1990. Things, however, did not work as expected, and in the following years a growing number of analysts came to recognize that the magnitude of the problem had been seriously underestimated. By 1987 it was becoming increasingly clear that the debt burden had greatly reduced the incentives for reforming the region's economies and was seriously affecting the ability of the debtor nations to grow. Between 1985 and 1987 net resource transfers—defined as net capital inflows minus interest and dividend payments to the rest of the world—were significantly negative, averaging almost 28 percent of exports.

In March 1989 a fundamental breakthrough in the official approach toward the debt crisis took place, when the creditor nations and the multilateral institutions recognized that, in many cases, it was in everyone's interest to provide (some) debt forgiveness. The basic idea was that, for countries facing a very high implicit marginal tax on foreign exchange earnings, partial forgiveness of the debt would be equivalent to lowering the implicit tax and thus would encourage the type of market-oriented reform conducive to higher exports and faster growth. In March of that year U.S. secretary of the treasury Nicholas Brady announced a new initiative based on *voluntary* debt reduction. This basic proposal amounted to exchanging old debt for new long-term debt, with a lower face value. The exact conversion ratios, and the detailed characteristics of the new instruments, were to be negotiated between the debtor countries and their creditors. In order to make this new approach feasible and attractive to creditor banks, the advanced nations and the multilateral institutions devoted substantial resources—on the order of US$30 billion—to guarantee the new "Brady" concessional bonds. Typically, principal payments on these new securities were backed by thirty-year zero-coupon U.S. Treasury bills, and interest payments were subject to rolling three-year guarantees.

Starting in 1989, then, the official approach toward the crisis combined two basic mechanisms for alleviating the debt burden. First, the use of debt reduction schemes based on secondary market operations was actively encouraged. Although this technique for reducing the debt had been used since the mid-1980s, it acquired special momentum after 1988, when, in a number of countries, debt-equity swaps became an important mode for privatizing state-owned enterprises. Second, direct debt reduction agreements between creditors (commercial banks) and individual countries became increasingly common after the introduction of the Brady plan. Between 1989 and 1997 Costa Rica, Mexico, Venezuela, Uruguay, Argentina, Brazil, and Peru reached agreements with their creditors to reduce their debt burdens.

In order for countries to be eligible for Brady plan negotiations they had to show willingness "plus some prior action" to engage in serious market-oriented economic reform. From an incentive point of view this new initiative was intended to have two effects. First, it was seen as a way of rewarding countries truly committed to implementing modernization reforms, and second, it was expected that in some countries it would lift the debt overhang burdens associated with extremely high payments. In 1989 Mexico and Costa Rica were the first countries that, within the Brady plan framework, reached broad agreements with their creditors to reduce the value of their debts. Venezuela and Uruguay followed in 1990 and 1991, and Argentina and Brazil signed draft agreements in 1992. In 1996 Peru became the latest country to come to terms with its creditors within the context of the Brady plan. Table 1.1 contains the details of selected Brady deals.

By 1990 the vast majority of the countries in the region had embarked on market-oriented reforms. Although programs varied across countries, they exhibited three common components: (1) Stabilization programs were implemented aimed at reducing inflation and generating a sustainable current account balance. In most countries fiscal retrenchment, including major tax reform, was at the heart of these programs. (2) Economies were opened to

Table 1.1   Brady Debt Reduction Agreements in Selected Latin American Countries (millions of U.S. dollars)

Country and Date of Agreement	Face Value of Eligible Debt	Buyback[a]	Discounted Bonds[a]	Par Bonds[b]	New Money[b]	Total Debt, December 1991[c]
Argentina, 1993	23,160[d]	n.a.	n.a. (35)	n.a. (35)	0 (4–6)[e]	56,273
Brazil, 1993	44,000[f]	0	n.a. (35)	n.a.[g]	n.a.[g]	118,148
Mexico, 1989	48,089	0	20,851 (35)	22,427 (6.25)	4,387 (LIBOR + 13/16)	98,263
Venezuela, 1990	19,098	1,411 (55)	1,794 (30)	10,333 (6.75)	6,060 (LIBOR + 7/8)	34,081

Source: World Bank, several country-specific reports.

Note: n.a. = not available.

[a]Numbers in parentheses are percentage discounts.

[a]Numbers in parentheses are interest rates.

[c]Includes IMF and net short-term debt.

[d]Estimated. In addition, there are $8.6 billion in arrears, including imputed interest.

[e]Interest rate increases from 4 percent in the first year to 6 percent in the seventh year; 6 percent from then on.

[f]Estimated. In addition, there are $6 billion in arrears, including imputed interest.

[g]Several par bonds are offered, with different maturities/grace periods, interest rates, and collateral: Option A, 30/30 years, rate is 4 to 6 percent in the first seven years, 6 percent from then on, full collateral principal, twelve-month interest. Option B, 15/9 years, rate is 4 to 5 percent in the first six years, LIBOR + 13/16 from then on, twelve-month interest collateral for six years. Option C, 20/10 years, LIBOR + 13/16, but interest above the rate in bond B is capitalized, no collateral. Option D, 20/10 years, 8 percent and interest above the rate in bond B is capitalized, no collateral. Option E, 18/10 years, LIBOR + 7/8, no collateral; under option E, new money is equivalent to 18.18 percent of debt tendered for debt conversion bonds.

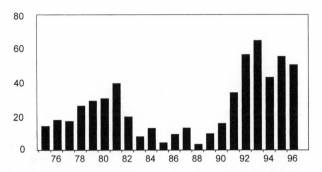

Fig. 1.1   Total capital inflows to Latin America, 1975–96 (billions of U.S. dollars)

international competition. While every country reduced its trade barriers substantially, the approaches to capital account liberalization were very diverse. In some nations, Mexico and Argentina for example, capital controls were abolished; in others, such as Brazil, Chile, and Colombia, some forms of capital controls were maintained. (3) Major privatization and deregulation programs were undertaken aimed at reducing the importance of the state in economic affairs. As the reforms proceeded, many countries added the implementation of social programs benefiting the poor as a fourth component of the new development strategy (Edwards 1995b).

The Resumption of Private Flows: Magnitudes and Some Issues

Starting in 1991 the majority of the Latin American countries were able, once again, to attract private capital. By 1992 the net volume of funds had become so large—exceeding 35 percent of the region's exports—that a number of analysts began to talk about Latin America's "capital inflow problem" (Calvo, Leiderman, and Reinhart 1993; Edwards 1993). To many analysts this sudden change from capital scarcity and negative resource transfers to foreign capital overabundance was surprising and reflected a surge in speculation in international markets. To others the fact that merely a dozen years after a major crisis these countries were able to tap the international market reflected the success of the market-oriented reforms. If the market is willing to reward these countries with plentiful funds, the argument went, it must mean that the reforms are bearing fruit.

Figure 1.1 presents the evolution of net total capital flows (in billions of dollars) to Latin America during the period 1975–96. Figure 1.2 presents data on net resource transfers as a percentage of exports for the same period. Finally, figure 1.3 presents the evolution of net official capital inflows as a percentage of exports during 1980–96. Several interesting aspects of the Latin American experience emerge from these figures. First, the cyclical—almost paranoid, one could say—nature of capital inflows to Latin America comes out clearly. Figure 1.1 shows the abundance of the late 1970s and early 1980s, the

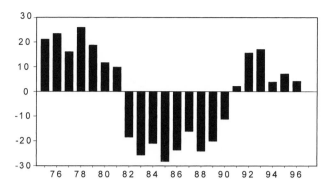

Fig. 1.2   Net resource transfers to Latin America as percentage of exports, 1975–96

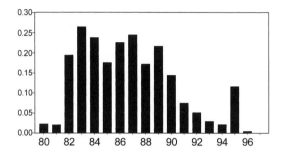

Fig. 1.3   Net official capital inflows as percentage of exports, 1980–96

following collapse in inflows during most of the 1980s, and the remarkable return to abundance in recent years. Figure 1.2 shows the severity of the crunch in the 1980s, when the region as a whole was transferring (in net terms) almost 30 percent of its exports to the rest of the world. And the data in figure 1.3 show a new reality in the 1990s, when official capital flows—and in particular funds coming from such multilateral institutions as the IMF and the World Bank—have declined significantly in relative terms. Notice, however, that this figure shows a large jump in net official flows in 1995, when in response to the Mexican crisis, the IMF, the World bank, the IDB, and the U.S. government transferred large amounts of funds to Mexico. This picture is a vivid reflection of the significant change in the role of official financing during the past few years. It has gone from being the most important provider—and in some countries the sole provider—of foreign funds to being a provider of stabilizing funds. The multilateral official institutions have become insurance companies of sorts, whose main role is providing relief when a disaster occurs.

Figure 1.4 presents data on *net* capital inflows for eight selected countries. Figure 1.5 contains data on the composition of capital inflows to these Latin

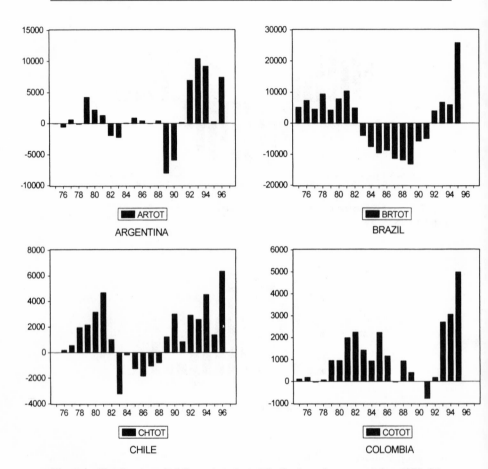

Fig. 1.4   Total net capital flows to selected Latin American countries, 1975–96 (millions of U.S. dollars)

American countries for 1975–96. Three types of flows are distinguished: (1) *DFI*—these flows reflect, at least in principle, a long-term commitment on the part of the investor in the host country. (2) *Portfolio investment*—this category includes transactions in equity and debt securities. (3) *Other types of flows*—this rather broad category includes trade credit (both long and short term) and official (bilateral and multilateral) loans. Several important trends emerge from these figures. First, portfolio investment is a relatively new phenomenon in these countries. Until the late 1980s "other" constituted the dominant form of inflow to most countries. Second, in some countries portfolio flows were by far the dominant form of inflow after 1991. This has been particularly the case in Argentina and Mexico. Figure 1.5 also shows that Brazil has experienced a tremendous surge in portfolio funds in the past few years. These portfolio flows take two basic forms: equity acquisitions—mostly in the form

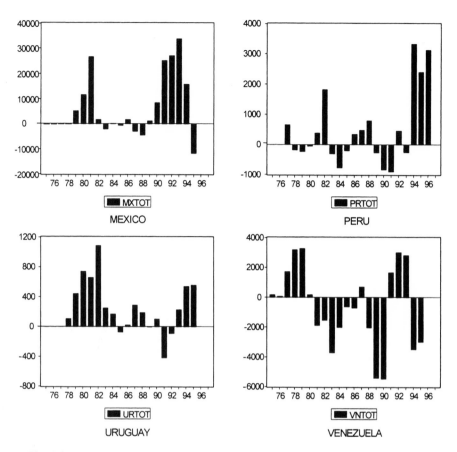

Fig. 1.4   **(cont.)**

of American Depository Receipts (ADRs)—by foreign investors and bond issues in international markets. The World Bank (1997) has reported that an
increasing number of institutional investors (including pension funds) in the
advanced countries are adding emerging economy equities to their portfolios.
This heavy reliance on equities and bonds contrasts with the 1970s, when syndicated bank loans constituted the dominant form of private capital inflow to
Latin America. Third, figure 1.5 shows that the importance of DFI varies
greatly across countries. Chile, Colombia, and Peru have received particularly
large volumes of DFI in the past few years. In all three cases these funds have
been largely devoted to natural-resource-intensive sectors—mining in Chile
and Peru and oil in Colombia.

The recent surge in capital inflows—and particularly in portfolio inflows—
to Latin America has been the result of two basic forces: First, developments
in international financial conditions, and in particular the decline in U.S. inter-

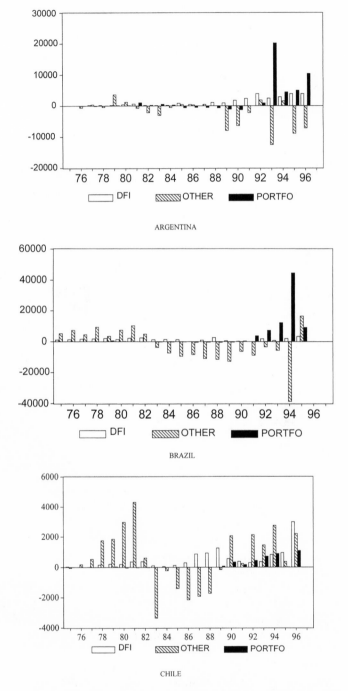

Fig. 1.5 Composition of capital flows to selected Latin American countries, 1975–96 (millions of U.S. dollars)

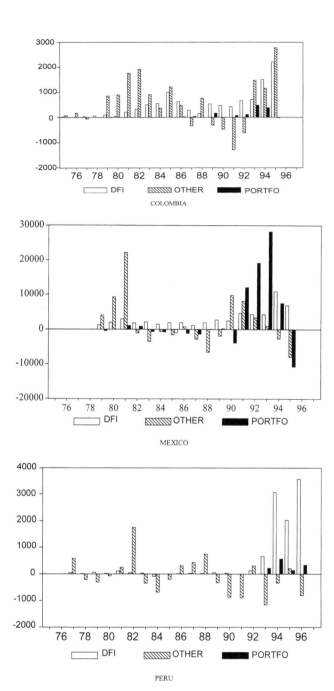

Fig. 1.5   (cont.)

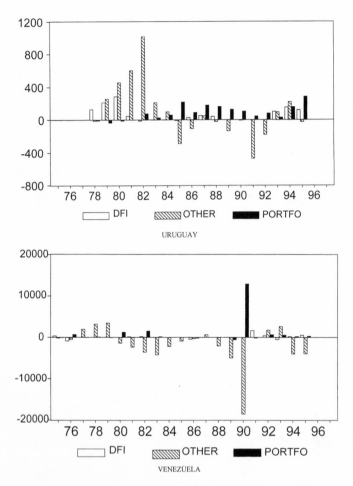

Fig. 1.5   Composition of capital flows to selected Latin American countries, 1975–96 (millions of U.S. dollars) (cont.)

est rates since 1990–91, have encouraged investors in the advanced countries to seek higher returns in other markets, including Latin America. Calvo et al. (1993) provided an early, and very influential, study of the determinants of capital inflows to the region. These authors argue that cyclical external factors have been by far the most important determinants of these flows. These results have recently been confirmed by the World Bank's (1997) massive study of private capital inflows to developing countries. Second, the improvement in Latin America's economic prospects—including the reduction in country risk that has been associated with the implementation of market-oriented reforms—has increased the attractiveness of these countries to international investors. In an extension of the Calvo et al. (1993) study, Chuhan, Claessens, and Mamingi (1993) found that the recipient country's own fundamentals were as important as cyclical factors in explaining the surge in portfolio flows to Latin America. In a recent analysis of the determinants of capital inflows to Chile, Larrain, Laban, and Chumacero (1997) argued that, while interest rate differentials play a key role in determining short-term flows, they are unimportant in determining longer term ones. Long-term flows to Chile are affected by longer term structural variables, and in particular by the country's impressive market-oriented reforms.

The prominent role played by external cyclical factors suggests that, once external conditions change, there may be massive flow reversals. Although it is too early to know whether this will indeed be the case, some evidence already indicates that flow volatility has declined somewhat. First, quarterly inflows to the large countries are far less variable than in the past. For example, for the 1980s the coefficients of variation of quarterly aggregate net inflows to Argentina, Brazil, and Mexico were 5.4, 3.1, and 9.3, respectively. For 1990–97 these coefficients had declined in all three countries, to 2.1, 2.6, and 1.3. Second, it seems that the extent of cross-market contagion has declined significantly. This was apparent in the aftermath of the Mexican and Brazilian currency crises of 1994 and 1999, when in stark contrast with previous episodes—including the debt crisis of 1982—the international financial community did not stampede out of Latin America. In fact, this time around, international investors were quick to realize that there are significant differences among Latin American countries, and after a brief hesitation, they even increased their exposure in those countries with strong fundamentals. Both of these developments suggest, then, that in spite of the importance of cyclical elements in determining the direction of capital flows, countries with strong fundamentals—including modern bank supervisory systems—will not face imminent collapse once international financial conditions change.

In recent years a number of analysts have become concerned about the very low level of saving in the region: on average, Latin America saves 19 percent of GDP, compared with 32 percent in East Asia (see Edwards 1996). This concern has grown after the Mexican peso crisis of 1994. The surge in capital inflows experienced by Mexico in 1991–94 allowed Mexican nationals to increase their expenditure greatly. Starting in 1990, the country experienced a consumption boom that put additional pressure on an already appreciated real exchange rate and contributed to the creation of a large current account deficit. This rapid increase in consumption had as a counterpart a steep decline in domestic saving, from almost 20 percent of GDP in 1988 to 16 percent of GDP in 1993. In the 1993 *Trends in Developing Economies,* the World Bank staff already expressed its apprehension in vivid terms and stated that "in 1992 about two-thirds of the widening of the current account deficit can be ascribed to lower private savings. . . . If this trend continues, it could renew fears about Mexico's inability to generate enough foreign exchange to service debt or remit dividends" (330). After 1993 the decline in saving became more serious, as fiscal policy was relaxed somewhat. The extent to which capital inflows—or more specifically the accompanying current account deficits—crowd out domestic saving has long been a subject of inquiry among authors interested in understanding saving behavior. In a recent study of saving in Latin America Edwards (1996) found that an increase in the current account deficit of 1 percent of GDP is associated with a decline in private saving of only 0.2 percent of GDP. Interestingly enough, however, these results suggest that in Latin America higher current account deficits have a somewhat greater crowding-out effect on public sector saving.

1.1.3   The "True" Degree of Capital Mobility in Latin America

For many years most Latin American countries restricted international capital mobility through a variety of means, including taxes, administrative controls, and outright prohibitions. Legally speaking, then, and as the IMF documented year after year, most countries in the region had closed capital accounts. From an economic point of view, however, what matters is not the *legal* degree of capital restrictions but the actual or "true" degree of capital mobility. Ample historical evidence suggests that there have been significant discrepancies between the legal and the actual degree of controls. In countries with severe impediments to capital mobility—including countries that have banned capital movement—the private sector has traditionally resorted to over-invoicing imports and underinvoicing exports to sidestep legal controls on capital flows. The massive volume of capital that fled Latin America in the wake of the 1982 debt crisis showed clearly that, when faced with "appropriate" incentives, the public can be extremely creative in finding ways to move capital internationally. A number of authors have resorted to the term "semiopen" economy to describe a situation in which the existence of taxes, licenses, or prior deposits restricts the effective freedom of capital movement. However, the questions of how to measure, from an economic point of view, the degree of capital mobility and the extent to which domestic capital markets are integrated in the world capital market are still subject to some debate.

In two early studies Harberger (1978, 1980) argued that the effective degree of integration of capital markets should be measured by the convergence of private rates of return to capital across countries. He used national accounts data for a number of countries—including eleven Latin American countries—to estimate rates of return to private capital and found that these were significantly similar. More important, he found that these private rates of return were independent of national capital-labor ratios. Harberger interpreted these findings as supporting the view that capital markets are significantly more integrated than a simple analysis of legal restrictions would suggest. Additionally, Harberger (1980) argued that remaining (and rather small) divergences in national rates of return to private capital are mostly the consequence of country risk premiums imposed by the international financial community on particular countries. These premiums, in turn, are determined by the perceived probability of default and depend on a small number of "fundamentals," including the debt-GDP ratio and the international reserve position of the country in question.

In trying to measure the effective degree of capital mobility, Feldstein and Horioka (1980) analyzed the behavior of saving and investment in a number of countries. They argue that, under perfect capital mobility, changes in saving and investment will be uncorrelated in a specific country. That is, in a world without capital restrictions an increase in domestic saving will tend to "leave the home country," moving to the rest of the world. Likewise, if international capital markets are fully integrated, increases in domestic investment will tend to be funded by the world at large, and not necessarily by domestic saving. Using a data set for sixteen OECD countries Feldstein and Horioka found that saving and investment ratios were highly positively correlated and concluded that these results strongly supported the presumption that *long-term* capital movement was subject to significant impediments. Frankel (1989) applied the Feldstein-Horioka test to a large number of countries during the 1980s, including a number of Latin American nations. His results corroborated those obtained by the original study, indicating that saving and investment have been significantly positively correlated in most countries.

In a recent comprehensive analysis of the degree of capital mobility Montiel (1994) estimated a series of Feldstein-Horioka equations for sixty-two developing countries, including fifteen Latin American nations. He argued that the estimated regression coefficient for the industrial countries should be used as a benchmark for evaluating whether a particular country's capital account is open or not. After analyzing a number of studies he concluded that a saving ratio regression coefficient of 0.6 provides an adequate benchmark: if a country regression coefficient exceeds 0.6, it can be classified as having a "closed" capital account; if the coefficient is lower than 0.6, the country has a rather high degree of capital mobility. Using this procedure he concluded that most Latin American nations exhibited a remarkable degree of capital mobility—indeed much larger than an analysis of legal restrictions would suggest. Table 1.2 contains the estimated Feldstein-Horioka *b* regression coefficients reported by Montiel (1994). As may be seen, for a large number of these countries the regression coefficient is below the 0.6 cutoff level.

Although Harberger and Feldstein-Horioka used different methodologies—the former looking at prices and the latter at quantities—they agreed on the need to go beyond legal restrictions in assessing the extent of capital mobility. In a series of studies Edwards (1985, 1988b) and Edwards and Khan (1985) argued that time series on domestic and international interest rates could be used to assess the degree of openness of the capital account (see also Montiel 1994). Using a general model that yields the closed and open economy cases as corner solutions, they estimated the economic degree of capital integration. They argued that capital restrictions play two roles: first, they introduce divergences into interest rate parity conditions, and second, they tend to slow the

Table 1.2   Feldstein-Horioka Regressions for Latin American Countries: Coefficient of the Saving Ratio, 1970–90

Country	Ordinary Least Squares	Instrumental Variables
Argentina	1.08[a]	0.88[a]
Brazil	0.58[b]	0.27[b]
Chile	0.51[b]	0.40[c]
Colombia	0.07	0.03[c]
Costa Rica	−0.28	0.57[a]
Dominican Republic	0.81[b]	0.51[b]
Ecuador	0.42[b]	0.73[a]
El Salvador	0.29[b]	0.50[b]
Guatemala	0.23	0.54[b]
Honduras	0.53[b]	0.80[a]
Mexico	0.28[b]	0.20[c]
Paraguay	0.52[b]	0.60
Peru	0.43[b]	0.53
Uruguay	1.10[a]	0.58
Venezuela	0.70[b]	1.88[b]

Source: Montiel (1994).
[a]Different from zero at the 5 percent level.
[b]Different from both zero and one at the 5 percent level.
[c]Different from one at the 5 percent level.

process of interest rate convergence. The application of this model to a number of countries (Brazil, Colombia, and Chile) confirms the result that in general the actual degree of capital mobility is greater than the legal restrictions suggest. Haque and Montiel (1991) and Reisen and Yeches (1991) expanded this model to allow the estimation of the degree of capital mobility even in cases when there are not enough data on domestic interest rates and when there are changes in the degree of capital mobility through time. Their results once again indicated that in most Latin American countries "true" capital mobility has historically exceeded "legal" capital mobility.

1.1.4   Capital Mobility, Real Exchange Rates, and International Competitiveness

The new growth strategy embraced by the Latin American countries since the late 1980s is largely based on achieving export-led growth. This requires, in turn, maintaining competitive real exchange rates, that is, real exchange rates that do not become overvalued. Starting in 1991–92, however, a surge in capital inflows has allowed the Latin American countries to increase substantially aggregate expenditure, generating significant pressure toward real exchange rate appreciation and, thus, a loss of international competitiveness. This phenomenon has generated concern among academics, policymakers, and fi-

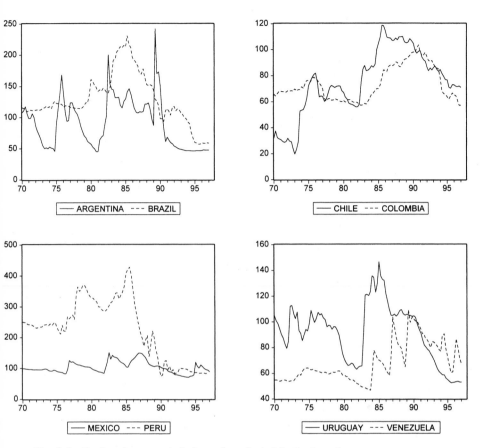

Fig. 1.6   Real exchange rate indexes for selected Latin American countries, 1970–97

nancial sector operators. As Calvo et al. (1993) have pointed out, however, real exchange rate appreciation generated by increased capital inflow is not a completely new phenomenon in Latin America. In the late 1970s most countries in the region, and especially the Southern Cone nations, were flooded with foreign resources that led to large real appreciations. The fact that this previous episode ended in a debt crisis has added drama to the current concern about the possible negative effects of these capital flows.

Figure 1.6 presents the evolution of bilateral real exchange rate (RER) indexes for a selected group of Latin American countries for the period 1970–1997:1.[5] An increase in the value of such an index represents a real depreciation and thus

---

5. These are bilateral indexes relative to the U.S. dollar and have a base of 1990 = 100. In their construction the U.S. producer price index and each individual country consumer price index were used.

an increase in the country's degree of international competitiveness. A number of characteristics of RER behavior in Latin America emerge from these figures. First, RERs have historically been very volatile in Latin America. Comparative analyses of RER behavior have indeed shown that, for long periods of time, RER variability has been greater in Latin America than in almost any other part of the world. Second, these figures show that in all eight countries the RER depreciated drastically after the 1982 debt crisis, only to experience a very large appreciation in the 1990s. These downward swings in RERs were largely caused, as I will argue later, by the surge of capital inflows in the 1990s. Third, these figures show that for most countries in the sample the appreciation trend has slowed in the past two or three quarters and, in some countries, it even seems to have ended.

Figure 1.7 shows the relationship between aggregate (net) capital inflows and the RER for a selected group of countries.[6] As may be seen, in all the countries there is a negative relationship between capital inflows and the RER: increases in capital inflows have been associated with RER appreciation, while declines in inflows are associated with RER depreciation. I explore this relationship further in table 1.3, where I present correlation coefficients between a proxy for quarterly capital inflows and the RER index. As may be seen, in every one of the seven largest Latin American countries there is a negative relationship between capital inflows and the RER, and in some the coefficient of correlation is quite large (in absolute terms). This table also includes results from a series of causality tests. These show that in seven out of the eight cases it is not possible to reject the hypothesis that capital flows "cause" RERs; in three of the seven countries it is not possible to reject two-way causality; and in none of the seven cases analyzed is it found that RERs cause capital inflows. These results, then, provide some support for the view that the recent surge in capital flows has been (partly) responsible for generating the loss in real international competitiveness reported above.

The exact way in which capital inflows translate into RER appreciation depends on the nature of the nominal exchange rate system. Under a fixed exchange rate regime, the increased availability of foreign resources will result in international reserve accumulation at the central bank, monetary expansion, and increased inflation. This, in turn, will put pressure on the RER to appreciate. As is discussed in greater detail in section 1.1.5, many countries have tackled this problem by attempting to sterilize these flows. Under a flexible exchange rate regime, on the other hand, large capital inflows will generate a nominal—as well as real—exchange rate appreciation.

A number of analysts have argued that the appreciation of the RER following a surge in capital inflows is an equilibrium phenomenon—that is, one gen-

6. These are the countries for which the IMF provides quarterly data on aggregate capital inflows. In order to have a larger sample, in table 1.3 I have used quarterly changes in international reserves as a proxy for capital inflows.

erated by fundamentals—and thus should not be cause for concern. This was, for example, the position taken by the Mexican authorities during 1991–94 when a number of independent observers argued that the real appreciation of the peso was not sustainable and was bound to generate a major currency crisis.[7] The view that an increase in capital flows leads to an appreciation of the RER is correct from a simple theoretical perspective. Indeed, in order for the transfer of resources implied by higher capital inflows to become effective, a real appreciation is *required*. A limitation of this interpretation, however, is that it fails to recognize that the rate at which capital was flowing into Mexico in 1991–93—at levels exceeding 8 percent of GDP—was clearly *not* sustainable in the long run. This means that at some point the magnitude of the flow would have to be reduced, requiring a reversal in RER movement.

Although there are no mechanical rules for determining the volume of capital that can be maintained in the long run, there are some helpful guidelines that analysts can follow in order to detect departures from capital inflow sustainability.[8] In general, there is an "equilibrium" level of a country's liabilities that foreigners are willing to hold in their portfolios. Naturally, this "equilibrium portfolio share" is not constant and depends, among other variables, on interest rate differentials, the perceived degrees of country and exchange risk, and the degree of openness of the economy. Moreover, when countries embark on (what is perceived to be) a successful reform program, the equilibrium level of the country's liabilities that is willingly held by international investors is likely to increase because they will be eager to take part in the country's "takeoff." In a recent paper Calvo and Mendoza (1996) argued that in a world with costly information it is even possible for very large volumes of capital to move across countries on the basis of rumors. They estimated that, in the case of Mexico, belief in a change in domestic returns by 0.5 percent could result in capital movements of approximately US$14 billion.

The following simple framework provides a useful way for approaching the capital inflow sustainability issue: assume that in equilibrium international investors are willing to hold in their portfolios a ratio k^* of the home country's (Mexico's, say) liabilities relative to its GDP.[9] This ratio depends on a number of variables, including the country risk premium and interest rate differentials. If, for example, the perceived degree of country risk goes down, and the country is seen as more stable, k^* will increase. This approach has two important implications. The first has to do with the long-run sustainable level of capital inflow and, thus, of the current account deficit. This depends on two factors: (1) international demand for the country's securities and (2) the real rate of growth of the economy. If, for example, foreign investors are willing to hold

7. For discussions of Mexico's RER appreciation in 1991–94 see, e.g., Dornbusch (1993), Dornbusch and Werner (1994), and Edwards (1993). On Mexico's official position regarding these developments see, e.g., Bank of Mexico (various years).
8. On the issue of current account sustainability see, among others, Reisen (1995).
9. Ideally this is a forward-looking measure of GDP.

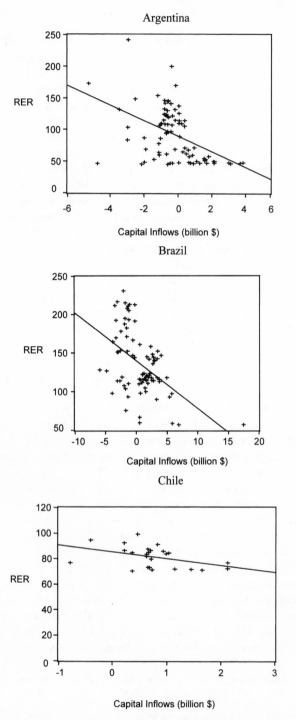

Fig. 1.7   Real exchange rate indexes versus capital inflows for selected Latin American countries, 1970–97

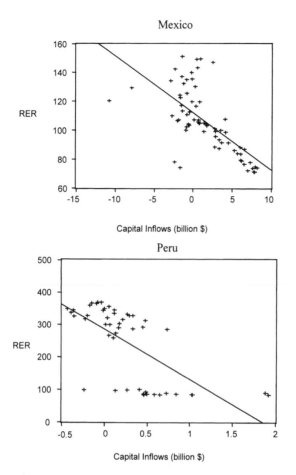

Fig. 1.7   (cont.)

national securities amounting to 50 percent of the country's GDP and the rate of growth is 4 percent per year, the long-run sustainable deficit is 2 percent of GDP. If, however, the demand for the country's securities is 75 percent of GDP, the sustainable current account deficit is 3 percent of GDP. More specifically, long-run sustainable capital inflow as a percentage of GDP is given by the following equation:[10] $C/y = g\,k^*$, where C is the current account deficit, y is GDP, g is the real rate of growth of the country, and k^* is the ratio to GDP of the country's liabilities that are willingly held by international investors. According to Bank of Mexico data, at their peak foreign holdings of Mexican securities reached approximately 50 percent of the country's GDP. Growth, however, averaged less than 4 percent during the first four years of the 1990s. These figures

10. This assumes that no international reserves are being accumulated.

Table 1.3   **Capital Inflows and Real Exchange Rates in Selected Latin American Countries: Some Basic Statistical Relations, Quarterly Data, 1980–97**

Country	Correlation Coefficient	Do Capital Inflows "Cause" Real Exchange Rates?	Do Real Exchange Rates "Cause" Capital Inflows?
Argentina	−0.723	Yes	No
Brazil	−0.727	Yes	Yes
Chile	−0.382	Yes	Yes
Colombia	−0.145	No	No
Mexico	−0.656	Yes	No
Peru	−0.478	Yes	Yes
Venezuela	−0.146	Yes	No

Note: Quarterly changes in international reserves were used as a proxy for capital inflows. Granger causality tests were performed. The results for Colombia and Venezuela are sensitive to the sample considered. If 1985–97 is used, the correlation coefficient is larger (in absolute terms), and in the case of Colombia it is not possible to reject the hypothesis that capital inflows "cause" real exchange rates.

indicate that Mexico's long-run sustainable current account deficit was in the neighborhood of 2 to 3 percent of GDP, significantly below the 7 to 8 percent levels actually attained during this period. On the other hand, in a country such as Chile, with a rate of growth of approximately 7 percent per year, the sustainable level of capital inflow is much larger. If, for instance, the steady state foreign demand for Chilean liabilities is 65 percent of the country's GDP, the sustainable inflow of capital is almost 6 percent of GDP.

The second implication of this framework is related to the dynamic effects of capital inflow on the current account and the RER. Transitional issues are particularly important when there are large shifts (positive or negative) in international portfolio demand for a small country's liabilities. If, for example, the country's degree of country risk drops, or if the country in question opens to the rest of the world, foreigners will increase their demand for the country's securities. In the short run—while the newly demanded securities are accumulated—capital inflow (and the current account deficit) will exceed in the short run, that is, it will overshoot, the level predicted by the preceding long-run analysis. Once portfolio equilibrium is regained, however, and investors hold in their portfolios the desired amount of the country's securities, capital inflow (and the capital account balance) will again revert to its long-run equilibrium level. In most instances this adjustment process will not be instantaneous. In some cases it will even take a few years. Historically, episodes of capital inflow surges have been characterized by increases in the demand for the small country's securities on the order of 20 to 30 percent of GDP, and by peak annual inflows on the order of 7 to 9 percent of GDP. Table 1.4 contains data on accumulated and maximum inflows during recent surges in Latin America.

One of the most important dynamic effects of the transition described above

Table 1.4   **Net Private Capital Inflows to Selected Latin American Countries, 1990s**

Country	Inflow Episode[a]	Cumulative Inflow at End of Episode[b]	Maximum Annual Inflow[b]
Argentina	1991–94	9.7	3.8
Brazil	1992–95	9.4	4.8
Chile	1989–95	25.8	8.6
Colombia	1992–95	16.2	6.2
Mexico	1989–94	27.1	8.5
Peru	1990–95	30.4	10.8
Venezuela	1992–93	5.4	3.3

Source: World Bank (1997).
[a]Period during which the country experienced a significant surge in net private capital inflow.
[b]Net long-term international private capital as a percentage of GDP.

is on the RER. As capital flows in, expenditure increases and the RER appreciates. Once capital stops flowing in, or even when the rate at which it flows slows down, the RER will be "overly" appreciated, and in order to maintain equilibrium, a massive adjustment may be required. The dynamics of capital inflow and current account adjustment will require, then, that the equilibrium RER first appreciate and then depreciate. And whereas during the surge in inflow the RER appreciates without impediment, when the availability of foreign capital declines nominal wage and price rigidity will make the required real depreciation difficult under a pegged exchange rate.[11]

Naturally, the situation is even more serious if, as a result of external or internal developments, the international portfolio demand for the country's securities *declines*—as was the case for Mexico after 20 December 1994 and for Argentina in the first half of 1995. Under these circumstances, the capital account balance suffers a very severe contraction—and the current account may even have to become positive—during the transitional period toward the new equilibrium. As is well known by now, whereas Mexico was unable to maintain the peg under the new circumstances, Argentina decided to stand firm and to engineer a major aggregate demand adjustment that generated a major hike in the rate of unemployment.

The effects of changing capital flows on the equilibrium RER, the current account, and reserve accumulation can be analyzed using simple numerical simulations. Edwards, Steiner, and Losada (1996) presented results based on a model of a small open economy with tradables and nontradables. In this framework, an increase in capital inflow allows residents of the country in question to increase expenditure on both types of goods. As a result of the surge in

11. This type of analysis has been made in relation to the sequencing of reform debate. See, e.g., Edwards (1984).

capital inflow the current account deficit rises and the RER appreciates. The specific magnitudes of these effects depends on the price and expenditure elasticities of demand and supply of nontradables. This analysis suggests that, under plausible values for the relevant parameters, an increase in the international demand for a small country's securities equivalent to 20 percent of the country's GDP generates an inflow of capital that will peak at approximately 8 percent of GDP; note that these figures correspond closely to Latin America's historical experience reported in table 1.4. In turn, this inflow of capital will generate (under the assumed elasticities) an RER appreciation of almost 10 percent. Perhaps the most important aspect of this analysis is that it clearly shows that after capital inflow has peaked and begins to decline to its new level, the RER *has* to depreciate until it achieves its new equilibrium level. In a fixed exchange rate regime, this real depreciation can only be achieved by means of reducing domestic inflation to a rate below foreign inflation, or, in terms of the framework developed by Edwards et al. (1996), by actually reducing the price of nontradable goods.

The above discussion suggests that the relevant question regarding events in Mexico was not, as some analysts incorrectly thought during 1994, whether the inflows observed during 1991–93 were sustainable but how and when Mexico was going to adjust to a lower availability of foreign resources. Mexico's clinging to its rigid exchange rate system made a smooth landing increasingly unlikely as the events of 1994 unfolded.

1.1.5 Capital Mobility and the Effectiveness of Monetary and Exchange Rate Policy

Most Latin American countries have tried to minimize the macroeconomic—and in particular, the RER—consequences of capital inflow surges. Basically, three approaches have been used to deal with this phenomenon: (1) Some form of capital controls are imposed in order to slow the rate at which foreign funds come into the country. Brazil, Chile, and Colombia have relied on these types of controls. (2) Sterilized intervention is attempted in order to offset the monetary—and inflationary—consequences of capital inflow. Almost every country in the region has tried this approach. (3) Nominal exchange rate flexibility is increased. While, strictly speaking, the adoption of a more flexible exchange rate regime does not avoid the real appreciation, it accommodates the required real appreciation without a surge in domestic inflation. Chile is the only country that has used this mechanism to any serious extent—and for a long period of time. In addition to these three mechanisms there have been discussions in a number of countries about using fiscal adjustment to compensate for the monetary impact of capital inflows on the RER. In no country, however, has this discussion actually become implemented into policy. In this section I review some of the Latin American country experiences with these policy responses.

Table 1.5   **Restrictions on Capital Inflow to Chile**

Type of Capital Inflow	Restriction
Direct foreign investment	Minimum stay of one year. No restrictions on repatriation of profits.
Portfolio inflows: issuing of American Depository Receipts (ADRs)	The issuance of ADRs by Chilean companies is strictly regulated. Only companies that meet a certain risk classification requirement (BBB for nonfinancial companies and BBB+ for financial institutions) can issue ADRs. There is also a minimum amount requirement: until September 1994, this was US$50 million; at that time it was lowered to $25 million; and in November 1995 it was further reduced to $10 million.
Other portfolio inflows	All other portfolio inflows—including secondary ADR inflows, foreign loans, and bond issues—are subject to a nonremunerated 30% reserve requirement. This reserve requirement is independent of the length of stay of the inflow. In the case of loan and bonds, the recipient may choose to pay the financial cost of the reserve requirement.
Trade credit	Credit lines used to finance trade operations are also subject to the 30% deposit.

Source: Budnevich and Lefort (1997).

Capital Controls in Chile and Colombia

Chile and Colombia have relied on capital controls in an effort to avoid some of the destabilizing short-term effects—in particular, RER appreciation—of capital inflow surges. In their current form capital controls were introduced in 1991 in Chile and in 1993 in Colombia.[12]

In Chile these restrictions have taken two basic forms: minimum stay requirements for DFI flows and nonremunerated reserve requirements on other forms of capital inflow. Table 1.5 contains details on these regulations, as of the third quarter of 1997. In Colombia, on the other hand, capital controls have taken the form of a variable reserve requirement on foreign loans—except trade credit—obtained by the private sector. Initially, this reserve requirement was set at a rate of 47 percent and was only applicable to loans with a maturity shorter than eighteen months. During 1994, as the economy was flooded with capital inflows, the reserve requirements were tightened. In March they were extended to all loans with a maturity below three years; in August they were extended to loans of five years or less. Moreover, the rate of the reserve requirement became inversely proportional to the maturity of the loan: thirty-day loans were subject to a stiff 140 percent reserve requirement—which was vir-

---

12. It should be noted that both of these countries had a long tradition with capital controls before the 1990s. See, e.g., Edwards (1988b).

tually prohibitive—while five-year loans had to meet a 42.8 percent deposit. See figure 1.8 for the actual reserve requirements for various loan maturities.

In both Chile and Colombia restrictions on capital movements act as an implicit tax on foreign financing. The recent studies by Cardenas and Barreras (1996) and Valdes-Prieto and Soto (1996) calculated the tax equivalence of these controls in order to analyze the effects of these restrictions on capital movements. In particular they estimated a number of capital inflow equations to investigate whether these mechanisms have succeeded in affecting the rate at which capital has flowed into countries. These authors found that aggregate capital inflows have not been sensitive to this tax equivalence factor and concluded that these capital restrictions have been ineffective in slowing capital movements. In both countries, however, capital controls have resulted in a change in the composition of capital inflows, with flows not affected by these implicit taxes growing faster than they would have otherwise (see Budnevich and Lefort 1997 and Larrain et al. 1997 for similar results). Valdes-Prieto and Soto (1996) persuasively argued that, in the case of Chile, the existence of capital controls has actually had an important negative effect on welfare for two reasons. First, to the extent that trade credit is subject to reserve requirements, these requirements are also an implicit barrier to free trade, and the economy is subject to the traditional welfare consequences of protectionism. Second, by introducing a wedge between domestic and foreign interest rates these controls result in a misallocation of intertemporal consumption and discourage investment.

In view of the questionable effectiveness of capital controls, policymakers in a number of countries have considered alternative mechanisms to smooth the volume of *net* capital inflows. Some analysts have argued that the relaxation of restrictions on capital *outflows* from developing countries provides an effective way of achieving this goal (Budnevich and Lefort 1997; World Bank 1997). According to this view, if domestic residents can freely move funds out of the country (for portfolio diversification or for other reasons), net inflows will be lower, and so will the pressure on money creation, inflation, and the RER. Laban and Larrain (1997), however, argued that a relaxation of restrictions on capital outflows may further complicate macroeconomic management. This will be the case if investors interpret the new policy as reducing the overall cost of investing in the country. This, in turn, will make investment more attractive than before and (perhaps paradoxically) will generate an increase in net capital inflows to the country.

Sterilized Intervention: Is It Possible? How Costly Is It?

Most countries in Latin America have tried to offset (at least partially) the monetary impact of the recent capital inflow surge. Several mechanisms have been used to this end, including increasing commercial banks' marginal reserve requirements, transferring public sector deposits to the central bank, which is equivalent to imposing a very high reserve requirement on this type of deposit, and undertaking sterilized intervention on behalf of the central

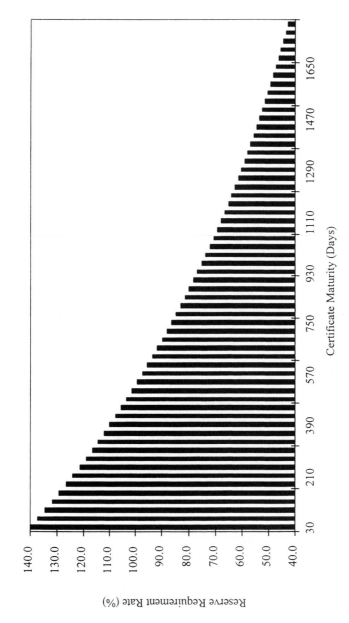

Fig. 1.8 Reserve requirement rate versus certificate maturity in Colombia, 1996

bank. The last mechanism has been used in almost every country in the region and is usually carried out through the sale of central bank securities to the public at large. Figure 1.9 illustrates the extent of sterilization in Argentina, Colombia, and Mexico. As may be seen, in each of these countries changes in reserves have been associated, in the past few years, with changes in the opposite direction in domestic credit (during the same quarter).

A problem with sterilized intervention, however, is that it can be very costly for the central bank. This is because interest earnings on international reserves are rather low, while the central bank has to pay a relatively high interest rate to persuade the public to buy its own securities. Calvo (1991), for example, argued that this cost can become so high that it may end up threatening the sustainability of the entire reform effort. Moreover, as Frenkel (1995) pointed out, in an economy with capital mobility and predetermined nominal exchange rates it is not possible for the monetary authorities to control monetary aggregates in the medium to long run. This view has been confirmed by econometric estimates of the monetary "offset" coefficient for a number of countries (see, e.g., the studies in Steiner 1995).

Colombia's experience during the early 1990s illustrates very clearly what Calvo (1991) called "the perils of sterilization." In 1990 newly elected President Gaviria announced a trade liberalization program aimed at eliminating import licensing and greatly reducing import tariffs. At the same time a twenty-year-old exchange and capital control mechanism was eliminated. By March 1991, however, it was becoming clear that trade reform was not having the effects the economic team had anticipated. Perhaps the most surprising fact was that imports were not growing and that, as a result of it, the country was experiencing a growing trade surplus. This, in conjunction with larger inflows of capital, was putting pressure on the money supply, making macroeconomic management very difficult. As inflation increased, the RER began to lose ground, and both exporters and import-competing sectors began to lose competitiveness. The Banco de la Republica reacted to this situation by implementing a series of policies that in retrospect appear to have contradicted each other. First, an aggressive policy of sterilizing reserve accumulation was undertaken. This was done by issuing indexed short-term securities (the OMAs). In the first ten months of 1991 the stock of this instrument shot up from US$405 million to $1.2 billion, or 85 percent of the total monetary base. Naturally, this policy resulted in an increase in domestic (peso denominated) interest rates and a significant interest rate differential. This attracted further capital into the country, frustrating the sterilization policy itself. Second, the authorities decided—as they had in the past when facing coffee booms—to postpone the monetization of export proceeds. For this reason, in 1991 the monetary authority stopped buying foreign exchange in the spot market. Instead, it started issuing "exchange certificates" (*certificados de cambio*) in exchange for export foreign currency proceeds. These certificates could be transacted in the secondary market and initially had a three-month maturity, which was later extended to one

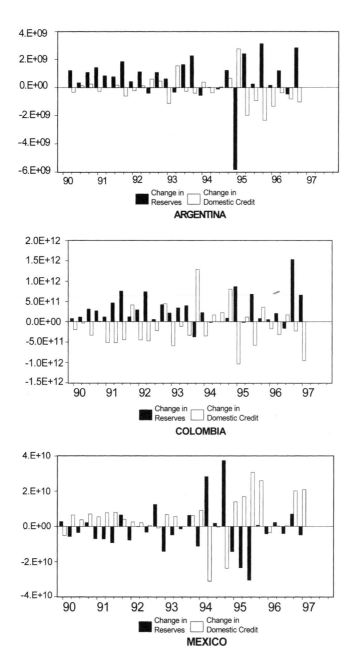

Fig. 1.9   Sterilized intervention in selected Latin American countries

year. Moreover, the central bank established a maximum discount for the certificates in the secondary market of 12.5 percent. All of this, of course, amounted to an attempt at controlling too many variables—the spot and future exchange rates, the nominal interest rate, and the stock of money—at inconsistent levels. During the first ten months of 1991 Colombia was trapped in a vicious circle: a very rapid process of reserve accumulation generated high inflation and RER appreciation; but the policies put in place to combat these phenomena created incentives for capital inflows and further appreciation of the RER. These events generated two political problems for the Gaviria administration. First, exporters and import-competing sectors were becoming increasingly unhappy about the real appreciation of the peso; second, the lack of progress against inflation was a black spot in an otherwise quite positive picture.

Nominal Exchange Rate Flexibility: Chile's Band Experience

After a major and protracted macroeconomic crisis, in early 1986 Chile adopted a nominal exchange rate system based on a crawling band system. The band was originally quite narrow, allowing fluctuations of ±2 percent around a backward-looking crawling central parity. Through time, however, two innovations were introduced into the system. First, the band became wider, reaching ±12 percent in 1997; second, the central parity was defined relative to a three-currency basket. The latter measure was based on the idea that basket pegging would add some uncertainty to the system, discouraging (very) short-term speculators. Throughout, however, the rate of crawl of the band has been backward looking and is determined as the previous month's rate of domestic inflation minus an estimate of international inflation. The adoption of this band was an integral part of an economic program aimed at achieving very fast rates of growth—mostly driven by export expansion—while reducing inflation.

Figure 1.10 presents the evolution of Chile's band and actual exchange rate since 1989. Four important features emerge from this figure. First, given the alterations introduced into the system the Chilean band has been, de facto, nonlinear relative to the U.S. dollar. Second, throughout much of the period the actual rate was at the bottom of the band. This has been the direct result of very large capital inflows, which created an abundance of foreign exchange. From all practical points of view, then, during this period the band acted as an effective floor for the nominal exchange rate. There is, in fact, little doubt that if it had not been for the band the nominal value of the peso would have appreciated significantly during the period. Third, the form of the band has given significant flexibility to the system, allowing the economy to accommodate external shocks, such as the (short lived) scare following the Mexican crisis of 1994. And fourth, the band has allowed the peso to remain very stable in nominal terms in the last eighteen to twenty-four months, taking away inflationary pressure from the system. Some evidence, however, suggests that the widening of the band added uncertainty to the economy and resulted in an increase in domestic interest rates.

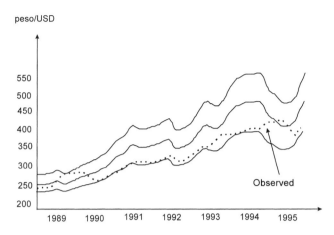

peso/USD

Fig. 1.10   Chile's band

Although the Chilean band it has not prevented RER appreciation, it has maintained it at a relatively controlled level. In fact, a new World Bank (1997) study indicated that the Chilean peso is still slightly undervalued. Moreover, the band has allowed the gradual reduction of inflation—in 1997 it will be approximately 5 percent. In fact, in spite of having an elaborate indexation system, Chile has been able to reduce the degree of inflationary inertia significantly. Given the relative success of the Chilean band system, it is surprising that more countries have not adopted this type of regime.

1.1.6   The Role of the Domestic Banking Sector

The resurgence of capital inflows to Latin America has raised some important questions: Will there be another reversal? Are institutional investors likely to behave in a herd fashion, as in the past? How vulnerable are the Latin American countries to a contagion effect coming out of East Asia or other emerging markets? The analysis presented in the preceding sections suggests that the conditions behind capital flows have changed. These appear to be less volatile than in the past, and investors are becoming more sophisticated and understand that there are significant differences among regions and countries. However, the issue of vulnerability remains. What makes the situation particularly difficult is that in many Latin American countries commercial banks—which (ultimately) intermediate capital inflows—continue to be financially weak, even in the aftermath of the Mexican crisis. Moreover, in most nations supervisory systems are inefficient and unable to monitor effectively the quality of the portfolio and the extent to which banks indeed abide by existing rules and regulations.

Latin America's own history justifies the current concern about banks' vulnerability. As previous episodes in the region have shown, when banks fail the effects of financial crises are greatly magnified. Past experiences in Chile and

Mexico illustrate this point vividly. Banks were at the center of the Chilean crisis of 1982. After intermediating very large volumes of capital inflows during 1978–80, commercial banks became increasingly vulnerable to negative shocks stemming from the international economy. In mid-1981, as international interest rates increased rapidly, asset prices in Chile began to fall and the demand for deposits experienced a significant decline. Some firms had trouble paying their debts, and in November 1981 two major banks—Banco Español and Banco de Talca—ran into serious difficulties and had to be bailed out by the government. During late 1981 and early 1982 aggregate production collapsed, domestic interest rates continued to increase, and the number of bankruptcies increased greatly. In the first half of 1982 deposits in the Chilean banking system, especially deposits by foreigners, continued to decline steeply. During the first five months of 1982 alone, foreign deposits in commercial banks dropped by 75 percent. An interesting feature of the Chilean episode was that most commercial banks were owned by large conglomerates (the so-called *grupos*), which received major loans from the banks themselves. Many times these loans were made sidestepping financial criteria and were guaranteed by assets with highly inflated prices. In June 1982 the government decided to devalue the peso, in the hopes of alleviating speculative pressure on the economy. The devaluation, however, affected negatively the financial condition of many firms that had borrowed heavily in dollars. Depositors decided to fly from peso-denominated assets, commercial banks continued to accumulate bad loans, and the central bank had to inject large amounts of funds into the economy. In January 1983 the government concluded that the cost of this muddling-through strategy was too high and pulled the rug from under some of the major commercial banks. By mid-1983 a number of banks had gone bankrupt, and Chile's financial crisis was in full swing. At the end of the road the massive bank bailout that followed cost the country (in present value terms) in excess of 20 percent of GDP.

What makes this story fascinating is its parallel to the 1997–98 crises in Indonesia and Korea. All the key elements are there—a rigid exchange rate policy, marked overvaluation, a high current account deficit, reckless lending by conglomerate-controlled banks, poor bank supervision, and a major asset bubble. In fact, one cannot avoid thinking that, had watchers of East Asia studied the Chilean financial crisis of 1982, they would not have been so shocked by the turn of events in the countries once called Asian "tigers."

Similarly, it is possible to argue that both the magnitude and timing of the 1994 Mexican crisis were affected by the behavior of the banking system. Throughout 1994, as international interest rates increased and Mexico was hit by a series of political shocks, the Mexican authorities made great efforts to maintain domestic (peso denominated) interest rates at a relatively low level. A two-prong approach was followed: on the one hand, a cap was imposed on peso-denominated interest rates; on the other, the authorities issued increas-

ingly large amounts of dollar-denominated securities—the so-called Tesobonos. The investment house J. P. Morgan summarized this state of affairs
in its 22 July 1994 newsletter: "Half of the 28-day and 91-day Cetes [peso-
denominated securities] were issued; the central bank would not accept the
high yields required by the market to auction the full amount." And on 23 July
the *Economist* pointed out that "the central bank has also had to issue plenty
of tesobonos—dollar linked securities that are popular with investors that
worry about currency risk." This strategy—which in retrospect has mystified
so many analysts—partly addressed the Mexican authorities' concerns regarding the financial health of Mexican banks. This concern had begun in late 1992,
when a large increase in past-due loans became evident. In 1990 nonperforming loans were estimated to be only 2 percent of total loans; that ratio increased to 4.7 percent in 1992, to 7.3 percent in 1993, and to 8.3 percent at the
end of the first quarter of 1994. With the fourth largest bank—Banca Cremi—
in serious trouble, the authorities tried to buy additional time as they worked
out an emergency plan. By the end of the first semester the state development
banks had developed a relief program based on some write-offs of commercial
banks' past-due interest and government-issued loan guarantees. In the belief
that the peso was sustainable and that they had superior information, Mexican banks engaged in aggressive derivative operations, accumulating sizable
dollar-denominated off-balance-sheet liabilities (Garber 1996). On 19 December 1994, however, with the Bank of Mexico having virtually run out of reserves the Mexican authorities decided to widen the exchange rate band. It was
too little, too late. In the months to come it became increasingly clear that a
key element in the stabilization policy would be to contain—or at least minimize—the extent of the banking crisis.

1.1.7 Concluding Remarks

This paper has dealt with Latin America's experience with capital flows during the past decade and a half. It has covered a number of issues of increasing
interest to academics and international observers, including the effect of capital inflows on domestic saving, the effect of capital mobility on the ability to
engage in independent monetary policy, and the effectiveness of capital controls. The data analysis presented in section 1.1.2 shows that the Latin American countries have gone through wild cycles. In the mid- to late 1970s they
benefited from the recycling of petrodollars and were flooded with private capital. After the eruption of the Mexican debt crisis in 1982, the international
capital market dried up for every country in the region, and net private capital
inflows became significantly negative. Things changed in 1991, when once
again private capital began to pour into the region. Although this turn of events
has largely been welcomed, it has also generated some concern among analysts
and policymakers. In particular there are still questions about the sustainability

of these flows, as well as about the extent to which the region will be affected by the still developing East Asian crisis. In early 1998 the consensus seems to be that this time around Latin America has strong fundamentals and is facing the crisis from a strong footing. This view is nicely summarized by the following quote from ING Barings: "Latin America is relatively insulated from the direct contagion effect of Asia. . . . The policy response of the Latin authorities to the recent turbulence in the emerging world has been impressive and the general resilience of Latin America to a more difficult global economic backdrop has much to do . . . with an improving microeconomic base" (1998, 7).

References

Bank of Mexico. Various years. *The Mexican economy.* Mexico City: Banco de Mexico.
Bruno, Michael. 1995. Currency crises and collapses: Comment. *Brookings Papers on Economic Activity,* no. 2:205–56.
Budnevich, Carlos, and Guillermo Lefort. 1997. Capital account regulations and macroeconomics policy: Two Latin American experiences. Working Paper no. 6. Santiago: Banco Central de Chile.
Calvo, Guillermo A. 1991. The perils of sterilization. *IMF Staff Papers* 38, no. 4 (December): 921–26.
Calvo, Guillermo, Leonardo Leiderman, and Carmen Reinhart. 1993. Capital inflows and real exchange rate appreciation in Latin America: The role of external factors. *IMF Staff Papers* 40 (March): 108–51.
Calvo, Guillermo, and Enrique Mendoza. 1996. Rational herd behavior and the globalization of security markets. College Park: University of Maryland. Mimeograph.
Cardenas, Mauricio, and Felipe Barreras. 1996. On the effectiveness of capital controls in Colombia. Washington, D.C.: World Bank, International Finance Division. Processed.
Chuhan, Punam, Stijn Claessens, and Nlandu Mamingi. 1993. Equity and bond flows to Latin America and Asia: The role of global and country factors. Policy Research Working Paper no. 1160. Washington, D.C.: World Bank, International Economics Department.
Dornbusch, Rudiger. 1988. Our LDC debts. In *The United States in the world economy,* ed. Martin Feldstein. Chicago: University of Chicago Press.
———. 1993. Mexico: How to recover stability and growth. Chapter 17 in *Stabilization, debt, and reform.* Englewood Cliffs, N.J.: Prentice-Hall.
Dornbusch, Rudiger, Ilan Goldfajn, and Rodrigo Valdes. 1995. Currency crises and collapses. *Brookings Papers on Economic Activity,* no. 2:219–93.
Dornbusch, Rudiger, and Alejandro Werner. 1994. Mexico: Stabilization, reform and no growth. *Brookings Papers on Economic Activity,* no. 1:253–315.
Edwards, Sebastian. 1984. The order of liberalization of the external sector in developing countries. Princeton Essays in International Finance, no. 156. Princeton, N.J.: Princeton University, International Finance Section.
———. 1985. Money, the rate of devaluation, and interest rates in a semi-open economy: Colombia, 1968–82. *Journal of Money, Credit and Banking* 17 (1): 59–68.
———. 1988a. *Exchange rate misalignment in developing countries.* Baltimore: Johns Hopkins University Press.

———. 1988b. The United States and foreign competition in Latin America. In *The United States in the world economy,* ed. Martin Feldstein. Chicago: University of Chicago Press.

———. 1993. *Latin America and the Caribbean: A decade after the debt crisis.* Washington, D.C.: World Bank.

———, ed. 1995a. *Capital controls, exchange rates and monetary policy in the world economy.* Cambridge: Cambridge University Press.

———. 1995b. *Crisis and reform in Latin America: From despair to hope.* New York: Oxford University Press.

———. 1996. Why are Latin America's savings rates so low? An international comparative analysis. *Journal of Development Economics* 51 (1): 5–44.

Edwards, S., and M. Khan. 1985. Interest determination in developing countries: A conceptual framework. *IMF Staff Papers* 32, no. 3 (September): 377–403.

Edwards, Sebastian, Roberto Steiner, and Fernando Losada. 1996. Capital inflows, the real exchange rate and the Mexican crisis of 1994. In *Stabilization and reforms in Latin America: Where do we stand?* ed. Hermann Sautter and Rolf Schinke. Frankfurt: Vervuert Verlag; Madrid: Iberoamericana.

Feldstein, Martin, and Charles Horioka. 1980. Domestic saving and international capital flows. *Economic Journal* 90 (June): 314–29.

Frankel, J. 1989. Quantifying international capital mobility in the 1980s. NBER Working Paper no. 2856. Cambridge, Mass.: National Bureau of Economic Research, February.

Frenkel, Jacob. 1995. The order of liberalization. In *Economic policy in a world of change,* ed. K. Brunner and A. H. Meltzer. Amsterdam: North-Holland.

Garber, Peter. 1996. Managing risk to financial markets from volatile capital flows: The role of prudential regulation. *International Journal of Finance and Economics* 1 (July): 150–69.

Haque, Nadeem, and Peter Montiel. 1991. Capital mobility in developing countries: Some empirical tests. *World Development* 19 (October): 91–98.

Harberger, Arnold. 1978. Perspectives on capital and technology in less developed countries. In *Contemporary economic analysis,* ed. M. Artis and A. Nobay, 151–69. London: Croom Helm.

———. 1980. Vignettes on the world capital markets. *American Economic Review* 70, no. 2 (May): 331–37.

ING Barings. 1998. *Global investment strategy.* New York: ING Barings, first quarter.

Laban, Raul, and Felipe Larrain. 1997. Can a liberalization of capital outflows increase net capital inflows? Development Discussion Paper no. 584. Cambridge, Mass.: Harvard University, Harvard Institute for International Development.

Larrain, Felipe, Raul Laban, and Romulo Chumacero. 1997. What determines capital inflows? An empirical analysis for Chile. Development Discussion Paper no. 590. Cambridge, Mass.: Harvard University, Harvard Institute for International Development.

Montiel, Peter. 1994. Capital mobility in developing countries: Some measurement issues and empirical estimates. *World Bank Economic Review* 8, no. 3 (September): 311–50.

Morgan Guaranty and Trust Company. 1987. World financial markets. New York: Morgan Guaranty International Economics Department.

Ocampo, Jose Antonio. 1989. Colombia and the Latin American debt crisis. In *Debt, adjustment and recovery,* ed. Sebastian Edwards and Felipe Larrain. Oxford: Blackwell.

Reisen, Helmut. 1995. Liberalizing foreign investments by pension funds: Positive and normative aspects. *World Development* 25, no. 7 (July): 1173–82.

Reisen, H., and H. Yeches. 1991. Time-varying estimates on the openness of the capital account in Korea and Taiwan. OECD Development Centre Technical Paper no. 42. Paris: Organization for Economic Cooperation and Development, August.

Steiner, Roberto. 1995. *Flujos de capitales en America Latina.* Bogota: Tercer Muno-Fedesarrollo.

Valdes-Prieto, Salvador, and Marcelo Soto. 1996. New selective capital controls in Chile: Are they effective? Santiago: Catholic University of Chile, Economics Department. Processed.

World Bank. 1997. *Private capital flows to developing countries: The road to financial integration.* New York: Oxford University Press.

2. Francisco Gil Diaz

I would like to speak based on Mexico's recent experience, by which I mean especially the post-crisis period, and to compare it with the precrisis behavior of short-term capital flows. Some hypothesis is needed as to why they were so volatile and so large before the crisis, and why they have apparently shown such stable behavior after the crisis.

Mexico's recent and varied experience with international capital flows may throw some light on the interaction between such flows and different exchange rate regimes. To do so, it will be profitable to go from the present back to the past, by inspecting the behavior of a flow category that has worried policymakers because of its short-term nature and high volatility, especially given the speed and liquidity that characterize today's financial markets. The concern about short-term foreign capital flows is well founded, because of the sometimes ravaging effects of their injection and withdrawal on the financial stability and short-term output behavior of many economies.

To start the analysis with the most recent figures, consider the stock amounts invested by foreign residents in Mexico's money market between December 1995 and 8 October 1997. These quantities correspond to foreign resident purchases of government securities or commercial banks' money market instruments. The period chosen is significant because prior to December 1995 the figures are substantially contaminated by the liquidation by Mexico's federal government of the outstanding amounts of Tesobonos, the now infamous dollar-linked peso securities first issued at the end of 1991.

At the end of December 1995, the stock amount, not the flow, of these investments in Mexican government securities and private financial money market instruments was $3.8 billion. In December 1996, the amount was $3.9 billion, essentially the same number. And by the end of the first week of October of this year, it was $4.3 billion. So over the course of almost two years the increase has been a mere $500 million, or nothing. The figure has stayed basically the same.

The ups and downs of this concept over the twenty-three-month span, as well as its change from the beginning to the end of this period, were minimal.

This behavior is remarkable given the large influx of other categories of foreign resident capital into Mexico over the same period: during the past two years, the country has been the second largest recipient of foreign direct investment in the world, second only to China. It has also received large amounts channeled toward equity purchases, as well as a resumption of foreign bank loans and the floating of private liabilities in international money markets. In 1997, these flows will have contributed to financing a current account deficit of about $7 billion, plus an increase in international reserves in excess of $10 billion.

That is a flow of $17+ billion for this year, and yet the increase in short-term money entering Mexico was insignificant. Not only has the amount of foreign money channeled to Mexican monetary instruments remained stationary over this period, but its term to maturity is considerably longer than the forty-eight-hour investments that flowed in large quantities prior to the 1995 crisis. The instruments now being purchased by foreign residents tend to have a maturity of at least three months, with six months to one year being the favorites.

The shift in the exchange rate regime between the precrisis and postcrisis periods may explain the radical change in the nature of foreign capital flows into Mexico. The current lack of volatile capital flows may, in turn, hold the key to understanding the remarkable stability of the exchange rate over this recent period, as well as the perilous situation into which the Mexican economy fell before 1995. The fixed, or quasi-fixed, exchange rate that prevailed at the time, without the automatic self-adjusting processes of a currency board, generated diverse pathological market behaviors.

First, when the exchange rate veered toward the floor of its initially narrow peso-dollar band, it attracted large volumes of short-term capital inflows, because as long as the exchange rate stuck to its floor, investors would continue to obtain the high yields that had attracted them in the first place. But investors knew that the higher yields were possibly transitory under such circumstances, because the availability of hard currency, despite the implicit promise of convertibility, had as a limit some percentage of the international reserves of the central bank. The interest rate required to bring capital in, given those uncertainties, had therefore to contain some premium, and the term for which money market investors were willing to commit their capital had to be extremely short, allowing them to keep one foot inside and the other outside, so to speak.

Second, the other extreme possibility was for the exchange rate to be at its peso-dollar ceiling, sustainable as long as the central bank had sufficient international reserves. But when the exchange rate drifted toward the top of the peso-dollar band, the incentive for investors was to try to be the first out of the local currency, in a situation so desperate that virtually no interest rate could be high enough to encourage them to stay.

An exchange rate system with bands, therefore, appears likely to generate two polar possibilities. One is to attract vast foreign inflows invested in extremely short-term instruments; the other, to have investors trying to fly away as quickly as possible.

But this is old stuff, of course. That exchange rates tend to veer off to their allowable extremes, and that, once there, the system has all the flaws and dangers of a fixed exchange rate, was pointed out several decades ago by Harry Johnson. Otherwise, if the exchange rate does not stick to either of its extremes, the system behaves as a floating exchange rate. So why contaminate it with bands? Unfortunately, it seems necessary to continue rebottling old wines for the consumption of some economists, as well as for policymakers.

A careful empirical study performed by Trigueros provides some interesting statistical results along this line of reasoning. He concluded that foreign direct investment, portfolio investment, and foreign currency deposits issued by commercial banks, as well as the direct credit they obtained, exhibited remarkable stability in Mexico after the onset of the crisis. The opposite is true of foreign exchange inflows to the Mexican money market prior to the crisis, when in the period from 1990 to September 1994 $40 billion in short-term capital poured into Mexico.

The immediate postcrisis period, that is to say 1995, is atypical, because during that year the Mexican government decided to stop issuing Tesobonos and to liquidate those outstanding. The behavior of short-term capital from December 1995 up to the present has already been detailed above.

Another question related to the interplay between economic crisis and international capital flows is whether the latter are the outcome of capricious movements of fickle investors whose behavior has to be molded through multiple equilibria, which have multiple trajectories and multiple landing strips, or whether the flows respond rather to fundamental causes within the economies that become subject to attack.

Historical evidence recently presented by Michael Bordo and Anna Schwartz, and the contemporaneous experiences of some Asian countries, together with the roots of the Mexican crisis, point to a rational, if sometimes belated, response on the part of investors. The Mexican crisis and the recent problems in Thailand, Malaysia, and Indonesia bear some striking similarities.

Credit growth in the private sector was astronomical in Mexico prior to the crisis, 25 percent per year in real terms for six years. The quality of the expenditures financed was poor or nonexistent in large part, even before the situation was aggravated by the blows inflicted on borrowers, as interest rates rose and the exchange rate depreciated after December 1994. The capitalization of some banks was thin or completely transparent. The quality of the human capital of banks had eroded considerably because of the years spent under government ownership. The liberalization of the banking system, which, among other changes, freed banks from the obligation to finance some sectors, liberated interest rates and eliminated reserve requirements. All these changes combined with suddenly copious resources to induce an increase in aggregate demand that would widen quickly and excessively the deficit in the current account of the balance of payments.

We know now that the Asian countries that collapsed also experienced vast credit expansions of dubious quality. The similarities between the Mexican and Thai crises, and others, include as well an astronomical increase in real estate prices. Real estate prices in Mexico City rose 17.6-fold between December 1987 and December 1994, while the consumer price index over the same time span rose 3.6-fold; and an excessive expansion of mortgage credit into housing and office building booms artificially supported the asset price bubble. More fundamentally, because of their exchange rate systems, both countries attracted fatal amounts of short-term money. The similarities end there, however, because the export growth of some of the Asian countries had petered out by the time of their crises, while Mexico's nonoil exports were growing in 1994 at a pace of 20 percent, over an already very high base.

Contrary to some widely held perceptions, information concerning the behavior of the Mexican economy was available to anyone who wanted to see it. Data on the balance of payments, the nature, size, and volatility of capital flows, the size and speed of the expansion of credit, and the growth of the non-performing portfolio of the banks were there for anyone to see, with a timeliness and quality equaled even then by few countries.

As we realize the nature of Mexico's and of other recent crises, a fundamental question arises: What should economists watch?

Another issue is the appropriate exchange rate regime. Some may opt for what I believe are the increasingly futile bands, others for flexible exchange rates. Experience suggests that the answer may be found at either of two extremes: either no autonomous issuing of currency at all—with the currency board as an approximation of this solution—or a flexible exchange rate. However, it is important to set out the conditions for a well-functioning flexible exchange rate. It is not sufficient to simply let it loose. Among other ingredients, coverage mechanisms are essential, but especially in immediate postcrisis periods. Institutions that allow for cover may not be sufficient, however. Investors have to be assured of the delivery of hard currency at the end of the leg of a transaction. The importance of this ingredient was evident at the outset of the Mexican crisis. Despite the existence of a deep market in forward contracts, the foreign exchange market did not contribute to the stabilization of the peso and of local interest rates until delivery became guaranteed with the appearance of futures transactions on the Chicago Merchantile Exchange.

Having expanded on the pros and cons of alternative exchange rate regimes and other implications for the attraction of particular capital flows, I should pay tribute to the obvious. Recent currency stability in Mexico may have been aided by the different elements detailed in this paper, but it would not have been possible without the deep adjustment made in the government budget, without wage revisions that have not outstripped gains in productivity, or without political stability.

I would like to end by quoting a remark James Meigs made at this week's

CATO conference: "The only way to avoid an accident when your ship is heading windward onto a reef in the middle of a storm, is not to get into such a situation in the first place."

Let me add something to what I said before, and that is about the Fed tightening in 1994.[1] I most certainly agree that the Fed tightening in the early 1980s is an important part of the explanation of economic behavior at the time. Rates went up dramatically. It had a big impact on the U.S. economy. It had a big impact on export prices from Latin America. But did the 1994 change really matter that much to Mexico, or did the political shocks of that year trigger the crisis, together with the fact that Mexico's current account was getting so far out of line? How important are those, in retrospect, relatively small movements of U.S. interest rates in 1994 as a driver of what happened to the peso-dollar exchange rate?

Edwards's comments on the movements in the yield of the thirty-year bond are on target. Such movements are often premonitory of tightening by the Fed, as is the expectation of tightening by the Fed. Now that we are floating, these effects take about fifteen minutes to take hold—they are like an electric charge to the market. The moment we have the price of a thirty-year Treasury bond falling, right away we have our exchange rate depreciating and our interest rates rising, and vice versa when the price rises. I don't know if anyone has found a correlation between these hourly movements, but it doesn't really matter. We feel it every day by the hour.

But in 1994, Edwards is quite right, these effects took somewhat longer. Maybe it was because, as Fraga was saying, there was a lot of confidence in the economic team. Whatever the reason, it took somewhat longer, and I think it was the political events that had the first impact, although sooner or later rising interest rates also had an effect on the flows out of Mexico.

Peter Garber asked about the capitalization, the price paid for the banks and how that impinged on their performance. There were three kinds of banks, or three groups or tiers of purchasers of banks. One tier immediately started figuring out how to conduct fraudulent operations with their banks. It isn't a question of bad loans; it's a question of black holes in their accounts, money that hasn't been found. You can go up to several billion dollars when you're looking at those operations. So it wasn't an isolated case of maybe a loan or a sour operation. Some of these small and medium-sized banks, which were in the hands of people who are now being prosecuted or who are abroad facing extradition by the Mexican government, lost funds that were simply channeled to their owners' private uses.

The next tier raised the money needed to bid for the banks by convincing many people that they would enjoy large capital gains and telling them that as soon as they had control of the bank, investors would obtain loans to pay for

---

1. The remainder of this comment addresses points raised during the discussion.

the shares they were committing to buy. So in those cases it wasn't a problem of having paid too much for the banks, but often of having paid too little or nothing, because once you consolidated the assets with the liabilities there was no capital left in some cases.

Third is the tier where the two big banks are situated, as well as some others, some very small ones actually. In this tier you find that real capital was put in, and there were no fraudulent schemes; but even in these cases there was some poor lending, although most of this bad lending took place before the banks were privatized.

The reason is that before the liberalization of the financial system came a reduction in government debt. Internal government debt went down from 20 percent of GDP to 5 percent of GDP over a couple of years. Five percent is still a large amount, as Fraga says, because 5 percent of GDP is a lot of money. Nevertheless, the internal debt of the government fell by 75 percent as the proceeds of the privatization of all kinds of firms, as well as some government surpluses, went to pay off that debt. That created a huge amount of leeway for banks to lend, and that activity was already happening when the banks were still in the government sector. The successful renegotiation of the government's external debt was concluded before the banks were privatized, and this fact alone allowed the banks to obtain substantial amounts of foreign resources. So credit started to increase very quickly at that time, and bad loans were being generated even then.

The other question that Garber raises goes beyond the numbers I presented, because I state that the amounts invested by foreigners in money market instruments have not changed much, but he says that the system can be shorted in several other ways, and that maybe such movements are not reflected in those statistics. And he is quite right. I don't think anybody knows. The amounts that investors can move around by using derivatives are much larger than the amounts I mentioned, although presumably there have not been very wide swings, given the stability of the exchange rate over recent years. I did not want to downplay this factor but rather to emphasize the useful information that is available. Moreover, regardless of information not available, I think you should worry if you see a bank whose portfolio is increasing by leaps and bounds, and more so when you see a whole system behaving that way. That's a rule of thumb for anybody analyzing a banking system, or an individual bank. And that's what was happening. We provided that information every month, with a three-month lag, which is a very short lag for information about a whole banking system.

We had, of course, current account data. And while, just as Paul Krugman suggested, I wouldn't worry too much about the current account per se, I would perhaps about the relationship between the current account deficit as a proportion to GDP and the growth of GDP—the sustainability issue raised by Edwards—because it is not so much the current account, but how much debt you are incurring. If your current account is small enough in relation to your growth, then, if that money has been well invested, you are not necessarily getting into a more precarious situation. But in the case of Mexico, the ratio of the current account to GDP was growing much faster than GDP. And also the structure of its financing, because of many factors that combined to produce that structure, was so short term and so volatile that eventually we got into problems.

Now I would like to say something about international reserves, because even though Agustín Carstens and I wrote and published a paper about them, I think we haven't got the point across. The number that was provided for the amount of international reserves of the central bank, which was already quite low, was released in November 1994 at the bankers' convention, and it was widely published and widely known. So we were not hiding anything. Maybe nobody wants to acknowledge it today, but we certainly did release that number, and it was accurate. Now we publish it every week and nobody follows it any more.

Andrew Crockett raised the question of optimal exchange rate strategy, and somebody else mentioned, I think it was Fraga, that the Argentine mechanism worked not because it was automatic, but because there was support. I certainly agree with that. No system can withstand a massive and persistent currency attack, a speculative attack, or can resist it without any effects on the system. I suppose that a currency board and a flexible exchange rate are ways of making things more transparent and more immediate, but there are certainly no vaccines against crisis if an attack is strong enough. What would be the optimal strategy for South America? I have very little knowledge.

Finally, related to current account information, I would like to end by commenting that some years ago Milton Friedman said that current account figures shouldn't be published. They should be abolished. So he concurs completely with Krugman's point of view.

3. Arminio Fraga

In my remarks I will take the viewpoint of a practitioner, which is what I have been for many years. First, a bit of background. I fully agree with Sebastian Edwards's view that capital flows to Latin America have been hot and cold, or up and down as he says. That has certainly been the case for a long time, as a wonderful book by Carlos Marichal (1989) clearly demonstrates.

In most crises reviewed by Marichal swings in the supply of funds played a very important if not key role. Work by Calvo, Leiderman, and Reinhart (1993) on this subject highlights and supports this view. Their research presents evidence that factors external to a country's domestic fundamentals frequently drive the flow of funds to and from the country. For instance, when monetary policy is loose in the main financial centers, the developing countries tend to have easy access to capital. Conversely, countries typically face problems following a Fed tightening, a financial crisis, a war, and so forth. Recent examples include the Fed tightening engineered by Volcker in the early 1980s followed by the debt crisis and the more recent Mexican crisis, which came on the heels of the relentless tightening of 1994.

Some vulnerability was present in the first place in all of these cases. This vulnerability is often a product of the excesses of the boom years, again in classic fashion, à la Kindleberger (1978). Some of the signs that trouble may be brewing include drastic real exchange rate appreciations, as well as complacency in the financial sector associated with loan growth that outstrips real GDP growth several times over. These and other signs are commonly associated with periods in which capital comes too easily.

Naturally each crisis has a slightly different flavor. For example, in the 1980s, in Latin America, one could argue that the crisis was driven by foreign borrowing, which was financing budget deficits. A lesson was learned: that was not a good idea. Then perhaps we could say in the 1990s that capital flows were financing consumption. Again, not a very good idea, because it doesn't generate any capacity to repay. And one could argue in the case of Asia more recently that overinvesting also ends up exposing the borrower to the risk of a crisis.

One factor, however, seems to be there every single time. This is my own undocumented experience, or somewhat documented; I have studied the crises of the 1980s and the 1930s. That factor is short-term debt. The danger signal for us investors that seems to be clear—maybe clearest of all, next to banking abuses—is the excessive accumulation of short-term debt. It usually comes toward the end of a credit cycle, again in standard Kindleberger fashion.

From a conceptual standpoint it is somewhat puzzling why the maturity profile of a country's debt is important. In a world where derivatives are available maybe it shouldn't matter that much. But it seems that it does matter.

One explanation that is consistent with a world where investors can create their own interest rate and currency risk profiles (by engaging in transactions such as swaps, forwards, futures, or options) is the fact that the production function for derivatives requires the use of balance sheets of banks and other institutions. And when the stock of short-term debt outstanding is large, financial intermediaries have no difficulty producing derivative instruments to sell short a given currency: they simply borrow the short-term instruments and sell them in the marketplace.

Take the Mexican case as an example. It was very hard to sell the peso short during the period that preceded the crisis because the Mexican authorities strongly discouraged Mexican banks from offering currency forwards. However, with the large stock of outstanding peso-denominated treasury bills (known by their Spanish acronym CETES) shorting the peso was not impossible: one could borrow Cetes and sell them short, thus effectively shorting the peso. To conclude, excessive short-term debt is risky not only because of the standard rollover risk it entails but also because it allows investors to take short positions more easily even in the presence of other restrictions. If a large stock of short-term debt had not been there, perhaps Mexico would not have been so vulnerable.

This brings me to an interesting question, and an important one. Somebody is borrowing short term, and one can come up with a lot of reasons why. Governments, for example, tend to have short horizons. They typically don't care much beyond their own administrations. But what about investors? Why do they finance these financial parties? Why do they stick around for so long? I guess one could invoke some sort of disaster myopia, in the style of what used to be the explanation for the debt crisis of the 1980s. Additionally, one can observe in the markets what could be characterized as trend-following behavior, whereby investors ride their winners. Financial flows tend to follow good performance. Derivatives also tend to generate this pattern, as we learned from the research on the portfolio insurance practices of some years back.

Another element that deserves to be highlighted in the context of this discussion is the role of governments and their policies in the process. Governments, for whatever reason, usually for political reasons, often try to defend situations that are clearly unsustainable. And when governments have a history of success and are good at telling their story, investors tend to hear it, at least for some time. This further delays the needed adjustment. The recent crisis in Thailand is a perfect example. Were it not for the spectacular successes of Thailand in the previous decade it would not have been possible to build the imbalances that eventually caused the Thai collapse in 1997.

The market patterns observed in the Mexican and Thai crises are fairly standard. The story typically begins with good fundamentals initiating a positive trend. There then follows a phase of complacency in which the trend continues despite the surfacing of economic and financial excesses. Moreover, in both these countries policies in place at a microeconomic level created incentives for a rapid build-up of foreign and domestic indebtedness. Finally, reality catches up with the markets and the trend is broken, frequently in violent fashion. Then we start over again . . .

I would now like to discuss some cases in Latin America. I'll start with Mexico—very briefly because I generally agree with the presentation by Francisco Gil Diaz. For Mexico, the break came with the devaluation of 1994–95. Before the crisis Mexico displayed a growing current account deficit and a declining rate of saving. This meant that inflows of external capital were in effect financing consumption. These inflows, in turn, were increasingly characterized by short maturities, a clear vulnerability as discussed above. As if that was not enough, Mexico was then hit by two exogenous shocks: the Fed tightening and the political events and assassinations of 1994. These were some of the key causal ingredients of the crisis.

An interesting question to me is, Why did it take so long? That brings us to the first trend, the one that went all the way to the cliff. There were a lot of reasons for the longevity of this trend, starting with the high quality of government officials in Mexico, who really did a great job up until the very end. Until 1993 the Mexican story made a lot of sense, despite the growing current account deficit. Additionally, as mentioned above, it was difficult to sell the peso short. The government of Mexico was always informally on top of the situation, trying not to allow a market for peso derivatives to develop. That may have been a case where partial liberalization worked against Mexico, because while it was easy to bring short-term capital into Mexico, it was hard to hedge it. Perhaps the absence of foreign banks in Mexico also led to what Gil Diaz described as a poorly managed banking system, after the privatization, when the banks were basically bought by brokers.

Mexico's response to the crisis and the support package it received are well known. The recovery came swiftly and brought with it a renewed sense of stability, as discussed by Gil Diaz. This stability is in large part due to the prudent management of fiscal and monetary policies, which in turn lead to the absence of short-term debt. One consequence of this successful adjustment has been a continuous appreciation of the peso in real terms. One potential risk to be monitored in this context is that if the currency appreciates all the way back to where it was before the crisis, we may see the same movie again. This is a very difficult policy issue that many governments face in a world where capital flows are prone to bouts of enthusiasm and depression. What can be done about this problem?

We have talked about capital controls and how they can perhaps be used on a temporary basis. But then what else can be done? Fiscal policy is just not an alternative. Governments don't have fiscal policy as a button they can push. It takes time; it's hard to do. The right policy response to what is known as the capital inflow problem is still a subject of debate.

Brazil is now in its third year of not having inflation. Brazil had been a monetary alcoholic for most of its history. I as a Brazilian grew up in that environment. It really feels strange to have 5 percent inflation down there, and I think it is quite an achievement. But the achievement came with a few imbalances that naturally pose some risk of future problems.

After stabilizing and implementing an impressive array of structural reforms (trade liberalization, privatization, banking reform, etc.), Brazil finds itself in a situation where inflation is low but it has to deal with twin fiscal and current account deficits. The nominal budget deficit, though declining from the heights of the high-inflation era, remained at 6 percent of GDP in 1997 (4 percent in the operational concept, i.e., in real terms), while the current account deficit has reached about 4.3 percent of GDP. Brazil has chosen a gradual approach to handling these problems that, although not free of risks, seems feasible. The budget deficit is being gradually reduced, to the tune of 1 percent of GDP a year. Further progress depends on proposed civil service and social security reforms, both of which require constitutional amendments. To address the current account deficit the exchange rate is being depreciated at a rate that will generate a real devaluation of about 5 percent a year.

The gradualist approach on the fiscal and balance-of-payments fronts is likely to succeed because it is being compensated by aggressive monetary and privatization policies. The policy of very high interest rates is possible because banking sector problems were tackled early. Also, at this point there is very little leverage in the Brazilian economy. For instance, loans to the private sector add up to less than 25 percent of GDP, compared to 150 percent of GDP or so in Thailand, Malaysia, and Korea. Brazil can therefore can afford to run a very tight monetary policy for some time, at the cost of postponing a long overdue resumption of fast and sustained economic growth.

In terms of capital flows, Brazil has moved away from short-term financing. During the first year after the Real plan, Brazil was flooded with hot money. Since then the share of short-term financing of the current account has been shrinking. Already in 1996, some 50 percent of the deficit was financed by foreign direct investment and equity portfolio flows. Equities are inherently more stable because they have an automatic stabilizing factor. If investors decide to leave, prices go down, and investors change their minds. That is not the case with short-term money, which allows for exit at close to par under all but the most extreme circumstances.

On the issue of capital controls, I tend to agree with Sebastian Edwards. Capital controls may play a useful role in the short term, particularly when employed to support and reinforce good economic policies. In the long term, however, they are distortive and ineffective. Here I draw on my brief but illuminating experience at the central bank of Brazil. We spent one and a half years there trying to reduce or rationalize an extensive set of capital controls. I left the central bank convinced that long-term capital controls had harmed Brazil more than they had helped. They gave policymakers a false sense of security and probably allowed Brazil to avoid or postpone a number of important macroeconomic policy changes and structural reforms.

References

Calvo, Guillermo A., Leonardo Leiderman, and Carmen M. Reinhart. 1993. Capital inflows and real exchange rate appreciation in Latin America. *IMF Staff Papers* 40 (March): 108–51.

Kindleberger, Charles. 1978. *Manias, panics and crashes.* New York: Basic.

Marichal, Carlos. 1989. *A century of debt crises in Latin America.* Princeton, N.J.: Princeton University Press.

Discussion Summary

Sebastian Edwards noted that capital controls may become a central topic of discussion at the upcoming Summit of the Americas because few disagreements remain on trade issues. He cited evidence that although capital controls have become permanent fixtures in many countries, including Chile, Colombia, and Brazil, they are largely ineffective. Edwards also drew attention to the centrality of sustainability in considering the current account deficits that are common in Latin America. For example, Chile's 4 percent current account deficit may be manageable given the size of incoming foreign direct investment flows and their productive potential.

David Folkerts-Landau noted that dismissing capital controls is equivalent to depriving countries of an instrument with which they can manage their external position. *Moeen Qureshi* also noted the irony that when capital flows were minimal in the 1950s and 1960s, the IMF recommended capital controls to countries. Now capital flows are orders of magnitude larger and the IMF is recommending the dismantling of capital controls.

Peter Garber suggested that this contradiction is resolved by noting that historically most countries had capital controls and so the policy recommendations of the IMF reflected this common practice. He inquired about the financing methods used in the privatization of banks in Mexico and about the role these methods may have played in the crisis. Garber also questioned the emphasis on short-term debt given the ability of derivatives to transform risks across the maturity spectrum. More generally, he emphasized the liquidity of the markets rather than the duration of the existing obligations.

Francisco Gil Diaz replied that there were three types of bank purchases. First, some banks were purchased by individuals who perpetrated fraud. In these banks, bad loans per se were not an issue because these banks simply became black holes. Second, some purchases were structured to minimize capital infusions leaving them highly vulnerable to losses. Third, for the two largest banks and other smaller ones, the purchases involved real capital infusion and did not involve fraud. In these cases, very poor lending decisions made them vulnerable to failure.

Folkerts-Landau noted that both Gil Diaz and Fraga minimized the role of information dissemination while the IMF had emphasized this issue in the months following the crisis. He concurred with the speakers that aggregate data were available but questioned whether detailed data allowing investors to understand the financial exposure of the system were available in a timely fashion in the cases of Mexico and Thailand. *Martin Feldstein* also questioned Fraga about the information advantages that might lead certain speculators to behave more aggressively in foreign exchange markets.

Gil Diaz suggested that the relevant information on the banking system and reserve position in Mexico was available but went unheeded. While *Arminio Fraga* agreed with the general emphasis of the IMF on improved information disclosure, he concurred with Gil Diaz that the Mexican situation was one where enough information was available either through public disclosure or through informal channels.

Paul Krugman noted that the emphasis on certain statistics, such as current account deficits, leads to inappropriate conclusions without consideration of the investment opportunities within a country. He recalled a quote from James Callahan, a former chancellor of the exchequer for the United Kingdom, who suggested that the absence of statistics had allowed the British to emerge from previous crises unscathed. *Feldstein* countered that presumably a country runs out of reserves at some point. *Krugman* replied that, nonetheless, the emphasis on statistics may obscure underlying subtleties to an economic situation.

David Mullins noted that all central bankers would appreciate this call for opaqueness. *Qureshi* supported Krugman's point that certain types of information are being emphasized at the expense of a subtler understanding of the larger economic situation. He referred to the recent emphasis on the strength of the financial sector, for example, and questioned how fundamental this is to a country's prospects. *Gil Diaz* recalled that Milton Friedman had suggested that current account figures not be published. *Krugman* responded to this comparison by retracting his initial suggestion.

Andrew Crockett suggested that currency boards or flexible exchange rates provide for more stability than fixed exchange rates. He emphasized, however, that linkages created by common trade areas, such as Mercosur, could create spillovers when exchange rate regimes are distinct. Thus, the question of the optimal strategy within trade zones that feature distinct exchange rate regimes is extremely important. *Feldstein* noted that these problems are common to all countries pursuing stable relations with their trading partners. *Gil Diaz* agreed that flexible exchange rates, while superior to fixed regimes, are no vaccine against crisis and that no system can resist a speculative attack given the linkages in the world economy through trade and capital flows.

In contrast to Fraga's conclusions about Brazil, *Edwards* expressed concern about its short-term debt position. He suggested that massive increases in reserves would be needed over the next several years for Brazil to emerge unscathed. *Mullins* noted that if privatization proceeds are required for Brazil to emerge from its current predicament, its prospects are tightly linked to the future of the U.S. equity market. Finally, *Garber* noted that in the Brazilian case, some foreign direct investment was used to disguise short-term inflows as firms circumvented capital controls by buying small firms and purchasing commercial paper.

Fraga agreed that there exists little room for error in Brazil's situation. However, he suggested that the gradual process of annual 5 percent real devaluation now under way could prove successful. He also noted that much of the remaining short-term debt is domestic and that much of the short-term foreign money has already left Brazil. Fraga was therefore cautiously optimistic about

Brazil's prospects for emerging from its current difficulties without a severe discontinuity.

Edwards suggested that political events were more central to the Mexican crisis than were Federal Reserve actions. Fed tightening began in February 1994, suggesting large and unreasonable lags for it to have played a large role in the crisis. Similarly, *Mullins* noted, the recent Asian crisis featured a very benign backdrop of low interest rates and a booming stock market. In a similar vein, *Feldstein* noted that while steep increases in U.S. interest rates in the early 1980s may have had an important effect around the world, he disagreed that the gradual tightening of 1994 could have had such a dramatic effect. Instead, he highlighted the political events and the current account situation for the Mexican crisis.

Gil Diaz suggested that large changes in the long end of the term structure in the United States were premonitory of tightening and that these effects were felt immediately in Mexico. More generally, he agreed that political factors were most important and interest rate changes were secondary.

2 Capital Flows to Eastern Europe

*1. Hans Peter Lankes and
Nicholas Stern
2. W. Michael Blumenthal
3. Jiří Weigl*

1. Hans Peter Lankes and Nicholas Stern

Capital Flows to Eastern Europe
and the Former Soviet Union

2.1.1 Introduction

Net capital flows to eastern Europe and the former Soviet Union built up
rapidly during the 1980s, reaching around US$5 billion per annum in the sec-
ond half of the decade. This was largely in the form of commercial bank loans
and trade finance to state-owned foreign trade banks subject to sovereign guarantees. The dramatic changes of the early transition period saw a large rise in
the share of Western official lending, while private capital was initially hesi-
tant. Most of the old loans have, indeed, been subject to default. Now, seven or
eight years into the transition, capital flows have increased sharply and new
flows are predominantly to (and from) private entities.

The Berlin Wall fell in the autumn of 1989 and the countries of central Europe embarked very quickly on programs of liberalization, privatization, and
institutional change. Serious attempts at market reform did not take place in
the former Soviet Union until after its breakup in the autumn of 1991. Capital
flows started to pick up with a two- or three-year delay and were directed to

The authors are grateful for the assistance of Avyi Sarris. Kasper Bartholdy, Steven Fries, Joel
Hellman, and Ricardo Lago provided helpful comments.

those countries that were clearly more successful in their market reforms and at macroeconomic stabilization.[1] Flows to the western parts of the former communist region, indeed to the region itself, have been dominated by those to the Czech Republic, Hungary, and Poland. However, in the past year or two, capital flows to Russia have picked up sharply. For 1997 it is likely that foreign direct investment (FDI) in the region will be around US$15 to $18 billion, with other net private flows around twice that level.

The buildup of FDI has been fairly steady as investor confidence has grown and prospects have become clearer. There have, however, been very strong surges coinciding with major privatizations of infrastructure, for example, in Hungary in 1995. The most recent surge in FDI has been in Poland and Russia. The movement of portfolio investments into the region as a whole has been rather less steady, with very strong acceleration in the past one to two years, as the perception of risk has adjusted sharply.

In this paper, we examine some of the determinants and consequences of capital flows to the region. We conclude that FDI is driven primarily by progress in transition and macroeconomic stability. It is these factors that allow the huge potential of the region to be unlocked. That potential is itself based on strong endowments of human capital and natural resources together with advantageous geographical position. FDI was initially oriented to establishing positions in domestic markets, but as reforms advance, countries attract more FDI and the type of FDI they attract is more integrated into international production networks. Because portfolio flows have grown only very recently, there is less firm analysis of their determinants. They would, no doubt, be influenced by underlying factors similar to those affecting FDI. However, in the case of FDI commitments have responded gradually to the changing circumstances, whereas the recent past has seen some very dramatic changes in perceptions driving portfolio flows. Indeed, movements in the underlying process appear steadier than those in perceptions. It therefore seems unlikely that the recent acceleration in portfolio investment will be maintained, as the adjustment in perceived risk and the rearrangement of portfolios it entailed should probably be seen as a one-off event.

The impact of capital flows to the region is of fundamental importance to the economic transition. These flows bring new methods of business organization, new technologies, and powerful influences on the building of financial, regulatory, and other institutions. They help establish the financial discipline that is crucial to the effective functioning of a market economy. Thus their impact goes far beyond the simple availability of resources.

The structure of the remainder of the paper is as follows. In section 2.1.2 we

---

1. They were, however, slowed in countries such as Poland, where there were worries about earlier problems of large indebtedness (Poland's gross external debt was almost 80 percent of GDP in 1990). This did not apply to the Czech Republic, where inherited debts were small, or to Hungary, where the perceived probability of default was low (and indeed Hungary has been the only country with heavy debts that has not defaulted).

describe capital flows as they have developed over the past two decades. In section 2.1.3 we look more closely at some of the patterns involved and consider the key determinants of FDI, commercial bank lending, and portfolio flows. In section 2.1.4 we comment briefly on some consequences for the host economies, and in section 2.1.5 we consider prospects and policy questions facing host governments and international financial institutions. Table 2.1 provides summary statistics on the twenty-six countries of the region, which has a population of 400 million people and a combined GDP of around US$1,000 billion.

2.1.2   Capital Flows before and after 1989

Pretransition Period

The central planners were no strangers to international capital markets. Since the late 1970s, various governments developed active borrowing programs. These may be seen as part of efforts to sustain consumption in the face of ever-increasing investment targets as the productivity of capital continued its decades-long decline. The USSR, Poland, Yugoslavia, Hungary, and later Bulgaria approached the syndicated loan market, generally through their foreign trade banks, and expanded the use of export credit and short-term trade finance.[2] East Germany relied more on its ability to extract bilateral credits from the Federal Republic. Equity finance was foreign to socialism, and the decentralized nature of bond finance was not in favor with the powers that were. The sovereign risk of these economies was well regarded, as evidenced by their ability to raise rapidly their levels of indebtedness, although Yugoslavia and Poland underwent a series of debt restructurings as early as the late 1970s and early 1980s, respectively. Net medium- to long-term capital flows to the region averaged US$1.2 billion per year in 1976–80, $1.8 billion in 1981–85, and $5 billion in 1986–90 (table 2.2). The USSR continued to have access to large-scale commercial bank lending until its breakup in 1991. Except for Czechoslovakia and Romania, these countries entered the transition process with heavy debt burdens on which—apart from Hungary—they eventually defaulted.[3]

Economic Performance and Risk

The transition process changed radically both the volume and the composition of external capital flows. Capital flows from 1989 to 1993 were shaped by the determination of Western governments to support and protect the profound political and economic changes that were taking place. Private sources of funds, however, understandably took a wait-and-see approach. Country and

2. *Forfeiting*—a way of securitizing trade credit—developed into an art in Comecon trade finance, perhaps more so than in any other part of the world.
3. The problem of East German debt "resolved" itself with unification.

Table 2.1   Economic and Structural Indicators in Eastern Europe, the Baltics, and the Commonwealth of Independent States

Country	Population, 1996 Estimate (million)	Real GDP, 1997 Projection[a] 1989 = 100	Real GDP, 1997 Projection[a] % Change	Consumer Prices (year-end), 1997 Projection (% change)	FDI (net), 1996 Estimate Million US$	FDI (net), 1996 Estimate US$ per Capita	External Debt, 1996 Estimate (% of GDP)	Preferred Creditor Debt, 1996 Estimate (% of total)	Country Risk as of September 1997 (S&P's/Moody's)	Average Transition Indicator 1997	Average Transition Indicator 1994
Albania	3.3	73	−15.0	42	90	28	29	35	n.a.	2.6	2.5
Armenia	3.7	39	5.8	19	22	6	39	54	n.a.	2.5	1.8
Azerbaijan	7.6	41	5.2	7	661	72	16	26	n.a.	2.0	1.3
Belarus	10.3	66	3.0	99	75	7	7	57	n.a.	1.6	1.7
Bosnia-Herzegovina[b]	4.2	n.a.	35.0	0	n.a.	n.a.	n.a.	n.a.	n.a.	n.a.	n.a.
Bulgaria	8.4	63	−7.0	592	100	12	111	18	n.a./B3	2.8	2.5
Croatia	4.8	74	5.0	4	349	73	25	14	BBB−/Baa3	3.0	3.2
Czech Republic	10.3	97	1.0	9	1,264	123	38	3	A/Baa1	3.5	3.5
Estonia	1.5	76	7.0	12	110	71	8	59	n.a./Baa1	3.4	3.3
FYR Macedonia	2.1	56	2.0	8	39	20	32	50	n.a.	2.6	2.8
Georgia	5.4	34	10.5	9	25	5	30	26	n.a.	2.7	1.3
Hungary	10.2	89	3.0	17	1,986	196	62	8	BBB−/Baa3	3.7	3.3
Kazakhstan	16.3	58	2.0	17	1,100	67	19	31	BB−/Ba3	2.7	1.7
Kyrgyzstan	4.5	60	6.0	24	31	7	43	50	n.a.	2.8	2.8
Latvia	2.5	54	3.4	8	230	92	9	55	BBB/n.a.	3.2	2.8
Lithuania	3.7	44	4.5	10	152	41	12	47	BBB−/Ba2	3.1	3.0
Moldova	4.3	34	−2.0	11	56	13	43	55	n.a./Ba2	2.6	2.2
Poland	38.6	110	5.5	15	2,741	71	30	6	BBB−/Baa3	3.4	3.3
Romania	22.6	86	−1.5	116	210	9	21	26	BB−/Ba3	2.7	2.7
Russia	147.5	57	1.0	14	2,040	9	28	14	BB−/Ba2	3.0	2.7
Slovak Republic	5.3	94	4.5	7	177	33	41	9	BBB−/Baa3	3.3	3.3
Slovenia	2.0	99	4.0	9	180	90	22	8	A/A3	3.2	3.2
Tajikistan	5.8	36	−3.0	110	13	2	93	10	n.a.	1.6	1.7
Turkmenistan	4.6	51	−15.0	44	129	28	26	n.a.	n.a.	1.5	1.2
Ukraine	51.2	37	−3.0	15	500	10	21	36	n.a.	2.4	1.3
Uzbekistan	23.0	86	1.0	40	50	2	17	27	n.a.	2.2	2.0

Source: EBRD.

Note: Data for 1990–96 represent the most recent official estimates of outturns as reflected in publications from the national authorities, the IMF, the World Bank, the OECD, PlanEcon, and the Institute of International Finance. Data for 1996 are preliminary actuals, mostly official government estimates. Data for 1997 represent EBRD projections.

[a]Based on official estimates. Unofficial economic activity has been estimated to account for between 20 percent (eastern Europe) and 45 percent (CIS) of "true GDP," and relative prices have changed radically between 1989 and 1997. These indexes should therefore be interpreted with caution, with relative values across countries probably more reliable than levels.

Table 2.2 Net Capital Flows to Eastern Europe and the Former Soviet Union (millions of U.S. dollars)

	Annual Average			1989	1990	1991	1992	1993	1994	1995	1996	1997 Projection
	1976–80	1981–85	1986–90									
Total flows	1,179	1,805	4,871	4,032	3,396	14,464	24,874	23,520	17,463	32,921	40,976	60,076
Private flows	862	973	3,935	2,866	−8,355	−6,409	6,213	13,947	13,620	28,427	33,653	51,997
Equity investment	15	18	152	458	571	2,464	3,996	5,449	5,537	14,010	12,315	18,400
Direct equity investment	15	18	122	187	431	2,143	3,657	4,126	4,065	11,647	7,756	12,000
Portfolio equity investment	0	0	30	271	140	321	339	1,323	1,472	2,363	4,559	6,400
Commercial banks	694	680	76	908	−15,089	−8,226	996	2,450	2,576	8,845	10,337	6,790
Other private creditors	153	275	3,707	1,500	6,163	−647	1,221	6,048	5,507	5,572	11,001	26,808
Official flows	317	831	936	1,166	11,751	20,873	18,661	9,573	3,843	4,494	7,323	8,079
International financial institutions	204	625	−126	−1,143	1,112	5,729	3,607	3,101	2,940	3,414	3,523	6,368
Official bilateral creditors	113	206	1,062	2,309	10,639	15,144	15,054	6,472	902	1,080	3,800	1,711

Sources: Institute of International Finance, except direct equity investment from EBRD; portfolio equity calculated as residual.

Note: Data cover Bulgaria, the Czech Republic, Hungary, Poland, Romania, and the Slovak Republic.

commercial risk was, and was perceived to be, extremely high. The extreme dislocation meant that the macroeconomic position was very weak. When economic performance improved and the transition progressed, private capital began to enter the market, first timidly, then with great speed. Before discussing the evidence on capital flows it is important to have a picture of the economic circumstances in the early transition years. These varied substantially across countries with strong implications for risk and performance.

In the early years of transition, beginning around 1989–90 in eastern Europe and 1992 in the former Soviet Union,[4] central economic coordination (such as it was) was lost, with markets only gradually taking its place. Macroeconomic conditions were highly unsettled, relative prices adjusted sharply, and political uncertainty was severe, particularly in the former Soviet Union and Yugoslavia. Output contracted until 1993–94 in eastern Europe and the Baltics and until 1997 in the Commonwealth of Independent States (CIS),[5] for cumulative declines of 20 and 44 percent, respectively.[6] In 1992, only six economies in the region, out of twenty-six, recorded inflation of less than 100 percent. Macroeconomic conditions, in terms of inflation, improved rapidly in eastern Europe after 1993, and in the CIS from about 1995. In 1997 economic growth is returning to the region as a whole. Only seven countries are experiencing economic decline—largely those where structural reforms have been lagging—and eleven are experiencing GDP growth in excess of 4 percent. In only three countries is inflation expected to be at triple-digit levels in 1997. The turn-around in growth is primarily due to the end of economic contraction in Russia, the region's largest economy, which is expected to show small but positive growth this year. Performance has not improved consistently across the region. Some major setbacks, for example, recently in Albania, Bulgaria, and Romania, demonstrate the fragile nature of the recovery. Nevertheless, with a combined GDP of around US$1,000 billion—one-sixth of aggregate developing country GDP, or 3 percent of the world economy—the region is rapidly establishing itself as a major "emerging" market.[7]

After some degree of uniformity in the very early transition, individual

4. The initiation of price and trade liberalization is taken here as indicating the "starting point" of the transition.

5. Eastern Europe includes the twenty-six countries in table 2.1 less those of the former Soviet Union. The CIS includes the former Soviet Union less the Baltic countries (Estonia, Latvia, and Lithuania).

6. This calculation is based on official statistics and covers the period of contraction (1989–93 in eastern Europe and the Baltics and 1989–97 in the CIS). There are, of course, serious measurement issues in terms of earlier rationing, quality change, changes in reporting incentives, changes in official procedures, etc. Informal, mostly private, economic activity was estimated to account for about 20 percent of actual GDP in eastern Europe and more than 40 percent in the CIS (excluding central Asia) in 1995 and is only partly reflected in adjustments to official GDP data; see EBRD (1997, chap. 4).

7. It has around 7 percent of the world's population, and thus GDP per capita a little under half the world average. The countries are all middle income according to the World Bank classification, except for Albania, Armenia, Azerbaijan, Georgia, Kyrgyzstan, Bosnia-Herzegovina, and Tajikistan, which are low income (less than US$755 per capita in 1995).

countries quickly began to differ across the various dimensions of reform. So too did risk perceptions. Most countries moved rapidly to liberalize prices and markets. Progress on privatization was more uneven, but it is now fairly advanced in a majority of countries. In much of the region governments are now engaged in a "second phase" of direct sales of banks, infrastructure, and "strategic" companies, after an emphasis on speed in the "mass privatizations" of the first phase. A few transition economies now have private sector shares in GDP that are similar to many developed market economies. The greatest differences among countries are in the more qualitative aspects of transition, the building of sound financial and other market-supporting institutions, and the restructuring and governance of enterprises. Central European reformers are making some progress on these dimensions. But they still have far to go, and further east and south progress remains limited.

Investment and lending risk are closely associated with progress in transition. Figure 2.1 displays the results of a European Bank for Reconstruction and Development (EBRD) survey among actual and potential investors in the region, conducted in 1995 (for details, see appendix B). Note that, among five sources of risk presented to investors in the survey, regulatory and macroeconomic risks were judged to be most significant (by far) whatever the perceived risk level. It is evident from the figure that there is a close (negative) association between progress in transition and perceived country risk: there is a rank correlation coefficient of $-.89$ for the host countries included in the survey (see also table 2.1 for recent credit ratings).

Capital Flows and the Transition

Reflecting Western official support for the transition as well as the developments discussed above, capital flows to the region have followed a distinct sequence, with official funding, FDI, commercial lending not guaranteed in the countries of origin, dedicated equity funds, and finally direct local stock and money market investments entering successively at one- to two-year intervals (table 2.2 and figs. 2.2 and 2.3).[8] In important respects this may be seen as a "telescoped" version of the recent history of capital flows elsewhere, compressed into a much shorter period of time. It must be kept in mind, however, that there are serious data problems with measures of capital flows in the transition economies. Commercial bank syndicated lending and bond issues tend to be reasonably well covered by the Euromoney databases (Bondware and Loanware), but measures of FDI and, in particular, of portfolio equity and money market investments can differ enormously. For aggregate flows we rely here on information on a subset of countries compiled by the Institute of International Finance, but we supplement this with FDI estimates prepared from

---

8. Note that this sequence refers to increases in net exposure; gross flows of bank lending not guaranteed in the country of origin, largely to refinance existing official debt, were present throughout the early transition phase.

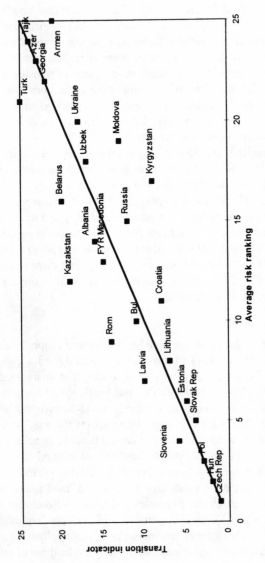

Fig. 2.1 EBRD transition indicators (1995) versus perceived country risk

Note: Countries are ranked by perceived country risk (*horizontal axis*) and level of transition (*vertical axis*). Interviewees were asked to assign the countries that they felt confident assessing to one of four risk groups ranging from 1 (low risk, comparable to risk in OECD countries) to 4 (unacceptably high risk). The data reported here represent the average of ratings. The measure of progress in transition is taken from the EBRD's annual *Transition Report*, with 1995 results used here for consistency with the risk assessments. The rankings are based on simple averages of scores—ranging from 1 (little progress) to 4 (advanced transition)—on the EBRD's eight transition indicators for 1995: extent of privatization (two indicators), extent of enterprise restructuring, scope and openness of markets (two indicators), progress in financial sector reform (two indicators), and progress in the creation of legal and institutional frameworks supporting private sector activity.

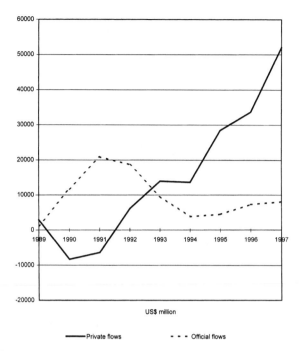

Fig. 2.2   Eastern Europe and former Soviet Union: net private and official capital flows, 1989–97 (millions of U.S. dollars)
Source: Institute of International Finance.
Note: Data cover Bulgaria, the Czech Republic, Hungary, Poland, Romania, Russia, and the Slovak Republic. The figure for 1997 is a projection.

balances of payments (mostly drawn from the International Monetary Fund—IMF) and EBRD information on equity funds.

Beginning in 1989–90, official funding, and funding guaranteed by Western export credit agencies (ECAs), increased sharply, while private sources of funds were largely absent from the region. A large share of the official capital flows were on account of German transfers to the former Soviet Union as part of the German unification agreement (e.g., housing for repatriated USSR soldiers), but substantial official support was forthcoming from a range of bilateral and multilateral sources (e.g., international financial institution contributions to the stabilization fund for Poland in 1991).[9] Net official flows to the seven largest recipient countries covered by table 2.2 peaked in 1991 at US$21 billion.[10] After 1993, they declined both as a share of the total and in absolute terms. Private flows to these countries began to exceed net official flows in 1993 and

9. In addition, Paris Club reschedulings were granted to Poland (1991, concessional terms), Bulgaria (1991, 1992, 1994), and Russia (1993, 1994, 1995, 1996).
10. Bulgaria, the Czech Republic, Hungary, Poland, Romania, Russia, and the Slovak Republic. Data from the Institute of International Finance.

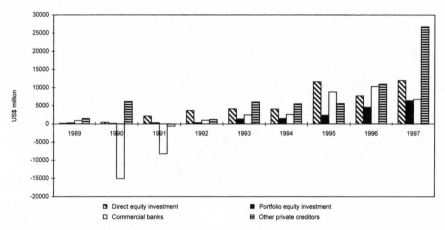

Fig. 2.3   Eastern Europe and former Soviet Union: composition of private capital flows, 1989–97
Source: Institute of International Finance.
Note: Data cover Bulgaria, the Czech Republic, Hungary, Poland, Romania, Russia, and the Slovak Republic. The figure for 1997 is a projection.

by 1996 accounted for $34 billion out of $41 billion in total net capital flows (excluding net resident lending abroad). This represented 14 percent of aggregate net private flows to developing countries.[11] In 1997, net private flows are projected to rise to $52 billion, or more than 5 percent of the GDP of the region. After a relatively minor presence as a destination in earlier years, Russia has, since 1996 and especially in 1997, increasingly dominated private flows of all types and may at present account for more than half of all flows. While foreigners have invested in Russia, however, Russians have increasingly transferred funds abroad, an estimated total of $29 billion in 1996. The main channels have been the nonrepatriation of export proceeds (accounting for perhaps $18 billion) and currency purchases by the population (IMF 1997).

The following provides a brief description of developments in different categories of private capital flows.

Foreign Direct Investment

The entry of private nonguaranteed capital was led by FDI (table 2.3). Hungary was the first country to receive significant FDI flows in 1991, mostly in the form of acquisitions under the Hungarian privatization program, and to a lesser extent Czechoslovakia (whose primary method of privatization was through vouchers). Poland, Russia, and Kazakhstan, and some smaller countries (Estonia and Slovenia) began to attract FDI over the period 1992–94. In 1995–96, FDI flows surged and began to cover a broader range of countries. In those two years (cumulatively), FDI in the transition economies accounted

11. With the transition economies included in the total for developing countries.

Table 2.3   **Foreign Direct Investment (inflows recorded in the balance of payments)**

	Total (million US$)									Per Capita (US$)		
	1989	1990	1991	1992	1993	1994	1995	1996 Revised	Cumulative FDI Inflows, 1989–96	Cumulative FDI Inflows, 1989–96	FDI Inflows, 1996	FDI Inflows as a Percentage of GDP, 1996
Albania	—	—	8	32	45	53	70	90	298	93	28	3
Bulgaria	—	—	56	42	40	105	82	100	425	51	12	1
Croatia	—	—	—	13	74	98	81	349	615	129	73	2
Czech Republic	—	120	511	983	498	1,024	2,720	1,264	7,120	692	123	2
Estonia	—	—	—	58	156	212	199	110	735	477	71	3
Hungary	187	311	1,459	1,471	2,339	1,097	4,410	1,986	13,260	1,300	195	4
Latvia	—	—	—	43	51	155	165	230	644	258	92	5
Lithuania[a]	—	—	—	—	30	31	72	152	285	76	41	2
FYR Macedonia	—	—	—	—	—	24	13	39	76	38	20	1
Poland	—	—	117	284	580	542	1,134	2,741	5,398	140	71	2
Romania	—	18	37	73	97	347	404	210	1,186	52	9	1
Slovak Republic	—	—	—	—	134	178	134	177	623	117	33	1
Slovenia	—	-2	41	112	111	131	170	180	743	372	90	1
Eastern Europe and Baltics	187	447	2,229	3,111	4,155	3,997	9,654	7,628	31,408	273	66	2
Armenia	—	—	—	—	—	3	19	22	44	12	6	1
Azerbaijan	—	—	—	—	20	22	284	661	987	130	87	19
Belarus	—	—	50	7	18	10	7	75	167	16	7	1
Georgia	—	—	—	—	—	8	6	25	39	7	5	1
Kazakhstan	—	—	—	—	473	635	859	1,100	3,067	187	67	5
Kyrgyzstan	—	—	—	—	10	45	61	31	147	33	7	2
Moldova	—	—	—	—	14	18	73	56	161	37	13	3
Russia	—	—	—	700	498	584	2,021	2,040	5,843	40	14	0
Tajikistan	—	—	—	8	9	12	13	13	55	10	2	1
Turkmenistan	—	—	—	—	79	103	233	129	544	118	28	5
Ukraine	—	—	—	170	200	100	300	500	1,270	25	10	1
Uzbekistan	—	—	—	9	48	73	-24	50	156	7	2	0
CIS	—	—	50	894	1,369	1,613	3,852	4,702	12,480	44	17	1
Total	187	447	2,279	4,005	5,524	5,610	13,506	12,330	43,888	110	31	1

Sources: IMF, central banks, and EBRD estimates.

[a]FDI figures for Lithuania are only available from 1993. For 1993 and 1994, figures cover only investment in equity capital.

for about 13 percent of aggregate FDI outside the developed market economies. In 1995, Hungary attracted the largest amount of FDI per capita of any country outside the developed market economies, and the share of FDI in its GDP exceeded 10 percent. Poland developed into the top destination in 1996 (with FDI doubling two years in a row), and large privatizations with foreign participation in the telecommunications and oil sectors have strongly increased inflows to Russia in 1997. One-quarter of the region's total FDI in 1997, which we expect to reach US$15 to $18 billion, is likely to flow to each of Poland and Russia. There is also concentration among countries of origin. By 1996 about one-third of cumulative FDI flows to eastern Europe had originated in Germany, while a similar proportion of the flows to the CIS is of U.S. origin (with hardly any German investment at all).

Commercial Bank Lending and International Bond Finance

By 1993, commercial bank lending and international bond issues began to pick up. Figures 2.4 and 2.5 provide a graphic representation of developments in these markets by subregion. After an initial "getting-to-know" period, these flows have surged in 1997. The share of the former Soviet Union in the total, large in 1990 and 1991 before the breakup of the USSR, remained relatively low from 1992 to 1996 but has been rising very strongly in 1997. Funding for the more advanced countries of eastern Europe grew at a more steady rate over the same period.[12] While sovereign and other public sector issuers have been particularly prominent on international bond markets—with Russia, the cities of Moscow and St. Petersburg, Ukraine, Lithuania, Moldova, and Kazakhstan making debut public offerings since the beginning of 1997—significant issues have also been made by "blue chip" commercial entities and banks, especially in the advanced countries of central Europe. Several Russian regional authorities, municipalities, and enterprises are expected to launch international bonds during the remainder of 1997. Since 1995, private borrowers have dominated the commercial loan market, the vast majority in the form of bank-to-bank loans and project financing. Again, borrowers from Russia have been particularly active on this market recently. Syndicated loans to twenty-one Russian banks for a total value of US$1.2 billion were registered in the first half of 1997 alone, usually with maturities of one year or less.

Along with rising volumes, terms have generally improved, but there are cases of rapid reversal that demonstrate the fragility of these markets and the information problem still faced by investors.[13] Issue spreads of 375, 325, 100, and 80 basis points over U.S. Treasury bills were recorded in 1997 bond issues by Russia (June, ten-year maturity), Ukraine (August, one year), Poland (June, twenty years), and Croatia (February, five years), respectively. As of mid-September, effective spreads were 312, 283, 120, and 152 basis points, sug-

---

12. The "blip" in bond issues to eastern Europe in 1993 is due to the Bank of Hungary's issuing twenty-one bonds to finance growing current account deficits.

13. Information on terms is drawn from the Euromoney Loanware and Bondware databases.

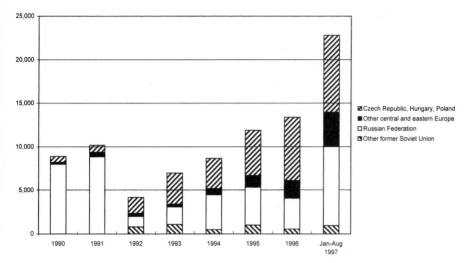

Fig. 2.4 Syndicated lending by commercial banks by subregion (millions of U.S. dollars)
Source: Euromoney Loanware.
Note: "Other central and eastern Europe" includes the Baltics.

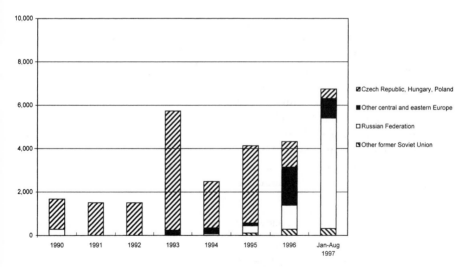

Fig. 2.5 International bond issues by subregion (millions of U.S. dollars)
Source: Euromoney Bondware.
Note: "Other central and eastern Europe" includes the Baltics.

gesting improved confidence in the former two countries and slightly deteriorating confidence in the latter two. Figure 2.6 describes the movement over time of average maturities and spreads of syndicated loans to public sector borrowers in the Czech Republic, Hungary, Poland, Romania, and Russia.[14] It shows that spreads fell first in the Czech Republic in 1994–95, whereas a more generalized decline in spreads came only in 1996–97.[15] It is interesting to note that Russian public sector borrowers continue to pay a far higher premium than the old Soviet Vneshekonombank used to be charged in 1990–91.

Portfolio Equity

Dedicated country and regional equity funds entered the region quite early, focusing primarily on central Europe, but their period of rapid expansion came in 1993–94 (table 2.4). As of September 1997, there were 170 portfolio funds (investing in listed securities) and 64 direct equity funds (unlisted shares), with cumulative investments of US$11 and $2.2 billion, respectively.[16] The vast majority of funds, including regional funds, have been invested in Russia and Poland, with estimates of around one-half and one-fifth, respectively, of the total. Closed-end funds were prevalent in the earlier stages of transition, but an increasing number are now open ended. While Western pension funds and other institutional investors account for much of the capital of the portfolio funds, the capital of private individuals is more prominent in funds specializing in unlisted shares.

Over recent years, eastern European and Russian corporates and banks have increasingly taken the direct route to overseas equity markets, although this group still represents a small share of aggregate flows. Issues have generally taken the form of ADRs/GDRs and private placements,[17] but there have also been direct listings on the London Stock Exchange. International equity issues, primarily in conjunction with privatization, were initially dominated by Hungary, which issued US$837 million in shares abroad over the period 1994–96. Poland had issues of $218 million in 1995, but it was in 1996 that this form of finance took off, with a total of $1.3 billion in share issues from seven countries. Russia ($800 million) again dominated this segment.[18] Overseas issues are viewed increasingly as an attractive option by large companies in the region

14. Fig. 2.6 only draws on those commercial bank loans for which pricing information is available on Euromoney Loanware.

15. Data refer to the first half of 1997.

16. Disbursements as measured in the EBRD Database, Early Stage Equity team.

17. American and Global Depository Receipts spare nonresident investors the settlement and custody problems of what are still weak institutional infrastructures for capital markets in the region.

18. The largest single issue in a transition economy was from Russia's Gazprom (US$430 million ADR). Lukoil of Russia plans to raise $1 billion in New York this year. In central Europe, MATAV, the Hungarian telecommunications company, will likely be the largest issue so far, with a value of perhaps $0.5 billion.

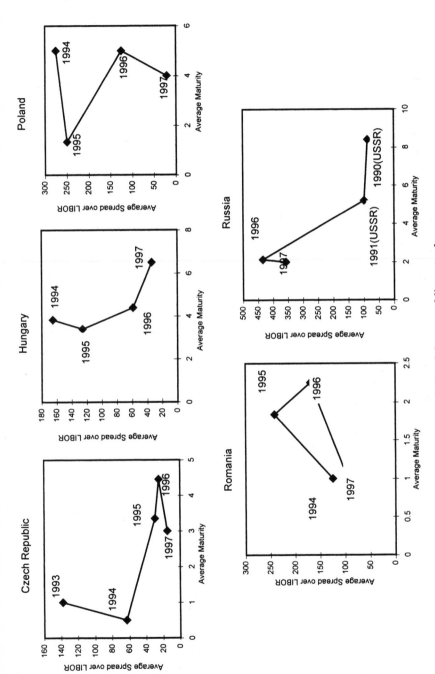

Fig. 2.6 Average spreads and maturities of commercial bank loans: public sector borrowers

Source: Euromoney Loanware.

Note: Spreads are in basis points, maturities in years.

Table 2.4 Equity Funds in Eastern Europe, the Baltics, and the Commonwealth of Independent States (millions of U.S. dollars)

Portfolio Funds (Listed Securities): Amount Invested as of 30 September 1997

Target	1989	1990	1991	1992	1993	1994	1995	1996	1997 (9 months)	Cumulative Total since 1989
Region										
Central and eastern Europe										
Central Europe		135	28	12		570	275	370	30	1,257
CIS		380				1,200	280	760	15	2,418
Baltics					1,400	440	60	80	10	2,370
Central Asia				18		82	5	45	10	150
Country										
Albania										0
Bulgaria								20		20
Czech and Slovak Republics				105	400	100	140	70	20	835
Hungary		270		10						294
Poland			19	320	5	9		190		529
Romania								15		15
Russia				140	180	550	520	1,300	350	3,040
Ukraine									60	60
Total invested		785	47	605	1,985	2,951	1,280	2,850	495	10,998
Total number of funds		8	3	6	7	42	14	56	34	170

Direct Equity Funds (Unlisted Securities): Amount Invested as of 30 September 1997

Region / Country									Total
Region									
Central and eastern Europe	50					80	100		230
Central Europe			120	40	40				200
CIS				40	120		50		210
Baltics					10	5			15
Central Asia					30	10			40
Country									
Albania						5			5
Bulgaria			50						50
Czech and Slovak Republics				50	20				70
Hungary		60	16	8	12				96
Poland	30	260			70	95	40		495
Romania					25			20	45
Russia					290	150	240	30	710
Ukraine					40		5		45
Total invested	80	320	186	138	657	345	435	50	2,211
Total number of funds	2	3	5	5	21	13	11	4	64

Source: EBRD.

because of the lack of depth and liquidity of domestic equity markets. Some fifteen Russian corporates had launched ADR programs by the spring of 1997, and at least as many others were preparing such issues.

Money Market Investments

Inflows to local markets for short-term securities (a similarly recent phenomenon) have made an equally spectacular start and are again dominated by Russia. Inflows to the Russian T-bill (GKO and OFZ) market have been prompted by the gradual relaxation of restrictions on purchases by nonresidents since early 1996, which has been partly motivated by the authorities' desire to lower the cost of public debt.[19] Nonresidents purchased US$5.6 billion in T-bills through "S" accounts in 1996, and $5.4 billion in January–April 1997 alone. By April, they held approximately one-quarter of outstanding issues through these official channels, with additional stakes held as the result of "gray market" operations with Russian intermediaries. Since mid-1997, with yields on GKOs having declined significantly (from 89 percent annualized in early 1996 to 28 percent in April 1997), foreigners have been entering the more "exotic" Russian regional and municipal bond markets in search of higher yields (e.g., Orenburg[20] T-bills yielded 600 basis points over GKOs in August). Unhedged positions are now being taken in rubles.

The experience of Ukraine and Bulgaria demonstrates the impact that foreign inflows have had on market conditions (see figs. 2.7 and 2.8). In both countries, foreign investors were all but absent from the domestic securities markets until late 1996. Foreign hedge funds and proprietary traders of various investment banks began to enter the Ukrainian hryvna T-bill market in massive volumes in January 1997 and contributed to driving down yields by about 25 percentage points (annualized) within a matter of two weeks and by a further 10 percentage points by mid-July. In Bulgaria, annualized yields on four-week T-bills fell from 600 to 100 percent within the first three weeks of April after the government signed an IMF program. They declined further to less than 6 percent in July. Foreigners accounted for 20 percent (or US$98 million) of the outstanding stock of T-bills at the end of August, up from virtually nil in March. In addition, over the same period $225 million was invested in Bulgarian bank recapitalization bonds with a twenty-five-year maturity (indexed to the U.S. dollar but payable in leva), driving the market price up from around 40 to 75 percent of nominal value.

19. Since early 1996, nonresidents have been allowed to open so-called ruble "S" accounts at designated Russian banks to buy government paper, but profits have to be repatriated through contracts involving a cap on dollar yields. This requirement is gradually being phased out and markets are set to be fully liberalized by early 1998. "Gray market" purchases involving Russian intermediaries have played on the large arbitrage margins between resident and nonresident markets.

20. A Russian *oblast* (region).

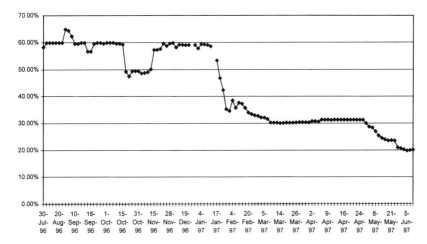

Fig. 2.7   Ukraine: annualized yield on six-month treasury bills, July 1996 to June 1997

Source: Salamon Brothers International.

Note: Gaps indicate no data, holiday, or halt in trading.

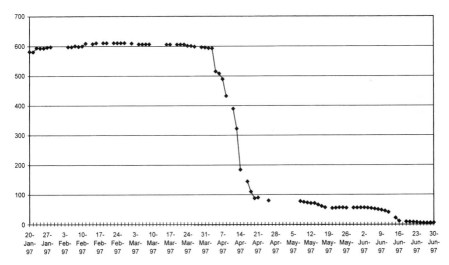

Fig. 2.8   Bulgaria: annualized yield on four-week treasury bills, January to June 1997 (percent)

Source: Salamon Brothers International.

Note: Gaps indicate no data, holiday, or halt in trading.

2.1.3   Capital Flows: Patterns and Determinants

Private capital flows to the transition economies have a short history. The recent surge in net inflows means that, by the end of this year under current projections, almost two-thirds of all private capital will have entered the region during 1996 and 1997. Combined with the paucity of detailed data, this makes a formal analysis of the determinants—let alone the consequences—of these inflows difficult. As mentioned, FDI has a slightly longer history in the transition economies than most other forms of capital flow, and we are able to draw on survey evidence and EBRD experience to discuss its motives and impact. As we shall see, FDI may also be a particularly important form of capital flow for the region because it goes well beyond the provision of finance in its ability to cement and promote the transition process. Our discussion of the patterns and determinants of portfolio flows will be shorter and will rely on more circumstantial evidence.

Our main result is that the level, location, and motive of FDI in the region are all closely associated with progress in transition. In other words, the basic human, natural resource, and geographical endowments are strong, implying that potential returns will be high if economic policies and institutions allow. While portfolio movements appear to be dominated by shorter run developments, these flows have essentially the same determinants and have recently "caught up" with reforms in the sense of investors' (rapidly) adjusting their perceptions of risks and returns. The markets have now recognized that gradual improvements in the structural and institutional fundamentals have gone a long way. Other factors, particularly macroeconomic stability, will have their role to play, but the progress in transition is and will be the driving force in integrating these economies into global markets.

Location of Foreign Direct Investment

As we have emphasized, Hungary and other eastern European destinations were the first to attract significant inflows of FDI. Russia and the oil economies of the CIS followed with some delay. Several countries of central Asia, the Caucasus, and southeastern Europe have so far failed to prove attractive to investors. The transition process first got under way in central Europe, and these economies continue to lead both in the depth of their reforms and in the volume of investment. It is tempting to compare measures of progress in transition with FDI per capita. Leaving out the three oil and gas economies of central Asia (Azerbaijan, Kazakhstan, and Turkmenistan), the rank correlation coefficient for twenty-two countries between the EBRD's average transition indicator in 1996 and cumulative FDI per capita over the period 1989–96 is .88 (it is .86 for FDI per capital in 1996 alone).[21] This association supports the conclusion that it is

21. See table 2.1 for the EBRD's transition indicator. The measure used here is the average of scores, on a scale from 1 to 4, along eight dimensions of transition, including large and small enterprise privatization, enterprise restructuring, price liberalization, trade and foreign exchange

Table 2.5   Obstacles to Doing Business: Survey Results

	CIS	World	Developing Countries	Developed Market Economies
High taxes or tax regulations	80	59	62	50
Policy instability	52	32	36	12
General uncertainty about costs of regulations	44	29	30	17
Crime and theft	48	38	43	11
Corruption	84	47	54	18

Source: World Bank (1997b).
Note: Table reports percentage of respondents reporting a "strong obstacle."

the reform process that opens opportunities for profitable investment and that, through its impact on risk (as discussed in section 2.1.2), motivates investors to take advantage of them. It also suggests that direct equity investors have evaluated the economic environment and made informed choices.[22]

Continued reforms can therefore be expected to elicit additional growth in investment. These reforms have far to go, especially in the CIS. Both the practical experience of the EBRD and recent World Bank (1997b) survey evidence suggest that shortcomings in the implementation of reforms, and in particular in the way the business of government is conducted, remain a deterrent to private investor activity. The survey evidence relates to the CIS, but it is consistent—though the problems are less intense—with EBRD experience even in the more advanced economies in transition. Key messages from the survey include the following: taxes and tax administration are major problems (vague tax laws with little rationality across firms, and haphazard and sometimes corrupt implementation), laws and regulations are seen as burdensome and ever changing, there is continuing uncertainty about the institutional and regulatory regime, and there is little confidence in the ability of the administration to enforce property rights and contracts or to control crime and corruption.

The survey was conducted among enterprises worldwide and therefore allows comparisons of the severity of these investment deterrents with those for other regions. The results reproduced in table 2.5 confirm that the transition economies of the CIS still face significant challenges in improving their investment climate—for domestic investors but even more so if they are to compete successfully with other locations for FDI. The consequences that (largely transition specific) deficiencies in the administrative and regulatory environment

---

regime, competition policy, banking reform, and development of securities markets and nonbank financial institutions.

22. As we argue in section 2.1.4 below, the high degree of correlation between progress in transition and FDI may also partly result from causality running the opposite way, from FDI to progress in transition.

can have for investors are also demonstrated by the EBRD's experience, which is described with the help of examples in appendix A.

Additional factors that are hard to separate from our measure of transition are likely to have played a role in location decisions. They include in particular the proximity (both physical and cultural) of investment locations to Western markets and the prospects for market (and political) integration with the European Union. These factors, which are particularly relevant for cost-motivated investments (as opposed to those seeking new markets), are themselves closely associated with the achievements in market-oriented reform, partly because the prospect of accession to the European Union has served to stimulate the reform commitment, and partly because Association Agreements with the European Union have brought early benefits of market access and massive technical assistance. This close relationship between prospects for EU accession and the depth of reforms may also contribute to the motives for FDI, which we analyze in the following section.

Motives for Foreign Direct Investment

The distinction between market and cost motives for foreign investment has been central to a variety of surveys of FDI in the economies in transition. One pattern that emerges very clearly is the predominance of market seeking as the prime investment motive. Factor cost considerations appear to be of less importance for the majority of investments. However, an EBRD survey (described in appendix B) shows that, while market seeking is indeed the dominant motive for a majority of the investments in the sample, the type of FDI varies significantly according to the host country's progress in economic transition.[23] FDI projects in countries that are more advanced in transition are more likely to be export oriented, more integrated into the foreign parent's multinational production process, and more likely to exploit the comparative advantage of the host economy.[24]

In examining the relationship between project function and host country characteristics (using a multinomial logit model), the host country transition indicator was found to be a significant determinant of the functional mix of projects operating in each country.[25] Results are reported in table 2.6, which

23. The following discussion draws on Lankes and Venables (1996), which describes the EBRD survey results in greater detail.

24. In light of our earlier discussion about the investment climate it is useful to note that a country's level of transition relates also to the likelihood of successful implementation. One point "up" in the transition indicator of a country is associated with an 80 percent fall in the chance of a project's being eventually abandoned or postponed.

"Export-oriented" investors stress the importance of production cost reduction in general and the availability of cheap *skilled* labor in particular—this is the single most important motivating factor in their investment decision. In the sample, salaries of skilled workers in export investments are at 16 percent of their Western (parent company) level, while productivity is reported to be, on average, 72 percent of the Western level. Since other, unspecified cost factors are less advantageous, overall unit costs of exporters represent 67 percent of those in western Europe.

25. The EBRD's 1995 transition indicators were used in these calculations for consistency with the timing of the survey (EBRD 1995).

Table 2.6   **Host Characteristics and Functional Type**

	Local Supply/ Distribution	Export/ Distribution	Export/ Local Supply
Relative probability at mean	3.0	1.8	0.61
Percentage change in relative probability per unit change in transition indicator	115 (1.2)	596 (2.5)	224 (1.9)

Note: Number of observations is 140. Numbers in parentheses are *t*-statistics.

presents the changes in relative probabilities associated with a one-point increase in the transition indicator. Increasing the transition indicator increases the probability that the project is engaged in local supply relative to distribution. It also increases the probability that it is export oriented, relative to either local supply or distribution; the latter effect is particularly large and is statistically significant.[26] These results may be partly explained by the relation between costs and flexibility in production and the depth of reforms. Administrative discretion and trade barriers raise direct costs and can complicate logistics. The survey suggests that first-mover advantage is an important strategic motive among investors aiming at serving local markets. Efficiency-seeking export investors, on the other hand, focus more on costs and may therefore wait for the obstacles that raise costs (and risks) to recede.

A further result throwing some light on the process of integration into international production networks—especially if viewed in conjunction with the association between transition and export orientation—is that a project's position within the production chain of its multinational parent corporation differs by project function. An export investment is somewhat further "upstream" within the multinational's production chain and sells almost half its product within the corporation (i.e., to the parent company or other subsidiaries), while for a "market investment" the share is only 3 percent. In both cases, input supply is roughly one-third from within the corporation (imports). "Vertical FDI"—that is, the cross-border relocation of parts of the production chain—seems to be particularly prevalent among German investors, who, as mentioned in section 2.1.2, have concentrated almost exclusively on central European locations.

Portfolio Investments and Commercial Bank Lending

As we have seen, bond purchases and commercial bank lending were the first to follow FDI into the region in significant amounts, with equity funds next in line and money market investments and direct offers of equity abroad much more recent phenomena. Again, the central European advanced reformers led the way, but the recent explosive growth in these markets is very much

26. Alternative specifications were investigated, allowing for the effect of measures of country size and controlling for industrial sector. These variables were not significant and did not change the signs or significance levels of results reported in table 2.6, which seem robust.

dominated by Russia. We shall argue that bank lending has built on relationships established over time with counterparts in the region and on the techniques of structured finance, while perceptions of short-term risk and return opportunities in the region's financial markets have played a greater role in portfolio flows. As mentioned, our discussion of the determinants of these flows in the following has to rely primarily on circumstantial evidence, much of it drawn from the lending experience of the EBRD.

Commercial banks were the main source of external funds for eastern Europe and the USSR during the 1980s. During that period, close working relationships were built with foreign trade banks. These relationships survived the uncertainty and debt defaults of the early transition years, though the volume and nature of lending changed. Commercial banks participated in export finance insured by export credit agencies and provided short-term trade finance collateralized with balances on correspondent accounts. By 1992–93, as trade flows between central and western Europe surged, terms on these transactions began to soften for central European obligor banks (see table 2.7 for confirmation fees on letters of credit). Collateral requirements were gradually replaced by uncovered forms of documentary credit and medium-term refinancing facilities. Between 1993 and 1994, for instance, Komercni Banka, a prominent Czech bank, was able to lengthen maturities on export refinance transactions from eighteen months to three years while spreads fell sharply. While Japanese banks made their first significant entry on that market in those years, contributing to greater competition, most of the lending operations were conducted with western European banks that had long-standing relationships with Komercni and other large Czech institutions. Project finance developed during that period in the context of FDI projects and syndications with international financial institutions such as the EBRD. This was assisted by improvements in the legal basis for secured lending.

Nonguaranteed bank-to-bank operations with the countries of the former Soviet Union took more time to develop, partly because of the more unsettled macroeconomic and regulatory environments and partly because—unlike in eastern Europe—new private banks quickly came to dominate the banking sectors in these countries and relationships took more time to rebuild.[27] Again, cash-collateralized trade finance was often the first step in this process. By 1996, on the basis of lengthening track records, Russian bank-to-bank lending and project finance had become well established, though other CIS countries, generally with weaker banking systems, were lagging behind.[28]

When commercial bank lending expanded rapidly in 1995–97, this was mostly on the basis of such previous relationships. As we noted in section

27. Except for Vneshekonombank, successor to the former Soviet trade bank, which continued to enjoy privileged access to funding from its established Western banking partners.
28. From 1996, demand for EBRD trade guarantee facilities, which insured counterparty risk for Western confirming banks by way of standby letters of credit, gradually declined from some of the larger new Russian banks.

Table 2.7   **Indications of Confirmation Fees on Letters of Credit for Transition Economies, 1995**

Country	Indication of Confirmation Fees (CILC)	Availability
Albania	Case by case	Very difficult
Armenia		Nothing available
Azerbaijan		Nothing available
Belarus	Case by case	Very difficult
Bosnia-Herzegovina		Nothing available
Bulgaria	5% or more p.a.	Up to 360 days for two main banks
Croatia	Varies by bank	Up to 3 years possible for certain banks
Czech Republic	1% p.a.	Up to 7 years available
Estonia	5% or more p.a.	Up to 5 years possible
Georgia		Nothing available
Hungary	2% p.a.	Up to 5 years possible
Kazakhstan		Nothing available
Kyrgyzstan		Nothing available
Latvia	5% or more p.a.	Up to 3 years, certain banks only
Lithuania	5% or more p.a.	Up to 3 years, certain banks only
FYR Macedonia	Case by case	Up to 1 year possible
Poland	1% p.a.	Up to 7 years
Moldova		Nothing available
Romania	5% p.a.	Up to 5 years
Russia	5% p.a.	360 days maximum, certain banks only
Slovak Republic	1% p.a.	Up to 5 years
Slovenia	1% p.a.	Up to 7 years
Tajikistan		Nothing available
Turkmenistan		Nothing available
Ukraine		Nothing available
Uzbekistan		Nothing available
Yugoslavia/Serbia		Nothing available

Source: Jardine Credit Insurance Ltd.

2.1.2, bank-to-bank lending appears to have dominated the surge. In addition, privatization in many countries moved into a new phase with infrastructure and large enterprises increasingly on offer. Privatization revenues for the region as a whole increased from US$3 to $4 billion in 1992–94 to $9 billion in 1995.[29] Together with FDI, this has vastly increased the opportunities for project finance. Infrastructure financing raised from foreign banks, for instance, grew from $960 million in 1994 to $3 billion in 1995 (World Bank 1997a, table 2.2). The improvement in terms that has accompanied this process over the past two years, especially in some countries of eastern Europe, would appear at times to have gone further than could be justified by the underlying risk. The sharp increase in competition from other sources of capital inflow has been the main driving force of the fall in spreads. This perception is shared by some of the

29. World Bank (1997a, table A.6.3). Regionwide data for 1996 are not available.

EBRD's Western banking partners, who nevertheless aim to maintain and develop long-term lending relationships and build market share in a promising market beyond what is viewed as a problematic but transitory phenomenon (implying low returns in relation to risk).

Apart perhaps from some of the equity funds that have long been operating in the region, supplies of portfolio flows and bond finance have, by their nature, relied less on direct relationships built over time and more on highly structured transactions. As in other markets they are motivated in part by the well-established benefits of portfolio diversification. However, three additional factors are likely to have played an even greater role in explaining recent rapid movements. The first factor is closely linked with the transition process itself. The rapid change associated with transition and the immaturity of local capital markets (both in terms of regulation and liquidity) has opened opportunities for short-term arbitrage and has generated lags and leads in the perception of underlying risk. The region does not have a history of credit ratings, and the first formal ratings came, for most countries outside central Europe, at a time when reforms had already progressed. This rating has put these countries "on the map" over the past two years. In 1996–97, the first credit assignments by Moody's and Standard & Poor's were given to Russia, Romania, Kazakhstan, Latvia, Lithuania, Moldova, Bulgaria, Croatia, and the cities of Moscow, St. Petersburg, and Nizhny Novgorod. Partly as a result, international fund managers "discovered" the region, and it is interesting to note how the most aggressive funds have moved from one security to the next successively in search of new arbitrage margins (such as from Russia to Ukraine and Bulgaria, or from Russian federal T-bills to regional ones).[30]

The second factor is the liquidity in global markets. Because yields in industrialized countries have remained low, and emerging market finance has recovered as memories of the Mexico crisis fade, liquidity has reinforced the greater interest in the opportunities offered by the region. A third important factor, finally, has been tensions within the macroeconomic policy mix of several countries, including Poland in 1995 and the Czech and Slovak Republics and Russia in 1996–97. Significant uncovered interest differentials emerged as the result of tight monetary policies, combined with loosening fiscal stances. These offered investors in money markets (particularly bank deposits) opportunities for short-term gain.

Referring to our discussion of the relation between risk and progress in transition, fundamentals on the side of demand for finance and of credit quality have moved far too gradually to be the explanation for the recent surge in short-term capital flows.[31] Of the factors reviewed above, information lags have, in

---

30. A Banque Nationale de Paris brochure (1997) refers explicitly to Russian GKOs as being "close to their sell-by date." It goes on to state that "by shopping around, you can equip yourself with the necessary breathing apparatus to keep climbing from here."

31. The softening of restrictions on foreign participants in the Russian T-bill market since early 1996 has clearly been an additional trigger, but there have been no such policy changes in countries

our view, been the most important in motivating the surge. International liquidity, macroeconomic policy, and, in Russia, remaining restrictions on security markets have reinforced this factor. This suggests that herding may have played a role and raises the prospect of macroeconomic instability associated with possible volatility in these flows, problems that are discussed in a little more detail in the next section.

2.1.4   Capital Flows: Consequences

Capital flows to the transition economies will be of great value in realizing the region's growth potential. The potential productivity (and profitability) of new capital is likely to be higher than in more settled market environments. The physical and human capital stock in transition economies is large by the standards of middle-income countries but inefficiently employed and partly obsolete. Investment for restructuring, combined with improved management and Western technology, offers opportunities for raising the yield of some of the existing capital at relatively low cost. At the same time, domestic financial systems are able to offer only limited support to investors, and savings are lower than under the earlier regime, especially during the recovery from the transition recession when future earnings expectations stimulate consumption. Capital flows have, as discussed in section 2.1.2, contributed significantly to lowering financing costs. Net capital inflows and associated current account deficits can therefore play a useful role in the region's development if channeled into quality investment. However, they also create obligations that will have to be serviced, and recent current account deteriorations and rising consumption have, in some countries, reached worrisome proportions.

In this section we argue that FDI, in particular, has the qualities most likely to stimulate transition and growth. Other forms of capital inflow can also contribute to the transition process, but they are likely to generate lasting benefits only if combined with cautious fiscal and monetary management.

Broadly speaking, the transition is about placing economic interactions on a market footing and promoting private and entrepreneurial initiative. Accordingly, one can identify three dimensions in the transition process: (1) the creation, expansion, and improvement of markets; (2) the establishment and strengthening of institutions, laws, and policies that support the market (including private ownership); and (3) the adoption of behavior patterns and skills that have a market perspective.

Apart from its role in capital accumulation, FDI tends to have a "package" of attributes that can make a significant contribution to transition along these dimensions through upstream and downstream linkages and demonstration effects. It can, for instance, force modern standards of product quality and supply

---

that have, on a smaller scale, attracted a similar surge in interest (Bulgaria, Croatia, Romania, and Ukraine).

reliability on local producers through its procurement management. This can both provide learning externalities from which other purchasers can benefit and promote market-oriented behavior. In monopolized markets, often a remnant of the command system, FDI may have the muscle to impose greater competition. Standards of behavior, including in relation to corporate governance, and technology can be transmitted via demonstration effects. And advanced marketing methods can have an impact on distribution systems and market logistics as well as competition. In the financial sector, FDI in banks (and equity funds) can have particularly broad effects by bringing credit skills and a strong element of financial discipline.

The EBRD assesses transition impact in the context of its investment projects. Traditional methods of project appraisal proved ill suited to the task. The spotlight in the analysis of transition falls precisely where cost-benefit analysis is weakest. Transition focuses on processes rather than outcomes. Of course, one looks to processes (here those of the market) that are thought likely to produce good outcomes, but the scope and depth of the changes make explicit modeling of outcomes intractable. We have developed an approach in which the type of impact of a project is assessed and checked against areas in a country or sector in which the transition challenge appears particularly great. A checklist of transition impact appears in appendix C. Figure 2.9 reviews the structure of transition impact of the EBRD's Russia portfolio and pipeline across the seven dimensions of transition impact identified in the checklist. Restructuring and competition are particularly relevant in private sector projects, while an emphasis on institution building and policies underpinning market efficiency represent key purposes of the EBRD's involvement in the state sector.

Bank lending, in the form of project finance, trade credit, and interbank lending, can contribute to the transition process through some of the same channels. In particular, it can transfer financial technologies and the learning effects associated with financial discipline. Similarly, equity flows and the issuing of corporate bonds can strengthen disclosure, shareholder rights, and other elements of corporate governance. A recent example is the legal battle over minority shareholder rights in Russia's Novolipetsk steel mill, which was won by foreign portfolio investors against management. The city of St. Petersburg overhauled its finances and took steps toward the commercialization of certain municipal services in the context of its international bond issue earlier this year.

Nevertheless, there are dangers associated with the rapid rise in capital flows. Combined with domestic demand-led growth, and partly fueling it, they have contributed to a significant deterioration in current account balances over the past two years (fig. 2.10). This raises the question of the vulnerability of balances of payments to sudden reversals in short-term flows if risk perceptions change. Two areas are of particular concern. First, the financial institutions and markets that intermediate part of these funds are still highly immature in many countries in transition. Greater liquidity, combined with weak regulation, can

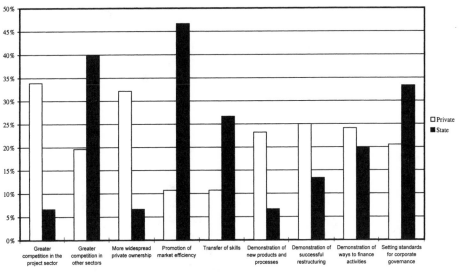

Fig. 2.9   Russia: transition impact by class of borrower, stock of projects as of April 1997 (percentage of projects associated with each impact)
Source: EBRD.

stimulate the accumulation of poor lending portfolios. Over recent months, we have seen banks even in the advanced transition countries rushing into transactions without due diligence. Simultaneously, the growing stability in the macroeconomic environment and the capital inflows themselves have reduced earlier sources of easy income for banks on the government securities and foreign exchange markets, and foreign funds compete with local banks by driving down margins on "blue chip" lending. This heightens the risk of bank failures and associated dangers of volatility in capital flows.

Second, the size of the current account imbalances could lead to volatility in expectations if the associated growth in the debt burden is judged to be unsustainable. Table 2.8 provides a grouping of countries into broad categories around some indicators of financial imbalance: the sizes of the current account and fiscal deficits and the ratios of external debt to exports and GDP. In such a broad-brush categorization, the cutoff points for "low," "medium," and "high" are necessarily somewhat arbitrary. Also, the fiscal deficit criteria should ideally be expanded to cover "quasi-fiscal deficits" resulting from the state's influence over the activity of banks and enterprises. The accounts of Belarus and Turkmenistan, for instance, would then look far worse. Nevertheless, table 2.8 offers some useful insights. With very few exceptions, the external debt burden is not high by international standards. For instance, the Latin American average ratio of gross debt to exports (including goods and nonfactor services in the denominator) was 203 percent in 1996 (World Bank 1997a), a level surpassed

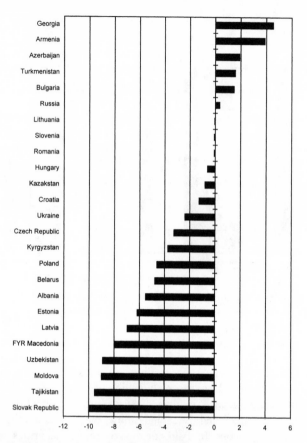

Fig. 2.10   Deterioration in trade balances, 1996 (percentage of GDP)
Sources: IMF, national authorities, and EBRD estimates.

among transition economies only by Armenia, Bulgaria, and Georgia. The average for all developing countries was 146 percent, compared with 121 percent for the transition economies.[32]

However, while external debt is not (yet) high, it has been growing very rapidly, and current account deficits have been associated with significant budgetary imbalances in several CIS countries. Together with evidence of low public investment activity (Kapur and van der Mensbrugghe 1997), this suggests that a large proportion of foreign funding may serve to meet current outlays that do not improve those countries' future repayment capacity. Foreign borrowing was in some cases explicitly earmarked to reduce budgetary pensions and wage arrears (e.g., a recent Russian bond issue and a planned Kazakh

32. Weighted averages. The ratio was almost the same in eastern Europe and the Baltics (123 percent) and in the CIS (118 percent).

Table 2.8   Indicators of Debt and Deficits, 1996

Current Account Balance[a] (% of GDP)	Fiscal Balance[b] (% of GDP)	Gross External Debt/ Current Account Revenues[c]	Net External Debt/ GDP[d]
		Low	
Russia (2.2)	Belarus (−1.6)	Albania (82.1)	Albania (20)
Bulgaria (1.3)	Croatia (−0.5)	Azerbaijan (66.4)	Armenia (28)
Poland (−1)	Czech Republic (−0.7)	Belarus (16.3)	Azerbaijan (10)
Slovenia (0.3)	Estonia (−1.5)	Croatia (58.9)	Belarus (4)
Turkmenistan (−0.7)	FYR Macedonia (−0.4)	Czech Republic (67.3)	Croatia (13)
	Latvia (−1.4)	Estonia (11.8)	Czech Republic (15)
	Slovak Republic (−1.2)	Kazakhstan (69.3)	Estonia (−7)
	Slovenia (0.3)	Latvia (29.4)	FYR Macedonia (25)
	Turkmenistan (−0.2)	Lithuania (34.8)	Georgia (27)
		Slovak Republic (70.2)	Kazakstan (9)
		Slovenia (36.9)	Latvia (−4)
		Turkmenistan (36.0)	Lithuania (4)
		Ukraine (45.5)	Moldova (27)
		Uzbekistan (61.7)	Poland (17)
			Romania (16)
			Russia (26)
			Slovak Republic (24)
			Slovenia (9)
			Turkmenistan (−19)
			Ukraine (17)
			Uzbekistan (1)

(continued)

Table 2.8   (continued)

Current Account Balance[a] (% of GDP)	Fiscal Balance[b] (% of GDP)	Gross External Debt/ Current Account Revenues[c]	Net External Debt/ GDP[d]
Medium			
Albania (−4.7)	Azerbaijan (−2.6)	FYR Macedonia (128.9)	Hungary (40)
Belarus (−6.7)	Georgia (−4.4)	Hungary (143.7)	Kyrgyzstan (35)
Georgia (−4.9)	Hungary (−3.5)	Kyrgyzstan (141.0)	
Hungary (−3.8)	Kazakhstan (−3.1)	Moldova (100.2)	
Kazakhstan (−3.8)	Lithuania (−3.6)	Poland (145.3)	
Lithuania (−4.4)	Poland (−3.1)	Romania (110.5)	
Romania (−5.9)	Romania (−3.9)	Russia (125.9)	
Ukraine (−2.7)	Ukraine (−3.2)	Tajikistan (186.0)	
High			
Armenia (−26.6)	Albania (−12.0)	Armenia (211.4)	Bulgaria (105)
Azerbaijan (−23.6)	Armenia (−9.3)	Bulgaria (204.0)	Tajikistan (90)
Croatia (−7.6)	Bulgaria (−13.4)	Georgia (331.0)	
Czech Republic (−8.1)	Kyrgyzstan (−6.4)		
Estonia (−10.3)	Moldova (−6.7)		
FYR Macedonia (−7.8)	Russia (−8.3)		
Kyrgyzstan (−23.7)	Tajikistan (−5.3)		
Latvia (−7.2)	Uzbekistan (−7.3)		
Moldova (−13.1)			
Slovak Republic (−10.2)			
Tajikistan (−10.9)			
Uzbekistan (−7.9)			

Sources: IMF; national authorities, and EBRD estimates.

[a]Categories are "low," current account deficit is less than −2 percent; "medium," between −2 percent and −7 percent; and "high," greater than −7 percent.

[b]The fiscal deficit refers to the general government. Categories are "low," fiscal deficit less than −2 percent; "medium," between −2 and −5 percent; and "high," greater than −5 percent.

[c]Categories are "low," ratio of gross external debt to current account revenues smaller or equal to 100; "medium," between 100 and 200; and "high," greater than 200. Current account revenues include merchandise exports and exports of nonfactor services. In the case of Armenia, Azerbaijan, Belarus, Bulgaria, FYR Macedonia, Georgia, Kazakhstan, Kyrgyzstan, Latvia, Lithuania, Moldova, Romania, Tajikistan, Uzbekistan, the gross external debt is divided only by merchandise exports.

[d]Net external debt equals gross external debt net of gross reserves of the monetary authorities. Categories are "low," ratio of net external debt over GDP smaller or equal to 30 percent; "medium," between 30 and 50 percent; and "high," greater than 50 percent.

issue).[33] The association between budgetary and external imbalances is particularly worrying if viewed against the background of weak fiscal revenue performance across much of the CIS. The vast majority of CIS debt is owed by sovereign or sovereign-backed borrowers. Problems of fiscal sustainability are perhaps the most likely source of external instability in the future.

2.1.5   Prospects and Policies

A discussion of prospects for capital flows to the region takes us very quickly to a discussion of the prospects for transition and to economic policies. We have seen that flows have been predominantly to countries at more advanced stages of transition and to countries with better records on macroeconomic stability. Thus the underlying advantages of the region are strong in terms of market potential, low cost, and proximity to European markets. It is rapid transition and sound economic policies that unlock this potential.

Over the past two years or so the markets have realized the opportunities that are available. There has been a rapid adjustment in perceptions and a major acceleration in flows. Thus FDI has more or less tripled between 1994 and 1997, with an even more dramatic rise in other flows. FDI in the region is now running at around US$40 to $50 per capita, or 2 to 3 percent of GDP. In some countries it is more than $200 per capita. It is natural to ask whether this acceleration of flows will continue. In our judgment it is likely that over the next few years FDI in the region will grow further. Growth of output is now positive in nearly all economies of the region and is returning in Russia. The rise in real exchange rates that has brought a 50 percent increase in the region's GDP in the past three years (notwithstanding zero or negative real output growth) is likely to continue, albeit at a slower rate. Thus the next few years will see strong market growth. The presence of significant human capital, together with the scrapping of much obsolete capital stock, makes the potential return on investment high. As we have emphasized throughout, the crucial additional ingredients are continued transition and sound policy.

The prospects for other capital flows are more difficult to judge. The rapid acceleration of the past two years is, however, unlikely to be maintained since it is, as we have suggested, in some part due to a one-off adjustment in perceptions. It should also be kept in mind that the transition has far to go, and in some respects, for example financial institutions, it is fragile. There is little doubt that political commitment has been remarkably strong through difficult times and changing governments, but one must expect setbacks and crises on the way. The very high balance-of-payments deficits that have emerged in the past year or two (together with capital inflows) are likely to cause problems before too long and may result in sharp reactions from the markets. The future

---

33. And, in fact, certain state-owned enterprises are said to have borrowed abroad to meet their tax liabilities. This is a reflection of the liquidity crisis in the enterprise sector of the CIS.

of very large capital outflows, particularly from Russia, is also hard to predict. It is to be hoped that those Russians seeking returns outside Russia will also have greater confidence in the high returns to be obtained from domestic investment.

Subject to continued advance in the transition, and greater security of their assets through the legal and administrative systems, investors will be looking particularly closely at fiscal policies. It has been monetary policies that have led the way in restoring macroeconomic stability with, at times, extraordinarily high real rates of interest. If the macroeconomic position is to be secured, the fiscal position must be put on a sound long-term basis. In many countries there are still difficult adjustments to make on both the revenue and expenditure sides. As a broad generalization we can say that in the western part of the region the challenges will be particularly severe in controlling expenditure, and in the east in raising revenue. As on most dimensions of the transition, improving policy on the fiscal front requires careful attention not only to building institutions but also to promoting and enforcing responsible behavior both inside and outside government. While the first phase of the transition can be seen in terms of liberalization and privatization, the next phase involves the building and deepening of these institutions and behavior. These processes will take time, but in most countries of the region the next phase of transition is under way.

Appendix A
Obstacles to Investment: The EBRD's Experience

Each year, the EBRD invests about US$3 billion in over 100 projects. Including the investments made by sponsors of these projects and other financial investors, the total investment in Bank-supported projects amounts to about $10 billion per year. This figure corresponds to roughly 5 percent of total fixed investment in the Bank's countries of operations. Since the Bank is active in all its countries of operations, this participation in investment throughout the region generates a considerable body of experience that underpins its analysis and understanding of the obstacles to growth that are associated with failures in the investment climate.

Perhaps the most fundamental lesson from the Bank's experience for private investment is its severely limited scope in the absence of macroeconomic stabilization and of basic structural reforms (such as price and trade liberalization, privatization of small-scale enterprises, and elimination of directed credits and interest rate controls in credit markets). In such a climate for investment, financially viable private investment projects tend to be restricted to those that operate as enclaves within the local economy. Such projects are often capital-intensive projects in the natural resource sector, where the capital inputs are sourced from abroad and the output is exported. The main locally provided inputs are labor and transportation services. This type of private investment, while it can be of real value, has only limited linkages to the local economy and is unlikely to generate the types of commercial interactions that yield significant spillovers on the productivity of the local private sector.

With progress in macroeconomic stabilization and basic structural reforms, however, the EBRD has been able to expand significantly its support for private investment projects, particularly in the local private sector. Nevertheless, the Bank often encounters a number of obstacles related to government policies and practices. The examples that follow serve to illustrate our experiences. While they have been expressed in general terms to avoid reference to specific projects, they are based on concrete and sometimes painful experiences.

Corporate Taxation

A pervasive problem in private investment projects throughout the region is the lack of predictability of tax rules (a problem that can be exacerbated by the retroactive implementation of some measures) and the arbitrary and discriminatory enforcement of taxation (e.g., many domestic enterprises accumulate tax arrears and enjoy exemptions while compliance by enterprises that are not so favored, including foreign companies, is strictly enforced). The level of taxes for the honest taxpayer who is not privileged with exemptions can be punitive, and many potentially viable projects do not come to fruition for this reason.

A second set of problems related to corporate taxation is the inability to deduct certain legitimate business expenses (e.g., part of interest payments, training, and travel) and the distortions that arise from the structure of depreciation allowances. The Bank is involved in a number of projects in the region (which are viable over the medium term) that are currently running at a loss according to International Accounting Standards but that are nevertheless paying substantial profit taxes because of the peculiarities of the accounting and tax systems. In one case, these taxes amount to close to US$100 million.

Product Markets

Barter transactions among enterprises are prevalent in some countries and sectors. It appears that barter transactions serve to conceal profits and to stifle competition. The use of barter can be exacerbated by sometimes severe liquidity problems and prevents the financial viability of otherwise viable projects.

Enterprises (Including Infrastructure and the Environment)

Excessive licensing and regulation of businesses often contribute to bureaucratic obstacles to business formation and investment. For example, one

EBRD-supported project required seventy signatures from officials to clear all applicable licensing and regulatory hurdles. Such government policies and practices fuel corruption and inhibit investment.

EBRD support for the privatization of some enterprises has placed it in the position of minority shareholder with the government retaining an influential role in corporate control. In some investments, governments have used their residual ownership stakes to pursue noncommercial objectives, including political patronage. This has involved privileged sales of shares at special prices to enterprise managers after outsiders have been sold shares at higher prices and the manipulation of share registers. Such actions cut against the objective of instilling a strong commercial orientation in enterprises through privatization. Also, they obviously discourage outside investors from buying shares, thereby eliminating an important source of finance and corporate governance.

Many dominant infrastructure enterprises remain largely unreformed, despite the potential for de-monopolization and for increasing competition in the provision of services. In addition, the structure of infrastructure tariffs continues to place a heavy burden on business customers, with the structure of tariffs often inverted (i.e., with businesses paying tariffs that are five and six times those paid by households, despite the higher costs of delivering services to households; see, e.g., EBRD 1996).

The region has relatively little experience with regulatory institutions and practices, and only a handful of countries in the region have established independent regulatory agencies. Several EBRD-supported and other commercial infrastructure projects have been adversely affected by arbitrary regulatory actions and by adverse court rulings, contributing to investor caution. These actions have included the withdrawal of previously agreed licenses, the failure to implement agreed tariff increases, and the imposition of misguided restrictions on competition.

The tolerance of payments arrears in the energy sector (primarily by large state-owned industries and local governments) severely curtails the financial viability of projects, as does the extensive use of barter. It is also limited by the failure to implement tariffs that reflect the incremental costs of production and the financial constraints of government (although the EBRD recognizes that there are social constraints to the instantaneous introduction of such tariffs). Taken together these problems have inhibited the flow of private investment into power generation and distribution. As a result, EBRD activity in this sector has also been held back.

Financial Markets and Institutions

In some countries, governments have sought in effect to nationalize financially viable private banks with which the EBRD was associated through directed mergers with state-owned banks. Such actions are in conflict with the transition objective of achieving a strong commercial orientation through private ownership of commercial banks, and the possibility of such actions inhibits investment in the sector.

Connected lending by commercial banks remains a pervasive practice in the region and has been a principal cause of several bank failures.

Accounting standards remain inadequate from the perspectives both of internal financial control of banks and of prudential regulation. Rapid movement to International Accounting Standards remains a priority.

Failure of government to implement effectively the prudential regulation of banks and other financial institutions has contributed to financial instability that has adversely affected the performance of otherwise sound banks with which the EBRD is involved.

Legal Institutions

In contrast to the countries in eastern Europe and the Baltic region, those in the CIS have no prewar experience with commercial and civil codes. While such codes have now been established in much of the region, this lack of commercial traditions has meant that there is relatively little understanding of the functioning of these codes. This in turn may contribute to a lack of respect for the laws, weak judicial enforcement, and reliance on private enforcement of agreements. Some EBRD projects have experienced a range of arbitrary interventions by local government—for example, attempting to expropriate the project company's output and to prevent its export.

Appendix B
EBRD Investor Survey

In January 1995, the EBRD conducted an investor survey.[34] They contacted 11,000 firms worldwide. Of the 1,435 firms that responded, 628 indicated that they were willing to be interviewed at the senior executive level. Executives from 117 of these firms with 145 investments in eastern Europe and the former Soviet Union were interviewed between June and November 1995. To qualify for the survey, a company needed to have an operational, planned, postponed, or abandoned project in the mining or manufacturing sector of an EBRD country of operation; in addition, its headquarters had to be in western Europe. The 145 surveyed investments cover sixteen economies in transition, employ 39,000 workers, and have a total foreign equity contribution of US$2.8 billion. A summary description of investment projects in the survey is presented in table 2B.1.

---

34. A fuller presentation of the survey is contained in Lankes and Venables (1996).

Table 2B.1   Summary Description of Investment Projects in EBRD Survey

Country (Group)		Status		Function		Control Mode	
Czech Republic and Hungary (Group I)	44	Planned	38	Distribution and services	24	License or subcontract	16
Poland, Baltics, and other eastern Europe (Group II)	57	Operating	91	Supply of regional or local markets	72	Joint venture	72
Russia and other CIS (Group III)	44	Postponed or abandoned	16	Exports from the region	44	Wholly owned by foreign parent	53
Total	145		145		140		141

Appendix C
Qualitative Aspects of Transition Impact of Projects: A Checklist

The following checklist covers only those potential effects of a project on the host country that relate to the conversion from a command economy to an economy driven by well-functioning markets. It does not cover direct income and resource effects of a project, and it covers environmental impact only indirectly to the extent that it is a consequence of the broadening and deepening of markets. Applications of the checklist should therefore be viewed in conjunction with an analysis of the financial and economic rate of return and of the wider environmental impact of a project. The checklist is "generic" in the sense that, in principle, its categories fit all project types (e.g., small and medium-sized infrastructure projects and technical assistance).

Project Contributions to the Structure and Extent of Markets

1. *Greater competition in the project sector:* A project can promote greater competition in its sector of activity. Increased competitive pressure is likely to improve the efficiency with which resources are utilized, demand is satisfied, and innovation is stimulated. However, in some circumstances a project might lead to a slackening of competitive pressure on market participants, including the project company itself.

2. *Expansion of competitive or market interactions in other sectors:* A project can help to set business relationships in other markets on a more competitive footing. The benefits for the transition process would be similar to those described under point 1 above. There are two important ways in which markets can be extended and their functioning improved by projects: (i) through interactions of the project entity with suppliers and clients and (ii) through project contributions to the integration of economic activities into the national or international economy, in particular by lowering the cost of transactions.

To have a structural effect, these contributions should not be one-off but should enhance competitive market interactions on a sustained basis. This would generally be achieved either through the formation of actors, methods of work, policies, and institutions that last, or through interactions that have a strong demonstration effect.

Project Contributions to the Institutions and Policies That Support Markets

3. *More widespread private ownership:* A project may result in increased private ownership through privatization, or new private provision of goods and services. This can generally be expected to strengthen market-oriented behavior, innovation, the pool of entrepreneurship, and, more generally, commitment to the transition. Private ownership is also in itself part of the transition objec-

tive. With the right kind of business standards, regulation, and legal environment, private ownership is complementary to, and often a condition for, the expansion and improvement of markets.

4. *Institutions, laws, and policies that promote market functioning and efficiency:* A project may help to create or reform governmental or private institutions, policies, and practices whose function is to enhance entrepreneurship and the efficiency of resource allocation. This is particularly relevant where not only the project entity itself but also other economic activities benefit. Four types of contribution are of particular importance here: (i) the creation and strengthening of public and private institutions that support the efficiency of markets; (ii) improvements to the functioning of regulatory entities and practices; (iii) project contributions to government policy formation and commitment, promoting competition, predictability, and transparency; and (iv) contributions to laws that strengthen the private sector and the open economy.

Project Contributions to Market-Based Conduct, Skills, and Innovation

5. *Transfer and dispersion of skills:* Projects can directly contribute to providing and improving the skills required for well-functioning market economies. This may include management, procurement, marketing, financial, and banking skills. Such a transfer represents a relevant transition impact only when the skills are likely to be spread so as to benefit nonproject entities (otherwise they are simply costs like any others). Skill transfers are often complementary to other transition-related project impacts such as institution building, market expansion, and demonstration effects.

6. *Demonstration of new replicable behavior and activities:* A project may lead the way by showing other economic actors what is feasible and profitable and thereby inviting replication. Three types of demonstration effect are of particular importance here: (i) demonstration of products and processes that are new to the economy, (ii) demonstration of ways of successfully restructuring companies and institutions, and (iii) demonstration to both domestic and foreign financiers of ways and instruments to finance activities.

7. *Setting standards for corporate governance and business conduct:* By implementing high standards of corporate governance and business conduct in entities supported by the EBRD, projects may contribute to the spreading of behavior and attitudes that enhance the legitimacy and functioning of the market economy. This is a form of demonstration effect that functions by establishing reference points for other firms and individuals concerning businesses that they wish to invest in or interact with. Where role models for business conduct and corporate governance are rare, such pressures are less likely to materialize. A difference with institutional change, as discussed under point 4, is that such behavior may not be codified in a formal way.

References

Banque Nationale de Paris. 1997. *Eastern European markets.* Paris: Banque Nationale de Paris, Eastern European Investment Banking Group, August.

EBRD (European Bank for Reconstruction and Development). 1995. *Transition report.* London: European Bank for Reconstruction and Development.

———. 1996. *Transition report.* London: European Bank for Reconstruction and Development.

———. 1997. *Transition report.* London: European Bank for Reconstruction and Development.

IMF (International Monetary Fund). 1997. Staff report on Russia. Washington, D.C.: International Monetary Fund, May.

Kapur, I., and E. van der Mensbrugghe. 1997. External borrowing by the Baltics, Russia and other countries of the former Soviet Union: Developments and policy issues. IMF Working Paper no. 97/92. Washington, D.C.: International Monetary Fund, European II Department, June.

Lankes, H. P., and A. Venables. 1996. Foreign direct investment in economic transition: The changing pattern of investment. *Economics of Transition* 4 (2): 331–47.

World Bank. 1997a. *Global development finance 1997.* Washington, D.C.: World Bank.

———. 1997b. Improving the environment for business and investment in the CIS and Baltic countries: Views from entrepreneurs and World Bank country economists. Background paper presented at the annual meeting of the European Bank for Reconstruction and Development.

2. W. Michael Blumenthal

When our chairman used his seductive methods and superior persuasive powers to talk me into coming here and I accepted in a fit of absentmindedness, I wondered what it was that I could contribute. Since he asked me to tell war stories, that is what I now propose to do; so you're going to hear something that is very much at the microlevel, not at all macro as all the presentations so far have been.

Gil Diaz touched on country-specific factors that are sui generis and have to do with elements we don't immediately think about, such as the quality of human resources, the people we work with. He referred to that in connection with what is happening in banks and mentioned historical factors in the way that people relate to each other and how they work together. I agree that when you talk about the functioning of capital flows, it eventually comes down to what happens with very small groups of actors in the economy and their interactions.

I shall only talk about one country, Russia. First of all, I want to stress that when you consider capital flows to Eastern Europe and the former Soviet Union, you are often lumping together countries that are really quite different. Second, even within Russia, it is extremely difficult to generalize. I noticed

Martin Feldstein wrote an op-ed piece called "Russia's Rebirth." If he's responsible for this title, I warn him: Just because you wander around the streets of Moscow you can't conclude anything definitive about what is happening in, for example, the places where we operate in the Pacific part of Russia—Khabarovsk or Sakhalin Island. That's a different world altogether, and you need to look at these places as well, to get some sense of what is happening in the country as a whole. Moscow and St. Petersburg are not like the rest. The Far East is not like European Russia; Siberia's smaller towns are very, very different, both in the way in which they are run and in the way in which business is conducted.

The third point I want to make with regard to Russia is that it is a country of enormous contrasts. You can find anything you want there. One reads a lot about crime in Russia, and there certainly is a tremendous amount of that. Yet there are also instances of sublime honesty in Russia, and a lot of things you can do that could only be accomplished with hardworking, honest people. It is easy to lose lots of money on Russian investments. But there are also huge opportunities to make lots of money (I will give you a couple of examples to illustrate both experiences). More and more people are better off, and one notices this, particularly among younger people. But there are as many or more Russian citizens who are still substantially worse off than they used to be, particularly the older ones.

Let me tell you something about the environment in which the U.S. Russia Investment Fund (TUSRIF) operates. I shall then say a few words about TUSRIF itself and cite a few examples of both successes and failures we have experienced in our operations.

First of all, the positives. We find much in Russia today that is a lot better than when we started up three years ago. In 1992 inflation was 2,500 percent; in April of this year it was 15 percent. They're talking about a budget—and I should say, numbers in Russia are very, very iffy; statistics are orders of magnitude—that projects only about 5 percent inflation. Well, if it's 12 or 15 percent, it's still pretty good from where we've come, and it's clearly gone in the right direction. The budget deficit has been reduced. There was huge negative growth a few years ago. Now it's level, or maybe it's up a percent or two, and that's tremendous progress. One hundred and twenty thousand enterprises have been privatized in Russia in a very short period of time, and many, many more (we don't know how many) start-ups were launched. If you walk around any of the cities you see the kiosks and the new stores. All of that has to be counted in. Much of it did not exist before. We estimate that one-third of the population lived below the subsistence level three or four years ago. The number is still large, but it's much less now, maybe 20 percent. There are other indications of progress. Unfortunately, perhaps, car registrations are one index; those have doubled in two years. Russia now expects to be registering 1.5 million new cars each year over the next couple of years. A lot of capital is also suddenly flowing in. Russia has become exciting and fashionable for speculators and general investors. The stock market is booming; it tripled in eighteen months. There is more direct investment of the kind we're making. Clearly, things have moved faster than anyone would have expected two to three years ago.

But there are still huge long-term problems. They will be slow to resolve. The result is that the risk-reward ratio works with a vengeance, unlike anyplace else in the world I've ever seen. The tax system is a mess. Taxes are high, and jurisdictions overlap. There is total uncertainty about what will hit you. Tax administration is arbitrary; official promises and commitments are broken. Local authorities don't pay attention to the center and vice versa, and direct investment under those circumstances requires a strong stomach. There is large-scale evasion of taxes, which makes it very difficult for an outside honest investor because you compete with others who do not pay their taxes. On the other hand, for a non-Russian investor to make the right investments and to engage in the same kind of evasion that Russians do would carry particular risks, which certainly we and our fund cannot accept. That is something any private investor has to consider very carefully.

Moreover, the judiciary is often corrupt and generally underpaid. Laws and regulations are a morass, arbitrarily enforced or not enforced at all. Sometimes they are illegally enforced. It is very difficult to enforce your rights once you've signed a contract. For example, you can find your equity interest suddenly heavily diluted, contrary to a prior agreement, with your partners selling stock without telling you. Also, there are no dependable financial data. Audited statements are hard to come by. Bureaucratic inertia and late payment of debts is common.

Some of you may have read a long article about a place named Leninsk Kusninsky, which is reputed to be run by gangsters. It is a rather large city, where the most important man is a fellow with the interesting Russian title of "Killer." He uses this English word to describe what he does to keep things in line. That's an extreme example, of course. Petty crime is much more common. We tried to invest in a string of sandwich shops in the subways of Moscow, for example. In the end we didn't because we found that those places have to pay for protection and we didn't feel we could be a part of that. There are, of course, also plenty of instances of crime or corruption at a very high level, where assets were picked up for practically nothing as they were privatized.

Why then, would anybody invest in Russia under those circumstances? The reason simply is that the potential is great, for those who are greedy and willing to take risks. Arminio Fraga asked, Why would anybody stick around? The answer is greed—the potential for very large returns.

Turning now to TUSRIF. What is it? It is an acronym for the U.S. Russia Investment Fund. It grew out of 1993 U.S. commitments made in the course of G-7 meetings in Vancouver and Tokyo to help in the restructuring of Russia. TUSRIF is one of the U.S. enterprise funds that were originally organized for Poland and Hungary back in the Bush administration. The Clinton administration had the good sense to pick up these programs and to continue them. The fund is organized and funded by the U.S. government but operates like a private investment fund, with a private board of directors. The chairman is appointed by the president, as are the directors. The fund reports to the government—our contact point is the Agency for International Development—but operates independently with minimal or no interference. We report, of course, both to the Congress and to the executive. We presently have an authorized capitalization of $440 million, of which less than half has as yet been funded. Our offices are in Moscow, St. Petersburg, Yekaterinberg, Rostov on the Don, Khabarovsk, Vladivostok, and Sakhalin.

To date we have invested about $100 million in 22 large and medium-sized businesses, $10 to $15 million in 135 small businesses, $5 million in a microlending program, and about $1 million in technical assistance money connected with our various projects. Total employment in the various enterprises is about 20,000 people, and the projects cover many industries, from communications to publishing, beverages, textiles, wood manufacturing, retailing, food processing, and consumer services.

Let me now cite three examples to illustrate how these kinds of investments in Russia can work, both those that did well and the ones that went sour.

An investment of the first type is a bottled water company. We invested $2 million in equity. (Incidentally, we can make equity or debt investments, or a combination of the two.) The company's revenue in 1995 was $3 million, in 1996 $10 million, and in the first six months of this year $11 million. We think it'll be about $25 million for the year as a whole. So we've gone in two years from $3 million to $25 million. Profits were $200,000 in 1995 and will be about $2 million this year, and we hope to double them again next year. Our partner is the Russian Orthodox Church, and it makes sure that nobody holds us up. The Church, thus, is a good partner. Bottled water is a consumer product much in demand in Russia. We think we could already sell our stake for a multiple of the $2 million we invested. So that has been a very good and successful story for us.

A second good story concerns a pharmaceutical distributor. Same kind of situation: the first year saw $37 million in revenue, second year $60 million, and this year $100 million; quadrupling of profit and lots of opportunity to make more money in the future.

The third success story concerns a string of breweries. Net sales in 1994 were $43 million, in 1995 $108 million, in 1996 $180 million, and in the first six months of this year $150 million, so we'll do over $300 million. Profits: we had a loss in 1994, $370,000 in 1995, $3.7 million in 1996, and we estimate higher numbers this year. These are obviously very attractive results.

But perhaps you are more interested in our failures, which illustrate some of the problems you can run into in Russia.

We invested in a supermarket chain in the Far East, a joint venture among the former Ministry of Fisheries, a Russian chain of small stores, the free economic zone of Nachotka, a Russian bank, and a U.S. supermarket chain. We committed $8 million and began with a bridge loan of $3 million to the enterprise, which we have since written off. What happened? We found that the management lacked the skills to run such an activity. We found that they withheld the truth from us, hid their problems, and sent us inaccurate numbers. Cash disappeared or was wasted. Wrong equipment was bought.

Then the partners disagreed with each other. The U.S. partner wouldn't deliver. And there was large-scale pilfering in the region where they were operating. As the company was going down, the Russian bank, which is one of the smallest creditors, filed suit. Our office is in Moscow, and our lawyers are in Moscow, but the bank is right there in Vladivostok and knows the judiciary. The court grabbed the assets to which the bank had a substantially subordinated claim, even though the bank had made an agreement with us acknowledging that we had a superseding claim, which it did not tell the judge about. The judge, when he heard about the agreement, said it was not relevant. We appealed in Moscow, because in theory the Moscow courts have jurisdiction. Moscow agreed with us but has so far been unable to get the relevant parties in Vladivostok to answer the telephone. We have written off the $3 million.

The second example of a problem case is a $2.5 million investment in a very nice plywood manufacturing activity in a place called Kostroma. Based on technical expertise from a British plywood manufacturer, we financed the equipment. Everything was going along swimmingly—we were exporting the product and making a profit. The local tax authorities, I guess, needed money and decided that they would pay the value-added tax rebate on exports, no longer on the basis of documentary evidence that the product has been exported, but only after the product has been received in the foreign country, which, moving by ship, takes quite a while. To get the actual documentation back and *then* to encounter a delay of roughly four to six months costs the company $2 to $3 million in cash flow. It's a small company; it doesn't have $2 to $3 million, so unless its investors have deep pockets and are willing to come in and finance that, the company will go bankrupt. There is no appeal for this kind of thing. We don't have the Russian Orthodox Church, in this instance, to come and help us, and we now face a very difficult problem of what to do. We are looking for a solution.

Finally, you run into tax avoidance schemes and questions all the time. It is customary in Russia to pay off the import and customs authorities so that they will allow you to bring in equipment without paying full duty. It's done all the time, but we don't do it. It's also common to use short-term dummy corporations, which are later abandoned, in order to avoid taxes, or to set up an offshore purchasing company to buy the raw material, sell it to the manufacturing company, and accumulate most of the profit offshore, which is then never reported, or to use a short-term dummy corporation to avoid paying the value-added tax. We looked at a manufacturing company that showed $10 to $15 million in revenue, was able to generate $4.5 million in cash, but never really paid any taxes. The problem for an honest foreign investor is how to compete with that.

I would end by saying that a country as large as Russia, with no historical memory of operating a free enterprise system, with seventy years' experience with a bureaucratically run socialist system, but with many wonderful human and natural resources, will have a substantial impact on international capital flows. That is beginning with the stock market, but it can move very quickly in either direction. As you assess the opportunities and the impact on the global system, it is important to look behind the global numbers at the reality of the problems that have to be faced within a country, in order to judge which direction things are likely to move.

3. Jiří Weigl

I have to point out at the beginning that the paper by Lankes and Stern includes an excellent amount of information regarding the capital flows to my region, and I appreciated reading it, not only from the point of view of personal interest, but as background for my work at the prime minister's office. I think it is a very good analysis. It allows a better understanding of what is going on, so the EBRD is doing a very good job.

Surprisingly, I am going to cover the same topic that was discussed here for an hour and a half. It is the exchange rate issue and the introduction of convertibility in the transforming economies of central and eastern Europe. I would like to concentrate on the Czech case, which I know best. I think it represents a case study of successful and far-reaching transformation, but on the other hand, this year it became popular for a different reason. It hosted the first example of a currency shake-up coming from international capital markets, quite a new phenomenon in the transforming economies in central and eastern Europe.

Before I start, I would like to stress that my remarks and conclusions do not necessarily reflect the official positions of my government.

Back to the exchange rate problem. A radical opening of the economy through the liberalization of current account transactions was considered one of the cornerstones of our transformation, and the selection of an appropriate exchange rate regime was a precondition for the success of this initial phase of the transformation. At that time—the beginning of the 1990s—the prevailing economic advice we received propounded the advantages of anchoring the economy to one fixed point: the exchange rate. This would be the firm point according to which all the volatile variables would settle down and somehow stabilize, and it would enable us to weather the turbulent initial phase after the collapse of communism. We had some misgivings about that arrangement, but eventually we accepted it in cooperation with the people from the IMF. The system functioned, remained stable for seventy-six months (until recently), and worked surprisingly well. The empirical evidence shows that fixing the exchange rate has brought about rapid disinflation and stabilization of the economy, which was crucial to the success of the transition process as a whole.

Another key factor in our economic development was the rapid broadening of Czech koruna convertibility. It started as so-called internal convertibility for commercial transactions, which restricted capital accounts, and then in 1995 expanded to full current account convertibility, under IMF Article VIII, together with significant liberalization of capital account transactions. So in terms of the degree of convertibility, the Czech Republic has become a frontrunner among the central and eastern European transforming economies, and this policy, together with the general results of the transformation, has had a significant impact on capital flows to the country. The economy within the past several years, after the transformation shakeout and the accompanying decline in production, has started to grow quite rapidly, at a rate reaching 5 percent in 1995–96. The inflation rate has achieved single digits. The unemployment rate, about 3 percent, is among the lowest in Europe, and the budget has been kept balanced every year. Extensive mass privatization has been successfully accomplished. Furthermore, the country has enjoyed remarkable political stability, and up to now has been governed by a reform-minded, conservative government, with strong popular support and a good international reputation. These factors, together with low external debt, were reflected in the country's strong credit ratings from rating agencies. Moreover, the Czech Republic was the first of the central and eastern European countries to be admitted to the OECD. International financial markets appreciate these developments, and the country has enjoyed easy access to foreign capital. By the end of last year foreign direct investment exceeded $7 billion, foreign portfolio investments are about $5 billion, and enterprise debt has multiplied several times in the past several years.

So generally speaking, for a long time the Czech economy has produced confidence and optimistic expectations. Nevertheless, it was my country that this year was the first central European transitional economy to become a victim of a wave of currency speculation, similar to that occurring in Asian emerging markets. Thus we have to ask ourselves how it could happen. I would return to the exchange rate question. I think the fixed exchange rate regime was one of the factors at work. Its effects were quite controversial. On the one hand, I have already mentioned its stabilizing role, and I can add its function as an efficiency tool, putting pressure on exporters to improve efficiency and competitiveness because of the inflation differential between the Czech economy and its main trading partners. But on the other hand, long-lasting fixed exchange rates practically eliminate exchange rate risk and create very attractive conditions for foreign capital, especially speculative flows. Starting with the rapid economic recovery in 1993, capital flows were pulled by very strong investment demand, as a result of both the necessary restructuring after the privatization of the enterprise sector and, on the government side, the launching of many environmental and infrastructural projects that were required by international treaties or were simply a precondition for economic recovery, like telephones and so forth.

The extraordinarily high level of gross capital formation became more and more dependent on foreign capital inflow, which peaked in 1995 at 17.4 percent of GDP, when the share of national saving in GDP started to decline. This resulted in money supply growth of about 20 percent per year and inflationary pressure. Soon the symptoms of overheating in the economy became apparent. The situation posed a serious dilemma for economic policymakers. The first option was naturally an exchange rate adjustment, but as Moeen Qureshi has mentioned, we were confronted with unwanted appreciation pressures, so this option was not seen as a realistic solution because it would have exhausted the exchange rate cushion necessary for enterprises to survive this difficult restructuring. Maintaining the stabilizing role of the exchange rate fix was still seen as the number one priority.

The fiscal option was even less realistic, because the budget was balanced every year, and for political reasons it was practically impossible to achieve a fiscal surplus large enough to sterilize the extensive capital inflow. We did not want to introduce excessive capital controls, so the central bank was in quite a difficult position: what to do? Passive sterilization and high interest rate policy only worsened the problem and led to a vicious circle with no solution. High interest rates under a regime of extensive capital account convertibility gave banks and companies easy access to foreign debt instruments, and in this environment the effect of domestic interest rate policy was weakened, and competition from cheap foreign debt instruments created serious problems for local banks fighting with a growing burden of bad loans. So to escape this policy deadlock, the central bank widened the fluctuation band of the koruna, in order to increase exchange rate risk for speculators, and followed by greatly liberalizing capital account transactions, enabling capital outflow from the country. These actions temporarily terminated the speculative short-term inflows, but another, more important challenge started to emerge.

Since 1995, the current account deficit had grown progressively, driven especially by the rapid growth in investment I have already mentioned. The investment ratio in 1996 reached the extreme of 33 percent. The growth in investment had the shape of a massive wave, starting from a relatively low initial rate, and it was necessary to expect a relatively long time lag between the demand-generating and capacity-generating effects of the investment. Also, the specifics of privatization played an important role in this development. In the Czech Republic, where the voucher method of privatization had been extensively used, a turbulent process of ownership concentration was launched and became a relatively long-lasting phenomenon. These conditions affected the emerging domestic stock market, which has not functioned predominantly as a tool for capital mobilization, but instead has served mainly to redistribute existing stock holdings. This has made the Czech stock market a nonstandard place for foreign investors, damaging the credibility of the country.

An attempt to address the problem of increasing external imbalance using monetary tools produced a rapid fall in the rate of growth, as a result of a severe increase in reserve requirements by the central bank last year; and the decline in output had serious budget consequences, while the current account deficit kept worsening, reaching 8.6 percent of GDP in 1996. High interest rates prompted a resumption of the inflow of speculative capital and pushed the exchange rate up to the appreciation limit, thus further hurting current account development. These events, together with the more delicate political balance in the wake of the 1996 elections, eroded the confidence of international financial markets at a time when the Thai bhat crisis was approaching.

In the spring of this year, the longtime prevailing exchange rate appreciation was reversed, and in mid-May the level was pushed to record lows by speculative short selling, despite central bank interventions and dramatic highs in interest rates. Eventually, the fixed exchange rate regime was abandoned and replaced by a floating rate, and the koruna depreciated by some 12 percent on average. The currency shock led to a government reshuffle and an economic policy revision, based on drastic fiscal tightening and a public sector wage freeze, along with a set of systemic measures such as stock market reform, energy and rent control liberalization, and a speeding-up of privatization.

Five months later the situation has more or less stabilized, despite the devastating floods that hit parts of the Czech Republic in July. Also growth is estimated to slow down to about 1.5 to 2 percent. Inflation is still about 10 percent, 2 percent higher than last year, but the current account deficit will definitely end up visibly better this year than in 1996. The speculation against the koruna stopped almost immediately after the currency regime was changed.

My question is about the substance of these developments. Were they a manifestation of real economic crisis, or mere turbulence, or only a temporary loss of confidence by international financial markets? Some analysts describe the Czech case as an eastern European Mexico. I think this is an exaggerated parallel. We could hardly match Mexico's full-blown economic crisis generated by all-around weak fundamentals: Foreign debt, estimated at about 39 percent of GDP, remains moderate by the region's standards, and the debt-servicing ratio remains around 10 percent. About 70 percent of liabilities consist of long-term debt incurred chiefly by the private sector. Foreign reserves stood at comfortable levels before the crisis, with an import cover of four months. Unlike Mexico, the Czech Republic is facing its most serious difficulties financing the current account deficit, and moreover—and this is unique—the fiscal deficit is not a problem.

So when searching for the reasons why the recent shock happened, I think we are justified in asking whether the exchange rate fix was not kept too long, and whether the degree of currency convertibility adopted in the Czech Republic was not too high, whether it was not introduced too early, and whether it was adequate to the depth of changes produced by the transformation process in the economy. The enhanced liberalization of capital accounts was not able to compensate for the negative effects of the fixed exchange rate regime, which disarmed monetary policy. On the contrary, the extensive liberalization of capital accounts in circumstances of increased international uncertainty made the domestic currency particularly vulnerable to speculative attack.

One phenomenon illustrates the degree of convertibility of the Czech currency, which exceeds regional standards: The Czech koruna has become the only Eurocurrency within the region, and starting in 1995, about fifty-five Eurobond issues were placed in the market. On the one hand, this can be interpreted as a sign of confidence in the Czech economy; on the other hand, I think it increases the volatility of the currency and weakens the control of the central bank over the money supply.

The Czech experience shows that a credible exchange rate fix offers important advantages in the *early* stages of transition, but in my opinion, the fix should disappear in the medium term. The Czech Republic made this necessary shift late, and under pressure from speculation, which increased the cost. The introduction of currency convertibility was correct in terms of sequence, but too fast in terms of timing. The combination of a fixed exchange rate and extensive currency convertibility proved to be, in my opinion, a very risky arrangement at a time when the degree of current account imbalance, and the concern of international markets about the sustainability of the situation and the government's ability to react, was high. The coincidence of this development with the changing view in international markets of some, especially Asian, emerging markets provoked speculators to test the Czech currency. The shock was strong but short, and after a visible policy shift, the situation has returned to normal. The confidence of the international markets has not been substantially shaken, which is proved by the exceptionally favorable conditions of credit that our central bank was able to mobilize to replenish its international reserves, depleted during its hopeless attempt to intervene in the market during the attack.

Judging from these facts, I would call the developments in my country this year a terrible short-term crisis, serious turbulence that could be repeated if things go wrong. The koruna was attacked not because problems in the Czech economy were much worse than in other postcommunist economies. The attack was, in my opinion, partly a side effect of the strong speculative wave that hit other emerging market currencies and was made possible by the degree of convertibility of the Czech currency and because preventive exchange rate policy action was not taken in time.

There are arguments that such turbulence has some positive effects. I agree: it effectively disciplines economic policy and mercilessly forces changes in unsustainable trends. From this perspective, the far-reaching opening of the Czech economy, which allowed this automatic disciplining mechanism to function and, through international markets, to punish economic policy mistakes, can be seen as a fundamental vehicle for successful transformation. These arguments have strong potential, but we should also ask about the costs of this volatile adjustment mechanism, and especially whether and when the transforming economies can afford it.

The problems the Czech economy faced this year are not unique within the region. Trade deficits are becoming a general problem among the transitional economies in Europe, and the importance of foreign capital inflows is increasing. The process of liberalizing and broadening the convertibility of currencies is on track and is closely linked to the obligations of new central European OECD members. It creates a lot of space for the inflow of private capital but also makes these relatively weak economies more vulnerable to speculation and the risk of capital flight. The scope and speed with which the former communist countries have opened their economies and adopted currency convertibility has been much greater than similar processes after World War II in western Europe. Generally, this is regarded as an important sign of progress, and in my opinion, it undoubtedly is. But far-reaching openness also means great vulnerability to volatile capital movements and high risk for the still relatively weak transforming economies. So I would argue that the degree of convertibility and the pace at which it is introduced in these countries should correspond to progress in transformation, and the governments and central banks should fine-tune the process very carefully, together with a responsible exchange rate policy. Otherwise, the price that the small open industrial, ex-communist economies will pay for premature capital account liberalization could be quite high.

The enterprise restructuring question is very important.[1] Institutional bottlenecks still exist within the Czech system: the functioning of the court system, bankruptcy procedures, limited protection of creditors, and things like that, which simply prolong the lives of companies that should have gone bankrupt a long time ago. Sometimes people exaggerate the role of state ownership of the banks. In our case, the state is a very passive owner. The problem within the banking sector is not that the state somehow intervenes and pushes banks to extend loans but that corporate governance as such is lacking; the state is not able to exert its power, either for good or for bad. That is why privatization of the banks is one of the priorities of my government these days, but it is of course very controversial. I think there is no secret that our friends from Nomura Securities are bidding for the third largest bank in our country, and I wish them good luck. The government has already approved it. We are waiting for audits only. It is one component of the package that was adopted after the currency crisis, to accomplish systematic reform and to accomplish the privatization of such key institutions as the banks.

The capital market is another weak point, especially in the Czech Republic. It has been the subject of criticism for many years, and I was one of those pushing for rapid standardization. I think some defects arose naturally because

---

1. The remainder of this comment addresses points raised during the discussion.

of the voucher scheme. An artificial market was created to enable petty share-holders to trade their shares. It was a very nonstandard place and regulation was poor, so fraud and illegal practices and insider trading became not the exception but the norm. Methods that are unmentionable in developed markets have been used quite often, and of course it has become a political problem. The government recognizes it and is making it one of the priorities for the beginning of next year. An independent commission will be established to exert control over transactions, and there will be strong reporting requirements, as well as legal changes that will divide the mutual funds and banks that came into existence during the voucher privatization and created nontransparent structures wherein enterprises have natural links with banks. The banks own companies and extend them credit at the same time, and on the other hand, the companies own banks. It's a very nontransparent system, and it has to be changed and standardized.

Discussion Summary

Nicholas Stern noted that Michael Blumenthal's observations regarding Russia mirror the experiences of the EBRD. Stern said that the pace of change in the region has been remarkable but that there are reasons for caution. Previously, the EBRD encouraged investors to partner with them in order to convince them that "it's not really as risky as you think." Now, the rationale for partnering with the EBRD is that "it's rather more risky than you think." In particular, Stern drew a distinction between the fundamentals underlying much of the foreign direct investment to the region and the enormous drop in spreads accompanying portfolio flows. Moreover, the region is now characterized by high current account deficits and real exchange rate appreciation. The appropriate management of these conditions represents a substantial challenge to policymakers in the region.

Moving from the macroeconomic perspective to the day-to-day realities of business, Stern noted that organized crime is pervasive and extremely efficient in Russia today. The mafia visits companies immediately after registration and carefully monitors them to ensure that steady payments are extracted. Nonetheless, Stern emphasized that private investing in the region, while risky, can be extremely lucrative.

Sebastian Edwards disagreed with the emphasis on portfolio flows in precipitating crises and suggested that the combination of governance and the quality of the financial system are determining factors. In fact, if the IMF characterization of the Mexican crisis is correct, he noted, domestic investors took out as much money as foreigners did.

Arminio Fraga commented that banks, and particularly state banks, are central to the understanding of these situations. In particular, he noted that while private banks are difficult to monitor, public banks are impossible to monitor given the interests of bureaucrats and politicians. Consequently, public banks should be carefully monitored and supervised or, better yet, closed.

Jiří Weigl responded that state ownership of banks is problematic in the Czech Republic because of the passive role of the state as an owner and not because of excessive intervention. As a consequence, there exists no effective governance in state-owned banks. He noted that the privatization of banks remains central to the future of systemic reform in the Czech Republic.

Comparing the Czech and Mexican situations, *Francisco Gil Diaz* noted that the outcome in Mexico may have been more violent as the result of the combination of a tenuous reserve position and the overhang created by the issuance of the Tesobono bonds.

Bernard Wasow drew attention to the fact that a number of unviable Czech enterprises are still being supported by the state and that this policy of sustaining employment in the Czech Republic has not been addressed fully.

Weigl replied that a number of bottlenecks exist in the restructuring of state-owned enterprises. Notably, the legal system and the intransigence of creditors are prolonging the lives of companies that are no longer sustainable. He also noted that the voucher privatization system has hindered the growth of capital markets because it has created an artificial environment in which nonstandard behavior is the norm. Therefore, better oversight and standardization of procedures within capital markets are also important parts of the reform agenda.

Robert Feenstra noted that for foreign direct investment to flow into the region, foreign investors must perceive a viable exit opportunity through the existence of robust domestic capital markets. Accordingly, the creation and supervision of such capital markets should be foremost on the agenda for attracting foreign investment.

Blumenthal downplayed the importance of capital markets for attracting greater foreign direct investment. Instead, he noted that the most important determinant of future FDI flows would be a legal framework that provides predictability and stability. Such a framework is growing in the region, and companies are responding by investing more. In turn, Blumenthal suggested, capital markets will grow to accommodate the needs of the expanding firms.

3

Capital Flows to East Asia

1. Takatoshi Ito
2. Kathryn M. Dominguez
3. Moeen Qureshi
4. Zhang Shengman
5. Masaru Yoshitomi

1. Takatoshi Ito

Capital Flows in East and Southeast Asia

3.1.1 Introduction

The currency crises in Southeast Asia in the summer of 1997 have shown that even Asian "miracle" countries are not immune to the problems of volatile capital flows. From July to September, the four major currencies in the region depreciated by 20 to 30 percent, and stock prices continued declines that had started earlier. Although weak economies and financial sector problems are underlying causes of weakness, a speculative attack seems to have triggered the crises. A sharp exchange through the media between George Soros and Prime Minister Mahathir highlighted some frequently asked questions about the benefits and costs of free capital mobility and speculation.

This paper reviews and analyzes capital flows to Asian countries in connection with past growth and current pain in these economies. There is no doubt that capital inflows to most Asian countries accelerated their industrialization. Part of high economic growth was financed by foreign capital and technology. Capital inflows to Asian countries were considered to be managed relatively well in the first half of the 1990s. Even at the time of the Mexican peso crisis (December 1994 to 1995), "contagion" effects in Asian countries were short-lived and less serious.

This chapter was written with information available up to the time of the conference, October 1997. The crisis in East Asia, particularly in Indonesia and Korea, became much more serious. However, that topic needs another paper. Footnotes partially update events in Thailand.

In late 1996, exports from Asian countries started to slow and economic growth started to decelerate. The high-flying stock prices in Southeast Asian economies turned downward too. Since most Asian currencies were "effectively pegged" to the U.S. dollar, they were considered to have become overvalued. In 1997, pressure intensified. The Thai baht came under attack in February, March, and May. In July, the Thai authorities decided to float the currency. The Malaysian ringgit, the Indonesian rupiah, and the Philippine peso followed suit soon after the baht devaluation.

Capital flows to the Asian region provide an interesting case study in economic development and growth. The summer 1997 episode of currency crises in Asia contains lessons as significant as those learned from the Mexican crisis of 1994–95. The rest of the paper is organized as follows. Section 3.1.2 gives a historical overview of capital flows with an emphasis on Asia. Section 3.1.3 explains how capital flows helped economic growth in Asia. Section 3.1.4 surveys the literature on the problems associated with too much capital inflow. Section 3.1.5 gives a concise account of what happened in Thailand in 1997. Section 3.1.6 concludes.

3.1.2 Capital Flows to Asia

Net private capital flows to developing countries are estimated to have increased more than fivefold in the past six years. In 1990, total capital flows to emerging markets (developing countries and transition economies) were about $50 billion, of which half went to Asia and one-third to Latin America. By 1993, total capital flows rose to $160 billion, of which slightly less than 40 percent went to Asia and slightly more than one-third to Latin America. A majority of flows to Asia took the form of direct investment and an overwhelming portion of flows to Latin America took the form of portfolio investment. The large ratio of portfolio flows to Latin American countries in 1991–93 became a source of instability in the wake of—if indeed it did not trigger—the Mexican peso crisis. In 1994, capital flows to Latin American countries, especially in the form of portfolio flows, declined compared to the preceding two years, while capital flows to Asia continued to increase. In particular, in 1995, net portfolio investment in Latin America was negative. That is, there was net outflow from Latin America after the Mexican crisis. Capital flows to Latin America recovered sharply only in 1996, contributing to a new record high for the capital flows to emerging markets, exceeding $230 billion, of which about half went to Asia and one-third to Latin America. (For details, see table 3.1.)

Asian countries have in the past ten years tried to manage the rate of capital inflow. Technocrats and central bankers are well aware of the macroeconomic problems associated with too much capital *in*flow. However, the crisis in the summer of 1997 is the first test for the Asian countries of thinking in terms of managing capital *out*flow (or a decline in capital inflow).

Table 3.1   **Net Private Capital Flows to Emerging Markets (billions of U.S. dollars)**

Flows	1990	1991	1992	1993	1994	1995	1996
All countries							
Total	45.7	139.8	133.7	161.0	147.0	192.8	235.2
FDI	18.8	32.1	35.8	56.9	75.5	87.3	105.9
Portfolio	17.0	39.7	46.3	106.8	97.2	31.6	58.7
Others	9.9	68.0	51.7	−2.7	−25.7	73.9	70.6
Asia							
Total	21.4	37.7	22.4	59.5	75.1	98.9	106.8
FDI	9.5	15.2	17.2	35.2	44.6	50.7	58.0
Portfolio	−0.9	2.8	9.6	23.8	18.5	20.1	20.1
Others	12.9	19.7	−4.5	0.5	12.0	28.1	28.8
Latin America							
Total	10.3	24.9	55.5	61.7	44.9	35.7	77.7
FDI	6.6	10.9	12.9	13.4	21.5	19.9	29.9
Portfolio	17.5	14.5	30.6	61.1	60.8	−7.5	27.1
Others	−13.8	−0.5	12.0	−12.8	−37.5	23.3	20.7
Other regions							
Total	9.9	78.8	48.5	28.8	11.6	28.9	31.2
FDI	2.7	3.7	3.7	2.3	3.9	3.6	6.7
Portfolio	0.4	21.6	19.8	18.3	15.1	15.7	10.0
Others	6.8	54.7	25.0	8.0	−7.5	9.7	14.5
Transition countries							
Total	4.2	−1.6	7.1	10.9	15.4	29.1	19.4
FDI	0.0	2.4	4.2	6.0	5.4	13.1	11.3
Portfolio	0.0	0.8	−0.8	3.4	2.7	3.4	1.6
Others	4.2	−4.8	3.8	1.5	7.3	12.6	6.6

Source: Folkerts-Landau et al. (1997, 41).

Note: "Others" includes short- and long-term credit, loans (not including uses of IMF credit), currency and deposits, and other accounts receivable and payable. "Other regions" includes the Middle East, Europe, and Africa.

Even in Asia and Latin America, only a handful countries receive disproportionately large amounts of capital inflow. From 1990 to 1995, only eight countries have received more than $15 billion in net long-term private capital inflows: China (more than $160 billion), Mexico (more than $80 billion), Brazil ($60 billion), Korea ($50 billion), Malaysia, Argentina, Thailand, and Indonesia (World Bank 1997a, 12). The top three, China, Mexico, and Brazil, are relatively large countries. In ratio to GDP, Malaysia (1991–93) and Thailand (1989–91 and 1995) received the largest capital inflows (more than 10 percent) in the past several years. (For details, see table 3.2 and figs. 3.1 and 3.2.) Hence, relative to the sizes of their economies, some Asian countries have had to deal with much larger capital flow shocks than Mexico (and other Latin American countries).

Table 3.2   Net Capital Inflows (percent of GDP)

Country	Period	1988	1989	1990	1991	1992	1993	1994	1995	Cumulative
Indonesia	1990–95			2.5	1.9	1.3	0.2	1.1	3.6	8.3
Korea	1991–95				2.6	2.5	0.6	2.4	3.5	9.3
Malaysia	1989–95		2.9	5.7	11.1	15.3	23.2	1.2	6.6	45.8
Philippines	1989–95		2.1	3.9	4.4	2.3	4.4	7.9	5.2	23.1
Thailand	1988–95	7.4	10.4	12.3	12.3	8.6	7.7	8.3	12.1	51.5
Argentina	1991–94				1.3	3.8	2.9	3.1		9.7
Brazil	1992–95					2.8	2.3	1.9	4.8	9.4
Chile	1989–95		3.3	8.6	3.1	7.4	6.3	7.7	4.0	25.8
Colombia	1992–95					1.8	5.6	5.6	5.3	16.2
Mexico	1989–94		2.6	2.2	7.5	7.6	8.5	3.3		27.1
Peru	1990–95			3.9	5.4	5.3	4.6	10.8	8.2	30.4
Venezuela	1992–93					3.3	2.0			5.4

Source: World Bank (1997a, 175, table 4.1).

Country Experiences

The high intensity of capital flow, that is, exceeding 10 percent of GDP, that Thailand and Malaysia experienced in the late 1980s and early 1990s is truly remarkable. It is unparalleled among the Latin American countries, with only Peru reaching this volume in one year, 1994. Figures 3.1 through 3.4 show time series of ratios of net private capital flow to GDP for selected Asian and Latin American countries.

An examination of the details in table 3.3 reveals substantial differences among Asian countries. China receives the lion's share of capital flows, and most of them are in the form of direct investment, rather than bank credit or portfolio investment. Unlike other countries that attract capital inflows, China has recorded current account surpluses. This means China has very rapidly accumulated foreign reserves, because roughly speaking the sum of the current account surplus and capital inflow equals the increase in foreign reserves. These three aspects of the Chinese situation—that the current account is in surplus, that most capital inflows are in the form of direct investment, and that foreign reserves have been accumulated—mean that the risk of capital flow reversal is minimal in China.

In other countries (discussed below) capital inflows often finance current account deficits. For example, from 1993 to 1996, current account deficits increased sharply in Korea. The current account went from a small surplus in

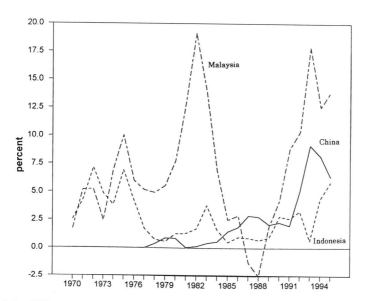

Fig. 3.1   China, Indonesia, and Malaysia: ratio of net private capital flow to GDP
Source: World Bank (1997b).

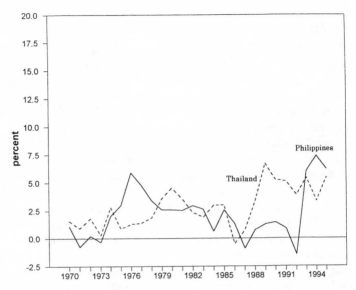

Fig. 3.2   Philippines and Thailand: ratio of net private capital flow to GDP
Source: World Bank (1997b).

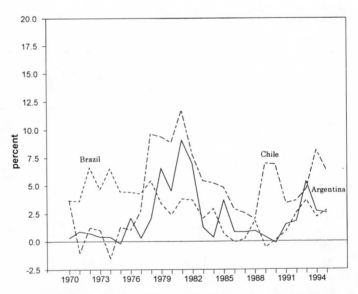

Fig. 3.3   Argentina, Brazil, and Chile: ratio of net private capital flow to GDP
Source: World Bank (1997b).

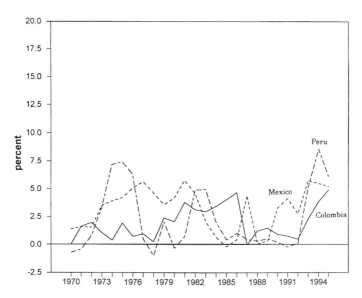

Fig. 3.4   Colombia, Mexico, and Peru: ratio of net private capital flow to GDP
Source: World Bank (1997b).

1993 to −5 percent of GDP in 1996. Capital inflows to Korea increased accordingly, most flows taking the form of bank credit.

Thailand has maintained relatively high current account deficits. Capital inflows have also been high and, up to 1996, more than offset the deficits, resulting in a steady increase in foreign reserves. Most capital inflows to Thailand took the form of bank credit, as in Korea. In fact, in 1993 Thailand opened an international offshore banking facility (Bangkok International Banking Facility), which became an intermediate point through which foreign banks could move funds into Thai domestic markets. This resulted in a threefold increase in bank credit inflows between 1993 and 1994. The size and characteristics of the capital inflows described here will be an important part of the backdrop to the baht crisis of 1997, described below.

Malaysia has also used capital inflows to finance current account deficits. However, the current account deficit in Malaysia is smaller than in Thailand, though larger than in Korea. The portion of bank credit in capital flows to Malaysia is much less than that to Korea and Thailand. Equity investment in Malaysia has been larger, probably because of its deep capital market (the ratio of stock market capitalization to GDP in Malaysia is the highest in the world), which attracts foreign equity investors.

Indonesia and the Philippines have also attracted increasing capital flows, though their size (in ratio to GDP) has not reached the level that Malaysia and Thailand experienced earlier. Both Indonesia and the Philippines have experienced modest current account deficits. Traditionally, both Indonesia and the

Table 3.3   **Type of Private Capital Flow (millions of U.S. dollars)**

	1992	1993	1994	1995	1996
			Asia		
China					
GDP	469,003	598,765	546,610	711,315	834,311
Current account	6,401	−11,609	6,908	1,618	7,243
Capital inflows	−250	23,474	32,645	38,674	39,966
Equity	7,922	24,266	34,208	36,185	39,981
Bank credits	4,008	2,146	3,786	8,405	10,625
Indonesia					
GDP	139,116	158,007	176,892	202,131	227,370
Current account	−2,780	−2,106	−2,792	−6,431	−7,663
Capital inflows	6,129	5,632	3,839	10,259	10,847
Equity	1,947	2,692	2,573	4,285	5,195
Bank credits	663	1,573	2,030	8,021	12,602
Korea					
GDP	307,938	332,821	380,822	456,356	484,569
Current account	−3,944	990	−3,867	−8,507	−23,006
Capital inflows	6,994	3,217	10,733	17,273	23,924
Equity	2,057	5,659	1,580	2,205	2,956
Bank credits	3,806	1,782	15,314	24,351	35,119
Malaysia					
GDP	58,310	64,180	72,506	87,315	99,169
Current account	−2,167	−2,991	−4,520	−8,469	−4,596
Capital inflows	8,746	10,805	1,288	7,639	9,479
Equity	5,439	11,664	8,986	4,604	5,361
Bank credits	2,001	4,518	−2,924	1,472	4,159
Philippines					
GDP	52,976	54,368	64,084	74,120	82,847
Current account	−1,000	−3,016	−2,950	−1,980	−3,953
Capital inflows	3,208	3,267	5,120	5,309	11,277
Equity	268	812	1,558	1,609	3,517
Bank credits	302	−2,843	115	1,513	3,875
Thailand					
GDP	111,453	125,575	144,525	168,355	185,047
Current account	−6,303	−6,364	−8,085	−13,554	−14,692
Capital inflows	9,475	10,500	12,167	21,909	19,486
Equity	1,538	4,337	259	3,238	2,718
Bank credits	4,630	3,964	11,490	17,828	9,531
			Latin America		
Argentina					
GDP	228,990	257,842	281,925	279,613	297,460
Current account	−5,462	−7,672	−10,117	−2,768	−3,787
Capital inflows	7,373	9,827	9,279	574	7,033
Equity	4,630	4,038	3,954	4,589	7,375
Bank credits	1,152	9,945	1,139	2,587	959

Table 3.3   (continued)

	1992	1993	1994	1995	1996
		Latin America			
Brazil					
GDP	446,580	438,300	546,230	704,167	774,868
Current account	6,089	20	−1,153	−18,136	−23,602
Capital inflows	5,889	7,604	8,020	29,306	33,984
Equity	3,147	4,062	5,333	8,169	15,788
Bank credits	11,077	4,375	9,162	11,443	14,462
Chile					
GDP	41,882	44,474	50,920	65,215	69,218
Current account	−958	−2,554	−1,585	−1,398	−3,744
Capital inflows	3,134	2,996	5,294	2,488	6,781
Equity	876	1,326	2,580	1,959	4,090
Bank credits	2,192	804	1,108	1,100	1,808
Colombia					
GDP	44,140	50,863	68,631	80,531	86,355
Current account	901	−2,102	−3,160	−4,365	−4,946
Capital inflows	183	2,701	2,770	4,485	7,098
Equity	744	913	1,532	1,384	3,416
Bank credits	813	1,453	1,483	2,503	3,564
Mexico					
GDP	363,608	403,194	421,721	286,697	330,044
Current account	−24,442	−23,400	−29,662	−1,576	−2,330
Capital inflows	27,039	33,760	15,787	−10,487	6,133
Equity	10,149	15,104	15,056	10,045	11,986
Bank credits	4,643	2,246	3,166	−58	−396
Peru					
GDP	41,739	−41,186	−50,287	−59,129	−61,002
Current account	−2,116	−2,327	−2,667	−4,314	−3,619
Capital inflows	451	−259	3,320	2,308	3,097
Equity	136	892	3,644	2,354	3,942
Bank credits	386	77	775	1,515	459
Venezuela					
GDP	60,422.69	60,047.78	58,417.47	77,389.42	70,537.85
Current account	−3,749	−1,993	2,541	2,014	8,914
Capital inflows	3,386	2,656	−3,203	−2,964	−1,784
Equity	644	−446	740	1,064	2,800
Bank credits	1,370	501	−500	−625	−740

Sources: GDP is nominal GDP converted into U.S. dollars at the annual average exchange rate and current account is current account surplus (negative means deficit); from IMF, *International Financial Statistics* CD-ROM (Washington, D.C., March 1999).

Capital inflows are net private capital inflows, equity is net equity investment including direct equity investment and portfolio equity investment, and bank credit is commercial bank, net credit flows; from Institute of International Finance, *Comparative Statistics for Emerging Market Economies* (Washington, D.C., December 1998).

Philippines have not relied on bank credit, but Indonesia recently received an increased level of bank credit.

Among Latin American countries, the ratio of capital inflow to GDP was highest in Mexico, before the peso crisis, and has recently become highest in Peru. However, the average level of this ratio among Latin American countries is lower than among Asian emerging market countries. The reason Asian countries did not experience a currency crisis or volatile capital outflows until 1997 is that growth rates were much higher there than in Latin America. When the growth rate is high, the future ratio of external liability to GDP is expected to be "sustainable." (See Milesi-Ferretti and Razin 1996 for the literature on current account sustainability.) For example, Mexico got into trouble when its current account deficit reached 8 percent with an economic growth rate of 3.5 percent in 1994, while Thailand with the same current account deficit ratio had no crisis in 1995 and 1996, when the Thai economic growth rates were 8.6 and 6.7 percent, respectively. Only when the growth rate declined sharply in 1997 did pressure on the baht become unavoidable.

Bank Credit

Since bank lending plays a large role in many countries in Asia, and to a lesser extent in Latin America, a more careful look at the nature and source of bank lending is necessary. According to Bank for International Settlements (BIS) data, as of the end of 1996, Asia in total had borrowed $367 billion from abroad (in all currencies and locally in foreign currencies; for details, see table 3.4, panel A). Latin American countries had borrowed $244 billion from abroad. Korea's cross-border liability amounted to $100 billion, while Thailand's reached $70 billion. Among Latin American countries, Brazil with $68 billion and Mexico with $61 billion were the largest. Both China and Indonesia in Asia had external bank liabilities of almost $56 billion, and Argentina had $45 billion in external bank liability.

Bank liability is important because currency crises are often associated with banking crises (as forcefully argued by Kaminsky and Reinhart 1996). Causality can go either way. The banking sector, which performs a clearing and settlement function for all transactions, is a key financial sector, so the government has to step in if a banking crisis develops. With a weak and vulnerable banking sector, a strong currency defense is impossible. Hence, the higher the ratio of external liability in the banking system, the more vulnerable is the banking system once a crisis develops. A banking crisis then results in a currency crisis as foreign investors withdraw funds. If the currency depreciates sharply, external liabilities, especially those denominated in foreign currencies, become a much larger burden. Hence, a currency crisis will develop into a banking crisis if external liability in the banking sector is unusually high. Put simply, the Mexican peso crisis caused a banking crisis in the subsequent months, while the Thai baht crisis was preceded by a banking crisis (to be precise, it was a financial market crisis, because the troubled institutions were not banks but finance companies).

Table 3.4   **International Bank Lending: International Positions of All Reporting Banks on Countries outside the Reporting Area, End of December 1996 (millions of U.S. dollars)**

A. By Maturity and Sector

Claims Vis-à-Vis	Total	Maturity of One Year or Less	Sector — Bank	Public	Nonbank Private
Developing countries	692,563	398,757	252,590	118,880	319,756
Asia	367,056	225,710	158,885	33,141	174,588
China	55,002	26,879	22,797	8,476	23,725
Indonesia	55,523	34,248	11,788	6,942	36,759
Korea	99,953	67,506	65,896	5,677	28,310
Malaysia	22,231	11,191	6,510	1,993	13,722
Philippines	13,289	7,737	5,246	2,723	5,319
Taiwan	22,363	18,869	12,924	475	8,955
Thailand	70,181	45,704	25,906	2,276	41,854
Latin America	243,608	131,320	59,934	67,533	115,639
Argentina	44,819	25,215	8,792	10,578	25,440
Brazil	67,954	42,835	20,978	17,849	29,102
Chile	15,155	7,762	3,701	1,689	9,765
Colombia	16,772	6,590	4,015	3,705	9,052
Mexico	61,335	28,080	12,953	22,305	26,069
Venezuela	11,082	3,150	796	5,654	4,627
Memorandum item for offshore banking centers	663,897	493,152	402,647	3,967	255,697
Hong Kong	207,164	170,867	135,474	1,084	70,020
Singapore	189,310	175,303	156,938	440	31,765

B. By Source Country: Japan and the United States

Claims Vis-à-Vis	Total	Japan	United States
Developing countries	692,563	138,317	106,468
Asia	367,056	118,576	34,241
China	55,002	17,792	2,688
Indonesia	55,523	22,035	5,279
Korea	99,953	24,324	9,355
Malaysia	22,231	8,210	2,337
Philippines	13,289	1,558	3,902
Taiwan	22,363	2,683	3,182
Thailand	70,181	37,525	5,049
Latin America	243,608	15,399	66,461
Argentina	44,819	1,789	13,242
Brazil	67,954	5,171	18,443
Chile	15,155	794	4,228
Colombia	16,772	1,310	4,125
Mexico	61,335	5,360	17,426
Venezuela	11,082	1,694	2,834
Memorandum item for offshore banking centers	663,897	219,690	35,617
Hong Kong	207,164	87,462	8,665
Singapore	189,310	58,809	5,727

Sources: Bank for International Settlements, "The Maturity, Sectoral and Nationality Distribution of International Bank Lending, Second Half 1996" (Basel, June 1997).

Note: Table reports consolidated cross-border claims in all currencies and local claims in nonlocal currencies.

The statistics also reveal that the public sector in Asian countries did not borrow much from foreign banks. Most cross-border borrowing went to either the domestic banking or nonbank private sector. Out of the $367 billion that Asian countries borrowed from abroad, only 10 percent went to the public sector. In contrast, one-fourth of the $243 billion that Latin American countries borrowed went to the public sector. Mexico has an external liability of $61 billion from abroad, of which one-third is owed by the public sector. In sum, Asian countries, most notably Korea and Thailand, relied on cross-border bank credit more than their Latin American counterparts. The domestic banking and nonbank private sectors were the major borrowers in Asia, while the public sector was also a substantial borrower in some Latin American countries.

In the BIS statistics on cross-border bank credit, it is also possible to trace the origin (lender) of funds (see table 3.4, panel B). For Asian and Latin American countries, substantial lending came either from Japan or the United States. Of the Asian liability of $693 billion owed to international banks, Japanese banks have lent $138 billion and U.S. banks $106 billion. In Latin America, U.S. banks have lent $66 billion, one-fourth of the total Latin American liability of $243 billion. Japanese banks lent only $15 billion to Latin American countries. Among Asian countries, Thailand is notable: of its $70 billion external liability to international banks, Japanese banks account for $38 billion, or more than half. No other major Asian or Latin American country has borrowed more than half its debt from the banks of a single country. This fact partly explains why Thai authorities particularly asked Japanese banks to keep the line of credit open during the baht crisis.

Foreign Direct Investment

Foreign direct investment (FDI) is often said to be a preferred form of investment for host countries. (Direct investment is usually defined as the purchase of more than 10 percent of the equity of a particular company.) Compared with bank credit, bank deposits, or bonds, it is more difficult and costly to withdraw investment that has become factories and other real assets. Moreover, with direct investment comes foreign management and technological transfers, which are expected to contribute to raising the industrialization level of the host country. In the beginning of the 1990s, Indonesia, Thailand, and Malaysia were the favored destinations of Japanese FDI. On average Indonesia has received more than 150 billion yen (about $1.3 billion) annually in the 1990s. By the mid-1990s, China had become the top host of Japanese FDI. In 1995, China received more than 430 billion yen (about $4 billion) of Japanese FDI.

Japanese FDI flows to Latin American countries were much smaller than those to Asian countries. Only Brazil has received more Japanese FDI than some Asian countries, such as the Philippines and Korea, in the 1990s (for details, see table 3.5).

Japanese FDI, mostly for the assembly of finished products, in Asia has stimulated industrialization. However, factories built by Japanese FDI continue

Table 3.5   **Flow of Foreign Direct Investment from Japan (billions of yen)**

Country	1990	1991	1992	1993	1994	1995	Average for 1990–95
Asia							
China	50.1	78.7	138.1	195.4	268.3	431.9	193.75
Indonesia	161.5	162.8	214.2	95.2	180.8	154.8	161.55
Korea	41.9	35.7	29.1	28.9	42.0	43.3	36.82
Malaysia	106.7	120.2	91.9	89.2	77.2	55.5	90.12
Philippines	38.3	27.7	21.0	23.6	68.3	69.2	41.35
Taiwan	65.3	55.4	37.6	34.3	29.2	43.9	44.28
Thailand	169.6	110.7	84.9	68.0	74.9	119.6	104.62
Latin America							
Argentina	30.4	5.5	2.4	3.9	2.1	11.0	9.22
Brazil	89.2	23.5	60.6	49.2	130.8	28.7	63.67
Chile	4.3	10.2	3.5	0.4	1.4	13.6	5.57
Colombia	8.9	0.5	0.0	0.0	2.4	2.1	2.32
Mexico	24.8	26.1	7.8	6.1	65.1	20.2	25.02
Venezuela	11.3	13.8	3.2	2.3	0.6	2.7	5.65

Source: Japan, Ministry of Finance, *Annual Report of the International Finance, 1996* (Tokyo: Kinyu Zaisei Jijo Kenkyukai, 1997), 436–37.
Note: FDI from Japan in these statistics is on the "reporting basis" of cross-border investment. It may not match actual disbursement because some reported investment may be canceled, and some will be carried out without reporting (no penalty). New FDI financed locally or reinvestment from past FDI is not covered by these statistics.

to require imports of parts and semifinished goods from Japan. Domestic production of parts has become a challenge for Asian countries that have recorded large trade deficits against Japan. (An exception is Indonesia, which records surpluses against Japan.)

3.1.3   Capital Flows and Economic Growth: Virtuous Circle

Until the Thai baht crisis of 1997, no one questioned that capital flows to Asian countries have contributed to accelerating economic growth. As the economies grew and industrialization proceeded, the funds needed to build more factories became larger every year. As domestic saving lagged behind high investment, capital inflows were used to fund investment. Unlike in Latin America, where capital inflows were often fueling a consumption boom, Asian capital inflows were either directly building factories (as in the case of "green field" FDI) or intermediated by the banking system to materialize in fixed investment.

Although Japan, Taiwan, and, to a lesser extent, Korea achieved their industrialization and high economic growth without foreign capital, the ASEAN countries—Singapore, Thailand, Malaysia, and Indonesia—relied heavily on foreign capital at least at the beginning stage of industrialization in the 1980s.

In the 1990s, China became a large importer of foreign capital. The authorities of these countries were keen on selecting industries for their economic development.

In the past fifty years, Japan has upgraded its industries from textiles to consumer durables, to heavy and chemical industries, to automobiles, and to high-tech products. Korea and Taiwan seem to be following a similar industrialization path, a few decades later. And the ASEAN countries are chasing Korea and Taiwan up the industrialization ladder, while themselves being chased by China and Vietnam. This pattern of staggered industrialization by the Asian economies is often nicknamed the "flying geese pattern" (see Ito 1996, 1997b for the concept and earlier literature of this pattern). Capital flows play an important role in this pattern of economic development. As some industries, say textiles, lose competitiveness as the result of wage hikes in one country, say Korea, a company will seek to move its factories to a lower wage country, say Thailand. If management skills are transferable to different countries, this will accelerate the industrialization process of the host country. The host country will develop its own industries as skilled workers and middle-level management become available through training at the foreign firms on domestic soil. Technological transfer has to occur sooner or later. Korea and Taiwan have already become capital exporters.

This explanation also points out that capital flows in Asia are related to trade. In some cases, exports are replaced by FDI, and in other cases, foreign investment is followed by more trade. Initially, parts and semifinished goods have to be imported by a host country, until they become available domestically, and then exports from the host country will increase as the firms become successful. This process took place in many industries in many countries in Asia.

3.1.4   The Problem of Too Much Capital Flow

Although capital inflows are essentially beneficial to a host country, emerging market countries sometimes face what the authorities consider "too much" capital inflow. Malaysia faced capital inflows that amounted to more than 10 percent of GDP in 1991, more than 15 percent of GDP in 1992, and more than 20 percent of GDP in 1993. Thailand also attracted capital flows that exceeded 10 percent of GDP in 1989, 1990, 1991, and 1995. In Latin America, Chile, Mexico, and Peru experienced capital inflows that exceeded 6 percent of GDP in the past decade. Capital inflows of this magnitude are difficult to manage (Khan and Reinhart 1995; Folkerts-Landau and Ito 1995, chap. 4).

Doing nothing in the face of large capital inflows will certainly appreciate the currency sharply. That will force some export industries out of business. Once an industry is lost, even if the exchange rate depreciates to the earlier level, production and exports of the industry may not recover. Because many industries require fixed investment, volatility in the exchange rate has an adverse effect on exports. Hence, unless the current account is in surplus, which is unlikely for most emerging market countries, the first macroeconomic response to large capital inflows is usually to intervene in the foreign exchange market to prevent a sharp nominal appreciation of the currency. If the exchange rate regime is de facto fixed, then intervention is not a choice but a must. Foreign reserves will increase as a result of intervention to keep the nominal exchange rate from appreciating too much. Foreign exchange intervention will increase the domestic monetary base. There then are two choices: the increase in monetary base can be offset by domestic open market operations (sterilized intervention), or the increase can be left alone (unsterilized intervention).

Suppose the case of unsterilized intervention. Unless an increase in money demand, which is sometimes observed in a rapidly growing economy, absorbs the increase in the monetary base, the result will be lower interest rates, overheating, and inflation. These are undesirable consequences. Suppose the case of sterilized intervention. It can reduce the risk of inflation, but it may lead to even larger capital flows. In order to see this, suppose that the initial surge in capital inflows takes the form of FDI and equity investment. Then one-to-one sterilization will likely increase the short-term interest rate (as opposed to keeping the same rate). This leads to an increase in short-term capital inflows, such as investment in interbank deposits, interbank lending, and short-term securities. From the viewpoint of a host country, capital inflows in short-term instruments are less desirable than FDI or equity investment. In fact, sterilized intervention may adversely change the composition of capital inflows.

If intervention, sterilized or not, is not a cure-all, what other options or combinations of options does the host country have? If overheating (e.g., as a result of unsterilized intervention) is a problem, the period of capital inflows provides an excellent opportunity for tightening fiscal expenditure. Thailand succeeded in reducing fiscal deficits during the 1989–91 period of large capital inflows. Emerging market countries tend to have current account deficits caused by imports of capital goods, and surges in capital inflows tend to worsen these gaps. In order to prevent current account deficits from increasing, domestic saving has to be promoted. Tax incentives for saving, or some more direct measure (introducing a compulsory pension plan), can help to prevent further deterioration in current account deficits.

If all these options are exhausted and capital inflows are still substantial, capital controls, a more controversial option, may be used. Capital inflows in short-term instruments can be discouraged by reserve requirements on bank deposits by nonresidents, a withholding tax on interest from bank deposits and short-term securities, or an outright ban on sales of short-term instruments to nonresidents. Reserve requirements on deposits by nonresidents and especially on those denominated in foreign currency can be justified as a part of prudential policy rather than foreign exchange capital controls. When capital flows are volatile and exchange rate risk rises, bank risk management has to be enhanced.

A tricky part of introducing capital controls is that the host country does not want to discourage long-term capital inflows or lose the confidence of investors in the long run. Changes in capital controls should be transparent and fair. It would be better to slow a liberalization process rather than eliminate capital control measures once and then reintroduce them. Capital controls, if implemented without loopholes, will make it possible for a host country to induce a shift in the composition of capital flows to more long-term instruments and will allow the monetary authorities to use the short-term interest rate for domestic purposes, such as keeping inflation in check.

Several Asian and Latin American countries have implemented capital controls. For example, in 1991–92 Chile introduced a withholding tax on borrowing from abroad; Brazil in 1994 introduced a tax on foreign investment in the stock market; Malaysia introduced a ban on the sale of short-term instruments to nonresidents in January–August 1994, and banks were required to place reserves at the central bank. Both Malaysia and Thailand maintained restrictions on the open foreign currency positions of banks (see Folkerts-Landau and Ito 1995, chap. 5; Dooley 1996).

3.1.5   The Baht Crisis of 1997

Economic growth in Thailand starting in the late 1980s has been one of the miracles of Southeast Asia. After staying at or above 10 percent from 1988 to 1990, the growth rate has been stable at 8 to 9 percent in the 1990s. However, in 1996 Thailand fell into a (growth) "recession," and the growth rate declined below 7 percent, a decline that continued in 1997. One of the reasons for this was a decline in export growth. The twelve-month export growth rate had become zero by the beginning of 1997. Suddenly, the engine of growth, namely exports, stalled, and several structural weaknesses in the economy became exposed. Since large current account deficits, 8 percent of GDP, were financed by capital inflows, a lower economic growth rate posed the question of sustainability. A high growth rate means that a country may be able to grow out of debt (in ratio to GDP), while a low growth rate means that debt (in ratio to GDP) will accumulate quickly. The difference in economic growth rate affects confidence among investors, even if the ratio of the current account deficit to GDP is the same.

Overvalued Currency

One of the reasons for the export slowdown was overvaluation of the currency. The Thai baht was under the basket system. However, an overwhelming weight was placed on the U.S. dollar. Thus it was de facto pegged to the U.S. dollar. The situation was similar in Malaysia and Indonesia. When the U.S. dollar depreciates against the Japanese yen (as when the yen went to 80 per dollar in April 1995), Southeast Asian goods sell well in the United States and Japan. However, when the dollar appreciates (as between April 1995 and late 1996, when the yen went from 80 to 125 per dollar), the price competitiveness of Southeast Asian exports is lost.

Since all of these countries have a significant trade relationship with Japan, and some Asian countries have products that compete directly with Japanese products in global (mostly U.S.) markets, fluctuation in the yen-dollar exchange rate affects their trade accounts. When the yen appreciated in the first half of the 1990s (from the 120s in 1993–94 to the peak at 80 yen per dollar in April 1995), these countries enjoyed a boom in exports. However, the subsequent depreciation of the yen (back to the 120s in 1995–96) sent the exports of these economies into a tailspin.

Japan accounts for one-third of total imports to Thailand. Most imports from Japan are in the category of parts and semifinished products. The goods then manufactured and assembled are exported mostly to the United States (accounting for 20 percent), Japan (15 percent), and other Asian countries (30 to 40 percent). Malaysia has a similar import and export structure. For Indonesia, Japan is the most important export destination (25 percent) as well as import origin (25 percent). Therefore, the dollar peg has gradually lost its justification for these countries. During the period of yen appreciation, the dollar peg served these countries well by providing gradual depreciation for export competitiveness. However, recent large fluctuations of the yen put these countries in an awkward position.

Another factor that indicates the strong linkage of the Asian economies to Japan as well as the United States is the ratio of yen invoicing in Japanese exports to and imports from East Asian countries. According to Ministry of International Trade and Industry statistics, the yen invoice ratio for Japanese exports to the region increased from 30 percent in 1981 to more than 50 percent at the beginning of the 1990s; the yen invoice ratio for Japanese imports from the region increased from 2 percent in 1983 to more than 25 percent in 1993. When prices are quoted in yen, while currencies are pegged to the dollar, fluctuation in the yen-dollar rate directly affects the trade accounts of these economies.

Property Sector Problems

The slowdown in economic growth was accompanied by the bursting of the real estate bubble. Some bank credit, which had increased in 1994, went to the real estate sector. Office buildings were overbuilt. As the financial bubble collapsed, stock prices and real estate prices declined sharply, and nonperforming loans increased. Finance companies (nonbank financial institutions lending heavily to the real estate sector) were particularly hard hit. In the spring of 1997, the Bank of Thailand had to start providing liquidity support to the troubled finance companies because funds started to flee institutions that were perceived to be weak. The earlier collapse of the Bangkok Bank of Commerce (eventually taken over by the government) created a background of pessimism about financial institutions. The central bank extended loans to finance companies through the Financial Institutions Development Fund (FIDF), which is vaguely similar to a deposit insurance system. By the time these finance companies were suspended (sixteen in June and another forty-two in August), 430 billion baht had been lent. These financial troubles weakened the confidence of foreign investors in the economy and the currency. As discussed in section 3.1.2, Thailand had large inflows to its banking sector. Hence the loss of confidence in the financial system among foreign investors had a much larger effect on capital flows and on the economy in general than would otherwise have been the case.

In order to alleviate the problem of nonperforming property loans, the Thai authorities set up the Property Loan Management Organization (PLMO) in the spring of 1997 to help restructure such loans. However, the operational details of the PLMO are still under discussion, and it is unclear to what extent the PLMO will be beneficial to developers and financial institutions. Open, transparent pricing of properties to be bought by the PLMO is crucial.[1]

Speculative Attack

When the banking sector is in trouble, the currency becomes vulnerable. The interest defense (increasing the interest rate in the hopes of stopping capital outflows or even attracting inflows) cannot be deployed when financial institutions are beset with large portfolios of nonperforming loans. Capital flight becomes a serious concern. Precisely at this moment, the probability of success in a speculative attack increases.

A massive attack on the baht took place in mid-May 1997.[2] Baht selling took place in the spot market and also in the forward market in the form of swap arrangements. Speculators hoped to cause devaluation by selling short the baht. When this strategy was countered by intervention, and the spot rate held, speculators went to sell the baht forward, through swap arrangements. The swap arrangements that speculators engaged in were essentially contracting to sell baht forward at the same time that they were buying baht in the spot market (probably squaring the position of earlier short selling in the spot market). When the central bank becomes a counterparty in swap deals, it is able to acquire dollars on the balance sheet (as a result of the spot transaction, the first leg of the swap arrangement) while having dollar liabilities off the balance sheet. The fact that the foreign reserve level changed little from May to June means that the central bank countered spot selling of the baht by intervening in the market, while engaging in swap arrangements similar in magnitude. Had the future liabilities of dollar selling (buying baht) been consolidated, the true foreign reserve level at the end of May would have revealed a substantial decline. At that point, keeping the de facto fixed rate would have become impossible. The Thai authorities must have hoped for some event that would allow

---

1. The resolution of bad debt needed a very radical solution in the end. Of the fifty-eight suspended finance companies, fifty-six were closed in December 1997. Assets from these companies were sold to the public in several auctions in 1998. See Ito (1998) for updates on the events in Thailand.

2. See Nukul Commission (1998) for exactly what happened during the speculative attack of May 1997.

the central bank to regain a comfortable level of foreign reserves before the forward liabilities became due, but no such event took place. Although the central bank managed to keep the fixed rate until 2 July, the game had been over by the end of May.

Market participants knew the fact that the central bank had engaged in the swap arrangements, but they did not have precise information on the size of the swaps in which the central bank had engaged. It was revealed in August (as part of the IMF loan conditions) that the Bank of Thailand had forward liabilities of more than $23 billion (about two-thirds of its foreign reserves). It was a shock to most market participants.

"Mai Thai" Hangover

In the aftermath of the Mexican crisis of December 1994, pressures on currencies and stock prices spread to other Latin American countries and even some Asian countries. Indeed, the "tequila effect" was felt as far away as Thailand in January 1995. In 1997 it was Thailand's turn to be at the epicenter of a shock, and effects on the region's other currencies—the Philippine peso, the Korean won, the Malaysian ringgit, and the Indonesian rupiah—have been considerable. All, including the Thai baht, are continuing to fall through September. I call this state of affairs the "Mai Thai" hangover (after the Mai Tai, a popular cocktail in Bangkok).[3]

Stock prices are also falling in these countries. Even Hong Kong, where the currency board arrangement fortifies the already strong financial system, experienced speculative attacks, and an interest rate hike intended to defend the currency triggered a sharp stock price decline.

The episode poses several questions: Why did the IMF rescue package fail to halt the decline in exchange rates and stock prices in Thailand and beyond? Are there similar fundamental conditions in the Southeast Asian economies that contributed to the spillover? What should be done in the region to prevent such crises in the future?

The IMF decided to offer $4 billion under a standby arrangement, and the Asian countries led by Japan contributed an additional $10 billion. The total package, including pledges from the World Bank and the Asian Development Bank, amounted to $16.7 billion by the time the IMF plan had been approved by its board. The amount was considered to be more than enough to offset the drain of foreign reserves expected to result from the Bank of Thailand's unwinding of its forward positions. The hope was that halting the slide of the baht would make the crisis less contagious, thereby restoring confidence in the region as a whole. The intended effect did not, however, materialize.

The IMF package was not immediately effective for two reasons. First, as part of the IMF standby agreement, the Bank of Thailand announced a larger than expected volume of forward contracts (or maximum size of foreign re-

---

3. This section draws heavily on Ito (1997a).

serve losses), causing the baht to slide further. The market reaction may not be fully justified, since some of the forward exposures (especially onshore contracts) were the result of providing baht to the market through swap agreements—just like government bond repurchase agreements—as a part of domestic open market operations. However, this point was too subtle to calm the market. The wisdom of "full" disclosure in this case is open to question.

Second, the IMF package did not directly address the problems in Thailand's financial sector. The balance sheets of many financial institutions, in particular finance companies, were damaged by declining property values. The monetary authorities in Thailand had taken several measures before the IMF package: the PLMO was created to buy nonperforming loans, and the worst finance companies, sixteen of them, were suspended in June, and an additional forty-two were suspended in August. However, the market apparently did not take comfort from the actions, partly because it was not clear at that point whether the merger or liquidation of these institutions would require any fiscal expenditure and whether the liquidity support to these institutions provided by the FIDF could be paid back in full. The market did not like the uncertainty about the fate of these institutions and its possible impact on fiscal positions in the future.

The Mai Thai hangover seems to have been more widespread, prolonged, and damaging (having forced countries to abandon their pegs) than the tequila effect. (To be fair, though, it took a month or two after the IMF package for Mexico was announced to stabilize Mexican financial markets.) General spillover of the Thai baht crisis to other currencies certainly suggests a common root of the problems. The region's economic structures may be so similar that one external shock rocks all countries. The yen-dollar exchange rate is a prime suspect for the external shock. All of the currencies of the emerging markets in the region were effectively pegged to the U.S. dollar. Even those countries that had basket systems, such as Thailand, put an overwhelming weight on the U.S. dollar in the basket. (Singapore was known to have put a relatively heavy weight on the Japanese yen.) As discussed earlier, the dollar peg, with yen-dollar fluctuation, led to weak export performance.

With the "big bang" of the Japanese financial markets, competition for financial business in Asia will become fierce. Now that Japan is awakening and will make a move, financial markets in the region will become more liberalized and efficient. Low interest rates in Japan are making Japanese investors seek opportunities outside. Capital flows are not scarce, despite the turmoil in the currency and stock markets in the region. In a sense, the current crisis is manageable in an environment where interest rates are low and liquidity is ample. The integration of financial markets will proceed. But danger may come the next time Japan raises interest rates. Its effect will be much more strongly felt in the region than before, because financial markets will be more integrated than before. Markets in the region have to prepare for an eventual rise in yen interest rates, once the current turmoil is over.

The simultaneous depreciation of the currencies in the region looks like a competitive devaluation. With the baht, Philippine peso, and ringgit depreciating, the rupiah has no choice but to depreciate in order to maintain its competitiveness. All this suggests that the monetary authorities of these countries may be well advised to consider pegging their currencies, with a wide band, to similar baskets—if not the common basket—in which the yen and euro are heavily weighted.

Given that these Southeast Asian economies have been integrated with the Japanese manufacturing and financial sectors, as well as with the U.S. economy and financial markets, the weights in the baskets to which their currencies are pegged should have been revised some time ago. Announcements and press releases from the IMF claim credit for having recommended "flexibility" in exchange rates well before the crisis. However, the IMF has not shown a safe way to exit from the peg. "Exit policy" has become a hot issue in discussions of exchange rate policy for emerging markets.

Both the Mexican and Thai crises teach the lesson that the financial sector (especially banks) is important in managing the economy. Banks in Thailand had borrowed short-term funds through an offshore facility and then lent to domestic industries. Some funds went to property markets, which had been booming. The bursting of the property bubble made these loans nonperforming, and then depreciation of the baht further troubled those institutions that had borrowed in dollars.

This compares, on one side, to the Mexican Tesobono problem and, on the other side, to the Mexican banks that suffered losses from the peso depreciation and subsequent recession. Tesobonos made it possible for Mexico to continue financing large current account deficits, while short-term bank loans played a similar role in Thailand. Thailand argued before asking for the IMF loan that Thai obligations were in the private sector, unlike the sovereign debt (Tesobonos) of Mexico. However, when the banking system is at risk, the government has to step in. Indeed, the Thai government had to guarantee the depositors (holders of promissory notes) of all suspended finance companies and even the creditors of the forty-two finance companies that were suspended in August in order to prevent a run on the remaining finance companies and banks. It might not make any difference in the end whether the "overborrowing" occurred in the private banking sector or the government sector. As with the Tesobonos, most creditors were bailed out in Thailand. International financial communities have not found a way to prevent moral hazard among international creditors (holders of Tesobonos and creditors of finance companies).

3.1.6 Concluding Remarks

This paper described the size and types of capital flows to Asia and analyzed their impact on the Asian economies. Capital flows bring both benefits and risk to a host country. Appropriate macroeconomic responses to manage the size and composition of capital flows are crucial. Domestic financial markets have to be deep and robust in order to minimize the risk from volatile capital flows. In particular, the banking system is crucial to keeping the economy away from a chaotic recession in the wake of currency turmoil. The Thai baht crisis proves that even Asian miracle economies can suffer the kinds of financial crises that have occurred in Latin America. Understanding the mechanism behind such crises and developing appropriate prudential policy to prevent them is a challenge for all of us.

References

Dooley, Michael. 1996. Capital controls and emerging markets. *International Journal of Finance and Economics* 1 (3): 307–20.

Folkerts-Landau, David, and Takatoshi Ito. 1995. *International capital markets: Developments, prospects, and key policy issues.* Washington, D.C.: International Monetary Fund.

Folkerts-Landau, David, Donald J. Mathieson, Garry J. Schinasi, et al. 1997. *International capital markets: Developments, prospects, and key policy issues.* Washington, D.C.: International Monetary Fund.

Ito, Takatoshi. 1996. Japan and the Asian economies: A "miracle" in transition. *Brookings Papers on Economic Activity,* no. 2:205–72.

———. 1997a. The "mai thai" hangover. *Nikko Capital Trends,* September, 1–2.

———. 1997b. What can developing countries learn from East Asian economic growth? Paper presented at the annual bank conference on development economics, World Bank.

———. 1998. The development of Thailand's currency crisis: A chronological review. *Japan Import/Export Bank Review* (September/October), 68–93.

Kaminsky, Graciela L., and Carmen M. Reinhart. 1996. The twin crises: The causes of banking and balance-of-payments problems. Washington, D.C.: Board of Governors of the Federal Reserve System. Photocopy.

Khan, Mohsin S., and Carmen M. Reinhart, eds. 1995. Capital flows in the APEC region. IMF Occasional Paper no. 122. Washington, D.C.: International Monetary Fund.

Milesi-Ferretti, G. M., and A. Razin. 1996. Current account sustainability. Princeton Studies in International Finance, no. 81. Princeton, N.J.: Princeton University, International Finance Section, October.

Nukul Commission. 1998. *The Nukul Commission report: Analysis and evaluation on facts behind Thailand's economic crisis.* Bangkok: Nation Multimedia Group.

World Bank. 1997a. *Private capital flows to developing countries: The road to financial integration.* Washington, D.C.: World Bank.

———. 1997b. *World development indicators.* Washington, D.C.: World Bank.

2. Kathryn M. Dominguez

The Role of the Yen

3.2.1 Introduction

Over 90 percent of American exporters sell their goods abroad using contracts denominated in dollars. Over 80 percent of German exporting companies denominate their sales in deutsche marks. Over 50 percent of French and British exports are denominated in francs and pounds sterling, respectively. This pattern of invoicing exports in domestic currencies is characteristic of most developed countries with a single, notable exception: Japan. Japanese companies are more likely to denominate exports in dollars than in yen.

This paper analyzes the role of the yen in international financial and commercial transactions. Over the past twenty-five years the yen has played a surprisingly small role in international markets. Far fewer commercial contracts, bonds, bank loans, and official reserves are denominated in yen than in U.S. dollars, and fewer in yen than in deutsche marks, in spite of the size and performance of the Japanese economy. Nowhere is this puzzle more apparent than in Japan itself, where Japanese companies and investors are more likely to transact in dollars than in yen.

There are several possible explanations for the apparent underutilization of the yen. The first is habit formation. After the Second World War the dollar replaced the pound sterling as the dominant currency in world trade. Although the U.S. economy has declined in importance, habit formation works to maintain the central role of the dollar. A second explanation is that a large and growing share of Japan's exports go to the United States, and U.S. imports are predominately invoiced in dollars. Third, the short-term capital market in Japan is relatively underdeveloped. For example, the size of the Japanese treasury bill market is much smaller than that in the United States. Foreign investors or importers receiving yen therefore have fewer opportunities to park their yen-denominated funds. Also, high transaction costs in the bankers' acceptance market limit the amount of trade financed in yen. A fourth explanation involves the role of Japan's large trading companies that handle the bulk of Japan's exports (and imports). It may be that these trading companies are able effectively to hedge the foreign exchange risks that arise when Japanese exports are denominated in foreign currencies.

The author is grateful to the NBER for financial support; to Martin Feldstein, James Hines, and Gunter Dufey for comments and suggestions; to Peter Boberg, Pat McGuire, and Heather Montgomery for help in translating Japanese documents; to Hidetoshi Fukuda for helpful discussions and for providing access to his survey results; and to Takatoshi Ito and David Weinstein for assistance in obtaining data.

Over time it should be the case that any impact of dollar habit formation on yen usage should diminish; similarly, any limitations on short-term yen investing and financing should have little long-run impact. Further, although these considerations might explain the dominance of the dollar over the yen, they apply equally well to Germany, yet the deutsche mark is much less dominated by the dollar than is the yen. The only explanation, of the first three, that distinguishes Germany from Japan is the bias in Japanese exports toward the U.S. market. Exports to the United States do not directly explain why Japanese companies invoice so rarely in yen, but this bias combined with "pricing to market" strategies often followed by Japanese firms may partly explain low yen invoice ratios.

Pricing-to-market models imply that firms set their export prices in foreign currencies if profits are at risk of falling sharply when the domestic currency appreciates yet profits rise only slowly when the foreign currency appreciates (in other words, profits are concave functions of the exchange rate). If the reverse is true (profits are convex functions of the exchange rate), then exporters will prefer to invoice in the domestic currency (see Krugman 1987; Giovannini 1988). Fukuda and Ji (1994) found empirical evidence supporting the hypothesis that the profits of Japanese firms generally fall more rapidly as the yen appreciates than they rise when the yen depreciates. However, this explanation ignores the possibility that exporters can hedge exchange rate risk. If hedging is possible and not too costly, invoicing can be separated from exchange rate risk management and pricing-to-market behavior will not necessarily be related to the choice of the invoice currency. The fourth explanation for the low yen invoice ratios is related to this point. If the large Japanese trading companies are able effectively to hedge the exchange rate exposure exporting firms face when invoicing in currencies other than the yen, then pricing-to-market behavior does not explain the low yen invoice ratios.

The final explanation, that large trading companies effectively hedge the foreign currency exposure of Japanese exporters, does not explain why the dollar remains the dominant currency used in Japan. If hedging is possible and relatively costless, then the denomination of the invoice currency is, in principle, arbitrary. On the other hand, the dollar remains the dominant currency in derivative markets, suggesting that the cost of hedging dollar exposure may be lower than for other currencies.

There are signs that the yen is being used more heavily in international capital markets even as yen invoice ratios remain low. The share of yen-denominated sovereign debt has risen dramatically, at the expense of the dollar, in certain Asian and Pacific countries. Over a quarter of new bond issues by developing countries and countries in transition are now denominated in yen. And the volume of yen transactions in over-the-counter foreign exchange derivative contracts now exceeds those denominated in deutsche marks.

What is the ultimate significance of the continued underutilization of the yen? In the short run, a case can be made that the low yen invoice ratios accentuate the slow adjustment of Japanese bilateral current account imbalances. The Japanese economy has run large and persistent current account surpluses with the rest of the world, and particularly with the United States. Theory indicates that such surpluses are unlikely to persist over prolonged periods. If exchange rates are flexible, then the value of the domestic currency should rise in response to a current account surplus, rendering export goods less competitive and imports more attractive so that, in equilibrium, a country's current account returns to balance. If exports are invoiced in the domestic currency, the automatic adjustment process is straightforward. However, if exports are invoiced in the foreign currency and relative prices remain unchanged (perhaps due to pricing-the-market behavior), the adjustment process is far from automatic. Of course, if the domestic currency strengthens and relative prices do not change, the profits of exporting firms (as denominated in the domestic currency) will fall. Eventually, relative prices must change if exporters are to stay in business. Price adjustment therefore implies that the significance of yen invoicing lies in its implications for short-run adjustments and not long-run resource flows.

This paper explores the reasons why the role of the yen has not kept pace with the rise in Japan's economic power in world trade, as well as the implications of this pattern for Japan and the rest of the world. The paper is organized in five sections. Section 3.2.2 reviews the history of Japanese inflation, the liberalization of the Japanese financial markets, and the international use of the yen. Section 3.2.3 explores the reasons why the yen is rarely used as an invoicing currency in international trade. Section 3.2.4 examines the practice of yen exchange rate risk management and shows how hedging techniques can be used by Japanese firms to offset the risks of invoicing in foreign currencies. Section 3.2.5 considers the relation between the international use of the yen and the Japanese balance of payments. Section 3.2.6 concludes the paper by analyzing the significance of the relatively minor role of the yen in international markets.

3.2.2 The International Role of the Yen

The U.S. dollar is the dominant international currency. The dollar is widely used in international trade contracts, it makes up the bulk of international reserves, and over 80 percent of the derivative market is dollar based. The German mark is second in importance after the dollar, while the Japanese yen is a distant third. Domestic and international currency demands depend on several factors that include the ease with which currency transactions can be made, the stability of a currency's purchasing power, regulatory oversight of the currency, and the investment opportunities available in the currency. This section reviews each of the factors that influence demand for the yen.

The Theory of International Currency Use

International currency uses are similar to national currency uses. An international currency is a medium of exchange, a unit of account, and a store of value outside the country in which it is issued. So, for example, the dollar is used to discharge financial obligations, used to denominate trade contracts, and serves as an investment asset for individuals, companies, and governments outside of the United States. An international currency is considered a "vehicle" if it is used to denominate and execute foreign trade and international capital transactions that do not involve direct transactions with the issuing country.

The same factors that determine whether a currency is used internationally also influence its use as a vehicle currency, although most international currencies are not vehicle currencies. For example, the Mexican peso is an international currency in that it is widely held and used by traders and investors outside of Mexico. On the other hand, the peso is not a vehicle currency in that it would rarely be used in transactions other than those involving at least one party from Mexico. Vehicle currencies are distinguished from international currencies by their relatively low transaction costs (see Krugman 1980; Black 1991). After all, parties to a transaction are unlikely to use a currency other than one of their own unless using the third currency is considerably cheaper than the alternatives. Transaction costs for currencies, in turn, are likely to be lowest for currencies that are heavily used. Moreover, once a currency emerges as a vehicle, economies of scale come into play, reducing transaction costs yet further (see Swoboda 1968; Krugman 1984).

Historical studies of the emergence of the pound sterling as the dominant vehicle currency during the second half of the nineteenth century and the rise of the dollar after World War II suggest that at least two conditions must describe an issuing country for its currency to achieve dominance (see, e.g., Cohen 1971; McKinnon 1979). First, the value of the currency should be relatively stable. Second, the country issuing a dominant international currency should have well-developed financial markets. The next two sections examine Japan's inflation history and the development of Japanese financial markets in order to determine whether Japan satisfies the two conditions needed for the yen to achieve vehicle status.

Japan's Inflation History

Monetary policy decisions in Japan are not made by an independent central bank. The Bank of Japan Law authorizes the Policy Board, which includes representatives of the Ministry of Finance (MOF), to formulate, direct, and supervise Japanese monetary policy. Over the past twenty years, MOF influence on Bank of Japan (BOJ) policy decisions has varied with changes in top personnel and economic conditions. Typically, when the BOJ wants to change monetary policy, it consults with MOF, the finance minister, and the prime minister before coming to a decision. The objectives of Japanese monetary policy have undergone substantial changes over the past two decades, focusing alternately on economic growth, the value of the yen, the balance of payments, and inflation. The BOJ has no legal mandate to maintain price stability.

In the early 1970s, partly as a result of the first oil price shock, the Japanese inflation rate exceeded that in the United States or Germany. From 1970 to 1975 Japan's inflation averaged over 10 percent, while inflation in the United States and Germany averaged 6 percent. In the second half of the 1970s Japanese inflation rates continued to exceed those in Germany but were, on average, slightly lower than inflation rates in the United States. In the 1980s inflation rates in all three countries were significantly lower; German and Japanese inflation rates were roughly comparable, and U.S. inflation was about 2 percentage points higher. More recently, Japanese rates of inflation have been well below those of both Germany and the United States; indeed, using some definitions of price changes, Japan is currently experiencing deflation.

Of the G-7 countries, Japan experienced the highest rate of inflation variability (6 percent) in the 1970s. In contrast, in the 1980s Japan had the third lowest rate of inflation variability, only 0.1 percent above that of Germany. These data suggest that markets might have doubted the stability of the yen's purchasing power in the 1970s, but for the past decade and a half Japan's inflation record has been comparable to that of Germany and slightly better than the U.S. record. Therefore, Japan's more recent inflation performance might more credibly establish the purchasing power stability of the yen. At the same time, however, that Japan's inflation rate has stabilized at a low level, so too have the inflation rates of the other G-7 countries. It may be that one of the impediments to greater international use of the yen is the wide array of other currencies that currently have strong records of low and stable inflation.

The Liberalization of Japanese Financial Markets

In the period after World War II and before the breakdown of the Bretton Woods system, the Japanese monetary authorities actively discouraged international use of the yen. Historical accounts suggest that Japanese policymakers were concerned that, if the yen were widely held outside of Japan, then the BOJ's ability to control the yen money supply would be substantially reduced. Consequently, Japanese financial markets were highly regulated and capital inflows and outflows severely limited. Moreover, the financial system was designed to encourage personal saving and to direct financial resources to chosen private and public investment projects.

In the mid-1970s Japan entered a recession along with most of the G-7 countries as a consequence of which the corporate sector demand for funds declined and large government budget deficits emerged for the first time in postwar Japan. The public sector became a net borrower of funds; the number of government bonds outstanding rose eightfold from 1974 to 1982 (see Eken 1984). Japan's bond markets grew dramatically over this period, and a rising share of bank portfolios consisted of government bonds. Further, in order to reduce the burden of the government debt, interest rates on new issues were kept below market levels. At the same time the Japanese financial community, and particularly Japanese banks, began to demand changes in the financial system. Japanese bank profits suffered as a consequence of the low interest rates they received on government debt and the highly regulated interest rates they were allowed to offer depositors. In order to compete with other financial institutions Japanese banks needed to be able to offer new financial instruments and to access international capital markets.

Deregulation of Japan's financial markets began in the late 1970s. Table 3.6 provides a chronology of Japanese financial market liberalization starting in the 1970s. One of the first measures taken was to allow resale of government bonds. As a consequence the primary and secondary government bond markets dramatically expanded. At the same time the Gensaki market (for repurchase agreements on government bonds) and the market for certificates of deposit were established. In 1980 the Foreign Exchange and Foreign Trade Control Law was enacted, under which capital flows were gradually liberalized although numerous restrictions on outflows and inflows remained. In 1984, in the aftermath of the Yen-Dollar Agreement,[1] and in part to allay U.S. and other G-7 concerns that the closed nature of Japanese domestic markets was artificially depressing the value of the yen, a new phase of financial market liberalization was initiated. A number of measures were taken to increase foreign access to Japanese financial markets and to allow Japanese capital to flow into the Eurocurrency markets. In June 1984 the conversion of foreign currencies into yen was completely decontrolled; in June 1985 the market for yen-denominated bankers' acceptances was created and the Japanese government was allowed to issue short-term bonds to refinance existing debt; in June 1986 foreign banks were given permission to issue Euroyen bonds; in December 1986 the Tokyo offshore market was created; and in November 1987 the Euroyen commercial paper market was decontrolled.

The implementation of BOJ monetary policy has undergone substantial changes in the past twenty years in conjunction with the deregulation of financial markets. The intermediate target of BOJ monetary policy shifted in mid-1978 from bank lending to a broadly defined money stock. Money market operations also shifted from "window guidance," or moral suasion, together with direct control of interest rates, to controlling the supply of reserves to the banking system and thereby indirectly influencing interbank interest rates. The discount rate in Japan is the rate at which commercial banks can borrow funds from the BOJ, and it is always lower than the interbank rate. Consequently, discount window lending is rationed by the BOJ.[2] The two-month bill discount

---

1. See Frankel (1984) for a detailed description of the Yen-Dollar Agreement.
2. Further, the level of discount window lending changes at the initiative of the BOJ, rather than at the initiative of private banks (as in the United States and Germany).

Table 3.6   **Chronology of Japanese Financial Market Liberalization**

Month and Year	Measure
March 1972	Japanese banks permitted to purchase foreign securities
December 1973	Abolition of limits on acquisition of Japanese bonds and equities by foreign investors
August 1974	Liberalization of acquisition of fiscal bills by foreign investors
May 1979	Foreigners permitted to engage in Gensaki market
December 1980	Foreign Exchange and Foreign Trade Control Law enacted
June 1983	Short-term Euroyen loans to nonresidents liberalized
April 1984	External yen loans liberalized
	Rules for yen bond issuance and management relaxed
	Guidelines for Euroyen bond issuance by residents relaxed
June 1984	Conversion of foreign currencies into yen completely decontrolled
December 1984	Guidelines for Euroyen bond issuance by nonresidents relaxed
	Market for Euroyen certificates of deposit (CDs) (with maturity of six months) created
April 1985	Withholding tax on resident Euroyen bonds abolished
	Medium- and long-term Euroyen loans to nonresidents liberalized
June 1985	Nonresident Eurobonds diversified (to include, e.g., dual-currency bonds)
	Market for yen-denominated bankers' acceptances created
October 1985	Temporary Interest Rates Adjustment Law (TIRAL) begins liberalization process of interest rates on large time deposits
April 1986	Maximum maturity of Euroyen CDs extended (from six months to one year)
	Restrictions on the recycling of Euroyen relaxed (mandatory holding period for funds borrowed in the Euroyen market reduced from 180 to 90 days)
June 1986	Foreign banks given permission to issue Euroyen bonds
December 1986	Tokyo offshore market created
April 1987	Medium-term Euroyen bonds (wtih maturities of four years or longer) deregulated
May 1987	Yen-denominated bankers' acceptances further liberalized (by lowering the minimum denomination from ¥100 million to ¥50 million and extending the maturity from six months to one year)
November 1987	Euroyen commercial paper issuance by nonresidents decontrolled
May 1989	Restrictions on Euroyen loans to residents relaxed
September 1994	Interest rates on demand deposits, with the exception of current deposits, liberalized (part of TIRAL)
	MOF lifts ban on issuance of asset-backed corporate bonds by Japanese firms overseas
December 1994	Tokyo Foreign Market Practice Committee abolishes the time limit on foreign exchange trading hours, thereby making twenty-four-hour trading possible in Tokyo
May 1997	Amendment of the Foreign Exchange and Foreign Trade Control Law passes the Diet
April 1998	Permission and prior notification requirements for all external settlements and capital transactions abolished

Source: Fukao (1990) and Tavlas and Ozeki (1992); original data from Bank of Tokyo, *Tokyo Financial Review* (various issues), and Bank of Japan, *Annual Review* (various issues).

rate, the interbank rate that serves as an intermediate target for the BOJ, often diverged from comparable market interest rates during the 1980s. For example, in the summer of 1988, Euroyen rates were markedly higher than comparable bill discount rates, suggesting that arbitrage between offshore and onshore markets was not then possible.

In November 1988 the BOJ introduced a number of measures intended to further liberalize Japanese domestic money markets. One of the more important of these measures consisted of shifting BOJ market interventions into markets for securities of shorter maturities, including the one- to three-week bill market and the overnight commercial paper market. One of the goals of the 1988 reform effort was to enhance interest rate arbitrage between the domestic and offshore markets, as well as arbitrage between the interbank and open money markets.[3] Since the reforms were implemented, the markets for shorter maturity instruments have grown dramatically and short-term interest rates are now more reflective of market conditions.[4]

By 1990 virtually all the restrictions on Japanese capital flows had been eliminated. However, a number of the new financial instruments introduced in the 1980s have yet to develop significant market depth. For example, complicated operating procedures have hampered the development of the yen bankers' acceptance market; trading in the Gensaki market is complex due to the tax on securities transactions; and the treasury bill market is relatively inactive. In November 1996 Prime Minister Hashimoto initiated a financial system reform plan to liberalize the remaining restrictions on Japanese financial markets.[5] A drastic revision of the foreign exchange law took effect on 1 April 1998. And in principle, permission and prior notification for all external settlements and capital transactions are no longer required.

Although Japanese financial markets have changed dramatically over the past twenty-five years, many of the important liberalization measures are relatively recent. It is clear that the highly restrictive financial market structure put in place immediately after World War II actively discouraged international use of the yen. Deregulation has reversed this policy, but the pace of financial market reform has been quite slow. Part of the reason the yen is so little used internationally may be the incompletely developed financial markets in Japan.

---

3. The maturities of collateralized commercial bills were extended on the short end to one week, so that their maturities now range from one week to six months, compared with one month to six months previously; the maturities of collateralized call trading now range from overnight to one week, compared with overnight to three weeks previously. Also, the maturities of uncollateralized call trading were lengthened to a range of overnight to six months. For further discussion, see Tavlas and Ozeki (1992).

4. Prior to November 1988 the daily variation in the two-month bill discount rate was typically very small, reflecting the smoothing operations of the BOJ. Since the reform, the variation in the bill discount rate, as well as other short-term rates, has markedly increased.

5. Details of the 1997 financial system reform are currently available on the MOF home page (www.mof.go.jp).

Stylized Facts about the International Use of the Yen

International use of the yen has increased steadily over the past two decades. This is not surprising given the relatively low base from which the yen market started in the early 1970s. Moreover, the share of yen-denominated instruments varies widely across financial markets. A small percentage of international bonds are denominated in yen, while the share of yen-denominated sovereign debt in selected countries is relatively high. This section examines data on the use of the yen as a medium of exchange, as a reserve currency in central bank portfolios, and as an investment currency.

The Yen as a Medium of Exchange

Information concerning the currency composition of the spot foreign exchange market is not readily available because physical markets for foreign exchange transactions do not exist. The foreign exchange market is decentralized, and data on the volume of global trading are not collected. However, starting in 1989 the central banks of twenty-one countries began a triennial survey of foreign exchange turnover in the interbank markets in an attempt to estimate global activity in the spot and various derivative markets. (The survey in 1995 included twenty-six countries.) Table 3.7 presents data on the currency

Table 3.7   **Selected Currencies in Global Gross Foreign Exchange Turnover (percentage share)**

Currency	April 1989	April 1992	April 1995
U.S. dollar	90	82	83
Deutsche mark[a]	27	40	37
Japanese yen	27	23	24
Pound sterling	15	14	10
French franc	2	4	8
Swiss franc	10	9	7
Canadian dollar	1	3	3
Australian dollar	2	2	3
ECU	1	3	2
Other EMS currencies	3	9	13
Currencies of other reporting countries	3	3	2
Other currencies	19	8	8
All currencies[b]	200	200	200

Source: BIS (1995, table F-3).

Note: Number of reporting countries in 1989: 21; in both 1992 and 1995: 26. Data for 1989 and data for Finland in 1992 include options and futures. Data for 1989 cover local currency trading only, except for the U.S. dollar, deutsche mark, Japanese yen, pound sterling, Swiss franc, and ECU. The figures relate to gross turnover because comparable data on a "net-gross" or "net-net" basis are not available for 1989.

[a]Data for April 1989 exclude domestic trading involving the deutsche mark in Germany.

[b]Columns sum to 200 percent because both buying and selling volumes are included.

Table 3.8   Currency Composition of Foreign Exchange Activity by Country, April 1995
                   (daily averages; millions of U.S. dollars)

Country	Total	Specified Currency against All Other Currencies				
		U.S. Dollar	Deutsche Mark	Japanese Yen	Pound Sterling	ECU
United Kingdom	463,769	387,914	164,677	92,180	74,167	18,118
United States	244,371	211,072	103,755	54,767	23,298	2,430
Japan	161,316	151,150	25,684	130,810	3,587	357
Singapore	105,421	95,818	33,597	29,460	8,015	518
Hong Kong	90,198	84,155	25,746	28,050	7,144	–
Switzerland	86,462	62,676	40,981	8,034	3,807	1,944
Germany	76,236	55,477	58,106	5,942	3,600	1,456
France	58,047	38,215	27,087	4,854	1,810	4,183
Australia	39,534	36,896	10,800	6,162	3,119	–
Denmark	30,543	21,673	11,248	749	571	379
Canada	29,814	28,793	4,754	1,762	1,259	–
Belgium	28,107	23,179	8,682	1,876	1,647	2,458
Netherlands	25,509	17,754	11,006	1,287	2,998	685
Italy	23,248	17,708	5,692	485	242	1,290
Sweden	19,947	13,141	9,881	665	342	111
Luxembourg	19,060	14,872	11,029	694	484	1,042
Spain	18,261	13,897	7,252	393	585	216
Austria	13,340	10,254	9,565	214	115	61
Norway	7,557	5,499	3,045	139	170	73
New Zealand	7,115	6,755	1,039	916	282	1
Finland	5,302	2,986	2,930	47	109	217
South Africa	4,979	4,737	815	210	176	20
Ireland	4,875	2,518	2,879	171	1,841	424
Greece	3,291	2,059	1,554	786	54	126
Bahrain	3,080	2,844	938	523	231	2
Portugal	2,382	1,397	1,074	199	37	74
Total[a]	1,571,785	1,313,440	583,816	371,375	139,689	127,234

Source: BIS (1995, table 1-D).

Note: Table reports spot, outright forward, and exchange swap transactions.

[a]Becaused two currencies are involved in each transaction, the sum of transactions in individual currencies comes to twice total reported turnover.

composition of global spot foreign exchange turnover from these central bank surveys. (These data are made available by the Bank for International Settlements—BIS.)

According to the BIS surveys, use of the yen relative to other currencies has actually declined over the past five years. While use of the dollar has fallen, it is the deutsche mark and other European Monetary System (EMS) currencies, rather than the yen, that have replaced the dollar in some markets. Table 3.8 indicates that yen trading tends to be concentrated in Asian and Pacific centers as well as in the United States and the United Kingdom. In these markets, major shares of yen turnover are reported (between 14 and 29 percent), but yen trading accounts for low single percentages in most other markets. Although practically all markets report some turnover in yen trades against domestic currencies, most yen transactions involve the U.S. dollar (85 percent), the pound sterling (6 percent), or the deutsche mark (5 percent). In contrast to London and New York, the range of currencies actively traded in Tokyo is limited: 76 percent of all turnover in Japan involves the yen and the U.S. dollar, up from 67 percent in 1992.

Unsurprisingly, the yen is used most heavily domestically, with the United Kingdom and the United States ranked two and three in terms of total transactions. In percentage terms, however, it is in Singapore and Hong Kong that the yen is used most heavily. Other than in Japan, the yen is always ranked behind the U.S. dollar, and with the exception of Hong Kong, the yen is also always ranked behind the deutsche mark in terms of total currency transactions in each of the countries.[6]

The Yen as a Reserve Currency

Central banks hold foreign reserves to facilitate trade and to affect exchange rates through interventions in foreign exchange markets. The importance of currencies as international media of exchange and stores of value can therefore be inferred from their relative shares in official reserves. Table 3.9 presents aggregate data on the currency composition of all official reserve holdings and, for available years, the holdings of selected Asian countries.[7]

The share of the yen in official reserve holdings has remained relatively low and stable over the past fifteen years for all countries, and it actually fell between 1985 and 1990 in selected Asian countries. The U.S. dollar remains the dominant currency held in aggregate by central banks, and the share of Asian central bank reserves denominated in dollars has risen, not fallen, in recent years.

The Yen as an Investment Currency

One of the characteristics of international currencies, and particularly vehicle currencies, is their use to denominate investments. Until the mid-1970s, most international bonds, Eurocurrency deposits, and international bank loans were denominated in dollars. Over the past twenty-five years the share of dollar-denominated investments has fallen, and depending on the particular form of investment, the relative shares of those denominated in deutsche marks and yen have risen.

The share of yen-denominated international bonds (Eurobonds plus foreign currency bonds) rose dramatically in the second half of the 1980s. Table 3.10

---

6. It should be noted that the Japanese yen reached a postwar peak against the U.S. dollar during the month in which the BIS conducted its 1995 survey, possibly biasing the 1995 numbers.

7. Garber made the case that these data may not fully reflect actual central bank reserve holdings: "The data suffer from an incompleteness of coverage, as some countries that may carry weight in the demand for yen reserves do not regularly respond to the IMF's inquiry" (1996, 8).

Table 3.9   Currency Composition of Official Reserve Holdings
                   (percentage share)

Currency	1980	1985	1990	1995[a]
Japanese yen				
All countries	4.4	8.0	8.2	7.5
Selected Asian countries	13.9	26.9	17.1	n.a.
U.S. dollar				
All countries	68.6	64.9	50.3	56.4
Selected Asian countries	48.6	44.8	62.7	n.a.
Pound sterling				
All countries	2.9	3.0	3.2	3.4
Selected Asian countries	3.0	4.1	4.9	n.a.
Deutsche mark				
All countries	14.9	15.2	17.4	13.7
Selected Asian countries	20.6	16.4	14.2	n.a.
French franc				
All countries	1.7	0.9	2.3	1.8
Selected Asian countries	0.6	0.9	0.2	n.a.
Swiss franc				
All countries	3.2	2.3	1.3	0.9
Selected Asian countries	10.6	4.9	0.5	n.a.
Netherlands guilder				
All countries	1.3	1.0	1.0	0.4
Selected Asian countries	2.8	2.1	0.5	n.a.
Unspecified currencies				
All countries	3.0	4.6	6.7	9.7
Selected Asian countries[b]	–	–	–	n.a.

Source: IMF, *Annual Report* (Washington, D.C., 1996), and Tavlas and Ozeki (1992).
[a]The holdings of selected Asian countries are not available for 1995.
[b]The holdings of unspecified currencies by the selected Asian countries have been negligible.

indicates that the yen share reached a peak in 1990 at 13.5 percent of the international bond market. By 1996, however, the yen share had fallen back to just over 8 percent of the market. Part of the explanation for the sudden rise and fall in numbers of yen-denominated bonds is that, in the early 1990s, many Japanese companies had difficulty raising funds in the stock market due to the fall in stock prices, and therefore they turned to international bonds for alternative financing (Taguchi 1994). The data suggest that this shift to bond financing reversed itself by 1996. Further, aggregate yen-denominated issuance of long-term international bonds contracted further in 1997, apparently due in large part to Japanese investors shifting their purchases of foreign securities away from straight Euroyen and dual-currency Samurai issues toward U.S. dollar and sterling bonds (BIS 1997).

Although the yen share in the overall international bond market is relatively low, yen-denominated bond issues by developing countries and countries in

Table 3.10   Currency Composition of International Bonds (percentage share)

Currency	1975	1980	1985	1990	1991	1996
U.S. dollar	50.6	42.7	60.6	33.3	28.5	43.0
Japanese yen	0.4	4.8	7.7	13.5	12.9	8.6
Pound sterling	0.2	3.0	4.2	9.5	9.1	8.8
Swiss franc	17.1	19.5	8.9	10.5	7.3	3.3
Deutsche mark	16.4	21.9	6.7	8.3	7.1	14.0
ECU	–	–	4.1	8.1	11.1	0.7
Other	15.3	8.1	7.8	16.8	24.0	21.6
Total	100.0	100.0	100.0	100.0	100.0	100
(billion US$)	(20.0)	(38.3)	(167.8)	(240.2)	(311.4)	(719.0)

Source: OECD, Financial Market Trends (Paris, various issues).

transition has risen dramatically; the yen's share in these issues rose from 13 percent in 1994 to 26 percent in 1995 (Ito and Folkerts-Landau 1996). The expansion of the yen market in bonds issued by developing countries is due to the relatively low interest rates prevailing in Japan and the elimination (in January 1994) of the ninety-day lockup period before which sovereign yen-denominated Eurobonds could be sold to Japanese investors after initial placement.[8]

Bank deposits of currencies held outside countries of issue are termed Euro-currency deposits. The volume of transactions in the Eurocurrency market is now well over $4 trillion on a net basis (netting out all interbank deposits). As a matter of accounting, a currency's share in the Eurocurrency deposit market rises as the currency appreciates against other currencies. Given the substantial appreciation of the yen in 1995, therefore, we might expect the yen share in the Eurocurrency market to have risen, but the data in table 3.11 indicate that the yen share has remained low. The share of yen-denominated Eurocurrency deposits has only risen 4 percentage points since 1980, when 1 percent of de-posits were denominated in yen. Table 3.11 shows that Eurodollar deposits make up over 44 percent of the Eurocurrency market, and mark-denominated deposits are ranked second at 15 percent. The other European currencies, in-cluding the ECU, have smaller than 5 percent shares in the Eurocurrency mar-ket. At the same time, Europe is the dominant region for Eurobanking (56 percent of the market in 1995). Japan's share in the Eurocurrency market was 9 percent, just below that of the United States (at 11 percent) in 1995.

Table 3.12 shows that while the share of yen-denominated international bank lending increased twofold from 1991 to 1995, the share of mark-denominated international bank lending increased fivefold. Shares of bank loans denomi-nated in U.S. dollars, pounds sterling, and Swiss francs fell over the period.

8. Most international yen bonds are either Euroyen issues or Samurai bond issues. Samurai bonds are issued by non-Japanese residents and sold to investors in Japan under Japanese regula-tions, while Euroyen bonds are issued in the international offshore market.

Table 3.11   Currency Composition of Eurocurrency Deposits (percentage share)

Currency	1980	1985	1990	1991[a]	1996[a]
U.S. dollar	61.3	67.7	52.9	50.8	44.8
Japanese yen	1.1	3.4	5.0	4.8	5.6
Pound sterling	2.3	1.9	4.2	3.6	3.2
Swiss franc	5.3	6.5	5.6	3.2	4.1
Deutsche mark	12.2	11.7	16.2	15.6	15.3
ECU	–	2.4	4.4	5.1	2.9
Other	17.8	6.4	12.6	14.9	24.9
Total	100.0	100.0	100.0	100.0	100.0
(billion US$)	(1,056)	(1,385)	(3,576)	(3,508)	(4,288)

Source: BIS, "International Banking and Financial Market Developments" (Basel, various issues).
Note: Foreign-currency-denominated cross-border positions by BIS reporting banks, shares are based only on liabilities.
[a]First nine months of 1991 and 1996.

Table 3.12   Currency Composition of International Bank Lending (percentage share)

Currency	1980	1985	1990	1991[a]	1995
U.S. dollar	66.3	64.6	49.8	49.6	23.9
Japanese yen	2.7	2.7	4.5	4.0	10.5
Pound sterling	2.2	5.7	11.2	11.6	5.8
Swiss franc	14.4	11.3	14.5	13.2	2.6
Deutsche mark	7.0	6.4	5.5	5.0	20.1
ECU	0.0	2.2	3.3	3.8	4.8
Other	7.4	7.1	11.2	12.8	32.3
Total	100.0	100.0	100.0	100.0	100.0
(billion US$)	(1,500.1)	(2,557.2)	(6,132.4)	(5,735.4)	(7,753.9)

Source: BIS, "International Banking and Financial Market Developments" (Basel, various issues).
[a]First nine months of 1991.

Although yen-denominated international bank lending has significantly lower volume than do dollar and deutsche mark lending, Japanese banks rank first in terms of international banking assets. In 1997 international lending by Japanese banks represented 22 percent of the world market, a thirteen-year low, but a share that nevertheless exceeds those of German banks (17 percent) and U.S. banks (11 percent). Japanese banks have reduced international lending since the early 1990s due to the new capital adequacy ratio requirements and the dismantling of restrictions on the domestic financial system (BIS 1997). In addition, the weakness of domestic credit demand and the recent poor performance of the Japanese equity market (which reduced the value of the latent reserves included in Japanese banks' core capital) resulted in a 3 percent drop in Japanese bank lending between 1996 and 1997.

    Although the overall share of yen-denominated loans is small, the proportion of yen-denominated debt in selected Asian and Pacific countries has risen dramatically in recent years. The increase is in part due to the appreciation of the yen in 1995 and the increase in official yen loans as part of an increase in official development aid (Taguchi 1994).

The yen share in sovereign debt issued by selected countries in Asia and the Pacific has also increased dramatically. Table 3.13 shows that, in the case of Thailand, over 50 percent of sovereign debt is denominated in yen, up from

Table 3.13   **Sovereign Debt Denomination (percentage share)**

Country	1980	1985	1989	1995
Indonesia				
Deutsche mark	7.8	6.3	5.2	4.6
Japanese yen	20.0	31.7	34.1	37.7
Pound sterling	0.8	2.1	1.5	0.9
U.S. dollar	43.5	30.7	25.0	20.3
Other currencies	28.0	29.3	34.2	36.5
Total (million US$)	15,019.9	26,845.2	44,255.0	63,848.0
Korea				
Deutsche mark	3.7	1.6	4.7	4.0
Japanese yen	16.6	16.7	31.5	32.2
Pound sterling	3.3	1.7	0.7	0.3
U.S. dollar	53.5	60.3	33.0	48.1
Other currencies	22.9	19.8	30.1	15.4
Total (million US$)	15,932.8	28,304.0	18,787.0	27,103.0
Malaysia				
Deutsche mark	3.3	6.0	11.7	8.0
Japanese yen	19.0	26.4	33.4	39.4
Pound sterling	3.6	1.8	1.5	2.5
U.S. dollar	38.0	50.6	30.7	21.6
Other currencies	36.1	15.3	23.2	28.5
Total (million US$)	4,007.5	14,686.5	14,173.0	18,578.0
Philippines				
Deutsche mark	2.0	0.6	1.5	1.4
Japanese yen	22.0	24.9	31.1	38.1
Pound sterling	0.2	0.2	1.0	0.3
U.S. dollar	51.6	47.8	35.9	30.3
Other currencies	24.3	26.5	30.5	29.9
Total (million US$)	6,367.8	13,782.6	24,076.0	29,577.0
Thailand				
Deutsche mark	4.7	2.5	3.6	2.3
Japanese yen	25.5	36.1	42.8	53.0
Pound sterling	0.2	0.5	0.4	0.2
U.S. dollar	39.7	25.5	17.8	24.4
Other currencies	29.8	35.4	35.4	20.1
Total (million US$)	3,903.8	9,836.0	12,570.0	16,672.0

Source: World Bank, *World Debt Tables,* vol. 2 (Washington, D.C., 1996), and Tavlas and Ozeki (1992).

Note: Entries represent percentages of each country's total sovereign debt.

only 25 percent in 1980. The shift into yen-denominated debt by these countries is largely at the expense of the dollar. The share of Asian sovereign debt denominated in deutsche marks and other European currencies is generally less than 5 percent.

The data presented in this section suggest that while the use of the yen in international capital markets has grown substantially since the early 1980s, the U.S. dollar and the deutsche mark remain the dominant currencies. The yen's market shares in international bonds, Eurocurrency deposits, external bank loans, and official reserves remain well below 20 percent. On the other hand, the share of yen-denominated sovereign debt among selected Asian and Pacific countries has risen dramatically, suggesting an emerging regional bias toward the yen.

3.2.3   The Role of the Yen as an Invoicing Currency

Exporters must determine the currencies in which to denominate their prices. Most firms in developed countries choose to invoice exports in domestic currencies. The advantage of this strategy is that the exporter's exchange rate exposure is thereby minimized. Since invoice prices are not easily changed when exchange rates fluctuate, export prices rise when domestic currencies strengthen relative to currencies of export destinations. To the extent that higher export prices reduce market shares, long-run profits may suffer. This line of reasoning suggests that, under certain demand conditions in foreign countries, invoicing in the currencies of destination countries may be preferable to invoicing in domestic currencies. This strategy of focusing on shares of foreign markets is termed "pricing to market," and it is this strategy that Japanese firms are alleged to follow. This section examines the roles of exchange rates and market structure in the invoicing decisions of Japanese firms.

The Choice of Invoicing Currency in International Trade

A study of Swedish companies in the 1960s found that the exporter's currency, rather than a common vehicle currency, was most frequently used to denominate international trade contracts (Grassman 1973, 1976). This observation, commonly known as Grassman's law, continues to describe most developed countries other than Japan. Recent empirical studies of international invoicing practices find the following additional patterns: (1) invoicing in the exporter's currency is more likely for differentiated manufactured products; (2) trade between a developed country and a developing country tends to be denominated in the currency of the developed country; (3) trade in primary products and transactions in financial investments are usually denominated in U.S. dollars; (4) exports to the United States tend to be invoiced in U.S. dollars; and (5) currency hedging by importers in forward markets is not common.[9]

---

9. Magree (1974), Marston (1990), Fukuda and Ji (1994); see Bilson (1983) and Tavlas (1991) for overviews.

When an exporting firm invoices in a foreign currency, company profits are affected by exchange rate changes. Likewise, from an importer's point of view, the cost of foreign products depends on exchange rates if prices are set in foreign currencies. Both exporters and importers, therefore, prefer to invoice trade contracts in their own currencies in order to minimize foreign exchange risk. Given this, why is it commonly observed that exporters (and not importers) invoice in their own currencies? One explanation is that, in the case of differentiated manufacturing products, exporters are likely to have some degree of monopoly power, as a consequence of which they will have more negotiating power than importers. Another explanation focuses on the ability of both sides to offset exchange rate risks. Importers may be in a better position to guard against currency fluctuations by shifting the burden of higher costs due to exchange rate changes to their domestic customers. This is most easily accomplished in the absence of competing domestic industries. This may be the reason trade contracts between developing countries (which are less likely to have competing domestic industries) and developed countries tend to be invoiced in the developed country's currency. McKinnon (1979) offered yet another explanation for observed invoicing patterns. He reported that importers often receive open account credits from exporters that allow importers some discretion in the timing of their payments in return for bearing currency risk.

Explanations of why primary products and capital assets are usually denominated in dollars rely on the role of market structure. Whereas exporters selling differentiated products are typically assumed to have some degree of market power, international capital markets and markets for primary products are more often highly competitive. Because prices in competitive markets tend to be relatively volatile, it is useful to denominate prices in numéraire currencies in order to make price changes as informative as possible (Swoboda 1968; Magree and Rao 1980). Further, the numéraire currency is likely to be an established vehicle currency, such as the dollar.

It is difficult to explain why hedging exchange rate risk is so uncommon among importers. McKinnon (1979) noted that prices of primary goods are determined by global demand and supply conditions, thereby providing importers an automatic hedge. If the value of an importer's currency falls, the homogeneous nature of the product ensures that the domestic currency price of the importer's inventories will rise by the same amount as the exchange rate change.

Recent Currency Invoicing Practices among the G-6 Countries

It is instructive to compare invoicing practices among the G-6 countries in order to place Japan in context. Table 3.14 presents domestic currency invoice ratios for exports and imports by G-6 countries in the years 1980 and 1988. Japan and Italy are outliers in the export panel of the table with the lowest domestic invoice ratios. In the import panel of table 3.14, Japan's domestic invoice ratio is well below those of the other G-6 countries.

Table 3.14   **Domestic Currency Invoice Ratios among the G-6 Countries, 1980 and 1988**

	1980			1988[a]		
Country	National Currency	Japanese Yen	Other	National Currency	Japanese Yen	Other
Exports						
France	62.5	–	37.5	58.5	0.5	41.0
Germany	82.3	–	17.7	81.5	0.5	18.0
Italy	36.0	–	74.0	38.0	–	62.0
Japan	29.4	29.4	70.6	34.3	34.3	65.7
United Kingdom	76.0	–	24.0	57.0	–	43.0
United States	97.0	–	3.0	96.0	1.0	3.0
Imports						
France	33.1	1.0	65.9	48.9	1.3	49.8
Germany	43.0	–	57.0	52.6	2.5	44.9
Italy	18.0	–	82.0	27.0	–	73.0
Japan	2.4	2.4	97.6	13.3	13.3	86.7
United Kingdom	38.0	–	62.0	40.0	2.0	58.0
United States	85.0	1.0	14.0	85.0	3.0	12.0

Sources: Page (1981), Alterman (1989), Black (1993), and Tavlas and Ozeki (1992); original data from the ministries of finance of France, Germany, Italy, and Japan and U.S. Department of Commerce, Bureau of Labor Statistics.

Note: Entries are percentages of G-6 trade invoices denominated in national currencies, the yen, or other currencies.

[a]1988 data are provided except for German exports and Italian exports and imports, for each of which 1987 data are provided.

Why Is the Yen Rarely Used as an Invoicing Currency?

The share of yen-denominated invoicing of trade contracts is low, especially when compared to dollar and deutsche mark shares. Not only is the yen rarely used by other countries to denominate trade contracts, the yen is also rarely used by Japanese firms. If we compare the use of the yen against the dollar (in table 3.15) in Japan's export or import contracts we find that, although the dollar share has fallen over the years, use of the dollar continues to outstrip that of the yen.

One of the explanations for the low ratio of yen usage in Japan's export and import contracts is that a large share of Japanese trade is with the United States. U.S. exports and imports tend to be denominated in dollars. In order to ascertain whether the low use of the yen is mainly due to U.S. dominance of Japan's trade, it is instructive to consider whether Japan's trade with other parts of the globe are more likely to be denominated in yen. Table 3.16 breaks out the share of yen invoicing in Japan's exports and imports to East Asia.

The data in table 3.16 suggest that the share of yen invoicing in Japanese trade contracts with firms in East Asia is indeed higher than the overall share and that, at least until 1993, the share was growing. Interestingly, the data show that the percentage of yen-invoiced trade contracts with East Asia fell in 1994 and 1995 but remained higher than those with the world as a whole.

Table 3.15   **Yen versus Dollar Invoice Ratios in Japan's Exports and Imports, 1970–91**

Year	Exports (%)		Imports (%)	
	In Yen	In Dollars	In Yen	In Dollars
1970	0.9	90.4	0.3	80.0
1975	17.5	78.0	0.9	89.9
1980	28.9	66.3	2.4	93.1
1981	31.8	62.8	–	–
1982	33.8	60.9	–	–
1983	42.0	50.2	3.0	–
1984	39.5	53.1	–	–
1985	39.3	52.2	7.3[a]	–
1986	36.5	53.5	9.7[a]	–
1987	33.4	55.2	10.6	81.7
1988	34.3	53.2	13.3	78.5
1989	34.7	52.4	14.1	77.3
1990	37.5	48.8	14.5	75.5
1991	39.4	46.7	15.6	75.4

Source: Tavlas and Ozeki (1992). Original data on exports until 1982 from BOJ, *Yushutsu Shin-yojyo Toukei;* after 1982, MITI, Export Confirmation Statistics. Original data on imports until 1980 from MITI, Yushutsu Shyonin, Todokede Houkokusho; 1981–85, MOF, Houkokushyorei ni Motoduku Houkoku; after 1986, MITI, Import Reporting Statistics.

Note: Entries are percentages of Japanese trade contracts denominated in yen and dollars. Percentages are the average over the calendar year, except where otherwise noted.

[a]Fiscal year average.

Beyond reporting aggregate statistics on currency invoice ratios, it is difficult to characterize fully the differences between Japanese behavior and that of firms elsewhere. However, a number of recent empirical studies of Japanese manufacturing firms found evidence of pricing-to-market behavior (Marston 1990; Fukuda and Ji 1994; Gagnon and Knetter 1995). Although this evidence helps to explain why dollar prices of Japanese goods have not changed one for one with the recent movements of the yen against the dollar, it does not explain the proclivity of Japanese firms toward invoicing in dollars. As long as Japanese firms hedge the exchange rate risk that arises when trade is invoiced in a foreign currency, pricing-to-market behavior does not depend on the use of a particular currency of invoice. In other words, Japanese firms could invoice in yen (or any other currency) and simply vary the yen price so that relevant exchange rate changes do not affect final destination prices. The fact that firms are able to hedge against adverse movements in the exchange rate effectively decouples the relationship between profits and the exchange rate and, in turn, weakens the relationship between profits and the invoicing currency. There remains a puzzle as to why Japan is an outlier among the G-6 in its trade invoicing practices.

Table 3.16   Yen Invoice Ratios in Japan's Exports and Imports to the World and
              East Asia, 1969–96

	Exports (%)		Imports (%)	
Year	World	East Asia	World	East Asia
1969	0.6	–	–	–
1979	24.9	–	–	–
1981	31.8	29.8	–	–
1985	39.3	47.3	7.3[a]	–
1986	36.5	37.5	9.7[a]	9.2[a]
1987	33.4	41.1	10.6	11.5
1988	34.3	41.2	13.3	17.5
1989	34.7	43.5	14.1	19.5
1990	37.5	48.9	14.5	19.4
1991	39.4	50.8	15.6	21.6
1992	40.1[b]	–	17.0[b]	–
1993	39.9[b]	52.5[b]	20.9[b]	25.7[b]
1994	39.7[b]	49.0[b]	19.2[b]	23.6[b]
1995	36.0[b]	44.3[b]	22.7[b]	–
1996	35.9[c]	–	20.5[c]	–

Source: Fukuda (1996). Original data on exports for 1969–82 from BOJ, Statistics of Export Credit; 1983–91, MITI, Export Confirmation Statistics; 1992, Report of Settlement Currency; 1993, Report on Export Currency Movement; 1994–96, Report of Export Settlement Movement. Original data on imports for 1969–80 from MITI, Reporting of Import Permit; 1985, MOF, Report; 1986–91, MITI, Import Reporting Statistics; 1992, MITI, Report on Settlement Currency Movement; 1993, MITI, Import Reporting Currency Movement; 1994–96, MITI, Report on Import Settlement Currency Movement.

Note: Entries are percentages of Japanese trade contracts with the world and with selected Asian countries denominated in yen. Percentages are averages over calendar years, except where otherwise noted.

[a]Fiscal year average.
[b]September only average.
[c]March only average.

Survey Evidence on Invoicing Practices from
Japanese Subsidiaries in the United States

In order to investigate the reasons why Japanese companies often prefer to invoice exports in dollars rather than yen, Hidetoshi Fukuda, an NBER researcher and former MOF official, conducted a survey of Japanese subsidiaries in the United States. Fukuda interviewed the vice-president or head of finance of each of twenty-one Japanese companies located in the United States. Although the scope of each interview varied, each consisted in part of a set of standard questions reproduced in the appendix to this paper. In all cases the companies agreed to be interviewed under the condition of confidentiality. Fifteen of the companies included in the survey are in the manufacturing sector, three are general trading companies, one is a special trading company, one is a financial services company, and one is an accounting firm.[10] The sample of

10. Eight of the companies are located in New York, three in Houston, and ten in Los Angeles.

firms surveyed was not selected randomly, and the responses are intended to provide suggestive, not statistical, evidence.

One of the goals of the survey is to learn whether there are particular circumstances in which Japanese companies are more likely to invoice exports in yen. Although the majority of the companies surveyed generally invoice their U.S. sales in dollars, those interviewed suggested a number of situations in which yen invoicing is likely to arise. Such situations include circumstances with unusually long production runs, such as when an export contract is signed at the R&D stage of production. Yen-denominated contracts are also more likely if (1) production requires a majority of inputs acquired from other Japanese companies under contracts denominated in yen, (2) the yen-dollar exchange rate is unusually volatile, (3) the U.S. importer requests invoicing in yen, (4) the exports are going to Asian countries rather than the United States, and (5) the exports are beef products.

When asked why their companies invoice in dollars, rather than in an alternative currency, most of the companies surveyed cited the competitive nature of U.S. markets. A typical response was that in order to maintain product price competitiveness it is necessary to price U.S. exports in dollars. Further, respondents indicated that management of exchange rate risk is in all cases left to the parent company in Japan. For most subsidiaries, exchange rate hedging is handled by the finance department of the Japanese parent company on an overall company-wide basis (as opposed to a transaction-by-transaction basis). Futures markets are heavily used for exchange rate hedging, and in some companies, options are also used.

In all of the companies surveyed the invoicing currency decision is made by the parent company, and there have been no changes in corporate invoicing policy in recent memory. A few of those surveyed indicated that there was some discussion of switching to yen invoicing in the early 1980s, when the yen was weak relative to the dollar. But since the major swing in the yen-dollar exchange rate in 1985 there has been no further discussion of changes in invoicing policies. When asked how companies have dealt with the recent wide swings in the yen-dollar exchange rate, some of the companies revealed that they include provisions in their trade contracts that allow adjustment of dollar prices during periods of "excessive" exchange rate volatility.

None of the companies anticipated increased use of yen invoicing in the near future. They suggested that a more likely change would be higher production levels and purchase of production inputs in the U.S. market. Interviewees also cited recent changes in the U.S. tax treatment of foreign exchange gains and losses that makes "netting" easier and, in turn, provides greater incentives to invoice in dollars.[11] One of the impediments to yen invoicing cited by a few of

11. "Netting" entails offsetting gains on one side of a transaction against losses in another. IRS regulations for 1996 permit netting within consolidated groups, thereby making it possible for hedging transactions undertaken by one subsidiary to offset risks undertaken by another subsidiary (or parent), with tax liabilities generated only by the net position.

the companies is the difficulty foreigners face in borrowing and investing yen assets in Japanese financial markets.

3.2.4 Hedging Yen Exchange Rate Risk

The data presented in section 3.2.3 show that the majority of Japan's trade contracts are denominated in U.S. dollars rather than yen. From a typical Japanese exporter's perspective this means that the firm receives dollar revenues but incurs most costs in yen. Likewise, Japanese importers need to make payments in dollars, although sales are likely to be denominated in yen. In both these situations Japanese firms face exchange rate risk. Over the past twenty-five years markets in numerous hedging instruments have been created in order to provide firms with opportunities to hedge against losses due to adverse exchange rate movements. This section examines the theory and practice of yen exchange rate risk management.

An Overview of Yen Exchange Rate Behavior

The yen appreciated by 250 percent against the dollar from 1970 to 1994. Among other major currencies, only the Swiss franc and the deutsche mark appreciated strongly against the dollar (by 225 and 125 percent, respectively) over the same period. The rise in the value of the yen relative to the dollar occurred in two stages. First, in the 1970s after the breakdown of the Bretton Woods system and in the wake of the 1973 oil shock, the yen strengthened from 360 per dollar to just under 200 per dollar. The dollar then strengthened considerably in the early 1980s (largely as a consequence of Volcker's tight money regime and Reagan's fiscal expansion), with the exchange rate above 200 yen per dollar until late 1985. In the fall of 1985, and in concert with G-5 intervention efforts to weaken the dollar, the yen began its second dramatic appreciation against the dollar, peaking in April 1995 at 80 to the dollar.

Dramatic movements in the yen-dollar exchange rate over the past twenty-five years leave no doubt that Japanese firms invoicing in dollars face substantial exchange rate risks. However, reports in the financial press in 1993 and 1994, before the yen had actually peaked against the dollar, suggested that Japanese firms anticipated yen weakening. The possibly widely held expectation that the yen appreciation against the dollar was temporary may explain accompanying reports that many Japanese firms were not adequately hedged against exchange rate risk in the early 1990s. After the volatility in the yen-dollar rate in 1995, however, it seems unlikely that Japanese firms exposed to exchange rate risk would choose to remain unhedged.

Exchange Rate Hedging Instruments

An exchange rate hedge provides insurance against adverse currency movements. A Japanese exporter invoicing in dollars is "completely hedged" if changes in the value of the yen relative to the dollar do not influence its yen profits. Such a hedge provides an offsetting cash receipt if the value of the dollar falls relative to the yen and requires an offsetting cash payment if the dollar rises relative to the yen.

The market for hedging instruments has grown dramatically in the past twenty years. There are many ways to manage exchange rate risk (and other forms of risk). The most basic exchange rate hedge involves a forward or futures contract that simply fixes the future price of a foreign currency. A slightly more sophisticated hedge involves an option contract that is left unexercised if currency movements are favorable. Further, many swap instruments allow firms to take advantage of differences in financing opportunities over time, geographic regions, and currency markets.

Exchange rate risk management can involve simple transaction-by-transaction hedging, overall balance sheet hedging, and more sophisticated hedging techniques that take into account the exchange rate risks that competitors face. Likewise, the instruments used to hedge exchange rate risks range from "plain vanilla" contracts to exotic derivative structures. However, the growth of derivative markets and the use of exotic products slowed dramatically in 1995 as a consequence of major losses experienced by some financial and nonfinancial firms.[12] The notional principal outstanding of exchange-traded derivatives rose by less than 4 percent in 1995, compared with an average annual growth rate of 40 percent during the past decade.

The Practice of Yen Exchange Rate Risk Management

Firms are not obliged to disclose the details of their hedging practices, and most hedges appear as off-balance-sheet items in company accounts.[13] Further, as Garber (chap. 7.2 of this volume) discusses, the use of derivative products does not necessarily imply that firms are attempting to reduce risks. Derivative products can be used to speculate as well as to hedge (or to enhance) risk. The existing anecdotal evidence on the hedging practices of Japanese firms suggests that, rather than using financial instruments to hedge exchange rate risks, firms have shifted production from Japan during periods of yen appreciation. For example, on 9 June 1993 when the dollar had fallen to the 113–114 yen per dollar range, the headline on the *Asian Wall Street Journal* read "Most Japanese Firms Hold Off Hedging Their Currency Needs." Numerous articles in the popular press in the past few years report that Japanese manufacturers

---

12. Procter and Gamble and Orange County, California, are two prominent examples.

13. In April 1994 MOF banned the use of a device known as "historic rate rollovers." These allowed Japanese companies to delay taking a hit on loss-making forward currency contracts— agreements to buy or sell a currency at a fixed rate in the future—by selling them to friendly banks before they expired. The banks avoided making a loss themselves by immediately selling the companies new forward contracts at the same rate. This accounting trick allowed some companies to disguise heavy losses. In 1993, e.g., Showa Shell Sekiyu, a Japanese affiliate of Royal Dutch/Shell, said it had discovered that its treasury department had covered up losses of ¥166 billion using this technique. The affiliate's chairman and president subsequently resigned (*Economist,* 26 March 1994, 96–97).

have shifted production to lower cost countries, including the United States.[14] On the other hand, many explain the fact that a majority of Japanese trade is handled by a small number of large trading companies by the greater ability of the trading companies to manage exchange rate risks effectively. Trading companies have the advantage of economies of scale, and they may be able to offset risk exposure from their export business with that from imports. Moreover, most of the respondents to Fukuda's survey of Japanese subsidiaries in the United States indicated that their parent companies engage in some form of exchange rate risk management.

Unfortunately, there are no aggregate data on the proportion of Japanese firms engaging in exchange rate risk management. But a 1996 survey of the use of derivatives by Japanese corporations by Nippon Life Insurance found that about 41 percent of the 493 corporations polled used derivative products. Dominguez (1998) examined the degree to which Japanese companies hedge by estimating their exposure to movements in the dollar using Japanese stock market data and an international version of the capital asset pricing model. The results suggest that approximately half of all publicly traded Japanese companies are hedged against dollar exposure.

The BIS provides survey data on the currency composition of derivative products typically used to manage risk. There is not necessarily a strong correlation between hedging practices and the use of a currency in derivative markets, but information on the size of the yen derivative market indicates something about the hedging opportunities available to Japanese firms.

The first systematic survey of over-the-counter (OTC) and exchange-traded derivative markets was performed in 1995 by the BIS. Table 3.17 presents BIS data on the currency composition of the four main categories of OTC exchange rate derivative contracts: outright forwards, foreign exchange swaps, currency swaps, and options.[15] Outright forward transactions are defined as the exchange of two currencies for settlement more than two business days after the conclusion of the deal. Foreign exchange swaps are transactions involving the exchange of two currency amounts on a specific date and a reverse exchange of the same amounts at a later date. A currency swap is a contract committing two parties to exchange streams of interest payments in different currencies for an agreed period of time and to exchange principal amounts in different currencies at a preagreed exchange rate at maturity. Finally, an exchange rate option gives the holder the right to purchase (in the case of a call) or sell (in the case of a put) a currency at a specified exchange rate during a specified period. The

---

14. See, e.g., the article in the *New York Times* on 29 August 1993 with the headline "Japanese Moving Production Abroad."

15. Only OTC data are presented in the tables because of the low quality of the BIS exchange-traded data. Data from exchange-traded derivative markets were collected from OTC firms dealing on exchanges (rather than from the exchanges themselves) only in notional values. Total reported notional values outstanding on exchanges came to roughly one-quarter of the comparable OTC figures.

Table 3.17   Currency Composition of Transactions in Over-the-Counter Foreign Exchange Derivative Contracts, 1995

Currency Pair	All Instruments (daily average, billion US$)	Composition (%)			
		Outright Forwards	Foreign Exchange Swaps	Currency Swaps	Options
U.S. dollar against					
Total other currencies	630	12	82	0	5
Deutsche mark	122	15	76	0	8
Japanese yen	169	13	78	1	8
Pound sterling	53	10	87	0	2
French franc	44	10	85	0	4
Swiss franc	39	13	84	0	3
Canadian dollar	27	16	80	0	4
Australian dollar	21	9	86	1	4
ECU	16	8	92	0	0
Other	139	10	88	1	1
Deutsche mark against					
Total other currencies other than U.S. dollar	39	30	48	1	21
Japanese yen	7	41	31	1	27
Pound sterling	5	27	44	0	29
French franc	7	23	48	1	28
Swiss franc	3	36	40	0	24
ECU	1	40	54	6	0
Other	16	28	58	1	13
Other currency pairs	19	43	45	2	8
Total turnover	688	14	79	1	6

Source: BIS (1995, table D-8).

Note: Data are incomplete because they do not include outstanding positions of market participants in the United Kingdom.

main foreign exchange hedging instrument not available in the OTC markets are futures contracts (and options on futures contracts), which are exclusively exchange traded. A futures contract is essentially the same as a forward contract, except that one party to the transaction is always the exchange, and cash flows are settled daily (marked to market) rather than settled at the maturity of the contract.

Table 3.17 indicates that in OTC derivative contracts involving foreign exchange, the yen has the second highest volume, well below that of the U.S. dollar, but greater than deutsche mark volume. The U.S. dollar is involved on one side of 92 percent of all foreign currency derivative contracts. The comparable figures for the yen and deutsche mark are 26 and 23 percent, respectively (BIS 1995, 30). In the exchange rate futures markets, dollar-yen contracts make up 31 percent of the market. However, OTC contracts on dollar interest rates represent only 27 percent of the market, followed closely by those on yen rates (23 percent). Moreover, yen interest rate contracts make up a relatively large proportion of swaps and options compared with interest rate contracts on other currencies.

The geographical distribution of OTC derivative trading is similar to the distribution of overall foreign exchange trading. Table 3.18 shows that the United Kingdom was the most active center, with about 30 percent of total market activity, and the United States and Japan the second and third most active. Further, the United Kingdom, the United States, and Japan accounted together for 56 percent of total trading. While Japan's share of the derivative market vastly exceeds that of Germany, yen-denominated instruments account for roughly the same share of the market as do mark-denominated instruments. As in the foreign exchange market, the two centers outside of Japan in which the yen is relatively heavily used to denominate derivative contracts are Singapore and Hong Kong.

The BIS data indicate that the market in yen-denominated derivative products is substantial and that foreign exchange swaps are the most heavily traded of the four categories of OTC foreign exchange derivative products. This, in turn, suggests that Japanese firms interested in hedging dollar-yen exchange rate risk have ample opportunity to do so.

One issue related to hedging opportunities is the available maturity structure of instruments. If trade contracts are set long in advance, then effective hedges may require hedging instruments with long maturities. For the OTC derivative products, 89 percent of forwards, foreign exchange swaps, and options are for products with maturities of up to one year. And among derivative products sold on futures exchanges, the most liquid contracts tend to be ones with maturities of less than six months. On the other hand, over 50 percent of currency swaps have maturities of one to five years, and roughly 24 percent of these contracts exceed five years.

These findings raise the question of why many Japanese companies choose not to hedge using derivative products. Their reluctance to hedge may have

Table 3.18   **Currency Composition of Over-the-Counter Foreign Exchange Derivative Activity by Country and Currency, 1995**

Country	Total	Specified Currency against All Other Currencies				
		U.S. Dollar	Deutsche Mark	Japanese Yen	Pound Sterling	ECU
United Kingdom	292,422	272,858	61,818	60,909	46,855	13,521
United States	131,835	122,146	40,318	32,987	11,701	1,454
Japan	112,202	107,265	13,324	93,730	2,138	307
Singapore	62,994	61,518	13,210	18,468	5,014	402
Hong Kong	56,391	55,808	10,868	19,989	4,204	–
Switzerland	44,246	39,245	12,990	4,000	1,605	658
Germany	45,104	35,422	30,416	3,947	2,306	866
France	36,070	31,613	8,105	4,739	1,323	2,503
Australia	22,902	22,349	4,225	2,678	2,029	–
Denmark	22,937	19,728	5,073	531	444	253
Canada	18,681	18,548	1,785	931	633	–
Belgium	22,407	20,562	4,137	1,714	1,454	2,073
Netherlands	15,501	13,292	3,695	728	1,760	436
Italy	10,755	9,180	1,604	250	92	701
Sweden	11,800	10,497	2,614	266	171	46
Luxembourg	11,700	10,495	5,361	461	338	663
Spain	11,214	10,336	2,118	161	46	116
Austria	4,488	3,510	1,781	59	36	34
Norway	4,193	3,705	665	89	115	36
New Zealand	4,069	3,917	279	324	125	–
Finland	2,898	2,241	705	20	43	168
South Africa	2,829	2,679	270	104	77	12
Ireland	1,726	1,276	479	49	346	36
Greece	1,272	955	300	413	7	38
Bahrain	1,337	1,283	283	320	67	2
Portugal	1,018	893	44	103	4	51
Total[a]	952,993	881,319	226,466	247,972	82,935	24,375

Source: BIS (1995, table 9-D).

Note: Entries are dollar-denominated volumes of derivative activity by country and currency.

[a]Because two currencies are involved in each transaction, the sum of transactions in individual currencies comes to twice total reported turnover.

several explanations. The first is that, while hedging opportunities exist, they are costly and may be perceived by company managers as too costly to justify the benefits. Even if managers are convinced of the value of hedging, they may find it difficult to justify to outsiders the purchase of derivatives in states of the world in which, ex post, such hedges lose money. A second reason may be that a company's ability to compete in domestic markets depends in part on what its domestic competitors do. If other Japanese firms do not hedge and the value of the yen changes in a way that greatly reduces the value of hedge positions, firms that hedge may not have the financial resources to remain competitive in domestic markets.

3.2.5   The Relation between Yen Exchange Rates and the Japanese Balance of Payments

Balance-of-payments accounts provide a detailed record of the composition of a country's current account balance (a country's net exports of goods and services) and the transactions that finance it. There is a well-documented tendency for a country's current account first to deteriorate and then improve, in a J-curve pattern, in response to a currency depreciation. The usual explanation for this phenomenon is that the majority of trade is contractual and contracts are often set long in advance of actual transfers of goods. It takes time for importers to adjust their orders in reaction to changes in relative prices, and in the interim, import values (as measured in domestic currency units) rise, thereby eroding the current account. In the case of an appreciation of the domestic currency, the reverse is true, with the current account initially improving and then deteriorating. Further, the J-curve dynamics of the current account in response to a change in the exchange rate are consistent with the use of the exporter's currency to denominate trade contracts (Grassman's law). For example, from the perspective of Germany, if most German exports are denominated in deutsche marks and a significant fraction of German imports are denominated in foreign currencies, then when the deutsche mark appreciates, the deutsche mark value of export earnings is not affected whereas the deutsche mark price of imports falls. Consequently, even if the real value of trade is fixed by preset contracts,[16] the German current account improves in the short term when the deutsche mark strengthens.

Japanese invoicing conventions are different. Japanese exports and imports are more likely to be invoiced in foreign currencies (specifically the dollar) than in yen, and pricing-to-market conventions are likely to lead to the maintenance of relative prices. Consequently, if the yen appreciates against the dollar, trade contracts are preset, and relative prices are left unchanged, the yen value of both exports and imports will fall. And if Japanese firms continue to maintain relative prices (rather than passing through the yen appreciation), trade volumes are unlikely to change, further delaying the expected negative influence of the yen appreciation on the Japanese current account. Hence, Japanese invoicing and pricing-to-market practices are likely to prolong the J-curve effect.

An Overview of Japan's Current and Capital Accounts

Japan has run current account surpluses since 1981. The ratio of Japan's current account surplus to GDP reached a peak of 4.4 percent in 1986, declined to 1.3 percent in 1990, rose again during the economic recession of 1991–93, and has declined as a share of GDP since that period. Table 3.19 presents data on

---

16. International trade contracts are generally negotiated three to six months before goods are delivered and nine to twelve months before invoices are paid.

Table 3.19   **Japanese Current Accounts and Capital Flows (billions of U.S. dollars)**

Item	1987	1989	1991	1994[a]
1. Current accounts	87.0	57.2	72.9	129.1
Trade balance	96.4	76.9	103.0	145.9
Exports	224.6	269.6	306.6	384.2
Imports	128.2	192.7	203.5	238.2
Service balance	−5.7	−15.5	−17.7	−9.3
Transportation	−6.1	−7.7	−10.5	−12.6
Travel	−8.7	−19.3	−20.5	−27.2
Investment income	16.7	23.4	26.7	41.0
Other	−7.6	−11.9	−13.9	−10.5
Transfers	−3.7	−4.2	−12.5	−7.5
2. Long-term capital	−136.5	−89.2	37.1	−82.0
Assets (Japanese capital)	−132.8	−192.1	−121.4	−110.2
Securities	−87.8	−113.2	−74.3	−83.6
Stocks	−16.9	−17.9	−3.6	−14.1
Bonds	−72.9	−94.1	−68.2	−64.1
Yen-denominated bonds	2.0	−1.2	−2.5	−5.5
Direct investment	−19.5	−44.1	−30.7	−17.9
Trade credits and loans extended	−16.7	−26.5	−9.2	−3.9
Other	−8.8	−8.3	−7.2	−4.7
Liabilities (foreign capital)	−3.7	102.9	158.5	28.2
Securities investment	−6.1	85.1	115.3	34.7
Stocks	−42.8	7.0	46.8	48.9
Bonds	6.7	2.4	21.2	0.5
External bonds	30.1	75.7	47.3	−14.9
Direct investment	1.2	−1.1	1.4	0.9
Trade credits and loans received	−0.1	17.8	38.1	−9.6
Other	1.3	1.0	3.7	2.3
3. Short-term capital	23.9	20.8	−25.8	−8.9
4. Monetary movement balances	29.5	33.3	−76.4	−20.4
Private bank sector	71.8	8.6	−93.5	−22.7
Official sector	−42.3	24.7	17.1	2.3
Foreign reserves	−39.2	12.8	8.1	−27.3
5. Errors and omissions[b]	−3.9	−22.0	−7.8	−17.8

Source: BOJ, *Economic Statistics Annual* (Tokyo, various issues).
Note: Negative entries in capital and monetary movement denote outflow of capital from Japan.
[a]Starting in 1995 Japan's balance-of-payments data were no longer provided in U.S. dollars.
[b]Errors and omissions are defined by line 5 = −(line 1 + line 2 + line 3 + line 4).

Japanese current account and capital account flows since 1987. Starting in 1995 the BOJ stopped reporting these statistics in billions of dollars, but trends in these accounts have been stable since 1994. The largest component of the current account is the trade balance, and the figures reported in table 3.19 show that import growth has outstripped export growth, explaining the slower growth of the Japanese current account surplus in recent years.

In the late 1980s Japan's imports of long-term net assets (line 2 in table 3.19) exceeded the current account surplus, the difference being made up by short-term capital (line 3). In other words, Japan financed long-term investment by borrowing short-term capital. In 1991, despite continued current account surpluses, there was an outflow of long-term and short-term capital. Ito (1994) describes this as the "unwinding" of capital; basically Japan repaid the short-term debt it had accumulated in the second half of the 1980s. By 1994 long-term capital was again flowing into Japan, but these assets no longer exceeded the current account surplus, so that Japan exported short-term capital. Further, the switch in the long-term capital account to outflow in 1991 seems to have been mainly caused by the investment decisions of foreigners. Foreign capital liabilities exceeded Japanese capital assets in 1991, but by 1994 this pattern had reversed itself. Looking further at the cause of the capital outflows in the early 1990s, it appears that foreign investment was concentrated in Japanese securities. In 1994 foreign investment in stocks rose marginally from their 1991 levels, but net foreign investment in Japanese bonds fell dramatically, presumably due to the low yields on Japanese bonds.

Implications of Yen Invoicing Practices for the J-Curve

It is difficult to reconcile the persistent Japanese current account surpluses documented in table 3.19 with the dramatic appreciation of the yen relative to the dollar (and most other major currencies) in the past decade. An increase in the value of a currency does not guarantee that the current account balance of the issuing country will deteriorate, but the expectation is that, over time, its export goods will become less competitive on world markets. There are, however, at least three reasons why export prices denominated in yen may take longer to rise in reaction to a yen strengthening. The first reason is the pricing-to-market behavior of Japanese manufacturing firms. The second reason is the foreign currency invoicing practices of Japanese firms. As described earlier, pricing-to-market behavior does not explain Japanese invoicing conventions, but in combination with invoicing conventions, this practice is likely to dampen the effect of any yen appreciation on Japanese export prices. The third reason is that, if Japanese firms hedge against yen appreciation, the costs of exports and imports will not be influenced by changes in the value of the yen.

When domestic firms attempt to maintain foreign market shares and trade invoices are denominated in foreign currencies, an appreciation of the domestic currency is likely to influence export prices even more slowly than in the standard J-curve dynamic. Of course, eventually, if domestic firms are to stay in business and the currency appreciation continues, export prices must rise. Consequently, any effect of pricing-to-market, currency invoicing, and hedging is inherently short run. In the long run we should expect the Japanese current account surplus to fall in reaction to any yen appreciation, and the Japanese balance-of-payments statistics suggest that this process has begun.

Long-Term versus Short-Term Capital Outflows from Japan

The large Japanese current account surpluses should foster the internationalization of the yen. Japanese financial institutions benefit from opportunities to invest the large accumulated surplus. However, the extent to which the current account surpluses have enhanced the role of the yen depends on how short- and long-term capital outflows have been invested. This section examines the portfolio preferences of Japanese institutional investors, the role of the Japanese banks in providing yen denominated liquidity, and the destination of Japanese foreign direct investment.

The Portfolio Preferences of Japanese Institutional Investors

The data in table 3.19 indicate that long-term capital outflows from Japan have been concentrated in securities, and most of these foreign securities are held by Japanese institutional investors (banks, insurance companies, and investment trusts). Table 3.20 presents data on the shares of foreign security holdings of institutional investors in Japan as compared to institutional investors in other countries. The portfolios of institutional investors in Japan, along with those of investors in the United Kingdom and the Netherlands, are far more internationally diversified than U.S. portfolios.[17] The currency composition of Japanese foreign security holdings are not available, but Fukao and Okina (1989) present data from the late 1980s showing that 57 percent of life insurance portfolios (which account for 33 percent of Japanese foreign security investments) were denominated in U.S. dollars and 22 percent were denominated in Canadian dollars. Further, according to Fukao and Okina (1989, 202), as of the late 1980s only about one-third of foreign security investment by Japanese institutional investors was covered by forward transactions or matching foreign currency liabilities. Consequently, institutional investors were an important channel of uncovered capital outflows from Japan.

The Role of Japanese Banks

What role do Japanese banks play in recycling Japanese current account surpluses? Tavlas and Ozeki (1992) argued that Japanese banks have not acted like world bankers, transforming liquid yen-denominated deposits into longer term yen-denominated loans and investments. Instead, Japanese banks have been involved mainly in maturity transformation, borrowing short-term funds overseas in foreign currencies and investing funds in long-term foreign-currency-denominated instruments. Prudential regulations limit the net foreign exchange exposure of Japanese banks. So that, while Japanese banks hold a

---

17. Japan conducted a series of deregulations of foreign investment by financial institutions in the 1980s. A brief chronology of these is provided in Fukao and Okina (1989, app. b). Although this deregulation clearly provided Japanese institutional investors greater opportunities to invest abroad, it is likely that the large scale of investment was due in large part to the high real interest rates in the United States in the 1980s.

Table 3.20   Foreign Security Investments by Institutional Investors across Countries (percent)

Country	1980	1985	1990	1991
United States				
Private pension funds[a]	1.0	3.0	4.2	5.2
Japan				
Life insurance companies	9.0	26.4	30.0	28.4
Non–life insurance companies	7.4	19.4	29.1	28.5
Trust accounts of banks	2.2	14.0	19.4	22.1
Postal Life Insurance	0.0	6.7	14.0	12.1
Norinchukin Bank	4.3	10.3	22.7	32.6
Canada				
Life insurance companies	2.1	2.2	2.3	2.7
Pension funds	6.1	6.6	6.0	7.6
Italy				
Life insurance companies	11.7	10.1	11.6	9.7
United Kingdom[b]				
Life insurance companies	6.9	17.3	20.7	–
Pension funds	6.1	17.8	23.6	–
Belgium				
Insurance companies and pension funds	1.7	3.3	3.3	–
Netherlands				
Insurance companies	5.2[c]	10.3	9.3	10.3
Private pension funds	10.6[c]	13.8	21.1	23.5
Public pension funds	1.7[c]	2.8	5.2	5.7
Sweden				
Insurance companies	–	1.5[d]	10.4	12.5

Source: Takeda and Turner (1992).

Note: Entries are percentages of institutional capital invested in foreign securities.

[a]Tax-exempt funded schemes (excluding individual retirement accounts).

[b]Pension funds exclude central government sector but include other public sector. Unit trust investment is allocated as follows: 50 percent at the end of 1989 (on the basis of partial survey results), other years calculated in proportion to changes in the measured share of foreign assets.

[c]1983 figure.

[d]1987 figure.

large number of foreign securities, these tend to be financed by foreign currency liabilities to avoid currency risks.

The data reported in table 3.21 show that prior to 1991 external assets of authorized foreign exchange banks were predominantly in foreign currencies (mostly U.S. dollars) rather than in yen. Starting in 1992 external yen-denominated assets exceeded those denominated in foreign currencies. Nevertheless, the fact that Japanese banks heavily borrow and lend in foreign currencies means that they provide limited yen-denominated liquidity to the financial markets. The combined evidence in tables 3.20 and 3.21 suggests that it is

Table 3.21   **External Assets of Authorized Foreign Exchange Banks**

	Level (billion US$)			Composition (%)		
	1985	1990	1996	1985	1990	1996
Foreign currency denominated	77.9	344.8	400.2	78	56	44
Yen denominated	21.7	268.4	500.9	22	44	56
Total	99.6	613.2	901.1	100	100	100

Source: MOF, *Economic Statistics Monthly* (various issues).

Note: The 1996 figures, reported in millions of yen, are translated into dollars at the average 1996 exchange rate: 115.98 yen per dollar.

Table 3.22   **Japanese Foreign Direct Investment by Region (percent)**

Country/Region	1985	1990	1992	1993	1994	1996[a]
Asia	11.7	12.4	18.8	18.4	23.1	19.9
(billion US$)	(1.4)	(7.1)	(6.4)	(6.6)	(9.7)	n.a.
Europe[b]	15.8	25.1	20.7	22.0	15.2	n.a.
United States	44.2	45.9	40.5	40.8	42.2	45.2
Other[c]	28.3	16.6	20.0	18.8	19.0	n.a.
Total	100.0	100.0	100.0	100.0	100.0	

Source: Nihon Statistical Association, *Japan Statistical Yearbook* (various issues). Original data are from MOF, International Finance Bureau; 1996 data are from Nihon Keizai Shinbusha, *Japan Economic Almanac* (1997).

[a]Fiscal year through March 1996; Japanese foreign direct investment in Asia totaled ¥1.19 trillion in March 1996.

[b]Excluding Luxembourg.

[c]Includes the following tax havens: the Bahamas, Bermuda, the Cayman Islands, the Netherlands Antilles, Luxembourg, and Panama.

Japanese institutional investors, rather than Japanese banks, who have played the largest role in recycling Japanese current account surpluses and facilitating the international use of the yen.

Japanese Foreign Direct Investment

Japan's foreign direct investment (line 2 in table 3.19) is a substantial component of long-term capital flows. Japanese foreign investments are defined as "direct" if Japanese owners control 10 percent or more of the foreign firm in which investment is located.[18] In 1994 direct investment was 16 percent of Japanese long-term capital. Table 3.22 presents data on the destinations of Japanese direct investments.[19] The share of Japanese investment in the United

18. Prior to 1 December 1979 Japanese foreign investment was considered "direct" if Japanese owners controlled 25 percent or more of the foreign firms.

19. Japanese foreign direct investment data are notoriously unreliable. Weinstein (1997) pointed out that foreign direct investment entries are recorded not on the date of investment but on the date

States has been remarkably stable over the years; just under half of Japanese foreign direct investment each year goes to the United States. A significant fraction of Japanese direct investment goes to Asia, and starting in 1994 investments in Asia surpassed funds bound for Europe. The yen appreciation against the dollar in the mid-1990s heightened the attractiveness of foreign direct investment for Japanese firms. Japanese manufacturing firms, in particular, have been strengthening production networks in countries with cheaper labor and procurement costs.

History suggests that direct investment, especially in developing countries, can enhance the international role of a currency. British direct investment in developing countries in the second half of the nineteenth century and U.S. direct investment in reconstructing countries after World War II led to the buildup of large external pound- and dollar-denominated balances. In the case of Japan, direct investment in Asia, and especially China in the past few years,[20] is substantial, but direct investment to developing countries overall makes up a relatively small share of net capital outflows. So that, with the possible exception of Asia, Japanese foreign direct investment is unlikely to lead to significant external yen-denominated balances.

The Role of Bank of Japan Foreign Exchange Rate Intervention Operations

A final measure of a currency's international role is its use by central banks to intervene in foreign exchange markets. Foreign exchange interventions are typically defined as official sales or purchases of foreign assets against domestic assets in the foreign exchange market for the purpose of influencing relative currency values. The BOJ actively intervenes in the foreign exchange market, and most BOJ operations involve the yen. Other than the BOJ, however, the only central bank that regularly intervenes using the yen is the Fed. In recent years the Fed has typically divided its interventions equally between the yen and the mark. Although, on some occasions, especially in 1995 when the yen-dollar rate was the focus of intervention operations, Fed interventions were exclusively against the yen. The dollar is the predominant intervention currency used by developing country central banks. Intervention within the EMS is carried out exclusively in European currencies. And non-EMS-related interventions by the German Bundesbank typically involve the dollar.

Although no data exist on the relative use of currencies in official interventions, the yen is likely to rank well behind the dollar, and perhaps the deutsche mark. Moreover, daily foreign exchange intervention operations by the G-3 countries are typically under $200 million. Therefore, even were the use of the

---

of acceptance by MOF (the 1980 Foreign Exchange and Foreign Trade Control Law requires firms to notify MOF prior to the investment). There is often a time lag between time of MOF acceptance and the cash disbursement. Further, the entire value of multiple-year investments are recorded on the MOF acceptance date.

20. Japanese direct investment in China jumped 61 percent in 1995 to ¥431.9 billion.

yen in intervention operations to increase dramatically, such operations are unlikely to have much impact on the international role of the yen.

3.2.6 Summary and Conclusions

The role of the yen in international financial markets has greatly expanded in the past two decades. International use of yen was tightly controlled by Japanese authorities prior to the mid-1970s, but since that time Japanese financial markets and institutions have been significantly deregulated. Likewise, the yen's purchasing power has remained strong and relatively stable over the past two decades.

Although use of the yen as a medium of exchange, a reserve currency, and an investment currency has grown substantially since the early 1980s, the U.S. dollar and the German mark remain the dominant international currencies. Moreover, few trade contracts are denominated in yen, in spite of rising Japanese economic power in world trade. This paper explored a number of possible explanations for low yen invoice ratios, including Japanese pricing-to-market behavior. But as long as Japanese firms hedge exchange rate risks that arise when trade is invoiced in foreign currencies, pricing-to-market behavior does not rely on the use of particular invoice currencies. Further, BIS data indicate that the market for yen-denominated derivative products is substantial, suggesting that Japanese firms interested in hedging yen-dollar exchange rate risk have ample opportunity to do so. Hence, there remains a puzzle as to why Japan is an outlier among the G-6 in its trade invoicing practices.

Japanese invoicing practices may be partly responsible for observed J-curves. If the yen appreciates against the dollar, trade contracts are preset, and relative prices are left unchanged, then the yen value of both Japanese exports and imports will fall. And if the fall in the value of imports outweighs that in exports, the yen appreciation will lead to an improvement in the Japanese current account. However, the influence of currency invoicing on the J-curve is inherently short run; over time, if Japanese firms are to stay in business, and the currency appreciation continues, export prices must rise. Over the long run, Japanese current account surpluses will fall in reaction to a yen appreciation— and Japanese balance-of-payments statistics suggest that this process has begun.

Large and persistent Japanese current account surpluses serve to enhance the internationalization of the yen. Interestingly, it appears to be Japanese institutional investors, rather than Japanese banks, who have played the largest role in recycling Japanese current account surpluses and facilitating the international use of the yen. However, foreign investments by Japanese institutional investors, as well as Japanese foreign direct investments, have predominantly gone to the United States, where the share of yen balances remains relatively small. The only region in which large external yen-denominated balances have begun to build is Asia.

The evidence suggests that there is little reason to expect international use of the yen to increase substantially from current levels. The United States and Germany have, over the past decade, established records of low inflation and deregulated their financial markets, thereby strengthening the positions of their currencies. The U.S. dollar, in particular, appears to be widely used in part due to its history as a vehicle currency. Moreover, introduction of the euro at the end of the decade is likely to establish a competitor to the yen even stronger than the current deutsche mark. Consequently, to the extent that the limited international role of the yen may be puzzling, this puzzle is unlikely to disappear any time soon.

Appendix

Survey Questions: The Currency Invoicing Practices of Japanese Corporations

I. Corporate Policy on Invoicing

In your firm, how is it decided in which currency to invoice exports and imports?
Is there a concrete policy (decision rules)?
Is there any Japanese government, central bank, or MITI policy on this subject? If so, what are they? Are they mandatory? Discretionary?
Who is responsible for this policy, your firm or your headquarters? (level within the company/name)
Is there any management discretion in making the determination? At what level in the company?

II. Factors That Determine Currency Denomination of Invoicing

In your firm, on what basis is the invoicing currency determined?
Does the determination depend on countries on the other side, type of product, timing, or other condition(s) in making the choice?
As for imports you may handle as a trading company, how is the invoicing currency determined? Which currency is your firm in the United States using to invoice exports and imports to and from headquarters or Japanese firms?
If U.S. dollar denomination is being used instead of yen, what is the reason? Why isn't the yen used? Which currency is your headquarters in Japan using to deal with U.S. firms? If it is using U.S. dollar denominations, what is the reason?
Must the billed and billing party agree in advance on the invoicing currency?

A. Inflation and Currency Fluctuations

Does the relative inflation performance of alternative currencies enter into the invoicing decision process?

If so, are there minimums, baselines, or floors?

Who determines them and what are they?

Is past or prospective exchange rate volatility a factor in the invoicing decision?

B. Price Competition

Does your firm attempt to stabilize the price of your export products measured in the buyer's currency?

Does your firm invoice in foreign currency in order to maintain a constant markup over invoice price?

C. Taxation

Are there tax reasons to prefer one invoicing currency to another?

Are these tax reasons unique to the business or trading company?

Does the type of product have a bearing (special tax treatment)?

Does the paired company or nation for billing have an effect?

Do you have an advanced pricing agreement on transfer prices (between your firm and headquarters) with the U.S. Internal Revenue Service? If so, why? If not, why not?

Is some of the ownership of your company located in a tax haven (low tax) country? Or does your parent company in Japan hold 100 percent ownership?

What determines whether you reinvest your profits or remit them as dividends? How important are tax considerations in that decision?

III. Hedging Foreign Exchange Risk

When you do invoice in foreign currencies, do you hedge the consequent foreign exchange risk?

Does your company participate in currency hedging operations? Is this your responsibility or is it done elsewhere in the company?

How does your company decide if currency hedging is necessary?

Are there time limits associated with hedging—out 30, 60, 90 days? More?

If you hedge, do you hedge on an individual transaction (or contract) basis or for a bulk value of sales over a particular period?

Do you use derivative products for hedging or only forward currency contracts? If you use derivative products, what kind of products do you generally use? For 100 percent of the risk? How and who decides?

Do you generally borrow from your parent company or from foreign lenders? Does the currency in which you borrow influence your invoicing preferences?

IV. Factors That Might Lead to Changes in Current Invoicing Policy

What factors would lead your firm to change the invoicing currency denomination of your products?
What factors might lead you to invoice more in yen?
What factors might lead you to invoice more in foreign currency?
Has your company's invoicing policy for exports or imports changed recently?
Do you foresee any changes to the current invoicing policies in the near future?

References

Alterman, William. 1989. International economic transactions: Issues in measurement and empirical research. Paper presented at the Conference on Research in Income and Wealth, Washington, D.C., November.
Bilson, J. 1983. The choice of an invoice currency in international transactions. In *Economic interdependence and flexible exchange rates,* ed. J. Bhandari and B. Putnam, 384–401. Cambridge, Mass.: MIT Press.
BIS (Bank for International Settlements). 1995. Central bank survey of foreign exchange and derivatives market activity. Basel: Bank for International Settlements.
———. 1997. International banking and financial market developments. Basel: Bank for International Settlements, May.
Black, S. 1991. Transactions costs and vehicle currencies. *Journal of International Money and Finance* 10:512–26.
———. 1993. The international use of currencies. In *International finance: Contemporary issues,* ed. Dilip Das, 553–65. London: Routledge.
Cohen, B. J. 1971. *The future of sterling as an international currency.* London: Macmillan.
Dominguez, K. M. 1998. The dollar exposure of Japanese companies. *Journal of Japanese and International Economies* 12:388–405.
Eken, S. 1984. Integration of domestic and international financial markets: The Japanese experience. *IMF Staff Papers* 31:499–548.
Frankel, J. 1984. The yen/dollar agreement: Liberalizing Japanese capital markets. Policy Analyses in International Economics, no. 9. Washington, D.C.: Institute for International Economics.
Fukao, M. 1990. Liberalization of Japan's foreign exchange controls and structural changes in balance of payments. *Monetary and Economic Studies* (Bank of Japan) 8:101–65.
Fukao, M., and K. Okina. 1989. Internationalization of financial markets and balance of payments imbalances: A Japanese perspective. *Carnegie-Rochester Conference Series on Public Policy* 30:167–220.
Fukuda, S. 1996. The structural determinants of invoice currencies in Japan: The case of foreign trade with East Asian countries. In *Financial deregulation and integration in East Asia,* ed. T. Ito and A. O. Krueger, 147–63. Chicago: University of Chicago Press.
Fukuda, S., and C. Ji. 1994. On the choice of invoice currency by Japanese exporters: The PTM approach. *Japanese and International Economies* 8 (4): 511–29.

Gagnon, J., and M. Knetter. 1995. Markup adjustment and exchange rate fluctuations: Evidence from panel data on automobile exports. *Journal of International Money and Finance* 14 (2): 289–310.

Garber, P. 1996. The use of the yen as a reserve currency. *Monetary and Economic Studies* (Bank of Japan) 14:1–21.

Giovannini, A. 1988. Exchange rates and traded goods prices. *Journal of International Economics* 24:45–68.

Grassman, S. 1973. A fundamental symmetry in international payment patterns. *Journal of International Economics* 3:105–16.

———. 1976. Currency distribution and forward cover in foreign trade. *Journal of International Economics* 6:215–21.

Ito, T. 1994. On recent movements of Japanese current accounts and capital flows. In *Macroeconomic linkage: Savings, exchange rates, and capital flows,* ed. T. Ito and A. Krueger, 31–52. Chicago: University of Chicago Press.

Ito, T., and D. Folkerts-Landau. 1996. *International capital markets: Developments, prospects, and key policy issues.* Washington, D.C.: International Monetary Fund, September.

Krugman, P. 1980. Vehicle currencies and the structure of international exchange. *Journal of Money, Credit and Banking* 12:513–26.

———. 1984. The international role of the dollar: Theory and prospect. In *Exchange rate theory and practice,* ed. J. Bilson and R. Marston, 261–78. Chicago: University of Chicago Press.

———. 1987. Pricing to market when the exchange rate changes. In *Real financial linkages among open economies,* ed. S. W. Arndt and J. D. Richardson, 49–70. Cambridge, Mass.: MIT Press.

Magree, S. 1974. U.S. import prices in the currency-contract period. *Brookings Papers on Economic Activity,* no. 1:117–68.

Magree, S., and R. Rao. 1980. Vehicle and nonvehicle currencies in international trade. *American Economic Review* 70 (May): 368–73.

Marston, R. 1990. Pricing to market in Japanese manufacturing. *Journal of International Economics* 29:217–36.

McKinnon, R. I. 1979. *Money in international exchange.* New York: Oxford University Press.

Page, S. A. B. 1981. The choice of invoicing currency in merchandise trade. *National Institute Economic Review* 98 (November): 60–72.

Swoboda, A. K. 1968. The Euro-dollar market: An interpretation. Princeton Essays in International Finance, no. 64. Princeton, N.J.: Princeton University, International Finance Section.

Taguchi, H. 1994. On the internationalization of the Japanese yen. In *Macroeconomic linkage: Savings, exchange rates, and capital flows,* ed. T. Ito and A. Krueger, 335–55. Chicago: University of Chicago Press.

Takeda, M., and P. Turner. 1992. The liberalization of Japan's financial markets: Some major themes. BIS Economic Paper no. 34. Basel: Bank for International Settlements, November.

Tavlas, G. 1991. The internationalization of the yen. *Finance and Development* 28, no. 2 (June): 2–5.

Tavlas, G., and Y. Ozeki. 1992. The internationalization of currencies: An appraisal of the Japanese yen. Occasional Paper no. 90. Washington, D.C.: International Monetary Fund.

Weinstein, D. E. 1997. Foreign direct investment and keiretsu: Rethinking U.S. and Japanese policy. In *The effects of U.S. trade protection and promotion policies,* ed. R. Feenstra. Chicago: University of Chicago Press.

3. Moeen Qureshi

Capital Flows and the East Asian Financial Crisis

Let me try to follow in Michael Blumenthal's (chap. 2.2) footsteps by saying that what I am going to give you is the perspective of someone who, at least these days, is a practical operator. I remember Keynes's dictum that all practical men are the slaves of some defunct economist. With apologies to that unknown defunct economist, let me start with a thumbnail sketch of what has happened in terms of capital flows to East Asia, and in that connection, I want to thank Taka-toshi Ito for providing an excellent background paper. It encompasses most of the major problems, as well as most of the data that one really needs.

In very brief terms, there has been a sixfold increase in total capital flows to the emerging markets in the 1990s. All of the increase has been in private capital flows. In 1996 these amounted to $265 billion, if you include Korea. Official capital flows dwindled to less than $10 billion last year. East Asia has absorbed more than one-half of total private capital flows. East Asia and, within East Asia, China have had the lion's share of these resources.

The next important point is that there has been a major change in the structure of capital flows, with foreign direct investment now accounting for almost one-half of total private capital flows (prior to 1990, about two-thirds of private capital flows were essentially commercial bank lending). East Asia has been receiving, therefore, a great deal more than its proportionate share. This growing share of foreign direct investment has helped bring in new technology and modernization.

Why has East Asia been so favored? My own, perhaps simplistic, answer to that is the following:

First, East Asia has enjoyed political stability for almost the past two decades. Whenever new governments have come in—and some new governments have come in—they have not reneged on the promises of previous governments, and therefore, essentially all contractual agreements reached with foreign investors have been maintained and continued.

Second, over the past two decades, the region has had macroeconomic stability.

Third, the environment has been very investor friendly.

Fourth, and in my view perhaps most important, the governments of this region have been totally dedicated to economic development as a primary objective of policy. And they have recognized that they could only achieve this objective by liberalizing their economies and integrating them with the global economy. And they have actively pursued this goal.

I recall talking with the leaders of China, in fact with the prime minister of China, about eight or nine years ago. He told me that they had reached a collective decision to assign the highest priority to the task of economic growth, with the objective of achieving a standard of living comparable to that of the Japanese within a space of perhaps a quarter-century. And in order not to be distracted from achieving that objective, they intended to move swiftly to resolve their outstanding territorial disputes with the then Soviet Union and with India. And they proceeded to do so. In the process, they gave up an enormous amount of territory that had been in dispute with the Soviet Union for nearly a quarter-century. Similarly, their forces withdrew from the border with India, and they tried to settle that dispute as well.

If you look at the history of Southeast Asia, a similar sense of dedication to development can be observed in the other countries. I have had a modest role in trying to contribute to that objective—a very modest role—basically by organizing a fund that provides direct investment for infrastructure projects in Asia.

But how has this favorable picture changed? Over the past two months, East Asia has changed from the preferred destination for private foreign capital to the epicenter of a major financial and currency crisis. The East Asian countries have recently experienced a precipitous decline in currency values. I was just told that the Malaysian market fell further because of some of the steps the authorities have taken to restrict the freedom of market transactions. They have also seen a massive reversal of capital flows during this period. Why has this occurred?

Except in Thailand, the reason is not really a failure of macroeconomic policy. In a recent World Bank study of private capital flows that examined the impact of the Mexican crisis on other emerging markets, the authors extolled the virtues of the macroeconomic policies of the Asian tigers. The report pointed to the rapid rate of economic growth achieved together with overall monetary and fiscal stability and explained that this was the reason these economies were not much affected by the Mexican crisis.

More recently, attention has gravitated—some of the background papers make this very clear—to problems in the financial sector as the central issue. They seem to have triggered the crisis. These problems include, of course, the poor regulatory framework. They also include the excessive, and often speculative, involvement of financial institutions in intermediating capital flows.

In my view, while financial sector deficiencies have certainly contributed to—and aggravated—the financial crisis in East Asia, these deficiencies have existed for a long time. They have been known for a very long time, and the markets have happily ignored them, also for a very long time. I lean toward Paul Krugman's view, expressed in his excellent paper on currency crises (chap. 8.1), that foreign exchange crises typically occur, at least in today's environment of massive capital movements, not when economic fundamentals suddenly change, but when for one reason or another—whether it be an economic reason or a political reason, such as the issue of succession in Indonesia or of leadership in Malaysia—currencies suddenly look vulnerable. That is when crises most often occur.

Like others here, I was at the recent annual meetings of the IMF and the World Bank in Hong Kong. The issue of Southeast Asia's currency crisis was clearly in the forefront of discussions there. What really dominated the talk on the cocktail circuit—where most of the business gets done at these meetings—was the confrontation between Mahathir and George Soros. On one side, Mahathir blamed all Malaysia's troubles on Western speculators and manipulators and alleged that Western governments are behind their machinations. He identified George Soros as the real devil who had manipulated the market. On the other side, most Western observers claimed that the source of Asia's problem lay squarely at home. Soros put it bluntly: he said Mahathir was a menace to his country, and all Malaysia's problems were entirely due to Mahathir and his policies. What certainly is true is that Mahathir's pronouncements have not helped. Every time he makes a speech, the ringgit falls.

However, if this was all there was to the debate, it could be characterized as a confrontation between two very flamboyant and rather egocentric people. But there is more important fallout from this crisis. This crisis has substantial political and economic implications for the region, and it has already seriously damaged the growth and economic prospects of some Asian countries. If you look at the opportunity costs in terms of economic growth foregone, it runs to trillions of dollars. Therefore, we must understand the issues involved and their judicious management if we are going to continue to move toward globalization and liberalization of capital flows—the kind of liberalization that the IMF would like to achieve by modifying its Articles of Agreement.

Unfortunately, the debate has become polarized, between those who, to use Camdessus's phrase, are seeking to demonize free capital and currency markets and those who are seeking to portray them as the epitome of perfection. Of course, neither of these perspectives is correct. As Paul Krugman says in his paper, there have been, in the past six or seven years, three crises, in Europe, in Latin America, and in Asia; and prior to each crisis, it was well known that there were latent financial problems in the particular countries affected. But when the crisis came, it came very suddenly, and it came with herdlike behavior among investors.

There is also the issue of contagion. It is hard to see why, during the Mexican crisis, Thailand's stock market should be affected. It is equally hard to see why Indonesia should be so greatly affected by the Thai crisis. No country is perfect, but Indonesia's economic fundamentals are about the strongest you can find in a developing country today.

All this is to say that foreign exchange markets are really not as efficient as they are presumed to be, and if this is the point that Mahathir is trying to make, then he's absolutely right: there are indeed imperfections in market behavior. However, the fact forgotten in the East Asian context is that whether markets are efficient or not, it is precisely by tapping the vast resources of global capital, and the associated technology, that a country such as Malaysia advances to its current stage of economic development and modernization. And the same is true of the other East Asian countries. In this context Mahathir's inclination to go back to a system of capital and currency controls is tantamount to giving up the source from which the international community and the East Asian region have derived such great benefits.

I think Mahathir is right, though, that capital flows today are so large, and the contagion effects can be so rapid and so overwhelming, that even countries with sound policies can see much of their good work go down the drain when a crisis comes. He is also right when he says that small countries are particularly vulnerable to this type of economic disruption, and to use his phrase, it is difficult to establish a level playing field when you have a fight between a giant and a midget.

Moreover, it would be wrong to dismiss the political import of Mahathir's statement. Asia, too, has its protectionist lobby, which harbors a sneaking admiration for the David and Goliath type of confrontation at which Mahathir excels. It was no accident that despite his support for free markets, Li Peng, the Chinese prime minister, found it necessary to express some sympathy with Mahathir's position.

Now what can be done about managing these currency crises and, in the future, perhaps preventing them? The economist's answer is to go to freely floating rates. I am in no sense an advocate of fixed exchange rates, but having had some experience in managing a country for a certain period of time, I can tell you that giving total primacy to a policy of freely floating exchange rates creates such conflicts with domestic economic objectives that, politically, most governments cannot sustain such policies for any length of time.

Others have asserted that Asian markets should develop shock absorbers and mechanisms to respond to instability. But the remedies suggested are the same ones: financial sector reforms and fiscal flexibility. While these are obviously desirable, it is difficult to see how they would prevent, or even substantially mitigate, the kind of crises that currently affect the Asian countries. Selective capital controls are slightly more effective; but they're controversial, and they raise the specter of governments all too easily retreating into a world of controls.

At the recent IMF/World Bank meetings, a proposal that I thought very constructive was unfortunately sidelined, if not completely torpedoed: that of trying to put together a regional fund. It was torpedoed by fears that the IMF's turf was being invaded. Unfortunately also, this proposal was handled extremely clumsily by its promoters. However, I can tell you that no Asian leader whom I talked with—and I talked with several—intended to exclude the IMF, or the United States, from such a regional fund. Quite the contrary. Nor was there any intention, especially on the part of Japan, which was one of the leaders of this particular proposal, to make it into an "unconditional" facility.

The United States and the Chinese, in particular, were scared by this proposal because they thought the Japanese were trying to create a yen-denominated zone in which they could rule the roost. The Asian proponents of the proposal felt that the decisions of the fund would tend to be dominated by two or three countries. Since the Asians would be contributing the bulk of the resources, they should have a bigger say in the way the fund is operated. There are precedents to establishing such facilities; it has been done in Europe in the form of the General Agreement to Borrow. In any event, the Asian countries do wish to work closely with the IMF. Perhaps the best thing would be to have the IMF manage such a facility, and perhaps APEC could also be given some role in it because it has little else to do that is substantive.

My personal preference—and it would be delightful to organize it—would be for the private sector to try to put together an insurance fund. Indeed, I'd like to fly this kite a little bit higher: It is about time that we get the governments to move out of the way on some of these major financial issues and let the private sector handle them. Of course, the governments would have to cooperate. If you look at the East Asian region, you've got $500 to $600 billion in reserves among the Southeast Asian countries. You could easily pledge 10 percent of these reserves to provide collateral for such a fund. With that kind of financial support, it would not be difficult to get some business leaders to put together a fund that would be available to foreign investors in times of financial crisis. This is just one additional idea to titillate the imagination of some of my friends here, particularly those from official circles.

I think that the current situation, in which it is virtually impossible for a country to restore confidence and get out of a crisis without the IMF stepping in and putting its seal of good housekeeping on it, is very dangerous. Since the markets have only a vague, or somewhat confused, idea as to what is wrong with the country to begin with, everything now depends on the IMF's coming in and pouring its holy water over the country. Thus the country gets religion—and unless this happens, it is impossible to put Humpty Dumpty together again.

In a broader context, we must recognize that today more financial transactions are done outside the framework of national regulatory standards than within. Therefore, we should not be surprised if the excessive volatility that characterizes the system is often disruptive, rather than constructive. Accordingly, I think that there is a very important, more activist role for the IMF, and possibly for the International Trade Organization: to begin to evolve international standards and procedures for banks and financial institutions that operate in the international arena. I believe this process has already begun.

Reverting to Southeast Asia, my conclusion is that, like most issues that create conflict, the Asian issue is a combination of money, real estate, and politics. If you focus on the first, strictly limit the second, and completely avoid the third—that is, avoid politicizing the issue—you should do all right.

4. *Zhang Shengman*

As globalization continues, the world's production and trading patterns will undergo fundamental change. In this inevitable process, capital flows will play a central role. Indeed, looking ahead, if there are constraints to further rapid growth of such flows, they are not likely to be found on the supply side due to the likelihood of continued moderate interest rates in the industrial countries, the increasing competitive pressures limiting the margin of potential return to capital, and the small share of portfolios that emerging markets still represent. Constraints are more likely to be found on the demand side, where there is a question about the capacity of developing countries to attract, absorb, and manage these flows.

In this context, given the crisis in Thailand and its contagion effect on other Southeast Asian economies, it would be highly relevant to continue thinking about some of the questions raised, such as why the crisis was not avoided, since it was largely foreseen; how a crisis like this could happen in one of the world's most dynamic centers of investment and growth; and why the crisis was as contagious as it was in countries with some of the strongest fundamentals. Of course, there is no shortage of suspects—as already cited by various parties. These include a significant currency appreciation, a large current account deficit, increasing reliance on short-term borrowings, the authorities' delay in responding, and so on.

These possible causes are, of course, all relevant, interconnected, and cumulative in the sense they all contributed in some way to the collapse in confidence that is the stark characteristic of the crisis. What is sobering, however, is the fact that many of the same factors played a role in the Mexican crisis some two and a half years earlier. Indeed, one could say with reasonable certainty that the crisis in Thailand was due to a combination of cyclical and structural factors, three of them being particularly noteworthy.

The first factor is the remarkable deceleration of exports during the twenty months prior to the onset of the crisis. The deceleration appears to be at least in part a reflection of more deep-seated problems of competitiveness than just the exchange rate appreciation. One could argue that a very large current account deficit, which implies very rapid growth in net foreign liabilities, need not worry the markets if exports are growing just as rapidly, but the markets would worry if exports are not keeping pace. Clearly, the coupling of unexpectedly weak export performance and a large current account deficit raised basic questions about the sustainability of the country's external position, especially when much of the buildup in liabilities took the form of short-term borrowing.

A second factor is the precarious state of the financial system linked to the political economy of the country. According to Goldman, Sachs, the Thai system scored worst on a set of factors believed to contribute to banking crises in the region. In particular, credit expanded very rapidly in relation to GDP, and the size of bank loans relative to GDP in the country is one of the highest in a large sample of countries—suggesting that problems in the banking system could have especially severe repercussions. In fact, from 1993 to 1996, domestic credit to the private sector grew by more than 20 percent annually. According to Lewis Preston, the former president of J. P. Morgan and of the World Bank, continued annual growth of more than 15 percent for a financial institution is a recipe for disaster.

The third factor I would like to cite is the perception in the markets that the determination, urgency, and sophistication needed for a quick and adequate policy response was lacking on the part of the government, resulting in greater loss of market confidence. Indeed, by some accounts, there was a lag of more than six months between the onset of the confidence problems and the initiation of policy actions. This then may be one area where market perceptions differ from those that followed the crisis in Latin America several years ago.

When one analyzes the Thai and Mexican crises, one common conclusion is that continuous large capital inflows place enormous demands on the capacity of regulatory institutions and the soundness of macroeconomic policies. Even if some aspects of the system are solid (in Thailand, a very high rate of domestic saving and investment), a crisis can still be precipitated by the weaker links of the chain. As is said, the team is only as strong as the weakest member.

While it is too early to provide a certain set of prescriptive answers to the Thai crisis, it is, nevertheless, clear that notwithstanding the growing complexity associated with economic development in an increasingly integrated world economy, fundamentals remain of fundamental importance. Indeed, if anything, more so than ever before. To successfully manage the size, composition, and probably the direction of capital flows, appropriate and sound macroeconomic policies are indispensable.

With this backdrop, let me now turn to China, the largest recipient of capital flows in the developing world during the past four years. I will talk briefly about three aspects in this regard: the path China has traveled so far, how China has managed the large flows, and the challenges China still faces.

The Path China Has Traveled So Far

China formally adopted the open-door policy in 1979, and the first joint venture with foreign partners was set up in 1980, that is, seventeen years ago. Since then, the country has gone through basically three phases in the way it attracts capital flows.

The "mutual learning" period took place from 1979 to 1986. Just as China was ignorant, so investors were afraid. It was a period of getting to know each other and learning from each other. It is no wonder that practically all flows were from Hong Kong and Macao going largely to adjacent southern China. Furthermore, these limited flows financed mostly simple processing ventures.

The "getting ready" phase took place from 1987 to 1991. During this period, essential laws and regulations were enacted and attractive incentive measures adopted. The result was a fair, but gradual, expansion both in the number of economic sectors and of geographic locations into which flows were directed. However, the amount remained small; the scale of individual ventures was not large, nor was the level of technology transferred high.

The "rapid increase" period started in 1992 and continues, partly accompanying the rapid transformation of China's planned economy to increasingly a market economy and partly benefiting from the worldwide surge in private sector investment in emerging markets. The achievement in this period has been remarkable, as we all know. Suffice it to say that as much as 85 percent of total capital inflows have occurred during this period. Indeed, as of now there are more than 300,000 ventures involving foreign flows, close to the number of existing state-owned enterprises, with more than 140,000 already in operation. Almost $500 billion has been committed, with over $200 billion actually used—$53 billion in 1995 and $42 billion in 1996 alone—coming from over 160 countries and areas. Foreign direct investment (FDI) ventures—which employ 18 million people—now account for almost half of China's merchandise foreign trade and 10 percent of government tax revenue. Finally, of the 500 largest multinational corporations (MNCs), about 300 have ventures of various kinds in China, producing everything from consumer goods to durables to high-tech products.

By any measure, China's record in attracting capital flows is impressive. Here it is necessary to look further at some of the characteristics underlying these flows. One such characteristic is the large absolute amount of flows, up to $57 billion in 1995 alone and $43 billion in 1996, of which private flows accounted for 86.1 and 95.8 percent, respectively. Capital flows are primarily FDI. Portfolio flows (5.7 percent in 1995 and 9.6 percent in 1996) are a small share of the total, as are official flows, which accounted for less than $8 billion in 1995 and less than $2 billion in 1996. Another characteristic of China's capital flows is their high concentration, both in terms of investor origin and geographic destination. Twelve coastal areas accounted for over 90 percent, some 60 percent came from Hong Kong, and the top ten sources provided over 95 percent of all flows to China. And, finally, there was a gradual opening-up. This cautious approach applies to both economic sectors and geographic regions. China conducted a localized experiment before extending nationwide.

How China Managed These Large Flows

Normally, we know that with sustained large inflows, one tends to experience several macroeconomic effects, for example, expansion of the domestic money supply, upward pressure on prices and exchange rates, and widening of current account imbalances.

When looking at China since 1990, however, it appears that except for 1993 current accounts have remained positive throughout; price increases have been moderate (apart from the period 1993–94) or lately decelerating. Indeed, the latest figures for September 1997 showed practically zero inflation, and the economic growth rate, on average, was high, ranging from 9.5 to over 12 percent.

In short, there was little sign of the kind of instability in the domestic financial system commonly associated with large inflows. The question to ask, therefore, is why. A quick answer is that the Chinese have managed well under the circumstances. Among others, the following examples are noteworthy.

The Chinese pursued parallel policies of domestic monetary contraction, primarily through controls on aggregate credit. Specifically, the central bank managed to offset the increase in domestic money supply needed to absorb the inflows by reducing the credit available to domestic financial institutions and the government. Although nominal exchange rates remained more or less unchanged during the period, real effective exchange rates did appreciate substantially—by some accounts, over 25 percent from 1992. This appreciation, one would argue, helped to bring the trade balance to a more sustainable level in face of the large capital inflows.

In contrast to monetary policy, fiscal policy was not actively used; the government deficit level remained fairly stable. However, by controlling or constraining fixed capital investments, indeed by not increasing the deficit, fiscal policy played an effective supportive role in not putting additional pressure on the money supply.

Furthermore, China kept the domestic financial system insulated from these inflows by various means. A limitation was set on the entry of foreign banks and their engagement in local currency transactions both in nature and volume. China established surrender requirements and convertibility restrictions on the foreign currency transactions of domestic financial institutions. It also established separate categories of ordinary shares for foreign and domestic investors, and restrictions against foreign participation in domestic fixed income security markets. Unlike for current account transactions, all income from capital account transactions must be maintained in foreign-currency-denominated accounts and cannot be converted into domestic currency without permission. Hence, the related impact on the domestic money supply is thereby minimized. Of course, these restrictions had a cost in terms of economic efficiency: the point is that their intended purpose seemed to have been well achieved.

China adopted targeted incentive policies for FDI, putting the country's advantages to effective use. Incentives include a large market size, high economic growth, low production cost, competitive skilled labor, continued social stability, and a strong government with clear development objectives.

The result is that four out of every five dollars that flowed into China were in the form of FDI, and a large part of them were in turn spent on buying foreign rather than domestic goods, mainly machinery. This perhaps explains why, although from 1992 to 1996 cumulative inflows totaled some $165 billion, net foreign assets in the central bank and deposit money banks increased only by $70 billion.

The Challenges China Still Faces

The fact that you have done well does not guarantee that you will continue to do well, although admittedly it does help in terms of having had a successful experience and laid a necessary foundation. In China, while there is certainly no more debate about the necessity and usefulness of capital inflows, success itself has created its own problems and led to debate about them. A typical debate relates to the emerging dominance of foreign products in an increasing number of industries or sectors. As I and my colleagues in the World Bank see it, China will have to handle several important issues well if it is to continue to be successful in attracting capital flows and putting them to good use.

First, China will have to sustain strong macroeconomic performance through necessary reforms. One such reform would ensure continuation of balanced macropolicies by proceeding with effective state-owned enterprise reforms and financial sector reforms consistent with the government's regulatory and institutional capacities. The government will need to move to the right and strengthen its appropriate role in a growing market economy. China must achieve full convertibility of the domestic currency and create a level playing field for all, including foreign investors. In a way, China will have to place less emphasis on granting financial incentives to individual ventures and more on providing opportunities for global integration.

Second, China must strive for a more desirable distribution of capital flows, both geographically (more to the interior) and sectorally (more to some service sectors, retailing, banking, insurance, etc.). Here more innovative and original ideas will be needed concerning financial incentives, market access, majority ownership, and so forth. The issues of cascading from coastal to internal regions should also be investigated further given the complementary advantages of existing endowments and differential levels of development.

Third, China must increase the diversity of FDI sources—not so much to reduce flows from Hong Kong, Macau, and other Chinese-based sources as to increase flows from other sources. The result would be that as China integrates more with the world, capital flows would be on a more sustainable path and generate more of the expected benefits, such as global production, marketing links, and introduction of advanced technologies, as well as managerial practices.

To conclude, China has done extremely well in attracting and managing capital inflows, even allowing for its unique and distinct advantages. However, to continue to do well China faces challenges, not the least of which is the need to learn how to manage in an increasingly open and volatile environment, both in terms of regulatory infrastructure and institutional capacity. But prospects are encouraging, judging both from the government's recent policy indications and the evolving economic generation of educated Chinese who have come back from abroad or are expected to come back.

5. Masaru Yoshitomi

I am not a practitioner, or an academic expert, but I am somewhat concerned with the Asian financial crisis. I am now teaching at the Wharton School at the University of Pennsylvania. At the same time, however, I wear another hat, that of the Long Term Credit Bank of Japan. My bank is in trouble not only because of its large domestic nonperforming assets but also because of its heavier involvement in the banking crisis in Asia.

First, in discussing the banking and currency crises in Asia, many commentators stress that the engine of growth behind the Asian miracle has suddenly stopped. That is, in 1996 the growth rate of exports in many Asian countries, including China, slowed to just around 2 percent, and in the case of Thailand, down to −1.5 percent or so. Until 1995, export growth had been around 15 to 20 percent for most Asian countries. What, then, initiated this decline in exports? There are two schools of thought.

One school emphasizes the adverse effects of the Chinese currency devaluation in early 1994, up to 35 percent with regard to its official exchange rate. Because Thai exports compete with exports from China and other Asian countries in the same category of products, Thailand's failure to upgrade its export structure is a basic reason its engine of growth stopped, this school claims.

The other school of thought claims that the loss of international competitiveness is due to the maintenance of a fixed exchange rate with the U.S. dollar, despite the strong appreciation of the U.S. dollar in 1996–97 on top of high inflation in Asian countries. Asian currencies became overvalued, depressing exports and encouraging imports.

In this context, however, I cannot erase my memory of April 1995, just after the peso crisis, when my bank organized a seminar at Pataya Beach near Bangkok, inviting central bankers and officers from the treasury to discuss currency issues. The main concern at that time was the extraordinary appreciation of the yen against the U.S. dollar (up to 80 yen per dollar) and the weak dollar. The major complaint was the wide fluctuations of the exchange rate between these two major currencies. The Thai authorities didn't like seeing the two elephants dancing on their delicate grass.

Today in 1997, in sharp contrast, we hear that the fixing of the Thai baht to a strong U.S. dollar resulted in a large overvaluation that hurt Thai exports. But in 1996, the annual average exchange rate of the yen was 108 yen per dollar. Exchange rates of 100 to 110 yen per dollar are a reasonable zone for purchasing power parity in the tradable sector in Japan. Only in 1997 has the yen deviated from that sort of equilibrium exchange rate. In other words, though the yen depreciated sharply against the U.S. dollar in 1996, it was from the extraordinary overvaluation of the yen in 1995, and the *level* of the yen-dollar exchange rate in 1996 was quite normal. Nevertheless, Thai exports performed very poorly that year. Therefore, I cannot figure out how in such a short time

Thailand and other Asian countries suffered from the stalling of their engine of growth. At the same time, if Thailand had adopted a floating exchange rate in the context of its excessive capital inflows, which substantially exceeded the current account deficits in preceding years, then the Thai baht would have appreciated considerably. Such an appreciation could be interpreted as short-run overshooting, but in light of the excessive capital inflows for several years, the consequence could have been a prolonged misalignment in the exchange rate. Such a misaligned exchange rate could have imposed another difficult problem on the Thai authorities.

Furthermore, as you know, the Thai economy is still in an early stage of development, and therefore, its financial markets are not well developed. A floating regime under massive international capital movements can result in extreme gyrations in the exchange rate. The shallowness of the Thai financial market could not have coped with the volatility of international capital flows.

In 1994–95, when the Mexican peso crisis took place, we all discussed whether a contagious run could hit the Thai baht. Many people, including those at the IMF and the World Bank, concluded that all Thailand's macroeconomic fundamentals were quite good: low inflation, a balanced budget, a high saving rate, and a high potential growth rate. Inflation may have been accelerating, but from 5 percent to at most 7 percent. So we were satisfied with the stability of the baht.

Only two years later, we confront a banking crisis and currency crisis in Thailand and other Asian economies. Something new must have happened after early 1995, or must have already been happening around 1995, when we got together at Pataya Beach.

One such change occurred in the composition of international capital inflows to Thailand, which shifted from foreign direct investment to international bank credit. That is, short-term international bank loans became dominant in capital inflows. This shift was related to the fixed exchange rate, which had been maintained more than a decade, long enough for investors to forget the foreign exchange risk. Very few people were actually skeptical about the fixity of the exchange rate between the Thai baht and the U.S. dollar. The dollar interest rate was around 5 to 6 percent, and the baht interest rate was around 12 to 13 percent. Local financial institutions enjoyed this large interest rate differential, given the fixed exchange rate.

The other such change, one we did not recognize at the time, occurred in how and where international bank loans were being used. We only looked at the macroeconomic fundamentals and paid less attention to the sectoral allocation of domestic credit, the aggregate of which was increasing rapidly because of the massive inflow of international bank loans. Much more important, however, domestic credit to the real estate sector was expanding most rapidly. (This was also the case in Japan in the 1980s. I was in charge of macroeconomic policy in the Japanese government, and we paid a lot of attention to the fundamentals. The growth rate of the Japanese economy was 5.5 percent. The inflation rate was only 1.5 percent. Innovation was going on in microelectronics. The key policy issue was how to reduce Japan's external surplus. The continued good macroeconomic fundamentals may have produced a sort of euphoria. But in the midst of it, very few people could recognize that it *was* euphoria and a bubble. There were available many theoretical and empirical justifications for such optimism during the bubble period.)

At the same time, the Thai external deficit was widening in 1995–96. I had already warned at the Pataya Beach meeting that the external deficit was approaching 6 to 7 percent of GDP, more half of which was financed by international bank loans. Earlier in the 1990s, however, net capital inflows substantially exceeded the current account deficits. The resultant increases in foreign reserves and hence in the money supply—that is, excess domestic demand—produced increasing external deficits rather than higher domestic inflation, since the latter did not accelerate much. In other words, the excess net capital inflows *caused* the current account deficit to increase, rather than simply financing the increased external deficit. This issue requires deeper analysis.

The next question is whether the current account deficit mattered or not. The Thai current account deficit eventually accounted for 8 percent of GDP in 1995–96. Malaysia had an external deficit of similar magnitude, but it did not trigger a crisis. The Indonesian current account deficit was less than 4 percent of GDP, just half of the level in Thailand, but similar to the level in the Philippines. The current account deficit may not have mattered much, but what did matter was how the deficit was financed. This is because what made possible the sudden reversal from capital inflow to outflow, which should account for the suddenness of the currency depreciation, must depend on the characteristics of the capital inflow. Another important question is, What triggered such a reversal? A domestic banking crisis apparently triggered it.

Thus we come to the need to analyze the nature of banking crises. Over the past 10 to 15 years we have had banking crises in every country in the world. I was talking with George Kaufman in Chicago just a few weeks ago. When I said, "Every country has experienced a banking crisis these days," he said, no. He showed me a map produced by the IMF, published in 1996. Kaufman continued, "Here in these areas we have not had a banking crisis yet." Such areas were colored white on the map. "In the white colored areas, they don't have banks yet," he laughed.

Every country that has implemented financial liberalization has experienced a banking crisis, so that many analysts now claim that banking crises must be related to financial liberalization. In Thailand, the offshore market opened in 1993. Japanese banks, including my bank, were attracted to the offshore market because the Thai authorities promised to give foreign banks full banking licenses if they showed good performance, that is, extended a large amount of international credit in the offshore market. The offshore market in turn lent to local banks and finance companies, which were heavily engaged in lending to the real estate market.

The excess supply of domestic bank credit did not seriously accelerate domestic inflation in the general market of goods and services but instead fueled inflation mainly in the asset markets, particularly in real estate. This indicates that the sectoral allocation of bank credit is much more important than the monetary aggregate of either total bank credit or the money supply. (This problem happened in Japan in the 1980s. The aggregate money supply was indeed somewhat excessive, but the magnitude of that excess could not account for the tripling or quadrupling of asset prices in the decade.) What accounts for this kind of sectoral concentration of the extension of bank loans? That is a difficult question. In general, we can say that their declining franchise, in the face of financial liberalization and tougher competition from nonbanks, forced the banks to find new outlets. For example, demand for bank credit declined on the part of large borrowers, who could rely on the liberalized capital market in addition to greater self-financing of their business investment through retained income.

In particular, in the case of Thailand, banking behavior in the 1990s should be analyzed more carefully. The key issues are whether ex ante monitoring was done well by the banks, particularly in order to avoid adverse selection, and whether the banks monitored borrowers once loans were extended, in order to avoid moral hazard on the part of the borrowers.

We often emphasize that when we liberalize financial markets, we should at the same time improve prudential measures and supervision of banks, that is, improve the regulatory framework within which financial institutions operate. Prompt corrective action (PCA) centering on capital ratio regulations is a key.

Here we have some difficulty, however. Why do we need rule-based rather than discretion-based bank regulations? PCA can avoid the moral hazard of near insolvent banks, but only after the bursting of a bubble. Such moral hazard takes the form of offering higher interest rates on deposits to invest in riskier projects, to gain extra profits for writing off nonperforming assets, given the deposit insurance scheme. Also, the authorities are engaged in "forbearance policy." To avoid those two serious problems, moral hazard and forbearance policy, we should introduce PCA. The purpose of this rule-based measure is to close down potentially insolvent institutions as early as possible while they still hold positive capital, so as to minimize the expenditure of public money, which after all comes from taxes levied on the public. Public money must be used if necessary to bail out depositors but not to support insolvent institutions. However, a big question is whether PCA can prevent a bubble from taking place rather than simply preventing moral hazard and forbearance policy after the bursting of the bubble. It may be very difficult to prevent a bubble from being generated using the bank's capital ratios, because capital ratios move in a procyclical manner.

To sum up, the currency and banking crises in Asia should be analyzed from the following three economic policy angles:

1. How can we get exchange rate policy right in the face of massive capital

flows? Asian countries wanted to keep international price competitiveness, by fixing their exchange rates with the dollar. Over the past ten, fifteen, or twenty years, the dollar has continued to depreciate against the yen; therefore, by fixing to the dollar, the Asian economies were able to maintain reasonably good competitiveness. So it must have been very difficult for them to switch the currency basket by changing the weight between the U.S. dollar and yen or to switch from a fixed to a floating regime. The question is when they could have switched in an orderly manner, particularly in the context of shifts in the composition, size, and speed of international capital movements.

2. How can we get banking behavior right under the protection of deposits? We can talk about prudential measures and regulatory frameworks, but after all, it is very difficult to classify bank loans according to credit risk due to the nature of bank credit. It remains very difficult to evaluate bank credit risks and hence to securitize bank credit. It could be done by using credit derivatives, but that is still limited.

3. How can we counteract the financial–cum–real estate cycle? This is the hardest area to analyze. We do not have enough knowledge about what causes this cycle and how to stem such a cycle in the future. Moreover, it remains very difficult, in the midst of euphoria, to identify a bubble as such.

Finally, the critical question is what kind of policy package can cope with "twin" financial crises—for example, the currency crisis and banking crisis that have been reinforcing each other in the Asian countries. Current IMF packages may not be sufficient, as indicated by the continued depreciation of the Asian currencies, even after the packages were announced. We have to see whether the IMF packages can take care of both banking and currency crises effectively and simultaneously, without high cost to Asian economies.

Discussion Summary

Takatoshi Ito observed that China is generating both a sizable current account surplus and sizable capital inflows resulting in the rapid accumulation of foreign reserves. He wondered whether this is a conscious strategy and if the currency would be allowed to appreciate ultimately. *Paul Krugman* concurred, suggesting that this combination results in the recycling of capital inflows and, consequently, these flows are not financing domestic economic growth. Krugman characterized this as a precautionary macroeconomic policy but a curious developmental policy.

Zhang Shengman said this policy of accumulating reserves reflects an overall conservative economic approach by the Chinese. He suggested that reserves would reach approximately $140 billion by the end of the year, and he forecast a continued increase, although at a less dramatic pace. This reduced pace would be a function of reduced inflows following the removal of import duties, a slight loosening of monetary policy, policy changes required prior to membership in the World Trade Organization, and some signs of increasing outflows. He also noted that existing debt of $130 billion reduces the magnitude of the reserves.

Ito inquired about the health of the Chinese banking system. Some indicators seem stable while others show possible trouble ahead. Given the centrality of the banking sector to other crises, he asked about the specifics of the Chinese situation.

Zhang replied that this question is related to the overall issue of how to handle state-owned enterprises. While the economics of this situation are well understood, the implementation issues regarding employment and social implications provide a number of difficulties. He noted that four of the largest state-owned banks have nonperforming loan ratios of approximately 20 percent. The current policy response is to strengthen prudential discipline and to address the quality of state-owned enterprises directly. While there are over 350,000 state-owned enterprises in China, 1,000 enterprises account for 70 percent of their combined asset value. Focusing on the largest state-owned enterprises will allow for a gradual resolution of these difficulties.

James Hines asked why the Chinese government is worried about the geographic and sectoral concentration of foreign direct investment. Furthermore, he noted that any fiscal incentives to stimulate diversification may have significant efficiency consequences. *Robert Lipsey* inquired about the character of the huge foreign direct investment flows to China. In particular, given the importance of Hong Kong as a source, he asked about the magnitude of roundtripping flows that actually originate in China. More generally, he inquired about the nature of the flows from Hong Kong given their large size.

Zhang replied that the effort to guide foreign direct investment is equivalent to leveling the playing field. He noted that coastal areas had initially attracted flows through preferential treatment. Furthermore, transportation costs are extremely high for the westernmost parts of China, suggesting that incentives and infrastructure will be needed to guide foreign direct investment there. *Martin Feldstein* suggested that guidance to such regions may introduce the distortions alluded to by Hines. *Zhang* also noted that current estimates of the magnitude of roundtripping are at approximately 15 percent of inflows. Furthermore, the fact that Hong Kong provides 60 percent of all inflows reflects investment channeled through foreign subsidiaries based in Hong Kong and investment originating in Taiwan.

Kathryn Dominguez questioned the rationale for an Asian regional fund. Noting that Argentina had not averted a crisis with its currency board system of fully backed reserves, she suggested that the ability to resist a crisis is not a function of the amount of reserves a country has access to. *Stanley Fischer* further noted that the IMF has sufficient reserves and that a regional fund may not be able to enforce the same level of conditionality rendered by the IMF.

Moeen Qureshi replied that the rationale for a regional fund is twofold. First, a regional fund would allow access to more reserves. Second, a regional fund would address the perception that the political decision-making process of the IMF is still dominated by two or three countries and, consequently, does not reflect the fact that some Asian countries have come of age. Furthermore, he suggested that Japan, within the context of an Asian regional fund, would enforce conditionality terms that are as stringent as those of the IMF.

Ito emphasized the moral hazard lessons of these currency crises. In particular, he inquired about the potential consequences if the Mexican government had forced involuntary rollover of the Tesobonos or if the Thai government had forced finance companies to default on their obligations. Such punishment of investors that search for yield may serve to avert such crises in the future.

Masaru Yoshitomi responded that these questions are related to the validity of the too-big-to-fail doctrine. While punishing selective investors may be attractive, the systemic nature of these financial–real estate crises makes selective punishment difficult and introduces systemic risks. Moreover, given the euphoria and irrationality associated with these bubbles, he was sympathetic with the use of the too-big-to-fail doctrine.

Krugman noted that the absence of a forward discount on the Thai baht until May suggested that there was a great deal of irrationality as investors entered the market. As such, the irrationality was more pronounced during the entry of these investors in markets rather than on their departure. Krugman further noted that the real consequences of these bubbles present a significant challenge to the economics profession because no good macroeconomic models exist of the implications of a financial bubble on the real economy.

Arminio Fraga concurred that irrational behavior characterizes entry into a bubble and that such financial bubbles have real consequences. Furthermore, he noted that in many cases adjustment to reality happens in an instant with the arrival of information on government policy responses. For example, the Thai policy response to the growing crisis disturbed many investors and led to the disorderly depreciation. Fraga further noted that the Indonesian case was interesting in this vein because it felt like a real run. *Feldstein* responded that the high level of external debt may have accounted for the actions of investors. *Fraga* noted that the composition of the debt was weighted toward exporters and that much of the economy was still relatively healthy.

Ito suggested that the Thai and Mexican crises were distinct in an important way. In the case of Mexico, he argued, many investors were surprised by the devaluation and the banking crisis followed the currency crisis. In contrast, Ito characterized the Thai situation as one where the devaluation was expected and the financial sector crisis precipitated the currency crisis.

Sebastian Edwards disagreed with this characterization, suggesting that weakness in the banking sector in Mexico was apparent as early as 1992. Moreover, weakness in the domestic financial sector led to the issuance of the Tesobonos, which aggravated the situation and ultimate crisis. *Francisco Gil Diaz* concurred with Edwards and noted that the banking crisis was apparent prior to the exchange rate crisis. He noted that the distinction between which investors—Mexican or foreign—took money out during the crisis was a dubious one. In fact, many nationals were holders of Brady bonds, making any study of which investors deepened the crisis inconclusive. *Feldstein* noted, however, that the evidence is that the Mexican equity markets moved before the New York markets, suggesting that Mexican investors may have moved first.

Qureshi reiterated his conclusion that floating exchange rates create domestic pressures on politicians that can, in turn, create other distortions. For example, floating exchange rates create demand for subsidies from exposed sectors and employees who are not protected by the exchange rate regime. He also noted that the emphasis on the financial sector in these crises may not always be appropriate or distinct from sound macroeconomic policy. *Krugman* concurred, noting that both the U.S. savings and loan crisis and the Thai experience with finance companies can be characterized as covert fiscal expansions rather than as examples of poor oversight of financial systems. *Qureshi* also distinguished the experience of Thailand, which was a classic IMF case, from the experience of Indonesia and Malaysia, where political dimensions were magnifying smaller macroeconomic problems.

4 The Evolving Role of Banks in International Capital Flows

1. Bankim Chadha and
David Folkerts-Landau
2. Mervyn King
3. Roberto G. Mendoza

1. *Bankim Chadha and David Folkerts-Landau*

4.1.1 Introduction

The role of commercial banks in intermediating cross-border financing has been fundamentally transformed during the past twenty-five years. The traditional international financing role of these institutions as the dominant providers of long-term on-balance-sheet syndicated credits and trade financing has during the past ten years shifted toward one in which they are the dominant providers of short- to medium-term structured finance. Such "tailor-made" financing is designed to meet a variety of specific cross-border sovereign and corporate financing needs, including project and trade finance, bridge finance, and liquidity and risk management facilities. Banks' international financing activities have been supported by the export into local currency markets of their expertise in capital markets, trading, and risk management. These changes in the type of cross-border financing have coincided with far-reaching changes in the way international banks organize themselves and in their menu of products and activities. In particular, a more liberal regulatory environment has made it possible to exploit obvious complementarities among the areas of banking, security markets, and risk management, which has led to various types of cross-border financing activities—balance sheet lending, capital market fi-

The views expressed in this paper are the authors' own and do not necessarily reflect those of the International Monetary Fund. The authors thank Anne Jansen and Ken Wood for excellent research assistance.

nancing, off-balance-sheet risk management, and liquidity standby facilities—being combined within globally integrated financial intermediaries. Hence, the pure commercial bank of the 1970s has largely disappeared from international markets.

Section 4.1.2 of this paper reviews the changes in the role of banks in international financial flows. Section 4.1.3 discusses forces that are driving the changes in cross-border banking. Section 4.1.4 reviews the role of banks in the growth of global derivative markets. It also discusses the role of banks in providing credit to leveraged players such as hedge funds, and their role in currency crises. Section 4.1.5 discusses the challenges for policy created by the transformation of cross-border finance and the emergence of the universal global banking firm. Section 4.1.6 concludes.

4.1.2   The Changing Role of Banks in Cross-Border Lending

The flow of OPEC current account surpluses into deposit liabilities in the 1970s and early 1980s created the means for banks to play a lead role in intermediating international financial flows, leaving the direct capital markets relatively unused by cross-border borrowers. A number of institutional and financial market features gave banks a competitive edge, relative to capital markets, in the pricing of credit and further promoted a lead role for bank lending (see Folkerts-Landau 1985). These included, first, a growing perception during the recycling of the OPEC surpluses that financial authorities in the mature markets were increasingly ready to protect the deposit liabilities of large money center banks—the too-large-to-fail doctrine emerged. The cost of deposit liabilities for banks, therefore, became largely independent of banks' choice of assets, which provided incentive for banks to expand into new areas of lending, particularly as it was combined with low capital requirements. Second, in the syndicated loan market, international bank lenders were able to form credible coalitions through the use of restrictive loan covenants (cross-default and pari passu clauses) that could exert credit discipline by denying delinquent borrowers access to refinancing in the banking markets. This mechanism raised the cost of default to borrowers, encouraging renegotiation rather than outright default on bank debts in the event of borrower distress, leading to the view that "countries don't default." The higher expected salvage value of bank loans then allowed banks to charge lower margins on their loans than was acceptable in capital markets without enforcement mechanisms.

The late 1980s and 1990s witnessed a sea change in the composition of international financial flows. In 1980, medium- and long-term syndicated bank loans represented the bulk of international lending, accounting for over half—around 55 percent—of the total of global international primary market financing flows (syndicated loan plus security issuance) (fig. 4.1A). The share of syndicated bank loans then declined steeply, falling to around 20 percent of total financing in 1996, while the volume of international bond issuance grew to exceed that of syndicated bank loans, accounting for about 30 percent in 1996.[1] Relative to the overall volume of flows, international equity placements have remained modest; they accounted for less than 5 percent of total financing in 1996.

Reliance on bank lending over the period has been greater for emerging market borrowers than for those from the mature markets, and the growth in importance of direct borrowing from international capital markets has been a more recent phenomenon. For emerging market borrowers, medium- and long-term syndicated bank lending continued to account for over half of their total borrowing through the 1980s, representing 55 percent of total international fund-raising in 1990 (fig. 4.1C). But capital market financing by emerging market entities soared during the 1990s, with bond issuance, for example, rising to 40 percent by 1993 and international placements of equity to 10 percent, while the share of syndicated bank lending to emerging market borrowers declined to about 30 percent. It is notable that international placements of equity by the emerging markets, reflecting large privatizations of public enterprises, have been a more substantial component of international fund-raising than that by entities from mature markets.

As the Mexican peso crisis and subsequent tequila effect caused a deterioration in the perceived credit quality of emerging markets in late 1994 and early 1995, the share of capital market borrowing contracted, and the share of syndicated bank lending rose again during 1994–95. Although the share of such bank lending fell back again in 1996, to around 40 percent, its share in total flows remains sizable and is double that for entities from mature markets. The increased recourse to the syndicated loan market during times of credit deterioration reflects, as it did in the previous decade, the greater ability of banks to resolve debt problems flexibly. Furthermore, it also reflects the fact that the deterioration in the banks' own credit ratings means that banks are more likely to find it profitable to provide on-balance-sheet financing to borrowers of lower credit quality. With the resolution of the crisis in emerging markets, direct borrowing by emerging markets on international capital markets once again exceeded syndicated bank lending in 1996.

Across the major emerging market regions, there have been substantial differences in the composition of flows reflecting the differing use of funds in the regions (figs. 4.1D and 4.1E). The predominant share of syndicated lending to emerging markets in recent years has been to Asian emerging markets, with the share of syndicated lending flows to emerging markets destined for Asia rising from around 30 percent in the early 1980s to an average of around 60 percent during 1993–96. Asian emerging markets have continued to rely on syndicated bank lending as the dominant source of external primary market financing. Since 1993, the share of syndicated bank lending has been relatively

---

1. Note that to conserve on words we often use "syndicated loans" to refer to medium- and long-term syndicated bank loans, although "short-term" facilities are also syndicated. While the former represent actual lending flows comparable to those on capital markets, as discussed below, the latter are predominantly credit facilities that may or may not be drawn down.

A

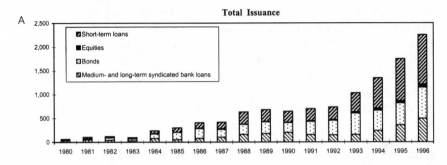

B

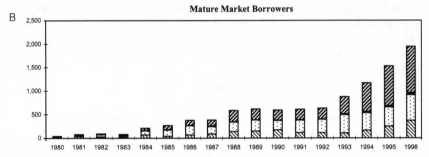

C

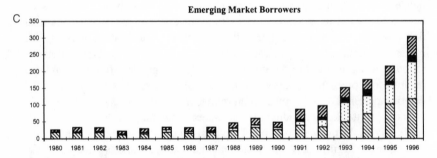

Fig. 4.1   International primary market activity, 1980–96 (billions of U.S. dollars)
Source: Capital Data, Ltd.

steady, rising modestly to account for about 50 percent of total financing in 1996. The relatively more modest securitization of external primary market financing flows to the Asian region, and the greater reliance of the region on syndicated bank lending, has reflected the comparative advantage of international banks vis-à-vis international bond markets to tailor the features of credit to meet the needs of infrastructure and project finance, which remains the main source of demand for external funds in the region.

Bank loans continue to be critical elements of structured and project finance packages, and project finance has been a significant component of international bank lending flows over the period, with the ratio of international project-

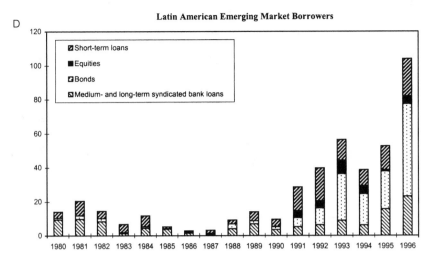

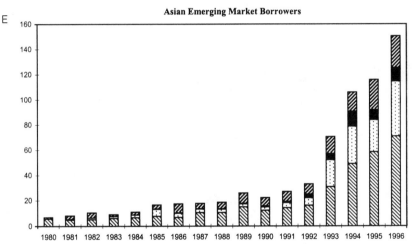

Fig. 4.1   (cont.)

finance-related lending to medium- and long-term syndicated bank lending for all borrowers averaging almost 10 percent between 1980 and 1996 (fig. 4.2). Spurred by deregulation, privatization, the greater need for infrastructure, and rapid economic growth in emerging markets, project finance has both represented a relatively larger ratio of syndicated bank lending to emerging markets—averaging 22 percent over the period—and, since 1992, accounted for a larger share of global project finance than in mature markets. The main driving force for these developments has come from Asia, where rapid economic growth put existing infrastructure under strain. During 1994–96 project financing to Asian emerging markets exceeded $20 billion a year.

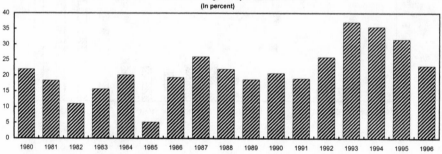

Fig. 4.2   Project financing, 1980–96
Source: Capital Data, Ltd.

A notable change in the composition of financing flows over the period has been the rapid growth in importance of loans classified as "short term." These loans are essentially liquidity-related credit consisting of trade credits, term loans with maturities of less than one year, and revolving credits. The share of short-term loans in total international financing has risen steadily from around 20 percent in 1980 to 45 percent in 1996. Since 1985 the volume of such short-term loans has in each year exceeded the volume of medium- and long-term

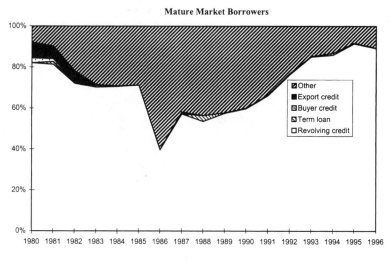

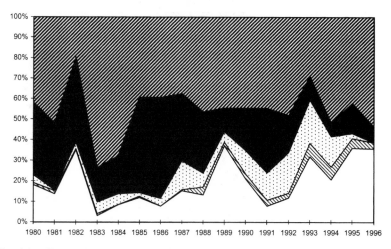

Fig. 4.3   Composition of short-term loans, 1980–96
Source: Capital Data, Ltd.

syndicated bank lending, and since 1993 it has been more than double the volume of medium- and long-term syndicated bank lending.

Figure 4.3 details the composition of "short-term" loans, dividing them into revolving credits, term loans with maturities of less than one year, buyer credits, export credits, and "other." The bulk of international short-term loans for entities from mature markets has been in the form of revolving credit facilities (90 percent), while short-maturity term loans and buyer and export credits have had very modest shares. For entities from emerging markets, revolving credits

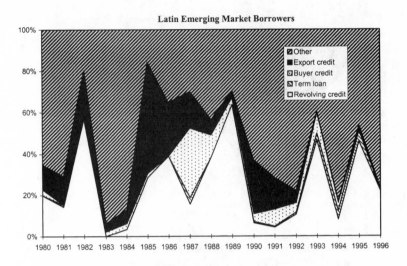

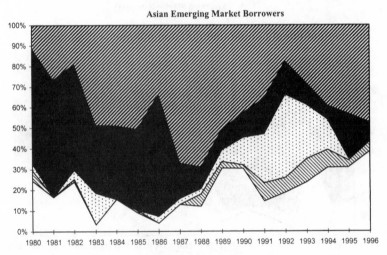

Fig. 4.3   Composition of short-term loans, 1980–96 (cont.)

have represented a much more modest share of around 35 percent, while trade credits—buyer and export credits—represented 10 percent of short-term loans during 1995–96.

The rapid growth of credit facilities, and in particular the increasing importance of revolving credits, illustrates the changing role of bank lending from the provision of medium- and long-term finance to the provision of contingency finance or liquidity insurance. This growth has been encouraged both by the securitization process itself, with contingency finance providing insurance for the borrower's debt securities, and by the regulatory advantage of lower capital cost to banks for off-balance-sheet financing than for traditional on-balance-sheet lending. Contingency finance or lending facilities can take a number of forms. A revolving credit facility, for example, is a contract that obliges the bank to provide funds, on demand, up to a certain maximum amount and for an agreed period under an agreed interest formula. The bank earns an up-front commitment fee for standing ready to lend, whether or not such lending actually occurs.[2] Such lending represents a backup line of credit to the borrower that serves to assure investors in the borrower's debt securities that liquidity will be available to the borrower when the security matures, and in the event the borrower has difficulty rolling over these securities on capital markets. The insurance provided by the presence of such facilities, therefore, reduces the cost of funds to the borrower on capital markets, with part of this difference being earned by banks in the form of commitment fees for the provision of the insurance service.[3]

4.1.3   The Forces behind the Change in Cross-Border Bank Lending

A number of factors propelled the growth of direct capital market borrowing and the changing composition of bank lending toward shorter term and structured finance. These changes were largely driven by developments in financial markets in the major industrial countries.

An important reason for disintermediation from the international banking sector into international capital markets was the decline in the credit standing of banks in mature markets relative to that of corporate and sovereign borrowers. The erosion of the asset quality of banks due to the developing country debt crisis of the 1980s and country-specific business and credit quality cycles in the United States, Europe, and Japan acted to raise the cost of funds to banks to the point where sovereigns, public sector entities, and highly rated borrowers were increasingly able to obtain financing on capital markets more cheaply than could be provided by banks. The deterioration in the credit quality of banks and their present credit standing relative to (potential) borrowers is illustrated most starkly by the number of AAA ratings of banks. Banks have ceased to be the highest rated entities, and therefore, their ability to intermediate international capital flows across their balance sheets for the high end of the market has been increasingly limited relative to direct capital market lending. In the view of all the major credit rating agencies that rate banks—Moody's, Standard and Poor's (S&P's), and IBCA—the credit standing of (major global) banks has continued to deteriorate over the past ten years.[4]

---

2. For a listing and discussion of various lending facilities, see Lewis and Davis (1987) and Smith and Walter (1997). Lending facilities are also distinguished into "committed facilities" and "uncommitted facilities," which are not legally enforceable and have lower fees.

3. Rating agencies such as Moody's and Standard & Poor's, e.g., require issuers of commercial paper to have such facilities in place.

4. The following table is from IBCA (1997). This list does not include a number of German Landesbanks that have AAA ratings due to a constitutional maintenance guarantee.

	Number of AAA Banks	
	1989	1996
Moody's	24	3
S&P's	10	3
IBCA	9	5

Of the twenty-four banks rated AAA by Moody's in 1989, ten have fallen into the AA category and eleven into the A category, and by 1996 only three banks retained a AAA rating. With the recent downgrade of Union Bank of Switzerland by S&P's there is now exactly one major global bank—the Rabobank from the Netherlands—with a AAA rating from all three agencies. This compares with nine sovereigns that are universally rated AAA and fourteen corporates that earn such a rating.[5]

Regulatory changes provided additional incentive for securitizing international syndicated lending. The imposition of risk-based capital requirements on banks in the late 1980s forced more precise accounting of how capital was used, increasing pressure to charge higher spreads and fees in order to recover the increased cost of capital, thereby reducing the competitive price advantages of bank loans. Table 4.1 shows that for most countries the ratio of commercial bank capital and reserves to the size of total balance sheets increased over the period. For France, Germany, Japan, and Switzerland, the capital and reserve ratio peaked in 1994, the last year of the sample, rising between 0.9 percentage points (Switzerland) and 1.6 percentage points (Japan) relative to 1985. For commercial banks in the United States, the capital and reserve ratio peaked in 1993, having risen a full 2 percentage points above the ratio in 1985. The one exception to the general trend of increased capital ratios is the United Kingdom, where capital ratios increased in the mid-1980s, peaking in 1988, but declined afterward.[6]

As the relative credit quality of banks deteriorated, increasing their own cost of funds, and risk-based capital requirements increased the costs of lending, the composition of bank borrowers changed dramatically during 1980–96. Governments, public sector entities, and highly rated corporate issuers turned away from bank lending and began to borrow directly on international capital markets, where they could obtain funding at better rates than banks could offer. The share of borrowing on the syndicated bank lending market by sovereign

5. The universally AAA rated sovereigns are Austria, France, Germany, Japan, Luxembourg, Switzerland, the Netherlands, the United States, and the United Kingdom. The corporates identified with international long-term AAA ratings are Siemens, Hitachi, Toyota, Shell, Unilever, CIBA, Nestlé, Novartis, Marks and Spencer, Amoco, Exxon, General Electric, Johnson and Johnson, and Merck and Company. The count excludes separate subsidiary and joint venture ratings.

6. The behavior of the aggregate capital ratio in the United Kingdom may reflect differing coverage of banking sectors across countries—see the notes to table 4.1.

Table 4.1   Composition of Bank Balance Sheets: Capital and Reserves, Securities, and Loans, 1985–94 (percent of year-end balance sheet total)

Country	1985	1986	1987	1988	1989	1990	1991	1992	1993	1994	Change over Period	Peak Relative to 1985[a]
Capital and Reserves												
Canada	4.7	5.2	5.0	5.4	5.5	5.7	**6.0**	5.5	5.5	5.3	0.6	1.3
France	–	–	–	2.5	2.2	2.4	2.6	2.4	3.7	**3.8**	1.3	1.3
Germany	4.4	4.8	5.0	4.7	5.2	5.2	5.1	5.3	5.2	**5.5**	1.1	1.1
Japan	2.0	1.9	2.2	2.5	2.7	2.9	3.1	3.4	3.6	**3.6**	1.6	1.6
Switzerland	5.9	6.0	6.1	6.1	6.5	6.3	6.3	6.2	6.4	**6.8**	0.9	0.9
United Kingdom	4.5	5.2	5.4	**5.7**	5.0	4.8	4.6	3.8	3.8	4.1	-0.4	1.2
United States	5.1	5.3	4.7	5.3	5.1	5.4	5.8	6.8	**7.4**	7.1	2.0	2.3
Securities												
Canada	10.2	10.9	9.4	10.4	10.2	10.2	13.2	15.6	17.9	**18.7**	8.5	8.5
France	–	–	–	7.6	7.7	10.4	15.9	16.5	19.9	**20.4**	12.8	12.8
Germany	14.0	14.1	13.0	11.8	12.3	12.3	12.4	13.0	**17.3**	17.2	3.1	3.3
Japan	10.5	10.8	10.9	10.7	11.0	11.0	10.8	11.8	11.9	**12.7**	2.2	2.2
Switzerland	13.0	13.0	12.1	9.7	10.4	11.3	11.8	13.0	17.3	**17.6**	4.6	4.6
United Kingdom	6.7	7.1	7.8	6.6	6.9	7.5	8.5	13.0	16.1	**17.5**	10.7	10.7
United States	12.2	13.8	14.4	14.1	14.6	15.3	18.2	20.8	**23.1**	19.6	7.5	10.9
Loans												
Canada	73.4	71.9	74.9	75.9	77.0	**77.7**	75.5	73.2	71.1	69.3	-4.1	-8.3
France	–	–	–	45.1	46.5	47.0	**47.8**	45.9	44.0	44.7	-0.3	-3.1
Germany	53.6	54.2	54.6	56.7	56.8	57.2	**60.5**	58.4	55.4	53.8	0.2	-6.7
Japan	52.7	52.5	52.9	51.3	49.6	54.1	57.6	62.9	63.5	**63.7**	11.0	0.0
Switzerland	46.2	45.3	47.7	52.9	59.4	61.1	**63.4**	62.3	58.2	58.3	12.1	-5.1
United Kingdom	59.5	57.1	59.3	61.2	62.0	**62.1**	60.5	58.2	54.5	52.0	-7.5	-10.1
United States	65.1	64.2	63.8	64.7	65.3	**65.7**	63.3	61.4	60.6	60.3	-4.8	-5.4

Source: OECD (1996).

Note: Coverage, extent of consolidation of bank balance sheets, and timing of fiscal years, for which the data are reported rather than the calendar years noted above, differ across countries. For Canada and the United Kingdom, the data cover commercial banks. For France, Switzerland, the United States, Germany, and Japan, the data cover the large commercial banks. For details see source. Numbers in boldface are peaks.

[a]For loans, change from peak.

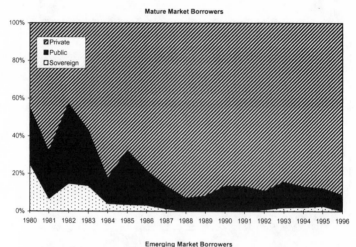

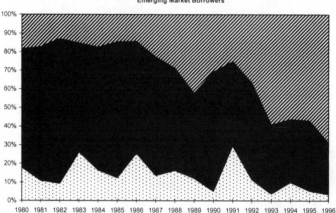

Fig. 4.4   Borrower mix of medium- and long-term syndicated bank loans, 1980–96
Source: Capital Data, Ltd.

entities from mature markets fell from around 25 percent in 1980 to below 3 percent in 1996 and has remained below this level since (fig. 4.4). The share of borrowing by private sector entities from mature markets, on the other hand, has risen from 45 percent in 1980 to 90 percent in 1996. The composition of emerging market entities borrowing on the international medium- and long-term syndicated loan market has evolved in a similar manner, though the decline in the shares of sovereign and public sector issuance occurred later—in the 1990s—and may not yet have run its course. The share of public sector entities also remains sizable at almost 30 percent in 1996, while private sector borrowing accounted for around 65 percent.

The decline in the relative credit quality of banks and the regulation-induced

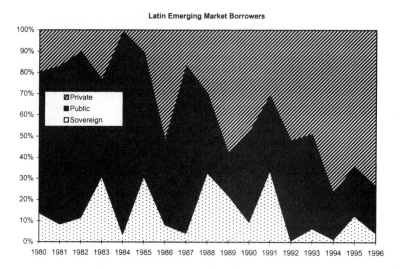

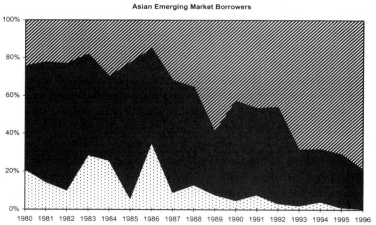

Fig. 4.4   (cont.)

increase in the cost of leveraging bank capital in lending, which prompted banks to shift the focus of their lending activities lower down the credit spectrum in search of higher yields, are evidenced by the behavior of spreads charged by banks. Average interest margins on international medium- and long-term syndicated bank lending, which averaged about 70 basis points during 1980–84, rose uninterruptedly during the latter half of the 1980s, almost doubling to around 130 basis points by 1989 (fig. 4.5). It is notable that the sustained increase in interest margins during 1984–89 was accompanied by relative stability in the average maturity of such loans. While average spreads

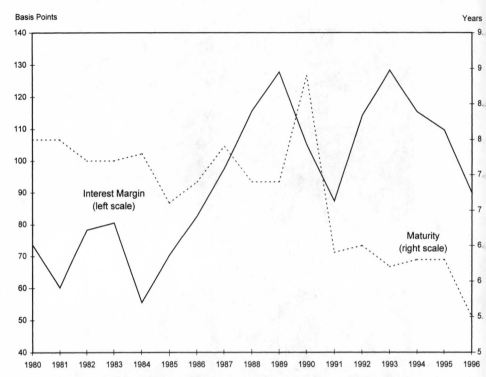

Fig. 4.5   All borrowers: terms of international medium- and long-term syndicated bank loans, 1980–96
Source: Capital Data, Ltd.

have fluctuated during the 1990s, reflecting a host of factors and in particular competitive pressures, they have remained at much higher levels than during the early 1980s.

Some of the pressures for securitization have been technical, spurred by efforts by the banks themselves to better manage their liquidity and risk exposures. The move toward capital market borrowing was also facilitated by improved disclosure standards for borrowers, advances in information technology that increased the public availability of information on borrowers, and an expansion of the universe of entities rated by international credit rating agencies, all of which reduced the value of superior or inside information in conventional bank lending contracts.

The changes in the composition of international financial flows coincided with structural changes in the financial industry. The severe competitive pressures on banks created by the liberalization of domestic markets—including the removal of restrictions on interest rates, the introduction of negotiated brokerage commissions, and shelf registration—the shift in individual investor preferences away from bank deposits, the cyclical deterioration in the quality of bank balance sheets, and the increased cost of leveraging capital in bank lending as compared to participation in direct capital market lending activity, in secondary market trading, and in asset management services forced an unprecedented wave of mergers and acquisitions in the banking industry. The easing of restrictions on the lines of business and geographical location and operation of financial businesses encouraged consolidation and concentration across segments of the financial industry and across international borders. Spurred in the 1990s by the ongoing process of globalization, international portfolio diversification, and growing demand for risk management products, the universal global banking firm—combining traditional on-balance-sheet deposit taking and lending with fee-based security market, risk management, and asset management activities—has emerged as the dominant global financial intermediary.[7]

The decline in the relative importance of traditional bank lending activity is reflected in changes between 1985 and 1994 in the relative contributions of interest and noninterest income to total commercial bank income, and in the shares of bank balance sheets devoted to security holdings and loans. For commercial banks from Canada, France, Switzerland, the United Kingdom, and the United States, there is a clear secular downward drift in the contribution of net interest income to total gross income over the period (see table 4.2).[8] For Canadian and French banks the decline has been particularly sharp, with the ratio declining over the period by over 20 percentage points, while it has been significant for British and American banks, for whom the ratio has declined by a little less than 10 percent.

The evolution of the share of commercial bank balance sheets devoted to security holdings is relatively uniform across countries, with the shares for each country increasing over the sample period and peaking in the last two years (1993–94) for which data are available (table 4.1). The increase is more notable for Canada, France, the United Kingdom, and the United States, with the shares for these countries increasing by between 8 and 13 percentage points. The increase has been more modest for Switzerland (5 percentage points), Germany (3 percentage points), and Japan (2 percentage points). The share of bank balance sheets devoted to loans in each of the countries, with the exception of Japan, peaked in 1990–91 and has fallen since by between 3 percentage points (France) and 10 percentage points (United Kingdom; table 4.1). In Japan, the share of commercial bank balance sheets devoted to loans continued to increase over the period.

7. On the decline of traditional banking in the United States, see Edwards and Mishkin (1995); on the changing borders of banking, see Borio and Filosa (1994) and Bisignano (1997); on the evolution of the universal global banking firm, see Smith and Walter (1997); and on the leading role played by a limited set of "core" integrated global financial firms, see Group of Thirty (1997).

8. For the United States, Edwards and Mishkin (1995) showed that noninterest income from fees and trading as a proportion of the total income of American commercial banks rose from an average of 19 percent in 1960–80 to 35 percent in 1994.

Table 4.2 Relative Contributions to Gross Income of Commercial Banks: Interest versus Noninterest Income, 1985–94 (percent of gross income)

Country	1985	1986	1987	1988	1989	1990	1991	1992	1993	1994	Change over Period	Change from Peak or Trough
						Net Interest Income						
Canada	**76.3**	75.3	71.7	72.6	70.8	69.1	69.9	69.0	67.8	55.0	−21.3	−21.3
France	–	–	–	**75.1**	68.6	66.8	66.8	70.6	50.5	55.1	−20.0	−20.0
Switzerland	51.8	50.3	48.7	**52.6**	49.7	49.1	48.8	49.9	49.6	45.4	−6.4	−7.2
United Kingdom	**65.5**	63.7	62.6	63.8	62.1	61.1	59.3	57.5	55.5	56.8	−8.7	−8.7
United States	**68.0**	64.0	62.4	62.7	60.0	59.1	58.3	58.3	56.3	59.6	−8.4	−8.4
Germany	68.9	**72.5**	69.9	68.6	66.4	65.1	71.3	67.6	65.4	70.5	1.7	−1.9
Japan	73.4	75.5	67.8	60.0	62.8	64.1	81.9	94.2	98.8	**100.6**	27.2	0.0
						Noninterest Income						
Canada	**23.7**	24.7	28.3	27.4	29.2	30.9	30.1	31.0	32.2	45.0	21.3	21.3
France	–	–	–	**24.9**	31.4	33.2	33.3	29.5	49.5	44.9	20.0	20.0
Switzerland	48.2	49.8	51.3	**47.4**	50.3	50.9	51.2	50.1	50.5	54.6	6.4	7.2
United Kingdom	**34.5**	36.3	37.4	36.2	37.9	38.9	40.7	42.5	44.5	43.2	8.7	8.7
United States	**32.0**	36.0	37.6	37.3	40.0	40.9	41.7	41.7	43.7	40.4	8.4	8.4
Germany	31.2	**27.5**	30.1	31.4	33.6	34.9	28.7	32.4	34.6	29.5	−1.7	2.0
Japan	26.6	24.5	32.2	40.1	37.2	35.9	18.1	5.8	1.2	**−0.6**	−27.2	0.0

Source: OECD (1996).

Note: Coverage, extent of consolidation of bank balance sheets, and timing of fiscal years, for which the data are reported rather than the calendar years noted above, differ across countries. For Canada and the United Kingdom, the data cover commercial banks. For France, Switzerland, the United States, Germany, and Japan, the data cover the large commercial banks. For details see source. Numbers in boldface are peaks for net interest income and troughs for noninterest income.

Out of these developments has emerged a set of highly competitive international banking firms, almost all headquartered in the G-5 countries, that are supported by an effective regulatory, supervisory, legal, and payments and settlement infrastructure and that have over the past five years gained a strong competitive advantage in international financial intermediation. The choice of cross-border financial instrument, ranging from syndicated bank loans to structured bank finance to long-term bond or equity finance, is now more likely to be made on the basis of technical financial and economic criteria relating to liquidity and risk management concerns.

Hence, while the organization and the activity mix of global bank intermediaries has changed significantly in response to changes in the financial environment, these institutions have remained key participants in intermediating international capital flows. Their strong presence has been supported by a number of factors. First, bank lending remains important as a source of cross-border structured finance—custom tailored to the needs of the international sovereign and corporate borrower. The flexibility of international bank lending in drawdown and repayment terms remains an important advantage in project and bridge finance, as well as trade finance. Similarly, such flexibility of financial terms remains important in short-term lending to finance merger, acquisition, and leveraged buyout transactions, as well as leverage finance for hedge funds and other high-leverage participants in international markets.

Second, while there has been a decline in the role of medium- and long-term syndicated bank lending in global financial flows, money center banks have increasingly exploited their comparative advantage as flexible suppliers of liquidity. The growth of foreign currency external liabilities has brought with it a growing demand for cross-border contingency financing—backup lines of credit, revolving credits, and standby credit facilities. Much like in the domestic markets in the United States, banks stand ready to lend when access to capital markets dries up temporarily or when the rolling over of short-term international obligations meets with resistance. This suggests a changing emphasis in the role of banks (as lenders) from providers of medium- and long-term finance to providers of contingency liquidity finance.

Third, the development of over-the-counter derivative markets—risk management finance—during the past ten years has been an important source of fee income for internationally active banks. Banks have been able to compete effectively with the organized futures exchanges by supplying hedging products that are tailored to clients' needs. Banks have become the main suppliers of derivatives—particularly swap contracts—used to modify the risk characteristics of international capital flows. Hence, even though banking entities have lost some of their advantages in extending on-balance-sheet commercial and industrial loans, they remain at the core of the financial industry, albeit embedded in larger financial service firms.

Fourth, while local restrictions continue to apply in some markets, on a global basis, the investment banking arms of the larger international universal commercial banks have played an important role as underwriters of international security issues, again suggesting an undiminished if evolving direct role for commercial banks in the international financial intermediation process. The dominance of the global universal banking firms in international primary market finance is apparent from table 4.3.[9] The majority of firms in the table have significant market share in arranging international loans and in the underwriting of debt and equity securities, that is, in both banking and investment banking. Three firms—J. P. Morgan, Deutsche Morgan Grenfell, and Credit Suisse First Boston—rank in the top ten firms in terms of market share in each of the loan, bond, and equity subsectors. The table also indicates that the international primary market finance industry is heavily concentrated, with the top two firms accounting for almost a fifth of business, the top five for a third, the top ten for a half, and the top twenty-five firms for 70 percent of the industry. It is also dominated by twelve U.S. firms, which take all five of the top positions in terms of total market share, represent one-half of the top twenty-five firms, and account for almost half (47 percent) of the global market.

Fifth, banks have not only facilitated the process of securitization, they have also become increased proprietary investors in (both domestic and) international securities and foreign exchange. Also, as asset managers and advisers, either directly or through their subsidiaries, commercial banks play an important role in the international allocation of funds.

Sixth, international banks have become key participants in domestic local currency markets, not only in emerging markets but also in other industrial countries. This internationalization of local currency markets has provided an important vehicle for the transfer of financial expertise in the capital market area, in trading, and in market infrastructure (settlement and market making). Indeed, internationally active institutions, operating in a well-regulated and supervised home jurisdiction with strong legal and market infrastructure have a major comparative advantage in the intermediation business, and this advantage is allowing them to make significant inroads into the intermediation business outside the major industrial countries.

We have discussed various forces driving the change in the composition of international primary market financing flows away from syndicated bank lending toward direct capital market lending. We would emphasize, however, that there are many similarities between syndicated bank lending and debt securities. Syndicated bank lending can, in fact, be characterized as a hybrid between traditional bank lending—that is, relationship and privileged information bank lending—and debt securities. The syndicated bank lending market has many features in common with that for debt securities. Risk is shared between a num-

---

9. These tables can be, and are, often constructed in a variety of ways, such as full credit to lead manager, etc. The proportional credit method adopted here avoids double counting when there is more than one lead manager, e.g., and yields measures of industry size comparable to the primary market financing flows presented in fig. 4.1.

Table 4.3   Global Wholesale Banking and Investment Banking Industry, 1996

Bank	Country	Loans[a] Rank	Loans[a] Amount (million US$)	Bonds[b] Rank	Bonds[b] Amount (million US$)	Equity[b] Rank	Equity[b] Amount (million US$)	Total[c] (million US$)	Share (%)
1. Chase Manhattan Bank NA	United States	1	251,174	26	5,700			256,874	11.7
2. J. P. Morgan & Co.	United States	2	130,998	3	38,308	10	1,484	170,791	7.8
3. Citicorp	United States	3	126,618	22	6,820	73	12	133,450	6.1
4. Bank of America	United States	4	110,002	0	0	0	0	110,002	5.0
5. NationsBank	United States	5	80,322	0	0	0	0	80,322	3.6
6. Deutsche Morgan Grenfell	Germany	6	44,308	9	26,305	9	1,499	72,112	3.3
7. Credit Suisse First Boston	Switzerland	8	37,153	8	27,245	4	3,809	68,207	3.1
8. Union Bank of Switzerland	Switzerland	9	36,599	11	23,625	13	1,261	61,485	2.8
9. SBC Warburg	Switzerland	22	14,103	4	38,084	3	6,757	58,944	2.7
10. Merrill Lynch & Co.	United States	68	2,151	1	51,671	5	3,672	57,494	2.6
11. Lehman Brothers	United States	16	23,088	7	28,872	6	2,382	54,342	2.5
12. Goldman Sachs & Co.	United States	54	2,999	5	35,607	1	10,866	49,472	2.2
13. Morgan Stanley & Co. Inc.	United States	94	1,111	2	39,138	2	7,456	47,705	2.2
14. NatWest Markets	United Kingdom	10	35,938	27	5,227	23	569	41,734	1.9
15. BZW	United Kingdom	7	37,379	0	0	–	0	37,379	1.7
16. Nomura Securities Co. Ltd.	Japan	77	1,493	6	33,796	28	345	35,634	1.6
17. First Chicago NBD Corp.	United States	11	33,323	–	0	–	0	33,323	1.5
18. ABN-AMRO Bank NV	Netherlands	12	33,309	–	0	–	0	33,309	1.5
19. Société Générale SA	France	20	16,287	20	8,816	41	141	25,244	1.1
20. Bank of Nova Scotia	Canada	13	26,561	0	0	–	–	26,561	1.2
21. Salomon Brothers Inc.	United States	0	–	10	23,719	12	1,412	25,131	1.1

(continued)

Table 4.3   (continued)

| Bank | Country | Loans[a] | | Bonds[b] | | Equity[b] | | Total[c] | Share (%) |
		Rank	Amount (million US$)	Rank	Amount (million US$)	Rank	Amount (million US$)	(million US$)	
22. Bankers Trust Co.	United States	14	24,153	42	2,388	–	0	26,541	1.2
23. HSBC Group	United Kingdom	25	10,878	17	11,282	19	807	22,967	1.0
24. CIBC Wood Gundy	Canada	15	23,741	47	1,675	–	–	25,416	1.2
25. ABN AMRO Hoare Govett	Netherlands	–	–	13	18,853	14	1,212	20,065	0.9
Industry totals			1,500,922		638,989		61,419	2,201,330	100.0
Top 2 (% of total)			25.5		0.0		0.0		19.4
Top 5 (% of total)			46.6		7.9		2.4		34.1
Top 10 (% of total)			55.5		34.1		30.1		48.6
Top 20 (% of total)			69.6		57.8		65.5		66.1
Top 25 (% of total)			73.5		66.8		71.1		71.5

Source: Capital Data, Ltd.

Note: Dashes indicate amounts less than $1 billion.

[a]Proportional credit to arranger.

[b]Proportional credit to book runner.

[c]Loans, bonds, and equity combined.

ber of participants. Pricing is competitively determined through an auction-type format, again involving a number of participants. There is secondary market trading, albeit mostly among a restricted class of investors, other banks. While an informal interbank market for loan participation has existed since the inception of the syndicated loan market, negotiability has been aided by the increased use of transferable participation certificates, which allow lenders to sell and transfer their shares in a loan and register the change in ownership legally. Nearly 20 percent of syndicated loans issued in 1995–96 were transferable, compared to 3 percent in 1985–86. Finally, since participation in a syndicate typically involves numerous banks, information regarding the loan contract is usually public knowledge.

At least three institutional characteristics distinguish syndicated bank lending from capital market financing, however: distinct investor classes for the two instruments, allocation of interest rate risk between borrower and lender, and the type and severity of restrictions imposed on borrowers in covenants. These differences have affected the relative importance of the two forms of finance in primary market financial flows, and changes in these characteristics will drive their future evolution.

First, participation in syndicated loans and investment in debt securities is undertaken by behaviorally distinct investor classes. The primary participants in syndicated loans have (so far), of course, been banks. Investors in debt securities represent a much broader class of participants—including retail investors, large institutional investors, and banks. These investor classes are fundamentally distinct both in their appetite for gauging and bearing credit risk and in their ability to salvage value in the event of borrower distress or default. Syndicated bank lenders consist of a relatively homogeneous set of creditors credibly able to form coalitions that can impose substantial costs on borrowers by denying them access to the international banking market, thus raising the cost to borrowers of defaulting to them. In the event of default, similarity of interests among members of the syndicate increases the incentive for cooperation among creditors. Some of the incentives for cooperation among creditors in the event of default are institutionalized in syndicated lending contracts. These include "sharing clauses," which require that any member of the syndicate receiving payments from a defaulting borrower share these with members of the syndicate who have not received similar amounts, including the proceeds of any litigation. In contrast, due to the relatively large number and diversity of investors in debt securities, and the absence of contractual incentives for cooperation, it is in general much more difficult to develop a common negotiating position that is in the collective interest of the bondholders.[10] The expected salvage value of debt securities in the event of borrower distress is, therefore, lower.[11]

---

10. The specific legal rights of international bondholders are determined by the local jurisdiction in which bonds are issued and can vary greatly.

11. Moody's (1996) reported recovery values during the 1990s (per $100 face value) of $71 for defaulted senior secured bank loans, $57 for senior secured bonds, $46 for senior unsecured bonds,

Second, international syndicated lending is at floating rates of interest, quoted as a spread over some rate representing banks' own cost of funds, while the majority of bonds are fixed coupon bonds. During 1980–96, for example, fixed rate bonds made up 76 percent of total issuance, floating rate notes (FRNs) 19 percent, and convertibles 5 percent. It should be noted further that the market for FRNs is dominated—on both sides—by financial institutions and can, therefore, be thought of as being to a considerable extent an interbank market.[12] Thus the bulk of interest rate risk is borne by the (nonfinancial corporate or sovereign) borrower on the syndicated loan market, while it is borne by the lender (investor) on bond markets.[13]

Third, one of the features of conventional bank lending that distinguishes it from direct capital market lending is the lack of public disclosure requirements as compared to direct borrowing on capital markets through security issuance. This feature of bank lending has survived the transformation from relationship to wholesale syndicated lending. The difference in public disclosure has traditionally been compensated for by stronger restrictions imposed on borrower behavior in covenants in bank lending—such as restrictions on the gearing ratio of the borrower and the double pledging of assets as collateral—than in security issuance.

In our view, the difference in appetite for risk between the two sets of investor classes, the relative allocation of interest rate risk between borrowers and lenders in the two instruments, and the relatively more burdensome covenant restrictions on syndicated loans have naturally strengthened the incentives for borrowers to access capital markets directly in "good times" and revert to bank borrowing in "bad times," heightening the role for banks as lenders of "next to last resort." During good times borrowers favor direct borrowing on the capital markets, for example through bond issuance, because it typically implies lower interest rate risk to the borrower and less burdensome covenant restrictions than bank lending. When borrowers face bad times, the lower tolerance for risk among investors in capital markets causes the terms of such lending to shift more sharply against borrowers, who then revert to bank lending. As discussed above, some of the change in the role of banks from providers of medium- and long-term financing to contingency financing has been formalized by the rapid growth of revolving credits and longer term credit facilities. In our view the medium- and long-term syndicated lending market also stands ready to extend new credit when borrowers face bad times.

---

and $34 for subordinated bonds. While these estimates are consistent with our hypothesis, we would emphasize that they underestimate the higher relative salvage value of bank loans compared to bonds because earlier and more frequent renegotiation of bank loans prevents actual defaults.

12. Financial institutions accounted for 71 percent of net FRN issuance in 1995 and 76 percent in 1996. Nonfinancial corporate issuers meanwhile accounted for 17 and 13 percent, respectively. See Bank for International Settlements (1997).

13. Banks do bear the more modest interest rate risk between repricing dates. They also bear the risk of changes in the average level of spreads over the duration of the loan.

While evidence for this hypothesis requires examples of good and bad times for individual borrowers, the aggregate patterns of borrowing by Latin American emerging markets during the 1990s boom in capital inflows to the region provide support for this view. Figure 4.6 presents quarterly data for external primary market financing for Latin America during the Mexican crisis. From the upper panel it is evident that despite the sharp contraction in total flows to Latin America in the first quarter of 1995, following the devaluation of the Mexican peso in December 1994, syndicated bank lending actually rose. The lower panel, which plots the shares of bonds, equities, syndicated bank lending, and short-term loans, indicates that during the first quarter of 1995, the share of international bond and equity issuance from the region reached its lowest point in the 1990s, with no equity issuance during the quarter. The share of syndicated lending, on the other hand, reached its highest point during the 1990s, accounting for about 50 percent of total flows. The price response was much more severe in bond markets than in loan markets. With regard to pricing, average spreads on new medium- and long-term syndicated sovereign loans to the region remained unchanged, at a little over 60 basis points, between the first quarter of 1995 and the last quarter of 1994.[14] In bond markets, on the other hand, the stripped yield spreads on Latin Brady bonds rose from around 750 basis points in October 1994 to 1,750 basis points in March 1995.

With regard to prospects for change in the institutional features that distinguish syndicated bank lending from debt security markets, we offer some observations. First, a number of new participants—institutional investors and, in particular, insurance companies and mutual funds—have recently begun to enter the syndicated loan market as suppliers of funds. As noted, these institutions have very different appetites for risk because they do not have a base of insured deposit liabilities as banks do. Nor are they subject to the same regulations and supervision. It is still, however, somewhat early to judge how their entrance will affect the syndicated loan market, and how it will affect banks. Second, competition—among banks for mandates within the syndicated bank loan market, between banks and other financial intermediaries, and between the syndicated loan market and capital markets—has in recent years created pressure for the relaxation of covenants on bank lending, bringing them, in a sense, closer to those embodied in debt securities. The relaxation of loan covenants has been most evident at the high-yield end of the market, such as on loans to emerging market entities, and in mid-1996, for example, three unsecured loans by Argentine companies were reportedly put up for syndication without any financial covenants (Loan Pricing Corporation, various issues). These developments prompted the U.S. Office of the Comptroller of the Currency (1996) to express concerns last year about the relaxation of lending standards to higher risk borrowers.

---

14. Average maturities also remained relatively stable at around three years.

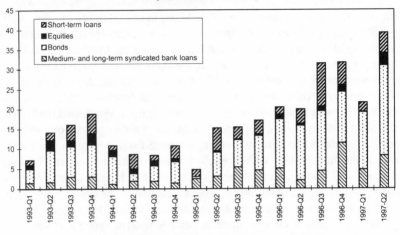

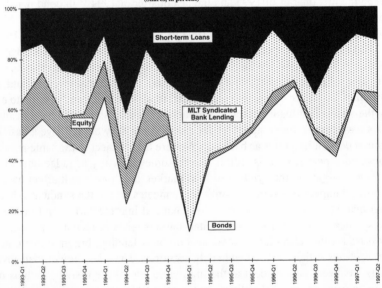

Fig. 4.6   Mexican peso crisis, 1993:1–97:2
Source: Capital Data, Ltd.

4.1.4   Cross-Border Derivative Transactions

Arguably the most significant development accompanying the globalization of international capital markets in the 1980s and 1990s has been the proliferation of financial derivative products, with profound implications for international capital flows. First, the use of derivatives has revolutionized the ability of participants in international capital markets to unbundle and manage risks—interest rate and currency risks and increasingly now credit risks as well—thereby greatly enhancing the attractiveness of cross-border investments. Second, as a ready means for arbitraging differences in funding costs and returns across market segments and international borders, derivatives have increased pressures for the integration of world capital markets.[15] Third, by lowering the transaction costs of carrying out complicated investment and hedging strategies, which would otherwise require several transactions in the underlying instruments, derivatives have increased the efficiency of international capital markets. It is interesting to note that out of a total volume of $47 trillion (in March 1995) of over-the-counter derivative products, $22 trillion, or about half, involved a cross-border counterparty; hence derivative markets are to a large extent international.[16] The enormous volumes measured in terms of notional principal suggest that derivative transactions have in many cases displaced transactions in the underlying markets, and although the use of derivatives does not increase net financing flows, it has been responsible for a massive increase in gross flows. Indeed, the extensive use of cross-border derivatives is obscuring the meaning of the traditional capital account categories in balances of payments. Existing capital accounts data are likely to be strongly compromised by the extensive use of derivatives. Fourth, derivatives are being used extensively to circumvent remaining domestic financial regulation in countries, particularly emerging market countries, and they thereby achieve a closer integration of these markets into the global market (see Folkerts-Landau and Garber 1998). For example, a bank constrained by regulation from taking on domestic equity price risk can acquire a U.S. government security position and enter into a total return swap with an investor who is allowed to buy the equity risk but who wants to hold a position in U.S. government securities. An international bank will most likely act as principal intermediary.

Swap contracts represent the predominant and pervasive derivative product (see table 4.4). The familiar method by which swaps provide a ready tool for arbitraging funding differentials between markets is that associated with the issuance of debt securities. Swaps used in conjunction with international bond financing lower the cost of funding by exploiting the comparative advantage of counterparties in the swap across segments of international capital markets that may exist for a variety of reasons. It is estimated, for example, that Eurobond transactions involving swaps have sometimes made up more than two-thirds of new issues (see Smith and Walter 1997). More recently, swaps have facilitated the "repackaging" of securities to arbitrage yield differentials across

---

15. For evidence on the integration of world capital markets during the period, see Goldstein and Mussa (1993).

16. These data are based on the Bank for International Settlements survey carried out in March 1995—see Bank for International Settlements (1996). They do not conform with the time-series data provided in table 4.4, which are based on reporting by members of the International Swaps and Derivatives Association.

Table 4.4   Markets for Selected Derivative Financial Instruments: Notional Principal Amounts Outstanding, 1986–96 (billions of U.S. dollars)

Instrument	1986	1987	1988	1989	1990	1991	1992	1993	1994	1995	1996
Exchange-traded instruments	618.2	729.9	1,304.7	1,766.9	2,290.3	3,519.3	4,634.4	7,771.1	8,862.5	9,188.2	9,884.5
Interest rate futures	370.0	487.7	895.4	1,200.8	1,454.5	2,156.7	2,913.0	4,958.7	5,777.6	5,863.4	5,931.1
Interest rate options[a]	146.5	122.6	279.2	387.9	599.5	1,072.6	1,385.4	2,362.4	2,623.6	2,741.8	3,277.8
Currency futures	10.2	14.6	12.1	16.0	17.0	18.3	26.5	34.7	40.1	38.3	50.3
Currency options[a]	39.2	59.5	48.0	50.2	56.5	62.9	71.1	75.6	55.6	43.2	46.5
Stock market index futures	14.5	17.8	27.1	41.3	69.1	76.0	79.8	110.0	127.3	172.2	198.6
Stock market index options[a]	37.8	27.7	42.9	70.7	93.7	132.8	158.6	229.7	238.3	329.3	380.2
Over-the-counter instruments[b]	—	865.7	1,657.1	2,489.0	3,450.3	4,449.5	5,345.7	8,474.6	11,303.2	17,712.6	21,069.0
Interest rate swaps	—	682.9	1,010.2	1,502.6	2,311.5	3,065.1	3,850.8	6,177.3	8,815.6	12,810.7	15,584.2
Currency swaps[c]	—	182.8	319.6	449.1	577.5	807.2	860.4	899.6	914.8	1,197.4	1,294.7
Interest rate options[d]	—	0.0	327.3	537.3	561.3	577.2	634.5	1,397.6	1,572.8	3,704.5	4,190.1

Sources: Bank for International Settlements, "International Banking and Financial Market Developments" (Basel, various issues), and International Swaps and Derivatives Association, Inc. (ISDA).

[a]Calls and puts.

[b]Data collected by ISDA only; the two sides of contracts between ISDA members are reported once only.

[c]Adjusted for reporting of both currencies; includes cross-currency interest rate swaps.

[d]Caps, collars, floors, and swaptions.

investor bases. For example, on the market for emerging market debt, which remains particularly segmented, issuers have bought and transferred Brady bonds to offshore trusts or special purpose vehicles, which have then issued asset-backed securities in Germany, where demand for emerging market credit denominated in deutsche marks has been particularly strong. By swapping the income from the Brady bonds into deutsche mark, the investor can lock in the yield differential.

International banking firms are the main suppliers of over-the-counter (OTC) derivatives, particularly swap contracts. Relatively scarce before 1980, cross-border swaps and their family of related products (forward swaps, collars, caps, swaptions) and transactions have come to represent a substantial component of international financial market activity. Banks have a natural demand for swaps to take advantage of swapping opportunities across their loan books, as a means of lowering funding costs, in managing funding gaps, for improving lending profits, and in managing interest rate and currency exposures from their loan or investment portfolios. Banks are also naturally positioned as counterparties in derivative transactions through their ability to supply liquidity to this market when needed.

Global derivative markets have grown exponentially over the past decade (table 4.4—based on reporting by members of the International Swaps and Derivatives Association). This has been the case for both exchange-traded and OTC products, though the flexible customized nature of OTC contracts and regulatory advantages have led to the increasing concentration of activity in the OTC market. According to a comprehensive survey conducted by the Bank for International Settlements in early 1995, the notional value of outstanding OTC derivative (including foreign exchange, interest rate, equity, and commodity) contracts totaled $47.5 trillion (after adjusting for double counting and including estimated gaps in reporting) at the end of March 1995 (see Bank for International Settlements 1996). About 98 percent of this total was accounted for by interest rate derivatives ($28.9 trillion) and currency derivatives ($17.7 trillion). In addition to OTC derivatives, intermediaries who were involved in the survey reported that they were engaged in a further $16.6 trillion of exchange-traded derivatives. In aggregate, therefore, respondents to the survey (from twenty-six countries) revealed that (after adjusting for double counting) they were involved in about $64 trillion, by notional principal, of derivative contracts. To put this in perspective, the aggregate market value of all bonds, equity, and bank assets in Japan, North America, and the fifteen EU countries totaled $68.4 trillion at the end of 1995, which is only about 7 percent larger than the size of derivative markets as measured by the above survey.

We would emphasize two other roles of banks that stem from their being the primary providers of credit to the international financial system, which have fundamentally altered its operation and the dynamics of financial crises. First, international bank lenders are the main suppliers of credit used to leverage the capital of high-risk, high-return investors, such as the macro–hedge funds, proprietary traders, and risk-tolerant mutual funds, imparting an aggressive speculative bent to a formidable quantity of international capital flows. Registered offshore (Bermuda, Cayman Islands), macro–hedge funds are subject only to the regulatory requirements in the markets in which they operate and are not subject to the disclosure and fiduciary regulation customary in the major capital markets. These funds are increasingly able to circumvent local prudential restrictions through the use of off-shore derivative transactions. It is estimated that speculative macro–hedge funds have about $100 billion under management. With an average leverage ratio of about ten, their total resources exceed $1 trillion. Without such leverage the impact of this new investor class in global financial markets would be more limited.

Second, banks play a key role in exchange rate crises, with obvious severe implications for capital flows. Speculation against a currency requires domestic currency credit, either implicitly (off balance sheet) or explicitly (on balance sheet), and banks are the major source of this credit. Speculation against a currency can be carried out directly by taking a position on the forward market—selling the currency forward—typically to a domestic bank as counterparty, who then bears the investor's credit risk, and the forward contract represents an implicit or off-balance-sheet extension of credit. As the domestic bank then hedges its position, entering into an offsetting transaction with the central bank or acquiring foreign exchange on the spot market, these transactions create pressures for the forward and spot rates to depreciate and for domestic interest rates to rise. Settlement of forward sales of a currency by a foreign speculator also typically involves the extension of domestic currency credit. Speculation against a currency can also be carried out by the use of explicit domestic currency credits that, when converted into foreign currency, create a short position in the domestic currency. The conversion of domestic currency credit into foreign currency represents a capital outflow, placing downward pressure on the spot exchange rate, and to the extent that these pressures are offset by central bank intervention, they result in a loss of reserves. Derivatives, such as structured and equity-linked notes, increase the channels through which leveraged positions can be taken against the domestic currency (see Garber and Lall 1998).

4.1.5 Policy Challenges

Resolution of Sovereign Debt Crises

The concentrated nature of syndicated debt holdings has been helpful in the resolution of international sovereign debt problems. History has amply demonstrated that the likelihood of achieving a negotiated debt workout and the provision of additional liquidity funding, without debilitating legal attachment of sovereign assets with disruption of international trade and finance, is much higher in the syndicated loan market than in international bond markets. During earlier periods of high capital mobility—in the nineteenth century and the interwar years—when international flows predominantly took the form of bond finance, free rider problems among bondholders made the provision of new money, which required large numbers of diverse individual investors to go along, difficult, and outright defaults were common (Eichengreen and Portes 1989; Eichengreen 1991). The readjustment of defaulted debts involved protracted negotiations that were complicated by the multiplicity of bondholders and by uncertainty about their representation, often requiring up to a quarter-century to complete. Furthermore, the fact that trade finance was provided by the banks, while long-term loans were extended by individual investors, separated the interests of the creditor groups and severely restricted the sanctions that bondholders could bring to bear against defaulting borrowers. Hence, the recent shift, or reversion, from bank to bond finance is likely to have made future debt crises more protracted and severe, unless better mechanisms can be found to achieve speedy and orderly workouts in international bond markets.

Regulatory Challenge

The emergence of a small group of highly innovative, adaptive, and competitive global banking institutions poses a major challenge to banking and securities supervisors. These institutions intermediate—on and off balance sheet—a significant portion of total international cross-border flows. They have the ability to book transactions in jurisdictions with low tax and regulatory restrictions. Their overall net firmwide exposures are difficult for supervisors to assess. The concern, therefore, is that these international institutions still lean heavily on the public sector financial safety net without being effectively constrained in their risk-taking activities.

The recent restructuring of the Basle risk-weighted capital requirement to allow for greater use of firms' own risk management models in arriving at regulatory capital requirements is removing a distortion from the risk-taking behavior of the firms, but whether capital requirements based on value at risk (VAR) models sufficiently restrict aggregate risk taking by international banks is an open question. Indeed, one might ask whether capital requirements that are sufficiently high to force banks to internalize the negative externalities of a solvency crisis—that is, pricing the financial safety net efficiently—might not make banking so unprofitable as to force most if not all banking business into nonbank financial institutions.

Derivatives

The already extensive and still growing practice of using cross-border derivative transactions to circumvent domestic financial regulation is contributing to the integration of emerging market countries and the smaller industrial countries into global capital markets. However, it is wresting control over the speed of deregulation away from policy authorities. It also raises prudential problems, since banks in these countries use derivative transactions with international banks to circumvent domestic prudential restrictions on their leverage and risk positions. In the absence of sophisticated risk management systems such position taking may undermine the stability of the domestic financial system. It is difficult, if not impossible, to avoid this problem, except to make sure that the domestic supervisory and regulatory architecture is sufficiently strong to ensure the integrity of the domestic financial system (Folkerts-Landau and Lindgren 1997).

Exchange and Financial Crises

International banking firms are the main providers of leveraged finance to highly leveraged macro–hedge funds. These funds have been heavily involved in taking leveraged positions when there is reason to believe that asset prices, including exchange rates, are out of line with underlying fundamentals. Although such pressure may be useful in forcing an adjustment in prices, it frequently precipitates adjustment far more rapidly than might be considered optimal. The question, therefore, arises whether the financing extended to high-leverage speculative position takers can, or should be, restricted through prudential regulation in the interest of international financial stability.

4.1.6   Conclusions

The international financial system is undergoing a major structural change, with the emergence of a small set of globally active financial firms, which have captured a large part of the international intermediary business. The composition of financial flows is shifting from medium- and long-term syndicated bank lending to greater direct capital market financing, and bank financing is shifting toward shorter term structured finance, including off-balance-sheet contingent liquidity and risk management finance. These changes have been driven by a deterioration of bank creditworthiness, increases in regulatory capital requirements, and significantly greater competition from nonbank financial institutions.

These developments have made the workout of sovereign debt difficulties far more difficult, and hence they have increased the potential disruptive impact of such crises. The evolving environment also poses major regulatory challenges. Is and can the financial safety net still be adequately priced without greatly diminishing the size of the banking business as it currently operates? International financial institutions have been the main suppliers of leverage finance for the speculative macro–hedge funds, thereby raising the issue of whether such financing is contributing to greater volatility in international markets.

References

Bank for International Settlements. 1996. Central bank survey of foreign exchange and derivatives market activity, 1995. Basel: Bank for International Settlements, May.
———. 1997. International banking and financial market developments. Basel: Bank for International Settlements, August.

Bisignano, Joseph. 1997. Toward an understanding of the changing structure of financial intermediation: An evolutionary theory of institutional survival. Paper prepared for the Expert Meeting on Institutional Investors in the New Financial Landscape, OECD, Paris, July.

Borio, Claudio E. V., and Renato Filosa. 1994. The changing borders of banking: Trends and implications. Working Paper no. 23. Basel: Bank for International Settlements, Monetary and Economic Department, October.

Edwards, Franklin, and Frederic Mishkin. 1995. The decline of traditional banking: Implications for financial stability and regulatory policy. *Federal Reserve Bank of New York Economic Policy Review* 2 (July): 27.

Eichengreen, Barry. 1991. Historical research on international lending and debt. *Journal of Economic Perspectives* 5, no. 2 (spring): 149–60.

Eichengreen, Barry, and Richard Portes. 1989. Settling defaults in the era of bond finance. *World Bank Economic Review* 3:211–39.

Folkerts-Landau, David. 1985. The changing role of international bank lending in development finance. *IMF Staff Papers* 32, no. 2 (June): 317–63.

Folkerts-Landau, David, and Peter Garber. 1997. Derivative Markets and Financial Soundness. IMF Working Paper. Washington, D.C.: International Monetary Fund, January.

Folkerts-Landau, David, and Carl Lindgren. 1998. *Toward a framework for financial stability.* Washington, D.C.: International Monetary Fund.

Garber, Peter, and Subir Lall. 1998. Derivative products in exchange rate crises. In *Managing capital flows and exchange rates: Perspectives from the Pacific Basin,* ed. Reuven Glick. New York: Cambridge University Press.

Goldstein, Morris, and Michael Mussa. 1993. The integration of world capital markets. Paper presented at the conference Changing Capital Markets: Implications for Monetary Policy, sponsored by the Federal Reserve Bank of Kansas City, Jackson Hole, Wyo., 19–23 August.

Group of Thirty. 1997. *Global institutions, national supervision and systemic risk.* Washington, D.C.: Group of Thirty.

IBCA. 1997. Who rates the raters? A comment on ratings of major international banks. London: IBCA Banking Analysis Ltd., February.

Lewis, Mervyn K., and Kevin T. Davis. 1987. *Domestic and international banking.* Cambridge, Mass.: MIT Press.

Loan Pricing Corporation. Various issues. *Gold sheets.* New York: Loan Pricing Corporation.

Moody's Investors Services. 1996. Defaulted bank loan recoveries. New York: Moody's Investors Services, November.

OECD (Organization for Economic Cooperation and Development). 1996. *Bank profitability: Financial statements of banks, 1985–1994.* Paris: Organization for Economic Cooperation and Development.
———. 1997. *Institutional investors: Statistical yearbook.* Paris: Organization for Economic Cooperation and Development.

Smith, Roy C., and Ingo Walter. 1997. *Global banking.* New York: Oxford University Press.

U.S. Comptroller of the Currency. Administrator of National Banks. 1996. *Survey of credit underwriting practices*. Washington, D.C.: National Credit Committee, September.

2. *Mervyn King*

At the annual IMF and World Bank meetings, there is intense competition to produce the most bland official pronouncement. Following an economic crisis, countries face "policy challenges." There are several policy-challenged governments around the world, and international capital movements seek them out.

Such capital movements are large. Net private sector capital flows to emerging markets in 1997 will, in all likelihood, exceed $250 billion. That is around 1 percent of world GDP, a not insubstantial figure. Those flows have increased substantially over the past decade. And many of them involve banks. But as the paper by Chadha and Folkerts-Landau illustrates, the role of banks has been diminishing. Bank-intermediated flows this year are sharply down over 1995 and 1996, especially to Asia. As Chadha and Folkerts-Landau argue, "The pure commercial bank of the 1970s has largely disappeared from international markets." Nevertheless, banks, and the health of the banking system more generally, are central to the diagnosis of the causes of the recent crises, such as that in Thailand, and have played a major part in the discussion at this conference.

At the risk of being too provocative, I want to pose three questions. First, are we in danger of focusing too much on banking supervision of individual institutions—which is rapidly becoming the mantra of international meetings of officials—rather than on an analysis of the risk exposure of the banking system as a whole? Second, should we not focus on the net risk exposure of a country's financial system as a whole rather than simply the banking system? Third, how should we think about and organize any international lender-of-last-resort facility?

Banks can be dangerous institutions. They engage in massive maturity transformation. Borrowing short and lending long can be a good way to make money. But it is also risky. A large enough capital base can provide some insurance against the risk of a run on an individual financial institution. That is why banks are prudent—the good ones by choice and the bad ones at the invitation of the regulator. But when the financial system as a whole hits trouble, a number of banks, indeed the system as a whole, may find themselves unable to meet the demands of their creditors, and a major financial crisis ensues. That is usually bad news for taxpayers. All finance ministries should carry a sign saying "Banks can be dangerous to your wealth."

All this is fairly obvious. But the issue is normally discussed in a domestic setting. Now we see it raised in the international context. It is striking that the common theme to almost all of the international financial crises that we have seen in the era of floating exchange rates involves a crisis of the banking system. Or, to be more precise, it involves a crisis of institutions with significant mismatch—of either maturities or currencies.

At one level, the solution is straightforward. Sound banking supervision combined with an international lender of last resort should both minimize the risk of a crisis erupting and provide a means of dealing with it when it occurs. And over the past two or three years significant progress has been made in extending both elements of the safety net. The Basle Committee, working in association with a number of emerging market countries, has enunciated twenty-five core principles for banking supervision, and the resources of the IMF have been significantly increased (with its new Emergency Financing Mechanism and the creation of the New Arrangement to Borrow—EFM and NAB, respectively), enhancing its ability to act as an international lender of last resort. But the question that should concern us all is the moral hazard that results. By that I do not mean that the borrowers themselves—sovereign borrowers in this context—are likely to pursue significantly inferior macroeconomic policies as a result of the existence of the IMF, although the recent suggestion of an Asian Monetary Fund creates doubts in my mind that a regional body would impose such tight conditionality as can a less political international body such as the IMF. No, the real moral hazard is that of the lenders. Are international capital markets lending to emerging markets or to the G-10?

In the domestic context, the classic statement of the lender-of-last-resort role was provided by Bagehot (1873): "In time of panic it [the central bank] must advance freely and vigorously to the public out of the reserves. . . . These loans should only be made at a very high rate of interest. This will operate as a heavy fine on unreasonable temerity and will prevent the greatest number of applications by persons who do not require it." The key principle is the willingness of the central bank to lend freely against good collateral. Where the proposed collateral takes the form of marketable securities, it is easy to calculate the appropriate degree of collateral that should be provided. But where collateral takes the form of illiquid loans and investments in nonmarketable assets, a central bank rarely has the opportunity to value with any precision the collateral offered. Rather, lender-of-last-resort support becomes a public investment to reduce the risk of a systemic crisis. But if the lenders know that the authorities will step in whenever such financial institutions—mainly banks—get into trouble, then there is little incentive to price such loans appropriately.

To remove the moral hazard requires a way of penalizing the creditors in such a situation. As a matter of public policy we have not been very successful in ensuring that lenders suffer some of the loss. Deposit insurance is often extremely generous in the case of domestic banking systems. And internationally, the various rescue packages have protected the investments of foreign investors who lent to either governments or the domestic banking system in foreign currency loans. Here the maturity mismatch has two components. First, in several instances, such as Thailand recently, the domestic banks borrowed short to invest in rather dubious long-term assets such as speculative real estate ventures. Second, lending in foreign currency protected the overseas investors from a consequence of a crisis that led to a sharp fall in the exchange rate. In contrast, investors who put their money into the equity market did indeed lose a great deal, because of both the fall in the equity market and the change in the exchange rate.

The mere existence of international rescue packages creates a moral hazard for lenders. Investors are encouraged to channel funds to emerging markets via forms of investment that are more likely to receive assistance. Following the Mexican crisis, the G-10 set up a working party to produce proposals that would convince private sector markets that bond finance was not underwritten by the G-10. Plans for workouts of private bond finance were published and put forward for discussion by the market. They have largely been ignored. And over the past two years secondary market spreads on international bonds have fallen significantly. Spreads on Brady bonds have halved, and in some cases have more than halved. Even with a widening of spreads on some Asian bonds following the flotation of the Thai baht, spreads on bonds in other regions continued to decline. In Thailand many of the overseas investors were able to lend in foreign currency, and their investments have been underwritten by the international rescue package. In those circumstances it is not surprising that the true risk is not priced into private sector loans. That encourages excessive short-term capital flows.

Many of these crises are associated with, or exacerbated by, banking crises. One of the main lessons of the background papers is that in too many parts of the world the banking system is weak. For example, in their background papers Sebastian Edwards (chap. 1.1) shows that the Chilean crises of 1982–83 and the Mexican crisis of 1994 were associated with problems in the banking system and Peter Garber (chap. 7.2) shows that the Mexican banks had little incentive to price Tesobono risk properly. The conventional conclusion, and indeed the universal recommendation of all official meetings in recent years, is that banking supervision must be improved. Although I would not wish to argue that supervision should be *less* rigorous, is it not time to ask whether the implicit government guarantee is not itself an important part of the cause of the problem because of the moral hazard created?

There is only one logical end to continuing increases in the degree of banking supervision—and that is public ownership of the banks. It is simply unrealistic to expect supervisors to regulate all capital transactions unless they end up managing the institutions themselves. And even then the managers seem to have difficulty controlling what goes on. Are we expecting supervisors to perform the impossible? Perhaps the time has come to consider whether or not governments should step back somewhat from the regulation of such a wide swath of the financial services industry.

The experience of emerging markets in recent years surely shows that the high degree of maturity transformation associated with the banking system is not a free good. Undoubtedly it conveys benefits. But it certainly involves costs. Some risks faced by banks are subject to the law of large numbers. Some default risks and the risk of individuals withdrawing deposits because they need cash may be uncorrelated. But important risks are highly correlated. These include the impact of the business cycle on default risk, the impact of changes in interest rates on values of long-term assets, and the risk of having to refinance short-term liabilities at different interest rates. In the era of global capital movements with flexible exchange rates and much greater competition between financial intermediaries, volatility and risk are higher. Banks no longer have large margins protected by oligopolistic positions with which to rebuild capital after an adverse shock. As Martin Hellwig has written persuasively, we have paid too little attention to the risks of the system as a whole and too much to those of individual institutions. Suppose, for example, that each bank borrows at a given maturity and lends at a maturity of only one year greater. The regulators may feel that there is rather little maturity transformation being undertaken by any given individual institution. But with forty banks in the system, short-term call money can be transformed into a forty-year mortgage on real estate. The banking system helps to reallocate risks among agents in the economy, but those risks have in the end to be borne by somebody. The monetary authorities need to understand the nature and size of those risks. To quote Hellwig (1995): "The interest rate risk exposure of the system as a whole is not visible to the individual institution unless it knows that it is but an element of a cascade and that credit risks in the cascade are correlated." Hence the focus on banking supervision misses an important aspect of the authorities' responsibility for financial stability. It is important to assess the net position of the financial system vis-à-vis the rest of the world. Looking at individual institutions is not enough. Information of that kind, especially with respect to currency and maturity exposure of the system as a whole, would have been helpful in the case of the Mexican crises, and no doubt the same applies in the case of Thailand and will apply in the case of future crises.

At the recent IMF meetings in Hong Kong, the G-10 started to ask itself what we could do to reduce the moral hazard associated with the existence of government intervention in financial markets. That was not just a comment on the crises in Thailand, or even on the Mexican crisis and the prospect of other international crises in the years to come. It was also a reflection on the role of intervention in our domestic financial system. In an era of free capital markets, it is essential that flows of capital move at prices that reflect the risks involved and are not underpriced because of the belief that the government will step in and rescue failed institutions. As Stanley Fischer argued at the meetings, the private sector must bear some of the costs of the risk involved. That requires a careful analysis of the sources of the moral hazard. The large number of creditors means that it is difficult to impose costs on bondholders. That lay behind the observation of the G-10 working party referred to above. Bank finance too can involve a moral hazard if the public sector underwrites the banking system, although in some cases, such as the debt crises of the 1980s, it is possible to impose losses if the number of banks involved is not too large. In contrast, equity holders bear the full cost of losses. So attention needs to be focused on the flows of bond and bank finance.

I shall leave for discussion the three questions I posed at the outset. But one conclusion is clear. Any measures that reduce the need for the public sector to intervene in the event of a financial crisis would reduce the extent of moral hazard. The aim should be to reduce the externalities arising from a financial crisis. Two measures would help in this respect. First, the promotion of real-time gross settlement systems for payments and settlements would reduce the potential knock-on effects of any given institution failing. Second, the contagion that we have seen in financial markets from one country to another in the wake of both the Mexican and Thai crises might be reduced by improving the information flow about policies that are followed in the countries that might be at risk. Transparency and disclosure can help to reduce contagion. It was appropriate for the IMF to ask Thailand to publish its forward book revealing the extent of the central bank's foreign exchange exposure. But it is hard to see how the G-7 can lecture other countries on the need for transparency if they themselves do not provide a lead. My own government has set an example by deciding to publish Britain's foreign exchange reserves, both spot and forward. Hitherto the forward book was kept secret.

It is perhaps somewhat incautious of me to break the central bankers' union rules by arguing both that banks can be dangerous institutions and that clarity and transparency is a good thing. But as Bagehot observed in his classic *Lombard Street,* "Many years since, I remember seeing a very fresh and nice-looking young gentleman, and being struck with astonishment at being told that he was a Director of the Bank of England. I had always imagined such Directors to be men of tried sagacity and long experience, and I was amazed that a cheerful young man should be one of them. I believe I thought it was a little dangerous."

References

Bagehot, Walter. 1873. *Lombard Street: A description of the money market.* London: Clowes.
Hellwig, N. 1995. Systemic aspects of risk management in banking and finance. *Swiss Journal of Economics and Statistics* 131:723–37.

3. Roberto G. Mendoza

In addressing the topic of the evolving role of banks in international capital markets, I would like to deal with an issue we've not yet discussed—the effect of technology. Financial technology, in the form of front-end analytics and back-office processing, has truly revolutionized the banking role.

First—this is in no particular order—technology has forced dramatic de facto regulatory change by redistributing the information advantage that the classic commercial bank intermediary enjoyed. With this resource taken away from banks, regulatory change had to occur, or banks would have gone out of business. In the United States, the breakdown is most noticeable between banking and securities activities. Globally, it's happening among banking, securities, and insurance.

Over the course of this conference, we've heard banks described as both obsolete and dangerous—an awful combination. But it's true. What many of us grew up thinking of as the traditional role of banks—to intermediate credit on the balance sheet—is simply not a worthwhile activity on a wholesale basis in any developed market, despite the implicit subsidy provided to commercial banks by the various guarantee systems to which Mervyn King just referred.

The second result of technology advances, securitization, has already been mentioned. We now have the technology to make the enormous computations necessary to securitize anything from mortgage-backed securities to commercial loans to the royalty rights to David Bowie's songs. Indeed, one could argue that in the future all financial assets—and a great many nonfinancial assets—will be securitized, which has profound implications for the financial system and the global economy. I will return to this later.

Third, technology has permitted the exponential growth of derivative markets. This also has profoundly changed and even enhanced—or so bankers like to think—the role of banks because derivatives allow financial intermediaries to aggregate, segment, and distribute risk, as opposed to assets, on an effective basis. I will argue in a moment that derivative markets enable the financial system and its banking component to lower the aggregate risk in the economy, whether at a national or international level, by permitting investors to diversify their portfolios more effectively, along the efficient frontier.

So these three effects—massive regulatory change, a securitization process that is becoming ever more efficient, and growth in derivative markets—have changed the role of banks in the evolving international markets.

Traditionally, banks recycled assets across their balance sheets in a manner that was visible and controllable and could be regulated by governments and central banks. But now we have three types of banks that we need to consider.

The first, which was described in the excellent paper by Chadha and Folkerts-Landau, is the universal bank, which performs a global, wholesale risk intermediation function. This kind of bank does much more than take deposits and make loans; it also provides advisory services, makes proprietary investments in debt and equity, and acts as an underwriter and agent in debt and equity transactions and as a counterparty in derivative markets. In effect, a universal bank is an extremely efficient agent for allocating capital and risk. Universal banks include not just the obvious names, such as DMG, Chase Manhattan, and CSFB, but all of the global securities firms, which now, as a practical matter, perform the same functions as a result of the breakdown in regulatory barriers.

The second category of banks is the one we have talked about a great deal with respect to Thailand and Mexico: primarily local and importantly retail. Such a bank is not a global asset allocator but rather an intermediary between saving and investment in the domestic market and between external and domestic markets. We have been focusing on the second role, in which a local Thai or Mexican bank may engage in maturity or currency transformation by funding itself in international markets to finance local activities such as real estate investment.

The third category—and perhaps the one with the greatest influence—is All Other. All Other has one significant characteristic; namely, All Other is not regulated. All Other includes obvious entities such as hedge funds and less obvious entities such as governments themselves playing a role as investors. But the enormous swings in capital flows facilitated by the first category, universal banks, and sometimes channeled through the second category, the local intermediaries, often represent the investment decisions of All Other, the unregulated. The fact that they are unregulated, and therefore can be highly leveraged, accounts for many of the issues discussed this morning.

Let's return to the change in role of traditionally defined banks: intermediating risk, not assets. The new role means banks need less economic, as opposed to regulatory, capital because of the securitization process. And they will need even less capital in the future. Instead, they will facilitate the transmission mechanism between financial events in a particular geographic sector and others, or between particular asset classes. To the extent that there is any true economic linkage, those effects are transmitted in a nanosecond across markets as a result of the efficiency of these global institutions and, primarily, their derivative activities.

The implications for the financial system are highly positive. The growth in derivative markets lowers aggregate risk and allows banks to manage themselves in a more prudent manner, thereby requiring a smaller cushion of capital. Derivative markets have another very important characteristic: they increase the transparency of the pricing of assets and liabilities. Both assets and liabilities can now be segmented according to their economic characteristics. The options embedded in them are stripped out and distributed to the natural holder of such a position or to the one for whom it has greatest value because of the balance of risks and rewards in the rest of its portfolio.

Another effect of derivative markets is that, almost by definition, they reduce the cost of capital. On a secular basis, the cost of capital is declining because of the more efficient distribution of risk in the financial system. Some even argue that the lower cost of capital accounts for the otherwise inexplicable heights equity markets have reached in some developed countries.

In essence, the effect of securitization is to turbocharge the influence of derivative markets in lowering the cost of capital. Capital not only costs less but earns greater returns because it is no longer a static concept of a certain amount of capital applied to a certain amount of assets. In the future, capital will primarily be used to support the intermediation process: the acquisition of assets, their segmentation into appropriate risk pools, and their distribution. So you need less of it; it has lower costs; and it provides greater returns.

These factors increase rather than decrease the stability of the system. This is the only point where I would respectfully take issue with Chadha and Folkerts-Landau's paper, which argues that, as a result of a move from bank financing to capital market financing, there will be greater risk, or greater severity, in future crises.

I would, as a counterpoint, suggest that when a crisis erupts, whatever the reason, a cost occurs at that time. That cost can be recognized immediately or it can be recognized later. But what the derivative and security markets do is enable the cost to be crystallized immediately, thereby reducing the severity of any crisis and accelerating the institution of policies needed to rectify whatever the problem was in the first place. In general, these markets are a positive element but are considered threatening because they diminish the importance of governments, central banks, regulators, and multinational agencies. It is not rescue packages but the ability of the markets to crystallize cost immediately that leads to effective reform. In short, markets are better arbiters of stable growth policies by individual countries. Not only that, the technologically induced advances in the banking function allow markets to fulfill that role in an ever more efficient way day by day. Evidence of this can be seen in the convergence of the risk-adjusted real rates of return. It's not that we have a single real rate of return. Instead, the real rates of return adjusted for risk are converging on a global basis—a function of the greater efficiency and speed in the banking system.

Of course, there is the old saw about how you can't fight the markets. In an exchange rate crisis, the markets are on one side and a central bank on the other, and eventually the markets beat the central bank. But that's yesterday's story. Today's story suggests that the markets have even greater power: the power to force regulatory authorities, broadly defined, to recognize that many existing forms of regulation are simply outdated. The markets circumvent them or force reform, so that the notion of regulation in an institutional framework as opposed to a functional framework is being destroyed.

Second, the markets will absolutely prevent any government from trying to pursue an independent monetary policy in the context of a fixed or semifixed exchange rate and free capital flows. Something has to give, and what the increasing speed of the transmission mechanism through the universal banks and the All Other has done is essentially force governments to adhere to policies that are market sensitive.

Moeen Qureshi made the point that the primacy of floating exchange rates was a dangerous concept or something to be avoided when you are actually in power and have political responsibility. I would respond: That's the whole point. The markets are not going to allow people to make those political trade-offs. If they do, they'll be overwhelmed.

There are two risks. One of them is that the speed of the transmission mechanism can also turbocharge the effect of a shock in one geographic area or one asset class and create unintended results where there isn't a true economic link. I subscribe to the classic argument about markets overshooting. They *do* overshoot. And they correct very quickly. This doesn't mean there aren't going to be crises, but rather that even a crisis induced by overshooting, as Arminio Fraga argues is happening in Indonesia, is undesirable but will correct very quickly. In the course of history, this is a blip, and everything will be fine. The Mexican experience was tremendously painful for the Mexican people on every level: economic, financial, social, and political. Having said this, the crisis was a very effective corrective mechanism that has made Mexico much healthier than it might otherwise have been.

The other risk is that the speed of transmission can accentuate the severity of crises. I have already argued that the opposite effect occurs. Derivatives reduce risk; securitization increases the return on capital; markets have greater power than those with political agendas; and the net result is more stable growth and less volatility in worldwide markets.

A number of key issues remain:

1. To what extent are policymakers who accept this framework comfortable with the tendency of markets to overshoot?

2. Although the markets react very fast, the reaction time of the chief players in a country in financial crisis is slower, which poses a risk that argues for some type of cushioning mechanism.

3. There is often a difference between the strength of universal banks and All Other and that of the national banks in the middle that are the transmission mechanism. For example, many Mexican banks had bad assets on their books when they were privatized and then proceeded to add more, with a compounding effect. In this case, the transmission mechanism was a weakness.

4. Portfolio diversification has a downside. Derivatives reduce risk because they diversify portfolios, but portfolio diversification also increases the possibility of contagion. The issue of moral hazard has been very carefully described by Mervyn King, but I want to bring up one issue that relates to Qureshi's point about the subsidy implicit in guarantees. We believe that it would be perfectly possible for the private market to provide the equivalent of the

FDIC guarantee to the U.S. banking system. Not only is the capital available, but it would be an economically rewarding proposition. Indeed, a proposal has even been submitted to Congress. The problem is that the banks don't want it because their premiums in tough times would be higher than the subsidized price provided by the government. And government officials don't want it because they like the control. But it could be done.

5. Finally, there is a potential source of tension between this mobility of capital, which is almost instantaneous, and the much lower degree of mobility of labor, which causes trade friction.

My final comment relates to the future of banks. Banks in the first category, universal banks, and banks in the third category, All Other, have a very bright future. They will be the custodians of intellectual capital, segmenting and distributing risk more efficiently than their competitors. And they will marry that capital with the benefits of technology. That mix has potential for excitement, profits, and a contribution to less volatility.

With respect to the point about reduction versus redistribution of risk, I would respectfully stand by the point that derivative markets redistribute *and* reduce risk.[1] The reason is that risk is not an ethereal, stand-alone concept. Risk is a function of particular cash flows associated with that risk and of how the risk correlates with other risks belonging to its owner. The argument would be that more efficient redistribution puts risk in the hands of investors for whom that particular risk, while in and of itself very risky, might reduce the overall risk of their portfolios. The classic example: Does it make sense for an investment trust that only holds AAA bonds to acquire a catastrophic reinsurance contract? If it's completely unrelated, the likely answer is yes. That's an extreme case.

As to Kathryn Dominguez's point, I think that what happened in 1987 was a portfolio problem. Most of the things we do work in practice but not in theory. That one worked in theory but not in practice because of the gapping problem. This is not an indictment of derivatives but of a particular application, which, in retrospect, missed a fairly obvious danger.

Now, to speak to the debate we've been having about information. David Mullins whispered to me the same point I'm about to make. With hindsight, it is very easy to know what information made it obvious that a crisis was going to occur in Thailand or that the peso was overvalued. It was not so obvious at the time. There was lots of information swirling around—and lots of people who, while they might have thought something was going to happen in Thailand, didn't know when, and the "when" is as important as the "if." Many of those same people lost money in Thailand, and also took a hit in the 1980s.

On whether the provision of liquidity by the Fed is a sine qua non for the proliferation of these instruments: *The answer is, I don't know.* I would say that the Fed's role of providing liquidity is a very good thing. Also, the Fed makes

1. The remainder of this comment addresses points raised during the discussion.

money, as does the Bank of England, so it's not as if it were a charitable activity. I was in no sense arguing against the Fed's providing liquidity. Nor was I arguing against regulation. Indeed, I think that entities that create systemic risk need to be regulated.

With respect to the question of why we don't give up our banking license, I recognize that I can be accused of currying favor. William McDonough's response to the question eloquently describes why we like being regulated by the Fed.

With respect to the point about moral hazard, I agree with every single comment made except the last one: the problem with bonds is that you can't get all of these bondholders together and compel them to do something. That is not the problem with bond financing. On the contrary, that is the *benefit* of bond financing. It is precisely because of that feature that borrowers are going to think very carefully before defaulting. It prods them to put themselves in a position not to default in the first place. Up until now, banks have been quite unintelligent in the way that they have lent money. They have lent in such a way that allows them to be herded into a room and told what to do. I predict that won't be the case in the future. The commercial banking system is simply not going to make long-term, next-to-lender-of-last-resort commitments and loans to governments with clauses in them that don't allow the loan to be transferred. Instead, they're going to use liquid instruments with a secondary market, and therefore the nature of these instruments is going to be the same as that of bonds. Over time, this will be a market force leading to more virtuous behavior.

Can there be blips along the way? And can some countries completely default and be excluded from the markets? Yes, and it's happened to some countries already, Peru being one. And Peru came back fine. It was just very painful.

Discussion Summary

David Folkerts-Landau noted that the growth and functioning of derivative markets in the United States depends on the cooperation of the Federal Reserve. Through their provision of liquidity and in their smoothing of overnight rates, policymakers at the Federal Reserve are complicit in the growth of these markets. As evidence of this, Folkerts-Landau noted that the Bundesbank is not prepared to take such actions in the overnight markets, and, as a consequence, derivative markets in Germany are considerably smaller. He also noted that, consequently, maintaining a banking license in the United States is extremely important even if typical commercial banking functions are less important to financial institutions. *Peter Garber* concurred and asked whether the massive liquidity provided by the Fed should be priced more aggressively.

William McDonough agreed that because the U.S. dollar remains the major reserve currency, the actions of the New York Federal Reserve are crucial to the functioning of derivative markets and that these services are provided at a modest cost. He went on to highlight the major issues facing financial regulators today. While a number of industries have combined into the financial services industry, regulation is still fragmented in an anachronistic manner. In order to remedy this disjunction, McDonough proposed an umbrella supervisor that would regulate any institution that could create or reallocate risk. Such an umbrella supervisor would tailor capital requirements for a financial institution in the context of the specific business strategy and risk appetite of that institution. Such an approach would represent a step toward risk-based capital requirements. These decisions would be made on the basis of regular, detailed discussions with the CEOs of these institutions that would include discussions of capital adequacy and management succession. These umbrella regulators would need to be particularly firm when questions of integrity or the breakdown of internal control became apparent.

McDonough also noted that while financial services firms manage their books on a global basis, regulation continues to be segmented by legal jurisdiction. In a related vein, he considered the too-big-to-fail doctrine pernicious and suggested that any institution can be deflated. He noted, however, that such an approach requires a robust payments system to ensure the elimination of Herstatt risk. Efforts are under way that will result in the elimination within two years of such intraday settlement risk.

To the questions raised by Mervyn King's comments, *Andrew Crockett* responded that the emphasis on individual banks is still necessary because systemic risk is still a function of the risk of the individual institutions. He also noted that while risk exposure does extend beyond the banking sector, banks remain the key players and consequently must remain the center of supervision. Finally, Crockett noted that penalizing lenders who had made imprudent loans should be a central aspect of the resolution of these crises. *Garber* asked King specifically about the twenty-five suggested bank standards and their applicability in the emerging market context.

Mervyn King concurred with McDonough's emphasis on payments systems and settlement risk. Regarding the creation of umbrella supervisory agencies, he agreed that as the financial services industry expands, creating regulations that don't distort firms' incentives is a top priority. King noted, however, that the most important obstacle to such umbrella agencies is bureaucratic and political resistance from existing regulators reluctant to cede control. He also suggested that in order to meet the challenges of the changing industry, regulators must move from an emphasis on the specifics of regulations to more blue-sky thinking.

René Stulz alluded to the instructive example of Switzerland in considering the appropriate set of bank regulations. He speculated that Switzerland has avoided major banking crises not because of better supervision but because of the absence of implicit or explicit guarantees in the banking system.

Nicholas Stern voiced concern that the current spreads on loans to eastern Europe may not fully reflect the existing risks in the region. He noted that the question for regulators is whether, and how, to voice such concerns. In particular, Stern asked whether it is appropriate for supervisory agencies to voice such concerns quietly or loudly, and privately or publicly.

Stanley Fischer responded that the moral hazard aspect of these crises, while receiving increasing attention, is often misunderstood. First, he rejected the notion that private lenders in the Thai crisis, whose losses may have been minimized by government actions, are an example of a moral hazard problem. By this criterion, Fischer noted that any countercyclical monetary policy would be characterized as creating a moral hazard problem. He stressed that the policy objective is to arrive at a sustainable exchange rate and avoid the deepening of the crisis. Second, Fischer noted that in contrast to bank lending to governments, bondholders are much more difficult to coordinate. Furthermore, the covenants of these bonds include legal penalties that made moratoria on payments very difficult to undertake. *Martin Feldstein* inquired about the nature of these penalties and what makes them so severe. *Fischer* responded that they include seizure of property and restrictions on international trade and payments.

King noted that the covenants referred to by Fischer are an example of the need for a multilateral approach through the G-7 or G-10. While no individual borrower could insist on the removal of such covenants in negotiations, a multilateral agreement would be the best way to approach this issue. Similarly, greater information disclosure should be a focus of multilateral efforts as no individual country would necessarily undertake such steps.

Regarding the ability of private markets to overcome crises, *Fischer* noted that any position that accepts that markets sometimes overshoot and that economies and firms suffer from hysteresis cannot then automatically accept the prescription that private markets can solve these problems alone.

With respect to the proliferation of derivatives, *Kathryn Dominguez* noted that it was puzzling that Japanese firms, who could have been hedging against yen appreciation, in fact did very little hedging. She noted that there is little debate about the benefits of derivatives in calm markets. Instead, the disagreement is about how they functioned during crises.

Roberto Mendoza responded that derivatives both redistribute and reduce risk exposures and cited the inclusion of catastrophic reinsurance contracts in AAA portfolios as an example of the risk-reducing nature of derivatives. He suggested that the performance of portfolio insurance during the 1987 crash was not an indictment of derivatives in general but rather of that particular application. He also suggested that the coordination problems of bondholders are precisely the reason countries will try to avoid default and, as such, are a positive development.

5   The Role of Equity Markets in International Capital Flows

1. Linda L. Tesar
2. René M. Stulz
3. Stephen Friedman
4. George N. Hatsopoulos

1. Linda L. Tesar

The Role of Equity in International Capital Flows

5.1.1 Introduction

In 1980 the United States dominated the world's financial markets, accounting for more than 50 percent of the capitalized value of the world stock market. Only a small fraction of the U.S. equity portfolio was invested in foreign markets; estimates of the foreign equity holdings of U.S. investors suggest that roughly 98 percent of the total equity portfolio was invested at home (Tesar and Werner 1995). To the extent that U.S. investors ventured into foreign markets, they did so primarily to the familiar markets of Europe and Canada. Although most of the legal barriers to cross-border trading in foreign securities were dismantled with the abandonment of fixed exchange rates, the practical costs of transacting in foreign capital markets remained prohibitive.

Rolling the clock forward seventeen years, the world has indeed become a different place. Fueled by the privatization of state-owned enterprises in Europe, Latin America, and Asia and the liberalization and expansion of markets in developing countries, cross-border equity investment has become an important channel for international diversification among industrialized countries and a conduit for capital flows from industrialized to developing countries. In 1994, global investment in the equity of firms in developing countries reached $26 billion, accounting for nearly 20 percent of equity inflows worldwide (IMF 1996). One in four equity transactions in the United States now involves foreign equity or a foreign buyer or seller, and roughly 12 percent of the U.S. portfolio is held in foreign stocks.

This paper reviews recent developments in the globalization of equity markets. Section 5.1.2 begins by presenting some evidence on the growth in equity markets and the factors that help account for recent trends in cross-border equity investment.[1] On the supply side of global capital markets, the benefits of global diversification provide a significant incentive for investing across national borders. In addition, there has been a general shift in the allocation of savings from traditional bank deposits toward investment in equity through mutual and pension funds. These institutionally managed funds have increasingly turned to international markets as a source of higher returns. On the demand side, the capital needs of developing countries and countries making the transition from centrally planned to more market-based economic systems have brought a large number of firms to the global equity market as a means of raising capital. The barriers between savers residing in one nation and firms demanding capital located in another nation have been declining over time as communications technology improves and the process of eliminating of capital controls continues.

Section 5.1.3 takes a closer look at the volume and direction of cross-border equity flows in light of the recent growth in equity markets. Data on net equity flows suggest that there has been an increase in the net flow of equity investment from industrialized to developing countries. However, 80 to 90 percent of global equity investment originates and is invested in the developed markets of Europe, the United States, Canada, and Japan. From the perspective of investors in industrialized countries, the majority of their portfolios are held in domestic equity, although the degree of home bias is eroding over time. Between 1980 and 1996, the share of the U.S. equity portfolio invested in foreign stocks increased from 2 to 12 percent, though it still remains far from the "optimal" portfolio allocation suggested by basic portfolio theory.

Section 5.1.4 turns to the behavior of U.S. investors in foreign equity markets. Concerns have been raised about the risk of equity flows as a source of long-term external finance. Analysis of the determinants of U.S. portfolio allocation suggests that U.S. investors are primarily driven by signals about the local economy, increasing their portfolio holdings in markets when expected returns in that market are high. Global factors, such as swings in world interest rates, are not found to be significant in the allocation of the U.S. equity portfolio. This evidence suggests that equity inflows can be a reliable source of capital as long as local market conditions are consistent with long-run growth and stability.

---

1. Throughout, the term "equity investment" will refer to portfolio equity investment. For a discussion of the issues related to foreign direct investment, see chapters 6.1 by Robert Lipsey and 6.2 by Robert Feenstra in this volume.

Table 5.1   **Equity Market Capitalization, 1990–96**

Market	1990	1996	Percentage Change 1990–96
Malaysia	48,611	309,179	84.3
Taiwan	100,710	273,608	63.2
South Africa	137,540	241,571	43.1
Brazil	16,354	216,990	92.5
Korea	110,594	138,817	20.3
India	38,567	122,605	68.5
China		113,755	
Mexico	32,725	106,540	69.3
Thailand	23,896	99,828	76.1
Indonesia	8,081	91,016	91.1
Philippines	5,927	80,649	92.7
Chile	13,645	65,940	79.3
Argentina	3,268	44,679	92.7
Turkey	19,065	30,020	36.5
Emerging markets	611,278	2,161,657	210.1
Japan	2,917,679	3,088,850	5.9
United Kingdom	848,866	1,470,246	73.2
United States	3,059,434	8,484,433	177.3
Developed markets	8,782,267	17,951,705	104.4
World	9,393,545	20,177,762	114.8

Source: International Finance Corporation, *Emerging Stock Markets Factbook* (Washington, D.C., 1996).
Note: End-of-period values in millions of U.S. dollars.

5.1.2 The Growth in International Equity Markets

Since 1990, world equity markets have grown at a phenomenal rate. Table 5.1 shows the capitalized values of the equity markets in Japan, the United Kingdom, the United States, and the twelve largest emerging stock markets in terms of market capitalization at the end of 1996. Over the 1990–96 period the capitalized value of the global equity market nearly doubled, expanding from $9.4 to $20.2 trillion. In contrast, world economic activity over the same period grew by a mere 15.7 percent (IMF 1997). At the end of 1996 developed equity markets in Europe, Asia, and the United States accounted for over 90 percent of the global market, growing from $8.8 trillion in 1990 to $20 trillion in 1996. The share of developed equity markets in the world total has declined over time, however, due to the even faster rate of growth of equity markets in emerging markets. This section examines some of the factors that contributed to the expansion of global equity markets and the increase in cross-border equity investment.

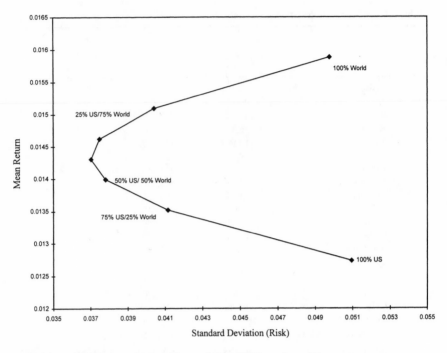

Fig. 5.1   Risk-return trade-off: portfolio of U.S. and world indexes, 1985:02–90:12
Source: Morgan Stanley Capital International.
Note: Monthly returns are in U.S. dollars.

The Benefits of Global Diversification

One obvious incentive for investing in foreign markets is the benefits of diversification across domestic and foreign securities. The potential benefits of diversification have been well known for decades. In a pair of articles written nearly three decades ago, Grubel (1968) and Levy and Sarnat (1970) demonstrated that the addition of foreign securities to a portfolio of domestic securities provides substantial risk reduction due to the relatively low correlation between domestic and foreign asset returns. To illustrate this point, figure 5.1 shows the trade-off in terms of risk and return of holding an index of U.S. stocks and the Morgan Stanley Capital International World Index over the 1985–90 period. The data are monthly returns in U.S. dollars. An investor holding a portfolio invested entirely in U.S. equities over this time period received a mean return of 1.27 percent (15.27 percent on an annualized basis) with a monthly standard deviation, or risk, of 5.09 percent, while the global portfolio earned a mean return of 1.59 percent (19.06 percent annualized) with 4.98 percent risk. The "bullet" shape in figure 5.1 illustrates the risk and return of holding different combinations of the two assets. The figure makes it clear that an investor who is averse to risk could have obtained higher returns and

Table 5.2   **Monthly Returns in Developed Equity Markets (percent)**

Market	Annualized Mean[a]	Risk[b]	Sharpe Ratio[c]
A. Sample Period: 1985:02–1989:12			
Canada	16.0	17.8	0.9
France	37.1	27.0	1.4
Germany	32.9	27.0	1.2
Italy	35.3	28.0	1.3
Japan	38.5	23.4	1.6
United Kingdom	27.6	24.5	1.1
United States	18.5	17.6	1.1
World	25.9	15.4	1.7
B. Sample Period: 1990:01–1997:06			
Canada	8.3	13.6	0.6
France	9.9	16.9	0.6
Germany	10.9	17.8	0.6
Italy	5.5	25.7	0.2
Japan	0.2	26.8	0.0
United Kingdom	13.8	16.1	0.9
United States	16.4	11.9	1.4
World	9.7	13.2	0.7

Source: Morgan Stanley Capital International.
Note: End-of-month total returns are in U.S. dollars.
[a]The annualized mean is the monthly percentage change times twelve.
[b]The annualized standard deviation is the monthly standard deviation times the square root of twelve.
[c]The Sharpe ratio is the annualized mean divided by the annualized standard deviation.

borne less risk by diversifying his portfolio away from U.S. stocks into the global portfolio.

Table 5.2 lists the annualized mean returns and the annualized standard deviations of equity returns in Canada, France, Germany, Italy, Japan, the United Kingdom, the United States, and the world index over the 1985:02–89:12 and 1990:01–97:06 periods.[2] The last column shows the Sharpe ratio, defined as the return per unit risk, for each of the markets. In the early period, the world index dominated investment in each of the individual country equity markets in terms of return per unit risk. Japan had the highest mean return and came close to matching the Sharpe ratio of the global index. In the later sample, Japanese equity returns declined dramatically and the global portfolio dominated investment in most national markets in terms of return per unit risk. Given the strong performance of the equity markets in the United Kingdom and the United States, however, investors in those countries actually earned higher risk-adjusted returns on investments in their home markets than by diversifying into the global market.

2. The annualized mean is the monthly mean return times twelve. The annualized standard deviation is the standard deviation of monthly returns times the square root of twelve.

The strong performance of particular markets ex post does not undermine the ex ante benefits of holding a portfolio of assets with less than perfectly correlated returns. Table 5.3 lists the unconditional correlations between monthly equity returns in the same set of countries. The data are broken into the same subsamples (1985:02–89:12 and 1990:01–97:06) to provide some indication of how the correlation structure has changed over time. Panel A of table 5.3 shows correlations ranging from .23 between the United States and Japan to .81 between the United States and Canada, with a cross-country average of .44. In the second subsample (panel B), the correlations are generally of the same magnitude, with an average of .40. However, a pairwise comparison of the correlations between the two subsamples suggests that the correlation structure between particular equity markets may not be constant over time.

Longin and Solnik (1995) developed an explicit model of the conditional correlation between equity returns for the seven countries shown in table 5.1 over the 1960–90 period. They concluded that the correlation between markets has risen over time and that the degree of co-movement tends to be higher during periods of higher volatility. Increased correlation across markets is consistent with—though not definitive evidence of—greater integration of financial markets. As markets become more tightly linked, global risk factors rather than country-specific factors become more important in determining asset prices. An analysis of the relationship between asset returns and market inte-

Table 5.3   **Correlations between Monthly Equity Returns in Developed Markets**

Market	Canada	France	Germany	Italy	Japan	United Kingdom	United States
A. Sample Period: 1985:01–1989:12							
Canada	1.00						
France	0.46	1.00					
Germany	0.26	0.69	1.00				
Italy	0.26	0.61	0.53	1.00			
Japan	0.27	0.46	0.25	0.46	1.00		
United Kingdom	0.63	0.53	0.43	0.38	0.36	1.00	
United States	0.81	0.50	0.34	0.27	0.23	0.60	1.00
Average correlation							0.44
B. Sample Period: 1990:01–1997:06							
Canada	1.00						
France	0.27	1.00					
Germany	0.28	0.67	1.00				
Italy	0.30	0.33	0.38	1.00			
Japan	0.25	0.40	0.30	0.36	1.00		
United Kingdom	0.43	0.63	0.58	0.22	0.47	1.00	
United States	0.63	0.44	0.37	0.23	0.24	0.56	1.00
Average correlation							0.40

Source: Morgan Stanley Capital International.

Note: End-of-month total returns are in U.S. dollars.

Table 5.4   **Composition of U.S. Household Assets, 1985–96**

Asset	1985.0	1990.0	1996.0	Percentage Growth 1985–96
A. Household Financial Assets by Type[a] (billion US$)				
Deposits	2,459.5	3,238.9	3,546.2	44.2
Credit market instruments[b]	805.5	1,501.4	2,003.8	148.8
Corporate equities	1,123.2	1,783.5	4,680.5	316.7
Mutual funds	197.9	467.8	1,582.8	699.8
Life insurance	257.0	380.9	590.2	129.6
Pension fund reserves	2,039.0	3,367.7	6,285.9	208.3
Equity in noncorporate business	2,272.6	2,628.6	2,740.7	20.6
Other financial assets[c]	551.8	838.5	1,411.1	155.7
Total financial assets	9,706.5	14,207.3	22,841.2	135.3
B. As a Percentage of Total Financial Assets[d]				
Deposits	25.3	22.8	15.5	
Credit market instruments[b]	8.3	10.6	8.8	
Corporate equities	11.6	12.6	20.5	
Mutual funds	2.0	3.3	6.9	
Life insurance	2.6	2.7	2.6	
Pension fund reserves	21.0	23.7	27.5	
Equity in noncorporate business	23.4	18.5	12.0	
Other financial assets[c]	5.7	5.9	6.2	

Source: Board of Governors (various years, table L100: Households and Nonprofit Organizations).
[a]Includes assets of private households and nonprofit organizations.
[b]Includes open market paper, U.S. government securities, municipal securities, corporate and foreign bonds, and mortgages.
[c]Includes security credit, investment in bank personal trusts, and miscellaneous assets.
[d]Percentages may not sum to 100 due to rounding.

gration is beyond the scope of this paper. Stulz, in chapter 5.2 of this volume, provides a detailed discussion of the impact of cross-border portfolio flows on asset prices.

Shifts in Private Saving

A second factor that can help account for the growth in global equity investment in the 1990s is the shift in private savings toward holdings of equity and bonds. Since 1980, the share of stocks and bonds—inclusive of indirect holdings through mutual funds—has increased from about 60 percent of total U.S. assets to over 80 percent, while the fraction invested in deposits and money market funds declined from 40 to less than 20 percent (Morgan 1994; Board of Governors, various years). Table 5.4 provides a decomposition of the assets of U.S. households by type over the 1985–96 period.[3] Over this period, the

3. The data are from the United States Flow of Funds. The figures include the assets of nonprofit organizations, which account for approximately 5 percent of total assets in the combined category of households and nonprofits.

fraction of total household assets accounted for by mutual fund investment grew from 2 to 7 percent, investment in corporate equities from 12 to 20 percent, and pension fund reserves from 21 to 28 percent.

Economists offer two explanations for the shift away from traditional banking deposits and money market funds toward other financial assets. First, low interest rates in 1990 and 1991 made these assets less attractive than stocks and bonds. Second, there is evidence that household investment in stocks and bonds is strongly correlated with the demographic structure of the U.S. population (Morgan 1994). It appears that investors of the baby boomer cohort are willing to exchange risk for return as a means of augmenting their savings for retirement. In a recent study, Heaton and Lucas (1997) found that even investors of retirement age have increased their holdings of stocks and bonds. They argued that such a shift is consistent with risk reduction because investors are substituting from private business ownership to a more diversified portfolio of stocks.

The shift in saving toward equity investment, particularly through pension and mutual funds, plays an important role in the increase in aggregate U.S. holdings of foreign equity. Competition among funds for the growing pool of savings has pressured fund managers to develop new products with better performance. In addition, by pooling large sums of money, fund managers are able to expand into new markets with lower transaction costs than were possible through individual stockholder investment. According to industry reports, over 10 percent of the net assets of mutual funds in 1996 was allocated to "international equity" (non-U.S.) and "global equity" (U.S. plus non-U.S.) funds (Investment Company Institute 1997). Although the evidence presented here has focused on the United States, there is some evidence that an aging workforce and concerns over the viability of public pension plans are having a similar impact on the allocation of saving in Europe (*Economist*, 29 March 1997). It should be noted that this shift toward equity investment does not imply that the total volume of saving has risen, but only that the composition of saving has shifted toward equity and bonds, which has in turn induced professional money managers to turn to foreign markets.

Raising Capital on Global Markets

Demographic shifts and potential gains from diversification help explain the increase in the supply of capital to global equity markets. On the demand side, the liberalization of markets and the privatization of state-owned enterprises in developing and transitional economies brought a growing number of firms to the global equity market as a means of raising capital. Table 5.5 shows the number of listed companies and the value of trading on equity markets in emerging and developed countries over the 1990–96 period. The growth in the number of listed stocks (panel A) reflects the remarkable rate of market reform in developing and transitional economies during this period. By 1996, the number of listed securities in developing countries had reached 22,263, ex-

Table 5.5   **Number of Listed Companies and Value Traded in Developed and
Emerging Markets**

Market	1990	1991	1992	1993	1994	1995	1996
		A. Number of Listed Domestic Companies					
Developed markets	16,403	16,315	17,227	17,431	19,064	19,467	20,141
Emerging markets	12,515	9,636	10,359	11,337	17,014	19,397	22,263
Emerging market percentage	43	37	38	39	47	50	53
		B. Value Traded (billion US$)					
Developed markets	4,617	4,411	4,166	6,634	8,446	10,633	12,011
Emerging markets	894	606	613	1,069	1,640	1,033	1,575
Emerging market percentage	16	12	13	14	16	9	12

Source: International Finance Corporation, *Emerging Stock Markets Factbook* (Washington, D.C., 1996).

ceeding the total number of listed stocks in the developed markets. The value traded (or turnover) on emerging market exchanges reached $1.6 trillion in 1996, about 12 percent of the total value traded.

The emergence of new markets broadened the scope of the gains from diversification for investors in industrialized countries. Table 5.6 shows the annualized means, standard deviations, and Sharpe ratios for a set of emerging markets over the period 1990:02–97:06. Comparing the figures with the returns in industrialized countries (table 5.2, panel B), it is clear that investment in emerging markets offers potentially high returns but also carries significant risk. The last column in table 5.6 shows the correlation with the U.S. return. The average correlation coefficient between the returns in emerging market equities with U.S. equity is about one-half the correlation coefficient between the equities of the industrialized countries, suggesting that there are significant diversification benefits to adding emerging market investments to a portfolio of equity from industrialized countries.

To further underscore the potential rewards as well as the hazards of investing in emerging markets, figure 5.2 shows the cumulated returns of one dollar invested in January 1990 in Japan, the United Kingdom, the United States, Mexico, an index of European, Asian, and Far East stocks (denoted EAFE), and an index of emerging markets (denoted EM).[4] As of June 1997, investors in Japanese equity had suffered a capital loss on their six-and-a-half-year investment, while investment in the EM and EAFE indexes earned modest capital gains. Investment in the United Kingdom and the United States yielded capital gains of 153 and 244 percent, respectively. But the most interesting story is the case of Mexico. The impact of the December 1994 peso crisis is clear; the value of the dollar invested in Mexican equity plummeted from a high of $5.11 in January 1994 to $1.58 in February 1995. However, investors who either held Mexican equity over the entire time period or purchased equity

---

4. The returns are not hedged and therefore contain currency risk as well as country risk.

Table 5.6   Monthly Equity Returns in Emerging Markets, 1990:02–97:06

Market	Annualized Mean[a]	Risk[b]	Sharpe Ratio[c]	Correlation with the United States
Emerging market index	5.96	18.90	0.32	0.35
Mexico	21.84	33.71	0.65	0.28
Malaysia	13.94	24.53	0.57	0.30
Taiwan	4.77	42.71	0.11	0.20
Brazil	39.13	57.51	0.68	0.25
Korea	−2.99	27.52	−0.11	0.19
India	16.10	35.66	0.45	−0.11
Thailand	4.71	32.48	0.15	0.25
Indonesia	7.90	29.30	0.27	0.37
Philippines	14.30	31.63	0.45	0.26
Chile	29.25	25.93	1.13	0.25
Argentina	44.27	52.86	0.84	0.28
Turkey	13.37	59.20	0.23	0.00
Average correlation				0.21

Source: Morgan Stanley Capital International and International Finance Corporation.
Note: End-of-month total returns are in U.S. dollars.
[a]The annualized mean is the monthly percentage change times twelve.
[b]The annualized standard deviation is the monthly standard deviation times the square root of twelve.
[c]The Sharpe ratio is the annualized mean divided by the annualized standard deviation.

following the crisis earned capital gains comparable to the U.S. market. Data on U.S. net purchases of foreign equity indicate that U.S. investors were net buyers of Mexican equity in December 1994 and January 1995. The data are not precise about the exact timing of the purchases within the month. If, however, U.S. investors purchased Mexican equity *after* the decline in prices, they may have been able to capitalize on an undervalued market. The link between net purchases of foreign equity and equity returns and the timing of investment in foreign equity markets will be discussed in more detail in section 5.1.4 below.

Financial Markets: Channeling Cross-Border Equity Flows

A number of factors have helped improve the flow of funds from savers located in one national market to firms located in another. In industrialized countries, explicit controls on cross-border equity investment have gradually declined and in most cases have been entirely eliminated. Equity markets in developing countries have also become more accessible to foreign investors as part of the general process of capital market liberalization and deregulation. At the same time, improvements in communications technologies have made investors more aware of opportunities available in foreign markets.

International stock exchanges have struggled to meet the growing appetites of domestic investors for foreign equities and the demand for access to capital markets on the part of foreign firms. In the United States, for example, differ-

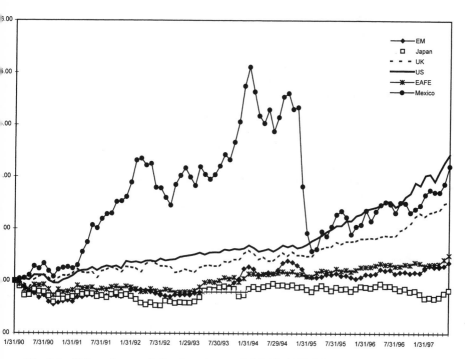

Fig. 5.2   Value of a one-dollar investment, 1990:01–1997:06

ences between accounting and disclosure requirements at home and in foreign countries have made it difficult for foreign firms to register their stock directly on U.S. exchanges. As a consequence, the majority of trading in foreign stocks by U.S. residents occurs either overseas or in over-the-counter, unregistered stocks. In 1994, 1,092 foreign stocks were issued on the combined AMEX, NYSE, and NASDAQ exchanges while 8,097 stocks were traded on Pink Sheets. The majority of American Depository Receipt (ADR) programs are also traded as unregistered securities on the over-the-counter market (Cochrane, Shapiro, and Tobin 1995).[5] It appears that U.S. investors' demand for foreign equities is large enough to bear the additional cost and potential risk of trading in stocks not under the regulatory control of the Securities and Exchange Commission.

5.1.3   Cross-Border Equity Flows

The demand for capital in emerging markets, the growing share of equity in the portfolio of savers, and the response of capital markets to facilitate cross-border investment have set the stage for increased capital flows from capital-

5. The Pink Sheets are listings of foreign stocks and their market makers. ADRs are certificates issued by a U.S. bank to represent ownership of foreign corporate shares.

rich to capital-poor regions of the world. This section discusses how investors have responded to this opportunity for global investment. It first examines the magnitude and direction of capital flows on a global scale then turns to the international investment choices of U.S. investors.

The Composition and Direction of International Capital Flows

To put the volume of cross-border equity investment in some perspective, table 5.7 shows the decomposition of international capital flows in industrialized and developing countries over the 1990–95 period. Among industrialized countries, portfolio investment (stocks and bonds) has been the largest channel of capital inflows, reaching a peak of $613 billion in 1993. Foreign investment in debt securities accounts for the bulk of portfolio investment in industrialized countries. The growing importance of equity markets as a means of external

Table 5.7   Composition of Global Capital Flows

	1990	1991	1992	1993	1994	1995
A. Inflows (billion US$)						
Industrialized countries						
Direct investment	169.6	112.9	117.7	136.5	139.5	208.9
Portfolio investment	213.6	410.9	385.3	613.4	316.2	541.5
Equity	−7.6	99.4	90.0	181.9	109.9	120.0
Debt	208.5	306.7	302.1	441.1	155.0	370.1
Other liabilities[a]	473.0	−57.4	177.5	123.0	274.4	209.9
Developing countries						
Direct investment	31.6	40.9	48.2	73.8	91.4	107.5
Portfolio investment	22.5	31.3	48.8	114.1	101.3	42.2
Equity	3.9	6.9	12.0	38.6	26.0	19.1
Debt	19.0	24.9	37.7	76.1	75.0	22.1
Other liabilities[a]	49.8	28.2	38.6	35.1	44.1	63.0
B. Outflows (billion US$)						
Industrialized countries						
Direct investment	−224.4	−186.7	−178.8	−206.5	−211.4	−278.3
Portfolio investment	−169.1	−317.0	−328.3	−537.7	−306.8	−398.4
Equity	−25.3	−90.6	−76.9	−153.8	−125.9	−100.6
Debt	−141.4	−212.1	−242.1	−357.5	−162.7	−289.3
Other assets	−325.0	−44.2	−160.7	−209.0	−65.5	−232.1
Reserve assets	−57.5	−14.1	3.1	−18.9	−35.6	−80.4
Developing countries						
Direct investment	−10.9	−6.7	−11.7	−15.4	−16.4	−19.0
Portfolio investment	−17.3	−11.4	−7.3	−10.2	−18.6	−11.4
Equity	−1.3	−1.6	−2.4	−10.8	−9.1	−8.6
Debt	−15.5	−10.3	−5.7	0.2	−10.0	−2.3
Other assets	−4.5	−4.2	−6.9	−2.2	−3.4	−3.1
Reserve assets	−35.0	−68.7	−61.1	−83.0	−71.0	−118.5

Source: IMF (1996).

[a]Trade credits, government and bank loans, currency, and deposits.

Table 5.8   **Net Cross-Border Equity Flows, 1994–95**

	Amount (billion US$)		Share of Global Equity Out/Inflows (%)	
	1994	1995	1994	1995
A. Net cross-border equity outflows from				
North America	55.0	54.0	40.7	49.5
United States	48.1	50.7	35.6	46.4
Canada	6.9	3.3	5.1	3.0
Japan	14.1	−0.2	10.4	−0.1
Europe	56.3	33.8	41.6	31.0
United Kingdom	0.7	16.0	0.5	14.7
Industrialized countries	125.9	100.6	93.1	92.1
Rest of world	9.1	8.6	6.7	7.9
B. Net cross-border equity inflows to				
North America	5.6	13.3	4.1	9.6
United States	0.9	16.4	0.7	11.8
Canada	4.7	−3.1	3.5	−2.2
Japan	49.0	50.7	36.1	36.4
Europe	47.1	30.0	34.7	21.6
United Kingdom	5.8	5.1	4.3	3.7
Industrialized countries	109.9	120.0	80.9	86.3
Rest of world	26.0	19.1	19.1	13.7

Source: IMF (1996).

finance is more obvious in developing countries. Between 1990 and 1995, equity inflows as a share of total portfolio inflows increased from 17.4 to 45.2 percent. On the asset side of the balance sheet, portfolio investment exceeds foreign direct investment as the main form of investment abroad by industrialized countries. Although the share of portfolio equity investment is rising, the bulk of foreign portfolio investment takes place through debt securities.

Table 5.8 provides more specific information on the source and the destination of cross-border equity investment during 1994 and 1995. The data confirm that capital markets play an essential role in reallocating capital from capital-rich countries to emerging markets. Panel A shows net equity outflows from the United States, Canada, Japan, Europe, and aggregate outflows for industrialized countries and the rest of the world. In 1994 and 1995 industrialized countries provided over 90 percent of all net equity outflows, with at least half of that amount originating in the United States. Panel B shows that the lion's share of capital outflows from industrialized countries remained as equity investment in other industrialized economies. As a percentage of global net capital outflows, over one-third was invested in equity from Japan in 1995 and one-fifth in Europe. However, there is some evidence of net capital outflows from industrialized countries to developing countries. In 1994, 93 percent of the supply of capital originated with investors in industrialized countries, and only

Table 5.9   Equity Inflows as a Percentage of Domestic Investment

Market	1990.0	1991.0	1992.0	1993.0	1994.0	1995.0
Developed markets						
Australia	2.5	4.0	0.2	13.1	11.8	4.1
Austria	5.5	1.8	1.7	10.8	10.8	8.1
Canada	−1.2	−0.7	0.8	9.3	4.7	−3.1
Finland	0.9	0.3	1.8	71.1	71.3	42.8
France	2.3	3.0	2.0	5.9	2.0	2.6
Germany	−0.6	0.4	−0.6	1.8	0.8	−0.3
Japan	−1.4	4.4	0.8	1.6	3.6	3.5
New Zealand	1.7	1.9	0.8	1.4	n.a.	n.a.
Singapore	4.6	−1.7	7.9	13.5	1.2	1.4
Spain	n.a.	2.2	2.9	n.a.	n.a.	n.a.
Sweden	n.a.	15.6	19.8	64.9	100.1	21.3
United Kingdom	1.5	2.6	10.9	18.1	3.8	3.0
United States	−1.8	1.3	−0.5	2.5	0.1	1.6
Emerging markets						
Chile	5.4	0.3	3.4	7.0	9.9	−1.7
Indonesia	n.a.	n.a.	n.a.	3.9	3.4	2.3
Korea	n.a.	n.a.	8.8	22.0	10.7	11.6
Mexico	3.9	11.4	7.0	14.3	5.0	1.1
Portugal	11.4	4.8	10.3	12.4	10.0	−3.5
South Africa	n.a.	−4.2	−4.1	4.8	0.7	5.9

Sources: IMF (1996) and IMF, International Financial Statistics, annual issue (Washington, D.C., 1996).

Note: Investment is measured as gross fixed capital formation.

81 percent was reinvested in equity from industrialized countries. Thus roughly 8 percent of the global supply of equity capital was reallocated from industrialized to developing countries. In 1995, the fraction invested in "rest of the world" equities had dropped from 19 to 14 percent, and the share reallocated across the two regions fell to 6 percent of the global total.

Table 5.9 shows the magnitude of equity inflows relative to domestic investment (as measured by gross fixed capital formation) in thirteen developed markets and six emerging markets. The data suggest that there is considerable volatility in equity inflows over time, even when expressed as a share of domestic investment. In some years the magnitude of foreign equity investment is as high as 70 to 100 percent of domestic investment (Finland in 1993 and 1994, and Sweden in 1994), though in most years the share of equity inflows is much smaller. The table also suggests that, at least for the sample of countries shown, the volume and volatility of equity investment in emerging markets is qualitatively similar to that in the developed markets.

Holdings of Foreign Equity: Is There Still Home Bias?

While investors have begun to exploit the gains from cross-border investment, the degree of international diversification is far from the level suggested by economic theory. As a benchmark for thinking about the "optimal" level of international equity investment, consider an environment in which investors from all countries have the same expectations about future returns, have the same degree of aversion to risk, face the same set of risks, have the same information about markets, and face no barriers or costs in undertaking international investment. Under these circumstances, all investors would choose identical portfolios. In equilibrium, the asset weights of the optimal portfolio would reflect the relative sizes of each national equity market. Table 5.10 shows the market capitalization shares for twenty-two developed equity markets and an aggregate of emerging markets for 1990, 1993, and 1996. In this idealized world, the share allocated to U.S. equity in the portfolio would have been about one-third in 1990 and would have increased to 42 percent by 1996. Japanese equity would also have had a weight close to one-third in 1990, but given the drop in equity prices in Japan, its optimal weight would have declined to 15 percent in 1996. By 1996, the optimal weight of emerging markets would have reached 11 percent of the total portfolio.

Estimates of the *actual* weight placed on foreign equities by investors in

Table 5.10   **Country Shares of Global Equity Market Capitalization**

Country	1990	1993	1996
Australia	1.14	1.46	1.55
Austria	0.12	0.20	0.17
Belgium	0.70	0.56	0.59
Canada	2.57	2.34	2.41
Denmark	0.42	0.30	0.36
Finland	0.24	0.17	0.31
France	3.34	3.27	2.93
Germany	3.78	3.32	3.33
Hong Kong	0.89	2.76	2.23
Italy	1.58	0.98	1.28
Japan	31.04	21.48	15.31
Luxembourg	0.11	0.14	0.16
Netherlands	1.27	1.30	1.88
New Zealand	0.09	0.18	0.19
Norway	0.28	0.20	0.28
South Africa	1.46	1.23	1.20
Singapore	0.37	0.95	0.74
Spain	1.19	0.85	1.20
Sweden	1.04	0.77	1.23
Switzerland	1.70	1.95	1.99
United Kingdom	9.03	8.25	8.62
United States	32.55	36.78	42.05
Developed markets	93.46	88.28	88.97
Emerging markets	6.54	11.72	11.03

Source: International Finance Corporation, *Emerging Stock Markets Factbook* (Washington, D.C., 1996).

industrialized countries fall far short of the market weights in table 5.10. Tesar and Werner (1995) found strong home bias in the portfolios of investors from Canada, Germany, Japan, the United Kingdom, and the United States. In 1990, the estimated weights on foreign equities ranged from 3.3 percent for investors from the United States to 23.5 percent for investors from the United Kingdom.[6] The degree of home bias in the U.S. portfolio does appear to be eroding, however. Using updated data, Bohn and Tesar (1997) found that the U.S. investment position in foreign equities roughly doubled between 1990 and 1993.

Figures recently released by the U.S. Treasury Department suggest that these estimated foreign portfolio shares for U.S. investors may have understated the magnitude of the U.S. investment position in foreign equity markets. The portfolio shares cited above are calculated by cumulating net purchases over time starting from an initial benchmark position, taking into account capital gains and losses. The benchmark position for U.S. portfolio investment in foreign markets was based on a survey of U.S. investors' foreign investment positions in long-term securities in 1943.[7] The Treasury Department recently surveyed 3,344 custodians and fund managers regarding the level of their holdings of foreign long-term securities as of 31 March 1994. Foreign long-term securities covered by the survey include all publicly and privately placed equity and long-term debt securities issued by non-U.S. firms, foreign governments, and international organizations. ADRs and Global Depository Receipts are considered foreign securities if the underlying securities are claims on firms located outside of the United States.[8] Based on the results of the new survey, the estimated U.S. investment position in foreign equities has been revised upward from its previous level of $228.5 billion[9] at the end of 1994 to $595.5 billion. Using the estimate of U.S. market capitalization as reported by the International Finance Corporation, a rough estimate of the share of the U.S. portfolio invested in foreign equities was 10.66 percent in 1993 and 11.75 percent in 1994.[10]

In principle, if net purchases accurately reflect transactions in equity between domestic and foreign residents, the estimates based on cumulated net purchases should provide a good approximation of the investment position regardless of the date of the benchmark survey. There are three reasons, however, to anticipate potentially large errors in the investment positions based on cumulated net purchases.

---

6. French and Poterba (1991) reported similar figures.

7. Surveys to measure the magnitude of foreign holdings of U.S. securities have been conducted every five years since 1974.

8. For a complete discussion of the survey methodology and the updated investment positions, see Pappas (1997).

9. Author's own estimates (see Bohn and Tesar 1997).

10. A more exact estimate of the portfolio share would be to adjust the denominator for U.S. holdings of foreign equities and foreign holdings of U.S. equity. It should also be noted that the measure of U.S. market capitalization reported by the International Finance Corporation has considerably larger coverage than the figures of market capitalization reported by either Morgan Stanley Capital International (MSCI) or the *Financial Times* (FT). The share of home equity in the U.S. portfolio would obviously be larger if the MSCI or FT market capitalization were used.

1. Innovations in telecommunications and computing technology and the elimination of capital controls in many countries have made it difficult for government agencies to keep track of the volume of transactions between domestic and foreign residents. Although this is a potentially serious problem, it would affect purchases as well as sales of foreign securities and may not substantially bias the data.[11]

2. The net purchases data provide no information about *which* securities investors are buying or selling. For lack of a better alternative, estimates of investment positions are based on the assumption that investors transact in foreign market indexes. To the extent that investors choose stocks that outperform the index, their investment positions in foreign stocks will be underestimated.

3. The data reflect net purchases cumulated during the month and therefore contain no information about the exact timing of transactions in foreign stock. If there are large changes in equity returns during a particular month, as in the case of the 1994 Mexican peso crisis, inaccuracies in the timing of net purchases can have a large impact on the estimated value of the investment position in that market.

Although the updated investment position figures reflect a substantial increase in U.S. holdings of foreign equity, a portfolio weight of 12 percent on foreign equity is still far below the level predicted by the simple economic model. There are a number of potential explanations for the home bias puzzle, though none have provided a definitive solution to the problem. The most obvious explanation for home bias is that there may be costs associated with transacting in foreign markets, such as explicit taxes on foreign equity investment, that would deter an investor from undertaking foreign investments and thereby skew the portfolio toward domestic assets. There is evidence that government restrictions have had an impact on asset prices in developing countries, which could explain the low U.S. investment position in emerging markets in the early 1990s (see, e.g., Bonser-Neal et al. 1990; Claessens and Rhee 1993). However, most explicit limits on holdings in foreign equity have either been eliminated or are well above observed portfolio shares and would therefore not restrict portfolio allocations. Transaction costs could also hinder cross-border investment but again would have to be implausibly large to explain the large and persistent degree of home bias. A recent study of the trading costs of institutional investors—inclusive of fees, commissions, and market impact effects—suggests that costs are indeed higher in emerging stock markets than in more developed equity markets. Interestingly, the cost of trading in NASDAQ stocks is higher than in many foreign markets due to market impact effects (Elkins/McSherry Company).

---

11. Biases would be more likely for countries that impose taxes on cross-border trading or on holdings of foreign assets. In comparing data sources on Canadian holdings of U.S. equity in 1990, Tesar and Werner (1992) found that the official figures reported by the Bank of Canada were smaller than the figures reported by the U.S. Treasury Department by a factor of four. One possible explanation for the discrepancy is that Canadian holdings were underreported to avoid Canadian taxes on foreign investment income.

The high-transaction-costs explanation for home bias also flies in the face of evidence on the volume of trading in foreign securities. Tesar and Werner (1995) found that the turnover rate on holdings of foreign equity by U.S. and Canadian investors in 1989 was at least double the rate of turnover on their home markets.[12] They also found that *foreign* investors' turnover rate on holdings of U.S. equity was 60 percent higher than the turnover rate on the U.S. market. Both findings suggest that transaction costs are not a deterrent to making frequent transactions in foreign stocks.

A second explanation for home bias is that investors in different countries face different risks and that the optimal "hedging" strategy against these risks is a portfolio skewed toward domestic securities. Shocks that affect purchasing power, such as changes in inflation or shifts in the supply of nontraded goods, have been shown in theory to produce home bias in national portfolios under some circumstances. When tested empirically, however, these factors have not been found to be important enough to generate portfolio weights consistent with those observed in most countries (see, e.g., Cooper and Kaplanis 1994; Baxter, Jermann, and King 1995; Tesar 1995). Baxter and Jermann (1997) developed a model that takes into account the impact of wages on the optimal investment portfolio. Because both labor income and domestic equity returns tend to be procyclical, they found that the optimal hedging strategy involves holding a *short* position in domestic equity, further deepening the home bias riddle.

Another explanation for home bias is that investors have better information about investments in their home markets than about investments in foreign markets and are thus cautious about trading against better informed foreign traders (see, e.g., Gehrig 1993). On the surface, such an information bias seems plausible. However, investors need little information to pursue a simple buy-and-hold strategy that would capture the gains from diversification. The information bias explanation for home bias is also inconsistent with the large volume of trading and turnover in foreign equities.

Rowland and Tesar (1998) examined the possibility that investment in multinational corporations provides indirect global diversification benefits, thereby reducing the need to purchase equity directly in foreign exchanges. Using data from Canada, France, Germany, Japan, Italy, the United Kingdom, and the United States over the 1984–92 period, they found weak evidence that multinationals may have provided diversification benefits for U.S. investors, though not for investors domiciled in the other six countries. In addition, they reported that even after taking the indirect diversification benefits into account, there remain significant benefits from diversifying internationally.

Each of these potential explanations for home bias probably contains more

---

12. The turnover rates are derived by scaling gross purchases and sales in foreign equity by holdings. The Treasury's revised figures for U.S. holdings of foreign securities reduce the aggregate turnover estimates of U.S. investors in foreign securities by about one-half.

than a kernel of truth. However, the extent and the persistence of home bias in the face of seemingly large benefits from diversification remains a puzzle for continuing research.

The U.S. Foreign Portfolio

The Treasury data also contain information about the allocation of the U.S. equity portfolio across foreign markets. Table 5.11 lists the twelve countries with the largest weights in the U.S. foreign portfolio as of March 1994. As a benchmark, column (1) shows each country's share of global market capitalization excluding the United States. Column (2) shows the estimated portfolio weights based on the cumulated net purchases series as calculated in Bohn and Tesar (1997). Column (3) lists the portfolio weights based on the Treasury's 1994 survey. In terms of market capitalization, Japan has the largest market share at 34 percent, followed by the United Kingdom at 13 percent, Germany at 5.25 percent, and France at 5.17 percent. Both the Bohn-Tesar and Treasury estimates place Japan's share in the U.S. portfolio at around 17 percent, about half of its market share, suggesting that U.S. investors are currently underweighting Japanese equity. U.S. investors tend to overweight equity from the United Kingdom, Canada, and Mexico with portfolio shares of 17.6, 7, and 6.1 percent (Treasury estimates), respectively. The factors that cause U.S. investors to adjust their portfolio weights over time are discussed below. By and large, the allocation of the U.S. portfolio across foreign stocks roughly corresponds to relative market sizes.

Table 5.11   **Allocation of U.S. Portfolio across Foreign Markets, March 1994**

Market	Share of World Market Excluding United States (1)	Estimates Based on Bohn-Tesar (2)	Estimates Based on New Treasury Survey (3)
Australia	2.3	1.5	3.0
Canada	3.7	10.7	7.0
France	5.2	6.0	4.5
Germany	5.3	5.0	4.5
Hong Kong	4.4	7.4	3.1
Italy	1.5	2.1	2.4
Japan	34.0	17.0	17.5
Netherlands	2.1	4.1	6.7
Sweden	1.2	2.2	2.1
Switzerland	3.1	5.2	3.7
United Kingdom	13.0	24.3	17.6
Mexico	2.3	8.0	6.1

Notes: Col. (1), Ratio of market capitalization to global market capitalization excluding the United States at the end of 1993. Col. (2), Portfolio shares estimated in Bohn and Tesar (1997). Col. (3), Based on Pappas (1997).

5.1.4   Long-Term Investment or "Hot Money"?

Foreign equity investment still accounts for only a fraction of the portfolio held by investors in industrialized countries. From the perspective of developing countries, however, the expansion of equity markets worldwide has resulted in a dramatic shift in external finance from official development and bank loans to private capital inflows. This growing dependence on private capital inflows has caused policymakers to question the reliability and sustainability of equity investment as a means of financing long-run development. Is the increase in equity investment abroad part of a long-run trend toward greater diversification or is it simply a short-run phenomenon that could reverse itself? Do investors take a long view in making foreign equity investments, or is equity investment "hot money," in pursuit of short-run capital gains? Do local factors have a significant impact on the allocation of investment, or are equity flows largely driven by global events outside of the control of local policymakers?

The behavior of U.S. investors in foreign equity markets provides some insight into these questions. Using monthly data on U.S. net purchases of equities in twenty-two countries, Bohn and Tesar (1996, 1997) identified the main determinants of foreign equity investment. In general, net purchases of foreign equity in a particular market were found to be positively related to the expected equity returns in that market.[13] In other words, U.S. investors tend to buy equity in a particular market if the signals about that market suggest that future returns will be high. This suggests that U.S. equity investment is not driven by fads, but that U.S. investors are responsive to local market conditions.

The behavior of U.S. investors in foreign markets also sheds light on the relative importance of global and local factors in explaining international capital flows. Calvo, Leiderman, and Reinhart (1993, 1996) argued that global factors—in particular, the fall in U.S. interest rates—induced investors to shift their portfolios away from domestic securities to seek higher returns abroad. Their study raised concerns that a subsequent increase in U.S. interest rates could just as easily cause investors to retreat from foreign markets. Bohn and Tesar (1999) found that U.S. interest rates do in fact play a role in explaining U.S. net purchases of foreign equity, but only through their impact on forecasted returns. After conditioning on expected returns and a linear time trend, they found no evidence that global variables have an independent influence on net equity purchases.

Finally, there is concern that increased foreign equity investment will produce "contagion" effects, that is, that a crisis in one market will spill over into other markets. The impact of portfolio flows on asset returns is discussed by

---

13. The forecastable component of future equity returns is obtained by regressing current returns on a set of predictor variables. Variables that are found to have out-of-sample explanatory power for foreign equity returns include lagged measures of the return on the local stock market in U.S. dollars less the U.S. safe rate, the local dividend yield, U.S. stock returns, the U.S. interest rate, the term structure of U.S. interest rates, and U.S. industrial production.

Stulz in chapter 5.2 of this volume. In terms of the transmission effects working through quantities, vector autoregressions of net purchases in one market on net purchases in other markets yield little evidence of a statistical relation between net purchases across markets. There is also no evidence that the Mexican peso crisis had an impact on U.S. investments in other Latin American or Asian markets.

5.1.5 Conclusions

Despite the acceleration in cross-border equity flows during the 1990s, the internationalization of capital markets is in fact only in its infancy. Of the total volume of global equity flows, only a fraction represents a net shift of capital investment from capital-rich to capital-poor regions of the world. There remains substantial home bias in the portfolios of investors in the wealthiest countries, suggesting that there also remain substantial gains from global diversification. Market reforms and the privatization of state- and family-owned enterprises in Europe, Asia, and Latin America are just beginning to take hold. For virtually all countries, the gains from increased access to international capital markets are sizable.

The recent crisis in Asia and its "contagious spread" to eastern Europe, Latin America, and possibly the United States has caused some economists and policymakers to question the benefits of globally integrated financial markets. Ironically, after decades of progress in dismantling capital controls, barriers to international capital flow have again become fashionable under the guise of restoring global economic order. While these policies may, in some circumstances, delay the swift transmission of economic crises, the chief consequence of capital controls will be to deny firms, individuals, and governments access to much needed capital for investment and growth. A better response to global uncertainty is to adopt policies that will strengthen domestic institutions, create greater transparency on the part of borrowers, and facilitate coordination among national governments.

References

Baxter, Marianne, and Urban Jermann. 1997. The international diversification puzzle is worse than you think. *American Economic Review* 87:170–80.
Baxter, Marianne, Urban Jermann, and Robert King. 1995. Non-traded goods, non-traded factors and non-diversification. Charlottesville: University of Virginia. Working paper.
Board of Governors of the Federal Reserve System. Various years. *Flow of funds accounts of the United States, flows and outstandings.* Washington, D.C.: Board of Governors of the Federal Reserve System.

Bohn, Henning, and Linda L. Tesar. 1996. U.S. equity investment in foreign markets: portfolio rebalancing or return chasing? *American Economic Review: Papers and Proceedings* 86 (2): 77–81.

———. 1997. The U.S. international investment portfolio and mean-variance optimization. Santa Barbara: University of California. Working paper.

———. 1999. U.S. portfolio investment in Asian capital markets. In *Managing capital flows and exchange rates: Perspectives from the Pacific Basin,* ed. R. Glick. New York: Cambridge University Press, forthcoming.

Bonser-Neal, C., G. Brauer, R. Neal and S. Wheatley. 1990. International investment restrictions and closed end country fund prices. *Journal of Finance* 45:523–48.

Calvo, G., L. Leiderman, and C. Reinhart. 1993. Capital flows and the real exchange rate appreciation in Latin America: The role of external factors. *IMF Staff Papers* 40 (1): 108–51.

———. 1996. Inflows of capital to developing countries in the 1990s. *Journal of Economic Perspectives* 10 (2): 123–39.

Claessens, S., and M. Rhee. 1993. The effects of equity barriers on foreign investment in developing countries. NBER Working Paper no. 4579. Cambridge, Mass.: National Bureau of Economic Research.

Cochrane, James L., James E. Shapiro, and Jean E. Tobin. 1995. Breaking down the barriers separating supply and demand. NYSE Working Paper no. 95-04. New York: New York Stock Exchange.

Cooper, Ian A., and Evi Kaplanis. 1994. Home bias in equity portfolios, inflation hedging and international capital market equilibrium. *Review of Financial Studies* 7: 45–60.

Europe's fund phobia. 1997.*Economist,* 29 March.

French, K., and J. Poterba. 1991. Investor diversification and international equity markets. *American Economic Review* 31:222–26.

Gehrig, T. 1993. An information based explanation of the domestic bias in international equity investment. *Scandinavian Journal of Economics* 1:97–109.

Grubel, H. G. 1968. Internationally diversified portfolios. *American Economic Review* 58:1299–1314.

Heaton, John, and Deborah Lucas. 1997. Savings behavior and portfolio choice: Which risks matter? Evanston, Ill.: Northwestern University. Working paper.

IMF (International Monetary Fund). 1996. *Balance of payments statistics yearbook.* Washington, D.C.: International Monetary Fund.

———. 1997. *International financial statistics,* annual issue. Washington, D.C.: International Monetary Fund.

Investment Company Institute. 1997. *The mutual fund fact book.* New York: Investment Company Institute.

Levy, H., and M. Sarnat. 1970. International diversification of investment portfolios. *American Economic Review* 50:668–75.

Longin, Francois, and Bruno Solnik. 1995. Is the correlation in international equity returns constant: 1960–1990? *Journal of International Money and Finance* 14 (1): 3–26.

McLiddon, Michael P. 1996. *Privatization and capital market development.* Westport, Conn.: Praeger.

Morgan, Donald P. 1994. Will the shift to stocks and bonds by households be destabilizing? Kansas City: Federal Reserve Bank of Kansas City.

Mutual funds: Savers flock to put cash into America's unit trusts. 1996. *Financial Times,* 6 June.

Pappas, Milton. 1997. United States long-term portfolio investment abroad. A special report on the Outbound Portfolio Investment Survey. Washington, D.C.: Department of the Treasury.

Rowland, Patrick F., and Linda L. Tesar. 1998. The gains from international diversification revisited. Ann Arbor: University of Michigan. Working paper.
Tesar, Linda L. 1995. Evaluating the gains from international risksharing. *Carnegie-Rochester Conference Series on Public Policy* 42:95–143.
Tesar, Linda L., and Ingrid M. Werner. 1992. Home bias and the globalization of securities markets. NBER Working Paper no. 4218. Cambridge, Mass.: National Bureau of Economic Research.
———. 1995. Home bias and high turnover. *Journal of International Money and Finance* 14 (4): 467–92.

2. René M. Stulz

International Portfolio Flows and Security Markets

For most of the period following World War II, the economic significance of net capital flows was small and net portfolio flows were even less important (see Feldstein and Horioka 1980). Over recent years, net capital flows have become much larger, especially to developing economies. Net portfolio flows are now a major component of net capital flows. Table 5.12 gives various estimates of the main components of net capital flows for developing countries. From 1977 to 1982, average annual net cumulative portfolio flows to developing countries were negative (−$10.5 billion). In contrast, in the year before the Mexican crisis, net portfolio investment of $85.8 billion exceeded net foreign direct investment of $76.3 billion. After recovering from the Mexican crisis, net portfolio investment fell again with the Asian crisis. Net portfolio flows turned negative for Asian developing countries, but they were not as important in the 1990s for these countries as they were for Latin America. To find a period in history when net capital flows were possibly as important as in the 1990s, one has to go back to the beginning of this century. Strikingly, however, while net flows were comparable to the recent experience before World War I, there are two important differences. First, to use the expression coined by Eichengreen and Fishlow, the current era is the "era of equity finance," which started at the end of the 1980s when "an unprecented volume and share of capital flows to developing countries began to take the form of equity purchases by individual investors . . . through their institutional representatives" (1998, 24). Second, gross flows are dramatically larger today than ever before. A good example of this is the turnover in foreign exchange markets which exceeds one trillion dollars a day (Bordo, Eichengreen, and Kim 1998).

Part of this paper was written while the author was a Bower Fellow at the Harvard Business School. The author is grateful for comments from Warren Bailey, Geert Bekaert, Cam Harvey, Martin Feldstein, Anthony Richards, Linda Tesar, Ingrid Werner, an anonymous referee, and conference participants.

Table 5.12   Capital Flows to Developing Countries (billions of U.S. dollars)

A. Net Capital Flows to Developing Countries, 1977–94 (yearly average)

	1977–82	1983–89	1990–94
Total net capital flows	30.5	8.8	104.9
Net direct investment	11.2	13.3	39.1
Net portfolio investment	−10.5	6.5	43.6
Other	29.8	−11.0	22.2

B. Net Private Capital Flows to Emerging Markets

	1994	1995	1996	1997	1998[a]
Net private capital flows	133.6	147.3	190.9	131.8	87.6
Net direct investment	76.3	86.3	108.6	126.7	106.2
Net portfolio investment	85.8	22.2	52.5	51.8	38.0
Other net investment	−28.6	38.8	29.7	−46.6	−56.6

C. Net Private Capital Flows to Asia

	1994	1995	1996	1997	1998[a]
Net private capital flows	64.8	91.7	100.2	21.5	−18.3
Net direct investment	44.4	51.0	60.2	60.2	45.1
Net portfolio investment	11.5	10.0	10.1	7.5	−6.5
Other net investment	9.0	30.8	29.9	−46.3	−56.9

Sources: Panel A, Folkerts-Landau and Ito (1995); panels B and C, IMF, World Economic Outlook and International Capital Markets (Washington, D.C., 1998).
[a]Numbers are estimates.

The increased relevance of net portfolio flows results first and foremost from the liberalization of financial markets in developing economies. This liberalization made it possible for investors from developed countries to invest in many emerging markets where previously they could not invest. As part of the liberalization, many countries engaged in large-scale privatization programs that increased the supply of equity from these countries. Even if investors from developed countries had kept their share of the capitalization of emerging equity markets constant, large capital flows would have taken place because of the increased capitalization of the emerging markets in which investors could buy securities as a result of the opening of markets and of privatization programs. However, investors also increased their share of the capitalization of emerging equity markets. The scope for further liberalization and privatization programs has narrowed, but large capital flows could result from increases in portfolio allocations to emerging markets. Currently, investors in major developed countries invest less than 1 percent of their assets in emerging markets. A 1 percent increase in this allocation corresponds to net capital flows of more than $120 billion.

Net portfolio flows should lower the cost of capital in many countries and facilitate the flow of capital to firms and countries that have the best investment opportunities irrespective of their locations. Overall, net portfolio flows should therefore be an engine of worldwide growth. This should be even more so because portfolio investments subject firms and countries to the discipline of capital markets. To attract and keep portfolio investments, firms and countries have to behave so as to maximize the value of these investments and are punished when they do not. As a result, firms and countries have greater incentives to invest efficiently. These arguments in favor of unrestrained portfolio flows are powerful, but many argue that they are flawed because investors are sometimes moved by "animal spirits" rather than rational thinking, so that portfolio flows have a dark side that can destabilize countries and reduce growth. The large net capital flows of the 1990s and the concomitant increase in the role of international investors in developing countries have led many to reconsider the benefits and costs of net portfolio inflows with some urgency.

The Mexican crisis has been an important cause of this reconsideration. It prompted many to worry about the stability of portfolio investments. Contrasting the Mexican crisis to the debt crisis of the early 1980s highlights why sudden changes in portfolio flows might be a source of concern. With the debt crisis, there were few key players in developed countries, their claims were illiquid, and they had strong incentives to work out solutions with the developing countries. With the Mexican crisis, coordination among portfolio investors was impossible. Even though collectively investors might have been better off committing funds to the Mexican government to resolve the crisis, individually each investor was better off selling out and could do so quickly because he was holding liquid securities. A number of economists have therefore argued that financing a country's growth through portfolio investment can expose it to sudden inflows and outflows that can destabilize an otherwise sound economy, force it into dramatic macroeconomic adjustments, and wreak havoc in its security markets. After worrying about the insufficient economic importance of net capital flows, some economists now worry that there might be too much portfolio investment. Sachs, Tornell, and Velasco aptly summarized this concern: "In today's world of fickle private capital movements, it is argued, large inflows leave a country exposed to the latest mood of Wall Street traders" (1996, 171). This leads economists such as Williamson to say that they "would not urge complete liberalization prior to (a) evidence that . . . controls have become completely ineffective (and hopelessly corrupting), or (b) the assurance that inflows will not be excessive" (1993, 14).

The Asian crisis has added fuel to this growing reconsideration of the benefits of capital flows. For instance, Stiglitz (1998) called for greater regulation of capital flows, arguing that "developing countries are more vulnerable to vacillations in international flows than ever before." Radelet and Sachs (1998) attributed the crisis to panic from foreign investors. Krugman (1998) summarized his view on the impact of capital flows in the East Asian crisis as follows:

"What turned a bad financial situation into a catastrophe was the way a loss of confidence turned into self-reinforcing panic. In 1996 capital was flowing into emerging Asia at the rate of about $100 billion a year; by the second half of 1997 it was flowing out at about the same rate. Inevitably, with that kind of reversal Asia's asset markets plunged, its economies went into recession, and it only got worse from there." He then went on to argue that the solution is to impose currency controls, finishing with an apocalyptic description of what would happen without them: "But if Asia does not act quickly, we could be looking at a true Depression scenario—the kind of slump that 60 years ago devastated societies, destabilized governments, and eventually led to war."

In this paper, we examine these concerns about the implications of net portfolio flows in light of the existing empirical evidence and theories of international portfolio investment. In section 5.2.1 we evaluate the impact of liberalization on equity valuations and on the cost of capital. In section 5.2.2 we address the issue of cross-country comovement in valuations and examine whether there is contagion in international financial markets. In section 5.2.3 we consider whether net portfolio flows can drive valuations away from fundamentals and make asset prices more volatile. Section 5.2.4 attempts to provide an assessment of the net benefits of openness to portfolio investment.

5.2.1   Capital Market Liberalization and Equity Valuations

The past twenty-five years in international capital markets have seen the dismantling of the restrictions on capital flows resulting from the two world wars. At the end of World War II, capital markets were essentially completely segmented. Because of restrictions on capital flows, investors mostly held assets from their home countries. International investment took the form of official capital flows. Some restrictions were soon lifted as currencies became convertible, but other restrictions were added periodically as governments in many countries tried to direct economic activity by reducing the role of markets. Since the 1970s, most of these restrictions have been removed. First, the markets of developed economies were deregulated. Countries removed obstacles to exchange rate transactions, agreed to tax agreements that reduced obstacles to international investment, and eliminated restrictions on foreign ownership that were often binding. Developing countries started to deregulate later than the developed countries, and many such countries have only taken timid steps in that direction. Nevertheless, many of these countries have eliminated obstacles to capital flows and promoted equity market deregulation actively.

Though economists in general are enthusiastic about the benefits of free trade in goods, they often seem surprisingly reluctant in their assessment of the gains from free trade in securities. For instance, Bhagwati (1998) stated: "This is a seductive idea: freeing up trade is good, why not also let capital move freely across borders? But the claims of enormous benefits from free capital mobility are not persuasive. . . . It is time to shift the burden of proof from those who oppose to those who favor liberated capital."[1] This is surprising because a country cannot take full advantage of the benefits of free trade in goods without full capital mobility. Capital mobility allows a country to produce more efficiently and enables the residents to bear fewer of the risks associated with domestic production. To understand these two effects of capital mobility, we consider a country with no capital flows that, for the sake of illustration, has a well-defined comparative advantage in producing coffee beans. We then consider the impact on that country of capital flow liberalization.

In the absence of capital flows, a country cannot have net trade flows. Consequently, residents have to bear all the country's risks. If they produce only coffee beans, any shock to the price at which they can sell coffee beans affects the country's income in direct proportion to the size of the crop. Any damage to the crop also affects the country's income directly. Since the price of coffee beans is quite volatile and crop yields can vary unexpectedly, the country's income would be quite volatile if it devoted all its resources to producing coffee beans. To avoid this volatility, the only solution in the absence of capital flows is to diversify production. This means that the country produces other goods even though it is less efficient at doing so. In the interest of smoothing its income, the country therefore limits the extent to which it takes advantage of the benefits of international trade.

In a country with a market economy, the channel through which production will be directed away from the coffee bean industry is the stock market. In the stock market, investors are rewarded for bearing risk with a risk premium. A stock's risk premium is the expected return of the stock in excess of the return of an investment that has no risk. For instance, the average annual risk premium on the U.S. stock market from 1926 to 1990 was 6.1 percent. Because coffee bean production leads to volatile returns, investors require a high risk premium to invest in that industry and a lower risk premium to invest in industries that provide diversification from the coffee bean industry. As a result, industries that provide diversification from the coffee bean industry are able to obtain capital at low cost. They can promise lower returns to investors because investing in them reduces portfolio volatility. The low cost of capital in industries that allow investors to diversify the return on their investments makes it possible for these industries to compete successfully against imports. As a result of this diversification effect, the country produces in industries for which it does not have a comparative advantage.

Consider now the impact on that country of allowing unrestricted capital flows and assume that there is no dark side to capital flows. Immediately, as investors learn that capital flows will be allowed, the risk premium in the coffee bean industry falls. As investors throughout the world invest in the country's coffee bean

---

1. Even before the recent crises, prominent economists advocated various kinds of taxes to limit international trade in securities in order to decrease speculative capital flows. See Summers and Summers (1989) and Tobin (1978).

production, they find that good events in that industry mostly offset bad events in their portfolios so that investing in coffee bean production actually reduces the risk of their portfolios. This means that the risks associated with coffee bean production are largely diversifiable internationally, so that the world capital markets require a much smaller risk premium to bear such risks and might require no risk premium at all. As the risk premium for the coffee bean industry falls, the country invests more in that industry. Simultaneously, the local industries that helped residents diversify their coffee bean production risks no longer offer that benefit to residents since residents can diversify internationally. Consequently, these industries may well contemplate an increase in their cost of capital and decreased investment. Once this process is completed, the country might specialize in the industry for which it has a comparative advantage.

We have shown that capital market liberalization leads to a reallocation of capital across industries. Obstfeld (1994) showed that this is not the whole story. Because the risks of a country's production can be diversified internationally after capital market liberalization, production technologies that were too risky before liberalization become advantageous because their risks can be diversified internationally. Hence, if riskier technologies are those with higher expected output, liberalization makes it possible for a country to shift to riskier production technologies and hence experience higher growth.

To have a better understanding of the transition from complete segmentation to a completely open capital market, it is helpful to use a numerical example. Suppose a country specializes in coffee bean production, the average annual value of the crop is $1 billion, and the annual volatility is $400 million. This means that each year there is a 5 percent probability that the country's income is below $340 million (assuming that the value of the crop is normally distributed). The country therefore experiences high income volatility. To simplify the discussion, let's assume that all the income accrues to capital. Because of the high volatility, suppose that investors require a risk premium of 10 percent for investments in the coffee bean industry and that the risk-free interest rate is 10 percent. This means that domestic residents are willing to invest in the coffee bean industry only if they expect to earn 20 percent annually, the sum of the rate that they receive on investments without risk plus the risk premium. The only way they can expect to earn 20 percent annually by investing in coffee bean production is if the value of the industry is the present value of a cash flow stream of $1 billion a year discounted at the rate of 20 percent. Consequently, the value of the coffee bean industry is $5 billion. An industry whose cash flows do not move with the cash flows of the coffee industry would have little risk for an investor heavily invested in the coffee bean industry and that investor would require a low risk premium to invest in that industry. Hence, that industry could raise funds promising an expected return to investors close to 10 percent. A dollar of annual average income from that industry is therefore worth $10.

Consider now the impact of an extremely successful liberalization, so that the risk of the production of coffee becomes a risk diversified in portfolios throughout the world. The risk premium on the coffee industry almost disappears, so that the present value of the perpetuity of $1 billion is now close to $10 billion. In other words, liberalization has a dramatic effect on the equity market capitalization. At the same time, however, the diversifying industry might now face a risk premium of 5 percent, so that its cost of capital increases from 10 percent to 15 percent. A dollar of average income in that industry falls from $10 to slightly more than $6. As with trade liberalization, not everybody benefits from capital market liberalization. However, as with trade liberalization, those who gain can compensate those who lose in such a way that everybody is made better off.

The decrease in the cost of capital has three effects on the coffee industry. First, it increases the value of the expected cash flows from existing investments since these expected cash flows are discounted at a lower rate. Second, it makes investments profitable that were not profitable at the higher cost of capital. Thus there will be an investment boom in the coffee industry. The third effect is that new investors will come to the industry and monitor firms in that industry.[2] These investors will have new ideas and will want to influence the actions of firms to make sure that their investments are profitable. Foreign investors will therefore improve corporate governance in the coffee industry, which will increase the value of the industry.

Our analysis of opening up security markets in a country has four empirical implications: (1) foreign investors acquire domestic securities; (2) domestic valuations increase; (3) the cost of capital falls; and (4) growth increases. We now consider the empirical evidence on these four implications. We focus on capital account liberalizations in developing economies both because of their intrinsic interest and because they constitute well-defined events.

Liberalization and Foreign Investment

Our analysis of liberalization assumes that foreign investors invest in the liberalized market rapidly. If this does not happen, no risk sharing takes place and asset prices do not increase. It is well known that holdings of foreign securities are small within portfolios of investors in developed countries.[3] Consequently, most of a developed country's equity is held by domestic residents. For instance, according to the NYSE 1996 fact book, foreigners held about 6 percent of U.S. equity at the end of the third quarter of 1996 (NYSE 1997, 59). This so-called home bias in portfolios implies that, even though portfolio flows have been large, domestic investors still have to bear a large fraction of the risks associated with domestic production. This limits the extent to which the cost of capital falls following liberalization.

Empirically, portfolio flows grow significantly as liberalization occurs. Kim

2. See Stulz (1999) for an analysis of the corporate governance benefits of globalization.
3. See Cooper and Kaplanis (1994), French and Poterba (1991), and Tesar and Werner (1994).

Table 5.13   Estimates of U.S. and Foreign Ownership for Selected
Emerging Markets

Country	U.S. Ownership (% of market capitalization)	Foreign Ownership (% of market capitalization)
Argentina	20	38
Brazil	6	–
Chile	4	17
Columbia	6	7
China	–	6
India	2	–
Indonesia	6	–
Malaysia	1	–
Mexico	21	25
Peru	–	38
Thailand	6	–
Venezuela	43	36

Source: Estimates of U.S. ownership are from Bekaert and Harvey (1999), who cumulate flow of funds data until the end of 1995. Estimates of foreign ownership are from Campollo-Palmer (1997).

and Singal (1993) documented that initially following liberalization there is a short period of net capital outflow, after which net capital flows turn positive and become large. This effect varies across countries. Liberalizations differ in degree across countries dramatically, so it is not surprising that foreign investors build larger stakes in some countries than in others. Table 5.13 provides estimates of U.S. equity investment and foreign equity investment in a number of emerging markets. For most countries, foreign ownership is difficult to estimate precisely. The table shows this vividly for Venezuela where the estimate of U.S. ownership exceeds the estimate of foreign ownership! Nevertheless, these numbers show that, on average, liberalization leads to substantial foreign equity holdings. These foreign equity holdings are generally large compared to foreign equity holdings in the United States. Consequently, the home bias has a somewhat different meaning for developing economies than for large developed economies. Because the capitalization of emerging markets is small, an investment corresponding to a small fraction of the capitalization of U.S. markets represents a large fraction of the capitalization of many emerging markets. One way to understand this is that in 1997 Bill Gates could have bought all the equity of Greece, Hungary, Jordan, Nigeria, Poland, Sri Lanka, Venezuela, and Zimbabwe—and would still have had $7 billion left to invest elsewhere.

Estimates of the Increase in Valuations Resulting from Liberalization

With our example, the capital market liberalization induces an increase in equity valuations and a decrease in the cost of capital, which leads to an increase in investment. Because of the home bias, the economic importance of these effects of liberalization is an empirical issue. It is relatively straightforward to look at stock market returns and evaluate whether they are unusually high at the time a country liberalizes. We will see that it is harder to figure out whether the cost of capital falls.

The large returns on emerging markets over the past fifteen years are well known. For instance, from December 1984 to December 1994 the real value of emerging market equity increased by 202 percent; in comparison, the S&P 500 increased by 93.5 percent. These large returns are in part responsible for the interest of portfolio managers in these markets. Since so many liberalizations took place during that period, the performance of emerging markets is consistent with the theoretical prediction of increases in equity valuations accompanying liberalization. However, stock market valuations are not affected by liberalization of capital flows only. Liberalization of capital flows is often accompanied by other events affecting the economy that liberalizes. For instance, the economy might have a new political regime that is market oriented and undertakes extensive domestic reforms that increase stock market valuations. Also, the performance of the stock market depends on how the economy is performing, so macroeconomic conditions have to be taken into account.

To assess the effect of liberalization on equity valuations, it is therefore important to pay close attention to other events that take place in the country that liberalizes its markets. This task is made more difficult by the fact that liberalization is rarely a one-shot event. Countries liberalize some aspects of their markets at one time and others at some other time. Henry (1999b) painstakingly identified individual economic reform and capital flow liberalization events that affected twelve emerging markets. Presumably, by the time the liberalization takes place, its effects are already incorporated in stock prices because investors have been aware of it for some time. It turns out that for the seven months preceding the first liberalization, equity returns are about 40 percent after adjusting for world market equity returns. However, once Henry (1999b) controlled for other events that affect these economies and for macroeconomic conditions, he concluded that the effect is on the order of 18 percent. He found an effect of 16 percent for subsequent liberalizations. This suggests a cumulative effect of about 37 percent.

The Impact of Liberalization on the Cost of Capital

The evidence of Henry (1999b) shows that capital flow liberalization has a large effect on equity valuations. In our earlier analysis, we argued that liberalization, by reducing the cost of capital, can have such an effect. The question that arises out of Henry's evidence is how large the impact of liberalization is on the cost of capital. Suppose that the reevaluation effect is 37 percent. In this case, the reevaluation takes $1 invested in a market and brings it to $1.37. This reevaluation captures all the effects of liberalization discussed earlier. Since the decrease in the cost of capital also makes new investments profitable, the

$.37 reevaluation is an upper bound on the impact of the decrease in the cost of capital. This upper bound implies that a country where the cost of capital for a project of typical risk was 20 percent now has a cost of capital of no less than 16.6 percent. In other words, the cost of capital of that country falls at most by 17 percent.

The sharp stock market increase associated with liberalization suggests that it might be straightforward to measure directly the impact of liberalization on the cost of capital. It turns out that this is not an easy task. The equity cost of capital is the expected return that investors anticipate from equity investments. As this cost falls, entrepreneurs can raise more funds for a project. Measuring the return that investors expect on equity is a difficult undertaking. One might be tempted to use past returns to forecast future returns. However, this strategy is not possible in the case of markets that undergo a liberalization. For such markets, the past returns are those appropriate for the segmented economy that no longer exists following liberalization. To complicate things further, past average returns for such markets are high for two reasons. First, segmented markets have higher risk premiums because domestic investors have to hold more domestic equity than they would in the absence of segmentation. Second, as discussed, liberalization boosts equity valuations as the cost of capital falls. Hence, the prospect of lower expected returns on equity has the paradoxical implication of increasing average returns on equity when measured over the liberalization period. This is because the expected cash flows on equity are discounted at a lower rate.

A second strategy to estimate the change in the cost of capital is to assume that following liberalization the expected return is determined by how the risk of equity is priced in global markets. To do this, one has to posit a model of how risk is priced in global markets and one has to assume that this model applies to equities of liberalized markets. For such an approach to make sense, one has to believe that it is reasonable to treat the world as if liberalized markets form one big market where capital flows freely across markets to equalize risk-adjusted returns. To proceed further, we therefore have to consider whether it is reasonable to think of the world of liberalized markets as one big market.

If investors can move capital freely across countries, they can diversify their portfolios internationally. This means that risks that are specific to small countries typically do not matter much in their portfolios. If their investments in one small country do poorly because of events specific to that country, their investments in another small country might be doing well. On balance, therefore, these risks offset each other. By diversifying internationally, investors can form a portfolio that has a lower volatility for a given expected return. Since investors would rather bear less risk than more, they should prefer this strategy. A reasonable measure of the gain that American investors can make by diversifying internationally was provided by DeSantis and Gerard (1997). They showed that as of 1994 a portfolio diversified internationally among ten major developed economies had the same volatility as a well-diversified portfolio of American equities but the annual expected return was higher by about 2.5 percent. Adding emerging markets to this portfolio would lead to further gains from diversification. For a portfolio to be well diversified internationally, however, its holdings have to be in the same proportions as the capitalization of securities from each country. A portfolio that holds the same proportion of the capitalization of each security in the world is called the world market portfolio. Hence, since emerging markets represent about 12 percent of world market capitalization, a well-diversified portfolio has an investment of about 12 percent in emerging markets.

An investor who holds a portfolio that is well diversified internationally measures the risk of a security by its contribution to the volatility of that portfolio. As the volatility of her portfolio increases, she bears more risk. Hence, she is only willing to hold a security that contributes significantly to the volatility of the portfolio if she receives enough of a reward in the form of a risk premium. A security contributes more to the volatility of her portfolio if that security moves more together with the other securities in the portfolio. Such a security has little diversification value since, if the portfolio performs poorly, that security is highly likely to perform poorly also. A security can have high volatility and yet have little co-movement with the portfolio. The investor will not be concerned about the volatility of such a security because most of the randomness of its return will be diversified away in the portfolio.

The part of the return of a security that cannot be diversified away is the part that moves with the return of the whole portfolio. Financial economists call this part of the return of a security its systematic risk. A simple model of the risk of securities in markets where capital flows freely is the international capital asset pricing model, which states that the return of a security in excess of the risk-free rate is equal to the systematic risk of that security times the risk premium on the world market portfolio.[4] The measure of the systematic risk of a security for a well-diversified investor is the degree to which it moves with the world market portfolio. For instance, if the world market portfolio has a 1 percent return, one can expect the U.S. market portfolio to have a 0.84 percent return while the Argentinian market portfolio is only expected to return 0.19 percent.[5] Consequently, the U.S. market portfolio has substantially more systematic risk than the market portfolio of Argentina and should earn a higher expected return. A security that covaries more with the world market portfolio must promise investors a higher expected return because it has more risk that investors cannot diversify away. With this model, the equity cost of capital is equal to the risk-free interest rate plus the systematic risk of the security times the risk premium of the world market portfolio. If we take the risk premium of the world market portfolio to be 6 percent, the Argentinian market portfolio

4. See Stulz (1995) for a detailed analysis of the theory and empirical tests of it.
5. These estimates are from Erb, Harvey, and Viskanta (1996).

would be expected to earn 1.14 percent in excess of the risk-free rate and the U.S. market portfolio 5.4 percent.

The international capital asset pricing model has been tested extensively with some degree of success, especially among developed countries. There is clear evidence that the returns of securities are related to their systematic risk. Countries whose markets covary more with the world market have higher equity returns on average, as predicted. At the same time, however, such a simple model has limitations. There are regularities that it cannot explain. For instance, it understates the required return from small firms and tends to overstate the required return from growth firms. Part of the difficulty for the model is that countries still have obstacles to capital flows. Nevertheless, the clear lesson from the empirical evidence is that, for countries whose capital markets are fairly open, the primary determinant of the valuation of securities is their risk as measured on international capital markets.

Like Argentina, most emerging markets have traditionally had little systematic risk. As these markets liberalize, the valuations of their securities are increasingly determined on international capital markets. As a result, valuations increase because the securities do not have much systematic risk. It is not the case, however, that these markets become completely integrated into world markets as soon as they liberalize. Liberalizations are generally partial, and there is always a risk that a country will adopt new restrictions on capital flows. Hence, the expected returns on emerging market common stocks are best described as a mix between expected returns determined on world markets and expected returns determined on local markets, with the mix changing over time.[6] If liberalizations were complete and credible and if there were no home bias, liberalizations would have a more dramatic effect on stock returns. Going back to our example where we argued that the empirical evidence suggests a fall in the cost of capital of 17 percent, one would expect the cost of capital to fall from 20 percent to about 10 percent rather than to 16.66 percent if the liberalized market became completely integrated into world capital markets. In this case, a liberalization would more than double equity valuations.

Bekaert and Harvey (1999) proposed a third approach to investigate the impact of liberalization on the cost of capital. They argued that the ratio of the dividend to the share price is a good proxy for the cost of capital. They then investigated how this proxy changes as a country liberalizes. Generally, they found that liberalization decreases the cost of capital by a relatively small amount (less than 100 basis points). Compared with the predictions one obtains from the applying the international capital asset pricing model, the estimates of Bekaert and Harvey (1999) are surprisingly small. Though the estimates implied by the work of Henry (1999b) are somewhat larger, they are also small compared to the predictions from the international capital asset pricing model. A plausible explanation is that the impact of liberalization on the

---

6. See Bekaert and Harvey (1995) for a model of how this mix changes over time.

cost of capital is limited because of the extent of home bias. If foreign investors do not buy the equity of liberalized countries, the cost of capital for that country does not decline.[7]

One last point should be made. As investors become better able to diversify their portfolios internationally, they bear less risk. If investors require more compensation to bear more risk, this means that the compensation for risk falls. Hence, greater globalization of capital markets implies a fall in the cost of capital everywhere because the risk premium on the world market portfolio falls.

The Impact on Growth

From our analysis, liberalization decreases the cost of capital. This should lead to an increase in growth because investment projects that were not advantageous before liberalization become advantageous afterward. Henry (1999a) provided direct evidence on this issue. He showed that liberalization induces an increase of 23 percent in private investment the year following liberalization and an increase of 24 percent the year after that. He also found that his estimate of the stock market effect of liberalization helps predict the increase in investment following liberalization.

We have seen that globalization increases stock market valuations, increases growth, and increases welfare. The question we have to address is whether there is a dark side of globalization that negates or even dwarfs these positive effects. We have proceeded as if capital markets work efficiently in allocating capital to its best uses. Instead, those concerned about capital flows are likely to believe Bhagwati's argument that "only an untutored economist will argue that, therefore, free trade in widgets and life insurance policies is the same as free capital mobility. Capital flows are characterized, as the economic historian Charles Kindleberger of the Massachusetts Institute of Technology has famously noted, by panics and manias" (1998, 8). The panics and manias are generally presumed to translate into contagion effects and volatility effects of capital flows. We therefore investigate the concerns about contagion in the next section and those about volatility in section 5.2.3.

5.2.2   How Do Changes in One Market Affect Other Markets?

With free capital flows, markets are connected. Investors who think that one market will have higher returns can move their investments to that market. Some have argued that this connection implies that markets move together more than they would if they were segmented. As investor sentiment changes in one large country, they argue, this change affects stock returns throughout the world irrespective of fundamentals. This view suggests that stock moves

---

7. See Stulz (1999) for a simple model showing the relation between the cost of capital impact of liberalization and the extent of home bias.

are contagious. To evaluate this claim, it is important to understand what moves stock prices. In section 5.2.1 we thought of stock prices as the present value of cash flows. Consequently, stock prices can change because expected cash flows change or because of changes in discount rates. The discount rate is the risk-free rate plus a risk premium. This means that the discount rate can change because of interest rates or risk premiums.

In global markets, the risk premium is determined globally. For instance, the risk premium on U.S. stocks is not determined in the United States alone. Chan, Karolyi, and Stulz (1992) documented that the risk premium on U.S. stocks and the risk premium on Japanese stocks are clearly connected, so that changes in the risk premium on Japanese stocks also affect the risk premium on U.S. stocks. This effect naturally induces co-movements in stock prices across the world, and it does not imply that investors are irrational or that stock prices disregard economic fundamentals. It does mean, however, that U.S. stock prices can change in circumstances where, if the United States were an isolated country, they would not change. We now examine stock price co-movements and whether they have changed as capital flows became less restricted.

Have Co-movements Increased over Time?

Much of the analysis of stock price co-movements has focused on one measure of co-movement, namely, the correlation of stock returns, which takes values between -1 and $+1$. Typically, well-diversified portfolios of U.S. stocks have a correlation close to one. Historically, however, correlations of foreign indexes with the U.S. market have been small, especially for emerging markets, where they often have been indistinguishable from zero. At the same time, though, these correlations change over time. This makes it difficult to figure out whether correlations are greater now than they used to be. This task is further complicated by the fact that these correlations are not well understood. Although many authors have tried to construct models that explain how they change over time and how they differ across countries, this literature has had little success. Table 5.14 provides a comparison of correlations of stock markets with the world market portfolio over two periods. One period is the sample period for which returns were available. The other period corresponds to the first five years of the 1990s (April 1990 to March 1995). Correlations have changed, but some increased and others decreased. The average correlation is .35 for the whole sample period and .41 for 1990–95. Hence, on average, correlations increased, but not by much. Many recent papers have looked at the issue of whether correlations have increased over time using sophisticated statistical techniques.[8] There is evidence of an increase in correlations, but the extent of this increase differs across studies and some studies do not report an increase. One important issue that affects the conclusions of the ex-

---

8. See Karolyi and Stulz (1996) for references.

Table 5.14   **Correlations between Countries and the World Market Portfolio (MSCI)**

			Correlation	
Country	Source	Sample Start	Full Sample	April 1990–March 1995
Argentina	IFC	October 1979	−0.01	0.12
Australia	MSCI	October 1979	0.52	0.49
Austria	MSCI	October 1979	0.30	0.54
Belgium	MSCI	October 1979	0.62	0.72
Brazil	IFC	October 1979	0.09	0.19
Canada	MSCI	October 1979	0.69	0.55
Chile	IFC	October 1979	0.07	0.12
China	IFC	April 1993	0.05	0.05
Colombia	IFC	October 1985	0.06	0.08
Denmark	MSCI	October 1979	0.51	0.63
Finland	MSCI	April 1988	0.47	0.51
France	MSCI	October 1979	0.65	0.73
Germany	MSCI	October 1979	0.56	0.66
Greece	IFC	October 1979	0.17	0.18
Hong Kong	MSCI	October 1979	0.43	0.47
Hungary	IFC	April 1993	0.45	0.45
India	IFC	October 1979	−0.05	−0.16
Indonesia	IFC	October 1990	0.12	0.25
Ireland	MSCI	April 1988	0.69	0.77
Italy	MSCI	October 1979	0.47	0.44
Japan	MSCI	October 1979	0.74	0.83
Jordan	IFC	October 1979	0.13	0.20
Malaysia	IFC	October 1985	0.41	0.47
Mexico	IFC	October 1979	0.24	0.29
Netherlands	MSCI	October 1979	0.75	0.77
New Zealand	MSCI	April 1988	0.39	0.56
Portugal	IFC	October 1986	0.41	0.62
Singapore	MSCI	October 1979	0.53	0.70
South Africa	IFC	April 1993	0.33	0.33
South Korea	IFC	October 1979	0.23	0.35
Spain	MSCI	October 1979	0.56	0.71
Sri Lanka	IFC	April 1993	0.01	0.01
Sweden	MSCI	October 1979	0.59	0.72
Switzerland	MSCI	October 1979	0.69	0.78
Taiwan	IFC	October 1985	0.22	0.33
Thailand	IFC	October 1979	0.27	0.34
Turkey	IFC	October 1987	0.06	0.05
United Kingdom	MSCI	October 1979	0.76	0.80
United States	MSCI	October 1979	0.77	0.70
Venezuela	IFC	October 1985	−0.08	−0.02
Zimbabwe	IFC	October 1979	0.08	0.11

Source: Erb, Harvey, and Viskanta (1996).

Note: IFC = International Finance Corporation. MSCI = Morgan Stanley Capital International.

isting studies is that some include the crash of 1987 and others do not. Over a short period of time in 1987, markets moved together by extremely large amounts. Including data from that period has the effect of increasing correlations. Hence one's conclusion about the evolution of correlations depends on whether or not one takes into account the crash. DeSantis and Gerard (1997) examined the correlation between the U.S. market and an equally weighted portfolio of nine other large developed markets. They used a statistical model to estimate monthly correlations. Their sample period was January 1970 through December 1994. The twenty lowest correlation estimates are all from before 1980. Sixteen of the twenty largest correlations are from after 1980. Their evidence shows that there is high correlation in periods of extremely low stock returns. Their average correlation is .56. However, the S&P 500 dropped by 29.42 percent from September to November 1987. They reported their highest correlation, .76, for that period. The second highest correlation they reported is during the period from January 1973 to September 1974, when the stock market dropped 45.06 percent. There is now considerable evidence that correlations are high in bear markets. It is difficult to attribute this to liberalization since correlations were high during the bear market of the 1970s also. This phenomenon creates concerns about the benefits of international diversification, however. Our analysis in section 5.2.1 argued that the benefit of international diversification is that some countries do well while others are doing poorly. If correlations are high during bear markets, this suggests that countries are more likely to do poorly at the same time, which reduces the benefits from international diversification.

What about correlations for emerging markets? In table 5.14 the average correlation for the emerging markets is .17 for the whole sample period, which is roughly half the average correlation for all countries and confirms that emerging markets have much lower correlations with the world market portfolio than developed economies. For 1990–95, the average correlation for the emerging markets is .22, which is still close to half the correlation for the whole sample. There is therefore an increase in correlations of emerging markets, but correlations among developed markets increased proportionally by roughly the same amount. In an interesting paper, DeSantis (1993) looked at the correlations of markets in the World Bank's emerging markets database over two periods. The first period was 1976–84 and the second 1984–92. He found that the average correlation is essentially the same for these two subperiods. Looking at the correlation of the United States with these markets, he found a slight increase. The average is a trivial .038 for the first subperiod and .132 for the second subperiod. The second subperiod contains the crash of 1987, however. Again, this evidence suggests a slight increase in correlations, but the increase seems slight enough that some might conclude there is no change. In a recent study, Bekaert and Harvey (1999) estimated a model that allows correlations between emerging markets and the world market to change over time. They then estimated correlations before and after liberalization. Out of seventeen emerging markets, they found the correlation with the world market to be higher for nine markets. This result seems to provide, at best, weak evidence that correlations increase after liberalization. We discuss below the increase in correlations during crisis periods. Adding the past two years, which correspond to a crisis period, to the samples of the studies discussed here would lead to higher correlation estimates.

Though there is little evidence of strong increases in equity return correlations before the Asian crisis, there is evidence of dramatic increases in correlations between bond yields. Goldstein and Folkerts-Landau (1994) provided correlations between ten-year yields in the seven largest developed economies and the U.S. ten-year bond yield. For the period 1970–79, the average monthly correlation excluding Canada is .41. This average correlation increases to .86 from 1980 to 1989 and to .88 from 1990 to 1994. Ilmanen (1995) showed evidence that there is a strong common factor in interest rate movements across developed countries. One view of this increase in correlations is that, as markets become more integrated, investors give little room to monetary authorities to pursue policies that lead to sharply divergent interest rate movements. It is unclear, however, why the growing integration of markets would affect nominal yields rather than expected real yields.

Is There Causation?

Many papers have been written trying to determine whether stock price changes in one market lead to stock price changes in another market. Initially, this research used monthly or weekly data. However, it quickly became apparent that such research is difficult to interpret. If prices adjust very quickly, there is little hope of finding relationships using infrequently measured data. If a shock to U.S. prices is transmitted to the rest of the world within twenty-four hours, this transmission is obscured by using monthly data. Weekly or monthly data might also yield spurious effects. Not all stocks trade frequently. Infrequent trading of some stocks can give the impression that one market leads another. To see this, suppose that the U.S. stock market drops by 20 percent during one month and one looks at whether this knowledge helps explain the return on foreign markets the following month. One would expect foreign stocks to fall contemporaneously to the extent that the U.S. stock market drop is brought about by some adverse event that affects the whole world. For instance, there could be bad news about the U.S. economy, which would reduce equity values throughout the world to some extent since firms would not be able to sell as much to the United States as expected. However, if some foreign stocks trade infrequently, the effect of bad news on their prices will be recorded only when they trade. Hence, if some foreign stocks do not trade when bad news occurs, they will record a drop subsequent to the drop in the United States, leading to the wrong impression that the U.S. drop caused the drop abroad, when in fact both drops were caused by the same bad news.

The difficulty of interpreting results using weekly and monthly returns has led to the use of data of much higher frequency. Some of this research focuses on returns for periods when stock markets are open and periods when they are closed. Other research measures returns over even shorter periods of time. The opening hours for the U.S. and Japanese stock markets do not overlap. Over a twenty-four hour period, the Japanese market opens first and closes before the U.S. stock markets ever open. Japanese returns contain information about U.S. stock returns because the markets are correlated. A rough estimate is that a 10 percent increase in Japanese markets on average corresponds to a 3 percent increase in U.S. markets. However, all the information contained in the Japanese return during trading hours should be incorporated in U.S. stock prices at the time that the market opens in the United States. This means that the 10 percent Japanese market increase of our example should have no information about the U.S. market return during the U.S. trading day. The evidence is that most of the effect of the 10 percent Japanese market increase will be incorporated in U.S. stock prices by the time the market opens.

This research has also examined whether unexpected increases in volatility spill over across markets. The question asked is whether unexpectedly high volatility in the United States, when the U.S. market is open, leads to high volatility in Japan. This seems to be the case. It seems further that this effect is symmetric across the world: unexpected volatility in the United States leads to higher volatility in Japan, and unexpected volatility in Japan leads to higher volatility in the United States. One might be tempted to attribute this volatility spillover to the increased flow of capital and hence to the greater connections across markets. However, this literature finds greater evidence of spillovers in data before the crash of 1987 than after. One possible explanation is that many of the spillover effects documented in the literature were spurious, resulting from infrequent trading. There is substantial evidence that since the crash information has been incorporated in prices much faster, at least in the United States.

The problem with both the return and the volatility evidence is that it is consistent with two hypotheses that have dramatically different implications for the efficiency of financial markets. One hypothesis is that the Japanese and U.S. markets have common components, and spillovers reflect these common components. Under this hypothesis, spillovers show that markets incorporate information efficiently. The second hypothesis is that spillovers are the work of uninformed investors who overreact to news in one market, corresponding to a change in sentiment.[9] They become more risk averse following bad news and less risk averse following good news, regardless of the fundamentals of their own market. With this view, there is contagion. The lack of spillover reversals is evidence against the uninformed investor hypothesis. Lin and Ito (1994) devised an additional test that makes it possible to distinguish between the two hypotheses. They pointed out that uninformed traders who become

9. De Long et al. (1990) developed a theory of uninformed investors moved by sentiment and showed that such investors can affect asset prices in equilibrium.

more or less risk averse trade to change their portfolios. Consequently, strong spillovers should be associated with high volume. They found no such evidence and argued that the evidence is more consistent with the view that markets impound information efficiently.

Contagion and Crises

We saw in the previous paragraph that there seems to be little evidence of contagion among developed markets under normal circumstances. However, we know that there are greater co-movements in bear markets. This could mean that there is contagion when it might be most damaging, namely, in periods of turmoil. There has been much discussion of contagion among emerging markets during the Mexican crisis and during the Asian crisis. Some have used this contagion to justify the help given to the Mexican government in 1994. For instance, Stanley Fischer states, "Of course, there was another justification: contagion effects. They were there and they were substantial" (quoted in Calvo, Goldstein, and Hochreiter 1997). Table 5.15 shows the performance of some emerging markets during January 1995. During that period, the markets performed poorly. Further, as documented in Calvo and Reinhart (1997), correlations among Latin American market equities and Brady bonds increased sharply around the crisis. Many have interpreted this as evidence of a contagion effect of the Mexican crisis. The view is that, as Mexico fell into its crisis, investors reassessed the prospects of emerging markets and grew pessimistic

Table 5.15   **Returns on Major Emerging Market Indexes during January 1995**

Country	Return (%)
Mexico	−22.2
Peru	−19.2
Brazil	−10.2
Chile	−6.9
Argentina	−5.8
Hungary	−21.1
Poland	−13
Turkey	−12.9
Pakistan	−13.4
Philippines	−13.2
China	−12.5
India	−12.2
Taiwan	−11.3
Hong Kong	−10.3
Thailand	−10.3
Malaysia	−9.2
Indonesia	−8.4
Singapore	−6.5
Sri Lanka	−2.3

Source: Khannah (1996).

even when there was no basis to do so. Flows to emerging markets slowed markedly immediately after the Mexican crisis, so that some have argued that this slowing was responsible for price drops. In the remainder of this section, we first discuss the economics of contagion and then examine some empirical evidence of the economic importance of contagion associated with the Mexican and Asian crises.

The traditional view of contagion has to do with banking panics. The idea is that a bank fails and depositors start withdrawing funds from other banks that are healthy, thereby weakening these banks. For emerging markets, the reasoning is similar, namely, that a shock in one market leads investors to withdraw funds from other markets because of irrational fears. It is certainly the case that some investors behaved that way. Stories of specific investors making obvious mistakes in their analysis of emerging markets have been repeated often.[10] Though such stories enliven conferences, they are irrelevant to an assessment of contagion. Market prices are the product of the actions of all investors, and the important question is whether aggregate outcomes are efficient. One would expect other investors to take advantage of the opportunities created by investors who panic. Hence, if there is plenty of arbitrage capital, contagion should not be a problem.

Unfortunately, the investment industry is organized in such a way that arbitrage capital to be used to take advantage of mispricings in emerging markets may be artificially scarce. Most investments in emerging markets are made by institutional investors. Typically, these investments are made because sponsors and clients designate emerging markets as an asset class in which they want to put funds. The investment industry responds to the demand for investment vehicles in an asset class by creating mutual funds and other investment vehicles. Consider now how institutional investors can react to lower stock prices brought about by panic selling from uninformed investors. Institutional investors who are not specialized in the emerging market asset class will find it difficult to suddenly start investing in emerging markets to take advantage of investment opportunities created by panicky investors. Institutional investors who are specialized in the asset class face a situation where their resources are weakened by the adverse shock that starts the contagion process and where they may find it difficult to liquidate assets to generate cash to exploit advantageous investment opportunities because of turmoil in the markets. Consequently, few institutional investors may be able to take advantage of the investment opportunities created by the actions of the uninformed investors. This lack of arbitrage capital creates a situation where valuations depend on the capital committed to an asset class and can create discrepancies between valuations across asset classes. For instance, Gompers and Lerner (1997) showed that valuations in the venture capital industry depend on the funds committed to the industry.

10. See, e.g., Wadhwani's comment in Calvo et al. (1997).

Institutional investors specialized in emerging markets face an additional problem that further limits their ability to take advantage of investment opportunities during periods of turmoil, namely, withdrawals of funds by clients. Shleifer and Vishny (1997) cogently argued that clients of institutional investors may not be able to easily assess whether an investment strategy is right and may therefore use short-term returns to guide their investment decisions. For instance, it may be quite difficult for the typical pension fund organization to assess the performance of an asset manager specialized in emerging markets. The manager may have a solid economic argument that explains why current valuations are too low and the best solution is to keep the portfolio unchanged. However, the client may find it difficult to assess whether this argument is correct and may simply change her allocation of funds to the manager based on his recent performance. Consequently, an institutional investor who thinks that stock prices are too low in a particular country may not be able to act on his judgment if his portfolio has done poorly because funds are being withdrawn. In fact, institutional investors may be forced by circumstances to aggravate the contagion rather than exploit it. Facing redemptions, they may have to liquidate assets in healthy countries because those markets are liquid and may therefore adversely affect capital flows in these countries. What creates the contagion in this case, however, is not an excess of speculative capital. Rather, it is that an insufficient amount of arbitrage capital is devoted to an asset class. The contagion arises because of a lack of investors who can provide liquidity to the institutional investors forced to withdraw from a country. Hence, leaders of emerging countries should not complain about the actions of hedge fund managers but rather should complain that there are too few hedge funds. As more institutional investors become authorized to shift funds between developed and emerging markets and across emerging markets, the possibility of contagion induced by forced liquidations of some institutional investors should disappear.

Contagion caused by panicky investors and forced liquidations is self-limiting in equity markets. As prices fall, it becomes more advantageous to hold on to an investment rather than liquidate it. However, in debt markets, the situation is more delicate for those who rely on short-term debt. If investors are reluctant to roll the debt over, promising higher yields may not solve the problem because these higher yields may imply too high a probability of default. As a result, a country or a firm might face a liquidity crisis and be forced to decrease investment because it was cut off from public markets. Obviously, firms and countries that find themselves in such situations chose an imprudent financing policy. Financing with short-term debt amounts to betting that one's credit will not deteriorate. Sometimes it does. When it does, those that finance with short-term debt face problems whether the change in the perception of credit quality is driven by contagion or not. If the change in credit quality is driven by poor economic prospects for a firm or a country, it should contract investment. However, if economic fundamentals are solid, contraction is not appropriate. Unfortunately, contagion can lead to costly liquidation of investments that represents a waste of resources.

When there are few creditors, they can get together and realize that the appropriate solution to a liquidity crisis is to restructure the debt. By doing this, the creditors make it more likely that they will be paid back. When the number of creditors is large, this coordination is no longer possible. A provider of liquidity of last resort can solve the problem by providing temporary loans. However, the existence of such a provider may lead to the problem in the first place. In the absence of such a provider, different funding strategies would be used to reduce the risk of a liquidity crisis. The existence of a provider of liquidity of last resort may also aggravate contagion. Presumably, the provider has limited resources; if these resources are deployed to help one country, they are not available to other countries. Consequently, a crisis in one country reduces the credit of other countries that might need the help of the provider of liquidity of last resort.

Empirical evidence derived by Calvo and Reinhart (1997) shows that the capital accounts of developing economies are negatively related to the U.S. ex post real rate of interest. This shows that there is a common factor in these capital accounts. The existence of common factors is not, however, evidence of irrational contagion. In the absence of a careful model that shows what the capital accounts of these economies would be in the absence of contagion, there is no way that correlations among capital accounts caused by the existence of common factors can be attributed to contagion. For instance, historically the U.S. stock market increases when interest rates fall. It could be perfectly rational for U.S. investors to invest more in developing economies when their wealth increases.

Contagion does not require changes in capital flows to sharply decrease the value of financial assets. This is because public information affects stock prices without trades in stocks. To see this, consider the Mexican crisis. All investors could observe the events taking place. When an adverse event has taken place, investors will not buy stocks at the prices prevailing before the event. On average, one would expect the price of the first trade taking place after the event to incorporate the information revealed by the event. At the very least, equity prices would reflect the event very quickly, and there is no reason for massive sales to take place for equity prices to reach their new value. If the stock price adjustment process is quick, it is very difficult to find evidence that information in one country caused markets in other countries to change value irrespective of fundamentals by trying to show that the change in one country preceded the other.

The literature often defines contagion to be an increase in correlations among country indexes in periods of crisis. The reasoning is that correlations among country indexes in noncrisis periods reflect fundamentals, so that if correlations during crisis periods are higher, this must reflect contagion. Rigobon (1998) showed why this reasoning is wrong. Correlations among security returns naturally increase when the volatility of a common factor that influences stock returns increases. For instance, if country indexes are related to the world market index, an increase in the volatility of the world market index implies that country indexes become more correlated with the world market index. Hence, comparing correlations among indexes for periods of different volatility would necessarily lead to the result that correlations are higher when volatility is higher. Consequently, higher correlations during crisis periods do not mean contagion. Forbes and Rigobon (1998) estimated correlation increases during the Mexican and Asian crises taking into account the natural increase in correlations during periods of high volatility. Using traditional estimates of correlations, they found that the correlation between Hong Kong and Australia was .356 during a period of stability and .865 during the Asian crisis period. The increase in correlation is statistically significant. Adjusting for the impact of the increase in volatility, they found the correlation during the crisis period between Hong Kong and Australia to be .561 rather than .865, and the correlation increase is not statistically significant. Looking at many countries, they found the same pattern, namely, statistically significant contagion when the estimate of the correlation increase ignores the impact of the volatility increase and statistically insignificant contagion otherwise. They found similar results looking at the Mexican crisis. For instance, the correlation between Mexico and Argentina was .382 during a period of stability and .859 during the crisis period when one ignores the impact of the increase in volatility. However, taking into account the impact of the increase in volatility, the correlation during the crisis period was .500 and is not significantly greater than the correlation during the period of stability. The analysis of Forbes and Rigobon showed that one cannot argue that the increases in correlations observed during crisis periods are evidence of contagion.

Using daily stock returns does not provide statistically significant evidence of contagion. Often, higher frequency data lead to more powerful tests. A recent study by Bailey, Chan, and Chung (1997) investigated the relation between changes in the peso-dollar exchange rate at half-hourly intervals from 21 December 1994 to 30 April 1995 and the returns of Asian and Latin American American Depository Receipts (ADRs) on the NYSE and country funds on the same exchange. They estimated the relation between the half-hour change in a stock and the contemporaneous change in the peso exchange rate as well as the change in the previous half-hour. Not surprisingly, they found a strong contemporaneous relation between the Mexican ADRs and the peso exchange rate, as well as a strong lagged relationship. However, they also found that a depreciation of the peso during a half-hour has a significant adverse effect on non-Mexican Latin American ADRs for the same period as well as for the next period. Essentially, a 1 percent depreciation of the peso is associated with a negative return on non-Mexican Latin American ADRs of −0.15 percent.

There is no effect on Asian ADRs. Looking at closed-end funds, they found a small but significant effect of peso depreciation on Asian country funds and a stronger effect on non-Mexican Latin-American country funds. A 1 percent depreciation of the peso is estimated to reduce the value of Asian country funds by 0.03 percent and the value of non-Mexican Latin American country funds by 0.18 percent. They also explored the impact of the intensity of news announcements on the volatility of ADRs and country funds. Again, they found that non-Mexican Latin American ADRs and country funds experience larger absolute returns when there is news about Mexico during a half-hour.

The findings of Bailey et al. (1997) provide evidence of a tequila effect on the NYSE. Unfortunately, the paper did not attempt to assess how much of the effect is due to information effects and how much is explained by the panic of uninformed investors. Lin and Ito (1994) argued that contagion associated with stock price decreases implies that high correlations are associated with high volume because uninformed investors liquidate their positions. Bailey et al. (1997) provided evidence that can be used to check whether contagion due to uninformed investors was important. They showed that news about the Mexican peso and other Mexican news had a strong effect on the volume of Mexican ADRs and closed-end funds. However, the same news had little effect on the volume of non-Mexican ADRs and closed-end funds, whether they were Latin American or Asian. From 21 December 1994 to 30 April 1995, Mexican news explained 5 percent of the variation in Mexican ADR volume and 9 percent in Mexican closed-end funds volume. In contrast, it explained nothing of the variation in Asian ADR or closed-end fund volume. For Latin American ADR and closed-end funds, Mexican news explained 1.1 percent of the variation in the volume of closed-end funds and 0.3 percent of the variation in volume of ADRs. Though it may be that using different measurement intervals would lead to different conclusions, this evidence is more supportive of the view that Mexican events provided useful information to markets rather than the view that a stampede of uninformed investors harmed valuations by sudden excessive cautiousness.

Another way to consider the economic importance of contagion was provided by Sachs et al. (1996). They examined the reaction of twenty emerging countries to the Mexican crisis. They argued that countries that suffered significantly from the tequila effect were weak to start with, in that they suffered simultaneously from a weak banking sector, an overvalued currency, and low reserves. In such countries, withdrawals of capital by foreign investors adversely affected the currency and endangered the banking sector as the value of foreign-currency-denominated liabilities increased in domestic currency. They argued that in the countries that did not suffer from these problems, the "Tequila effect left no hangover" (Sachs et al. 1996, 193). They found, however, no additional explanatory power in the magnitude and composition of capital flows before the crisis. In other words, large net portfolio flows did not make a crisis more likely.

5.2.3 Flows and Asset Returns

In section 5.2.1 we saw that liberalization increases valuations and decreases the cost of capital. In section 5.2.2 we saw that there is little evidence of large increases in cross-country co-movements with liberalization and that, while co-movements are larger in bear markets, it is quite difficult to distinguish contagion effects from information effects based on evidence from stock returns. In this section, we address the issue of whether changes in valuations can be traced directly to flows. In other words, we try to understand how an additional dollar of flow affects valuations. This issue is at the heart of the concern of whether flows can push up equity prices irrationally only to bring them crashing when foreign capital withdraws unexpectedly. In this view, flows increase prices when they come in and decrease them when they leave. Further, they make prices more volatile because they come and go on a whim. From reading some commentators, it would seem that there is little debate about this issue. For instance, Dornbusch and Park argued that "there is ample evidence that financial market opening is likely to increase the volatility of asset prices" (1995, 39). The mechanism they had in mind is that foreign investors buy more as prices go up, engaging in what is called positive feedback trading. As they do this, prices keep increasing. Further, they also argued that the interest of foreign investors makes markets more liquid, thereby facilitating speculative trades.

A long tradition in financial economics argues that demand and supply shocks that do not convey information about fundamentals are unimportant. This tradition got its start with Scholes (1972). He showed very carefully that sales of large blocks of stocks have a negligible impact on the stock price when these trades are made purely for liquidity reasons. The reason is straightforward. If the equity of an individual firm becomes underpriced, investors can make money by buying it. Similarly, if equity is overpriced, those who own that equity can make money by selling it. Trades undertaken purely for liquidity reasons provide no information about the value of the equity for investors and hence do not change investors' assessment of the value of the equity. If investors suspect that a large trade is undertaken on the basis of information about the firm, then the large trade will naturally have an impact on the value of the equity as buyers will only buy at a price that protects them from the adverse information the seller has. In this view, the demand for securities is perfectly elastic at given prices as long as information about the securities does not change. This view implies that capital inflows or outflows have an impact on valuations only if they are undertaken because of information that foreign investors have that is not yet incorporated in prices.

Are there any reasons to suspect that foreign investors at times are better informed than domestic investors? This seems unlikely. As already mentioned, it is well known that investors do not take advantage of international diversification as much as simple models would suggest. There are many possible explanations for this phenomenon, but a leading one is that investors are less well informed about foreign securities than about securities of their own country. They are therefore concerned that when they buy equity from foreign investors, they buy the equity that foreign investors believe to be overvalued. A natural protection for investors who diversify internationally is therefore to invest in firms for which information is more easily available. Typically, large firms are the ones for which most information is available.

Unfortunately, data are lacking to test the hypothesis that foreign investors favor large firms. Japan seems to be the only country where data on holdings of equity by foreign investors are easily available at the firm level. Kang and Stulz (1997) demonstrated that foreign investors have a considerable bias toward large firm stocks in Japan. Dividing Japanese firms each year into five groups according to firm size, they found that foreign ownership in the smallest firms is 1.8 percent on average from 1975 to 1991; in contrast, ownership in the largest firms is 7.66 percent. This large difference in ownership between small and large firms is not completely attributable to the decrease in the information advantage of local investors as firm size increases. Most international investment is done by institutional investors. As reported by Falkenstein (1996), institutional investors prefer shares of large firms. These shares have lower transaction costs, are more liquid, and enable investors to make larger trades without affecting share prices. The overall preference of foreign investors for large firms suggests that large firms should have a lower cost of capital. For the case of Japan, Kang and Stulz (1997) found weak evidence that shares in which foreign investment is large have lower average returns.

The Mexican crisis offers another piece of evidence that foreign investors are at an information disadvantage. Whereas some have blamed foreign investors for Mexico's troubles, careful examination reveals quite a different story. Capital outflows from residents took place throughout 1994, following the assassination of the presidential candidate Colosio on 23 March 1994. In contrast, foreign investors were net buyers of Mexican equity even in December 1994.

Frankel and Schmukler (1996) found an interesting way to look at this issue. They investigated the returns of Mexican closed-end funds that trade in the United States. A closed-end fund typically trades at a price that differs from the value of the portfolio that it represents. The value of the underlying portfolio is called the net asset value (NAV) of the fund. Frankel and Schmukler (1996) reasoned that the price of a fund moves because of its U.S. investors whereas the NAV moves because of Mexican investors since the underlying portfolio is a portfolio of Mexican stocks that trade in Mexico City. They found that the NAV moves before the price of the fund and causes changes in the price of the fund. Their interpretation was that Mexico City moves Wall Street's assessment of Mexican stocks rather than the reverse.

If foreign investors are less well informed than domestic investors, they will be more sensitive than domestic investors to public announcements. First, public announcements are less likely to be news to domestic investors because they are insiders. Second, since foreign investors are less well informed, their assessment of a country is less precise and hence can be altered more by public information. This makes capital flows sensitive to news. Brennan and Cao (1997) modeled this phenomenon and provide supporting evidence. Note that this sensitivity to news implies behavior that is not too dissimilar to that discussed by Dornbusch and Park (1995). If investors react to news strongly, they buy when stock prices are increasing and sell when stock prices are falling. This makes capital flows correlated with contemporaneous returns. However, there seems to be no clear evidence in Brennan and Cao (1997) that investors practice a positive feedback trading strategy in that there is no evidence that high returns are followed by high flows rather than accompanied by high flows. Tesar and Werner (1993) also looked at the issue of the determinants of equity portfolio flows. Unfortunately, they only reported correlations. Nevertheless, their data set also provides evidence of a positive contemporaneous correlation between returns and flows for most Latin American countries and some Asian countries.

Several recent studies examined whether foreign investors are positive feedback traders, namely, whether they buy following positive returns and sell following negative returns. Bohn and Tesar (1996) found evidence of positive feedback trading using monthly data for a large number of countries. Using daily data of trades from the investors who use State Street Bank & Trust as their custodian, Froot, O'Connell, and Seasholes concluded that "there is very strong trend following in international inflows. The majority of the co-movement of flows and returns at quarterly intervals is actually due to returns predicting future flows" (1998, 18). Using data from Korea, Choe, Kho, and Stulz (1999) found strong evidence of positive feedback trading among foreign investors in that country in 1997. Surprisingly, however, the evidence of positive feedback trading is weak for the last three months of 1997 when the Asian crisis hit Korea. It seems implausible therefore that the trading practices of foreign investors had much impact on the crisis. Perhaps more important, positive feedback trading need not be destabilizing. For instance, if markets are slow to incorporate information into stock prices, positive returns can be expected to be followed by positive returns. Consequently, positive feedback trading is profitable, but investors who trade that way make markets more efficient rather than destabilizing them since they accelerate the incorporation of information into prices.

If domestic investors are better informed than foreign investors, they will hold more domestic shares on average. The reason is that foreign investors discount share prices relative to domestic investors since domestic investors tend to sell if they have adverse information that is not incorporated in asset prices. This means that foreign investors do not take as much advantage of international diversification as they would if all investors had the same information. This home bias resulting from information asymmetries implies that the cost of capital in the domestic country is higher than it would be in the absence of these asymmetries because domestic investors bear more risk. As flows leave the country because of bad news, equity prices fall because domestic investors have to hold more domestic shares. Inflows have the opposite effect. This means that in such a model flows have an impact on the cost of capital. It is also the case that information asymmetries between domestic and foreign investors increase equity return volatility. There is no reason for flows induced by new information to be destabilizing. As information is revealed, investors change their holdings, which has a permanent effect on prices.

When shares are sold by domestic investors to foreign investors, the shares become held by investors who are internationally diversified and who do not view domestic shares to be as risky as domestic investors do. Unexpected changes in investor composition affect equity prices for two reasons, one permanent and one transitory. The permanent reason is the one discussed in the previous paragraph, namely, that investors requiring a lower risk premium buy the shares. As foreign investors come to the domestic country, however, there might also be a transitory effect, which is that as they seek to buy the securities, they have to offer domestic investors an inducement so that they will sell. This compensation only affects prices in the short run, and its size depends on the liquidity of the markets. In very liquid markets, the compensation is trivial. As markets become less liquid, it might be substantial. This liquidity compensation has to be paid by investors who seek to buy, as well as by investors who seek to sell. If an investor wants to get out of a country quickly, she has to offer a discount on the shares she wishes to sell. As shown by Campbell, Grossman, and Wang (1993), this liquidity compensation creates reversals in stock prices. When a large group of investors wants to get out of stocks in a market, they have to provide compensation to buyers of their shares in the form of a larger short-term return. Buyers can only obtain this return by buying the shares at a temporarily low price. There is evidence for the United States that such an effect exists, but there is also evidence that it becomes much weaker over time as markets become more efficient.[11]

This liquidity compensation is a cost that investors pay to trade and it affects their trading strategies. In the extreme case, an illiquid market has a lock-in effect: the discount to be paid to get out is too high and therefore investors do not sell and ride out the bad times. Illiquidity can also keep investors out, however. Not surprisingly, international investors tend to hold securities for which this liquidity compensation is small, namely, securities of large firms. Though some have argued that liquid markets promote short-term horizons on the part of investors, which hurt economies, going even so far as to argue that the liquid markets of the United States were a source of competitive disadvantage for the

11. Froot and Perold (1995) documented that the short-term behavior of stock prices is different in recent years from what it has been historically. Yesterday's stock returns have much less information about tomorrow's stock returns than they used to. Gagnon and Karolyi (1997) showed that the volume-return relation is much weaker after the crash of 1987 than before.

United States, it is important to remember that liquid markets facilitate purchases by investors. Investors who cannot sell in a country have no incentive to invest in that country.

We now look at the evidence of the impact of flows on returns. There is a paucity of empirical evidence at this point. Part of the reason for this is that good data on international flows are hard to find. Before turning to the international evidence, we first consider some evidence for the United States that uses high-quality data.

There is clear evidence from the United States that changes in the composition of investors can have a direct impact on the value of equity. Over the past twenty years, indexing has become tremendously important and the index chosen most often for index portfolios is the S&P 500. Consequently, when a stock joins the S&P 500, this immediately creates a demand for that stock from indexers. Standard and Poor's adds stocks to the S&P 500 based on public information, so that the fact that a stock is added to the S&P 500 does not reveal information about the true value of the stock. Further, indexers have to buy the stock irrespective of its price on the date that it joins the S&P 500. This means that no information is conveyed by the increased demand for the stock. According to the traditional finance model, there should be no price impact when a stock joins the S&P 500. Yet there is such a price impact. Shleifer (1986) and Harris and Gurel (1986) estimated this impact at 3 to 4 percent. Further, all the evidence suggests that this impact is permanent, corresponding to a decrease in the cost of capital for firms that join the S&P 500. The most sensible explanation for this effect is that the demand for the stock has increased. Existing investors in the stock do not have a perfect substitute for the stock that they are giving up if they sell, so that the total demand for the stock increases.

Adding a stock to the S&P 500 probably does not affect the overall demand for stocks. Rather, the existing demand gets redistributed across stocks and this redistribution has a price effect. One might argue that such an example understates the importance of changes in demand and that the situation of emerging markets facing an inflow of capital is more akin to what happens when new mutual fund money flows into the U.S. stock market. An inflow of mutual fund money is mostly money that was not invested in the stock market. In an interesting recent study, Warther (1995) argued that the impact of an unexpected flow of mutual fund money to the U.S. stock market is rather considerable. His estimates were that a 1 percent increase in mutual fund stock assets, which for his sample period corresponds to an inflow in the stock market of $4.57 billion, brings about an increase of 5.7 percent in stock prices. His concern was naturally whether this is a reversible price impact due to liquidity or a permanent price impact. Though he looked hard to find reversals, he was not successful. It appears that this effect is permanent. A plausible explanation is that a broadening of the shareholder base lowers the risk premium as risks are spread across more investors.

Flows move prices. One would expect this to be the case if the risk of stocks becomes spread across more investors. The alternative explanation is that flows move prices because they drive stock prices away from fundamentals. As investors flow into a market, they push prices up without regard for fundamentals, driven by some kind of feeding frenzy. Eventually, prices collapse. Clark and Berko (1996) attempted to distinguish between these two views in the case of Mexico. Mexico saw a dramatic increase in foreign ownership during their sample period. From 1989 to the end of 1993, foreign ownership of Mexican equities increased from a trivial amount to more than one-fourth of the Mexican market capitalization. Like Warther (1995), they found a strong effect of flows on returns. Their estimate was that an unexpected inflow equal to 1 percent of the capital of the market leads to a contemporaneous increase of 13 percent in prices. This estimate was actually smaller than Warther's (1995). They found no evidence of price reversals, suggesting that the impact of flows is permanent rather than transitory and cannot be explained by price pressure. They also found no support for the hypothesis of positive feedback trading. Therefore, their evidence is fully supportive of the investor base broadening hypothesis.

In an article discussing the difficulties of some Asian emerging markets, an economist at J. P. Morgan was quoted in the *New York Times* as saying: "One wishes the markets were less fickle." It could indeed be that flows have a permanent effect on prices but they are so volatile and fickle that, by coming and going, they keep inflicting shocks on prices. This is the concern often expressed about portfolio flows, that somehow equity investments are the wrong kind of investments for a country because they can leave a country rapidly. This view seems rather perverse in that, in the absence of contracting costs, there would be little reason to have direct foreign investment and all foreign investment would be portfolio investment. This suggests that portfolio investment is a more advanced and more efficient form of international investment. However, there are many ways to obtain financing through sales of securities. The risk of financing through short-term debt is that one might not like the conditions at which the debt can be refinanced. Portfolio flows should not be blamed when a country or a firm has chosen a financing strategy that leaves it exposed to refinancing risks.

Though well established, the view that portfolio investment is more fickle than other forms of investment seems to have little empirical basis. In a useful study, Claessens, Dooley, and Warner (1993) investigated the volatility of foreign direct investment, portfolio equity flows, long-term flows, and short-term flows for five developed economies and five developing countries. They also broke down flows by transactors, namely, foreign direct investors, banks, governments, and the private sector. The developing countries in their sample were Mexico, the Republic of Korea, Indonesia, Argentina, and Brazil. In all cases, they focused on net flows. Their results are surprising in light of the comments about fickle equity flows. They found no support for the notion that equity flows are somehow less stable than direct investment or official flows. They found that the label of flows provides no information about how they behave over time. Their conclusion was that "if presented with one time-series (statistics) only, one will likely be unable to tell the label of the flow" (Claessens et al. 1993, 26).

Liberalization opens the door to capital flows. These flows affect security prices. Another implication of the hypothesis that portfolio flows are excessively volatile is that portfolio flows increase the volatility of security returns. The risk-sharing hypothesis that predicts a decrease in the cost of capital suggests that opening up a country could well decrease the volatility of its security returns. Consider the example of our closed economy that has a comparative advantage in producing coffee beans. An adverse event that decreases the value of the coffee crop makes the country poorer. Suppose that poorer investors are more reluctant to bear risk. In this case, the adverse shock increases the risk premium and hence decreases stock prices even further. If this economy is an open economy, the adverse shock will be spread across investors throughout the world and hence will have only a trivial effect on the risk premium. With this analysis, opening up the economy decreases volatility. However, opening up the economy means that the risk premium on the coffee bean industry now depends on worldwide factors, so that shocks to the world risk premium affect the value of the coffee bean industry. If one thinks that risk premiums should be fairly stable on world markets, then opening up a country decreases volatility if investors who have become poorer are less willing to bear risk.

Let's consider the empirical evidence on volatility and liberalization. A number of different authors have examined this issue, using different approaches. Kim and Singal (1993) considered changes in volatility around liberalizations for a sample of sixteen emerging markets. In their study, they found that volatility in the first twelve months following a liberalization is not significantly different from volatility in the previous twelve months. However, they also found that after the first twelve months, volatility falls significantly on average. They provided other evidence that is consistent with an increase in volatility for some countries and no effect for most countries. Interestingly, the countries for which they found large significant increases were Argentina, Chile, and Mexico. Richards estimated volatility for emerging markets using weekly data and concluded that "the period 1992–1995, which saw foreign institutional investors playing a more significant role in emerging markets has been characterized by volatility that is marginally lower than the remainder of the sample period (1975 to 1992)" (1996, 473). His result is surprising in that it covers the period of the Mexican crisis. Bekaert and Harvey (1997) considered twenty emerging markets and examined stock return volatility before and after liberalization. Using a variety of approaches, they found in all cases that on average liberalization decreases volatility. The bottom line from these studies is that the claim that liberalization increases volatility is not supported by empirical evidence.

These volatility studies do not relate flows directly to volatility. Hamao and

Mei (1996) did this for the case of Japan using monthly data on equity purchases and sales by foreign investors. Foreign portfolio equity investment in Japan has been small over the past twenty years, peaking in 1984 at 10.31 percent but falling back to less than 5 percent in 1990. This means that evidence for Japan has to be viewed with caution on this issue. Nevertheless, they found that trades by foreign investors do not differ in impact on volatility from trades by other investors.

Folkerts-Landau and Ito (1995) computed volatility of emerging markets for periods that differ in the intensity of portfolio flows. Table 5.16 summarizes their evidence. They also showed evidence on the issue of whether a day of high volatility for the Dow Jones predicts high volatility the next day in an emerging market for periods where the nature of flows differ. Overall, their evidence is rather mixed. Mexican stock prices appear to be the least volatile when flows are most volatile. In contrast, however, the Hong Kong stock return volatility is higher when flows are most volatile. There seems to be evidence that local volatility is more strongly linked to the volatility of the Dow Jones in periods of more volatile flows. Models where foreign investors are less well informed than local investors and alter their holdings when they receive new information produce a positive relation between stock return volatility and flow volatility. However, in this case, this relation results mostly from flows and stock prices being driven by the same factors. The relation between flows and volatility would be a source of concern if it were due to temporary increases and decreases in stock prices. It is often argued that such temporary increases and decreases in stock prices can be the result of herding by institutional investors. The idea is that institutional investors behave alike, pouring in and out of stocks as a group. In the most detailed and careful study to date, Wermers (1998) investigated whether U.S. institutional investors herd and whether this behavior leads to temporary changes in stock prices. He found strong evidence of herding behavior, especially for smaller stocks. However, at the same time, he failed to find evidence that herding leads to temporary changes in stock prices. An increase in institutional ownership is associated with an increase in stock prices, but this increase appears to be permanent.

In a detailed investigation of the behavior of foreign investors in Korea in 1997, Choe et al. (1999) found that there is evidence of herding among foreign investors. Their data included all trades on the Korea Stock Exchange for 1997. For each trade, they had information on whether a party to the trade was a foreign investor and the country of origin of that investor. They showed that there is herding among investors from different countries. Further, herding measures for investors from the United States, though upward biased because of the nature of the data, seem extremely high. Surprisingly, however, they found that herding measures were smaller during the last three months of 1997, when the Asian crisis hit Korea, than before. To investigate whether foreign investors have a destabilizing effect on prices, they estimated the impact on prices of large purchases and large sales by foreign investors. They argued that

Table 5.16   **Flows and Volatility of Stock Returns**

Country and Period	Volatility of Daily Returns	Local Volatility Divided by Volatility of Dow Jones	Correlation between Local Squared Return and Previous-Day Dow Jones Squared Return
Hong Kong			
Low inflow			
(Jan. 1988–Aug. 1991)	1.61	1.52	0.068
High inflow			
(Sept. 1991–Oct. 1993)	1.31	1.98	0.023
Volatile flow			
(Nov. 1993–July 1994)	2.33	3.68	0.150
Korea			
Low inflow			
(Jan. 1988–Dec. 1991)	1.51	1.42	0.055
High inflow			
(Jan. 1992–June 1993)	1.18	2.55	0.029
Volatile flow			
(July 1993–July 1994)	1.14	2.31	0.120
Thailand			
Volatile flow			
(Jan. 1988–Apr. 1991)	1.19	1.74	0.296
Moderate inflow			
(May 1991–Oct. 1992)	1.69	2.14	0.115
High flow			
(July 1993–July 1994)	1.17	2.66	0.103
Mexico			
Low inflow			
(Jan. 1988–Apr. 1990)	1.99	1.88	0.048
Volatile flow			
(May 1990–Jan. 1993)	1.57	1.76	0.324
More steady inflow			
(Feb. 1993–July 1994)	1.61	2.57	0.003

Source: Constructed from tables I.13 and I.14 of Folkerts-Landau and Ito (1995).

if foreign investors destabilize prices, they should start runs on prices. Instead, most of the price impact of trades by foreign investors is incorporated in prices within ten minutes and nothing else happens following trades by foreign investors. In other words, there is no evidence that foreign investors start runs on prices. Roughly, the impact of large trades by foreign investors in Korea is no different from the impact of large trades by institutional investors on the NYSE.

5.2.4   Conclusions

The empirical evidence shows that international portfolio flows have a beneficial effect on countries that liberalize, by decreasing the cost of capital in these countries and enabling residents to share risks with other investors. Portfolio inflows seem to have permanent positive effects on valuations. There is no strong empirical support for the view that portfolio flows increase the volatility of security returns or otherwise adversely affect the performance of equity markets. In particular, there is little evidence that the opening of countries has led to substantial increases in the co-movement of their stock markets with the world market. There is evidence that investors find information about one emerging market useful in their assessment of other emerging markets. However, proponents of the view that there is extensive irrational contagion across emerging markets have yet to prove their case.

Opening a country to portfolio flows makes the country better off by enabling it to share risks with foreigners and to lower costs of capital for its industries. It positions the country to receive more capital when the country's investment opportunities improve. The only way a country can take advantage of these benefits is by understanding fully that in a market economy foreign investors pursue the best investment opportunities available as they see them. They have strong incentives to identify all good investment opportunities carefully, because any opportunity they miss lowers the return on their portfolio. Their behavior makes investors as unlikely to be swept away by irrational contagion as to stay passive when governments try to maintain exchange rates and interest rates that are not sustainable.

References

Bailey, W., K. Chan, and Y. P. Chung. 1997. Depository receipts, country funds, and the peso crash: The intraday evidence. Ithaca, N.Y.: Cornell University. Unpublished paper.

Bekaert, G., and C. R. Harvey. 1995. Time-varying world market integration. *Journal of Finance* 50:403–44.

———. 1997. Emerging equity market volatility. *Journal of Financial Economics* 43:29–77.

———. 1999. Foreign speculators and emerging equity markets. Durham, N.C.: Duke University. Working paper.

Bhagwati, J. 1998. The capital myth. *Foreign Affairs* 77 (3): 7–12.

Bohn, Henning, and Linda Tesar. 1996. U.S. equity investment in foreign markets: Portfolio rebalancing or return chasing? *American Economic Review* 86:77–81.

Bordo, M. D., B. Eichengreen, and J. Kim. 1998. Was there really an earlier period of international financial integration comparable to today? NBER Working Paper no. 6738. Cambridge, Mass.: National Bureau of Economic Research.

Brennan, M. J., and H. H. Cao. 1997. International portfolio investment flows. *Journal of Finance* 52:1851–80.

Calvo, G. A., M. Goldstein, and E. Hochreiter. 1997. *Private capital flows to emerging markets after the Mexican crisis.* Washington, D.C.: Institute for International Economics.

Calvo, S., and C. M. Reinhart. 1997. Capital flows to Latin America: Is there evidence of contagion effects? In *Private capital flows to emerging markets after the Mexican crisis,* ed. S. Calvo, M. Goldstein, and E. Hochreiter, 151–71. Washington, D.C.: Institute for International Economics.

Campbell, J. Y., S. J. Grossman, and J. Wang. 1993. Trading volume and serial correlation in stock returns. *Quarterly Journal of Economics* 10:407–32.

Campollo-Palmer, C. 1997. Equity investment in emerging markets. Paper presented at the NYSE Conference on the Globalization of Financial Markets, Cancun, Mexico.

Chan, K. C., G. A. Karolyi, and R. M. Stulz. 1992. Global financial markets and the risk premium on U.S. equity. *Journal of Financial Economics* 32:137–68.

Choe, Y., B. C. Kho, and R. M. Stulz. 1999. Do foreign investors destabilize stock markets? The Korean experience in 1997. *Journal of Financial Economics,* forthcoming.

Claessens, S., M. Dooley, and A. Warner. 1993. Portfolio capital flows: Hot or cool? In *Portfolio investment in developing countries,* ed. S. Claessens and S. Gooptu, 18–44. Washington, D.C.: World Bank.

Claessens, S., and S. Gooptu, eds. 1993. *Portfolio investment in developing countries.* Discussion Paper no. 228. Washington, D.C.: World Bank.

Clark, J., and E. Berko. 1996. Foreign investment fluctuations and emerging market stock returns: The case of Mexico. New York: Federal Reserve Bank of New York. Working paper.

Cooper, I. A., and E. Kaplanis. 1994. Home bias in equity portfolios, inflation hedging and international capital market equilibrium. *Review of Financial Studies* 7:45–60.

De Long, J. B., A. Shleifer, L. Summers, and R. J. Waldman. 1990. Noise trader risk in financial markets. *Journal of Political Economy* 98:703–38.

DeSantis, G. 1993. Asset pricing and portfolio diversification: Evidence from emerging financial markets. In *Portfolio investment in developing countries,* ed. S. Claessens and S. Gooptu, 145–68. Washington, D.C.: World Bank.

DeSantis, G., and B. Gerard. 1997. International asset pricing and portfolio diversification with time-varying risk. *Journal of Finance* 52:1881–1913.

Dornbusch, R., and Y. C. Park. 1995. Financial integration in a second best world: Are we still sure about our classical prejudices? In *Financial opening: Policy lessons for Korea,* ed. R. Dornbusch and Y. C. Park. Seoul: Korea Institute of Finance.

Eichengreen, B., and A. Fishlow. 1998. Contending with capital flows: What is different about the 1990s? In *Capital flows and financial crises,* ed. M. Kahler. Ithaca, N.Y.: Cornell University Press.

Erb, C., C. Harvey, and T. Viskanta. 1996. Expected returns and volatility in 135 countries. *Journal of Portfolio Management* 22:46–58.

Falkenstein, E. G. 1996. Preferences for stock characteristics as revealed by mutual fund portfolio holdings. *Journal of Finance* 51:111–35.

Feldstein, M., and C. Horioka. 1980. Domestic saving and international capital flows. *Economic Journal* 90:314–29.

Folkerts-Landau, D., and T. Ito. 1995. *International capital markets: Developments, prospects, and policy issues.* Washington, D.C.: International Monetary Fund.

Forbes, K., and R. Rigobon. 1998. No contagion, only interdependence: Measuring stock market co-movements. Cambridge: Massachusetts Institute of Technology, Sloan School of Management. Working paper.

Frankel, J. A., and S. L. Schmukler. 1996. Country fund discounts, asymmetric information and the Mexican crisis of 1994: Did local residents turn pessimistic before international investors? NBER Working Paper no. 5714. Cambridge, Mass.: National Bureau of Economic Research.

French, K., and J. Poterba. 1991. International diversification and international equity markets. *American Economic Review* 81:222–26.

Froot, K. A., P. G. O'Connell, and M. S. Seasholes. 1998. The portfolio flows of international investors, I. Boston: Harvard Business School. Working paper.

Froot, K. A., and A. F. Perold. 1995. New trading practices and short-run market efficiency. *Journal of Futures Markets* 15:731–65.

Gagnon, L., and G. A. Karolyi. 1997. Information, trading volume and international stock market co-movements. London: University of Western Ontario. Working paper.

Goldstein, M., and D. Folkerts-Landau. 1994. *International capital markets: Developments, prospects, and policy issues.* Washington, D.C.: International Monetary Fund.

Gompers, P., and J. Lerner. 1997. Money chasing deals? The impact of fund flows on private equity valuation. Boston: Harvard Business School. Working paper.

Hamao, Y., and J. Mei. 1996. Living with the "enemy": An analysis of investment in the Japanese equity market. New York: Columbia University. Working paper.

Harris, L., and E. Gurel. 1986. Price and volume effects associated with changes in the S&P 500 list: New evidence for the existence of price pressures. *Journal of Finance* 41:815–29.

Henry, P. B. 1999a. Equity prices, stock market liberalization, and investment. Palo Alto, Calif.: Stanford University. Working paper.

———. 1999b. Stock market liberalization, economic reform, and emerging market equity prices. *Journal of Finance.* Forthcoming.

Ilmanen, A. 1995. Time-varying expected returns in international bond markets. *Journal of Finance* 50:481–506.

Kang, J.-K., and R. Stulz. 1997. Why is there a home bias? An analysis of foreign portfolio equity ownership in Japan. *Journal of Financial Economics* 46:3–28.

Karolyi, A., and R. Stulz. 1996. Why do markets move together? An examination of U.S.-Japan stock return co-movements. *Journal of Finance* 51:951–86.

Khannah, A. 1996. Equity investment prospects in emerging markets. *Columbia Journal of World Business* 31:32–39.

Kim, E. H., and V. Singal. 1993. Opening up of stock markets by emerging economies: Effects on portfolio flows and volatility of stock prices. In *Portfolio investment in developing countries,* ed. S. Claessens and S. Gooptu, 383–403. Washington, D.C.: World Bank.

Krugman, P. 1998. Saving Asia: It's time to get radical. *Fortune,* 7 September.

Lin, W.-L., and T. Ito. 1994. Price volatility and volume spillovers between the Tokyo and New York stock markets. In *The internationalization of equity markets,* ed. J. Frankel. Chicago: University of Chicago Press.

NYSE (New York Stock Exchange). 1997. *NYSE facts for the year of 1996.* New York: New York Stock Exchange, May.

Obstfeld, M. 1994. Risk-taking, global diversification, and growth. *American Economic Review* 84:1310–29.

Radelet, Steven, and Jeffrey Sachs. 1998. The onset of the East Asian financial crisis. Cambridge, Mass.: Harvard University. Working paper.

Richards, A. J. 1996. Volatility and predictability in national stock markets: How do emerging and mature markets differ? *IMF Staff Papers* 43:461–501.

Rigobon, Roberto. 1998. On the measurement of contagion. Cambridge: Massachusetts Institute of Technology, Sloan School of Management. Working paper.

Sachs, J. D., A. Tornell, and A. Velasco. 1996. Financial crises in emerging markets: The lessons from 1995. *Brookings Papers on Economic Activity,* no. 1:147–217.

Scholes, M. 1972. The market for securities: Substitution versus price pressure and the effects of information on share prices. *Journal of Business* 45:179–211.

Shleifer, A. 1986. Do demand curves for stocks slope down? *Journal of Finance* 41: 579–90.

Shleifer, Andrei, and Robert W. Vishny. 1997. The limits of arbitrage. *Journal of Finance* 52:35–55.

Stiglitz, Joseph. 1998. Boats, planes and capital flows. *Financial Times,* 25 March.

Stulz, R. M. 1995. International portfolio choice and asset pricing: An integrative survey. In *The handbook of modern finance,* ed. V. Maksimovic and W. Ziemba. Amsterdam: North Holland.

————. 1999. Globalization and the cost of equity capital. New York: New York Stock Exchange. Working paper.

Summers, L. H., and V. P. Summers. 1989. When financial markets work too well: The cautious case for a securities transactions tax. *Journal of Financial Services Research* 3:261–86.

Tesar, L., and I. Werner. 1993. U.S. equity investment in emerging stock markets. In *Portfolio investment in developing countries,* ed. S. Claessens and S. Gooptu. Washington, D.C.: World Bank.

————. 1994. International equity transactions and U.S. portfolio choice. In *The internationalization of equity markets,* ed. J. Frankel. Chicago: University of Chicago Press.

Tobin, J. 1978. A proposal for international monetary reform. *Eastern Economic Journal* 4:153–59.

Warther, V. A. 1995. Aggregate mutual fund flows and security returns. *Journal of Financial Economics* 39:209–35.

Wermers, R. 1998. Mutual fund herding and the impact on stock prices. *Journal of Finance* 54:581–622.

Williamson, J. 1993. Issues posed by portfolio investment in developing countries. In *Portfolio investment in developing countries,* ed. S. Claessens and S. Gooptu. Washington, D.C.: World Bank.

World Bank. Various issues. *World debt tables.* Washington, D.C.: World Bank.

---

3. *Stephen Friedman*

These comments sketch out the following hypothesis: an important side effect of U.S. international equity flows is to assist in the development—and much needed transformation, over time—of the business and bureaucratic cultures underlying emerging country capital markets and economies. I will lay out my perceptions on this subject in the hope that you find them worth more rigorous and less anecdotal inquiry than I can bring to bear. For several reasons, my focus will be on the effect of equity flows from the United States to emerging economies throughout the world.[1] One reason is that I am most familiar with

---

1. Recent net equity market flows into the United States are relatively modest and not transforming in any conceptual sense. From 1990 through the first quarter of 1997, foreign net purchases of U.S. equities totaled only $46 billion, against a U.S. market value of almost one-half the total world stock market capitalization. Non-U.S. investors do hold about 6.5 percent of all U.S. shares, but their activities usually have only a small impact on market direction. During the same period, aggregate net U.S. flows into the equity markets of Latin America and Asia outside of Japan were about $78 billion—greater both absolutely and relatively than flows into the United States since the funds went into markets whose cumulative capitalization was only about 7 percent of the world total at midyear.

the U.S. investor. More important, I want to concentrate on the present and potential transforming influence of U.S. equity outflows—which, I believe, gives them a significance far greater than the quantity of dollars would suggest.[2]

First, however, some general background on the accelerated globalization of U.S. equity portfolios in the past decade. The volume of U.S.-owned foreign shares is currently over $1 trillion, equal to roughly 6 percent of the U.S. stock market capitalization, and these holdings are growing markedly faster than the value of domestic equities. Since the mid-1980s, these outflows have been evenly spread between industrialized countries and emerging markets, with flows to Asia and Latin America consistently positive. Demand has also generated its own supply, and the size, sophistication, and competitiveness of U.S. equity markets has led to explosive growth in the number of issuers attracted to our market: 20 percent of U.S.-based equity demand during the past decade flowed to the emerging stock markets of Asia and Latin America.[3]

Without attempting to go far back in history, prior to the 1990s U.S. equity portfolio flows to emerging nations offered a rather straightforward bargain: they afforded to a relatively small investor base some diversification (with low correlation of investment results to U.S. markets) plus acceptable returns— hopefully, higher returns than the S&P 500 to compensate for the increased volatility—in turn, foreign recipients were provided with an additional source of long-term funds and lower capital costs.

2. Equity portfolio flows from other advanced economies, particularly the United Kingdom (which, together with the United States, the French think of as the proponent of "Anglo-Saxon" style capitalism), would tend to have similar impacts.

3. From an October 1997 presentation: "The Globalization of U.S. Equity Ownership" (by Eric Dobkin, the chairman of Goldman, Sachs worldwide equity capital markets group). Dobkin went on to identify some reasons for the ongoing expansion in U.S. ownership of foreign equities:

1. Demise of communism, reducing event risk
2. Globalization of world economies, with a correlation between necessary and growing openness of economies, economic growth, and capital flows
3. Desire of U.S. savers to attain greater diversification into the slightly more than one-half the global market capitalization and 80 percent of world GDP lying outside the United States (pension fund and endowment advisors frequently support an allocation benchmark of 15 to 20 percent of equity holdings in foreign shares)
4. Exposure to superior growth potential in certain emerging markets, albeit at the cost of greater sector volatility
5. Returns generated from the emerging markets not very correlated with the S&P 500 (or among themselves) thus dampening potential volatility in the entire portfolio
6. Increased familiarity: becoming "comfortable with those foreign companies that looked and smelt like U.S. companies [and] were subject to the same or similar accounting principles"
7. Technology: "the structure and flexibility of the U.S. financing sector allows a more effortless passing of the baton from venture capital financing to the stock market than is the case in much of Europe or Asia. [This has] allowed U.S. investors to become early stage major shareholders in a number of foreign technology companies at a time when non-U.S. investors may not have felt entirely comfortable with the very nascent state of these revenues"
8. Familiarity with restructuring: given the industry-by-industry wave of restructuring and consolidation in the United States, and U.S. investors' resulting positive experience, they have learned to identify candidates for consolidation, cost cutting, and rationalization abroad

I suggest that, as the absolute size and relative importance of these flows has increased, and a critical mass of U.S. emerging nation investment has been reached, there has been a qualitative change in their impact. Analogous to the effect of open trade markets, sizable equity portfolio flows from advanced U.S. (and other "Anglo-Saxon" style) capital markets are accompanied by influential demands as to acceptable practices, by infectious cultural norms, and by role model and mentoring effects, which substantially affect the business cultures of recipient emerging countries and companies. This applies—albeit imperfectly—in varying degrees whether the recipients are emerging nations in Latin America, Southeast Asia, Russia, or eastern Europe.[4] In other words, as one influential investment banker summed it up: "If [particular emerging nations and their enterprises] want to compete for the money, they'll have to clean up their act."

In a different context, Paul Samuelson and William Nordhaus have discussed "external economies" and noted that the return to a nation from new innovation can be a multiple of the reward collected by the innovator. My central point is that, just as there is a very high "social return" to a nation from tangible, patentable invention, there can also be very high returns from the cultural transformation of enterprise work practices and norms: motivating people to change the way they think and, most important, influencing attitudes toward the very process of ongoing change.

This general principal is readily observable in action. For example, the transfer of "lean production" know-how from Japanese auto manufacturers and other industrial concerns to U.S. auto companies and other manufacturers— much of which accompanied Japanese direct investment in the United States— has been vastly beneficial to the United States.[5] According to management, supervisors, unionists, and blue-collar workers in positively affected plants, the prerequisite to many of these successful innovations was *not* hard technological innovation but "softer," cultural change: major shifts in attitude and relationships needed to occur between and among senior management, suppliers, managers of functional staff "silos," plant supervisors, and blue-collar workers. Much of U.S. industry ultimately accepted the need to make radical shifts in methodology due to twin pressures—from the showroom floors and, pertinent to this discussion, from institutional investors. From personal experience, I can

---

4. Lankes and Stern in chap. 2.1 note: "The impact of capital flows to [eastern Europe and the former Soviet Union] is of fundamental importance to the economic transition. These flows bring new methods of business organization, new technologies, and powerful influence on the building of financial, regulatory, and other institutions. They help establish the financial discipline that is crucial to the effective functioning of a market economy. Thus their impact goes far beyond the simple availability of resources."

5. I won't enter a dog in the fight over the extent of overall productivity improvement in the United States; however, clearly something of great value occurred when so many plants absorbed new work practices and—without additional capital and with sharply reduced hours of worker input—turned out markedly superior products.

testify that a similar transfer affecting work practices and productivity took place among British merchant bankers when U.S. investment banks set up "green-field plants" in the City of London that were (grudgingly) accepted as role models.

Knowledge transfer now accompanies not only global direct investment and open trade but also U.S.-style portfolio investment: encouraging "best practices" and—with greater or less success in different emerging markets—transmitting a benign virus attacking many dysfunctional traditional overseas governmental and business patterns. Over the long term, and we all know how long that can be, the most productive ideas tend to win out—*if* (and these are two big "ifs") markets and information flows make them accessible to potential adoptors *and if* competitive pressures overcome resistance to change (i.e., if fear of the future exceeds the pain of change).

So, I come to a question that has intrigued me for years: What are the "spillover effects" and "social returns" to a nation from encouraging U.S.-style portfolio equity inflows—through privatizing state-controlled corporations, promoting greater financial transparency, introducing more enlightened regulatory practices, and otherwise creating hospitable local equity markets? Can the social returns to the recipient nation be estimated? Can we estimate the value to an economy of more efficient equity markets, in terms of increased domestic savings, and more efficient channeling of money to areas of high productivity and return?

I will attempt to describe my perceptions as to some frequently overlapping, beneficial side effects of U.S. equity portfolio investment. (A caveat: developing U.S.-style capital markets in emerging economies is a very uncertain and long-term process with some backsliding; my views are anecdotally based and lap over into the predictive—and, perhaps even more suspect, into sociology!)

An increasingly vocal and influential, primarily "Anglo-Saxon," international investor constituency has arisen—with strong motives for encouraging positive change in the financial infrastructures and corporate practices of emerging nations. Even to an amoral equity speculator, "an act which badly needs cleaning up" creates risks and systemic distortions harmful to present investment and future opportunities. The "Washington consensus,"[6] with the addendum of a "Wall Street/City of London consensus," as to desirable macro- and micropolicies for emerging economies and capital markets is increasingly being accepted—at least at the technocrat level—by a new generation of highly educated (often in the United States) foreign government officials and private sector managers. Obviously, this acceptance has not occurred at some very important political and bureaucratic levels of certain emerging nation govern-

6. In remarks at the Roundtable on Financial Stability and Supervision in Emerging Markets (Hong Kong, September 1997), Jerry Corrigan touched on key points related to the conference topic on which there is general consensus and points for which important gaps in information or understanding exist.

ments (viz. current events in Southeast Asia and the recent IMF meeting), nor is one detailed prescription appropriate for all patients. Nevertheless, there is a broadening global understanding that autarky and bureaucratic allocation systems have failed to deliver growth and that many Western capitalistic norms must be embraced, including industrial competitiveness and open trade—and open capital markets.

The Wall Street/City consensus assumes that an open, flexible, and transparent equity market, and the financial and regulatory infrastructure underlying it, is a vital national asset for the United States and the United Kingdom and that its emulation in emerging nations would be a great boon to their own and the world's prosperity. In contrast, many emerging markets are characterized by widespread corruption, insufficient regulation of the safety aspects of financial systems (contrasted with top-heavy bureaucratic meddling to enhance political power), inadequate protection of legal rights, insecure clearance and settlement systems, and cronyist concessions from influential politicians to supporters.[7] There is a question of causation with respect to portfolio flows to emerging nations: emerging economies that better satisfy investor preferences are more likely to attract foreign capital, and those that do not meet those norms are unlikely to be large-scale recipients of flows. Which comes first, the money or the benign environment? I believe that what occurs is an iterative process in which adventurous "early adapter" speculators venture into a particular perilous emerging market when they perceive potential compensation in terms of extremely high returns; these investors then try to effect changes in the regulatory and normative environment in order to make their present and potential investments safer and more attractive. To the extent that they succeed, these speculative "pioneers" encourage other, less bold but still adventurous, "homesteaders" to speculate in equities in these emerging countries, with an attendant increase in the mass of voices demanding conformity with desired norms. To the extent that they are enlightened, host nations have a mutual interest with investors in the adoption of policies that reduce risk premiums[8]—and their costs of capital—and are associated with improved resource allocation, long-term growth, and competitiveness.

In Russia this process is in its very early stages and is highly uncertain (a later stage of development is playing out behind the turmoil and highly confrontational debates accompanying the recent IMF meetings in Asia). For example, in Russia today, early adapter equity investors are really on the frontier of the Wild East and must be corporate governance activists in order to protect their investments. Elementary protections—against managements usurping corporate opportunities or flagrantly cheating minority shareholders or against

---

7. Capital does not avoid risk per se—it readily accepts it if the potential rewards are there and it believes it can assess the playing field and the odds—but it generally avoids perils of an unfamiliar nature, even if the ultimate amount of risk is no greater.

8. According to Goldman Sachs research, a reduction in these risk premiums has been a key reason Latin America stocks have performed strongly in recent years.

fraud in share settlement and clearance systems—often do not exist and must be put in place.

A U.S. equity investment fund in Russia, in its own interest, may expend money, experience, and energy to vindicate minority shareholder rights in a merger, thereby setting a vital precedent for the embryonic commercial legal system; use its global relationships to seek a strategic foreign direct investment (FDI) partner for a portfolio company; and encourage local companies to use a Western custodian for their shares and to use a recognized accounting firm and accepted international auditing standards. As a spillover effect, in the future a state pension fund in the United States or a university endowment may, as a result of these efforts, be more likely to entrust its capital to a fund investing in Russian equity.

As another example, Indonesia also has a powerful incentive to listen to investors and take much needed steps to increase confidence. Thus, in a recent meeting cohosted by an American investment bank, high-ranking Indonesian officials met with foreign equity managers "to try to persuade them that the country is on the right track" (*Wall Street Journal,* 10 October 1997). Clearly, the international investors have influence—they vote with their feet—and strong motives to exert it.[9]

Important emerging market privatizations are typically designed to encourage local participation and develop habits of broader domestic equity ownership. Some privatizations, in Russia for example, have been on concessionary terms to powerful local barons. However, in most nations, the political and economic goal is to encourage the person on the street to begin investing and saving in equities, often a practice that is little understood. Western investment bankers and investors assist this process by making knowledgeable demands for an increase in shareholder protections. They typically insist, as the price of their participation—a very valuable good housekeeping seal for an equity issuer—that management evince a focus on creating value for all shareholders, rather than propping up weak entities for local political purposes or feathering managers' personal nests. These concepts, alien to many economies, are borne on the currents of open market capitalism and are contagious.[10]

Not only should investor-friendly equity markets be a magnet for increased domestic savings (which, outside of Asia, is a potential Achilles' heel for

9. Samuelson and Nordhaus (1986) in discussing the massive capital flows of the Pax Britannica period before World War I, including the "transfer [of] capital from place to place at [the] slightest whim," note that "those nationalistic countries which questioned private property were intimidated by a show of battleships or an army battalion." Today, equity markets, along with the bond and currency markets and FDI flows have these *in terrorem* effects. (Even in the United States, markets intimidate: note James Carville's hope to be reincarnated as the bond market "because everyone is scared to death of it.")

10. "Chinese officials hope that over the long run, releasing state companies into the free market will force a natural selection of viable businesses. 'We must have a system where the strong survive and the weak fail,' said China's Minister of the State Economic and Trade Commission, during a recent party Congress: 'That is the lesson of the market economy'" (*New York Times,* 5 October 1997).

emerging nations), but educating the public and giving them reason to be more comfortable with equity investment promises to allocate and channel savings more efficiently to the most productive and highest return investments.[11] Thus the ability of equity flows to develop an infrastructure and template for domestic equity investment—and provide a trusted imprimatur to well-run local corporations—is likely to be more important than the actual amount of U.S. dollar inflows into emerging markets. These inflows, while welcome, are modest compared to domestic savings. Thus, for example, in Latin America, there has been an explosion in private pension funds, which now manage about $130 billion, growing by about $1 billion a month. "Assets that once languished in inefficiently managed government pension plans are being channeled to asset management firms, whose holdings include a growing share of local stock . . . markets." The portion of Latin American equity deals, often led by Wall Street firms, that is sold locally, which averaged 10 to 15 percent a year ago, has grown to 20 to 30 percent of many issues, and in some cases all the equity can now be raised in the local markets. To the extent that Western investors are able to make the Russian stock market safer for minority shareholders, Russians— cynical observers of abuses in early privatizations—are more likely to take money from under their mattresses and buy equities. This will provide desperately needed working capital to domestic corporations and encourage the flow back to Russia of some of the immense amounts of earlier capital outflow.

More emerging nation domestic venture capitalists and risk-tolerant investors will emerge and invest in start-ups and high-growth young companies if maturing, vital domestic stock markets promise liquidity and exits. Meanwhile, U.S. venture capitalists and merchant bankers and some elite, domestic specialists in the emerging nations are investing aggressively in private, liquidity-short, high-growth ventures in these nations, often counting on a "takeout" down the road with a U.S.-led initial public offering (IPO).

With open equity markets, the opportunities for management measurement and benchmarking are dramatically enhanced; competition for capital and investor approbation "concentrates the mind wonderfully." With Anglo-Saxon equity flows come Anglo-Saxon-style money managers, security analysts, and investment bankers.[12] Newly privatized and other emerging market public companies now have public financial reports that can be compared to those of competitors or other industry participants across national boundaries, and voluminous analysts' reports abound with every conceivable comparative metric. Senior executives are anxious to tap into the information flow and learn what their domestic and international competitors are doing, not only from their

11. Outside the emerging markets, this process is already at work in western Europe. An immense volume of forthcoming telecommunications and vital infrastructure privatizations overhangs the market, and investment bankers count on the buying power of a relatively new class of domestic equity investors.

12. Whose incoming fees are a useful addition to U.S. "service" trade flows and whose advice is—arguably—a useful export!

subordinates—according to whatever particular agendas they have—but in private meetings or investor conferences with security analysts, money managers, and investment bankers. Good and bad performance is highlighted. Managements feel increased pressure to improve and to perform for stockholders—a focus that had rarely been their experience before—pressure to get a higher return on assets, to make their businesses more efficient, and to reduce redundant employment, rather than to be a source of politically convenient jobs.[13] Emerging nation equity market leaders recognize the need for security reform, improved settlement procedures, and more transparent accounting standards if their companies are to compete for much needed equity inflows. The financial industry trade press is replete with stories underscoring this point. For example, an article entitled "Market Reform: The Promise of Liquidity," in *World Equity* magazine, reports on how Middle Eastern regulatory authorities are assiduously responding to the specific criticisms of specialist equity managers (often U.S. and U.K. emerging market fund managers) to reform their markets, in order to be competitive in capital markets. This is a mentoring effect, similar to that from FDI.

Good security and country analysts provide much the same benefit as a free press, exposing obfuscation and cover-ups—generally with much greater insight. There is a growing watchdog effect in many emerging markets (though obviously, as indicated by recent events, often still without sharp enough teeth!). Road shows and meetings with analysts and money managers do not respect the cultures and motives of family conglomerate empires or statist corporations. A publicly traded industrial company that might wish to use its cash or borrowing capacity to speculate in real estate, or to accumulate ill-fitting subsidiaries for reasons of domestic power and prestige, will find it difficult over time to rationalize such decisions in a return-driven environment with more checks and balances. Appointments of senior bureaucrats, whose principal qualification is loyalty to those in power, to run key state-controlled public companies as a form of patronage and to ensure that politically acceptable people control assets will become more difficult to carry off. Unsavory practices—for example, family groups shifting funds from public vehicles they control to private vehicles they own outright—are more likely to be ferreted out, leading to less wasteful, less corrupt uses of capital. The use of political pressure to intimidate nominally private banks into funding politically motivated but economically unsound projects, or politically favored businessmen, will become less likely in such an environment, if markets send loud negative signals. This process is under way, albeit embryonically, in many emerging markets. However, as recent events in Southeast Asia make abundantly clear, steps to date in this direction have been inadequate.

With access to U.S. equity investors, and the more attractive financing this makes possible, privatized and newly public emerging market corporations

---

13. This, and numerous other insights in this paper, stem from the "firing line" experience of Mark Evans, co-chief executive of Goldman, Sachs's global equity capital markets thrust.

now have the currency to make sizable acquisitions. Stock prices permitting, they are likely to be participants in merger markets, leading to useful cross-fertilization and transactions and building economies of scale.[14]

I will now attempt to identify some very conceptual, fundamental cultural externalities that I believe will accompany U.S. portfolio equity investment over time in those emerging markets where the soil is ripe for entrepreneurialism. This is "soft stuff," but more and more smart managers understand that "culture is destiny." In my perception, culture is far more important in national and corporate development than differences in hard assets. So I'm going to dwell on this point.[15]

It's now axiomatic that—in an ever faster, more volatile, and more global world—economic success depends heavily on innovation and ready adaptability. Success goes to corporate cultures that strive to be in the information flows—the markets for new ideas—and that are more entrepreneurial and less hierarchical, embody the concept of constant improvement, are willing to cannibalize their own product lines and shelve past practices (a big psychological barrier), break down interior functional walls and inculcate greater interdisciplinary cooperation into their workforces (another major resistance point), and achieve greater fluidity in forming interfirm partnerships (to augment their own comparative advantages). Accompanying these norms should be an attitude more open to bold experiment—with the attendant risk of failure. (These attitudes are generally far better accepted and understood in the United States than in western Europe or Japan.) Underlying all of these cultural attitudes is the assumption that the greater short-term financial and career risks inherent in these approaches demand greater financial carrots. In other words, the successful risk taker deserves to get his or her financial head well above the crowd (which is not a very continental European, Japanese, or British approach, in general).

As another way of saying it: success in a world of global information revolution requires organizations that function as complex adaptive systems—in the Santa Fe Institute sense—highly motivated, regularly evolving human ecosystems, composed of constantly interacting, self-directing units—that come together in varying unit configurations to better adjust to changing environments. In Darwin's world, it helps a lot to be strong, swift, and smart, but survival—

14. E.g., Mexico's poultry leader, facing increased competition from U.S. firms, launched a U.S. IPO, the proceeds of which were in part intended to finance acquisitions to afford economies of scale (*Wall Street Journal,* 19 September 1997). Similarly, a major Argentine retailer, which received much of its early support from U.S. brokers rather than Argentine investors, went public in April 1996 and obtained capital to make consolidating acquisitions in the Latin American retail area, which faces increased competition from major global firms.

15. A parable teaches that "if you give a man a fish you feed him for a day, but if you teach him to fish you feed him for a lifetime." That, in a way, is what happens when a transfer of specific technical knowledge accompanies FDI. However—to beat the parable to death—I would argue that inculcating a U.S.-style capitalistic equity market orientation into emerging markets provides the infrastructure, incentive, and orientation for local entrepreneurial managers to work out for themselves new and better ways of fishing, perhaps even leapfrogging FDI patrons. No one has ever figured out a better framework for encouraging the "invisible hand."

and being a beneficiary and not a victim of "creative destruction"—ultimately depends on being adaptive.[16]

Sound "touchy-feely"? To me, it distinguishes the economic winners from the losers. I am suggesting a vision in which Microsoft, Hewlett-Packard, and Intel are epitomes of adaptive cultural success in our economic environment—for the present at least! (Also, take a look behind the glossy facades of successful U.S. investment banks. If they didn't behave as complex adaptive systems, they couldn't compete.) Economic institutions such as these place exceptional demands on their employees and cannot thrive without the lure of exceptional financial rewards to attract extraordinary effort from top talent.[17]

In the earlier industrial revolutions of steam machinery and electricity, great risk takers and entrepreneurs performed epic feats, built highly successful companies for the era, and were lavishly rewarded. In the current era, if one accepts what I've suggested are the attributes necessary for success—for example, flatter hierarchies and operations dependent on the initiative of larger numbers of motivated people—reward systems must reach further down into organizations. And—of immense importance—the reward system must align key employees' incentives with the stated goals of the enterprise (otherwise employees will tend consciously or unconsciously to game the system). Nothing achieves this goal better than employee ownership of stock and U.S.-style stock options (which, until recently, were not even legal in some major industrial nations). Anyone who spends time in the fastest paced and most vibrant parts of our economy[18] would be struck by the driving psychological force for employees of an ownership stake.[19]

The United States is particularly hospitable to entrepreneurial environments

---

16. One of the country's leading lawyers, whose practice deals with titanic corporate struggles, cites the Forbes 400 as a research tool for understanding the changing U.S. economy and the "new breed" of business leaders in the information age.

17. Such corporate successes constantly help to spawn even more entrepreneurial progeny. Indeed, just as Wall Street, Hollywood, Pittsburgh, Detroit, Chicago, and Toledo early became nests for fledgling finance, motion picture, steel, auto, meat packing, and tire companies, complex adaptive systems ready to deal with the challenges of the twenty-first century have sprung up in Silicon Valley, Austin, Seattle, Route 128, the Research Triangle, and San Diego.

18. E.g., the Internet; computer and biotech start-ups; fledgling companies in retail and service industries; "consolidations" seeking efficiencies through "roll-ups" of existing businesses; software companies developing solutions to dramatically enhance supply chain productivity, factory and warehouse efficiency, and targeted marketing strategies; new and more efficient health care ventures.

19. In one sense, this is just a modern-day example of the "invisible hand" at work, but in another sense, modern U.S.-style capitalism, replete with the holy grails of equity ownership—IPOs, stock options, etc.—provides the same attraction to highly energetic, talented people that administering Her Majesty's empire might have had in a prior century or working in FDR's New Deal earlier in our own. Of great importance is the fact that these entrepreneurial and wealth-creating U.S. environments also attract great talent from abroad, often from emerging nations—a form of mercantilism in which the United States imports great brains and exports high-value-added, sophisticated high-tech products, often software. Clearly, this phenomenon is hyped by an aggressive bull market, and a major downturn will bring substantial morale problems, but equity incentives have proved their value over many cycles.

and attitudes—a major advantage of the U.S. economy as we approach the twenty-first century. Such environments can no more be manufactured whole than the Amazon rain forest. However, with patience, incentives, and conscious transplanting of seeds, such environments can take root in some emerging markets. (In its own way, Hong Kong is very much the sort of environment I've described.) However, it would be a great aid to have U.S.-style equity markets to lure risk capital funders and to provide incentives to entrepreneurs (these incentives are delicately called "liquidity events"). (Certainly, this variable is insufficient in itself—Silicon Valley required much more than stock options in order to evolve as an archetype of such an environment.)

In many emerging nations, there will continue to be resistance from established political forces that want the capital that comes with FDI and portfolio investment, as well as the politically unthreatening, economy-boosting technological improvements that accompany it, but are uncomfortable with the gradual cultural changes, emerging entrepreneurial classes, and reduced governmental control that are likely to follow from U.S.-style equity markets. However, I'm betting that, over time, an idea that delivers demonstrable value will prevail.

---

4. George N. Hatsopoulos

I am going to say a few words about the mirror image of what was addressed by Stephen Friedman, namely, equity flows to the United States, which by all measures have been small. I have added them up over the past five years, over $45 billion, so they're not much compared to the size of the U.S. economy. But they have played a very important role in the development of Thermo Electron.

In general, much of the equity flow to the United States is the result of equity offerings that U.S. companies make in Europe and, to a lesser degree, in Asia. This activity usually takes place when the companies intend to raise capital. U.S. corporations want to enlarge their investor base, so they go to Europe or other parts of the world where investment funds are available.

Our company completed a large number of public offerings over the past five years. In total, we raised about $3 billion, of which 40 percent was in straight equity, and the remainder was kind of a hybrid of equity and debt known as convertible debenture. Another aspect of this aggregate is that about half the money was raised in Europe and half in the United States. That ratio is quite unusual. It's not accidental; it's very deliberate. We decided to raise only half of new equity or new subordinated debt in the United States, and the rest abroad. I would like to explain why Thermo Electron has followed this practice.

Some fourteen years ago, we decided to embark on the creation of a new corporate structure that has become known as the "spinout" structure. Pursuant to this effort, we incorporated virtually all of our distinctive business activities into subsidiaries and allowed each to raise the funds it might need from external equity markets, with the provision that each of these subsidiaries abide by the rules outlined in what we call the Thermo Electron corporate charter. The principal reason for introducing this spinout structure is to provide the management incentives addressed by Friedman, namely, some ownership in their own business by way of stock options and the responsibility of running their own company. Sometimes Thermo Electron owns as much as 90 percent of these spinouts, and although some spinouts are owned by the parent at a lower percentage, it is always a controlling percentage. The second reason for this structure is that we have been able to raise money at lower capital cost than if we were to raise it by selling shares of the parent company. Thermo Electron has always had a favorable price-to-earnings (P/E) ratio, between 20 and 30, which has usually been rather comfortable for raising equity capital—but not nearly as comfortable as raising capital with an infinite P/E ratio, which many of our subsidiaries have.

Let me now come to the reasons why we are intending to raise only half the capital in the United States. The first reason is that, when we started to examine the European market about twenty-seven years ago, especially in developed economies such as the United Kingdom, West Germany, Switzerland, France, and more recently Italy and Greece, we found we would be dealing with investors who in general have much longer investment horizons than do Americans. That is quite important to us because of our longterm goals and strategies. The second characteristic of Europeans is their much longer institutional memory. Right now, for instance, we know the people in maybe a dozen banks in Zurich. We know individuals in each of the banks who invested in our company back in 1971. This wouldn't be possible with American institutions. For a company like us, this characteristic is very important. The third aspect is that Europeans, and Asians as well, value safety more than high returns. This attribute suits us very well. For instance, for a subordinated debenture, American investors require a pretty high coupon. Of course, they give you an equivalent premium. But if we go to Europe and tell them, "We'll give you a lower conversion premium, but we want to pay only 3 percent," they will take it. This is much better for us because we know they're going to convert anyway, so why pay the higher interest rate?

What happens, incidentally, is that by starting the process in Europe to raise half the capital, we force the other half, which is in the United States, to buy the terms that we have negotiated in Europe. That has worked enormously well. We'll never go the other way around. If we start in the United States, negotiating with major institutions, we're going to get less desirable terms. So we start negotiating in Europe, where there is in each institution at least one person who has known us for a long time.

I thought you might want to hear about some of our experiences.

Discussion Summary

Linda Tesar noted that approximately 10 to 12 percent of the current U.S. portfolio of stocks is invested abroad. While this figure corresponds to recent large equity outflows, these figures remain relatively small from the perspective of the long-run diversification benefits afforded by investing abroad. Tesar noted that this increased diversification has the potential to lead to contagion as losses may be more easily transmitted across markets. Finally, she commented that it was extremely difficult to isolate contagion empirically.

Stephen Friedman responded that institutional investors differ in their appetite for international exposure, with some seeking to allocate 20 percent of their portfolios abroad. He also noted that contagions and crises, by definition, involve greatly shaken confidence concerning the stricken market. For this and other reasons, he was highly doubtful about the creation of a private insurance fund to cover the risk of currency crises, as had been suggested by one of the participants. These crises are typically characterized by overshooting and enormous emotionality, requiring early returning participants to the market to be confident bargain hunters. Finally, Friedman noted, markets can correct themselves relatively quickly as investors regain confidence.

Friedman speculated that the turnover rates of U.S. institutional investors are somewhat higher than in other countries. He noted that bankers can tailor offerings in a great variety of ways to satisfy the requirements of different issuers. *George Hatsopoulos* responded that the difference between the horizons of U.S. investors and European investors is small but perceptible. He noted that Thermo Electron had chosen a 50/50 mix between U.S. and European investors and found that mix to be optimal. Finally, Hatsopoulos commented that the spinout strategy employed by Thermo Electron is becoming a model for other firms. Other firms, however, are more sensitive to the disadvantages of such a strategy, particularly the greater transparency of such a structure.

6 The Role of Foreign Direct Investment in International Capital Flows

1. Robert E. Lipsey
2. Robert C. Feenstra
3. Carl H Hahn
4. George N. Hatsopoulos

1. Robert E. Lipsey

6.1.1 Introduction

The purpose of this essay is to provide some quantitative historical background to the question of what role direct investment plays in the broader story of international capital flows. The essay examines whether that role has changed over time, or changed for some groups of investing or receiving countries, and how that role differs among countries and types of countries.

International flows of capital perform a variety of functions in the world economy. For example, they permit levels of domestic investment in a country to exceed the country's level of saving. That has been the case for the United States for the past fifteen years and for most of the past twenty-five years. For rapidly growing economies, such as the United States and Argentina in the nineteenth century, inflows of foreign investment permit faster growth, or growth with less sacrifice of current consumption, than could otherwise take place. For countries generating large amounts of saving, international capital flows provide a means to invest where returns are higher than at home, as was the case for Great Britain in the nineteenth century and for Japan more recently.

These are long-term uses of what are, in some cases, prolonged periods of capital flow into or out of particular countries. Shorter periods of capital flow may serve some different functions, such as smoothing various types of cyclical or other economic fluctuations. For example, Edelstein (1982) has sug-

The author is indebted to Shachi Chopra-Nangia and Ewa Wojas for able research and statistical assistance.

gested that while inward capital flows to the United States during the nineteenth century were not large relative to domestic capital formation over long periods, they were much more important in shorter periods when capital formation spurted far ahead of more slowly growing saving levels, financing booms in capital formation that might otherwise have been strangled by rising interest rates. Countries heavily dependent on particular crops need capital flows to finance periods when crops fail or when crop prices fall drastically, permitting consumption, and perhaps capital formation, to be at least partially sheltered. International capital flows can also help to finance periods of war or of reparations, sometimes resulting from defeats in wars.

When these uses of international capital movements are studied, the flows of capital are usually measured net, as the difference between outflows and inflows, rather than by examining outflows and inflows separately. That is partly out of necessity, for lack of gross flow data. Most international capital flows during the nineteenth century are approximated by estimates of the net balance on current transactions, where it can be estimated, or even by the merchandise trade balance, where it cannot. One exception to this rule is that there have been many studies of flotations of foreign securities during the nineteenth century, particularly in the British capital market. Some of the components of the balance on capital account are, even now, usually observed in the form of net outflows or inflows; the simultaneous, or almost simultaneous, purchases and sales of different types of equity, of government securities, of private bonds, and of short-term debt are not observable for many countries.

Flows of direct investment capital are an exception to this netting out of outward and inward flows; for many countries, data are available separately for outward and inward flows. Outward flows are measured as the flows involving firms based in the reporting country, although these firms can, at times, repatriate their foreign investment, producing negative outward flows. Inward flows represent the activity in the country of firms based in other countries. The division reported now by the International Monetary Fund (IMF), following this practice, is between "investment abroad" and "investment in" a country.

A possible way to explain the different treatment of direct investment, aside from the problems of collecting data, is that direct and portfolio investment are related differently to the financial markets in home and host countries. In the markets for bank loans, government securities, and private company bonds and equity, many buyers and sellers are competing with each other to supply and acquire fairly standardized types of assets with fairly well defined prices in identifiable markets. Changes in flows can presumably be associated with changes in various interest rates in markets for these types of securities. It may matter little in the French and U.K. corporate bond markets whether, for example, the U.K. demand for French corporate bonds and the French demand for U.K. corporate bonds both increase equally at the expense of demands for each country's own bonds, or both decrease equally in favor of their own countries' securities, or whether there is no change in any of these demands.

Direct investment flows, on the other hand, do not enter any general financial market. They are internal to each firm, and an inflow is not simply offset by an outflow. Each flow brings something different to a country because it is attached to a specific firm. Equal direct investments from France to Germany and Germany to France do not simply cancel each other out; there has been an addition to the stock of French skills producing in Germany and an addition to German skills producing in France. Thus a comparison of net direct investment flows with aggregate net international investment misses much of the significance of direct investment.

This contrast should not be drawn too sharply. Portfolio investment may also flow in two directions at any given time. Investors in country 1 make portfolio investments in country 2 while investors in country 2 are making such investments in country 1. They may be seeking country or industry diversification in their portfolios even if their preferences and attitudes toward risk are the same. If they are not the same, investors in one country may be indulging a greater appetite for political risk or industry instability combined with higher returns.

The flow of direct investment is very much a two-way street among the top investing countries, even though direct investment is more concentrated among source countries than among recipient countries. The top ten exporters of direct investment capital accounted for over 90 percent of the world total in 1989–93 while the top ten recipients accounted for less than three-quarters of reported inflows. Nevertheless, six of the top ten exporters were also among the top ten recipients, and two of the other top recipients ranked just below the top ten as exporters (World Bank 1997). Another distinction between the exporter and importer groups was that the exporter group was a little more stable: eight out of the ten largest exporters of direct investment capital in 1969–73 were also in the group in 1989–93, while only six of the ten largest importers were still among the ten largest importers in 1989–93.

The data for the stock of outward and inward investment, which presumably reflect the cumulation of flows over many years, show similar concentrations. The top ten holders of direct investments abroad in 1995 owned 87 percent of the world total, while the top ten host countries were the location of about two-thirds of the stock. Six of the top host countries were also among the top ten holders (United Nations 1996).

6.1.2 The Definition and Measurement of Direct Investment: Control versus "Lasting Interest"

Direct investment is often discussed as if it consisted entirely of the investment associated with multinational corporations. Such a concept would match the theoretical literature on direct investment, but the data available do not follow it. Many aspects of multinational corporation activity are not included in measures of direct investment, and all past and present definitions of direct investment include transactions that do not involve multinationals.

The definition of direct investment and therefore its measurement have changed considerably over time. Definitions and measurements even now differ among countries despite the efforts of international agencies to push for uniformity.

The United States was a pioneer in surveying both outward and inward direct investment. The object of the surveys, as described in the 1937 inward investment survey, was to measure "all foreign equity interests in those American corporations or enterprises which are controlled by a person or group of persons . . . domiciled in a foreign country" (U.S. Department of Commerce 1937, 10). The term "equity interest" encompasses all holdings of common and preferred stock, advances, and intercompany accounts. No definition of "control" is provided, but control is the criterion for inclusion.

The outward survey for 1950 does provide a definition of direct investments, "the United States equity in controlled foreign business enterprises . . . as statistically defined for the purposes of this survey" (U.S. Department of Commerce 1953, 4). Four categories were covered:

1. "Foreign corporations, the voting securities of which were owned to the extent of 25 percent or more by persons or groups of affiliated persons, ordinarily resident in the United States."

2. "Foreign corporations, the voting stock of which was publicly held within the United States to an aggregate extent of 50 percent or more, but distributed among stockholders, so that no one investor, or group of affiliated investors, owned as much as 25 percent."

3. "Sole proprietorships, partnerships or real property (other than property held for the personal use of the owner) held abroad by residents of the United States."

4. "Foreign branches of United States corporations."

Three of these categories are part of current measures of direct investment, but the second one is not. An earlier definition had been even broader, including publicly owned companies with as little as 25 percent of stock in scattered U.S. holdings. The definition of control has been narrowed to mean ownership by a company, a person, or a small affiliated group. The change eliminated from the total of U.S. outward direct investment mainly Canadian companies, probably including such companies as Canadian Bell and Alcan Aluminium, that for historical reasons had large numbers of noncorporate U.S. holders.

The current definition of direct investment endorsed by the OECD (1996) and the IMF (1993) avoids the idea of control in favor of a much vaguer concept. "Foreign direct investment reflects the objective of obtaining a lasting interest by a resident entity in one country ('direct investor') in an entity resident in an economy other than that of the investor ('direct investment enterprise'). The lasting interest implies the existence of a long-term relationship between the direct investor and the enterprise and a significant degree of influence on the management of the enterprise" (OECD 1996, 7–8).

While this concept is a vague one, the recommended implementation is specific. "OECD recommends that a direct investment enterprise be defined as an incorporated or unincorporated enterprise in which a foreign investor owns 10 percent or more of the ordinary shares or voting power of an incorporated enterprise or the equivalent of an unincorporated enterprise. . . . An effective voice in the management, as evidenced by an ownership of at least 10 per cent, implies that the direct investor is able to influence, or participate in the management of an enterprise; it does not require absolute control by the foreign investor" (OECD 1996, 8).

The idea of control, which is behind much of the literature on multinationals, has been specifically abandoned. The fifth edition of the IMF *Balance of Payments Manual* points out that the concept of direct investment now used "is broader than the SNA concept of foreign-controlled, as distinguished from domestically controlled resident enterprises" (1993, 86). A single "direct investment enterprise" could be part of several different multinational firms, possibly from several countries. Duplication is avoided in investment flow and stock data, the main areas of concern to the OECD and the IMF, by allocating the financial aggregates to the various owners according to the extent of their ownership. However, data on the activities of multinationals, particularly those collected by home countries on, for example, the sales, employment, or output of their multinational firms or their overseas operations, could easily contain duplication if this 10 percent criterion is used.

6.1.3   Historical Background

Direct Investment before World War I

The history of multinational firms, and of the cross-border capital flows associated with them, foreign direct investment, goes back a long time. Mira Wilkins reminded us that "the origins of American multinational enterprises go back to the colonial period" and that "multinational enterprise headquartered in Europe has a longer history than American business abroad, going back to the middle ages" (1977, 577). She described "modern" American multinational corporations as dating from the 1850s and "investments over borders of modern European-headquartered manufacturing companies . . . to have accelerated in the late nineteenth and early twentieth centuries." She suggested that historical studies of international capital flows "often short-changed foreign *direct* investment."

It is striking, in view of the current interest in multinationals and foreign direct investment, that many descriptions of pre-World War I capital flows, perhaps the largest in history relative to total income or fixed investment, either did not discuss direct investment at all (Iversen 1936) or combined it with portfolio investment, as in the compilation in Palgrave (1910, vol. 2), without considering whether the determinants or effects were similar. However, Hobson did describe a half-century or more that "has witnessed an enormous rise in the importance of the international company, in railways, mining, tramways, water, gas, electricity, banking, insurance, finance, land plantations, and other enterprises" (1914, 125). "The international company has even extended to manufacturing, but there it is still somewhat rare." In one of his early books, John Dunning described the pre–World War I situation by the statement that "in 1914, 90 percent of all international capital movements took the form of portfolio investment—i.e., the acquisition of securities . . . issued by foreign institutions, without any associated control over, or participation in their management. . . . Several American and European companies . . . already owned sizeable foreign manufacturing ventures, but these were the exceptions rather than the rule, and they rarely accounted for a major part of the enterprises' total activities" (1970, 2).

The consensus was probably well summarized by Arthur Bloomfield's appraisal that "portfolio investment was a far more important component of long-term capital movements before 1914 than direct investment" (1968, 3), although Bloomfield noted one exception, China, among host countries, and one, the United States, among investing countries. Another apparent exception among investing countries, heavily weighted by investment in China, was Japan, with almost 90 percent of its foreign investment in the form of direct investment, as indicated in a number of sources cited by Mira Wilkins (1986). Bloomfield also noted that "before 1914 . . . the concept of direct investment (in its present-day sense) was not clearly distinguished from other (noncontrolling) equity investments in private foreign enterprises" (1968, 3–4).

The idea that direct investment flows were negligible before 1914 was challenged, at least as it applied to investment in developing countries, by Peter Svedberg (1978), who claimed that it was an illusion stemming from the typical methods of estimating flows and stocks. These relied heavily on compilations of government bond purchases and holdings and on London Stock Exchange and other similar flotations. They therefore missed many direct investments that did not pass through the exchanges. Also, by assuming that none of those that were publicly floated were bought by controlling interests, the estimates classified some direct investment as portfolio investment. After reviewing the data, Svedberg estimated that some 44 to 60 percent of the $19 billion of accumulated investment in developing (or "underdeveloped") countries in 1913–14 was in the form of direct investment. Furthermore, similar ratios could be found for investment in many different areas and by many different home countries and were not peculiar to investment by the United States.

Whatever the correct picture for the world before 1914, the history of U.S. inward international capital flows in that period conforms to the traditional picture. Foreign investment in the United States was overwhelmingly portfolio investment, to the extent that just before World War I about 80 percent of the stock of long-term investment in the United States was portfolio investment (Lewis 1938, 546). Federal, state, and local governments and railways were the chief borrowers, and most of the borrowing was in the form of bonds rather than equity.

On the other side of the balance sheet, three-quarters of the U.S. outward investment stock in 1914 was in the form of direct investment (Lewis 1938, 605). Thus, even if it is true that the worldwide role of direct investment before 1914 has been understated in the historical literature, its large role in U.S. outward investment was outside the range of other capital-exporting countries' experience and far greater than in other countries' capital exports to the United States.

The divisions between domestic and foreign financing and between direct and portfolio investment can be thought of as ways of dividing up risks among different types of investors and borrowers. One could imagine that in the early history of the United States, foreign capital might have financed risky types of capital formation that domestic investors would avoid. However, the nature of the projects financed by foreign capital does not support this idea. Early foreign investment went mainly into government securities, probably thought of as relatively safe, although some of them proved riskier than was expected. Later investment went heavily into railroads. A common feature, aside from lending to the federal government during the Civil War, was that foreign portfolio investment went to large, lumpy, social overhead capital projects—railroads, canals, and later public utilities—relatively safer investments and less dependent on local knowledge than the typically much smaller, and on that account, riskier enterprises in agriculture or manufacturing, which were left mainly to local financing (Edelstein 1982, 39–41, 237–38).

Many manufacturing enterprises were set up by foreign craftsmen or entrepreneurs with special skills. Since transportation and communication were so slow that it was impossible to manage these enterprises from abroad, the investment was therefore often accompanied by the migration of children or other relatives of the foreign investors to manage the enterprise. Although these enterprises were a form of direct investment, they were different from most direct investment now in that they were not controlled by parent firms as an outgrowth of their businesses, but by individual investors. Mira Wilkins (1989) referred to these as "free standing enterprises." Over time they tended to become more independent and often eventually lost the status of direct investments when their owners migrated to the United States.

The Dominance of Direct Investment in U.S. Investment Abroad and of the United States in World Outward Direct Investment

The United States has been, since its earliest days as a foreign investor, exceptionally focused on direct investment. An estimate for 1897, when the United States was still predominantly a recipient of capital from abroad rather than a supplier, showed more than 90 percent of U.S. outward investment to be direct investment. By 1914, the share had declined to three-quarters, still far above the proportion in foreign investment in the United States or in world investment as a whole (Lewis 1938, 605).

The period of World War I saw the first major U.S. portfolio investment abroad, including large loans to foreign governments that outweighed total private financing. By the end of 1919, direct investment had been reduced to a little over half of U.S. private investment abroad but to less than a quarter of total foreign investment including intergovernment loans (Lewis 1938, 447). The 1920s were characterized by rapid growth in both direct and portfolio private investment abroad but were unlike the earlier periods in that portfolio investment became the predominant avenue for U.S. investment, tripling in value while direct investment only doubled, and accounting for over 60 percent of the growth in private U.S. investment abroad. By 1929, the value of U.S. private portfolio investment exceeded that of direct investment for the first time (Lewis 1938, 450, 605).

The Great Depression reversed the change in the composition of the U.S. private foreign investment portfolio that had taken place in the 1920s. Half of the foreign loans extended in the late 1920s went into default (Mintz 1951, 6). U.S. holdings of securities, even valued at par, were reduced by almost 30 percent (almost 50 percent with defaulted bonds at market value), and short-term credits were cut almost in half (Lewis 1938, 454). By 1940, direct investment was back to 60 percent of U.S. private outward investment. It was a little more than that in 1950 and remained between 60 percent and two-thirds through 1970 (U.S. Bureau of the Census 1975, series U26–U39).

U.S. government loans to foreign countries had expanded further during World War II and by 1950 were almost twice the total of all private investment stocks. Thus the restored dominance of direct investment in 1950 applied only to private investment. After 1950, U.S. government loans did not increase greatly, and by 1970, more than 70 percent of U.S. international assets were private and almost half were direct investment.

The United States not only had much or most of its international investment in the form of direct investment but also accounted for a large part of the world's stock of direct investment. In 1960, almost half of all the outward direct investment was owned by investors based in the United States. No other country came close; the next ranking holder of direct investment was the United Kingdom at 18 percent, followed by the Netherlands at 10 percent and France at 6 percent (United Nations 1988, table 1.2). The large role of direct investment in U.S. foreign investment was associated with a large role for the United States in the world's direct investment universe.

6.1.4   The Importance of Foreign Direct Investment in Total International Investment Flows

The first question we attempt to answer here is about the size of direct investment flows relative to other forms of international investment. For almost all countries, a three-way division is published by the IMF, separating international investment flows into direct investment, portfolio investment, and other investment.

The definition of direct investment has been discussed above. Portfolio investment includes equity securities, debt securities in the form of bonds, money market instruments, and financial derivatives, such as options, all excluding any of these included in direct investment or reserve assets. The distinction between long and short term formerly made has been abandoned on the ground that original maturity is now of relatively little importance. The final category of "other investment" includes trade credit, loans, financial leases, currency, and deposits, mostly short-term assets.

The categories do not match those of the pre-1980 data we use, and some of the following tables therefore show an overlap for 1980–84. The data for years before 1980 are on a similar basis to later ones for direct investment, reported as "investment by," mainly outflows from the reporting country, and "investment in," mainly inflows to the reporting country. That is the case for most flows, but there can be reverse flows on both sides. A country's firms can repatriate accumulated earnings from their foreign affiliates or sell foreign operations to foreign buyers, resulting in a negative outflow (a positive entry in the balance of payments), and foreign firms in a host country can repatriate earnings or sell operations, producing a negative inflow of capital (a negative entry in the balance of payments).

For categories other than direct investment, the flows before 1980 are reported on a net basis, not distinguishing between changes in assets and changes in liabilities. There is thus no natural world total for those categories because every transaction should enter as both an asset change and a liability change, and the total should therefore be zero. For these categories we approximate gross flows very roughly by aggregating the net flows of those countries that report net outflows in that category in each year. That is, we aggregate all the negative balance-of-payments entries in each year under the headings of "portfolio investment, net," and "other investment, net." The alternative of aggregating positive entries should give the same result if the data were complete, but of course they are not. Judging by the 1980–84 overlap, the 1969–79 estimates for portfolio investment outflow are understated by almost 30 percent and those for other investment by almost half.

The amounts of the three major types of investment flows, by these imperfect measures, are shown in appendix table 6A.1. All types of international capital flows increased enormously. Since these are nominal values, they reflect the rise in world nominal income, which was, in 1990–94, about five and a half times as high as in 1970–74. All the forms of international capital flow grew faster than world nominal income. If we take the overlap in 1980–84 as an indicator of the underestimate of gross flows during 1970–79, we would conclude that the flow of direct investment grew the most and that other investment hardly grew faster than income (table 6.1). Since 1980, where we do have estimates of gross flows, portfolio investment has grown somewhat faster than direct investment, and other investment hardly grew until 1995, when it jumped ahead of the other two.

The long-term trend, if there is one, seems to have been an increase in the share of direct investment in total investment flows from 1980 through 1994, and possibly since 1970 (table 6.2). After 1994, the trend was apparently reversed, with a burst of portfolio and other investment, but the direct investment share remained well above that of the early 1970s.

All these statements have an important cloud over them. That is the persistent world current account deficit that has remained stubbornly close to $100 billion a year, instead of zero, as it should be. That deficit, which is really a discrepancy item, is so large that it implies that the correct figures for some of these entries could be very far different from those we are relying on to study and follow investment flows. The latest indicator of how far some of these numbers are from the facts they are supposed to represent is the results of the recently completed survey of U.S. portfolio investment abroad, which found that the market value of U.S.-owned foreign securities at the end of 1994 was $910 billion instead of the previously estimated $556 billion, an addition of 64 percent.

Table 6.1   Growth in Three Forms of Capital Outflow

Investment Type	Ratio
1990–94/1970–74	
Direct	61.7
Portfolio	49.6
Other	5.9
1990–94/1980–84	
Direct	5.24
Portfolio	5.97
Other	1.08

Source: Appendix table 6A.1, with 1970–74 estimated from 1980–84 overlap.

Table 6.2   Share of Direct Investment in Total Capital Outflow

Period	Share (%)
1970–74	5.8
1975–79	18.0
1980–84[a]	11.6
1985–89[a]	20.7
1990–94[a]	25.4
1990–94[b]	26.2
1994[b]	31.3
1995[b]	24.8
1996[b]	20.4

Source: Appendix table 6A.1, with 1970–74 and 1975–79 estimated from 1980–84 overlap.
[a]Excluding Hong Kong and Taiwan.
[b]Excluding Hong Kong but including Taiwan.

6.1.5   The Geography of International Investment Flows

Origins and Destinations of Direct Investment

Outward direct investment originates mainly in the highest income countries, as can be seen from appendix table 6A.2. The United States was the chief source of direct investment in 1970–74, larger than all the other regions shown here put together. Europe caught up in the second period and then far surpassed the United States. Japan caught up in 1985–89, and even exported more direct investment capital than the United States during those years, although it is a considerably smaller economy, with GDP less than three-quarters of that of the United States in nominal terms and less than 40 percent in real terms. After 1990, Japan faded as a direct investor and the United States resumed its position as the largest single supplier of direct investment.

The most rapid growth in outward direct investment was in the two developing areas, developing Asia and Latin America, especially the former. By 1990–94, according to the IMF data, the outflow from the developing Asian countries had reached over 85 percent of the Japanese level. However, these data grossly understate the contribution of developing Asian countries and its growth in recent years by omitting Hong Kong, even though they include Taiwan, decorously concealed under the title "Asia not specified." The addition of Hong Kong doubles the figure for the outflow from Southeast Asia in 1990–94. Hong Kong was a larger supplier of direct investment funds than Japan in 1994, 1995, and 1996 (United Nations 1997, annex table 13.2), and its addition to the developing Asia total brings that region to an important position as a direct investor. The timing of the growth in Hong Kong's outward investment is similar to that in China's inward investment, confirming the impression that much of the investment was going to China. Although there is no reported surge in Hong Kong inward investment, it is hard not to suspect that some part of the outward investment originated outside Hong Kong.

The flows to the main regional destinations for FDI are described in appendix table 6A.3. The two outstanding shifts in the destinations of FDI flows over the quarter-century were toward Asian countries, both China and Southeast Asia, and toward the United States. The flow to the United States reached a peak in the 1980s, when it was larger than the combined flows to all European destinations combined. After that, the flow to the United States receded somewhat, and in the next period the major growth was in the flow to Europe. Direct investment in developing Asia continued to grow rapidly and that in Latin America revived. In 1990–94, Europe resumed its earlier position as the main destination of direct investment. Most of the increase over the previous period was matched by similar growth in European outflows, an indication that a large part of the growth was in intra-European investment.

There is more direct evidence on the nature of European FDI. If Europe were treated as a single unit, its importance as a source and destination for FDI would be greatly reduced. Among the European countries that publish inward FDI position data, all except the United Kingdom had received 60 percent or more of their FDI stock from other European countries. And among those that published outward FDI positions, all except the United Kingdom had sent half or more of their FDI to other locations within Europe (OECD 1998).

Inflows to the United States have been volatile in the 1990s, first dropping to low levels in 1991 and 1992 and then rebounding strongly. Inflows to Japan, always small, turned negative in 1989 and, after a brief flurry in the early 1990s, stayed below $1 billion per year in 1993–96. Inflows to China, already far above earlier amounts, took off after 1991, reaching over $42 billion, almost ten times the 1991 level, in 1996 (United Nations 1997). There has been some suspicion that part of direct investment in China originates in China itself, routed through Hong Kong for various reasons including favorable treatment accorded to foreign-owned enterprises in China. If that is the case, such "round trip" investment does not appear to be substantially financed by reported Chinese direct investment in Hong Kong, which is quite small relative to inward direct investment in China.

The major elements of the net flows of international capital in these regions since 1969 are summarized in appendix tables 6A.4, 6A.5, and 6A.6. Negative numbers represent net outflows of capital and positive ones, net inflows.

Europe and Japan were consistent net suppliers of direct investment to the rest of the world and Latin America was a consistent absorber of such capital, as was developing Asia, especially in the last period (appendix table 6A.4). In 1993–95, China far surpassed Latin America as a net importer of direct investment (United Nations 1997, annex tables B.1 and B.2). One odd case here is the United States, which shifted from being the world's major net supplier of direct investment during the 1970s to being a large net recipient throughout the 1980s before returning to its traditional role. The shift is sometimes attributed to the devaluation of the dollar that started in 1985, and it is true that the inflow was at its largest in 1987–89, but the United States switched to being a net importer of direct investment capital much earlier, in 1981, and was a net importer through the period when the dollar was at its highest. Something more than exchange rates must have been at work. The other switch was in Southeast Asia, which, after absorbing direct investment on balance from 1969 to 1992, became a net supplier, mainly on account of Hong Kong, after that.

The net flow of portfolio capital does not show the same consistency of direction as the direct investment flow, and some of the fluctuations are very large (appendix table 6A.5). Japan has been a pretty consistent capital exporter in this category since the 1970s, while the other regions have mostly been importers. For the United States, portfolio inflows were particularly large in 1985–89, just when direct investment inflows were also at a peak. In this period, the high inflow to the United States almost exactly matched the outflow from Japan. The fact that the peak period in the United States was the same as for direct investment suggests that whatever led to the large inflows was not

Table 6.3   **Reported Net Inflows of Portfolio Capital, 1980–96 (millions of U.S. dollars)**

Country/Region	Inflow
United States	650,180
Japan	−506,320
Europe	276,200
Developing Asia	86,128
Latin America	273,771
Total	1,286,279

Source: See appendix tables 6A.2 and 6A.3.

peculiar to direct investment. In Latin America, also, the jump in direct investment inflows in the 1990s was accompanied by a large rise in portfolio capital inflows. For the whole period since 1980, the regions listed reported imports of portfolio capital reaching over $1.25 trillion, while the only net exporter in the list, Japan, reported less than half that amount in exports (table 6.3).

In the case of other capital flows, only one region, Europe, was consistent over time with respect to the direction of the flows, with inflows in every period (appendix table 6A.6). Every other region had periods of both inflows and outflows, sometimes with abrupt shifts from one to the other. The United States was a net supplier of funds through 1979–83 and then became a net recipient. Latin America was almost always a supplier of funds, and the other countries showed no consistent role.

The Regional Distribution of Total Net International Investment Flows

The combination of the various types of net capital flows is the total net international flow of capital. Japan has been a consistent supplier of capital on the international market throughout the whole period since 1980, while the United States has been a major net recipient of international capital flows, especially in the most recent years (appendix table 6A.7). Southeast Asia and Latin America have been pretty continuous recipients and were relatively large ones except when the United States began to absorb foreign capital on a large scale in 1983. Europe has mostly absorbed capital on net balance except in the 1985–89 period.

6.1.6   Differences in Behavior among Types of International Financial Flows

Volatility

As was mentioned in the discussion of historical aspects of international investment above, different types of financial flows can perform quite different functions for both investing and receiving countries. One difference among the types of flows that affects their functions, especially for the recipients, is in their volatility, a subject that has received increased attention since the Asian crisis began. We can compare flows of different types by asking how often net flows to or from a country change sign. That is, how often do inflows turn into outflows and outflows turn into inflows.

For direct investment, among the fifty-two countries for which we have long runs of data, and data for each type of capital flow, the average number of reversals was 2.50, indicating an average run in a single direction of over four years (table 6.4). The next most stable type was portfolio investment, with 3.60 reversals on average, an average run in one direction of over three years. Other capital flows reversed signs 4.2 times on average. Thus the general impression of the stability of direct investment, relative to the other types, is confirmed.

These comparisons take account of the direction of flows but not the size, which can vary sharply without any change of direction. We compare the types of flow with respect to their standard deviations in table 6.5.

Table 6.4   Frequency of Sign Changes in Capital Flows, 1980–95

Investment Type	No. of Sign Changes	Average Frequency of Sign Changes	Average Duration of Run
Net direct	130	2.50	4.29
Net porfolio	187	3.60	3.26
Net other	217	4.17	2.90

Source: IMF (1998).

Note: Number of countries is 52.

Table 6.5   Ratios of Standard Deviations to Means for Various Types of International Capital Flows, 1969–93

Country/Region	Net FDI	Other Long Term, Including Portfolio	Portfolio	Short Term
United States	1.302	1.469	1.188	1.297
Japan	1.307	1.371	1.473	1.636
Southeast Asia				
Unweighted average[a]	1.373	1.857	1.658	1.561
Aggregate[b]	1.455	2.265	1.835	1.179
Europe				
Unweighted average[a]	1.311	1.524	1.625	1.708
Aggregate[b]	1.008	1.911	2.102	1.823
Latin America				
Unweighted average[a]	1.072	1.792	2.228	1.478
Aggregate[b]	0.819	1.781	2.278	1.484

[a]Unweighted average of standard deviations for individual countries.

[b]Standard deviation of aggregate net flows to or from region.

In the case of the United States, both portfolio and short-term capital flows fluctuated less relative to the average flows than did net direct investment. The United States was unusual in this respect, however. For Japan and for the three regions, the average for individual country volatility, as measured by the ratios of standard deviations to means, was lowest for net direct investment. The volatility of the aggregates in two of the three regions confirmed the relative stability of direct investment. There is a particularly wide gap in Latin America between the volatility of net portfolio investment and the relative stability of net direct investment.

Relations among Capital Flows

If flows of direct investment respond to current economic conditions in each country, one might expect to find alternating periods of larger outflows than inflows and larger inflows than outflows and, therefore, a negative relationship between gross outflows and gross inflows. As table 6.6 indicates, for a selection of major exporters and recipients of FDI flows, that is not the case. By and large, where there is a significant relationship, it is a positive one; direct investment inflows to a country tend to be large when outflows from the country are large.

To some extent, this relationship may reflect trends, or simply the effects of growth, which we may partially remove by taking international flows relative to GDP. The trend influence is confirmed by the fact that fewer equations are significant, correlations are lower, and one significant negative relationship appears, for Brazil; but the overall result is still that outflows and inflows are positively related, where there is any significant relationship at all.

We can also ask how gross or net FDI outflows are related to flows of capital in other forms. The results for the thirteen countries used in the test are presented in table 6.7.

The strongest relationship is that between outward direct investment and outward flows of short-term capital. Large outflows of direct investment are accompanied by outflows of short-term capital as well. There is also a much weaker positive association with net flows of portfolio capital. Net outflows of direct investment are negatively correlated with net flows of all other long-term capital and also with that part of it that is portfolio capital. Little of the variability in one flow is explained by the other, but there is at least some suggestion here of substitution among types of long-term capital flows, especially between direct and portfolio capital flows.

The Importance of Retained Earnings in Direct Investment

One feature of flows of direct investment that distinguishes it from other forms of investment is that it can be, and often is, financed from the retained earnings of affiliates. The IMF and the OECD recommend that direct investment flows include "the direct investor's share of the company's reinvested earnings" (OECD 1996, 16). Unfortunately for our ability to make compari-

Table 6.6   **Summary of Equations Relating FDI by a Country to FDI in a Country, 1969–94**

	FDI By = f(FDI In)		FDI By/GDP = f(FDI In/GDP)	
	Coefficient of FDI In	Adjusted R^2	Coefficient of FDI In/GDP	Adjusted R^2
United States	.45	.16*	−.05	−.04
	(2.40)		(.18)	
United Kingdom	1.01	.66**	.73	.32**
	(7.02)		(3.53)	
Japan	4.13	.01	−3.68	.03
	(1.09)		(1.33)	
Germany	2.26	.60**	.51	.05
	(6.26)		(1.48)	
France	1.49	.85**	1.62	.71**
	(12.02)		(7.70)	
Netherlands	1.47	.83**	1.04	.47**
	(11.27)		(4.68)	
Sweden	1.11	.28**	1.20	.18*
	(3.26)		(2.51)	
Canada	.49	.36**	.06	−.04
	(3.81)		(.38)	
Brazil	−.01	−.04	−.06	.12
	(.14)		(2.06)	
Singapore	.14	.57**	.09	.07
	(5.40)		(1.59)	
All	.76	.38**	.09	.03**
	(12.55)		(3.03)	

Note: Numbers in parentheses are t-statistics.
*Prob $F < 0.05$.
**Prob $F < 0.01$.

Table 6.7   **Simple Regressions Relating FDI Flows to Flows of Other Types of Capital in Thirteen Countries**

	Coefficient of FDI	Adjusted R^2
Outward FDI × Short-term capital	.230**	.148
Outward FDI × Long-term capital excluding FDI	−.016	−.003
Outward FDI × Portfolio capital	.080*	.014
Net FDI × Short-term capital	.059*	.012
Net FDI × Long-term capital excluding FDI	−.097**	.039
Net FDI × Portfolio capital	−.121**	.059

*Significant at 5 percent level.
**Significant at 1 percent level.

sons across countries, many important capital exporters do not include reinvested earnings in their capital flow data. Among the OECD countries, Belgium, Canada, France, Italy, Japan, and Norway are in this group.

The United States is one country that has kept records of retained earnings of its firms' foreign affiliates over many years, although there have been some changes in their treatment in the balance of payments. The distribution, by type, of U.S. direct investment outflows in recent years is described in table 6.8.

Although there are large fluctuations in the proportions, reinvested earnings are clearly the predominant form of financing of U.S. outward direct investment. They account for more than half of investment over the whole period, in each subperiod, and in ten out of the fourteen individual years. The only year in which they were not larger than each of the other forms of investment was the severe recession year, 1982.

One reason for the importance of reinvested earnings in U.S. outward direct investment is that U.S. firms' foreign operations are relatively mature, having started earlier than most of those from other countries. However, the large role of reinvested earnings is an old one for the United States. During the late 1930s and through World War II they were virtually the only source of additions to direct investment, and even when the pace of investment picked up after the war, retained earnings still provided over 40 percent of the growth.

In the twenty-five years from 1950 through 1975, reinvested earnings accounted for more than half of the growth in the stock of U.S. outward direct investment, 60 percent in manufacturing and trade, and somewhat lower proportions in petroleum and in other industries including finance (table 6.9).

Some more recent data, for countries that keep such records, are summarized in table 6.10, for both home countries and host countries, 1989–95. The large contribution of retained earnings to growth in direct investment, a characteristic of U.S. outward direct investment for so long, is not a universal characteristic of direct investment, as can be seen in the large negative retained earn-

Table 6.8   **Distribution by Type of U.S. Outflows of Direct Investment**

Period	Equity Capital Outflows	Retained Earnings	Intercompany Debt Outflows
1982–86	26.7	84.9	−11.6
1987–91	23.6	64.6	11.8
1992–95	34.2	50.7	15.0
1992	37.6	41.8	20.6
1993	33.0	40.4	26.6
1994	24.8	62.4	12.8
1995	39.0	56.3	4.7

Source: U.S. Department of Commerce, Bureau of Economic Analysis, *U.S. Direct Investment Abroad: Balance of Payments and Direct Investment Position* (Washington, D.C., n.d.), diskette.

Note: Intracompany transactions with the Netherlands Antilles have been removed.

324   Robert E. Lipsey

Table 6.9   Cumulated Reinvested Earnings and Changes in U.S. Outward
                 Direct Investment Stock: Total and Selected Industry Groups,
                 1950–75 (billions of U.S. dollars)

	Change in Direct Investment Stock	Investment Stock 1975/1950	Cumulated Reinvested Earnings	Share of Reinvested Earnings
All industries	112	10.5	60	54
Petroleum	23	7.7	10	43
Manufacturing	52	14.6	31	60
Trade	12	16.4	7.5	62
Other, including finance	19	16.0	7	37

Source: U.S. Department of Commerce (1982).

ings on inward direct investment in the United States. The importance of retained earnings appears to be related to the age of the investments, the United States, the United Kingdom, Sweden, and Switzerland being direct investors of long standing. Much of U.S. inward investment, on the other hand, is a product of the late 1980s, and therefore very new during the period covered. Similarly, Germany is a relatively late entrant as a major direct investor, partly because much of its investment was confiscated after losses in two world wars.

Other factors may also play a role. During the period of exchange controls, many enterprises were not permitted to repatriate their profits, particularly from developing countries. There are also differences and changes in systems of taxation of overseas earnings that affect where profits are made, where they are accumulated, and if and when they are repatriated.

6.1.7 Summary

Direct investment, as a flow of capital, is only partly related to the activities of multinational firms. Most of what these firms do, and most of their impact, is unconnected with current capital flows, and parts of the capital flows are unconnected with multinational firms. Over time, the definition of direct investment has shifted from an emphasis on control across national boundaries to a vaguer notion of "lasting interest" and "significant" influence on management, and in the balance-of-payments data the enterprise is divided up statistically among owners of shares of 10 percent or more.

The history of cross-border ownership of enterprises is a long one, and its importance as a part of international capital flows before World War I a matter of some controversy. However, it is clear that direct investment was more important in total U.S. investment abroad than in total foreign investment by other countries and far more important than in foreign investment in the United States. As a result of this specialization in direct investment, the United States

Table 6.10   Outflows and Inflows of Direct Investment: Total and Reinvested Earnings for Selected Countries, 1989–95 (millions of U.S. dollars)

	Total Direct Investment Assets (Outward FDI)	Reinvested Earnings	Share of Reinvested Earnings (%)	Total Direct Investment Liabilities (Inward FDI)	Reinvested Earnings	Share of Reinvested Earnings (%)
United States	368,988	184,508	50.0	308,242	−47,582	−15.4
Germany	149,700	10,849	7.2	28,005	−6,687	−23.9
Netherlands[a]	86,549	9,159	10.6	48,025	8,225	17.1
Sweden	51,406	12,742	24.8	34,359	4,327	12.6
Switzerland	57,885	15,729	27.2	19,818	7,805	39.4
United Kingdom	184,230	108,908	59.1	153,375	32,047	20.9

Source: IMF (1996).

[a]1989–94.

was the dominant holder of direct investment assets in the decade or two after World War II.

It is hard to assess the relative importance of direct investment as a method of financing international investment flows because of the offsetting of one set of flows by another. In the gross flow data, direct investment has accounted for a little under a quarter of flows since 1989 and appears to have grown in importance since the 1970s.

The United States was by far the major source of direct investment outflows in the early 1970s, but Europe soon caught up and Japan almost did before fading out in the 1990s. Hong Kong became a major investor in the 1990s, investing heavily in China. The United States shifted from being the world's largest net supplier of direct investment to being a large absorber of such investment from other countries, especially in 1985–89, and then reverted to its earlier net supplier role. Latin America and Southeast Asia have been continuous net recipients of direct investment.

Portfolio capital has been supplied to the world steadily by Japan. The United States, at times, particularly in 1985–89, has absorbed much of this capital, on net balance, and Southeast Asia and Latin America have also been major borrowers.

Total international capital flows, of which the United States supplied a large proportion through 1983, have since then become a source of capital for the United States, as they have been for China and Southeast Asia in almost every period. Europe also has been a net absorber of capital in most periods, and Japan the only consistent supplier.

In recent years, capital flows among the developed countries, particularly the United States and Europe, have been dominated by portfolio capital. Direct investment has played the largest role in net outflows from Japan and especially in the inflows to Southeast Asia, China, and Latin America.

The different forms of international investment flows not only vary in importance among regions but have different characteristics in other ways. Direct investment flows have been the least volatile among the different types in most countries, the chief exception being the United States, which has flipped back and forth from being the dominant net supplier to dominant net recipient and back to dominant net supplier. For other countries, and particularly for developing countries, direct investment has been the most dependable source of foreign investment.

One reason for the relative stability of direct investment flows may be the importance within them of retained earnings. These do fluctuate, of course, with profits, but they rarely shift sharply into the negative once firms are well established. Retained earnings appear to be most important in outward U.S. and U.K. investment. There are some large negative retained earnings in recent years for foreign direct investment in the United States, relatively new and perhaps purchased at the peak of real estate markets, but the general relationship seems to be that older holdings of direct investment grow a good deal from retained earnings.

Appendix

Table 6A.1   **World Investment Flows (millions of U.S. dollars; five-year averages)**

Period	Direct Investment	Portfolio Investment	Other Investment	Total
	Old IMF Data, 1970–84			
1970–74	3,564	5,081	26,608	
1975–79	36,669	14,493	76,336	
1980–84	44,751	42,247	145,149	
	Current IMF Data, 1980–96			
1980–84	44,514[a]	59,316[a]	279,690[a]	383,520
1985–89	140,069[a]	188,670[a]	346,895[a]	675,634
1990–94	219,969[a]	352,784[a]	294,752[a]	867,505
1990–94	233,409	353,927[b]	303,104[b]	890,440
1994	276,443	330,662[b]	276,721[b]	883,826
1995	349,501	372,438[b]	684,525[b]	1,406,464
1996	348,992	587,069[b]	778,432[b]	1,714,493

Sources: IMF (1998), World Bank (1995, 1997), and United Nations (1996, 1997, 1998).
[a]Excluding Hong Kong and Taiwan.
[b]Excluding Hong Kong but including Taiwan.

Table 6A.2   **Sources of Direct Investment Outflows (millions of U.S. dollars; five-year averages)**

Period	United States	Japan	Europe	Developing Asia	Latin America
	Old IMF Data, 1970–84				
1970–74	8,670	1,042	6,968	23	31
1975–79	15,876	2,133	16,000	109	194
1980–84	10,117	4,280	24,889	240	358
	Current IMF Data, 1980–96				
1980–84	9,592	4,280	24,958	163[a]	262
1985–89	22,890	24,590	75,591	6,168[b]	411
1990–94	50,240	26,286	121,846	22,696[c]	1,625
1994	69,264	18,089	131,789	36,302[c]	2,936
1995	86,738	22,508	177,416	42,180[c]	2,797
1996	87,812	23,442	172,053	48,024[c]	3,770

Sources: IMF (1998), World Bank (1995, 1997), and United Nations (1996, 1997, 1998).
[a]Excluding Hong Kong and Taiwan.
[b]Excluding Hong Kong but including annual average outward direct investment by Taiwan over the period 1984–89.
[c]Including both Hong Kong and Taiwan.

Table 6A.3   **Destinations of Direct Investment Inflows (millions of U.S. dollars; five-year averages)**

Period	United States	Japan	Europe	Developing Asia	Latin America
		Old IMF Data, 1970–84			
1970–74	2,070	126	7,181	708	1,308
1975–79	6,092	123	11,474	1,423	3,270
1980–84	17,965	262	15,202	3,641	5,214
		Current IMF Data, 1980–96			
1980–84	17,965	262	15,536	4,716[a]	6,308
1985–89	47,773	101	46,226	11,512[b]	6,505
1990–94	36,507	1,371	91,489	36,182[b]	15,287
1994	45,678	912	84,642	59,753[b]	27,495
1995	67,527	39	138,030	68,385[b]	28,838
1996	76,955	200	120,109	77,995[b]	40,056

Sources: IMF (1998), World Bank (1995, 1997), and United Nations (1996, 1997, 1998).

[a]Including annual average figures for outward direct investment by Hong Kong and Taiwan over the period 1980–85.

[b]Including both Hong Kong and Taiwan.

Table 6A.4   **Net Inflows of Direct Investment (millions of U.S. dollars; five-year averages)**

Period	United States	Japan	Europe	Developing Asia	Latin America
		Old IMF Data, 1970–84			
1970–74	−6,600	−916	213	685	1,277
1975–79	−9,784	−2,010	−4,526	1,314	3,076
1980–84	7,847	−4,018	−9,688	3,401	4,855
		Current IMF Data, 1980–96			
1980–84	8,373	−4,018	−9,422	4,553[a]	6,045
1985–89	24,883	−24,489	−29,365	5,344[b]	6,094
1990–94	−13,733	−24,915	−30,357	13,486[c]	13,662
1994	−23,586	−17,177	−47,147	23,451[c]	24,559
1995	−19,211	−22,468	−39,386	26,204[c]	26,041
1996	−10,857	−23,242	−51,945	29,970[c]	36,286

Sources: Tables 6A.2 and 6A.3.

Note: Net flows are inflows minus outflows.

[a]Excluding Hong Kong and Taiwan.

[b]Including Taiwan and excluding outward investment from Hong Kong, but including inward investment.

[c]Including Hong Kong and Taiwan.

Table 6A.5   **Net Flows of Portfolio Capital (millions of U.S. dollars; five-year averages)**

Period	United States	Japan	Europe	Developing Asia[a]	Latin America
Old IMF Data, 1970–84					
1970–74	5,494	−292	−691	54	−18
1975–79	8,140	392	3,014	254	790
1980–84	12,449	−1,784	−4,521	576	1,568
Current IMF Data, 1980–96					
1980–84	12,449	−1,908	−12,981	810	1,661
1985–89	70,229	−69,458	23,802	1,749	−118
1990–94	14,380	−14,354	39,192	8,231	40,225
1994	79,091	−27,219	−66,265	13,408	65,989
1995	137,401	−36,575	51,246	14,593	4,827
1996	274,879	−41,145	−25,111	17,585	60,104

Sources: IMF (1998) and World Bank (1995, 1997).
Note: Net flows are inflows minus outflows.
[a]Including Taiwan.

Table 6A.6   **Net Flows of Other Investment (millions of U.S. dollars)**

Period	United States	Japan	Europe	Developing Asia[a]	Latin America
Current IMF Data, 1980–96					
1980–84[b]	−14,399	−5,428	42,073	20,639	22,477
1985–89[b]	29,093	36,522	1,468	9,769	2,895
1990–94[b]	85,088	−37,926	34,187	11,156	−9,412
1994	75,967	−40,714	89,957	9,973	−43,513
1995	35,579	−4,936	7,841	26,475	28,023
1996	−75,558	36,288	53,420	46,640	−22,922

Sources: IMF (1998) and World Bank (1995, 1997).
Note: Net flows are outflows less inflows.
[a]Including Taiwan.
[b]Annual averages.

Table 6A.7   **Total Average Annual Net International Capital Flows (millions of U.S. dollars)**

Period	United States	Japan	Europe	Developing Asia[a]	Latin America
1980–84	6,423	−11,354	19,670	26,002	30,183
1985–89	124,205	−57,425	−4,094	16,863	8,871
1990–94	85,735	−77,195	43,022	32,873	44,474
1994	131,472	−85,110	−23,455	46,832	47,036
1995	153,769	−63,980	19,701	67,272	58,891
1996	188,464	−28,098	−23,636	94,195	73,469

Sources: IMF (1998) and World Bank (1995, 1997).
Note: Net flows are outflows less inflows.
[a]Including Hong Kong.

References

Bloomfield, Arthur I. 1968. *Patterns of fluctuations in international investment before 1914.* Princeton Studies in International Finance, no. 21. Princeton, N.J.: Princeton University, International Finance Section.

Dunning, John. 1970. *Studies in international investment.* London: Allen and Unwin.

Edelstein, Michael. 1982. *Overseas investment in the age of high imperialism: The United Kingdom, 1850–1914.* New York: Columbia University Press.

Hobson, C. K. 1914. *The export of capital.* London: Constable.

IMF (International Monetary Fund). 1993. *Balance of payments manual,* 5th ed. Washington, D.C.: International Monetary Fund.

———. 1996. *Balance of payments statistics yearbook.* Washington, D.C.: International Monetary Fund.

———. 1998. *Balance of payments statistics yearbook.* Washington, D.C.: International Monetary Fund. Diskette.

Iversen, Carl. 1936. *Aspects of the theory of international capital movements.* Copenhagen: Levin and Munksgaard; London: Humphrey Milford and Oxford University Press.

Lewis, Cleona. 1938. *America's stake in international investments.* Washington, D.C.: Brookings Institution.

Mintz, Ilse. 1951. *Deterioration in the quality of foreign bonds issued in the United States, 1920–1930.* New York: National Bureau of Economic Research.

OECD (Organization for Economic Cooperation and Development). 1996. *OECD benchmark definition of foreign direct investment,* 3d ed. Paris: Organization for Economic Cooperation and Development.

———. 1998. *International direct investment statistics yearbook.* Paris: Organization for Economic Cooperation and Development.

Palgrave, Robert Harry Inglis, ed. 1910. *Dictionary of political economy.* London: Macmillan.

Svedberg, Peter. 1978. The portfolio-direct composition of private foreign investment in 1914 revisited. *Economic Journal* 88, no. 352 (December): 763–77.

United Nations. 1988. *Transnational corporations in world development: Trends and prospects.* New York: United Nations, Centre on Transnational Corporations.

———. 1995. *World investment report, 1995.* New York and Geneva: United Nations.

———. 1996. *World investment report, 1996.* New York and Geneva: United Nations.

———. 1997. *World investment report, 1997.* New York and Geneva: United Nations.

———. 1998. *World investment report, 1998.* New York and Geneva: United Nations.

U.S. Bureau of the Census. 1975. *Historical statistics of the United States, colonial times to 1970.* Washington, D.C.: Government Printing Office.

U.S. Department of Commerce. 1937. *Foreign investments in the United States.* Washington, D.C.: Bureau of Foreign and Domestic Commerce.

———. 1953. *Direct private foreign investments of the United States, census of 1950.* Washington, D.C.: Office of Business Economics.

———. 1982. *Selected data on U.S. direct investment abroad, 1950–76.* Washington, D.C.: Bureau of Economic Analysis.

Wilkins, Mira. 1977. Modern European economic history and the multinationals. *Journal of European Economic History* 6, no. 3 (winter): 575–95.

———. 1986. Japanese multinational enterprise before 1914. *Business History Review* 60 (summer).

———. 1989. *The history of foreign investment in the United States to 1914.* Cambridge, Mass.: Harvard University Press.

World Bank. 1995. *World data.* World Bank indicators on CD-ROM. Washington, D.C.: World Bank.

————. 1997. *World development indicators on CD-ROM.* Washington, D.C.: World Bank.

---

2. Robert C. Feenstra
Facts and Fallacies about Foreign Direct Investment

6.2.1 Introduction

Foreign direct investment combines aspects of both international trade in goods and international financial flows and is a phenomena more complex than either of these. As its name suggests, it first involves ownership of the assets of a firm: foreign direct investment (FDI) is often defined as the acquisition of 10 percent or more of the assets of a foreign enterprise. Second, it involves the choice of a host country for these assets. The choice of where to invest will depend on cost conditions and the extent to which investment gives preferential access to the local market, and both of these considerations depend on trade restrictions and other policies in the host country. In this respect, the decision of firms to invest abroad will be a counterpart to the international trade policies of the countries involved.

Third, FDI involves the choice of which activities to keep internal to a firm, and which to contract on the market: only the activities *internal* to a firm will be included in FDI, while other activities can be pursued by arm's-length transactions between unrelated firms. For example, a firm investing in a country might bring with it some knowledge that cannot be effectively leased or sold on the market. Instead, it will set up a plant for local production and also export, so as to profit from the knowledge it has; in this case FDI leads to a transfer of intangible assets (knowledge) from the parent to the foreign subsidiary. This argument can work equally well in reverse, whereby the acquisition of a foreign firm can bring with it some knowledge of value to the purchaser that could not be obtained by simply buying the products of that foreign firm. I will argue that increased inflows of FDI to the United States during the past decade have been motivated in part by the acquisition of knowledge.

These three features of FDI—ownership, location, and internalization—make up the so-called OLI framework for understanding FDI. This framework stresses the multifaceted nature of any decision to acquire a foreign firm. Because of the complexity of this decision, one should not expect any simple model to account for the trends in foreign investment as it occurs around the globe. Nevertheless, one might still expect the broad facts to be well under-

The author thanks Josef Merrill for excellent research assistance, and William Zeile of the Bureau of Economic Analysis for help with obtaining and interpreting the foreign investment data.

stood. In this paper I will argue that this is not the case, and on the contrary, there is a good deal of confusion about even the most elementary aspects of FDI, such as who is investing where, how much, and why. Some of this confusion is due to contradictory data, but in other cases, it represents genuine conceptual misunderstandings about FDI.

To present the arguments in the starkest manner, I will organize the discussion around four fallacies about FDI. This presentation runs the risk of having the reader reject the fallacies as simpleminded, and not believable in the first place. But I hope each reader will find some degree of plausibility in these fallacies, and indeed, each of them contains an element of truth. It is when they are taken as factual statements intended to hold quite generally that they become incorrect.

I begin the paper with a summary of the major trends in foreign investment over the 1980–95 period. Following that I present the various fallacies, dealing with the magnitude of foreign investment in Japan and the impact of FDI on the U.S.-Japan trade balance; the extent to which multinational corporations control U.S. trade; the impact of exchange rate movements on foreign investment flows; and, finally, the impact of FDI on the welfare of the host country. I conclude the paper with further analysis of recent trends in foreign investment, and their implications for the competition faced by U.S. firms in international markets. Taken together with what I learn from overturning the various fallacies, this analysis can serve as a guide to understanding movements in FDI today.

6.2.2   Trends in Foreign Direct Investment

Theories of FDI often emphasize the links between developed and developing countries. For example, the celebrated "product cycle" model of Vernon (1966) described how new products are created in the developed countries, where production first occurs, and then as the production process is standardized production will shift to lower wage developing countries. This shift in production need not occur within a multinational firm, but often it does, as Vernon rightly emphasized. While this is an insightful description of the dynamic process of product development and trade, it ignores the fact that the *majority* of foreign investment flows have been between developed countries. Thus about three-quarters of the world stock of direct investment is currently located in developed countries, with only one-quarter in developing countries. In table 6.11 I show the allocation of inward and outward FDI stocks between the developed and developing countries over the years 1980–95. These data are obtained from United Nations sources, which are the best available on a worldwide basis but still have some deficiencies that I will describe later.

Looking first at the inward stock in the upper half of table 6.11, the proportion of FDI located in developing countries fluctuated between 19 and 26 percent over 1980–95. Investment surged into the developed countries in the sec-

Table 6.11   FDI Stock, 1980–95 (billions of U.S. dollars)

	1980	1985	1990	1995
Total inward stock	481.9	734.9	1,716.9	2,657.9
Developed economies	373.6	538.0	1,373.3	1,932.7
Developed share (% of total)	77.5	73.2	80.1	73.9
U.S. inward stock	83.1	184.6	394.9	564.6
U.S. share of developed stock (%)	22.2	34.3	28.8	29.2
Developing economies	108.3	196.8	341.7	693.3
Developing share (% of total)	22.5	26.8	19.9	26.1
Chinese inward stock	0.0	3.4	14.1	129.0
Chinese share of developing stock (%)	0.0	1.7	4.1	18.6
Total outward stock	513.7	685.6	1,684.1	2,730.2
Developed economies	507.5	664.2	1,614.6	2,514.3
Developed share (% of total)	98.8	96.9	95.9	92.1
U.S. outward stock	220.2	251.0	435.2	705.6
U.S. share of developed stock (%)	43.4	37.8	27.0	28.1
Developing economies	6.2	21.2	69.4	214.5
Developing share (% of total)	1.2	3.1	4.1	7.9
Chinese outward stock	0.0	0.1	2.5	17.3
Chinese share of developing stock (%)	0.0	0.6	3.6	8.1

Source: United Nations, *World Investment Report* (New York, 239–48, 1996), annex tables 3 and 4.

ond half of the 1980s, during which time the stock of investment in developed countries nearly tripled from $538 billion to $1,373 billion. The magnitude of direct investment in the United States doubled between 1980 and 1985, and again between 1985 and 1990. Since 1990, the stock of investment located in the developing countries has grown more rapidly, which is in large part due to increased FDI in China. This country accounts for 18.6 percent of the inward stock of developing countries in 1995, up from 4.1 percent just five years earlier. The vast majority of FDI entering developed and developing countries alike comes from the developed countries, as detailed in the lower half of table 6.11.[1]

In comparison with these stock figures, about one-third or more of the inward *flow* of FDI in recent years has been going to developing countries, especially China. For example, in 1995 the United States was the largest recipient of FDI, with an inflow of $60.2 billion, but China was the second largest recipient with an inflow of $37.5 billion. Table 6.12 provides detailed information on the inward and outward flows of FDI for developed and developing countries. The surge in FDI flows during the second half of the 1980s both came from and was directed toward the developed countries: this flow reached $172 billion in 1989. This was followed by a fall in direct investment magnitudes

1. Note that the total world stock of inward FDI in 1995—$2.66 trillion—is less than the total stock of outward FDI—$2.73 trillion. This discrepancy is due to different accounting practices among countries in recording the value of FDI, as I shall discuss below.

Table 6.12   FDI Flow, 1983–95 (billions of U.S. dollars)

	1983–88[a]	1989	1990	1991	1992	1993	1994	1995
Total inflows	91.6	200.6	203.8	157.8	168.1	207.9	225.7	314.9
Developed economies	71.8	171.7	169.8	114.0	114.0	129.3	132.8	203.2
Developed share (% of total)	78.4	85.7	83.4	73.8	70.0	64.8	61.4	68.4
U.S. inflows	34.4	67.7	47.9	22.0	17.6	41.1	49.8	60.2
U.S. share of developed inflows (%)	47.9	39.4	28.2	19.3	15.4	31.8	37.5	29.7
Developing economies	19.8	28.6	33.7	41.3	50.4	73.1	87.0	99.7
Developing share (% of total)	21.6	14.3	16.6	26.2	30.0	35.2	38.6	31.6
Chinese inflows	1.8	3.4	3.5	4.4	11.2	27.5	33.8	37.5
Chinese share of developing inflows (%)	9.2	11.8	10.3	10.6	22.2	37.6	38.8	37.6
Total outflows	93.7	217.9	240.3	210.8	203.1	225.5	230.0	317.9
Developed economies	88.3	202.3	222.5	201.9	181.4	192.4	190.9	270.6
Developed share (% of total)	94.2	92.8	92.6	95.8	89.4	85.4	83.2	85.2
U.S. outflows	14.2	25.7	27.2	33.5	39.0	69.0	45.6	95.5
U.S. share of developed outflows (%)	16.1	12.7	12.2	16.6	21.5	35.9	23.9	35.3
Developing economies	5.4	15.6	17.8	8.9	21.6	33.0	38.6	47.0
Developing share (% of total)	5.8	7.2	7.4	4.2	10.6	14.6	16.8	14.8
Chinese outflows	0.5	0.8	0.8	0.9	4.0	4.4	2.0	3.5
Chinese share of developing outflows (%)	8.5	5.0	4.7	10.3	18.5	13.3	5.2	7.4

Source: United Nations, *World Investment Report* (New York, 1995, 1996), annex tables 1 and 2.

[a]Annual average.

from 1990 to 1991, with a recovery that was slow at first but has increased recently to reach $203 billion in 1995. The inflow of investment to China grew most dramatically from $4.4 billion in 1991 to $37.5 billion in 1995.

In addition to China, the inflows of FDI to the developing world are concentrated in a rather small number of countries. In table 6.13 I show the top ten recipient developing countries for both FDI stock and flow, for 1995. China has nearly 5 percent of the world stock of FDI in 1995, which is about twice as much as the next highest country, Mexico. At the same time, it is receiving nearly 12 percent of the world's flow of FDI, which is about five times as much as that entering Mexico. The other developing countries with substantial

Table 6.13   FDI in Top Ten Developing Countries, 1995

	Total (billion US$)	Share of World Total (%)	Share of Developing Total (%)
FDI Inward Stock			
All developing economies	693.3	26.1	100
China	129.0	4.9	18.6
Mexico	61.3	2.3	8.8
Singapore	55.5	2.1	8.0
Indonesia	50.8	1.9	7.3
Brazil	49.5	1.9	7.1
Malaysia	38.5	1.5	5.6
Bermuda	28.4	1.1	4.1
Argentina	26.8	1.0	3.9
Saudi Arabia	26.5	1.0	3.8
Hong Kong	21.8	0.8	3.1
All others	205.3	7.7	29.6
Total for top 10		26.08	70.4
FDI Inflow			
All developing economies	99.7	31.7	100
China	37.5	11.9	37.6
Mexico	7.0	2.2	7.0
Malaysia	5.8	1.8	5.8
Singapore	5.3	1.7	5.3
Brazil	4.9	1.5	4.9
Indonesia	4.5	1.4	4.5
Argentina	3.9	1.2	3.9
Hungary	3.5	1.1	3.5
Chile	3.0	1.0	3.0
Bermuda	2.9	0.9	2.9
All others	21.4	6.8	21.5
Total for top 10		31.6	78.2
Total excluding China		19.7	62.4

Source: United Nations, *World Investment Report* (New York, 1996), annex tables 1 and 3.

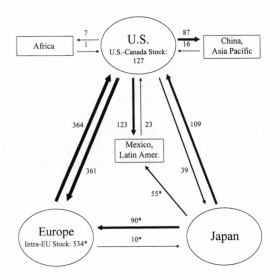

Fig. 6.1   Principal FDI bilateral stocks, 1995 (billions of U.S. dollars)
Source: U.S. Department of Commerce, Bureau of Economic Analysis, STAT-USA database.
*Estimated by author. Intra-EU stock is for 1994.

inward stocks and flows include Malaysia, Singapore, Brazil, Indonesia, and Argentina. Taken together, the top ten recipient countries account for 70 percent of the inward stock and nearly 80 percent of the inflow.

The principal bilateral stocks and flows of FDI in 1995 are represented in figures 6.1 and 6.2. I focus on the "Triad" countries: the United States, Europe, and Japan. Bilateral FDI between these regions accounts for fully one-third of the world stock (which is $2.7 trillion) or of the world flow (about $315 billion) in 1995. It is apparent that stocks and flows between the United States and Europe continue to dominate the world allocation of direct investment, in addition to intra-European FDI. Following these in magnitude are outward investment from Japan to the United States and Europe and outward investment from the United States to China, Mexico, and Latin America.[2] The large magnitude of FDI in the United States, and its steady increase during the 1980–90 period, should be seen as not that surprising in view of the tendency for FDI to concentrate in the industrial regions of the world. The exceptions are the recent flows of FDI to China and, to a lesser extent, Mexico and other areas of Latin America and Asia.

2. Direct investment from Japan to China and investment from Europe to Africa are not shown due to inadequate statistics.

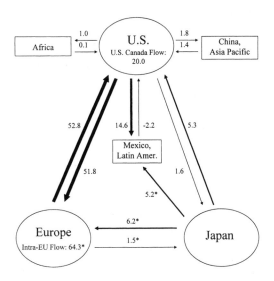

Fig. 6.2   Principal FDI bilateral flows, 1995 (billions of U.S. dollars)
Source: U.S. Department of Commerce, Bureau of Economic Analysis, STAT-USA database.
*Estimated by author. Intra-EU stock is for 1994.

6.2.3   Fallacies about Foreign Direct Investment

Fallacy 1: Foreign direct investment in Japan is less than 1 percent of assets, sales, or employment.

An often-cited figure is that foreign investment accounts for less than *1 percent* of the value of assets in Japan, or of the share of sales or employment. This figure has appeared in widely read studies of foreign investment (Graham and Krugman 1989, 25; 1993, 16; Lawrence 1993, 85), within a popular textbook (Krugman and Obstfeld 1994, 162), and even in the *Economic Report of the President* (1994, 216). The source of this figure is a study by Julius and Thomsen (1988), who reported data for 1986. The extremely low apparent share of FDI in Japan contrasts with the United States, where the share of FDI in assets, sales, or employment reported by Julius and Thomsen is 7 to 10 percent, and with European countries (France, Germany, and the United Kingdom), where it ranges from 13 to 27 percent.

The 1 percent figure for Japan used by Julius and Thomsen is consistent with that country's own statistics reported by the Ministry of International Trade and Industry (MITI). However, Weinstein (1997) examined these statistics in detail and found that they substantially understate the actual level of inward FDI. He cited several reasons for the understatement. Only about one-half of the firms surveyed actually respond, and only firms with 33 percent or more foreign ownership are even included in the survey: this percentage is far higher than the 10 percent criterion for foreign ownership used by the United States and other countries. Weinstein rejected the MITI data on foreign investment and instead constructed his own estimates using a published sample of foreign firms operating in Japan. Based on this sample, he estimated that the share of sales accounted for by these foreign firms is about 5.6 to 5.7 percent of total sales, or over *five times higher* than the numbers reported by Julius and Thomsen (Weinstein 1997, 86).[3] This figure can still be considered low in comparison with other industrial countries, but then again, it is quite comparable to the share of sales or employment in the United States accounted for by foreign firms.[4]

Unfortunately, the understatement built into the MITI numbers for foreign investment extends to other Japanese sources, particularly those of the Ministry of Finance (MOF) and the Bank of Japan, the latter of which are used for balance-of-payments purposes. Neither of these agencies collects information from smaller foreign firms, so there is some understatement for that reason. A more serious problem, however, stems from that fact that *reinvested earnings* are not included as a source of foreign investment. Thus, if an American firm in Japan funds additional investments from earnings, it would not be recorded as FDI. It should be noted that the exclusion of reinvested earnings from FDI, especially from data collected for balance-of-payments purposes, is a common problem in various countries (though not for the United States). This is one of the reasons for the discrepancy between the worldwide inward and outward FDI figures in table 6.11. The reason this problem arises is that balance-of-payments data only include transactions between domestic and foreign residents and therefore exclude investment due to reinvested earnings because there is no foreign exchange transaction. This type of financial activity could in principle be captured by surveys of firms, such as that conducted by MITI, but as we have seen this survey does not extend to all foreign firms in Japan.

To further illustrate the problems with the FDI reported by Japanese sources, in table 6.14 I focus on bilateral U.S.-Japan direct investment and contrast the Japanese MOF numbers with those reported by the U.S. Bureau of Economic Analysis (BEA). The BEA data are based on a mandatory survey of U.S. foreign affiliates, and they *include* investment from their earnings (Mataloni

3. Weinstein (1997, 85) also suggested that the stock of foreign assets in Japan as reported by MITI ($26 billion in 1992) should be at least four times higher (at least $100 billion).
4. In 1995, the share of total U.S. private industry employment accounted for by U.S. affiliates of foreign companies was 4.9 percent, the same as in 1994 (Fahim-Nader and Zeile 1997). The gross product originating in U.S. affiliates was $327 billion in 1995, which compares to U.S. GDP of $7,254 billion, giving a 4.5 percent share of value added. Eaton and Tamura (1994) argued that foreign investment in Japan is within the range of what one would expect from a "gravity" equation, given that country's size and distance from others.
    The government of Japan is currently engaged in various activities to promote inward foreign investment, including the establishment of Foreign Access Zones, the provision of low-interest loans by the Japan Development Bank, and various tax incentives such as the extension of a carryover period for initial losses on investment (see JETRO 1995a, 1995b).

Table 6.14   **FDI Stock and Flow between the United States and Japan (billions of U.S. dollars)**

	Reported by Japan	Reported by the United States
U.S. stock in Japan		
1993	12.17	31.10
1994	13.77	36.68
Japanese stock in the United States		
1993	177.10	100.27
1994	194.43	104.53
U.S. flow to Japan		
1993	0.93	1.63
1994	1.60	2.52
Japanese flow to the United States		
1993	14.73	1.06
1994	17.33	7.65

Sources: Japanese figures from Japan MOF as quoted on U.S. Department of Commerce, STAT-USA database, NTDB search queue. U.S. figures from U.S. Department of Commerce, Bureau of Economic Analysis, *U.S. Direct Investment Abroad,* http://www.bea.doc.gov/bea/usdia-d.htm, and *Foreign Direct Investment in the United States,* http://www.bea.doc.gov/bea/fdius-d.htm.

1995).[5] The first column of table 6.14 reports the stock or flow of FDI between the United States and Japan in 1993 and 1994, taken from MOF data, while the second column reports the comparable figure taken from BEA statistics. It can be seen that the Japanese MOF data substantially understate the BEA data on the inward FDI stock or flow from the United States, while they overstate the BEA data on the outward FDI stock or flow.[6] I have argued that the understatement is due to the omission of reinvested earnings from the Japanese statistics on inward FDI, and the overstatement on outward FDI appears to be due to the fact that the Japanese figures do not take into account depreciation or losses on investment.

To put the Japan-U.S. investment flows into perspective, in table 6.15 I report the bilateral FDI stocks and flows between the United States and a number of other countries. The Japanese inflows into the United States, such as the purchase of Rockefeller Center and Pebble Beach in Monterey, California, gained widespread attention in the popular press. However, the United Kingdom and the Netherlands have historically been even larger investors in the United States. By 1993, the Japanese stock of investment in the United States

5. Benchmark surveys conducted by the BEA every five years cover virtually the entire universe of U.S. multinationals. The annual and quarterly surveys are not as extensive in their coverage, but data for smaller firms not surveyed are estimated by extrapolating from the last benchmark survey. By including foreign investment due to reinvested earnings, the BEA is following the latest recommendations of the International Monetary Fund and the OECD (Mataloni 1995, 39–40).

6. It turns out that discrepancies of roughly the same magnitude can be observed in United Nations data on bilateral FDI flows between Japan and the United States, which is not surprising since these data are based on the Japanese MOF and U.S. BEA sources.

Table 6.15   FDI Inward Stocks and Flow for the United States by Source
Country (billions of U.S. dollars)

	1993		1994		1995	
	Amount	% of Total	Amount	% of Total	Amount	% of Total
	FDI Inward Stock					
Total	466.7		502.4		560.1	
Japan	100.3	21	104.5	21	108.6	19
Canada	40.5	9	42.1	8	46	8
Netherlands	71.9	15	68.2	14	67.7	12
United Kingdom	103.3	22	111.1	22	132.3	24
Germany	35.1	8	40.3	8	47.9	9
France	30.7	7	34.1	7	38.2	7
	FDI Inflow[a]					
Total	43.5		49.9		60.9	
Japan	1.1	2	7.7	15	5.3	9
Canada	3.8	9	4.0	8	4.5	7
France	6.8	16	4.0	8	3.7	6
Germany	7.7	18	6.6	13	8.2	13
Netherlands	3.0	7	−2.3	−5	−0.2	0
United Kingdom	13.2	30	11.1	22	22.1	36

Sources: U.S. Department of Commerce, Bureau of Economic Analysis, as quoted on STAT-USA database, www.bea.doc.gov/bea/fdius-d.htm#fdius-1.
[a]Negative values indicate a depreciation of investment values.

had surpassed that of the Netherlands and nearly caught up with that of the United Kingdom. But there has been a reduced inflow from Japan since that time, reflected in part by capital losses on investment.[7] The United Kingdom remains the largest single investing country in the United States, followed by Japan and then the Netherlands.

Fallacy 2: Multinational firms account for the majority of U.S. imports and exports.

Graham stated that "intrafirm trade by MNCs accounted for almost 50 percent of US exports and well over 50 percent of US imports of merchandise in 1991" (1996, 14). Numbers of this magnitude appear to confuse two types of trade by multinational corporations (MNCs): the trade that occurs between a parent and an affiliate—"intrafirm" trade—and the trade that occurs between a multinational and all other companies it buys from and sells to. The second type is just an example of arm's-length transactions between unrelated firms, and there does not seem to be any reason to treat it as special. The first type

7. E.g., Rockefeller Center was sold back to General Electric by Japanese investors at a very large capital loss, and similar losses were taken on U.S. investments purchased during the "bubble" economy in Japan.

includes only those products that are transferred internationally within a MNC. Since this movement of goods leads to issues of transfer pricing, which affects the tax liability of the corporation and tax revenues of the countries involved, there is good reason to focus attention on these trade flows.

The magnitude of trade by U.S. multinationals and foreign affiliates in the United States is shown in table 6.16. About one-third of exports and 43 percent of imports consist of intra-MNC trade, handled between a U.S. or foreign MNC and its affiliates. On the export side, twice as much is transacted within U.S. MNCs as by foreign MNCs. On the import side, intrafirm trade through foreign MNCs is somewhat more than through U.S. MNCs ($134 billion compared to $93 billion), but the majority of those imports by foreign MNCs are within wholesale and retail trade. A good example of this is imports of finished automobiles, where Japanese affiliates such as Toyota Motor Sales in Los Angeles handle the distribution of products into the United States.

Tyson (1991) added another twist on the issue of intrafirm trade by contrasting the patterns of American and Japanese firms. A substantial portion of imports to Japan are handled by Japanese MNCs, especially the large trading companies called *soga shosha*. For example, it is estimated that in 1990 the *soga shosha* handled more than two-thirds of Japanese imports and one-half of Japanese exports (World Bank 1994, 111). Tyson argued that this contrasts very strongly with the United States, where rather than having our own firms manage import and export trade, such trade is instead managed by *foreign* firms: "Foreign direct investment in wholesale and retail trade in the U.S. is so substantial, in fact, that by 1986 foreign affiliates accounted for 75 percent of total U.S. imports and nearly 70 percent of U.S. exports. So while Japanese firms

Table 6.16   **U.S. Imports and Exports through Multinational Corporations, 1992 (billions of U.S. dollars)**

Total U.S. merchandise exports	448.2	Total U.S. merchandise imports	532.7
Exports through U.S. MNC		Imports through U.S. MNC	
U.S. parent to foreign affiliates	104.7	Foreign affiliates to U.S. parent	92.6
U.S. parent to other foreign firms	140.8	Other foreign firms to U.S. parent	107.2
Other U.S. to foreign affiliates	15.6	Foreign affiliates to other U.S.	16.6
Exports through foreign MNC		Imports through foreign MNC	
U.S. affiliate to foreign parent	48.8	Foreign parent to U.S. affiliate	137.8
Manufacturing	11.6	Manufacturing	37.3
Wholesale trade	34.6	Wholesale trade	89.2
Motor vehicles and equipment	5.2	Motor vehicles and equipment	28.7
U.S. affiliate to other foreign firms	55.2	Other foreign firms to U.S. affiliate	46.7
Total intra-MNC exports	153.5	Total intra-MNC imports	230.4
Intra-MNC exports (% of total)	34.2	Intra-MNC imports (% of total)	43.3

Sources: Mataloni (1995, 48, table 7); U.S. Department of Commerce, Bureau of Economic Analysis, *Foreign Direct Investment in the United States: 1992 Benchmark Survey, Final Results* (Washington, D.C., 1995), tables H-25, H-27, H-31, and H-33.

control Japanese trade with the rest of the world, foreign firms dominate America's trade" (1991, 45).

As has been shown, a significant portion of Japanese exports to the United States are indeed handled by their MNCs, with investments in the wholesaling and retailing sector. But the magnitude of these flows are not nearly as high as suggested by Tyson. For example, in table 6.16 the magnitude of exports by U.S. affiliates of foreign corporations is $48.8 billion, which amounts to 10 percent of total U.S. merchandise exports. Of this amount, $29.6 billion, or 7 percent of total exports, is shipped to foreign parents in Japan. Similarly, the magnitude of imports by U.S. affiliates from their foreign parents is $137.8 billion, amounting to one-quarter of total U.S. merchandise imports. Of this amount, $71.2 billion, or 13 percent of total imports, is shipped by parent corporations in Japan.

Fallacy 3: Exchange rate changes do not affect the flow of foreign direct investment.

Of all our misconceptions, this is the one held with greatest vigor by economists, at least until recently. The reason exchange rates are presumed not to matter is that FDI is treated like the acquisition of a financial asset. The decision of a Japanese firm to purchase an American Treasury bill, for example, will depend on the expected rate of return on the Treasury bill. The need to first convert its yen currency to dollars, and later convert the dollar returns back to yen, would be handled in the spot and forward markets for foreign exchange at the time of purchase. Thus there is no risk involved in this currency transaction, and the exchange rates involved will effectively cancel out of the decision: all that matters is the expected return on the Treasury bill as compared to alternative investments for the firm, as well as the covariances between the returns on these various assets.

This theoretical independence from the exchange rate of FDI decisions seems to be contradicted by recent evidence for the United States, as illustrated in tables 6.17 and 6.18. Table 6.17 shows outlays by Japan and five other top investing countries for *acquisitions of existing plants* in the United States, while table 6.18 shows outlays for *new establishments*.[8] These tables show a very marked increase in acquisitions following the depreciation of the dollar in 1985, with a much smaller increase in Japanese outlays for establishments, and no variation at all in purchases of establishments by the other countries. The boom in acquisition lasted for about six years, slowing around 1991 but recovering since then for the United Kingdom and Canada. These numbers suggest that FDI for acquisitions is especially sensitive to the exchange rate.

To reconcile the theory with this evidence, several reasons why exchange rates *will* affect the foreign investment decision have recently been proposed.

8. These figures only use data on new investments and do not include the acquisition of additional equity in an existing U.S. affiliate by the foreign parent, or plant expansion (Quijano 1990, 31). Therefore, the data are less than total FDI inflows, such as shown for Japan in table 6.14.

Table 6.17   **Foreign Acquisitions in the United States by Source Country, 1980–96 (millions of U.S. dollars)**

Year	Japan	Canada	France	Germany	Netherlands	United Kingdom
1980	521	1,743	516	1,186	783	2,793
1981	469	5,100	801	800	408	5,309
1982	137	914	359	315	139	2,002
1983	199	718	167	378	360	1,448
1984	1,352	2,185	145	476	460	2,964
1985	463	2,494	593	2,142	579	6,023
1986	1,250	6,091	2,403	1,167	4,406	7,699
1987	3,340	1,169	1,949	4,318	204	14,648
1988	12,232	11,162	3,691	1,849	2,067	22,237
1989	11,204	4,196	3,295	2,216	3,351	21,241
1990	15,875	1,675	10,771	2,003	2,189	12,200
1991	3,413	1,191	4,706	1,828	1,543	1,808
1992	1,643	954	373	1,398	1,113	1,621
1993	1,359	3,234	1,143	2,347	1,345	7,841
1994	1,018	2,983	1,253	2,701	1,083	16,855
1995	1,893	6,037	358	13,657	624	9,428

Source: U.S. Department of Commerce, Bureau of Economic Analysis, *Foreign Direct Investment in the United States: U.S. Business Enterprises Acquired or Established by Foreign Direct Investors 1980–91 and 1992–95* (Washington, D.C., n.d.), tables 2, 5E, 6.1, 6.2, 6C, and 6D, diskette.

Table 6.18   **New Foreign Establishments in the United States by Source Country, 1980–96 (millions of U.S. dollars)**

Year	Japan	Canada	France	Germany	Netherlands	United Kingdom
1980	75	213	83	238	867	273
1981	147	984	104	349	163	869
1982	450	282	124	285	191	1,126
1983	193	354	128	206	132	918
1984	454	402	186	210	102	751
1985	689	420	161	127	192	708
1986	4,166	412	88	184	295	872
1987	3,666	107	96	347	188	494
1988	3,956	198	508	241	147	321
1989	6,206	206	174	219	279	1,806
1990	4,584	201	114	159	177	898
1991	1,944	2,263	271	95	118	361
1992	1,277	397	33	566	219	634
1993	706	563	106	793	730	397
1994	1,696	1,145	151	627	454	406
1995	1,865	444	859	498	261	249

Source: See note to table 6.17.

The first is due to Froot and Stein (1991) and depends on the idea that firms have less than perfect access to capital markets for loans. Since an appreciation of their exchange rates make the firms wealthier in terms of their purchasing power abroad, this will increase their ability to buy foreign firms. In particular, the appreciation of foreign currencies against the dollar after 1985 meant that foreign firms were better able to purchase U.S. plants or establish new plants here. Note that this argument applies equally well to acquisitions or new establishments, so that it does not explain why the largest increase in FDI in the United States after 1985 was of the former type.

A second reason why exchange rates matter has been advanced recently by Blonigen (1997) and helps to explain the particular surge in acquisitions in the United States. This argument builds on the OLI framework described at the beginning of the paper. The ownership implied by FDI allows a parent company to transfer knowledge to the subsidiary, but it equally well allows the parent to receive knowledge from the subsidiary. This knowledge can take the form of a product or process development, for example. Suppose that either of these can be usefully applied by the parent corporation in its own home market, leading to a stream of profits in that market. This will mean that the company purchases a firm in one currency (say, dollars) and receives a stream of profits in its own currency (say, yen) due to the investment. Given that revenues and costs are in different currencies, it is *certainly* the case that the exchange rate will affect the decision whether to acquire the U.S. plant, and an appreciation of the yen would make it more likely that the Japanese firm will make the investment. Blonigen (1997) has shown that this argument helps to explain the increase in FDI in U.S. manufacturing industries, especially those with high R&D.

Fallacy 4: If foreign direct investment occurs in response to trade restrictions, then it harms the host country.

The import substitution regimes that used to exist in Latin America and elsewhere led to inflows of foreign investment to "jump" the tariff barriers, and to counteract this, the countries imposed various restrictions on FDI. These restrictions have some, albeit limited, theoretical justification. Inward FDI *does* harm the host country when (1) trade restrictions in the host country take the form of tariffs, (2) foreign investment does not lead to any wage increase, or technology transfer, in the host country, and (3) foreign investment reduces but does not eliminate imports of the good (Brecher and Diaz-Alejandro 1977). Under these assumptions, the tariff will artificially raise the rate of return in the protected industry, and this return is earned by the foreign firms located there. Unless these artificially high profits are taxed by the host country, their withdrawal will be harmful to that economy.

Recently, however, a number of developing countries have recognized the potential benefits of FDI and loosened restrictions on these activities. For example, Mexico greatly liberalized the rules governing foreign investment during the 1980s, and these actions were taken even before discussion of the North America Free Trade Agreement (NAFTA). Together with the change in the policies of some developing countries, there has also been a growing awareness among economists that losses from FDI are the exception rather than the rule. One reason for this is that FDI generally does lead to wage increases in host economies, as well as providing benefits through technology transfer.[9] Another reason is that trade restriction in the host country often take the form of quotas or "voluntary" export restraints, rather than tariffs. In this case, even the limited theoretical case showing losses due to FDI no longer holds, because the inflow of foreign investment effectively reduces the need for imports, so the quota is no longer binding. A good example of this is the voluntary export restraint on U.S. auto imports from Japan during the 1980s. This import restriction led to a large inflow of foreign investment from Japan, which had the effect of lowering prices in the United States, thereby offsetting the initial cost of the trade restriction. In a world of rapid capital mobility, direct investment can offset the distortions created by trade restrictions and also offset their welfare costs.

6.2.4   Analysis of the Trends

It is easier to throw stones than dodge them, and this paper has taken advantage of that. Even among the most widely read popular writers in economics, there are some misconceptions about the magnitudes or implications of FDI. In the process of explaining these, I have tried to outline the trends in FDI as it occurs around the globe. In this section, I will provide further explanations and analyses of these trends.

Protection

Since the early 1980s there has been a very substantial increase in FDI in the United States. The reasons for this increase, and its implications, are still being debated. Among other factors, the inflow of FDI has been influenced by the threat of protection in various industries. This threat was triggered in part by the tight monetary policy, U.S. recession, and strong dollar of the early 1980s. Bhagwati, Dinopoulos, and Wong (1992) have coined the term "quid pro quo foreign investment" to describe the inflow of foreign investment in response to protectionist threats. As they state: "There is certainly some plausible, more-than-anecdotal evidence that the acceleration in Japanese FDI in the United States in the early 1980's was due to a mix of 'political' reasons: some partly in anticipation of the imposition of protection, and others partly to defuse its threat." They report a survey by MITI of Japanese firms undertaking

---

9. Lipsey (1994) showed that foreign-owned establishments in the United States pay higher wages, on average, than domestically owned establishments. Aitken, Hanson, and Harrison (1994) and Aitken, Harrison, and Lipsey (1995) documented the positive impact of investment inflows on wages for various developing countries.

foreign investment between 1980 and 1986, where it was found that many were motivated by "avoiding trade friction."

The threat of protection reflects the ongoing tendency for the United States to move away from a position of supporting undivided free trade, as it did in the postwar years as the hegemonic leader of the multilateral system, to a more activist position in using its trade policies to influence the behavior of its trading partners. The inflows of foreign investment resulting from such threats of protection should not be viewed as anything new, at least from the perspective of other countries: a substantial amount of U.S. investment entered Europe during the 1960s and 1970s, in response to the moral suasion of those governments. So while these flows have reversed direction in recent years, the reasons for the movement of capital has remained the same.

An empirical investigation of quid pro quo foreign investment was undertaken by Blonigen and Feenstra (1997). They examined the impact of Japanese FDI on the outcome of antidumping investigations in the United States and found that inflows of FDI tend to reduce the likelihood of antidumping duties being imposed. The same has been shown to hold for the application of antidumping duties in Europe (Barrel and Pain 1999). Goodman, Spar, and Yoffie (1996) described how the industry coalitions in the United States in automobiles, semiconductors, steel, and typewriters were affected by the entry of foreign firms; in most cases the eventual outcome was a reduction in the demand for protection. In sum, there is good empirical evidence that inflows of FDI have an impact on the demand for and the application of tariffs, and in most cases the impact is to reduce the use of tariffs. This means that FDI inflows can have a positive impact, over and above the benefits from increased wages and technology transfer.

Exchange Rates

In addition to the threat of protection, I have argued that the depreciation of the dollar has played a significant role in increasing the flow of FDI. I have relied on a new argument for the importance of exchange rates: that a foreign company purchasing a U.S. firm will be able to use the knowledge from this firm in its own home market, so that it purchases the firm in dollars but earns a return in its own currency. It is then certainly the case that the exchange rate will enter into the calculation of whether to purchase a U.S. firm or not (but not in the decision of whether to establish a new firm). I believe this argument is especially important in industries with high R&D expenditures and can explain the influx of foreign firms into Silicon Valley.

To complete this argument, however, it is necessary to ask why the U.S. plant in question did not enter the foreign market itself, either by exporting there or establishing a subsidiary of its own. This question is easily answered: the foreign market may have restrictions on imports and on inward foreign investment. In the presence of these restrictions, the foreign company will have preferential access to its own market and will be able to earn higher profits there from acquiring the U.S. firm than could the American firm itself. Indeed, there is evidence that foreign companies do pay a premium for U.S. firms when they are acquired (Swenson 1993), suggesting that some aspect of this acquisition is of greater value to the foreign firm.

This rationale for FDI therefore depends fundamentally on market imperfections, giving foreign firms preferential access to home markets and therefore increasing the value of intangible assets (such as knowledge of process or product innovations) they acquire from U.S. firms. It is essentially the reverse of the traditional argument for FDI, whereby a domestic firm would move its proprietary knowledge abroad. The idea that FDI in the United States is for the purpose of acquiring American knowledge may lead to the question of whether the companies involved are receiving the full value of that knowledge in their sale. While there is no reason to think that the markets are undervaluing these firms, it may be the case that *state subsidies* to FDI make these firms attractive targets for foreign takeover. A broad array of state-level subsidies are available to foreign investors, especially those investing in new establishments. It is quite possible that states compete against each other in an effort to attract foreign investment, ending up in a "prisoner's dilemma" whereby the subsidies offered are too high from a national point of view, but each state maintains these subsidies so that it does not lose out to others. For this reason, Reich (1991) proposed that an Office of the U.S. Investment Representative—analogous to the U.S. Trade Representative—should govern the use of state incentives to attract foreign investment.

Investment in Mexico and China

At the same time as capital from Europe and Asia is entering the United States, there has been a substantial outflow of FDI to Mexico and China. This outflow is explained by the more conventional reasons of access to low-priced labor and (for China) to large domestic markets. The flow from the United States to Mexico may have already stabilized following the establishment of NAFTA. But the flow of investment to China can be expected to continue for some time to come, though it will depend on the development of infrastructure and stable policies in that country. Japan and the newly industrialized countries of Asia have large and growing investments in China. Europe, by contrast, has relatively little FDI there.

There is an important difference in the rationale for FDI in China when it comes from elsewhere in Asia, rather than from the United States. Investment from Japan, Taiwan, Korea, and Hong Kong is largely for the "outward processing" of goods, whereby inputs are provided by those countries and certain stages of assembly and processing are done in China. The availability of low-priced Chinese labor reduces the overall cost of the final goods. Some of these products are quite sophisticated, such as computers or their components, and compete with American-made products on world markets. The use of China as an outward-processing region for goods developed elsewhere in Asia therefore increases the competition facing some American products on world markets.

How are American corporations responding to this challenge on international markets? It appears that their investment in China is not of the same type as that done by other Asian countries. Rather, large American firms investing in China are attracted in large part by the huge domestic market in that country. These companies see the population of 1.2 billion, with low but rising personal incomes, as a potential source of future sales. Companies such as Boeing, General Motors, and Motorola see their investments in China as part of a global strategy, designed to secure sales in China over the long term, but not necessarily resulting in short-term reduction of production costs.

This characterization suggests that the competitive challenge created by the outward processing of goods in China, originating in Japan, Taiwan, and Korea, will *not* be met by similar investment in China by American corporations. Rather, U.S. firms have the opportunity to meet this challenge by the outsourcing of production activities to Mexico, under NAFTA and the offshore assembly provisions of the U.S. tariff code. These provisions allow U.S. firms to export intermediate inputs, have them processed in Mexico or elsewhere, and then reimport the final products while only paying duty on the value added by the overseas activity. As tariff reductions continue to take effect under NAFTA, the incentives for outsourcing to the so-called *maquiladora* plants in Mexico will increase even more. These plants should be viewed as the counterpart to the outward processing done in China for other countries in Asia. In both cases, the outsourcing of assembly activities allows the parent firms to lower their costs of production and increase their ability to compete on world markets. The outsourcing by U.S. multinationals, especially to Mexico, and the outsourcing by multinationals from elsewhere in Asia, especially to China, creates two regionally based production networks that take advantage of the low-priced labor on each continent. The competition between these regional production networks is perhaps the most important outcome of foreign investment in the developing world and will continue to have fundamental effects on the pattern of trade and investment in the next century.

References

Aitken, Brian, Gordon H. Hanson, and Ann E. Harrison. 1994. Spillovers, foreign investment, and export behavior. NBER Working Paper no. 4967. Cambridge, Mass.: National Bureau of Economic Research, December.
Aitken, Brian, Ann Harrison, and Robert E. Lipsey. 1995. Wages and foreign ownership: A comparative study of Mexico, Venezuela and the United States. NBER Working Paper no. 5102. Cambridge, Mass.: National Bureau of Economic Research, May.
Baldwin, Robert E., and Fukunari Kimura. 1998. Measuring U.S. international goods

and services transactions. In *Geography and ownership as bases for economic accounting,* ed. Robert E. Baldwin, Robert E. Lipsey, and J. David Richardson, 9–48. Chicago: University of Chicago Press.

Barrel, Ray, and Nigel Pain. 1999. Trade restraints and Japanese direct investment flows. *European Economic Review* 43 (1): 29–46.

Bhagwati, Jagdish N., Elias Dinopoulos, and Kar-Yui Wong. 1992. Quid pro quo foreign investment. *American Economic Review* 82 (2): 186–90.

Blonigen, Bruce. 1997. Firm-specific assets and the link between exchange rates and foreign direct investment. *American Economic Review* 87 (3): 447–65.

Blonigen, Bruce, and Robert C. Feenstra. 1997. Protectionist threats and foreign direct investment. In *The effects of U.S. trade protection and promotion policies,* ed. Robert C. Feenstra, 55–80. Chicago: University of Chicago Press.

Brecher, Richard, and Carlos Diaz-Alejandro. 1977. Tariffs, foreign capital, and immiserizing growth. *Journal of International Economics* 7:317–22.

Eaton, Jonathan, and Akiko Tamura. 1994. Bilateralism and regionalism in Japanese and U.S. trade and foreign direct investment patterns. *Journal of the Japanese and International Economies* 8 (4): 478–510.

Economic report of the president. 1994. Washington, D.C.: Government Printing Office.

Fahim-Nader, Mahnaz, and William J. Zeile. 1997. Foreign direct investment in the United States. *Survey of Current Business* 77 (6): 42–69.

Froot, Kenneth, and Jeremy Stein. 1991. Exchange rates and foreign direct investment: An imperfect capital markets approach. *Quarterly Journal of Economics* 106 (November): 190–207.

Goodman, John B., Debora Spar, and David B. Yoffie. 1996. Foreign direct investment and the demand for protection in the United States. *International Organization* 50 (autumn): 565–91.

Graham, Edward M. 1996. *Global corporations and national governments.* Washington, D.C.: Institute for International Economics.

Graham, Edward M., and Paul R. Krugman. 1989. *Foreign direct investment.* Washington, D.C.: Institute for International Economics.

———. 1993. The surge in foreign direct investment in the 1980s. In *Foreign direct investment,* ed. Kenneth A. Froot, 13–33. Chicago: University of Chicago Press.

JETRO (Japan External Trade Organization). 1995a. Measures for promoting foreign investment in Japan. San Francisco: JETRO Information Service Department.

———. 1995b. Tax incentives and loan guarantees for foreign affiliates. San Francisco: JETRO Information Service Department.

Julius, DeAnne, and S. Thomsen. 1988. Foreign owned firms, trade and economic integration. In *Tokyo Club Papers,* vol. 2. London: Royal Institute of Economic Affairs.

Kimura, Fukunari, and Robert E. Baldwin. 1998. Application of a nationality-adjusted net sales and value-added framework: The case of Japan. In *Geography and ownership as bases for economic accounting,* ed. Robert E. Baldwin, Robert E. Lipsey, and J. David Richardson, 49–82. Chicago: University of Chicago Press.

Krugman, Paul R., and Maurice Obstfeld. 1994. *International economics: Theory and policy,* 3d ed. New York: Harper-Collins.

Lawrence, Robert Z. 1993. Japan's low levels of inward acquisitions: The role of inhibitions in acquisitions. In *Foreign direct investment,* ed. Kenneth A. Froot, 85–107. Chicago: University of Chicago Press.

Lipsey, Robert E. 1994. Foreign owned firms and U.S. wages. NBER Working Paper no. 4927. Cambridge, Mass.: National Bureau of Economic Research.

Lipsey, Robert E., Magnus Blomström, and Eric D. Ramstetter. 1998. Internationalized production in world output. In *Geography and ownership as bases for economic accounting,* ed. Robert E. Baldwin, Robert E. Lipsey, and J. David Richardson, 83–138. Chicago: University of Chicago Press.

Mataloni, Raymond J., Jr. 1995. A guide to BEA statistics on U.S. multinational companies. *Survey of Current Business* 75 (3): 38–55.

Quijano, Alicia M. 1990. A guide to BEA statistics on foreign direct investment in the United States. *Survey of Current Business* 70 (2): 29–37.

Reich, Robert B. 1991. Who is them? *Harvard Business Review* 69 (2): 77–88.

Rodrik, Dani. 1997. *Has globalization gone too far?* Washington, D.C.: Institute for International Economics.

Swenson, Deborah. 1993. Foreign mergers and acquisitions in the United States. In *Foreign direct investment,* ed. Kenneth A. Froot, 255–84. Chicago: University of Chicago Press.

Tyson, Laura D'Andrea. 1991. They are not us: Why American ownership still matters. *American Prospect,* no. 4 (winter): 37–49.

Vernon, Raymond. 1966. International investment and international trade in the product cycle. *Quarterly Journal of Economics* 80 (May): 190–207.

Weinstein, David. 1997. Foreign direct investment and *keiretsu:* Rethinking U.S. and Japanese policy. In *The effects of U.S. trade protection and promotion policies,* ed. Robert C. Feenstra, 81–116. Chicago: University of Chicago Press.

World Bank. 1994. *China: Foreign trade reform.* Washington, D.C.: World Bank.

3. Carl H Hahn

The changing role of foreign investment: Let me say first, "change" means for us Europeans something quite dramatic. At this time it means the end of privileges for Europeans that have lasted for more than 600 years, through the control of transport and capital, through superior firepower and know-how, through superior education, and so on. Today, access to know-how is universal. All that is needed is a high level of education, social consensus, and participation in the free market. More than 90 percent of the world has joined this club. We have a level playing field, more than some of us in Europe like.

To be a global company you must maintain one quality yardstick worldwide. Our VW cars are made in Germany, Mexico, China, or wherever. You segment not only your manufacturing processes. You segment your engineering and development processes as well. When you buy a Golf today, the transaxle might come from Argentina, the engine and the rear axle from Mexico. The vehicle might have been assembled, if it has four-wheel drive, in Bratislava, Slovak Republic, forty miles from Vienna, Austria. Component globalization requires an enormous degree of discipline, but it also reaps enormous benefits, taking advantage of regional cost differentials and permitting a high degree of specialization and division of labor. On the side, developing countries also benefit. They can attract world-class factories for global and not only local or regional demand, which optimizes the return on capital, one of the classical handicaps of investment in developing countries otherwise.

More and more the most modern factories we operate are enjoyed by workers in developing countries. Take our truck factory in Brazil, which is the latest one, and has all sorts of work processes that the German trade unions would not accept. Consequently, we employ only 300 people for an annual production of 30,000 trucks. Our 300 people do practically nothing but control quality and coordinate the vendors operating within our plant.

Let me try to tell you the core of what I think I can contribute from my point of view. Volkswagen is a relatively young manufacturer. As a matter of fact, we are the youngest automobile manufacturer in Europe besides our "stepbrother" Porsche. The VW Company and one of our products, the Beetle, still in production in Mexico, are both about half the age of our industry. As a rule, European automobile manufacturers are not even European in their philosophy or manufacturing structure, but rather national—far from global. Typically, the two U.S. manufacturers in Europe are European as well as, of course, global. The Volkswagen group, number four in the world and number one in Europe, South America, and China, is both European and global. According to the *World Investment Report 1997,* among the top 100 transnational corporations (TNCs) Volkswagen ranks sixth by foreign assets, close behind General Motors. Heading the list are Shell, Ford, General Electric, and Exxon. If we go not by assets but by an index made up of sales, employment, and assets abroad, Volkswagen is number one among automobile manufacturers, followed by Nissan, Mercedes, Toyota, Ford, and General Motors. This is just a rough idea how global we have become over the past thirty years.

How, you ask, has VW, the late starter, come to be so far ahead in so many races? In a nutshell, we have never enjoyed protection in our domestic market from the time the Royal Electrical and Mechanical Engineering Corps of the British Army started up the civilian life of our company in 1945. (We are certainly their most successful venture ever.) Moreover, after the war we lacked purchasing power at home, so we had to go abroad step by step as an exporter and as an investor in protected markets of interest. It is this latter role that I shall try to sketch, selecting three distinct examples: Brazil, the Czech Republic, and the People's Republic of China. I'm sorry not to select Mexico, but I am short of time.

Brazil

My first example is Brazil, the classic case for us. It turned out to be a very good experience, and I think for Brazil as well. The market potential at the time, the early 1950s, was small, and the minimum national competitive start-up volume and national investment accordingly. The local content volume required was almost prohibitively (uneconomically) high. At the time, the objective of governments in similar situations all over the Third World was expressed by the buzz phrase "Industrialization at any cost." There were few alternatives to industrialization, but these countries had to pay a certain (high) price as latecomers. In terms of automotive industrialization, I don't know of a single country that would have (could have) started without protectionism in the later, more developed period of the automobile. We were guaranteed closed borders and found an oligopolistic market with sleeping competitors, at that time, but certainly not anymore. Under these conditions, the price for the entrance ticket was not too high when you had the right vehicle, and it was affordable for us, starting with a first-year production of 20 Beetles in 1953. What we did not realize at the time was the outstanding potential of our Beetle, its extraordinary strength in the marketplace due to the numerous advantages of its longevity in every sense (no model change). Our reward was a 50 percent market share and the self-financing potential. Within a short time, we overtook all our competitors, who had mostly arrived after World War I. A local content close to 100 percent meant that our supply chain followed us from Europe to Brazil, even steel manufacturers.

Consequently, during most of the 1950s, as well as 1960s, the Brazilian economy lived through a period of rapid industrialization and growth. Industrial and product structures were simple. This was a time when you could repair your own carburetor. Consequently, the closed shop did not entail too many handicaps for the national economy at the time; on the contrary, I do not see any alternative.

For many external and mostly internal political reasons, almost twenty years of a mixture of stagnation and inflation would follow. Price controls never worked, but they were lovingly, repeatedly applied. To ease a growing external indebtedness, costly export subsidies, some as complex barter transactions—100,000 cars to Iraq for oil—were introduced, showing only short-term results at best. Enjoying high liquidity, as a manufacturer, as an industrialist, was a matter of survival in those days of instability. The economic policy of price controls induced capital to go in wrong directions. "Gray markets" developed and finally "exported" more and more capital abroad.

The successful merger of Ford and VW in Brazil and Argentina, as a defensive measure, was a creative answer to the political and economic situation of the countries in question. We established a safeguard, reducing the high risk of unpredictable government policies, which could expropriate your assets in weeks—for instance, by simply delaying permission for price increases by the respective authorities. It was easy to control the manufacturer, but not the entire value chain to the final consumer.

By our merger we had reached 50 percent market share and could attain our strategic objective of being the most cost-competitive manufacturer, in order to be "the last manufacturer to die." We accomplished this mostly by common platforms. Volkswagen models got Ford platforms, Ford got Volkswagen platforms. We closed consequently surplus factories, particularly in Argentina, where the market had shrunk to a fraction of its former size, increased working capital, and created liquidity—important competitive advantages during the final days of a regulated economy in a world governed more and more by market forces.

Reaching these objectives allowed us to exist without fresh money from the parents and to be profitable again. This all was viable, however, only up to the day of the introduction of a market economy Harvard-style in the 1990s. By then the industrial world had changed radically in complexity, in technology, and in sophistication. The Brazilian economy was unprepared for this new world; its industry was less competitive internationally than ever—a textbook case. Already by 1994, however, a $20 billion investment program in new plants and products over five years was the Brazilian automotive industry's response to sound economic policies. A new chapter of intense competition and rapid growth began instantly, partly also in response to the opening of the market to car imports. Enormous forces were set loose. The consumer was the great winner.

One of our most successful products in Brazil at the time, and still today, was a Volkswagen Bus type of multipurpose vehicle, which had a 1949 platform. Three new factories, meanwhile, two for Volkswagen, one for Audi, have already been put onstream. What a change, what a contrast.

Brazil has become the largest recipient of foreign capital in Latin America, with nearly $10 billion in 1996, up from $2 billion in 1992. These figures are indirect proof of the automotive industry's key role as a central driver in an economy. Brazil and Argentina will soon be able to enter the worldwide division of labor, one of the key elements for becoming competitive on a global scale.

However, a period of overcapacity can be expected for some time in Brazil and Argentina, intensified by new players and all-new model lines. Consequently, Brazil will become a highly competitive marketplace, with falling prices. Certainly, Brazil will become a big player in the league of the world automobile industry, searching, also for reason of overcapacity, for export markets, assisted by the global structure of the multinationals.

To summarize, in Brazil and most of South America the future has finally arrived. The year 2000 will see a new Brazil, forging as the largest economy of South America the integration of Mercosur—not an overnight process. I am also encouraged by the fact that the month before last we had for the first time no inflation in Brazil, at least for one month.

Czech Republic

My second example is investing in a former socialist economy, almost forty years later. Skoda or Tatra were known to us at Volkswagen for many good reasons. We had even volunteered to pay a royalty for the Volkswagen Beetle to Tatra. (The designer of the Beetle had come indirectly from Tatra.) We kept in touch with the Czech automobile industry during the Comecon days and were ready to go when the Iron Curtain came down. Thank God only two or three competitors followed at the time. Many were busy in Russia, tempted by Gorbachev. For a Western automobile manufacturer, however, there was in my mind no alternative to Skoda. Whoever owned Skoda would not only enjoy preferential access to the Czech Republic's market, inheriting a sales network in addition to the market share, but also to central and eastern Europe as well.

After buying a controlling interest in Skoda, we encountered managers much closer to the West, and products and factories head and shoulders above what we had found in the extremely run-down East German Trabi factories. The East Germans had had to operate under extremely adverse conditions and were never permitted to dialogue with us, being hermetically separated from the Western world, in contrast to their Czech neighbors.

In East Germany, near Zwickau, Saxony, we found, however, an extremely modern assembly plant built and finished one year before the Iron Curtain came down. On the day this factory "opened" it was mothballed. Within six months, the first VW left the assembly line. In Bratislava, Slovak Republic, forty miles from Vienna, Austria, we also "found" an automobile factory ten years old, with immediate access to the Danube, to rail, to superhighway; never used, mothballed. One hundred and fifty thousand VW passenger cars will be assembled in Bratislava in 1998, besides transmissions.

No question, this was a market- and cost-motivated investment by Volkswagen advantaged by the closeness to our factories in both western and now also eastern Germany and the markets of central Europe in general. The Czech people we had found at Skoda were determined to prove to the Germans how good they were. Vaclav Klaus showed shrewdness in introducing market-oriented reforms, as Jiří Weigl has described (chap. 2.3), and uniquely, quite a few politicians in the Czech Republic had prepared for the end of communism, even at universities in the United States and Great Britain.

Of course our investment entailed know-how imports in all fields, tangible and intangible assets, the opening of all our marketing channels worldwide, integration into our global division of labor, and the provision of benchmarks for every industrial activity or function—all this happened overnight, free of charge. In particular, access to our marketing channels, which took enormous capital and many, many years to create, made it a win-win situation.

In parallel, we educated the vendor industries of the Czech Republic and surrounding countries to Western standards, gave them chances to export, to integrate into our global sourcing process, and supplied the engineering and research know-how they needed to catch up. Their universities received grants from the Volkswagen Foundation and research projects from our engineering departments. We helped them to establish contacts with the universities where we operate.

Our expectations in eastern Europe have been fulfilled (except the quality and effectiveness of reforms in the former Soviet Union, which we had consequently to exclude from our FDI plans at the time, notwithstanding tempting offers by the governments). Our experiences as an investor in Poland, Slovakia, and Hungary have been equally good. In Slovakia and Hungary, the element of vertical integration allowed by component production in these locations played an additional important role in our investment strategy to improve our European cost structure, a process assisted by introducing common platforms for new designs and volume expansion, with a positive employment balance.

In 1996, the Czech Republic, Hungary, and Poland accounted for 68 percent of total inflows of FDI to central and eastern Europe, mostly privatization related, from TNCs not only from western Europe and the United States but also from Asia. In particular, the Republic of Korea moved into first place by foreign assets, among the top fifty TNCs based in developing economies. Summing up, it was possible to enter central Europe successfully through FDI during the reforms toward a free market economy. Setbacks and political changes, particularly in Poland and Hungary, did not discourage us. In some cases "communist" and socialist governments of a completely new type took over. They continued market-oriented economic reforms, trying to avoid the mistakes of their predecessor governments, which had disappointed the electorate in some of the reform countries.

In our case, we also obtained a new brand of strategic importance with international potential and historic value, a brand with a century of automotive tradition, quality people, marketing channels in central Europe, market share, virgin markets for the remainder of our automobile divisions, high-quality workmanship, manufacturing capacities, new vendors, and specialists very much at home in eastern Europe. This permitted us to create our fourth automobile division on a solid base.

In the first half of 1997, according to J. D. Power, a U.S. research firm probably known to you, Skoda was the number one European car in the United Kingdom in customer satisfaction. Today, you can produce quality virtually everywhere provided you conquer the hearts of your workers, train and motivate them, and give them the prerequisites for quality work through your design policies and engineering and by integrating them in all processes, benefiting from their experience and intellectual potential, as you do with your vendors.

China

My third point is about the People's Republic of China. We started negotiating with the Chinese government in the early 1980s. The communist leaders convinced us with the early and dramatic success of their clearly market-oriented reform policies. They practiced what they preached. I also took confidence indirectly but most importantly from the fact that almost every Chinese leader had not only more than one child but many studying in the United States—in my mind an insurance policy for the future political direction of the country and a strategic advantage for the United States of far-reaching importance.

We got to know each other well through frequent visits to Beijing and Shanghai. Zhu Rongji was the mayor of Shanghai in those days. The Chinese leaders on official or informal visits to Germany almost never left out Wolfsburg, our headquarters. This permitted us to underline our policies with hard facts. Eventually, we even traveled together to Mexico and Brazil, in order to demonstrate our policies in developing countries, showing our ability to adapt to local circumstances and to be a good corporate citizen. At the same time we pursued the careful contract negotiations that would establish the very detailed legal framework necessary because Western civil and commercial legislation is lacking in China. One of the shareholders in our 50/50 joint venture was the Bank of China, so we felt quite sure of the availability of foreign exchange, which we needed in the beginning.

In contrast to the tempting offers of the Russian perestroika leadership a short while before, we did not start with an initial capacity of hundreds of thousands, ending with one million units per annum within a short time, but with a trial assembly in the first year of 500, followed by 2,000 in the second year, doubling this number each year until we rapidly reached 250,000, always maintaining a market share of better than 50 percent.

Soon, a second joint venture would follow, not in Shanghai but in Changchun, province of Jiling, the former Manchuria, with the First Automobile Works (FAW), the birthplace of the Chinese auto industry in 1953. FAW was a stepping stone for many leading personalities of this country. Volume increases will gradually permit us to update our product program, which was kept simple initially to permit a successful learning curve. Soon volume will permit us to amortize new products in line with the international cycle of model change. This in turn will permit us to use this area as a base for exports to the Asia Pacific region with products made in China.

Let me summarize a few points, which I think, helped us greatly. Shanghai was able to reach a local content of 90 percent. Thanks also to the military industry, Norinco helped us to increase our local content rapidly, and to reach quality levels in line with our standards. We exported engines to Europe within three years. Of course this process was accompanied by vendor industries from Europe and the United States, representing an enormous inflow of capital and know-how. Changchun was supplied with CKD packs for Golf production from South Africa. The manufacturing equipment came from Westmoreland, Pennsylvania. CKD packs for the VW Santana, Shanghai, came from Brazil.

All this was proof that our global network was functioning in practice. We also benefit from a certain degree of component commonality between Shanghai and Changchun, with resulting savings in investment, higher volume, and lower cost. Audi became the government vehicle, replacing the Red Flag. A team of Chinese VW engineers and their Brazilian counterparts, connected via satellite, did most of the development work for a major facelift for the Santana, a vehicle that is produced in both countries.

We emphasized not only that we were prepared to give know-how in engineering and development but that we insist, in all countries where we operate, on mobilizing human intellectual talent and potential. We include the local workforce in our worldwide network of development and engineering activities. A German type of apprentice school in Shanghai with more than 200 pupils educates first-class craftsman from day one, and at any time there are at least 100 Chinese training in Wolfsburg, whether in bookkeeping, engineering, or manufacturing. Changchun was the first production site of our latest environmentally friendly five-valve engine. Nobody anywhere in the world produces a five-valve engine but our group, when I exclude Ferrari. Consequently, China is about to become one of the most advanced industrialized countries—and not only in skyscraper production—thanks to FDI. Furthermore, Chinese universities do research work for us and receive grants from the Volkswagen Foundation. Volkswagen has created an R&D center in China, besides doing development work in existing factories. During most of our time in China, the Shanghai factory was the "Joint Venture of the Year" and had a return on sales better than 10 percent according to official publications.

Early birds have a better chance to finance their investments partially by self-financing. The opposite is true for a latecomer. The price of entry increases constantly. No wonder China has been the largest developing country recipient of FDI since 1992, averaging $35 billion annually. China is attractive to all of us not only because of its size but because its economic growth potential, which will probably make it the world's number one economy by the early 2000s on the basis of their political stability and policies. Intelligence and hard work, not only low wages, make it an ideal platform for serving Asia Pacific markets, enjoying a healthy current accounts surplus situation. China is number one in dollar reserves already, even without including Hong Kong, which I feel complements Zhu Rongji's economic policies, considering the rate of GDP growth year after year and the low inflation rate.

No wonder Volkswagen continues to expand in China, taking advantage of the "socialist market economy" transition policy, under a communist government that has avoided the mistakes and tragedies we had to observe in the former Soviet Union. Naturally, there are risks, but I do not know of any entrepreneurial activity—or any kind of progress, for that matter—without risk, and I don't think that China tops the list of risky countries.

The entry of three billion people from Asia into the world economy with high potential qualifications; the gradual entry, slower than expected, of India; and hopefully one day the entry of Russia—together with what we observe in Latin America, these elements give us a chance no generation before us even dreamt of. As a consequence, globalization will take on new dimensions rapidly. Let us hope that politics will be able to master the new complexities and global risks, permitting us to harvest the fruits of FDI and its built-in know-how transfer.

Some final remarks on FDI in Europe: I can promise you there is almost no place in Europe where the investor will not be lured by subsidies. It's a sheer fight for investors via subsidies. A most unhealthy development, as you can imagine, more weakening than strengthening. There are all sorts of advantages you will be offered to come to central Europe as an investor as well. Not only do TNCs compete with each other, but all countries compete for investment from TNCs.

4. George N. Hatsopoulos

Of all economic issues of interest to noneconomists, I have found none that evokes more of a love-hate reaction than foreign direct investment. Most recognize the benefits it provides to a country, such as added financial capital as well as intangible capital in the form of technology or market presence. Many, however, worry about a real or perceived transfer of control and returns from domestic to foreign owners. In view of the vast changes that have happened in the world, I would like to raise the possibility that FDI, as it is currently measured, may become disconnected from its traditionally assigned attributes. I have no aggregate data to support such a hypothesis, only anecdotal information pertaining to Thermo Electron, the company I run.

Thermo Electron's FDI consists mostly of acquisitions of foreign-owned corporations. Only a small part of it, less than 5 percent, is invested to expand existing operations abroad. The motivation of the latter group of investments is not economic. Physical production, technology generation, and general management are done much more efficiently in U.S. locations. Labor laws that prevail in all other countries are the main cause of that disparity. Nevertheless, we need to invest small amounts in locations abroad to keep up the morale of our people there and maintain their ability to serve local customers.

Our acquisition program is substantial: in the past five years, we have acquired over eighty corporations at a cost of over $2 billion. So far this year, we have made twelve acquisitions at a total cost approaching $1 billion.

The first quarter of this year, we spent $0.5 billion to acquire a U.K. corporation called Life Sciences. In the flow-of-funds tabulation, this transaction will appear as FDI in the United Kingdom, implying that Americans increased their ownership of a manufacturing operation in the United Kingdom valued at $0.5 billion (out of $19 billion total outflow from the United States). The reality, however, is different for two reasons: first, two-thirds of Life Sciences plants are located in the United States, and second, one-third of the owners of Thermo Electron are not Americans. (These facts translate into FDI of only $0.11 billion.)

The situation just described is obviously exceptional. Nevertheless, it is less of an exception than it would have been twenty years ago, and current trends indicate that it will be even less of an exception twenty years from now. We have already witnessed a dramatic increase in the mobility of capital, goods, and services, as well as technology and know-how. We also see increased mobility of owners of capital. Is Mr. Murdoch really an Australian? To my knowledge, he invests mostly outside Australia where he also spends most of his time and money. These observations make me wonder whether the attributes historically assigned to FDI will continue to be valid for long.

Discussion Summary

Robert Feenstra commented that Hahn's description of Volkswagen's global sourcing procedures represent a substantial challenge to existing economic models. He went on to note that recent Canadian statistics suggest that 90 percent of Canadian trade is in intermediate inputs, further challenging the existing methods employed by trade theorists. Feenstra asked whether the technology transfer associated with foreign direct investment works in reverse, with host countries providing innovations that are transported through multinationals back to the home countries.

Carl Hahn replied that these global sourcing procedures have been fostered by technological advances in design processes, miniaturization, and a dramatic reduction in transport costs. For example, the cost of shipping a car from Europe to the United States is equivalent to the cost of transporting a car across the United States. As a consequence, some products, such as the new Beetle, will be assembled only in one place, Mexico, and transported to various destinations around the world. Furthermore, Hahn noted that the internal competition created under a global sourcing procedure is an enormous source of innovation and progress for Volkswagen. Regarding reverse technology transfers, Hahn saw great scope for such transfers. The only obstacle is the arrogance of acquiring companies, particularly U.S. companies, in assuming that local firms do not have important ideas to contribute.

George Hatsopoulos noted that reverse technology transfer is less likely to involve raw technology and more likely to be local market knowledge. Furthermore, this exchange of market knowledge and managerial expertise constitutes a major aspect of the value added of foreign direct investment for Thermo Electron.

Robert Lipsey noted that the cases provided by Volkswagen and Thermo Electron illustrate broader trends in foreign direct investment. American expansion in foreign direct investment came largely in the 1970s, and American firms have pulled back subsequently. In contrast, German and Japanese firms have become much more aggressive in the 1980s and 1990s. Lipsey also noted that the complexities illustrated by Thermo Electron's recent acquisition of Life Sciences are difficult for statisticians to capture in aggregate data. American data are unique in capturing these complexities as questionnaires inquire about ultimate ownership.

Hahn replied that U.S. firms are as aggressive as they have ever been. However, U.S. firms are now more likely to use their foreign affiliates, as in the case of GM-Opel, to make further investments. Similarly, *Hatsopoulos* suggested that Thermo Electron is expanding as aggressively and quickly as ever. Furthermore, he perceived the opportunities abroad to be greater than ever before.

James Hines asked whether Thermo Electron's financing strategy of seeking non-U.S. investors is related to its acquisition and expansion patterns throughout the world.

Hatsopoulos replied that these financing and investment plans are distinct because capital raised in Europe is raised in dollars and not used directly to finance European acquisitions. As such, the mix of equity capital is a function of the attributes of the capital providers rather than any particular expansion plans.

Nicholas Stern related the recent experience of the European Bank for Reconstruction and Development to the discussion. First, Stern observed that the apparent motivation for multinational investors in eastern Europe has shifted from market share concerns to a more cost-driven agenda. Second, he stressed the difference between the actual details of legal systems and the broader commitment to development that governments can convey to investors. In this vein, he wondered whether this commitment can provide a more convincing signal to investors than actual legal systems. Finally, Stern noted that 30 percent of investment in the eastern parts of the transition economies was provided by Germans while 30 percent of investment in the western parts was provided by American investors. He asked whether these trends are a function of different risk appetites or sectoral specialization and whether they related to the experience of Volkswagen and Thermo Electron.

Hahn denied the distinction between market share and cost motivations suggesting that the motivation is always the opportunity provided by a new market. Accessing these new markets quickly is the ultimate objective in order not to be left behind. He suggested that costs largely even out once up-front costs have been amortized. Hahn also noted that total costs rather than labor costs are of ultimate importance and wage differentials appear to be falling. Regarding the relative importance of legal systems and the commitment to development, Hahn explained that contracts with developing countries will often include the actual details of the German Civil Codes in order to protect Volkswagen's interests. He also noted that incentives for multinationals include a variety of policies from infrastructure provision to generous accounting treatment to facilitate investment and, finally, a variety of tax incentives. Finally, regarding the preference of Germans for the eastern parts of the transition economies, Hahn suggested that knowledge of these areas and historic relations account for these preferences. Current negotiations in Russia for Volkswagen are being conducted by Czechs because they are more familiar with Russian practices. Additionally, the historic weakness of Europeans in natural resource extraction may account for the late entry into Russia relative to U.S. firms.

Hatsopoulos concurred with Hahn on the question of labor cost motivations, saying that this had never been a motivation for a Thermo Electron investment. He further noted that productivity was of ultimate importance and that U.S. productivity, for Thermo Electron's product lines, is currently unmatched. In fact, he indicated a preference for keeping production within the United States and simply using affiliates for their local market knowledge.

René Stulz turned the discussion to the future of foreign direct investment. He proposed that foreign direct investment may become less important as portfolio flows increase. As transaction costs come down, such flows provide considerable diversification benefits to investors without some of the associated inefficiencies, including agency costs, of foreign direct investment. Accordingly, he suggested that portfolio flows may increasingly substitute for direct investment flows.

Stanley Fischer noted that Hahn's description of multiple sourcing reminded him of a description provided by Michael Blumenthal at one of the first practitioner-academic meetings he attended in the mid-1980s. At the time, Blumenthal stated that a Burroughs computer purchased in the United States had components manufactured in forty-two countries. Hahn's description of Volkswagen sourcing mirrored this very global process.

Arminio Fraga asked how currency volatility is handled by multinationals such as Volkswagen and Thermo Electron.

Hahn noted that he was expecting substantial improvement in currency stability with the advance of the euro and was optimistic about the stability provided by the dual dominance of the dollar and the euro. Hedging is not designed for asset positions but only trade flows for short periods, and this is not universal. More generally, Hahn expressed a preference for seeking balance in streams of merchandise as Volkswagen does with countries such as Spain, where there are sizable flows. Finally, Hahn noted that taking large foreign exchange positions and freezing exposure at certain levels is always risky. In this vein, he noted that the ability of U.S. firms to invoice in dollars represents a significant advantage given the built-in hedging opportunities afforded by such a strategy.

Hatsopoulos agreed that Thermo Electron does not try to predict exchange rate levels and aims instead to match costs and revenues to the greatest degree possible. In this vein, the use of debt financing in recent foreign acquisitions has facilitated matching to reduce exposure.

7

Risks to Lenders and Borrowers in International Capital Markets

1. Benjamin E. Hermalin and Andrew K. Rose
2. Peter M. Garber
3. Andrew Crockett
4. David W. Mullins, Jr.

1. Benjamin E. Hermalin and Andrew K. Rose

7.1.1 Introduction

This paper provides a framework for understanding the risks to borrowers and lenders in international capital flows. To isolate the features that are intrinsically international, we begin by analyzing the financial system in a purely domestic context. This allows us to focus on the extra effects associated with international activity.

All financial systems are fundamentally affected by two important and pervasive phenomena. First, borrowers and lenders are plagued by *asymmetric information*. Borrowers typically have better information about repayment prospects than do lenders, and they try to use this to their advantage. But lenders are aware of this risk and act accordingly, limiting their exposure and charging a premium for bearing this risk. The second fundamental imperfection is that borrowers cannot credibly commit to making repayments that lenders can collect at low cost. Since borrowers may choose to renege on their commitments, lenders bear the risk of not being repaid, but again, since lenders are aware of this possibility, *enforcement risks* end up being shared. Together, these

For comments, the authors thank Martin Feldstein, conference participants, and an anonymous referee.

frictions lead to low levels of financial activity, high interest rates, and insufficiently spread investment risks.

When we add the international dimension, both problems are exacerbated. Information is better inside countries than across international boundaries, and it is easier to use the legal system to back up contracts within a country than between countries. Consequently we expect to see relatively low amounts of international lending and borrowing, substantial premiums for international borrowing compared to domestic borrowing, and risks that are poorly spread across countries. Our framework makes it unsurprising then that we actually observe a low level of international (relative to domestic) financial activity. However, international lending can still be expected to occur between countries with dramatically different levels of wealth or different sources of systemic risk, or if competition from foreign capital improves the efficiency of the domestic financial system.

The differences between domestic and international financial systems are not merely microeconomic issues of information and enforcement. International capital flows are associated with two additional macroeconomic risks that are essentially absent in the domestic context. The first is *sovereign risk;* governments can choose to default on their international obligations. The second is the risk that international capital flows create macroeconomic instability through *monetary spillovers.* When capital flows internationally, the effects on the balance of payments spill out to the macroeconomy through the money supply and exchange rate, frequently with adverse effects.

In section 7.1.2 of the paper, we begin our analysis with a description of the financial system in a purely domestic setting. After identifying the fundamental sources of risk in this context, we move on in section 7.1.3 to an international setting. Section 7.1.4 provides an analysis of the macroeconomic effects of international lending that are absent in a purely domestic setting. The paper ends with a few brief conclusions.

7.1.2 The Domestic Financial System

We begin our analysis by considering the financial system at a relatively abstract level in a purely domestic context. This enables us to isolate the fundamental problems, which constitute extra risks to lenders and borrowers, that can, in principle, be avoided with a perfect financial system. In the next two sections, we consider what extra issues emerge in an international context.[1]

It is easiest to isolate the issues of interest with a thought experiment. Imagine an economy with a large number of farmers. The farmers are interested in borrowing seed (capital) to plant (invest) in their fields. A large number of individuals saving for the future are potentially interested in lending funds to the farmers, especially if the returns exceed the "safe" (risk-free) rate of return.

---

1. This section borrows from Eichengreen and Rose (1997) and Gertler and Rose (1994).

Consider, first, an idealized setting in which (1) all markets are competitive; (2) information is costless; and (3) borrowers and lenders can write credible contracts, guaranteed to be honored by both sides by a costless legal system, that cover all possible contingencies. The role of a financial system is to mobilize the savings of potential lenders and allocate these funds efficiently across the investment projects of potential borrowers. In our idealized economy, how well does the system work?

Flawlessly. In the frictionless setting, savers lend to farmers freely at the risk-free rate.[2] Market forces allocate the income of individuals efficiently between consumption and savings and then allocate savings across different farmers' investment projects. Each farmer borrows seed, signing a contract that specifies repayment plus interest to the lender under all possible circumstances. Since lenders compete to lend funds to borrowers, loan rates are driven down to the risk-free interest rate (arbitrage eliminates higher rates and no lender accepts less than the risk-free rate). Lenders do not have to worry about how much effort the farmer puts into tending crops—their repayment does not depend on the farmer's actions.[3] All farmers are able to borrow up to the point that the additional discounted expected return from capital just equals its price (the interest rate). There are no liquidity problems, and there is no need for precautionary savings. Government policy is unnecessary and would in general be counterproductive.[4]

This idyllic example is illustrated with dotted lines in figure 7.1. Perfect competition ensures that the supply of funds (measured on the x-axis) is flat at the risk-free rate, denoted r (interest rates are measured on the y-axis).[5] The demand for loans is downward sloping.[6] The point at which the two lines intersect gives the equilibrium quantity lent, x.

---

2. Given costless information, the farmers face an efficient market for insurance against the financial hazards incurred in farming (weather, price volatility, etc.). Hence, there is no reason for insurance to be bundled with financing. Since the farmers can obtain insurance and there is complete freedom of contracting, default risk is irrelevant in this idyllic setting. When, however, information is costly, economies of scale in information gathering can make the bundling of financing and insurance desirable vis-à-vis their separate provision. Consequently, we can expect to see lenders take on some insurance role through their willingness to face default risk. We develop this point in greater detail below.

3. The farmer's insurer will care about the farmer's efforts. Since, however, we are assuming costless information and freedom of contract, this will not pose a problem; i.e., there can be no moral hazard problem. Hence, any trade-off between insurance and incentives can be avoided.

4. If the rest of the world were also described by these assumptions, there would be no relation between domestic savings and investment; the identity and national origin of savers and borrowers would be irrelevant.

5. There is an implicit assumption that the market for farm capital is sufficiently small relative to the overall economy that the movement of funds to the farm sector does not cause the price of capital in other markets (i.e., the risk-free rate) to rise. I.e., we are assuming that *general* equilibrium effects are small.

6. This is a standard property of all factor demands.

Loan Rate

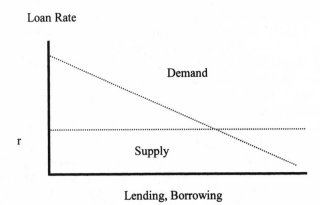

Lending, Borrowing

Fig. 7.1   Financial system with perfect information and credible commitments

Imperfect Information and Enforcement

Unfortunately, the idyllic situation portrayed in figure 7.1 is far from reality. Each of the assumptions we made is grossly unrealistic as a description of even advanced countries. There are barriers to entry in the financial system, information is unevenly distributed, and there are problems in enforcing contracts. Unsurprisingly, the predictions of the model are also not borne out in reality.

Our frictionless example is a poor description of reality for two fundamental reasons: imperfect information and difficulties associated with writing and enforcing contracts.[7] Information is costly to obtain, and the law imposes restrictions on the set of loan contracts that can be written (e.g., a debtor cannot waive his right to file for bankruptcy). Moreover, even within the set of legally enforceable contracts, the costs of using the legal system are high and uncertain.

The most critical legal limitations on loan contracts are those that limit the amount that can be seized from the borrower should the borrower default on the loan. Of these, the most important is the right to declare bankruptcy, which limits the debtor's liability. In the case of individual borrowers, personal bankruptcy laws, elimination of debtors' prisons, and prohibitions on slavery combine to make it almost completely impossible to seize the typical individual's most valuable asset, his human capital. In many states, his second and third most valuable assets—his house and car—also enjoy some protection against seizure.[8]

Limited liabilities laws and their ilk would not, per se, be directly relevant to lending in a world of full (symmetric) information. The borrower could take care of default risk by purchasing insurance from a third party, much in the

---

7. We think of imperfect competition in the financial system as being less important; it usually results either from policy or from information and enforcement problems.

8. See, e.g., Aghion and Hermalin (1990) for an economic analysis of such laws.

way some mortgage covenants require the borrower to obtain mortgage insurance and homeowner's insurance. In the real world, however, information is typically asymmetric, with the borrower having better information about his prospects than a lender or insurer. Here, default risk becomes directly relevant to lending. As is well known (see, e.g., Rothschild and Stiglitz 1976), when the insured have better information than the insurers—a situation known as *adverse selection*—insurance markets do not work efficiently. In particular, risks will not be fully insured. Consequently, a lender will ultimately face some default risk. This has a number of consequences for lending.

First, because the lender is exposed to default risk, the lender will have to charge a higher interest rate as a means of being compensated for bearing this risk. Hence, the interest rate will be higher than it would be absent default risk.

Second, because the lender will want to know the extent of this risk, the lender will be forced to acquire information about the borrower. Since information acquisition is costly, it is inefficient for two parties, the lender and an insurer, to both collect this information. Consequently, efficiency dictates that the supplying-of-funds function and the insurance function be bundled together by a single entity. That is, the interest rate is the sum of two prices: the cost of funds plus an "insurance premium" that the borrower pays the lender for the latter to assume the default risk. Moreover, because of asymmetric information, the borrower's total cost of borrowing (the interest rate plus the premium) will be greater than it would have been given symmetric information. Hence, the volume of lending will be less relative to a symmetric information world.

Third, lenders will tend to be "large." Given that each loan is now risky, an individual would be reluctant to enter into a one-to-one lending arrangement; the individual would not want to absorb that risk. If, however, that individual pools his capital with the capital of others and this "syndicate" makes a variety of loans, they can diversify away much of the risk.[9] The need for financial intermediaries to be large, combined with government regulation of entry into this industry, will yield these financial intermediaries a certain degree of market power. Consequently, we can expect these financial intermediaries to price their loans above their cost, which will further reduce the volume of lending relative to a symmetric information world.

Fourth, asymmetric information can lead to both the misallocation of funds and an increase in interest rates due to a "lemons" problem (see Akerlof 1970). This problem is most readily illustrated by an example: Suppose that there are two types of farmers, high risk and low risk, who are equally represented in the population of farmers. A high-risk farmer will, with equal probability, produce either $13 worth of output or $0 worth of output. A low-risk farmer will produce $7 worth of output with certainty. Observe that the low-risk farmer

---

9. Since there are also significant economies of scale in raising capital, providing banking services (e.g., an ATM network), etc., diversification is not the only motive for large financial intermediaries to arise, but it is, nevertheless, a significant one.

has the higher *expected* return. Both types of farmer have negligible capital and must borrow $6 for seed. Although a farmer knows what type he is, a lender does not. Assume that the farmers are protected by limited liability— should they default on a loan the lender gets only the value of the output. Finally, assume the risk-free interest rate is 10 percent, so lenders will only make loans that have an expected value of at least $6.60. In this situation, the lender will require a payment of at least $8.80 to make a loan of $6; otherwise, because of default risk, the lender will certainly lose money on average.[10] But since the low-risk farmer only earns $7, he will certainly default; he would do better to exit farming and employ his negligible capital elsewhere—this despite the fact that were this a symmetric information world, he would want and could receive a loan of $6. Recognizing that the low-risk farmer will exit the market, the lender will demand to be repaid at least $13.20 to make a loan of $6 (since it knows it will be lending to high-risk farmers only, who have a 50 percent default rate). But then the high-risk farmer will also certainly default, and he too would exit farming. Viewed another way, the farm sector is starved of capital and hence ceases to function. Observe that although the high-risk farmer would be excluded from borrowing under symmetric information (his expected return of $6.50 means a lender could not earn a 10 percent return), the low-risk farmer would not. Hence, we see that asymmetric information will lead to higher interest rates and the misallocation of capital.[11]

Fifth, because the lender absorbs some of the risk—essentially provides partial insurance to the borrower—the borrower's incentives can be dampened. Because what the borrower receives in good (nondefault) outcomes is only a portion of his project's return, his incentive to work for good outcomes is reduced. A related problem is that because the borrower is not gambling with his own money, his incentive under worsening financial conditions could be to "double up" on his bets—attempt to borrow more or pursue riskier, asset-dissipating behavior—in a desperate attempt to generate cash. That is, because it's not his money on the margin, the desperate borrower feels no compunction against throwing good money after bad. Asymmetric information—the high cost of monitoring the borrower—makes it difficult for the lender to guard against such *moral hazard* problems.

Although the discussion so far paints a somewhat dire picture, it needs to be remembered that both lenders and borrowers can take measures to mitigate

10. Let B be the amount to be repaid (the face value of the debt). Suppose the lender could expect to receive B 100 percent of the time from low-risk farmers (who make up half the population). Clearly, however, it can only expect repayment 50 percent of the time from high-risk farmers (who make up the other half of the population). Hence, its probability of repayment would be only 75 percent; so it would need to ask for a 33 percent premium to be insured against default risk (i.e., $.75 \times B \geq 6.60$ only if $B \geq 8.80$).

11. If we changed the high-risk farmer's good outcome from $13 to $13.50, then the low-risk farmer, who would still have the higher expected return, would still be blocked from borrowing, but the high-risk farmer would now be able to borrow (at an effective interest rate of 120 percent). Here, then, capital would be diverted from a high-return use to a lower return use.

Table 7.1   **FDIC-Insured Lenders' Debt Collateralized by Real Estate**

Year	Percentage
1995	21
1994	21
1993	22
1992	22
1991	21
1990	20
1989	19
1988	18
1987	17
1986	15
1985	13
1984	13

Note: The apparent trend toward increased collateralization with real estate may be misleading. Following the savings and loan (S&L) crisis of the 1980s, FSLIC, the deposit insurer of S&Ls, was eliminated and FDIC took over insuring S&L deposits. Since S&Ls do a higher proportion of their lending on real estate than banks, the apparent trend could be due to this change in the population mix, rather than to any trend in lending.

some of the problems caused by asymmetric information. Lenders can, for instance, monitor borrowers and employ methods of screening poor credit risks from good credit risks. They can also demand collateral (in fact, roughly 20 percent of lending by FDIC-insured institutions is collateralized with real estate—see table 7.1—suggesting the importance of limiting default risk in lending). Since lenders presumably undertake these measures to reduce the costs to which they would otherwise be exposed from asymmetric information, these measures should serve to lower the cost of lending relative to a situation of "pure" asymmetric information. We note, for later, that these methods often benefit from (and may even require) proximity between lender and borrower. Borrowers too can attempt to mitigate problems of asymmetric information by taking actions that signal information about themselves (such as offering collateral). Unlike lender screening and monitoring, however, signaling does not necessarily lower borrowing costs. The reason is that there is something of a "rat race" component to signaling; for a signal to convince a lender of the borrower's creditworthiness, it may have to be "extreme." Consequently, total borrowing costs (interest plus cost of signaling) can be greater than in a world in which borrowers are prohibited from signaling.[12] This further increase in borrowing costs will, of course, lead to even less borrowing and an even smaller capital market.

The information and enforcement frictions between lenders and borrowers lead to two general conclusions. First, borrowers will pay a premium for "external finance," that is, noncollateralized borrowing. This premium compen-

12. See Aghion and Hermalin (1990) for details and examples.

sates lenders for default risk, with the size of the premium being affected by the observable risk, the unobservable risk due to moral hazard, and the lemons problem (offset, somewhat, by the lender's efforts to screen for creditworthiness and monitor existing loans). Second, as a consequence, investors are able to borrow less than they would with perfect (symmetric information) financial markets. The scale of financial activity is smaller than it would be in the absence of these problems.

To make this more concrete, let us return to the farming example. Even with a perfect financial system, the harvest will be a result of many factors, some controlled by the farmer (e.g., the amount of effort spent tending the crops), some the result of the financial system (the amount of seed planted), and others more random still (weather). If it were costless to monitor the actions of farmers and to collect the payments specified in an all-encompassing and costlessly enforced contract, a saver could lend funds directly to farmers without any financial intermediary. In return, savers would receive a fixed return. But in reality, the farmer has better information than potential investors about soil quality, pest problems, and so forth. Furthermore, it is impossible to specify the amount of effort the farmer should apply in all circumstances; and even if it were, it would be impossible to monitor how much effort is actually applied. Court costs are far from negligible, and the farmer will also have the right to declare bankruptcy and walk away from his debt in sufficiently bad circumstances. Financial intermediaries, which can exploit economies of scale to reduce information and enforcement costs and can diversify risk, will come into existence—with possibly some reduction in lending competition—and all financial activity will be channeled through them; the cost advantage of intermediaries will eliminate direct loans from savers to borrowers. Intermediaries will only advance funds to a farmer at a loan rate higher than the risk-free interest rate. The farmer will accordingly borrow less than he would have chosen at a lower loan rate.

As a result, the investment decisions made by the farmer will depend on the farmer's financial situation. The farmer will first use internal funds to buy seed and only rely on external finance (e.g., bank loans) where necessary. The farmer will not maximize the value of the farm; crops will not be planted to the point where the risk-adjusted cost of funds equals the marginal expected gain from planting seed. Investors and farmers, consequently, lose out on profitable investment opportunities not undertaken, and the farmers further lose in that they bear too much idiosyncratic risk.

The effects of asymmetric information and enforcement problems are readily observed in figure 7.2. Both the demand for seed capital and the supply of savings are affected; the more realistic schedules are portrayed with solid lines (otherwise the figure is identical to fig. 7.1). The supply of funds is unaffected at low levels of lending activity. Up to the point of the farmers' collateralizable net worth, farmers can simply self-finance investment projects or

Loan Rate

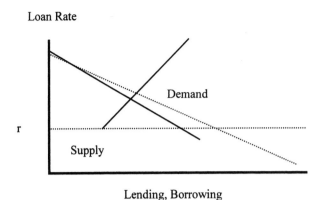

r

Lending, Borrowing

Fig. 7.2   Financial system with imperfect information and enforcement problems

provide collateral for any net borrowing.[13] But after this point, finance from other lenders—"uncollateralized external finance"—is required. Assuming a decreasing-returns-to-scale screening and monitoring technology, the supply curve then rises, reflecting the rising marginal cost of originating loans. The demand curve shifts in as well, since signaling behavior and the removal of full insurance raise the farmers' cost of borrowing.

Policy

Policy toward the financial sector matters because it can make business more or less costly for financial intermediaries. The more costly lending is, the greater the premium intermediaries will demand and, as the price of funds increases, the less borrowing there will be.

Policy can also protect—or harm—the precarious balancing act financial intermediaries must perform: The fact that their assets (deposits) are less liquid than their liabilities renders their financial condition delicate, and confidence is thus essential to their stability. If confidence wanes for any reason, the fact that demand for funds is met on a first-come, first-served basis gives creditors an incentive to liquidate their deposits at the first sign of trouble. Such a run means a contraction of lending activity.

For these reasons, governments wish to avoid disruptions in the financial sector. A number of standard policies can be taken to strengthen the financial sector. These include (1) deposit insurance for banks, (2) reserve requirements, (3) capital requirements, (4) restrictions on the riskiness of assets held by financial firms, (5) direct supervision, and (6) provision of lender-of-last-resort facilities. These policies can help to ensure the stability of the financial sector,

---

13. However, self-financing means that farmers may bear too much idiosyncratic risk.

thereby reducing the underlying enforcement and information problems. By reducing risks they can encourage more efficient, inexpensive, and widespread financial activity.[14]

7.1.3   How Does International Lending Exacerbate Information and Enforcement Problems?

Both of the fundamental problems we encountered in the financial system are exacerbated when we consider international lending. Local intermediaries are likely to have better information about local investment opportunities and risks than foreign intermediaries; they are also more likely to know how to squeeze payments from local borrowers.[15] In contrast, foreign intermediaries suffer from less information; hence, the problems of asymmetric information discussed above will be worse than for domestic lending.

The history of financial intermediation in the United States offers some evidence that domestic lenders have advantages over foreign lenders. Although partly due to restrictions on interstate banking and state restrictions on branch banking, most credit organizations in the United States have tended to be local operations despite the obvious risk reduction advantages to geographic diversification. This was undoubtedly due to the high cost of obtaining information about geographically distant borrowers.[16] Indeed, even *social* distance proved sufficient to restrict many savings and loan societies to operating within a single local immigrant group. More recently, evidence from the operation of savings and loans in the 1980s finds that those that made "long-distance" loans were outperformed by those that did not.[17]

A related problem is that foreign intermediaries often must compete against domestic intermediaries. As we have just noted, domestic intermediaries will have an information advantage vis-à-vis their foreign competitors. There are two consequences of this advantage. First, domestic intermediaries will, for reasons discussed previously, enjoy a cost advantage over foreign intermediar-

14. Of course, such policies can have inadvertent and perverse consequences. E.g., providing deposit insurance reduces the incentives of depositors to monitor intermediaries' activities. In addition, deposit insurance—coupled with limited liability—turns intermediaries into giant "put options" for shareholders: the shareholders receive the upside gain but can "put" the intermediary to the deposit insurer in bad states. This can lead intermediaries to behave in a risk-*seeking* manner with corresponding inefficiencies and misallocations of resources (for empirical estimates of this effect in the context of U.S. savings and loans, see Hermalin and Wallace 1994, 1997).

15. This point is often made in the development literature, where it is argued that a good way to deliver credit to rural farmers is to use village elders and chieftains as agents because of their superior knowledge of creditworthiness and their greater ability to force repayment (e.g., by threatening social sanctions). See Fuentes (1996) for more on this point, as well as references to empirical confirmation.

16. This could also reflect *within*-firm information problems exacerbated by geographic distance (e.g., it could be harder to control a local agent of the firm the farther he is from headquarters).

17. See Hermalin and Wallace (1994) for evidence on this matter.

ies. This allows them to be tougher competitors, which squeezes the foreign intermediaries' profits. Indeed, the cost advantage could be sufficient that foreign intermediaries are unable to capture enough of the market to cover the fixed costs of entry, so they are kept out of the domestic credit market altogether. The second consequence is that because a domestic intermediary is able to offer better rates than a foreign competitor, foreign competitors will be second-choice lenders for domestic borrowers. That is, foreign intermediaries could face an adverse selection of borrowers who have been denied credit by the better informed domestic intermediaries. This adverse selection means that foreign lenders are exposed to even greater risk.

There is some empirical evidence to support these conjectures. When U.S. savings and loans were allowed by deregulation to pursue lines of business previously restricted to commercial banks, those that took advantage of these new powers were greatly outperformed by those that chose to stay with traditional lines of business.[18] A plausible interpretation of this result is that those savings and loans that strayed from traditional lines had an information disadvantage vis-à-vis commercial banks. Consequently, they made lower profits and suffered higher rates of loan defaults.[19]

Given these information disadvantages faced by foreign lenders, the observed low levels of international financial activity seem unsurprising. This is especially true when we add the impact of enforcement problems.

Enforcement can be harder across international borders than within national boundaries. First, an alien legal system means that a foreign lender's domestic expertise on enforcement is of lower value; the foreign lender may, therefore, need to make expensive investments in acquiring the necessary expertise or become reliant on expensive local expertise. Second, in countries where the rule of law does not always function well, such as some developing countries or some postcommunist states, enforcement can be hampered by the borrower's ability to employ extralegal methods to deter enforcement (harass auditors, spirit assets away, etc.). Third, the legal system could exhibit a nationalistic bias, making enforcement by a foreign lender more difficult than it would be for a domestic lender.[20] These problems add either directly to the foreign lender's cost of lending or, by increasing the foreigner's risk, indirectly to the cost of lending. Higher costs, in turn, mean the foreign supply of funds shifts in, raising the interest rate and lowering the total amount of lending.

A further problem with international lending is that international banking policy is less well developed than domestic banking policy. Many of the policy

18. This result controls for pre-deregulation performance, so this is not the case of incompetent thrifts, unable to compete in their traditional lines, going looking for greener pastures.

19. See Hermalin and Wallace (1994) for a complete discussion.

20. This is a problem within the United States in lender liability suits where juries often favor local debtors (the plaintiffs) against distant banks (the defendants). See Fischel (1989).

institutions that serve to reduce the risks in the domestic financial sector do not exist at the international level.[21] Deposit insurance, for instance, is essentially absent internationally.[22] Lender-of-last-resort facilities are a very uncertain business at the international level.[23]

On the other hand, financial intermediaries can benefit from a lack of regulation. Government-imposed reserve requirements and bank supervision are largely absent at the international level, and requirements on capital adequacy and asset riskiness are much more difficult to monitor. This gives intermediaries greater flexibility, which, in theory, should allow them to make greater profits. The U.S. experience with savings and loan deregulation, however, suggests that greater flexibility may not be associated with greater profits in practice. The reasons for this are relevant to international lending. Intermediaries may respond to greater flexibility by rationally pursuing riskier strategies; but then the rate of failure can be expected to go up. Because intermediaries are themselves debtors (their deposits, recall, are loans from depositors) protected by limited liability, they receive upside gains but can walk away from downside losses. This, in turn, can give them risk-*seeking* preferences; that is, they could prefer a lower expected return, but riskier venture to a higher expected return, but safer venture.[24] Consequently, average returns could be lower than they would have been under tighter regulation.

In addition, the perception that international financial activity is risky may become a self-fulfilling prediction if governments create barriers to international capital flows. Historically, many governments have viewed international borrowing and lending as a source of more risk than opportunity and have accordingly erected international capital flow barriers.

The effects of international lending can be portrayed using the same conceptual apparatus as we applied in section 7.1.2. To clarify things, figure 7.3 illustrates the effects of allowing either only domestic *or* foreign lending to finance investment projects. Both information and enforcement problems are exacerbated by international lending; the relevant demand and supply schedules are graphed with dashed lines. The supply curve is higher and to the left of the domestic case, since the collateralizable net worth of the borrower is lower to foreign lenders than it is to domestic lenders (because of additional enforce-

21. The absence of these institutions is part of the raison d'être for the offshore financial sector. "Eurobanks" began to flourish in part because of the cost advantages that stemmed from the lack of regulation and reserve requirements.

22. This may also restrict foreign lenders to lending domestically raised funds. Since the source of funds is not as well diversified as it would be were the lender able to attract nondomestic funds, the lender is exposed to greater risks—such as duration mismatches—which raises its cost of business (although this cost is incurred regardless of where it lends).

23. While the Basle Committee has improved the supervision of multinational banks (most famously of late through bank capital measures), there are still many ambiguities, especially in the lender-of-last-resort facilities.

24. Hermalin and Wallace (1994) found evidence that deregulation resulted in many thrifts' switching to riskier, but lower expected return lines of business from their traditional lines of business.

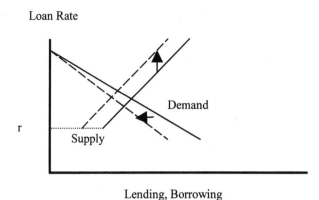

Lending, Borrowing

Fig. 7.3   Financial system with only foreign lending

ment and information problems). If borrowers are further restricted in the amount of insurance they are allowed to purchase, they may react to this increased risk bearing by reducing their demand for funds, shifting the demand curve in.

The differences between international and domestic financial activity are simply a matter of the degree to which information and enforcement problems bite. They need not be large; indeed, they need not exist at all. In principle, both enforcement and information problems could be less serious for international lending.[25] Still, the fact that international capital flows have historically been small—see tables 7.2 and 7.3 for evidence, and chapters 1.1 by Edwards, 3.1 by Ito, and especially 5.1 by Tesar in this volume—is consistent with our arguments that enforcement and information issues are worse for international lenders.[26]

International lending is more difficult than purely domestic lending; but international capital flows do exist and are in fact growing more rapidly than purely domestic activity. Why? The situation portrayed in figure 7.3 is too pessimistic since it ignores two important factors. First, it compares two different supply curves—one with only domestic savings, the other with only foreign savings. In reality, countries that allow international capital flows can finance investment projects with either or both. In this case, the aggregate supply-of-savings curve is unambiguously flatter than the purely domestic curve.

25. It is easy to think of counterexamples. Foreign expertise about export sectors can easily be superior to domestic information. Investors in recently deregulated or emerging sectors may benefit from foreign experience, providing an information advantage to foreigners. And foreigners may find governments and judicial systems more sympathetic to their claims than to those of domestic residents.

26. Table 7.2 contains data on the outstanding stocks and new issues of domestic debt in the OECD countries; table 7.3 contains the analogous data on international debt. While there are technical problems involved in a direct comparison, there seems to be little doubt that the overwhelming amount of financial activity is purely domestic in nature.

Table 7.2   Stocks and Net Issues of Domestic Debt (billions of U.S. dollars)

Country	1993	1994	1995
Total OECD[a]	19,714.5	22,171.4	24,110.0
United States	9,340.2	9,963.1	10,726
Japan	3,976.7	4,750	4,958.6
United Kingdom	440.8	524.6	598.7
Canada	469.6	463.6	503.3
Net issues	1,604.4	1,474.4	1,680.3

Source: Ito and Folkerts-Landau (1996, 59).
[a]Excluding Iceland and Turkey.

Table 7.3   Stocks and Net Issues of International Debt (billions of U.S. dollars)

| | Stocks | | | Net Issues, |
Country	1993	1994	1995	1995
All countries	2,037.8	2,441.7	2,803.3	313.2
Industrial	1,650.3	1,976.4	2,277.8	261.8
United States	176.9	209.3	272.8	60.6
Japan	340.1	360.6	356.7	7.3
Developing	121.8	162.1	192.9	31.3

Source: Ito and Folkerts-Landau (1996, 57).

Allowing capital flows can only reduce capital market imperfections, lowering interest rates and raising lending activity.

Second, the situation portrayed in figure 7.3 implicitly compares two identical countries. But countries differ in many ways; some—developing countries in particular—are capital poor. A small developing country with a relatively low endowment of capital faces a steeper supply-of-domestic-funds curve than it does if foreign capital is allowed to flow in. Since Northern countries are well capitalized, they will tend to have fewer investment opportunities with high rates of return, as most such opportunities are exploited as they emerge. Hence, the North will be willing to lend funds at a rate of return lower than required by Southern residents. Foreigners need not even be better endowed with capital if their presence creates more competitive domestic capital markets. And the systemic risks that affect countries can be different, providing a potentially important argument for international diversification. As a result, interest rates can fall and loan activity rise with international capital flows.

Figure 7.4 provides an illustration of this case for a capital-poor country or a country with an uncompetitive domestic financial sector. As in figure 7.3, to clarify the argument we compare financing all investment projects with either domestic or foreign savings. Because of information and enforcement problems, foreigners have access to a lower level of collateralizable net worth; the

Loan Rate

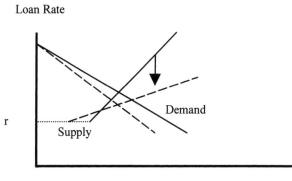

Lending, Borrowing

Fig. 7.4   Foreign lending for a capital-poor country

foreign supply curve starts to rise at a lower level. On the other hand, since foreigners have a larger (or more competitive) financial system because of their abundance of capital, the foreign supply curve is flatter than the purely domestic supply curve.[27] The net result is ambiguous. Interest rates may be lower and total financial activity higher with only foreign finance, as depicted. If the country is relatively well endowed with capital, or the domestic financial system is relatively efficient, then the more pessimistic situation of figure 7.3 will prevail.

It is not unreasonable to assume that foreign capital systems are more efficient than domestic financial structures in many countries. Offshore capital markets are large and very competitive, as can be seen in tables 7.2 and 7.3. International financial activity is large compared to domestic financial sectors for all except the largest industrial countries.

Finally, we should not forget that because foreign lending offers intermediaries geographic diversification of their loan portfolios, an intermediary in country A could value a loan in country B more than a country B intermediary.

The growth of international capital flows is, arguably, a manifestation of policies that have systematically reduced information and enforcement problems. For instance, the Bank for International Settlements (BIS) rules can be viewed as an attempt to reduce information problems on the strength of banks viewed from an international perspective. The accession of countries to the international economic community—say by membership in the International Monetary Fund (IMF), the World Trade Organization, and regional trade agreements—can be viewed as devices to lower enforcement costs. In addition, policies that allow for foreign control of domestic intermediaries mean that capital-rich foreign intermediaries can more easily team up with expertise-

27. Foreign capital may also be supplied more elastically than domestic capital if systemic risks vary by country, so that international diversification effects are important.

rich domestic intermediaries, and this control means they can reduce their risks.[28] Finally, although not solely the result of government policy, high-speed computers, a globally improved telecommunications infrastructure, and greater competition in transportation have reduced the costs of long-distance monitoring and screening of loans.

In summary, two fundamental problems are responsible for imperfect financial systems: imperfect information and the difficulty of writing credible and enforceable contracts. Foreigners are likely to have worse information about domestic investment projects; they are also likely to find it more difficult to write enforceable contracts at low cost. Since foreign intermediaries are usually at a disadvantage compared to domestic intermediaries, we would be surprised to see large amounts of international financial activity. There are, however, three caveats: large differences in capital abundance, a desire for systemic risk diversification, and an inefficient domestic financial structure can all induce large capital flows.

7.1.4 Macroeconomic Aspects of International Lending

We have discussed the financial imperfections at the heart of financial systems from a purely microeconomic viewpoint thus far. But an internationally integrated financial system also differs from an autarkic domestic system in two important macroeconomic aspects. First, borrowing countries can choose to default on foreign debt. The possibility of *sovereign risk* must be taken into account by potential lenders. Second, the domestic monetary regime is strongly affected by the presence of capital flows. This also has important implications for the monetary system of a recipient country, adding *monetary instability* to the potential risks borne by borrowers.

Sovereign Risk

In any society, firms and individuals occasionally find themselves unable or unwilling to meet their financial obligations, often for reasons beyond their control. A declaration of bankruptcy typically then gives creditors the right to seize the assets of the debtor. Sovereign risk differs from ordinary bankruptcy risk because enforcing this right beyond the jurisdiction of the creditor's government requires the cooperation of another government (Eaton 1990). If the defaulting agent is itself a government, it is unlikely to hand over domestic assets to foreign creditors, and those creditors will have little or no legal recourse. Sovereign risk constitutes an important impediment to international financial activity.[29]

---

28. In particular, the foreigners can reduce the "agency" problems—insufficient screening and monitoring by the domestic intermediary, misallocation of funds, etc.—that could arise in an arm's-length relationship. It is, however, reasonable to expect that even *within*-intermediary agency problems could be exacerbated by geographic distance (consider, e.g., Nick Leeson and Barings Bank). For more on agency issues, see Williamson (1985).

29. In a theoretical sense, sovereign risk can be viewed as an enforcement problem.

Table 7.4   **Countries in External Payments Arrears, End of 1995**

Albania	Egypt	Russia
Angola	Equatorial Guinea	Rwanda
Antigua and Barbuda	Eritrea	São Tomé and Principe
Azerbaijan	Ethiopia	Senegal
Belarus	Guatemala	Seychelles
Benin	Guinea	Sierra Leone
Burkina Faso	Guinea-Bissau	Sudan
Cameroon	Jordan	Suriname
Cape Verde	Kenya	Syrian Arab Republic
Central African Republic	Liberia	Tajikistan
Chad	Mali	Tanzania
Comoros	Mauritania	Turkmenistan
Congo	Myanmar	Ukraine
Costa Rica	Nicaragua	Venezuela
Côte d'Ivoire	Niger	Vietnam
Croatia	Panama	Zambia
Dominican Republic	Paraguay	
Ecuador	Peru	

Source: IMF, *Annual Report on Exchange Arrangements and Exchange Restrictions* (Washington, D.C., 1996).

Table 7.4 contains a list of countries in official payments arrears at the end of 1995, as tabulated in the IMF's 1996 *Annual Report on Exchange Arrangements and Exchange Restrictions.*[30] Long as this list is, it still understates the importance of sovereign risk. First, the very threat of sovereign risk has reduced international lending. Second, the list does not account for the effects of external rescue packages of the sort that prevented defaults by, for instance, Mexico and Argentina in 1994–95 and Thailand and Korea in 1997. Third, arrears have been much higher in the recent past, as any bank exposed to Latin debt in 1980s is painfully aware.

The possibility of sovereign default is clearly an important risk borne by international borrowers and lenders. Still, it must be of limited importance in practice; if it were not, debtor countries would never pay back foreign creditors. Since repayment is the norm, there must be important reasons for governments not to default. What are they?

One way to limit sovereign default risk is for creditors to threaten to seize the overseas assets of debtor countries. This incentive is of obviously limited importance if the borrower is a net debtor.[31]

A more important reason why debtor countries continue to pay their international obligations is that creditor countries can refuse to engage in trade with

30. External payments arrears include arrears that have been caused by exchange restrictions on current payments or transfers, as well as overdue arrears on financial obligations of which the obligor is the government or a resident in the country in question.
31. A "common pool" problem could also exist: if there is more than one creditor, a given creditor can be frozen out if other creditors attach the overseas assets first. Although this does not affect the deterrent effect of seizure for the debtor nation, it does increase the risk for its creditors.

debtors. Trade credit can be cut off, boycotts begun, and goods can be seized, thereby reducing the welfare of debtor countries.[32] Such sanctions can be important, especially for small countries with large gains from trade. Still, these sanctions are also limited in scope, since creditor countries also lose from disruptions in international trade. Creditor countries may lack the will to impose sanctions, particularly when the trade sectors have more political clout than the financial sector. Furthermore, to be most effective, the creditor countries must put up a common front; however, the temptation to cheat on such a boycott could be large (particularly when the exports of the creditor countries are in competition), making united action difficult. Finally, the trading partners could not all be creditor countries, which would mitigate the disruption (e.g., the defaulting nation could find substitute providers of critical imports and it could use these other trading partners to transship goods).

Another potential way to limit sovereign risk is for lending countries to diversify their risks by spreading loans across debtor countries. Complete diversification, however, requires negative correlation across default risks (e.g., as default risk in Mexico increases, default risk falls in Brazil). Yet, as shown by the Latin American experience of the 1980s, positive correlation would seem more likely than negative correlation.

An often-cited limit to sovereign risk is the "reputation effect." A country that anticipates needing foreign capital in the future will find it easier to borrow if it earns a reputation as a good credit risk by continued repayment.[33] After all, defaulting countries can be cut off from future borrowing by creditors or charged higher rates of interest than they would otherwise face. The empirical importance of this seems dubious, however. Many countries have defaulted on their international obligations only to reenter international credit markets shortly thereafter; the most dramatic recent examples are the Latin countries since the debt crisis of 1982.[34]

Yet, reentry into the credit markets does not necessarily disprove the logic of the reputation effect. While it is true that early game-theoretic models of the reputation effect assumed infinite punishment of transgressors (i.e., being infinitely barred from borrowing),[35] more recent models have realized that the logic applies even if the penalties are of finite length. In particular, if the transgressor plays a "penance strategy" (i.e., inherently suffers from its transgres-

32. The limiting case would be for the creditor country to make political threats; i.e., sovereign default can be met by gunboat diplomacy. For various reasons, this limit is rarely reached these days.

33. Important to this discussion is the assumption that the debtor nation wishes to remain in the international financial community. The literature has also considered the situation in which a debtor nation has the alternative of entering financial autarky. In our analysis, we assume that no debtor nations would actually find it in their interest to enter into such a state.

34. At a more abstract level, Bulow and Rogoff (1989) have shown that it is not generally worthwhile for small countries to establish a reputation for repayment.

35. A "grim strategy." For more on the game theory behind reputation effects, see Fudenberg and Tirole (1991).

sion), then the punishment phase need last only a short time. Given the financial disruptions associated with a major default, it could be argued that something resembling a penance strategy is being played after a default, which could help to explain why defaulting countries are soon welcomed back by the international financial community.[36] In short, then, reputation effects serve as a principal—but by no means perfect—way of enforcing repayment.

If reputation effects are indeed important, it might seem strange that we ever see sovereign default. In particular, why can't the creditor and debtor renegotiate when default is anticipated, thereby avoiding the costs incurred by actually defaulting? In fact, we do observe such negotiations in many instances (the equivalent of private workouts in the domestic context). A case could even be made that were creditor and debtor *symmetrically* informed about the debtor's circumstances, we should always see renegotiation rather than default. The problem is that once again asymmetric information makes it difficult for the debtor to communicate its circumstances convincingly. Consequently, the creditor worries that the debtor is trying to get away with repaying less than it actually could. The creditor, therefore, takes a harder stance in many instances than is warranted, leading ultimately to a default. Although the parties have an incentive to cooperate—analogously to partners in a game of bridge—they misread each other's signals, resulting in disaster. Nonetheless, the ability to renegotiate in advance of default can lessen the costs of default and reduce the impact of sovereign risk. Moreover, as the creditor's information about the debtor improves, this risk-reducing benefit is enhanced.

In summary, sovereign risk is a significant problem in international lending, one without an obvious analogue in domestic lending.[37] Direct enforcement is impossible. Direct punishment (seizing the debtor nation's assets abroad, trade boycotts, gunboat diplomacy, etc.) is likely to be applied in a haphazard way, at best, and so create few incentives for debtor nations to repay. The primary incentive, therefore, for repayment is reputation effects. In a world of certainty and symmetric information, reputation effects would be sufficient to deter all default; however, in the real world of uncertainty and asymmetric information, defaults will still occur.

Monetary Spillovers

In an autarkic country, the monetary regime is controlled by the central bank. The level of interest rates (the "risk-free" rate in the discussion above) is

36. Another, technical point is that much of the early reputation models predicted that there would be no transgressions in equilibrium. More recent work on "trigger strategies" has developed models in which, due to uncertainty, some transgressions occur in equilibrium (see, e.g., Green and Porter 1984).

37. Actually, given the rules of Chapter 11 bankruptcy, it could be argued that the managers and shareholders of a company in debt have some ability to frustrate their creditors' attempts to seize assets in the case of default. After default, a company coming out of Chapter 11 is often like a defaulted debtor nation; both are allowed to return to the capital markets. In this way, sovereign risk might not be so different from the risk faced in the domestic context.

determined by the authorities; additional risk premiums that compensate for information and enforcement problems are determined by market forces. The aggregate level of short-run real interest rates is a purely domestic matter.[38]

The situation is dramatically different in a country with free international capital mobility. While foreign capital can provide a healthy tonic of competition for domestic financial markets, it also compromises the ability of the central bank to conduct monetary policy from a purely domestic perspective.

The relationship between international lending and macroeconomic instability stems from two simple relations. First, the domestic monetary base—the most important component of the aggregate money supply—is composed of domestic credit and international reserves. Second, the balance-of-payments accounting identity links international flows of goods, services, and capital to changes in international reserves. Exogenous foreign shocks result in capital flows that lead to shifts in reserves and corresponding movements in the domestic money supply and the macroeconomy.

To make this concrete, consider a country's balance of payments:

Current account + Net capital flows = Net reserve flows.

Countries with net capital inflows that more than compensate for any current account deficit are in "balance-of-payments surplus" and experience rising levels of international reserves. But reserve flows are linked to the money supply since

Money supply = International reserves + Domestic credit.

So increases in international reserves lead to increases in the money supply, unless they are deliberately counteracted by the monetary authorities. The greater the degree of capital mobility, the faster and larger the reaction of net capital flows and the greater the impact on the money supply. Since the money supply is an important determinant of macroeconomic stability, undesired capital flows can compromise macroeconomic performance.

The first fundamental choice for a country with a nonzero balance of payments is whether to stem the imbalance or allow it to continue. For the sake of simplicity, we consider the case of a country with net capital inflows, which results in increasing international reserves.[39] To further sharpen our focus, assume too that the current account is balanced, and capital begins to flow into a country for purely foreign reasons.[40]

Allowing the capital to flow in might seem, at first blush, to be the obvious choice. After all, the country receives international reserves that can be kept for many purposes (e.g., defending the country's currency in the future). But the increase in international reserves raises the money supply if domestic credit

---

38. We assume that the monetary authority cannot alter real interest rates in the long run.

39. A number of Latin and Southeast Asian countries have been in this situation in the 1990s.

40. The first assumption is made purely for convenience; the second is far from uncommon. For instance, the reduction of capital flows to Mexico resulting from increases in American interest rates is often viewed as an underlying cause of the 1994 Mexican crisis.

policy is left unchanged. This loosening of monetary policy can result in undesirable future inflation. It can also fuel bubbles in asset prices, especially stock, bond, and real estate prices. If domestic banks become heavily exposed to asset price risk, either through design or neglect, popping asset bubbles can bankrupt the financial system, as Sweden and Japan found out in the early 1990s and Thailand more recently.

Still, even if the payments imbalance is allowed to continue it need not result in looser monetary policy. The central bank can offset increases in international reserves with a decline in domestic credit, usually sales of government bonds. This "sterilization" of reserve movements is not without its own perils though. Reductions of domestic credit tend to keep interest rates high. Since the government pays a higher interest rate on its bonds than it receives on its foreign (reserve) holdings, sterilization represents a nontrivial cost to the government. Sterilization also encourages continued capital inflows, so that the cause of the problem—the payments imbalance—persists. Further, sterilization is at best only a temporary policy, since it is naturally limited by the size of the credit base. The evidence to date indicates that while there is some scope for sterilization in the short run, there are few indications that sterilization is a viable policy over long periods of time.[41]

A third problem of allowing capital inflows to continue is that the international borrowing has to be repaid in the future (ignoring the sovereign risk considerations discussed above). Wisely invested, foreign capital can yield returns that pay back the original lenders while also providing domestic benefits. But if borrowing from abroad is used to finance consumption, perhaps by delaying painful but necessary fiscal adjustments, then repayment can be more difficult. Investing foreign capital in unprofitable projects with low returns is little better, as many Asian countries discovered in 1997.

Finally, it is always wise to remember that what has flowed in can also flow out. Foreign capital has an awkward habit of fleeing a country at the worst times, as many countries have rediscovered; Mexico in 1994, Argentina in 1995, and Korea and Thailand in 1997 are perhaps the most important recent examples.

Clearly, there are risks associated with allowing capital to continue to flow into a country for long periods of time.[42] The alternative is to stop the capital from coming in the first place.

There are two conceptually different methods of stemming capital inflows. The first is simply to restrict capital flows through administrative controls. Providing insulation from international capital flows through fiat has long been a standard tactic for developing countries (as a glance through the IMF's *Exchange Arrangements and Exchange Restrictions* indicates). Chile is often cited as a country that avoided the tequila effect of 1995 because of its controls on capital inflows. Indeed, many OECD countries imposed capital controls

---

41. See chap. 4 of Ito and Folkerts-Landau (1996) for references on this issue.

42. Deficits have comparable problems but are usually even less sustainable, since international reserves are smaller than domestic credit for most countries.

throughout the long post–World War II boom and have only removed them recently; France and Italy only reduced barriers in 1990.

But legal restrictions on capital flows come at a cost. While international financial activity may be "naturally" limited because of the enforcement and information reasons discussed above, it may still be enormously beneficial for capital-poor countries or countries that need competitive international markets to discipline domestic markets. Restricting access to foreign pressures over long periods can reduce domestic growth as a result. Moreover, countries are understandably reluctant to compromise their long-term access to international capital markets for short-term reasons.

Instead of permanently disrupting the linkage between the domestic and foreign financial systems, a more reasonable approach to countering a capital inflow may be to eliminate the underlying causes of the inflow. Both monetary and fiscal policy have important effects on the balance of payments and can be used to reduce or eliminate capital inflows. By lowering interest rates through the application of loose monetary policy, the monetary authorities can induce lower capital inflows directly. Alternatively, tighter fiscal policy can lower domestic absorption, thereby improving the current account and reducing net capital inflows; a fixed exchange rate can be devalued toward the same end.

While domestic policy instruments can be used to eliminate the underlying capital flows, the point remains: the independence of national macroeconomic policy is compromised as a result of international capital flows. In the case of unwanted capital inflows, either domestic monetary policy must be loosened or fiscal policy must be tightened. Neither policy may be desirable from a purely domestic perspective.

This argument is usually expressed in a more concise form that focuses on the purely monetary effects of capital inflows. Mundell's celebrated "Incompatible Trinity" states that international capital mobility, fixed exchange rates, and domestic monetary independence are mutually incompatible. A country may choose to stabilize its exchange rate for a variety of different reasons (e.g., to provide a nominal anchor for monetary policy or to encourage international trade by lowering exchange rate volatility). But once the country has decided to smooth its exchange rate, allowing unrestricted international capital flows comes at the risk of monetary instability. More precisely, the country relinquishes its ability to conduct monetary policy for purely domestic reasons because maintaining the exchange rate becomes the objective of monetary policy. As a result, the country bears higher risks of business cycle fluctuations. And if the country chooses instead to focus monetary policy on purely domestic objectives, this comes at the risk of unstable exchange rates and the instability that is associated with exchange rate variability.

In sum, reducing barriers to international capital flows may provide a number of microeconomic benefits, as discussed above. But the increased exposure to foreign capital means that the ability of the authorities to conduct independent policy oriented toward domestic objectives becomes more limited. Openness and external stability (of the exchange rate and balance of payments) come at the cost of the increased risk of domestic fluctuations.

Summary

Both sovereign risk and the monetary effects of net capital flows are macroeconomic issues that constitute extra risks from international financial activity. Sovereign risk is an issue of concern for both lending and borrowing countries. Net creditors face the risk of expropriation and default, but borrowers are affected because of the resulting higher interest rates and loan limits. Similarly, the monetary regimes of both lending and borrowing countries are fundamentally affected by openness to international capital flows; unwanted capital flows create macroeconomic instability.

7.1.5   Conclusions

In this paper we have provided a framework to analyze the risks to borrowers and lenders that are inherent in international financial activity. Microeconomic risks in all financial activity stem from two basic problems. Imperfect information compromises the ability of lenders to monitor the behavior of borrowers; the inability of borrowers and lenders to sign enforceable all-encompassing contracts at low cost also limits financial activity. Both of these problems are serious even in a purely domestic setting. And both are likely to be more problematic when financial activity takes place across international boundaries. At first glance, the low levels of international financial activity would seem to be unsurprising, except for countries with very different levels of capital, systematically different risks, or inefficient domestic financial sectors (the very countries that typically restrict international capital flows). This is especially true when we take into account two macroeconomic risks that have no analogue in a purely domestic setting: sovereign risk and monetary spillovers.

Still, many fundamental sources of risks are slowly being overcome. Information flows more easily than ever before, and the advantages that domestic residents have over foreigners in both enforcement and information are being eroded. Economic liberalization, increased dependence on foreign trade, and reduction in the state sectors of many countries reduce the risk of nations' defaulting on their debt or nations' using their sovereignty to thwart collection of debts from domestic firms. As these trends continue, we should see greater amounts of international capital flow and lower exposure to risk.

References

Aghion, Philippe, and Benjamin E. Hermalin. 1990. Legal restrictions on contracts can be efficient. *Journal of Law, Economics, and Organization* 6:381–409.

Akerlof, George. 1970. The market for "Lemons": Quality uncertainty and the market mechanism. *Quarterly Journal of Economics* 84:488–500.

Bulow, Jeremy, and Kenneth Rogoff. 1989. Sovereign debt: Is to forgive to forget?" *American Economic Review* 79:43–50.

Eaton, Jonathan. 1990. Debt relief and the international enforcement of loan contracts. *Journal of Economic Perspectives* 4:43–56.

Eichengreen, Barry, and Andrew K. Rose. 1997. Staying afloat when the wind shifts: External factors and emerging-market banking crises. NBER Working Paper no. 6370. Cambridge, Mass.: National Bureau of Economic Research.

Fischel, Daniel. 1989. The economics of lender liability. *Yale Law Journal* 99:131–54.

Fudenberg, Drew, and Jean Tirole. 1991. *Game theory*. Cambridge, Mass.: MIT Press.

Fuentes, Gabriel. 1996. The use of village agents in rural credit delivery. *Journal of Development Studies* 33:188–209.

Gertler, Mark, and Andrew K. Rose. 1994. Finance, growth and public policy. In *Financial reform: Theory and experience,* ed. G. Caprio, I. Atiyas, and J. Hanson. New York: Cambridge University Press.

Green, Edward, and Robert Porter. 1984. Noncooperative collusion under imperfect price information. *Econometrica* 52:87–100.

Hermalin, Benjamin E., and Nancy E. Wallace. 1994. The determinants of efficiency and solvency in savings and loans. *RAND Journal of Economics* 25:361–81.

———. 1997. Firm performance and executive compensation in the savings and loan industry. Berkeley: University of California. Mimeograph.

Ito, Takatoshi, and David Folkerts-Landau. 1996. *International capital markets*. Washington, D.C.: International Monetary Fund.

Rothschild, Michael, and Joseph Stiglitz. 1976. Equilibrium in competitive insurance markets: An essay on the economics of imperfect information. *Quarterly Journal of Economics* 90:629–50.

Williamson, Oliver. 1985. *The economic institutions of capitalism.* New York: Free Press.

2. Peter M. Garber

Derivatives in International Capital Flows

The explosive growth of derivative products in the past fifteen years has paralleled the growth of cross-border gross capital flows. The use of derivative products has been a major factor in the growth of cross-border capital movements for several reasons. First, by allowing the separation of various risks associated with cross-border investment, it makes such investment more attractive. Portfolio diversification becomes more likely, with a consequent increase in gross international flows. Moreover, impediments to movement of capital in search of higher real yields weaken, with a consequent increase in net flows. Various dimensions of risk can be moved across borders to markets that find them less unattractive. Indeed, such potential gains in the efficiency of the international allocation of capital has redefined a major, profitable segment of the international wholesale banking market.

The problems associated with the rise of derivatives stem partly from the same source as the benefits: the increased ability to separate and market risks means that some counterparties can assume riskier positions more readily than in the past. Coupled with the existence of weak financial systems and the inherent opaqueness of derivative positions due to obsolete accounting systems, slow reporting, and unprepared supervisors, derivatives can be used to leverage financial safety nets in efforts to double up lost financial bets. Often, such activity must move offshore to evade detection and naturally generates a gross international capital flow. Moreover, derivatives can be used readily to evade onshore prudential regulation and capital or exchange control, thereby generating yet more measured capital flows.

Interpretations of the causes and dynamics of the sudden capital flow reversals associated with balance-of-payments crises generally are based on on-balance-sheet information. In the presence of derivatives, however, such data can generate false inferences about the sources of a crisis and lead to misinformed policy prescriptions. They confound the sources of the crisis: whether it stems from foreign speculators, panicked green-screen traders, or domestic insiders armed with knowledge about weak fundamentals. In addition, in the presence of large volumes of derivatives, claims that crises are generated by such inappropriate policies as an excessively short maturity of the public debt can be mirages of on-balance-sheet accounting.

Even on-balance-sheet data for measuring the quality of international capital flows—the capital accounts of the balance-of-payments data—are obscured by derivatives used to enhance risk or evade controls or even for benign purposes. Subaccount data, such as portfolio investment, equity investment, foreign direct investment, or long- or short-maturity fixed interest rate lending, are illusory in the presence of substantial volumes of derivative products.

The remainder of this essay will provide general descriptions of some of the basic derivative products, along with recent data on the extent of the market in derivatives.[1] After a discussion of the positive effects of derivatives—the ability to refine the management of risk—the paper will examine the negative aspects of these products: their role in enhancing risk taking, in evading prudential regulations, taxes, and controls, in channeling the dynamics of currency and financial crises, and in obscuring the meaning of capital accounts data from the standard balance-of-payments accounts.

7.2.1   Some Basic Derivative Products

While the list of exotic derivative products expands almost daily, most derivatives outstanding are relatively simple, consisting mainly of *forward* contracts, *swaps,* and basic *options,* whose notional values are indicative of the magnitude of the market risks that are being acquired or hedged. *Structured notes,* however, are implicitly highly leveraged products whose notional values

---

1. The paper is an adaptation and expansion of ideas developed in Garber (1996), Garber and Lall (1996), and Folkerts-Landau and Garber (1997).

generally underestimate significantly the magnitude of the risks taken. Here I will concentrate only on a few types of swaps and structured notes.

A *generic swap of yields* is an exchange of the percentage return on one type of asset during a given period for the percentage return on another asset, multiplied by a predefined notional value to convert percentages to cash equivalents. Both returns are observable in security or banking markets. The swap may involve a periodic exchange of yields for a fixed period of time and settlement only of the net amount due. Specifically, for a given currency, an *interest rate swap* is an exchange of a fixed interest return for a floating return or perhaps one floating interest rate for another. An *equity swap* or *total return swap* generally is a periodic exchange of the return on a given share or equity index, including dividends and capital gains, for some interest yield, multiplied by a notional value in a given currency.

Interest and equity swaps do not involve initial and final payments of principal or notional value, although the counterparty with the greater credit risk may have to deliver some collateral. Currency and foreign exchange swaps do require initial and final delivery of principal. A *foreign exchange swap,* generally a very short term deal, is a combination of a spot sale of currency and a forward purchase—it packages in a single deal both foreign exchange market legs of the familiar interest rate parity arbitrage operation. Foreign exchange swaps coupled with spot exchange sales are the standard wholesale market technique for establishing forward currency positions. A *currency swap* similarly requires an initial and final exchange of principal amounts of the two currencies at predetermined forward exchange rates, but it is of longer maturity and involves periodic exchanges of interest on the principal amounts in the two currencies. A currency swap can be interpreted as a bundle of forward exchange contracts with sequentially lengthening maturities.

A structured note requires the delivery of a given amount of principal by the buyer to the seller, as in a standard bond purchase. The payoff of either interest or principal is set as a function of some underlying market value, such as an exchange rate or interest rate. Depending on the nature of the formula, the payoff may deliver multiples of the initial principal; or on the downside, the principal may be wiped out.

7.2.2   Data on the Extent of Derivative Markets

The 1995 Bank for International Settlements (BIS) survey of market participants in the major and many minor financial centers indicated that the notional value of over-the-counter (OTC) derivative products outstanding was $47.5 trillion in March 1995, and of this about 55 percent were cross-border transactions.[2] Most of this amount consisted of simple interest rate products such as

2. "The global nature of the markets is underlined by the large amount of business contracts with counter parties located abroad" (BIS 1995, 24).

In a survey of its members, the International Swap Dealers Association found that outstanding swaps had increased by 37 percent between 1995 and 1996, although this was not as comprehen-

swaps, and most cross-border transactions occurred between industrial countries.[3] For other derivative products, there are, nevertheless, large notional values outstanding in absolute terms—equity-based products and structured notes and options that may be quite complex—and these are also used to an ever expanding extent in key emerging market countries.

Of the $47.5 trillion in OTC notional values, 61 percent was in interest rate instruments, and 37 percent was in foreign exchange instruments, including outright forwards and swaps. Outstanding equity contracts amounted to 1.25 percent and commodity-related instruments were 0.75 percent of the overall notional value, or about $590 billion and $350 billion, respectively. Exchange-traded contracts outstanding amounted to $8 trillion, almost all of which were interest rate contracts. Gross market values or replacement costs were $2.2 trillion for OTC contracts, about 4.6 percent of the notional value.[4]

Of the interest rate products, 50 percent were cross-border; while 56 percent of foreign exchange products were cross-border, for an overall total of about $26 trillion (BIS 1995, 23, table D3). For equity products, cross-border position data are not reported by the BIS. For comparison, the total stock of domestic and international securities in the OECD countries was $26.3 trillion, and international banking assets excluding security holdings were $8.3 trillion in March 1995.[5]

Thus, if applied one to one to outstanding securities, the stock of both OTC and exchange-traded derivatives was sufficient to have repackaged the risk characteristics of all domestic and international securities and all international banking assets. Of the outstanding volume of OTC products, however, about 57 percent of the local and cross-border deals were between dealers to balance positions.

7.2.3 Why Derivatives Can Increase Cross-Border Movement of Capital

It is worthwhile at this point to consider a brief set of examples of derivative products. These examples will be used throughout the remainder of the paper to show how derivatives might aid in the diversification of portfolios, reduce or enhance risk, evade prudential regulations, and avoid capital controls and

---

sive a survey as that of the BIS. Exchange-based contracts outstanding were stagnant over the year, however. See BIS (1997, 130, 136).

3. Thus the problem of inferring market risk from balance-of-payments data applies especially with regard to the positions of industrial countries. Academic investigations of the lack of cross-border portfolio diversification based on capital account data are seriously compromised by this gap in these data.

4. Most derivative products are priced on initiation of the contract so that they have zero market value. As underlying market prices move through the life of a contract, the contract—which is a bet on the movement of the underlying prices—acquires positive absolute value. This value is called "replacement cost."

5. Notional amounts do not reflect payment obligations. They do reflect price exposure in the underlying markets, and they are useful for comparison with the underlying amounts outstanding. See (BIS 1995, 24).

taxes. In these activities, they can create gross international capital flows that otherwise might not have materialized, but they also can confound the nature of the cross-border flows that do occur. Some of the derivative types in the following examples were important in the Mexican exchange rate crisis of 1994–95, so they will be developed in the Mexican context, which is used as a backdrop for many of the succeeding conclusions; but they are generic products and are used worldwide for the same reasons they were used in Mexico.

Currency Swap

The initial example is a plain vanilla currency swap in its most common context. Suppose that IBM sells deutsche mark bonds in Germany to shave some basis points from its finance costs—German fund managers find IBM securities desirable for diversification purposes but insist on deutsche mark settlement. IBM wants dollar liabilities, however, because of the nature of its earnings stream. It enters a currency swap with a U.S. bank, equivalent to a stack of forward exchange contracts in which IBM pays dollars at predetermined exchange rates and receives the marks needed to cover its bond obligations. In its net position, IBM is then a dollar debtor, and the bank has acquired the currency risk. Similarly, Daimler-Benz also can save basis points by placing its bonds with a U.S. pension fund, which also seeks diversification of credit risk, but it must denominate the bonds in dollars. Another, opposite currency swap is born, perhaps with the original U.S. bank as the natural, ultimate counterparty. The U.S. bank makes the market and takes a spread but has no net currency position.[6]

There is no *net* international movement of capital, but the two bond issues appear on balance sheet as *gross* capital flows to be captured by the periodic snapshots of the balance-of-payments data. In the absence of the swaps, neither borrower may have found it beneficial to go to an offshore market and may have confined its borrowing to domestic lenders, leaving no tracks in the data on gross international capital movements. As off-balance-sheet items, the swaps are not reported and are not captured in balance-of-payments data, except to the extent that collateral is demanded by the market-making bank from one or both final counterparties.

Single Currency Interest Rate Swaps

It is natural that gross capital flows should arise from currency swaps, because a cross-border flow is at the heart of the swap deal. With interest rate swaps in a single currency, which account about 60 percent of the outstanding OTC notional value, the natural international aspect disappears. Nevertheless, such swaps are frequently associated with capital flows. Suppose that a highly rated U.S. company borrows fixed interest dollars in London and enters a swap

---

6. See Feldstein (1994, 13–14) for further analysis of net vs. gross movement of capital in the presence of derivatives.

as a floating rate payer with a bank—it will pay three-month dollar LIBOR multiplied by the notional value of the swap at the same maturity as its bond. On net, the U.S. company has converted its required service payments into floating rates, which it prefers. The bank's balancing customer might be a lesser rated Italian company that sells floating rate dollar-denominated securities in London but wants to pay fixed interest. In the absence of the swap, the U.S. company might have preferred to borrow at floating rates directly in the United States, but it is encouraged to borrow in London because the swap allows it to shave basis points from the deal, and similarly for the Italian company. The funds for the principal of the two loans have to come from somewhere. Whoever would have bought the U.S. company's potential U.S. bond issue—say a U.S. resident—will now buy its more attractive Eurobond issue, and similarly for the Italian company. Again, there are no net cross-border flows but positive gross flows. Before the advent of interest rate swaps, this gain from trade between the two companies would not have been possible, and the deals would have been financed directly from national sources.

Tesobono Swaps and Repos

The interest rate swaps described above involved exchanging fixed for floating rate yields in a single currency or fixed rate for fixed rate yields in two different currencies for relatively long maturities. Similar deals are made in large volumes for shorter maturities. Here, the *Tesobono swap* will serve as a useful example of such deals.

Tesobono swaps were offshore derivative operations used by Mexican banks as a means of leveraging Tesobono holdings, the notorious treasury bills of the Mexican government indexed to the peso-dollar exchange rate. In a Tesobono swap, a Mexican bank received the yield earned on Tesobonos and delivered dollar LIBOR plus some additional basis points, multiplied by a notional amount of dollars.

The leverage involved in Tesobono swaps can be most readily examined by analyzing first the nearly equivalent Tesobono repurchase agreement. As an example, consider a New York investment firm that is willing to lend dollars for one year against Tesobono collateral through a repurchase agreement. The firm engages in a repurchase agreement with a Mexican bank to buy Tesobonos at some agreed price and to resell them in a year at the original price plus a dollar interest rate.[7] In the example in table 7.5, a Mexican bank sells $1 billion of Tesobonos to a New York firm for $800 million with an agreement to repurchase the Tesobonos in one year for the original price plus the LIBOR plus 1 percent interest. The yield on Tesobonos is 8 percent while dollar LIBOR is 5 percent. Effectively, the Mexican bank has financed a $1 billion Tesobono position by borrowing $800 million, although official data on Tesobono holdings will indicate that a foreign address holds the Tesobonos. The gain to the

---

7. In the swap form of the deal, of course, only net amounts were due in each settlement period.

Table 7.5   Tesobono Repurchase Agreement

1. Tesobono yield = 8%
   LIBOR yield = 5%
   Maturity = 1 year
2. Mexican bank sells $1 billion of Tesobonos to New York firm for $800 million with agreement to repurchase in one year for $800 million × (1 + LIBOR + 1%)
3. New York firm funds 80% of Mexican bank's position—has $200 million of margin (20%)
4. New York firm is a foreign address holding $1 billion of Tesobonos
5. Mexican bank gets Tesobono return at 8% on $1 billion, finances 80% at LIBOR + 1%: 2% spread
6. New York firm borrows $800 million at LIBOR, lends at LIBOR + 1%

Table 7.6   Tesobono Swap

1. New York firm delivers Tesobono yield for LIBOR + 1% with Mexican bank on $1 billion notional principal
2. New York firm requires deposit of 20% margin—$200 million
3. To hedge, New York firm buys $1 billion of Tesobonos, financed by $200 million margin from Mexican bank, $800 million borrowed at LIBOR
4. Foreign address holds Tesobonos
5. Mexican bank puts up $200 million of own funds to get $1 billion of Tesobono yield

---

Mexican bank is that it pays LIBOR plus 100 to finance Tesobonos that may pay the equivalent of LIBOR plus 300. The gain to the U.S. lender is that it gets to place dollar funds at LIBOR plus 100 against good collateral while it borrows at LIBOR.

A *Tesobono swap* places both parties in the same risk position as a repurchase agreement. Table 7.6 indicates the positions taken if the financing of the Mexican bank's Tesobono position takes the form of a Tesobono swap. Suppose the New York firm swaps Tesobono yield in return for LIBOR plus 100 basis points against a $1 billion notional principal. It requires $200 million as collateral from its Mexican counterparty, that is, a margin deposit of 20 percent to guarantee compliance with the contract. The payoffs to the two counterparties are identical to those under the repurchase agreement. To hedge, the New York firm will purchase $1 billion in Tesobonos directly from the market, paid from the $200 million margin and $800 million borrowed at LIBOR. As before, the Tesobonos will be held by a foreign address, although Mexican domestic residents will bear the Tesobono risk.

In either form, these operations serve to channel a net flow of capital of $800 million into Mexico, which ultimately finances the government. Gross flow data picked up in the normal balance-of-payments operation will measure an inflow of $1 billion worth of Tesobono purchases and an outflow in the form of bank deposits for the collateral of $200 million. The swap, however, disguises the nature of the flow. Superficially, it appears that foreign lenders are buying Mexican government debt in the form of Tesobonos—that is, they are satisfied to hold the indexed T-bills at the maturities offered by the managers

Table 7.7	Equity Swap

1. New York firm delivers total return on Telmex for LIBOR + 3% with Mexican bank on $1 billion notional principal
2. New York firm requires deposit of 20% margin—$200 million
3. To hedge, New York firm buys $1 billion of Telmex American Depository Receipts, financed by $200 million collateral from Mexican bank, $800 million borrowed at LIBOR
4. Foreign address holds Mexican shares
5. Mexican bank puts up $200 million of own funds to get $1 billion of stock market risk

of the Mexican public debt. In fact, they are making short-term dollar loans, while Mexican residents are holding the Tesobono risk. On the national balance sheet—consolidating the government and domestic banking sectors—Mexico is a short-term borrower of dollars.

Equity Swaps

Table 7.7 presents an example to show that an equity swap establishes a leveraged position in shares, with funding coming from an offshore source. Again, a Mexico-based example will be used with an eye on later exposition, but such cross-border deals are commonplace.

Suppose that a Mexican bank agrees to swap the total return over one year on Telmex for dollar LIBOR plus 300 basis points on a notional amount of $1 billion. Its offshore counterparty, a New York securities house, requires $200 million in collateral. To hedge its short equity position, the New York firm then directly buys $1 billion worth of Telmex shares, thereby appearing as a foreign investor in Mexican shares. The New York firm is taking a long position in short-term dollar loans while the Mexican bank has a long position in Telmex shares and a short position in short-term dollar loans. The Mexican bank has acquired $1 billion of Telmex risk by putting up $200 million of collateral in New York.

Again, balance-of-payments accounts will report a gross inflow of $1 billion worth of equity purchases for portfolio investment or perhaps foreign direct investment and an outflow of $200 million in bank deposits. The Mexican bank—and therefore the national balance sheet—holds the equity risk, while the foreign address is only a short-term dollar lender.

Structured Notes

Structured notes exist in many forms, but the example studied here will determine the payoff on what might be described as a "bullish obligation on the peso," as presented in table 7.8.[8] For example, a Mexican bank or its foreign subsidiary might buy a note with a twenty-nine-day maturity from a New York investment house for $10 million. The coupon on the note and the principal on the note are payable in dollars. Suppose that the coupon offered on the note is

---

8. The description of this note was taken from an indicative term sheet issued by Donaldson, Lufkin and Jenrette on 22 March 1995.

Table 7.8   Bullish Obligation on the Peso

1. i_{cetes} = .85 annual
2. i_s = .05 annual
3. Maturity of contract = 29 days
4. Overall payoff of the note = Coupon + Principal
   $$= 1.95 * 7.0/P_m * 29/360 + 1 + 3\,[(7.0 - P_m)/P_m]$$
5. Some arithmetic to determine implied dollar and new peso (Npeso) positions:
   Payoff = $(-2 + 3.157 * 7.0/P_m) \times \$10$ million
   $= -\$20$ million $+ \$31.57$ million $* 7.0/P_m$
   $= -\$20$ million $+$ Npesos 221 million$/P_m$
   Present values:
   Current dollar position $= -\$19.92$ million
   Current Npeso $= 209.95$ million $= \$29.99$ million

195 percent annually multiplied by the ratio of the current spot value of the peso to the peso-dollar exchange rate at maturity. Interest rates on peso paper such as Cetes—peso-denominated treasury bills—are 85 percent per annum and 5 percent on dollar paper. The principal repayment also depends negatively on the peso value of the dollar at maturity—suppose it will be $[1 + 3 \times (7.0 - P_m)/P_m] \times \$10$ million, where 7.0 is the initial peso value of the dollar and P_m is the value at maturity. In an extreme case, if the peso has depreciated by 50 percent at maturity, from say 7.00 to 14.0 pesos per dollar, the principal repayment will be $-\$5$ million. The overall payoff is then $-\$3.25$ million.[9] Conversely, if the peso appreciates significantly, the payoff can be a multiple of the initial investment. Table 7.8 shows that this is the payoff structure of a position that is currently short about $19.92 million at a market dollar interest rate of 5 percent per year and long 209.95 million pesos at a market peso interest rate of 85 percent per year. Effectively, the initial $10 million investment has been leveraged threefold and invested in peso paper.

Overall, through the payoff formula, the New York investment house would have a position equivalent to being short 209.95 million worth of peso paper and long $19.92 million worth of dollar loans. In addition, it has the initial $10 million from the sale of the note. To hedge, it may wish to buy the peso by investing in one-month Cetes while simultaneously selling the dollars in the position. It would then appear in the on-balance-sheet accounts as a foreign buyer of a peso-denominated asset rather than as a dollar-denominated lender, which is its true position.[10]

If the seller of the note hedges the position, the balance-of-payments accounts will report a net inflow of about $20 million. This will result from a gross inflow of about $30 million in the form of portfolio purchases of short-

9. As a safety feature for the buyer, such structured notes cap the potential losses. E.g., in the actual "bullish obligation," in no case would the principal redemption plus coupon payment be less than zero. This adds a put option feature to the note.

10. As an additional feature, such notes contain clauses that state that the notes will pay zero if there is a "default event" on Cetes or an "exchange control event." This is a sort of poison pill that automatically wipes out part of domestic bank capital in a country that imposes such policies.

term, peso-denominated government paper and an outflow of $10 million in the form of a Mexican bank's purchase of a short-maturity, dollar-denominated note.

7.2.4   Circumventing Prudential Regulations and Capital Controls

In addition to their normal uses in portfolio diversification or risk reduction, derivatives can be used to increase risk—one side of the deal may be speculating. In weakly regulated, undercapitalized financial systems, derivatives provide a perfect opportunity for financial intermediaries to acquire risky positions in attempts to recover capital. This section will show how derivatives such as those in the examples developed earlier can be used to escape prudential regulation and capital controls.

Evading Prudential Regulation

Prudential regulations of varying stringency are well accepted across different financial systems, but they are especially important in the presence of large capital inflows. Such inflows, in particular, increase the potential to have systemic failures in the financial sector because of the rapid expansion of bank balance sheets into unfamiliar business. If capital suddenly flows into a country in quantity, there will be a general expansion of the financial system and investment projects; and it is not clear that a large fraction of the investments will be placed in "good" projects. There is a belief among regulators and academics that inflows are often the results of various investment fads—ultimately, investor disappointment over the payoffs from these investments will lead to an attempt to withdraw funds. Therefore, regulations are imposed—such as reserve requirements, limits on lending to individuals, firms, or sectors, liquidity requirements against domestic or foreign exchange liabilities, net foreign currency exposure limits, and capital requirements—which aim at channeling inflows away from banks and risky projects. Similarly, a ban on holding securities on margin or on short sales will mean that equity holders will not be forced to join the general scramble for cash in a liquidity crisis and thereby reduce the potential magnitude of the demand for cash. Nevertheless, bans on margin buying tend to push such activity offshore, through OTC derivative markets.

Banks can readily avoid regulations either in a straightforward manner or by going offshore or engaging in off-balance-sheet activities, which violate the intent, if not the letter, of regulations. We will examine how structured notes and equity swaps can be used to avoid such regulation.

Structured Notes

As shown earlier, structured notes are investment vehicles with coupon payments and principal repayments driven by formulas that can leverage the initial capital invested. Nevertheless, in value accounting systems they can be booked as normal investments and in the currency denominated in the prospectus.

More than simply magnifying the usual market risks associated with investment positions, structured notes provide an easy method for circumventing prudential regulations on currency positions or interest rate mismatches.

In the context of section 7.2.3's example, booked as claims of Mexican institutions with dollar principal and dollar payoffs, these notes in fact were currency bets that created a short dollar and long peso currency position to take advantage of positive interest rate spreads between peso and dollar money markets.[11] The notes were reported by Mexican banks as dollar assets, allowing them to offset short dollar positions in meeting regulatory limits on net foreign currency positions. In addition, some banks could count them to satisfy their liquidity coefficient required for foreign-currency-denominated liabilities because their short maturity allowed them to be classified as liquid deposits. In the event of a depreciation of the currency, banks might have a much larger net short dollar position and greater losses than regulators had realized.

Held in this way, the structured note of the example is a financial engineering device to circumvent prudential regulation. Only the principal was booked, in accordance with value accounting principles. The structured note payoff formula component was not booked—it is an off-balance-sheet item. That is the accounting trick—one can alter the nature of the booking through a complicated payoff formula. The use of the trick, however, requires an outflow of capital in the form of principal. Thus a net inflow of $20 million takes the form of a gross outflow of $10 million and a gross inflow of $30 million.

Equity Swaps

As a means of taking a position in stocks, the market in equity swaps can be used to avoid financial market regulations against such positions. Such regulations may ban buying securities on margin or short selling or limit the share positions of foreign addresses.[12] The benefits to market participants of the existence of this market are obvious. Speculators can leverage and gain larger positions, and hedgers of long positions held either directly or implicitly in the form of options can short stock to cover their positions. Again, net short-term dollar foreign borrowing for domestic stock purchases takes the form of a gross outflow in the form of dollar-denominated margin and a larger gross inflow in the form of a stock purchase by a foreign address.

Avoiding Capital Import Taxes or Controls

Taxes or outright bans on the acquisition by foreign addresses of domestic securities have emerged in recent years as a means of stemming capital inflows.

---

11. In Malaysia, these instruments, known as "principal adjusted coupon notes," serve the same purpose of providing leverage in domestic currency positions to foreigners through foreign exchange financing. Regulation precluded foreign addresses from directly holding short-term ringgit claims onshore.

12. Offshore equity swap markets also exist for Malaysia, Korea, and Thailand, among others, also in order to avoid curbs on short selling and leveraging.

They sometimes have been imposed differentially by maturity of asset and by type of asset. Often, such taxes have been successful in that they have placed a wedge between domestic and foreign yields on similar assets. They can be breached by the usual invoicing subterfuges, but market participants have also used financial engineering to circumvent the taxes. Specifically, suppose that an enforceable tax is placed uniformly on all forms of gross inflows. Then any positive net inflow will incur the tax, but gross transactions will move offshore. As an example, instead of acquiring an equity position directly, a foreign investor will buy an offshore equity swap from a domestic resident who can hedge without a tax. If the domestic resident has a lower credit rating, an export of capital in the form of margin will be recorded. There will be no taxable inflow, but foreigners can take risk positions in domestic assets.[13]

If the tax is differential across types of assets acquired from abroad, the net inflow will tend to take the form that incurs the lowest tax. Similarly, if differential controls are imposed allowing equity investment but limiting short-term fixed interest inflows, the flows will enter through the least restrictive door. The risk and maturity characteristics of the inflow can then be resculpted through offshore derivatives to a more desirable form. For instance, if equity investment is given better treatment than short-term fixed interest securities or bank deposits, the inflow will take the form of a stock acquisition together with an equity swap that converts it on net into a floating interest loan of foreign currency. Even the maturity of the loan can be adjusted with an attachment by the lender of a stringent margining provision that permits the offshore creditor to realize cash on call.

7.2.5   The Role of Derivatives in Crisis-Driven Capital Outflows

Where such markets exist, forward contracts are the speculator's instrument of choice in implementing an attack on a currency, the beginning of a sudden outflow of capital. Positions in forward contracts can arise suddenly or be built up gradually in the expectation of an impending devaluation. Such derivatives serve merely to effect a crisis that is emerging from other causes. Other derivative products, already outstanding in large volumes, may reflect an environment in which such speculation may be successful and may even determine the dynamics of the currency and financial crisis that ensues.

This section will show how forward contracts transmit an impending attack on a central bank's reserves through foreign exchange swap and spot exchange markets.[14] Next, using the examples developed earlier from the Mexican case,

---

13. In the case of Chilean equity, market sources report that offshore equity swaps are used regularly to permit trading in Chilean equity. They also report serious, though as yet unsuccessful, financial engineering research efforts to crack directly the Chilean tax on capital imports in the form of a uncompensated deposit requirement.

14. This section has been adapted from the exposition on the mechanics of speculative attacks from Goldstein et al. (1993) and notes written for Folkerts-Landau and Garber (1997).

it will show how the existence of these products operated to determine the dynamics of exchange markets leading into the currency crisis of December 1994, to determine the magnitude of the final attack, and to drive the foreign exchange market turbulence in the months after the attack.

The Mechanics of Speculative Attack

This section covers the mechanics of exchange market operations in speculative attacks. It shows how transactions in forward exchange work their way through the banking system and how they are financed. It discusses in particular the effect of reducing credit to speculators, either through interest rate increases or, more directly, through controls.

Speculators generally attack a weak currency by selling the currency through forward contracts to a bank at relatively long maturities, for example, thirty days.[15] Whether a customer speculates through a short sale or hedges a long position, the international banking system handles a forward sale of a currency in the same way. As standard practice to balance the long position in the weak currency that this transaction initiates, the counterparty bank will immediately sell the weak currency spot for the conventional two-day settlement. Although its currency position is then balanced, the bank still has a maturity mismatch in both currencies: it can borrow the weak currency overnight to cover settlement of the spot sale, but it will receive the currency in thirty days through the forward contract. It faces the opposite maturity mismatch with its strong currency position. To close this maturity mismatch, a bank typically will transact a foreign exchange swap. These are customary wholesale operations executed by banks writing forward contracts to customers, in both normal periods and speculative episodes.

Table 7.9 presents a concrete example of such a forward transaction. In this example, the weak currency is the baht and the strong currency is the dollar. Suppose that the forward and spot exchange rates between the dollar and the baht are 25 baht per U.S. dollar. In the first step, a customer sells 2,500 baht forward for $100 to a bank. This is an off-balance-sheet item for the bank, but it has payment implications like any on-balance-sheet transaction. The payment and receipt implications for the bank are displayed in the first panel. The bank will receive 2,500 baht and pay $100 in one month. These are the same movements of funds that the bank would face if it were long a baht Bank of Thailand bill and short a U.S. Treasury bill. To eliminate the currency mismatch, the bank immediately sells 2,500 baht for dollar spot exchange, the payment implications of which are combined with those of the forward con-

---

15. Forward sales may also be launched by hedging programs implemented by fund managers, nonfinancial corporations, and market makers. Speculators may also attack a currency by buying put options on the currency. From the perspective of the counterparty bank, this creates a long forward position in the weak currency in an amount indicated by the option pricing formula used by the bank. The bank's hedging program will respond in the same way as if the bank had entered directly into a forward contract with its counterparty. See Garber and Spencer (1995) on the effects of such hedging in a crisis.

Table 7.9   **Receipts and Payments to Counterparty Bank Arising from Forward Contract Operations**

Receipt	Payment
Step 1: Forward Contract = Currency Mismatch	
2,500 Baht in one month	$100 in one month
Step 2: Forward Contract + Spot Sale = Maturity Mismatch	
2,500 Baht in one month (forward)	2,500 Baht in two days (spot)
$100 in two days (spot)	$100 in one month (forward)
Step 3: Forward + Spot + Swap = Balanced Position	
2,500 Baht in one month (forward)	2,500 Baht in one month (swap)
2,500 Baht in two days (swap)	2,500 Baht in two days (spot)
$100 in one month (swap)	$100 in one month (forward)
$100 in two days (spot)	$100 in two days (swap)

tract in the second step. The currency positions are now balanced, but there remains a maturity mismatch in each currency—one-month baht are funded with rollover baht and rollover dollars are funded with one-month dollars. To eliminate the maturity mismatch, the bank immediately undertakes a one-month foreign exchange swap, exchanging $100 for 2,500 baht spot and 2,500 baht for $100 thirty days forward. The complete payment implications for the bank are displayed in the third step: the bank has eliminated market exchange and interest rate risk through these transactions.

This example indicates that a baht-dollar forward contract is equivalent to a foreign exchange swap combined with a spot exchange transaction. Also, on its origination, a forward sale of baht by the customer immediately generates a spot sale of baht by the bank.

Who is the ultimate counterparty in these transactions? In time of crisis, there are few spot market buyers of the weak currency, so a central bank defending an exchange rate level must appear as the counterparty through its exchange market intervention.

A customer in the forward market may be a central bank, which can intervene in the foreign exchange market to defend parity by buying its currency forward rather than spot. If the central bank's forward purchase of its currency matches a forward sale of some other customer of the banking system, all the swap and spot transactions of the banking system will balance; specifically, spot exchange sales will be matched with purchases at the parity exchange rate. Thus the central bank's forward intervention will absorb the spot sales of its currency without the central bank's having to intervene directly in the spot market. By entering a forward contract, the central bank implicitly supplies domestic currency credit directly to the short seller of its currency. The short seller in this example is obligated to deliver the weak currency to the central bank on the value date of the forward contract, effectively a loan from the central bank.

In a currency crisis, with the potential for a one-sided bet, few private parties would be willing net suppliers of weak currency credit. Nevertheless, to fuel a speculative attack, the world banking system must in aggregate provide credit in the weak currency to the short sellers. This is evident in the first step in table 7.9, where the bank's baht receipts from the forward contract embody a one-month baht loan to the short seller. If the central bank does not supply the credit directly through forward intervention, the credit must come either through its money market operations or its standing facilities. In any crisis, the baht provided by the banking system are a pass-through of credit from the Bank of Thailand, which must be the ultimate counterparty in both legs of the position-balancing transactions of the banking system. The bank in the example must find a counterparty bank to engage in the swap. By entering into a one-month baht foreign exchange swap, the counterparty bank effectively lends baht spot to be repaid in one month. When the baht are sold on the spot market, they are bought by the Bank of Thailand—and the other regional central banks that support it—in the campaign to defend the exchange rate. In lending spot baht through the swap, the counterparty bank acquires the baht needed for spot delivery either by discounting paper through the standing facilities of the Bank of Thailand or through outright sale or sale with repurchase through the Bank of Thailand's market operations.

Derivatives and the Dynamics of Capital Flow Reversals

Even in countries where currency forward contracts did not play a role in a sudden reversal in capital flows, other derivative products may be present in sufficient quantities to affect the dynamics of a crisis. The Mexican peso crisis of 1994 is such a case. Speculators did not use the forward market suddenly to short sell the peso. Rather, outstanding products of the sort outlined earlier drove the near-in movements of capital going into and coming out of the devaluation of the peso.

The derivative positions that drove the crisis were established by a weak banking system hungry for current income. The Mexican groups that had purchased the banks upon privatization in 1991–92 had financed the aggregate $12 billion price through substantial amounts of borrowing. Interest due had to be paid through current bank income, and this led the banks into taking increased credit risk through on-balance-sheet expansions and increased market risk through off-balance-sheet growth.

Tesobono Swaps

Industry sources in Mexico report that there was a stock of about $16 billion of Tesobono swaps at the time of the devaluation.[16] Of the $29 billion of Tesobonos outstanding on 19 December 1994, about $16.1 billion were held by

---

16. Such numbers are guesswork because no one aggregates such data. Nevertheless, similar estimates were given to me by market managers at the top two banks in Mexico, which did a large fraction of the business.

foreign addresses. Thus sufficient Tesobono swaps existed to repackage the entire foreign holding of Tesobono risk: foreigners held Tesobonos primarily to hedge Tesobono swaps and Mexican banks held the Tesobono risk.

When the crisis arrived, Tesobono market values in dollars suddenly fell. From December 1994 to January 1995, Tesobono yields jumped from 8 to 24 percent, and several of the interim offerings failed. The fall in market value reduced the value of the collateral and triggered margin calls to deliver dollars or close out the positions.

If the typical Tesobono fell by 15 percent in dollar value, the value of the collateral in the Tesobono swap of the earlier example would have fallen significantly; and a margin call would immediately have been sent to the Mexican bank. Alternatively, anticipating margin calls, the Mexican bank would immediately have sought dollar liquidity in preparation. To restore margin, the $16 billion in swaps would instantly generate $16 × .15 = $2.4 billion of demand for dollars by the Mexican banks.

Equity Swaps

Market participants have characterized the market in offshore Mexican equity swaps as very large, but they were not as explicit about orders of magnitude as in the case of Tesobonos, though several have claimed that up to $3 billion notional value of such contracts existed at the time of the crisis.

With the collapse of the peso, the stock market fell immediately by about 50 percent in dollars and by 66 percent within two months. With the margin in the equity swaps more than wiped out, margin calls or anticipations of margin calls again forced the Mexican banks to rush for dollar liquidity. Taking $3 billion as the notional value of outstanding equity swaps, this would have required the banks to find an additional $1.5 billion at the time of the 19 December 1994 devaluation. Mexican institutions and individuals engaged in these swaps had to sell pesos to get margin or close out their positions, adding to the turmoil of the exchange and stock markets.

The total of margin calls from Tesobono and equity swaps alone was about $4 billion. Coincidentally, this was approximately the amount by which the Banco de Mexico's reserves fell in the final attack just before the peso was allowed to float on 21 December 1994.[17]

Structured Notes

During 1994, Mexican financial institutions took large positions in structured notes with investment houses in New York.[18] Because the notes were reported by the banks as dollar assets, however, the accounting rules in Mexico allowed them to be booked as dollar positions, so that they were not counted

17. In addition, other Mexico-oriented derivative products, such as Cetes swaps and Brady bond swaps, also would have drawn margin calls at the same moment.
18. Most major New York financial engineering firms sold such products—e.g., Bankers Trust, Merrill Lynch, Bear Stearns, Donaldson, Lufkin, and Morgan Stanley.

against the regulatory net currency position limit of a maximum of 15 percent of capital.

The first group of these structures were known as Ajustabono structures and were first noticed when consolidated regulation was implemented in September 1994. The second group were similar to the structured note discussed earlier and came to the attention of authorities just after the December 1994 devaluation.

Ajustabonos are inflation-indexed Mexican government securities that had long been held by Mexican banks. In addition to paying a relatively fixed real interest return, Ajustabonos could be counted as foreign exchange assets in determining regulatory foreign exchange positions, so Mexican banks funded their Ajustabono positions with dollar borrowings. When real interest rates rose in 1992, Mexican banks found that their Ajustabono positions were frozen because they did not want to realize the capital losses on their investment portfolios. The solution was to contract structures with New York banks and investment houses through which the Ajustabonos could be used as collateral.

For example, a U.S. and a Mexican securities firm associated with a bank would jointly organize a company in the Caymans or in Bermuda that would agree to purchase Ajustabonos at face value, with the funding obtained from the sale of two series of securities, one senior and one junior, both denominated in dollars. Suppose that the deal involved a Mexican bank's selling $120 million par value worth of Ajustabonos to the company. The Mexican partner might put up $20 million and receive $20 million par value of the junior securities, which it would sell to the Mexican bank. Denominated in dollars, the junior notes could be counted as a foreign exchange asset in determining regulatory positions. The U.S. firm would invest $100 million and receive $100 million par value of the senior securities. The senior securities would be designed to pay a relatively secure dollar yield, which could be paid if the exchange rate did not depreciate excessively, and would be sold for LIBOR plus. The payoff on the junior securities was like that of a structured note—if the exchange rate did not depreciate, it would pay a high yield and make good the losses on the Ajustabonos. If the exchange rate depreciated, the yield or principal of the junior note would decline according to a predetermined formula.

When the banking authorities became aware that the return on the junior notes was correlated with the peso, they required that 100 percent of the notes be covered with foreign exchange. Market sources estimate that $2 billion of the junior notes were outstanding in 1994. The banks began to cover their positions in September 1994 and throughout the autumn, which contributed significantly to the drain on official reserves in the several months just prior to the devaluation.

The Banco de Mexico found out after the devaluation that the more general structured notes like that of the "bullish obligation" example existed in large amounts. Charged with enforcing the regulation on net foreign exchange positions of the banks, the Banco de Mexico immediately ordered the banks to cover their short dollar positions. This forced a scramble for several billion dollars of foreign exchange during the postcollapse floating period, leading to the highly volatile and illiquid foreign exchange market that dominated the first quarter of 1995.

Thus, taken in sequence, the Ajustabono structures, swaps, and structured notes account for most of the currency market dynamics in the months surrounding the collapse of the peso. The Mexican peso crisis is an example of a systemic crisis whose dynamics were driven by a structure of outstanding derivatives. The timing and magnitude of the near-in reserve drain, the final attack on foreign exchange reserves, and the postcollapse market turbulence are explainable by the automatic credit and market risk-covering programs attached to the contracts by counterparties and regulators themselves.

What Does "Proper Public Debt Management" Mean in the Presence of Derivatives?

Because Mexico had issued large amounts of short-term Tesobonos that could not be rolled over in the aftermath of the devaluation, subsequent analyses have pinpointed improper public debt management as a major cause of the crisis (see, e.g., Calvo 1996; Calvo and Mendoza 1996; Cole and Kehoe 1996). The consequent policy prescription has been to restructure the public debt to longer maturities in a modern version of the nineteenth-century British prescription for virtuous public debt management: "all consols—no bills."

The example of the Tesobono swaps, however, indicates that such a prescription can easily be circumvented. Even in the case of the relatively short term Tesobonos, the yield apparently was not sufficient to encourage foreign lenders to hold Mexico risk. Only the income-hungry Mexican banks wanted to hold the risk and were willing to accept the yields on Tesobonos that were unacceptable to foreign lenders. Thus, vis-à-vis the rest of the world, the Mexican national balance sheet was a borrower of callable dollars through the Tesobono-Tesobono swap operation. The Tesobono debt of the government was balanced by the Tesobono return claims of the Mexican banks, leaving on net only the dollar debt. The sudden calls on the Mexican banking system to deliver dollars to restore margin effectively converted the average maturity of the Tesobonos from six months to callable, and the only way to satisfy the call was to deliver official reserves.

Suppose that instead of the Tesobono issues, the Mexican government had structured its debt by issuing ten-year peso- or even dollar-denominated bonds. Foreign buyers, even more reluctant to absorb these issues than to absorb Tesobonos, would have required very high yields. Mexican banks, however, proved that they would have been willing to take the risk at lower yields than foreigners. The Mexican government, therefore, would have found a market for the longer term debt as follows. Mexican banks would have entered into total return swaps with foreign banks to receive the yield on the long-term debt and pay dollar LIBOR, delivering collateral to the foreign banks. Foreign banks would then have been willing to buy the long-term debt. Any decline in value of the long-term debt would have instantly triggered margin calls to deliver dollars. Effectively, these operations would have converted these long-term claims against the Mexican government into short-term, perhaps callable dollar claims against the national balance sheet.

If the foreign lenders' view of the risks is that they warrant only short-term lending, a prescription to lengthen the debt is an irrelevancy. Even if it is undertaken on balance sheet, it will be undone off balance sheet.

Of course, if the government has made a strong commitment not to bail out the banking system, the construction of a national balance sheet is irrelevant; Tesobono risk or the risk of government securities with any particular features would then be priced properly by the domestic banks, and their dollar margin requirements would not be met by the central bank. The public debt could then be truly lengthened, if that is desirable.

7.2.6   Effects of Derivatives on the Interpretation of Balance-of-Payments Accounting

Among the rationales for balance-of-payments accounting is to ascertain the stability of capital flows of on-balance-sheet movements of assets. Typically, balance-of-payments accounting data are used to measure how long capital will remain in a country—to distinguish "good" money from "hot" money.[19] Various categories of the capital accounts have been interpreted as indicative of the nature of capital inflows or outflows. Foreign direct investment, for example, has been considered a more stable form of investment than portfolio investment or the foreign acquisition of bank claims. Foreign acquisition of short-term fixed interest products is generally regarded as a speculative flow. Balance-of-payments accounts are also used to measure the foreign exchange position of a country's consolidated balance and, in times of crisis, to determine the potential outflow of foreign exchange through speculation or covering operations by holders of domestic liquid assets.

The revolution in global finance and notably the explosion in the use of derivative products have rendered the use of balance-of-payments capital account data even more problematic than it has been in the past.[20] Balance-of-payments accounting data use on-balance-sheet categorizations, and they are

---

19. Although balance-of-payments capital accounts are set up to measure cross-border changes in legal ownership of claims to assets and liabilities, the classification system for financial items is designed to bring out the motivation of creditors and debtors. See IMF (1994, xxii).

20. The usual problems concern omissions or miscategorizations of transactions. That these have been magnified in the presence of widespread use of derivatives has been duly recognized by authorities responsible for technical standards, as exemplified by the April 1996 meeting at the IMF of the Informal Group on Financial Derivatives. Nevertheless, technical discussions even now center on how to fit derivative-generated payments into standard categories such as interest vs. capital gains, the treatment of margin flows, and how to book repurchase agreements. The undermining of the meaning of the various asset categories of the capital accounts in the presence of unrecorded derivative products is not an issue under discussion.

based on value accounting principles to book and categorize asset values. They ignore almost completely the existence of derivatives and their role in reallocating who bears market risk. This would not be a problem of a magnitude greater than the normal caveats on balance-of-payments accounting data except that there has been an explosion in the use of derivative products and especially in the use of cross-border products.

For example, the acquisition of a large block of equity is classified as foreign direct investment, but a foreign buyer may be acquiring the block simply to hedge a short position in equity established through a derivative position. In the case of the equity swap described above, the foreign investment firm that sells the swap must acquire the shares to form a hedge. If the swap is large enough, the hedging operation may be booked as foreign direct investment because the offshore swap position is not included in the capital accounts, although the investment house in fact is making a short-term floating rate loan in foreign currency.

Declines in equity values or the exchange rate will then generate instantaneous exchange market pressure as margin calls are made or positions are closed. This is contrary to the general view among central banks that stock market investment will not likely generate exchange market pressure in a crisis because the losses will already have been absorbed in a resultant crash. Stock market money is therefore regarded as less hot. If the buyer of the swap is a domestic resident, the capital import effectively takes the form of short-term foreign-currency-denominated borrowing, but the leveraged equity risk, and even the long-term control, remains in the hands of the domestic resident. Thus the "direct investment" turns into the hottest of money. In a similar manner, direct investment in the form of reinvestment of profits can be converted into short-term funding through an equity swap.

Alternatively, a foreign program trader may acquire the domestic stock index in the cash market while selling forward in the offshore OTC index market. On net, he has a zero position in equities but in the balance-of-payments accounts appears as a portfolio investor in domestic equities. If the opposite positions are taken by domestic residents—a sale of equities in the cash market and a forward purchase in the derivative market—the net equity risk position for domestic residents is unchanged, though domestic residents are now in effect short-term foreign currency borrowers.

To the extent that they start with zero replacement values as in the case of swaps and forwards, derivative products do not affect measured net capital inflows or outflows, but they blur the information in subcategories of the capital accounts.[21] Specifically, they make a mockery of the use of capital account categories to attempt to measure the aggregate short foreign currency position of an economy.

---

21. An exception arises if a deposit of margin is required by a foreign counterparty; the margin will be counted as a capital export.

7.2.7 Conclusion

From the explosion in the use of derivative products has emerged a blind spot in both national and international surveillance of capital markets. Through derivatives both individual institutions and financial systems can be put at risk in magnitudes and from directions completely unknown to regulators. This problem arises because derivatives are ideal means of avoiding prudential regulations, given the universally slow adjustment of accounting principles to the advent of these products. On a more parochial level, the accounting principles on which the balance-of-payments data-gathering exercise is based are being made increasingly obsolete. For each country, the extent of the problem is unknown because comprehensive data on derivatives are gathered only at long intervals, and even the triennial BIS data are not broken down into those relevant for emerging market countries.

The optical illusion created by viewing the flow of capital only through the on-balance-sheet lens creates a dangerous potential for misinterpreting the implications of major events in capital markets. The information conveyed by the balance-of-payments accounts on the riskiness of the national balance sheet is confounded, so the susceptibility of an economy to capital flow reversals cannot be known. When capital flows suddenly reverse, it is difficult to know which players are driving the flows and therefore to determine the appropriate short- and long-term policy response.

This paper has provided several examples to illustrate how readily the existence of derivative products can change the meaning of capital flow data, how the derivatives may automatically generate liquidity demands in response to triggering events in financial markets, and how easy it is to attribute such responses to structural flaws elsewhere in the financial system.

References

BIS (Bank for International Settlements). 1995. Central bank survey of foreign exchange and derivatives market activity, 1995. Basel: Bank for International Settlements, May.
———. 1997. 67th Annual report. Basel: Bank for International Settlements, 9 June.
Calvo, Guillermo. 1996. Capital flows and macroeconomic management tequila lessons. Working Paper no. 23. College Park: University of Maryland, March.
Calvo, Guillermo, and Enrique Mendoza. 1996. Mexico's balance-of-payments crisis: A chronicle of a death foretold. Working Paper no. 20. College Park: University of Maryland, March.
Cole, Harold, and Timothy Kehoe. 1996. Self-fulfilling debt crises. Staff Report no. 211. Minneapolis: Federal Reserve Bank of Minneapolis, December.
Feldstein, Martin. 1994. Tax policy and international capital flows. Kiel: Institut fur Weltwirtscaft an der Universitat Kiel.
Folkerts-Landau, David, and Peter Garber. 1997. Derivative markets and financial sys-

tem soundness. In *Banking soundness and monetary policy*, ed. Charles Enoch and John N. Green. Washington, D.C.: International Monetary Fund.

Garber, Peter. 1996. Managing risks to financial markets from volatile capital flows: The role of prudential regulation. *International Journal of Finance and Economics* 1 (July): 183–95.

Garber, Peter M., and Subir Lall. 1996. Derivative products in exchange rate crises. Paper prepared for the Federal Reserve Bank of San Francisco's Conference on Managing Capital Flows and Exchange Rates: Lesson from the Pacific Basin, 26–27 September.

Garber, Peter, and Michael Spencer. 1995. Foreign exchange hedging with synthetic options and the interest rate defense of a fixed exchange rate system. *IMF Staff Papers* 42, no. 3 (September): 490–516.

Goldstein, Morris, David Folkerts-Landau, Liliana Rojas-Suarez, and Michael Spencer. 1993. *International capital markets. Part 1, Exchange rate management and international capital flows.* Washington, D.C.: International Monetary Fund, April.

IMF (International Monetary Fund). 1994. *Balance of payments annual.* Part 1. Washington, D.C.: International Monetary Fund.

3. Andrew Crockett

I will not rehearse at any great length in these remarks the advantages of international capital flows. They are obvious and they have already been discussed. Capital flows give countries with development potential access to foreign savings. They ensure the more efficient use of domestic savings because investment has to yield returns that are up to international standards. They discipline economic policy. And, last but not least, they help to share and diversify risks.

Risk is an inevitable part of all economic activity. An autarkic approach, in which each country would bear all of the risks of its own domestic investment choices, would clearly be inefficient. Therefore, allowing foreign investors to assume some of the risks of domestic investment, and allowing domestic investors to take profits from risk bearing abroad, helps improve welfare.

But while we all recognize these benefits and have indeed discussed them in the course of this conference, the fact is that recent experience is not particularly comforting. Consider events going back no further than, say, the 1970s. The lending boom to Latin America was followed by the debt crisis that started in 1982 and led to the "lost decade" for economic growth. More recently we had the Mexican crisis of 1994–95, and now we have the Asian crisis. These are all episodes in which the initial advantages of capital flows, which I think were real, were followed by very painful retrenchments, which cost a lot to the countries and the investors in the countries. They cost a lot, in some cases, to the lenders, too.

Typically, these episodes have had three distinct phases. In the first, inflows of capital have built up, lasted for a number of years, and often become very large. Economic liberalization and reform have usually acted as the initial spur to inflows. That was the case both in Latin America and in Asia. And in the general pattern, when these inflows begin and gather strength, the authorities resist currency appreciation, for understandable reasons, and accumulate reserves. Such a policy has the advantage of maintaining competitiveness better than it would otherwise be, but it also has drawbacks.

The first drawback is the cost of intervention. The interest paid on domestic currency liabilities is typically higher than that received on reserve assets, sometimes much higher. This is the so-called quasi-fiscal cost. The second drawback is that intervention can often lead to excessive domestic liquidity. Sterilization is generally not wholly effective, certainly not over prolonged periods of time. In Mexico, Malaysia, Thailand, and other countries intervention has contributed, directly or indirectly, to rapid expansion of domestic bank credit. A third drawback is that inflows may be too great, in such a short period of time, to be absorbed effectively in efficient, productive activities. They go either directly or indirectly to finance consumption—that has been the case in a number of Latin American countries—or they go into relatively low return infrastructure investment, which has been the case in certain Asian countries.

In the second phase of capital inflows, the tide begins to turn. Current account deficits widen, partly as a result of inflationary pressures driving up domestic costs and partly reflecting higher investment in infrastructure. At the beginning of this phase, authorities are not particularly worried. They may even be rather glad that the upward pressure on the currency is beginning to subside, and they may be happy to see some rundown of what they consider to be excessive reserves. Often the markets are not particularly worried in that initial turning phase either.

But then we come to the third phase of the three-phase process, which is when a crisis breaks out. At some point, the boom fades. It may be because exports or investment weaken, either from high rates to slightly lower rates, or from lower rates their growth may cease. It may be accompanied at some stage by a political trigger, but whatever it is, markets lose confidence, and there is a stampede for the exits. Countries that before had easy access to international capital markets at reasonable rates suddenly find they cannot raise capital at any price. The consequences of that can be, and have been, severe. The reduction in output below the trend level in Argentina and Mexico, for example, was probably in the region of 10 to 15 percent in the first year. A loss of confidence introduces very large risk premiums into interest rates and so strains the banking system of the countries concerned. Exchange rate adjustments may overshoot, raising the risk of inflation and increasing the debt service burden.

What I want to emphasize about this process is that the international financial markets have not exercised a progressive discipline, whereby a gradual increase in borrowing costs leads to progressively tighter constraints on the behavior of economic agents. What has happened is a discontinuity; a potentially catastrophic event that is judged to have low probability has initially not been factored into pricing and then has been recognized only when it is too late.

What should the reaction be to this three-stage development? Some, like Prime Minister Mahathir, have called for more restrictions on capital flows. I presume everybody at this conference would feel that is neither a desirable, nor indeed a feasible, response to the situation. We need to think more carefully about risk. The existing process has three important shortcomings that need to be addressed. They happen all to begin with "P."

One is perception: markets and others need to grasp the true dimensions of risk better than they do now. One is pricing: risks need to be properly priced. One is precautions: lenders and borrowers need to take measures both to reduce the risks of a crisis and to limit the damage when things go wrong.

Let me start with *perception.* Several factors can lead to inappropriate or inaccurate perceptions of the true risks involved in international capital flows. One is that markets underestimate the scale and duration of potential shocks, as well as the potential for destabilizing dynamics.

Nearly always, when economic agents are asked to think of where things could go wrong, they cite changes in financial market situations that are much smaller than can actually occur. If you spoke to observers of the Mexican economy in the pre-1994 period, even among the minority who were prepared to accept that something might go wrong a 10 or 15 percent depreciation of the currency was seen as the likely magnitude of a possible shock. Similarly in Asia, no one imagined the scale of the financial meltdown in the economies concerned.

So I think there is an unwillingness on the part of markets to contemplate the potential scale of a disruption they might subsequently face. It is also not fully appreciated how destabilizing dynamics can accentuate market reactions when it is the private sector that holds foreign currency debt. Once expectations change, for example, when those with dollar debt suddenly seek to hedge their positions, this can add enormously to the downward pressure on the exchange rate. That has been important in Indonesia, Thailand, and some other cases.

Moreover, it is often underestimated how much time it takes to reestablish confidence, and therefore extreme values of interest rates or exchange rates can persist for longer than is anticipated by market agents.

A second perception problem is that the nature of risks can change in the course of a crisis. For example, lenders may believe they are protected against interest risk or currency risk because loans are short term or denominated in foreign currency. They may not appreciate that extreme movements in interest rates and exchange rates can convert what was formerly an adequate credit risk into a poor credit risk. So the protections that are normally put in place to match interest rate or currency exposure may simply end up converting a market rate risk into a credit risk.

Last, linkages are not always fully grasped. Contagion spreads from one country to another. When conditions are calm policymakers in individual countries usually do not take enough account of how difficulties in a similarly placed country can affect them. However, markets that may seem to be loosely correlated in normal times can become much more closely correlated in a crisis. This needs to be borne in mind in assessing how effectively risks are diversified, in practice.

Another aspect is that external events outside the control of the country can create major common problems. For instance, if the shock is a change in the U.S. interest rate regime, then countries that consider themselves to be in distinct situations may find that they are similarly affected by developments in U.S. monetary policy.

Summing up, my point is that the first essential step is to make sure that the nature of risks is better assessed and perceived than it is at the moment.

Let me now pass on to the *pricing* of risk. Risk premiums do not appear to reflect greater risks even as a crisis approaches, but then they often overreact once the crisis strikes. Why don't they respond earlier? This is not an easy question to answer. A naive observer might expect that the greater depth and range of markets that exist nowadays would make risks more quantifiable, more tractable, and better priced than they were before. But for a number of reasons, markets are not pricing risks adequately in precrisis periods.

One such reason may be a variant of liquidity illusion. Individual investors believe that they can get out quickly, with only small losses. But in the aggregate, of course, they cannot. Paradoxically, the existence of hedging instruments may have encouraged firms to adopt riskier strategies, for example, through foreign currency borrowing, because they believe that they can hedge themselves effectively if a crisis appears imminent. A second element is the very familiar moral hazard question. There may be a greater expectation in markets that the authorities will somehow do "something" to prevent or cushion adverse developments. It is often not very clear in the minds of market participants exactly what that something is, but if there is such an expectation, the risks are seen as being less than they would be in the absence of expectations of official support.

I am sympathetic to the idea of a discontinuous regime shift of the kind that is referred to in Paul Krugman's paper (chap. 8.1). A situation that, up to a certain point, appears sustainable, and therefore attracts equilibrating behavior on the part of market agents, can, as a result of a relatively small change in the perception of the situation, result in behavior that tends to destabilize and bring about the crisis.

Last, it is worth mentioning an issue that is raised by Peter Garber (chap. 7.2): Does the greater range of derivative instruments help the unscrupulous to hide and disguise risks? It certainly could. There is a problem of opacity here, and the need to develop ways of enhancing effective disclosure, disclosure that really enables those who are observing the situation to gauge the risks that are being run.

Let me now come to the *precautions* that lenders and borrowers, in particular borrowers, can take to improve or to effectively contain the risks that are involved.

One is obviously prudent monetary policy. Crises are often preceded by earlier periods of monetary slackness. The precise signs vary. Sometimes it is too rapid expansion of bank credit, sometimes asset price bubbles, and sometimes a high level of dollar-denominated borrowing with a fixed exchange rate, which makes people think interest rates are low. It has been said at this conference that anything that grows at 15 percent (I think this was the figure used) is growing too fast. Whatever the precise figure, we have been naive in the past in looking at rapid rates of growth of variables that cannot grow indefinitely beyond the rate of the underlying economy and accepted for too long that they are sustainable. Then what happens is that there is a reluctance to tighten policy in a preemptive way when danger signals mount. Sometimes that is because of a commitment to the exchange rate, and the difficulties of getting out of such a commitment. But all of that unwillingness to react earlier makes the eventual crisis worse because the excesses accumulate longer.

I believe Lawrence Summers once said that a prudent response would be react to all adverse shocks as though they were permanent, and all positive shocks as though they were transitory. I am afraid that too often it has been the reverse, and the adjustment has not begun despite the mounting danger signals.

The second element of precautions has to be in the strengthening of financial systems, especially the banking system. Virtually all recent crises have been made worse by weak and overextended banking systems. In the end, the government typically pays for these mistakes. So there is a need to strengthen banking systems. The core principles of the Basle Committee have been mentioned. That is a start, but it is only a start. Mervyn King has reminded us why one needs to look beyond just the banking system, and beyond just banking supervision, in order to strengthen financial structures. Are enough precautions being taken to deal with worst-case scenarios? I doubt it, in many cases. Take loan-to-value ratios as an example. I have often been told by supervisors and monetary authorities: it's fine, we've enforced a loan-to-value ratio of 70 percent. Well, if the exchange rate falls by 30 percent and real estate falls by 20 percent, you've eaten up the 30 percent margin, very, very quickly.

Deeper and longer term financial markets are another important building block for a more robust system. An intrinsic problem in many emerging markets is that they are thin. They are also very short term. In Asia, long-term bond markets are not very developed. This can leave borrowers exposed to shifts in sentiment. But the development of large domestic pension funds should, over time, help to foster deeper and longer term financial markets.

Government must also avoid creating distortions that prevent the market from pricing risk properly. We have the example of the Tesobonos in Mexico, and the futures obligations in Thailand. In both cases, the market is demanding higher risk premiums, but the government is effectively underwriting the risks by issuing short-term dollar-denominated paper, or by forward sales of foreign currency, and so on. In both cases, the risk is not effectively coming through to influence private sector lender and borrower behavior.

There needs to be an increased ability for the market to become aware of risks at an earlier stage. We have talked about the importance of the publication of key indicators. I realize that indicators alone are not going to be sufficient. I do think, however, that better information is needed and that in certain cases it would have been easier for market participants to become aware of the risks that were growing if the data had been adequately available.

But more is still needed. I would cite two dimensions on which we might think about strengthening risk awareness. One is through a more effective use of credit rating agencies. Obviously it is not possible to tell credit rating agencies what to do, but I think they have often been too unwilling to adjust their ratings downward when danger has threatened. For example, the Japanese banks were nearly all AAA, right up until 1989. In hindsight, it seems clear that there were enough danger signals by 1989 that it would have been prudent to have done at least a modest downgrade before then.

Second is the question of whether official surveillance should somehow draw attention, more than it has done, to growing dangers. This is an issue that has come up in a number of forums. I would be interested in Stanley Fischer's comments on this in connection with the Thai crisis, where a number of official agencies saw the difficulties in advance. We did at the BIS, and so did the IMF. And I am sure we both said so to the Thai authorities. How much beyond that can you go? Is it possible to draw attention to unsustainable situations as they develop? I don't have a clear answer to that. Obviously it is not the answer to make a public speech that Thailand is about to face a crisis. But whether there is some intermediate response in which greater attention can be drawn at an early enough stage that a crisis is not likely to break out in a major way is I think an issue that deserves consideration.

I want to conclude by saying that we mustn't forget that one source of uncertainty for markets is whether effective official action to deal with a crisis will be taken. By that I mean that markets are uncertain about how strong the commitment of government is, both the political will and the economic understanding, to undertake necessary and timely measures to correct an unsustainable situation. In many episodes a loss of confidence in the government's ability to take decisive action, rather than just the underlying macroeconomic situation, has either initiated or prolonged the crisis.

There is also the question of international support. Much quicker IMF action is now available, supported of course by conditionality. The international financial community has to avoid creating an impression that the Seventh Cavalry will come to the rescue automatically. There is an important advantage to what I might have called "constructive ambiguity," if that term hadn't been criticized earlier. There is also much to be said for making it clear that, while the international community is there, it is there only under strict conditionality terms.

One of the potential dangers is excess liquidity. If we are indicating to markets that liquidity will be made available, either through national authorities, through the market itself, or through the international community, too easily, then we are not doing enough to make market agents internalize the risks. The objective must be to internalize the risks by the various measures I have talked about.

4. David W. Mullins, Jr.

I would like to explore some views and concerns surrounding the recent Asian crisis. This will also reinforce a number of points raised by others.

First, the generic setting, as I understand it. On the demand side, countries want to grow. They know how to grow. For the first time in seventy-five years, there is very little debate over the type of economic system that encourages growth. To grow requires capital, typically in excess of domestic savings, even in high-savings areas such as Asia. Some of the capital can take the form of foreign direct investment, but there are limits, including political limits. So high-growth countries typically rely to some not insignificant extent on portfolio investment. This is essentially the demand side of the equation.

The supply side is driven by deeply entrenched trends. The aging populations of developed nations produce large pools of savings in search of high returns. The mathematics and economics of international portfolio diversification produce benefits that are irrefutable, and ultimately irresistible. These are some of the factors driving the supply side of the market.

Supply and demand are brought together by markets. Of course in the past it was more likely financial institutions intermediating capital flows to emerging markets. Why have markets increasingly replaced direct lending by financial institutions? Driven by advances in technology, the flexibility, relative liquidity, and efficiency of markets have proved competitively superior to the older style financial system of direct investment by banks. There are even those who argue that market discipline is superior to direct lender discipline, pointing to the relatively quick recovery of Latin America from the market crisis in 1995, compared to the lost decade of development of the 1980s following the bank debt problems in Latin America. I think this comparison omits many factors. Still, the evolving market system has generally supported strong growth in countries, while providing investors diversification and attractive risk-adjusted returns. So what's the problem?

It has been suggested that, while markets generally work very well, they don't work perfectly. In particular, some have suggested that markets may be subject to imperfections, periods of instability that can damage the real economy. Some have suggested that markets in highly developed economies might get out of line every now and then. I would suggest there is enough concern to posit this possibility for discussion. In particular, with respect to emerging markets, it has been suggested that market discipline is highly imperfect, at times too lenient or too harsh; discipline is not well calibrated to the nature of the offense; and indeed, with contagion, harsh discipline is applied to the innocent.

A word about why contagion exists. Obviously one reason is redemptions by fund investors and the like. A more fundamental reason, though, is that contagion comes in part from sound risk management principles. An investor specializing in emerging markets who loses money in one country incurs a reduction in net worth and must reduce risk accordingly, by scaling back positions in other markets. This is in part what we call a behavioral correlation among countries that may have no fundamental economic linkages. This is simply a reality of the current market system.

Back to the issue of market dysfunction. One depiction of these emerging market crises starts with a period of what I would call "market forbearance," analogous to the manner in which banking regulators and bank lenders forbear. Investors, ignoring a country's problems, continue to invest, pushing prices higher, enjoying good returns. Why do they do this?

First, though aware of problems, professional investors may feel they must continue to invest and earn returns to keep up with competitors who are doing the same. Second, investors feel they are nimble enough to escape before the inevitable correction. And of course, typically following some triggering event, a change in government policy, currency regime, actions of some particularly aggressive market participants, or exodus by locals, when investors attempt to execute their escape in unison, the result is market overshooting, falling beyond the level seemingly warranted by fundamentals.

Lower market prices themselves produce economic damage, justifying lower prices, and this is the concern with overshooting. It is not benign, simply bouncing back. The concern is that the overshooting itself may produce damage and cause firms to go bankrupt, producing interruptions in production, and similar hardships, that actually damage the real economy. This is one scenario of market dysfunction. So even though markets generally work quite well, there is this concern of destabilizing market crises—runs—that may damage real economies, inflicting unwarranted pain and hardship. Accepting this possibility, what's the solution?

A number of government officials have argued, at least in private, that there is a very straightforward solution. They have argued an analogy with the earlier financial system, the banking system. That system too was subject to imperfections in the form of destabilizing bank runs that damaged the real economy. We found a solution to that imperfection. It began as the central bank as the lender of last resort, transmuted into deposit insurance, and evolved into the federal safety net for banking institutions. In the United States, following the banking collapse of the Great Depression, this solution produced a long period of financial stability, culminating in the not too destabilizing but very costly savings and loan and banking failures of the late 1980s and early 1990s. Academics of course are highly critical, almost unanimously opposed to the federal safety net. However, despite costly episodes of moral hazard, virtually every country relies on the federal safety net to combat the potential economic damage of destabilizing bank failures. In the period of the late 1980s during the savings and loan workout, and in the early 1990s when our banking system was weak, we were paying the wages of sin, the wages of moral hazard. Nonetheless, our colleagues in other countries were asking for technical help on how they too could develop a deposit insurance system, including in European countries. So this solution is fairly well established. Why not do the same to combat capital market instability? If governments can keep banks from failing, why shouldn't governments keep markets from falling, or at least from falling so fast or so far as to cause economic damage?

In my view, a government safety net is not likely to be an effective antidote to market instability. Compared to bank rescues, the direct cost of market rescues is likely to be much greater, and the probability of success much smaller. One instructive episode was the cost and outcome of the Europeans' attempt to sustain the Exchange Rate Mechanism in 1992, not an encouraging example. It is one thing to bail out one or a few banks, and quite another to confront the accumulated mass of a market. So in my view a government safety net market support system is neither a promising nor an appropriate solution to the problem of market instability. There seems to be a surprising degree of support underneath the surface of public debate for such a solution—support not only among some public officials but among investors. Similar attitudes were expressed following the Mexican problem in 1995 and after the 1987 stock market crash.

I will confess that our case against the government safety net would be stronger if we could offer a convincingly fail-safe alternative. As of yet we have none. In my view, we are still in the early stages of our experience with these episodes. We are learning, and making progress, and I shall review briefly some prescriptions that seem promising.

Among the remedies that have been suggested are the standard bromides. Indeed, around the time of the World Bank meetings, the *Financial Times* came out with an extensive supplement, giving its solution. One might characterize its solution to these problems as the stricture that governments should not make mistakes in managing their economies. I consider this a profound observation. It is certainly true that there are lessons on economic policy to be drawn from the recent crises. We have learned that contagion is a reality, and it is important that countries be aware of their neighbor's policies. This argues for regional consultation.

But I know from working in government that, under political pressures and economic shocks, mistakes will be made. All governments and countries are likely, if not destined, to experience some episodes of bad policy, bad management, and plain bad luck. So it would be useful to have an approach to market instability likely to be robust in the face of some of these possibilities.

The second preventative that has been discussed in detail here is increased surveillance, monitoring, and transparency. I couldn't agree more: I give a hearty two cheers for transparency, reserving the third cheer for an occasional application of opaqueness. I believe, though, that in recent episodes of market instability, the root cause was not that investors were unaware of the underlying problems. It is true that after the fact we can always specify the one critical variable, if we had only known. Let's specify these ahead of time.

While helpful, I am not overly optimistic that transparency alone will do the job, eliminating overshooting behavior. I should also mention that some countries argue the utility of limited capital controls that govern the inflow of portfolio investment. I am skeptical that capital controls will be found an effective and efficient mechanism, both to promote growth and inhibit market instability, although a number of countries seem to have performed pretty well with these controls. Those of us who oppose capital controls have a burden to explain more persuasively their disadvantages. There is growing support for limited controls, given the fact that a number of countries, for extended periods of time, seem to have done reasonably well. For a government safety net and limited capital control there is a surprising degree of support. It may be that just any approaches so universally opposed by economists can't be all bad.

There are several approaches that in my opinion would be useful. As others have noted, it would be useful for countries that depend on portfolio capital investment to focus on strengthening not only their financial policies, their currency regimes, but also their financial systems. Sound banking systems are especially important. This has been also explored by others, so I will not dwell on it.

Moreover, I believe countries dependent on portfolio capital investment should work to develop their capital markets. They need to erect the appropriate capital market infrastructure, to expand the diversity of investment vehicles including longer term investment markets as well. It is also useful for such countries to develop appropriate derivative markets, providing hedging and risk management vehicles. Such vehicles tend to weigh against mispricing, provide useful hedging opportunities for local institutions and firms, and tend to broaden the investor base, to attract investors who require such vehicles to manage risk. Derivatives also price risk and make risk more transparent. Derivatives clearly reduce the cost of risk. They allow different risks to be separated and segmented, and traded around the financial system to those willing and able to bear each risk at minimum cost. This reduces the overall cost of risk bearing. Derivatives also facilitate diversification, and diversification reduces risk. It's not this year's Nobel prize, but the earlier one given to Sharpe and Markowitz. Derivatives play a role in making markets more complete. Currently, in many emerging markets it is hard to get short, and this is one reason such markets may tend to get out of line.

More generally along these lines, some of the solutions to these problems can be found in the markets. Countries should seek to broaden and deepen the base of investors knowledgeable and confident in investing in their markets, especially those investors not themselves vulnerable to short-term capital withdrawals. After all, there is an attractive business investing in difficult market conditions, supporting markets, and seeking to profit when stability returns. The investors attracted to this strategy tend to have a longer term perspective and more stable sources of capital. I am suggesting that countries in effect work to recruit the other side of market disturbances, by actively developing their capital markets. Relevant here are a number of points that Stephen Friedman discussed (chap. 5.3), as well as Andrew Crockett's discussion about developing longer term markets (chap. 7.3).

If a country depends on portfolio capital investment, developing the capital markets is as important as developing the real economy because it will facilitate the development of the real economy. Continuing on the investors' perspective, in my view we are still in the early stages of the development of this global market system. Countries will still want to grow rapidly. We are certainly in the early stages of international diversification of investment portfolios. The overwhelming proportion of portfolios are still invested at home. We have a lot to learn.

This recent period of instability occurred against a quite benign market environment in developed countries. Despite all the setbacks and volatility, investors still view emerging markets as perhaps the most promising investment venue in the years ahead, unique opportunities in times of difficulty. Certainly those who invested in Mexico and Latin America in 1995 have done rather well. I recognize that region had the good fortune of close proximity to an impressive engine of growth, the U.S. economy, while the Asian region has a very formidable economic competitor emerging in the neighborhood in the form of China.

Still, at a time when asset prices in developed markets seem rather high, searching for value in emerging economies, countries seeking to recover from difficulties, is a most promising activity for investors—one that should be actively encouraged.

To summarize, there are real risks, both to the countries and investors, from these sorts of market disturbances. With contagion, following sound policies provides no guarantee of protection. Indeed, some countries in this crisis, which have followed the advice of enlightened economists, appear to have been hurt worse than other countries that have behaved badly.

While we have no fail-safe remedies to offer to the problem of market disturbances, I do not think the answer lies in retreating from the global market system, or in attempting to short-circuit markets with costly government protection of questionable efficacy. A better defense, and a good offensive strategy as well, is for governments not only to pursue sound economic policies but to develop and strengthen their financial systems and capital markets. Still, this is pretty cold comfort to countries that have tried to follow such policies and now face very painful adjustments in the real economy.

Discussion Summary

Martin Feldstein noted that two central policy questions had emerged from this discussion. First, what should surveillance agencies say and do in response to perceived mispricings of risk? Second, what are the advantages and disadvantages of capital controls in managing capital inflows?

Peter Garber commented that the source of the perceived mispricing of risks may be demand from domestic agents who are responding to the implicit protection afforded by domestic regulators rather than euphoria. In response to this implicit protection, domestic agents use derivatives to "double" their bets as their situation worsens. Accordingly, Garber agreed with the neutrality of derivatives in and of themselves but suggested that any prescription for the increased use of derivatives in developing markets is dangerous given these possibilities for the radical restructuring of risks and their associated opacity.

Paul Krugman noted that in recent crises, bank lending has been rational ex post given the packages of support provided to lenders. However, the obvious mispricing has been in domestic currency assets, as in Thailand, where little attention was paid to the possibility of a crisis until the last moment. Regarding the "James Dean" theory of investing noted by David Mullins, Krugman characterized this as the "greater fool" theory. In this vein, he recalled that when he asked an MBA student to ask banks that lent to Latin America in the 1980s why they lent, the common response was "We're lending short term so we're going to get out fine."

Roberto Mendoza suggested that crises make risks look mispriced ex post. However, it is far from clear that these risks were mispriced ex ante. Indeed, Mendoza noted that any supposed mispricing has to be measured within the entire range of assets and correlations ex ante. Furthermore, he suggested that markets should remove these mispricings if they truly exist and are persistent. Mendoza also noted that the notion that private lending has been safe in recent crises is not accurate. For example, U.S. banks and firms have suffered losses in the Thai crisis either through delayed payment or failed guarantees. Finally, Mendoza agreed with Mullins's characterization of derivatives as instruments that isolate and segment risks rather than increase systemic risks.

Feldstein recharacterized the question about derivatives as whether at the time of a crisis they allow governments or private agents to take actions that deepen the crisis. *Jeffrey Frankel* noted that the actions of the Thai government in the forward markets correspond to that description.

Garber acknowledged the advantages of derivatives in reallocating risk and making the price of risk more transparent. However, he noted that his emphasis was on private actors, such as local banks in over-the-counter markets, where their actions and net positions were made opaque as a result of using derivatives.

Feldstein characterized this as a disagreement between the advantages of derivatives in making the prices of risk more transparent and the use of derivatives in making the quantities or positions of economic agents more opaque.

Mullins suggested that even over-the-counter positions require manufacturing. Accordingly, the use of derivatives will make such positions more transparent.

Arminio Fraga suggested that the Mexican case may prove instructive for this question. He suggested that the absence of creditworthy counterparties was a major obstacle to shorting the peso. Consequently, there was not enough liquidity to drive down the price of the peso to reasonable levels. In fact, the entry of foreign banks in Mexico since the 1994 crisis has created much needed liquidity in that market. As such, this example suggests that the depth of derivative markets can mitigate potential crises.

Feldstein returned to the question of how we can recognize mispricing of risks and asked Andrew Crockett whether the BIS or IMF had inside information that led them to believe that mispricing existed.

Crockett responded that the BIS and IMF were concerned for a while about the Thai situation. Regarding the source of the mispricing, he suggested that many factors—including government interventions, informational symmetries, incentives, and price dynamics—can give rise to the prices of risk being wrong. Understanding these imperfections, while very difficult, is central to sorting through these questions. Additionally, derivatives exploit linkages between markets and therefore can magnify or spread these initial distortions and the associated mispricings.

David Folkerts-Landau returned to the benefits of using temporary capital controls within a program of broader economic liberalization. He suggested a parallel between the use of mandatory reserve requirements during extreme capital inflows and the use of limits on short positions or trading halts in developed capital markets. Such analogues should allow us to be more comfortable with the idea of capital controls.

Sebastian Edwards countered that while there may be an intellectual justification for temporary capital controls, this argument is very far from supporting the permanent fixture that such controls have evolved into in many Latin American countries. Edwards also agreed with Mullins's observation that the profession hasn't succeeded in making a convincing case that capital controls don't work as permanent fixtures. Edwards noted that there is some evidence that countries such as Chile have succeeded in spite of the presence of capital controls rather than because of them.

René Stulz emphasized that the expansion of derivative markets does face a natural limit in the need for counterparties that are sufficiently creditworthy. Additionally, he noted that a major benefit of derivatives had been overlooked. Derivatives allow firms to take additional production risks and thereby create additional value. Stulz also suggested that the questions of contagion and capital controls are intimately related. If we believe in contagion, then a substantial case can be made for capital controls. Nonetheless, contagion is easy to see but very hard to prove.

Takatoshi Ito concurred with Folkerts-Landau and suggested that there exists a consensus that short-term capital inflows can be dangerous when accompanied by rapid bank credit expansions. Accordingly, the emphasis should be on shifting the composition of inflows from the short term to long term by possibly adding sand to the gears in order to slow short-term flows.

Mullins suggested that contagion will continue to play a large role as long as markets are incomplete and individual portfolios are undiversified. Regarding the parallel between capital controls and circuit breakers, Mullins suggested that one of the lessons from his experience on the Brady Commission is that it is very difficult to stop temporary measures from becoming permanent. As a result, circuit breakers in the U.S. markets, which were intended to last two years, appear now to be permanent fixtures as are "temporary" capital controls in some countries. Regarding the Thai crisis, Mullins noted that, as in many stock bubbles, trying to short the underlying assets can prove extremely painful. Accordingly, completing markets and broadening the investor base provides the best remedy for overshooting.

8 Currency Crises

1. *Paul Krugman*
2. *Kenneth Rogoff*
3. *Stanley Fischer*
4. *William J. McDonough*

1. *Paul Krugman*

On 2 July of this year, after months of asserting that it would do no such thing, the government of Thailand abandoned its efforts to maintain a fixed exchange rate for the baht. The currency quickly depreciated by more than 20 percent; within a few days most neighboring countries had been forced to emulate the Thai example.

What forced Thailand to devalue its currency was massive speculation against the baht, speculation that over a few months had consumed most of what initially seemed an awesomely large war chest of foreign exchange. And why were speculators betting against Thailand? Because they expected the baht to be devalued, of course.

This sort of circular logic—in which investors flee a currency because they expect it to be devalued, and much (though usually not all) of the pressure on the currency comes precisely because of this investor lack of confidence—is the defining feature of a currency crisis. We need not seek a more formal or careful definition; almost always we know a currency crisis when we see one. And we have been seeing a lot of them lately. The 1990s have, in fact, offered the spectacle of three distinct regional waves of currency crises: Europe in 1992–93, Latin America in 1994–95, and the Asian crises still unfolding at the time of writing.

Currency crises have been the subject of an extensive economic literature, both theoretical and empirical. Yet there remain some important unresolved issues, and each new set of crises presents new puzzles. The purpose of this paper is to provide an overview both of what we know and of what we do not know about currency crises, illustrated by reference to recent experience.

The paper begins by describing the "canonical" crisis model, a simple yet suggestive analysis that was developed twenty years ago but remains the starting point for most discussion. Despite that canonical model's virtues, however, it has come in for justified criticism because of its failure to offer a realistic picture either of the objectives of central banks or of the constraints they face; thus the paper turns next to a description of "second-generation" crisis models that try to remedy these defects.

As it turns out, second-generation models have suggested a reconsideration of a basic question that the canonical model seemed to have answered: are currency crises always justified? That is, do currencies always get attacked because the markets perceive (rightly or wrongly) some underlying inconsistency in the nation's policies, or can they happen arbitrarily to countries whose currencies would otherwise have remained sound? The paper describes several different scenarios for currency crises that are not driven by fundamentals, including self-fulfilling crises in which endogenous policy ends up justifying investor pessimism, "herding" by investors, and the machinations of large agents ("Soroi"). Closely related to the question of arbitrary crises is "contagion," the phenomenon in which a currency crisis in one country often seems to trigger crises in other countries with which it seemingly has only weak economic links (e.g., Mexico and Argentina, or Thailand and the Philippines).

From there the paper moves to cases, considering in turn the three regional crisis waves of the 1990s (so far). Comparison of these waves turns out to raise a further puzzle: while the onset of crisis was similar in each case, the *consequences* of the crises seem to have been very different in the European as opposed to the Latin and Asian cases.

Finally, of course, we must ask the big question: is there any way to make crises less frequent, and if so what?

8.1.1   The Canonical Crisis Model

The canonical crisis model derives from work done in the mid-1970s by Stephen Salant, at that time at the Federal Reserve's International Finance Section. Salant's concern was not with currency crises but with the pitfalls of schemes to stabilize commodity prices. Such price stabilization, via the establishment of international agencies that would buy and sell commodities, was a major demand of proponents of the so-called New International Economic Order (NIEO). Salant, however, argued on theoretical grounds that such schemes would be subject to devastating speculative attacks.

His starting point was the proposition that speculators will hold an exhaustible resource if and only if they expect its price to rise rapidly enough to offer them a rate of return equivalent (after adjusting for risk) to that on other assets. This proposition is the basis of the famous Hotelling model of exhaustible resource pricing: the price of such a resource should rise over time at the rate of interest, with the level of the price path determined by the requirement that the resource just be exhausted by the time the price has risen to the "choke point" at which there is no more demand.

But what will happen, asked Salant, if an official price stabilization board announces its willingness to buy or sell the resource at some fixed price? As long as the price is above the level that would prevail in the absence of the board—that is, above the Hotelling path—speculators will sell off their holdings, reasoning that they can no longer expect to realize capital gains. Thus the board will initially find itself acquiring a large stockpile. Eventually, however, the price that would have prevailed without the stabilization scheme—the "shadow price"—will rise above the board's target. At that point speculators will regard the commodity as a desirable asset and will begin buying it up; if the board continues to try to stabilize the price, it will quickly—instantaneously, in the model—find its stocks exhausted. Salant pointed out that a huge wave of speculative buying had in effect forced the closure of the open market in gold in 1969 and suggested that a similar fate would await NIEO price stabilization schemes.

This basic logic was described briefly in a classic 1978 paper by Salant and his colleague Dale Henderson (their main concern in that paper was with the more recent behavior of the gold price, and in particular with the effects of unpredictable sales of official gold stocks). Other researchers soon realized, however, that similar logic could be applied to speculative attacks not on commodity boards trying to stabilize commodity prices but on central banks trying to stabilize exchange rates.

The canonical currency crisis model, as laid out initially by Krugman (1979) and refined by Flood and Garber (1984), was designed to mimic the commodity board story. The upward trend in the "shadow" price of foreign exchange—the price that would prevail after the speculative attack—was supplied by assuming that the government of the target economy was engaged in steady, uncontrollable issue of money to finance a budget deficit. Despite this trend, the central bank was assumed to try to hold the exchange rate fixed using a stock of foreign exchange reserves, which it stood ready to buy or sell at the target rate.

Given this stylized representation of the situation, the logic of currency crisis was the same as that of speculative attack on a commodity stock. Suppose speculators were to wait until the reserves were exhausted in the natural course of events. At that point they would know that the price of foreign exchange, fixed up to now, would begin rising; this would make holding foreign exchange more attractive than holding domestic currency, leading to a jump in the exchange rate. But foresighted speculators, realizing that such a jump was in prospect, would sell domestic currency just before the exhaustion of reserves—and in so doing advance the date of that exhaustion, leading speculators to sell even earlier, and so on. . . . The result would be that when reserves fell to some critical level—perhaps a level that might seem large enough to finance years of payments deficits—there would be an abrupt speculative attack that would quickly drive those reserves to zero and force an abandonment of the fixed exchange rate.

The canonical currency crisis model, then, explains such crises as the result of a fundamental inconsistency between domestic policies—typically the persistence of money-financed budget deficits—and the attempt to maintain a fixed exchange rate. This inconsistency can be temporarily papered over if the central bank has sufficiently large reserves, but when these reserves become inadequate speculators force the issue with a wave of selling.

This model has some important virtues. First of all, many currency crises clearly *do* reflect a basic inconsistency between domestic and exchange rate policy; the specific, highly simplified form of that discrepancy in the canonical model may be viewed as a metaphor for the more complex but often equally stark policy incoherence of many exchange regimes. Second, the model demonstrates clearly that the abrupt, billions-lost-in-days character of runs on a currency need not reflect either investor irrationality or the schemes of market manipulators. It can be simply the result of the logic of the situation, in which holding a currency will become unattractive once its price is no longer stabilized, and the end of the price stabilization is itself triggered by the speculative flight of capital.

These insights are important, especially as a corrective to the tendency of observers unfamiliar with the logic of currency crises to view them as somehow outside the normal universe of economic events—whether as a revelation that markets have been taken over by chaos theory, that "virtual money" has now overpowered the real economy (Drucker 1997), or as prima facie evidence of malevolent market manipulation.

Despite the virtues of the canonical model, however, a number of economists have argued that it is an inadequate representation of the forces at work in most real crises. These economists have developed what are sometimes known as "second-generation" crisis models, to which we now turn.

8.1.2 More Sophisticated Models

Perhaps the best way to describe what is wrong with the canonical crisis model is to say that it represents government policy (though not the market response) in a very mechanical way. The government is assumed to blindly keep on printing money to cover a budget deficit, regardless of the external situation; the central bank is assumed to doggedly sell foreign exchange to peg the exchange rate until the last dollar of reserves is gone. In reality the range of possible policies is much wider. Governments can and do try to condition fiscal policies on the balance of payments. Meanwhile, central banks have a variety of tools other than exchange market intervention available to defend the exchange rate, including in particular the ability to tighten domestic monetary policies. Obviously there are costs to such policies; but it may be important to recognize that the defense of an exchange rate is a matter of trade-offs rather than a simple matter of selling foreign exchange until the money is gone.

So-called second-generation models, perhaps best represented by Obstfeld (1994), require three ingredients. First, there must be a reason why the government would like to abandon its fixed exchange rate. Second, there must be a reason why the government would like to *defend* the exchange rate—so that there is a tension between these motives. Finally, in order to create the circular logic that drives a crisis, the cost of defending a fixed rate must itself increase when people expect (or at least suspect) that the rate might be abandoned.

Why might a government have a motive to allow its currency to depreciate? The general slogan here is "It takes two nominals to make a real." In order for a government to have a real incentive to change the exchange rate, *something* must be awkwardly fixed in domestic currency. One obvious possibility is a large debt burden denominated in domestic currency—a burden that a government might be tempted to inflate away but cannot as long as it is committed to a fixed exchange rate. (E.g., the attacks on the French franc during the 1920s were triggered mainly by suspicions that the government might try to inflate away its legacy of debt from World War I.) Another possibility is that the country suffers from unemployment due to downwardly rigid nominal wage rates and would like to adopt a more expansionary monetary policy but cannot as long as it is committed to a fixed exchange rate. (This was in essence the motivation both for Britain's abandonment of the gold standard in 1931 and its departure from the Exchange Rate Mechanism—ERM—of the European Monetary System in 1992.)

Given a motive to depreciate, why would a government choose instead to defend a fixed rate? One answer might be that it believes that a fixed rate is important in facilitating international trade and investment. Another might be that it has a history of inflation and regards a fixed rate as a guarantor of credibility. Finally, the exchange rate often takes on an important role as a symbol of national pride or commitment to international cooperation (as in the European Monetary System).

Finally, why would public lack of confidence in the maintenance of a fixed rate itself have the effect of making that rate more difficult to defend? Here there is a somewhat subtle distinction between two variants of the story. Some modelers—notably Obstfeld (1994)—emphasize that a fixed rate will be costly to defend if people expected *in the past* that it would be depreciated *now*. For example, debt holders might have demanded a high rate of interest in anticipation of a depreciation, therefore making the current debt burden so large that it is hard to manage without a depreciation. Or unions, expecting depreciation, might have set wages at levels that leave the country's industry uncompetitive at the current exchange rate.

The alternative (which to my mind seems much closer to what happens in real crises) is to suppose that a fixed rate is costly to defend if people *now* expect that it will be depreciated *in the future*. The usual channel involves short-term interest rates: to defend the currency in the face of expectations of future depreciation requires high short-term rates; but such high rates may either worsen the cash flow of the government (or indebted enterprises) or depress output and employment.

Suppose we take these three generic elements together: a reason to depreciate, another reason *not* to depreciate, and some reason why expectations of a depreciation themselves alter the balance between the costs and benefits of maintaining a fixed parity. As pointed out in Krugman (1996), it is possible to combine these elements to produce a general story about currency crises that is quite similar to that in the canonical model. Suppose that a country's fundamental trade-off between the costs of maintaining the current parity and the costs of abandoning it is predictably deteriorating, so that at some future date the country would be likely to devalue even in the absence of a speculative attack. Then speculators would surely try to get out of the currency ahead of that devaluation—but in so doing they would worsen the government's trade-off, leading to an earlier devaluation. Smart investors, realizing this, would try to get out still earlier . . . the end result will therefore be a crisis that ends the fixed exchange rate regime well before the fundamentals would appear to make devaluation necessary.

We can actually be more specific: given an inevitable eventual abandonment of a currency peg and perfectly informed investors, a speculative attack on a currency will occur *at the earliest date at which such an attack could succeed.* The reason is essentially arbitrage: an attack at any later date would offer speculators a sure profit; this profit will be competed away by attempts to anticipate the crisis.

It is important to notice an important point about this scenario. In the case just described—as in the canonical model—the crisis is ultimately provoked by the inconsistency of government policies, which make the long-run survival of the fixed rate impossible. In that sense the crisis is driven by economic fundamentals. Yet that is not the way it might seem when the crisis actually strikes: the government of the target country would feel that it was fully prepared to maintain the exchange rate for a long time and would in fact have done so, yet was forced to abandon it by a speculative attack that made defending the rate simply too expensive.

I think that it is fair to say that the standard reaction both of most economists and of international officials to currency crises is, at least informally, based on something like the scenario just described. That is, they recognize that the speculative attack, driven by expectations of devaluation, was itself the main proximate reason for devaluation; yet they regard the whole process as ultimately caused by the policies of the attacked country, and in particular by a conflict between domestic objectives and the currency peg that made an eventual collapse of that peg inevitable. In effect, the financial markets simply bring home the news, albeit sooner than the country might have wanted to hear it.

A significant number of economists studying this issue do, however, believe that the complaints of countries that they are being unfairly or arbitrarily attacked have at least some potential merit. So let me turn to the possible ways that—especially in the context of second-generation models—such complaints might in fact be justified.

8.1.3 Disputed Issues

I have just argued that although the detailed workings of a second-generation currency crisis model may be very different from those of the original models, the general result can be much the same: a currency crisis is essentially the result of policies inconsistent with the long-run maintenance of a fixed exchange rate. Financial markets simply force the issue and indeed must do so as long as investors are forward looking.

However, it is possible to conceive of a number of circumstances under which the financial markets are not as blameless as all that. The list below may not include all the relevant scenarios, but it seems to cover the cases most often mentioned.

Self-Fulfilling Crises

Suppose that, contrary to our earlier assumption, an eventual end to a currency peg is not completely preordained. There may be no worsening trend in the fundamentals; or there may be an adverse trend, but at least some realistic possibility that policies may change in a way that reverses that trend. Nonetheless, it may be the case that the government will abandon the peg if faced with a sufficiently severe speculative attack.

The result in such cases will be the possibility of self-fulfilling exchange rate crises. An individual investor will not pull his money out of the country if he believes that the currency regime is in no imminent danger; but he will do so if a currency collapse seems likely. A crisis, however, will materialize precisely if many individual investors do pull their money out. The result is that either optimism or pessimism will be self-confirming; and in the case of self-confirming pessimism, a country will be justified in claiming that it suffered an unnecessary crisis.

How seriously should we take this analysis? One obvious caveat understood by the economists studying this issue, but perhaps too easily forgotten by political figures, is that this analysis does not imply either that any currency can be subject to speculative attack or that all speculative attacks are unjustified by fundamentals. Even in models with self-fulfilling features, it is only when fundamentals—such as foreign exchange reserves, the government fiscal position, the political commitment of the government to the exchange regime—are sufficiently weak that the country is potentially vulnerable to speculative attack. A country whose government is expected to defend its currency firmly and effectively will probably not need to do so, while a country whose government is very likely to abandon its peg eventually in any case will almost surely find its timetable accelerated by speculative pressure. Or to put it a bit differently: one can think of a range of fundamentals in which a crisis *cannot* happen, and a range of fundamentals in which it *must* happen; at most, self-fulfilling crisis models say that there is an intermediate range in which a crisis *can* happen but need not. It is an empirical question (though not an easy one) how wide this range is.

It is also important to remember that a country whose fundamentals are persistently and predictably deteriorating will necessarily have a crisis at some point. Since the logic of predictable crises is that they happen well before the fundamentals have reached the point at which the exchange rate would have collapsed in the absence of speculative attack—indeed, as argued above, they happen as soon as an attack can "succeed"—it will always seem at the time that the crisis has been provoked by a speculative attack not justified by current fundamentals.

Let me add a conjecture here, which has not to my knowledge been addressed in the theoretical literature to date. A situation in which a crisis could happen but need not presents speculators with a "one-way option": they will reap a capital gain (or, if you measure it in foreign currency, avoid a capital loss) by selling domestic currency if the exchange regime collapses but will not suffer an equivalent loss if it does not. What, then, prevents them from fleeing the currency at even a hint of trouble? My conjecture is that microeconomic frictions—transaction costs, the difficulty of arranging credit lines, and so on—play an important role. Ordinarily we think of these frictions as being of trivial importance for macroeconomic issues, on the grounds that they are only a small fraction of a percentage point of the value transacted. However, currency crises unfold over very short periods, in which even small transaction costs can offset very large annualized rates of return. It may be small frictions that prevent a subjectively low-probability crisis from ballooning into a full-fledged speculative attack. If this is true, then the improving technical efficiency of markets may actually be a contributory factor to the frequency of currency crises in the 1990s.

If self-fulfilling crises are a real possibility, what sets them off? The answer is that anything could in principle be the trigger. That is, we are now in the familiar terrain of "sunspot" dynamics, in which any arbitrary piece of information becomes relevant if market participants believe it is relevant.

Herding

Both the canonical currency crisis model and the second-generation models presume that foreign exchange markets are efficient—that is, that they make the best use of the available information. There is, however, very little evidence that such markets are in fact efficient; on the contrary, the foreign exchange market (like financial markets in general) exhibits strong "anomalies" that can be reconciled with efficiency, if at all, only with layers of otherwise unpersuasive assumptions that irresistibly suggest the epicycles of pre-Copernican astronomy.

What difference might inefficient markets make to the study of currency crises? The most obvious difference is the possibility of "herding." In general, herding can be exemplified by the result found in Shiller's (1989) remarkable survey of investors during the 1987 stock market crash: the only reason consistently given by those selling stocks for their actions was the fact that prices were going down. In the context of a currency crisis, of course, such behavior could mean that a wave of selling, whatever its initial cause, could be magnified through sheer imitation and turn, quite literally, into a stampede out of the currency.

Aside from the (very real) biases and limitations of human cognition, why might herding occur? Theorists have proposed two answers consistent with individual rationality. One involves bandwagon effects driven by the awareness that investors have private information. Suppose that investor 1 has special information about the Thai real estate market, investor 2 has special information about the financial condition of the banks, and investor 3 has information about the internal discussions of the government. If investor 1 gets some negative information, he may sell, since that is all he has to go on; if investor 2 learns that investor 1 has sold, he may sell also even if his own private information is neutral or even slightly positive. And investor 3 may then end up selling even if his own information is favorable, because the fact that both investors 1 and 2 have sold leads him to conclude that both may well have received bad news, even though in fact they have not. Chari and Kehoe (1996) have argued that such bandwagon effects in markets with private information create a sort of "hot" money that at least sometimes causes foreign exchange markets to overreact to news about national economic prospects.

Another explanation focuses on the fact that much of the money that has been invested in crisis-prone countries is managed by agents rather than directly by principals. Imagine a pension fund manager investing in emerging market funds. She surely has far more to lose from staying in a currently unpopular market and turning out to be wrong than she does to gain from sticking with the market and turning out to be right. To the extent that money managers are compensated based on comparison with other money managers, then, they may have strong incentives to act alike even if they have information suggesting that the market's judgment is in fact wrong. (As an aside, herding by individual investors may well result from a similar kind of internal principal agent problem; as Schelling 1984 has argued, many aspects of individual behavior make sense only if viewed as the result of a sort of internal struggle between agents with longer term and shorter term perspectives. Put it this way: I will probably *feel* worse if I lose money in a Thai devaluation when others do not than I will if I lose the same amount of money in a general rout.)

A final point: anyone who has followed the currency crises of the 1990s must at least have speculated on what we might call reverse herding. In general, as described at greater length below, the markets seem to have been oddly complacent until shortly before the crises, even though there were ample reasons to think that there was at least some risk of such crises. Principal-agent-type stories might be one explanation of this passivity: money managers (or internal, subjective money management "modules") were less concerned about crisis than they should have been because they were acting the same way as everyone else.

Contagion

The currency crises of the 1990s have consisted of three regional "waves": the ERM crises in Europe in 1992–93, the Latin American crises of 1994–95, and the Asian crises currently in progress. But why should there be such regional waves—as Ronald Reagan said after visiting Latin America, they are all different countries, so why should they experience a common crisis? This is the issue of "contagion."

One simple explanation of contagion involves real linkages between the countries: a currency crisis in country A worsens the fundamentals of country B. For example, the Southeast Asian countries currently under speculative attack are, to at least some extent, selling similar products in world export markets; thus a Thai devaluation tends to depress Malaysian exports and could push Malaysia past the critical point that triggers a crisis. In the European crises of 1992–93, there was an element of competitive devaluation: depreciation of the pound adversely affected the trade and employment of France, or at least was perceived to do so, and thus increased the pressures on the French government to abandon its own commitment to a fixed exchange rate.

However, even in the European and Asian cases the trade links appear fairly weak; and in the Latin American crisis of 1995 they were virtually nil. Mexico is neither an important market nor an important competitor for Argentina; why, then, should one peso crisis have triggered another?

At this point two interesting "rational" explanations for crisis contagion between seemingly unlinked economies have been advanced (Drazen 1997). One is that countries are perceived as a group with some common but imperfectly observed characteristics. To caricature this position, Latin American countries share a common culture and therefore, perhaps, a "Latin temperament"; but the implications of that temperament for economic policy may be unclear. Once investors have seen one country with that cultural background abandon its peg under pressure, they may revise downward their estimate of the willingness of other such countries to defend their parties. (An observation: In 1982 the Latin countries suffered a crisis that, although it mainly involved dollar-denominated debt rather than domestic currency, was similar in form and psychology to a currency crisis. This crisis quickly spread from Mexico through the whole area. The Philippines, however, were at first unaffected, even though both its policies and its debt burden were quite as bad as those of Mexico, Argentina, and Brazil; it was not until almost a year after the original onset that investors seem to have decided that this former Spanish colony was in fact a Latin rather than an Asian country and attacked.)

Alternatively, one may argue that the political commitment to a fixed exchange rate is itself subject to herding effects. This is perhaps clearest in the European crises: once Britain and Italy have left the ERM, it is less politically costly for Sweden to abandon its peg to the deutsche mark than it would have been had Sweden devalued on its own.

One may also argue, of course, that contagion reflects irrational behavior on the part of investors, either because individuals are really irrational or because money managers face asymmetric incentives. South Korea has few strong trade links with the troubled economies of Southeast Asia; yet a fund manager who did not reduce exposure in South Korea, then was caught in a devaluation of the won, might well be blamed for lack of due diligence—after all, Asian currencies have been risky in recent months, haven't they?

As in the case of herding in general, there seems to be positive as well as negative contagion. During the wave of optimism that followed Mexican and Argentine reforms in the early 1990s, countries that had done little actual reform, such as Brazil, were also lifted by the rising tide; and the apparent myopia of markets about Asian risks seems to have been fed by a general sense of optimism about Asian economies in general.

Market Manipulation

Scenarios in which crises are generated either by self-fulfilling rational expectations or by irrational herding behavior imply at least the possibility of profitable market manipulation by large speculators. (Krugman 1996 proposed that such hypothetical agents be referred to as "Soroi.") Suppose that a country is vulnerable to a run on its currency: either investors believe that it will abandon its currency peg if challenged by a speculative attack, or they simply emulate each other and can therefore be stampeded. Then a large investor could engineer profits for himself by first quietly taking a short position in that country's currency, then deliberately triggering a crisis—which he could do through some combination of public statements and ostentatious selling.

The classic example of this strategy is, of course, George Soros's attack on the British pound in 1992. As argued in the case study below, it is likely that the pound would have dropped out of the ERM in any case; but Soros's actions may have triggered an earlier exit than would have happened otherwise.

In addition to being the classic example of how a market manipulator can generate a crisis, however, Soros's attack on the pound may be the *only* example in recent years. At any rate, it is hard to come up with any other clear-cut examples. This has not, of course, prevented politicians from blaming market manipulation in general and Soros in particular for currency crises, even when there is no evidence that they have played a role.

Why are such engineered speculative attacks rare? One answer is that the scope for self-fulfilling crises is actually rather limited: most currencies tend to get attacked soon after it becomes apparent that they are vulnerable to such an attack. As argued earlier, this will happen if a continuing deterioration in the fundamentals is predictable: knowing that an eventual collapse of the exchange regime is inevitable, investors will try to anticipate the collapse, thereby bringing it forward in time, and thus will tend to attack as soon as such an attack can succeed. In Krugman (1996) I also argued that the existence of Soroi itself tends to advance the date of speculative attack: since everyone knows that a currency that is vulnerable to a self-fulfilling attack presents a profit opportunity for large players, investors will sell the currency in anticipation that one or another of these players will in fact undermine the exchange regime—and in so doing investors will force the collapse of the regime even without the aid of a Soros.

Of course, if currencies spontaneously collapse as soon as a potential profit for Soroi appears, this will eliminate the opportunity for Soroi to make profits; but if nobody is playing that game, investors will no longer expect collapsible currency regimes to be collapsed. This paradox is essentially the same as that which arises in the context of struggles for corporate control: a takeover attempt will not be profitable if the potential gains are already in the stock price, but there will be no gains if there is no takeover attempt. From a modeling point of view this seems to suggest the absence of any equilibrium, unless one introduces sufficient "noise" into the story. In practical terms we may simply note that for whatever reason, the success of Soros at making money by provoking the pound's devaluation seems thus far to have been a one-time event.

8.1.4   Case Study 1: The ERM Crises of 1992–93

In the fall of 1992 massive capital flows led to the exit of Britain, Italy, and Spain from the Exchange Rate Mechanism of the European Monetary System. (Strictly speaking, they remained within the system itself.) In the summer of 1993 a second wave of attacks led to a decision to widen the exchange rate bands of that system, essentially to allow the French franc to depreciate without any formal exit. In subsequent years events have unfolded in somewhat ironic ways: France, having been given leeway for a somewhat weaker franc, chose not to use it, returning to the original narrow band against the mark; while the boom in the U.K. economy that followed the exit from the ERM has now pushed the pound *above* the rate at which it originally exited. Still, the ERM crises remain one of the classic episodes of speculative attack, and they are the most thoroughly studied such episode.

Part of what makes the ERM crises so classic is that they so clearly demonstrate the importance of second-, as opposed to first-, generation models. The European countries attacked in 1992 and 1993 did not fit the canonical crisis model at all. In all cases, governments retained full access to capital markets, both domestic and foreign. This meant, first of all, that they had no need to monetize their budget deficits; and indeed they did not have exceptionally rapid growth of domestic credit (Eichengreen, Rose, and Wyplosz 1995). It also meant that they were not suffering from any ironclad limitation on foreign exchange reserves: they remained able to borrow on foreign markets and indeed clearly retained the ability to stabilize their currencies had they so chosen simply by raising domestic interest rates sufficiently. Finally, all of the target economies had low and stable inflation both before and after the crisis.

What, then, provided the motivation for devaluation that we have seen is a crucial ingredient for second-generation models? The answer was clearly unemployment due to inadequate demand, and the resulting pressure on monetary authorities to engage in expansionary policies—policies that could not be pursued as long as the countries remained committed to a fixed exchange rate—was the essential fuel for the crises. Essentially we can think of European governments as facing a trade-off between the political costs of unemployment over and above its "structural" or "natural" level, on one side, and the political costs of dropping out of the ERM, on the other.

Behind the unemployment problem, in turn, was an unusual situation triggered by the interaction between the fall of the Berlin Wall and the role of the deutsche mark as the de facto key currency of the European Monetary System. The heavy expenditures by Germany on its newly reunited eastern Länder amounted to an expansionary fiscal policy for western Germany; the Bundesbank, like the Federal Reserve faced with the deficit spending of the 1980s, responded with a tight monetary policy. However, other European countries pegging to the mark found themselves obliged to match the tight monetary policy without the fiscal expansion; thus they were pushed into recession.

All the ingredients for crisis, then, were in place. However, four special aspects of the ERM crises should be noted. First was the role of a large actor— George Soros—in triggering the crisis. Soros had divined early in the game the possibility of a sterling devaluation and set about discreetly establishing a short position in the form of a number of short-term credit lines, totaling approximately $15 billion. He was thus in a position to profit from a collapse of the exchange regime and did in fact attempt by his own sales to precipitate that collapse. It remains unclear, however, how important a role his actions actually played; it is arguable that the fundamental reasons for the crisis would have set it off even without any action on Soros's part. A guess might be that he advanced the date of the crisis by only a few weeks or months.

Second, the crisis demonstrated the near irrelevance of foreign exchange reserves in a world of high capital mobility. The central banks of both Britain and Italy had substantial reserves and were also entitled under ERM rules to credit lines from Germany. Thus they were able to engage in direct foreign exchange intervention on a very large scale—Britain appears to have bought some $50 billion worth of sterling over the course of a few days. However, this intervention was sterilized—that is, it was offset by open market operations so as to avoid reducing the size of the monetary base. And it was clearly ineffectual. It became clear that sterling could be defended only by a domestic monetary contraction, and after only two (?) days of higher interest rates the Bank of England abandoned the fixed parity.

Third, retrospectives on the ERM crises turn up a surprising fact: the crises seem to have been virtually unanticipated by the financial markets. Rose and Svensson (1994) show that interest differentials against the target currencies did not begin to widen until August 1992—a month before the breakup.

Finally, a remarkable fact about the ERM crises is that the countries that "failed," and were driven off their pegs, did better by almost any measure in the following period than those that succeeded in defending their currencies. The United Kingdom, in particular, experienced a rapid drop in its unemployment rate without any corresponding rise in inflation.

8.1.5   Case Study 2: The Latin Crises, 1994–95

The Latin crisis of 1994–95 was similar to the ERM crises in some respects, quite different in others. Above all, its consequences were much more severe for the affected economies.

Claims that several Latin currencies, in particular the Mexican and Argentine peso, were overvalued were common among economists as early as the beginning of 1993 (see, e.g., Dornbusch 1994). These claims were based on one or more of three observations: purchasing power parity calculations, which suggested that costs and prices had gotten out of line with those of trading partners; large current account deficits; and slow growth (in the case of Mexico) or high unemployment (in the case of Argentina), suggesting that there would be room for monetary expansion if only the exchange rate were not a constraint.

In Latin America, however, as in Europe, these warnings appear to have been more or less ignored by financial markets. Government officials were adamant that devaluation was not under consideration, and the markets believed them. Through the whole of 1993 interest premiums on the pesos remained low, and the current account deficits were easily financed.

Mexico experienced a deteriorating situation over the course of 1994. Political uncertainty emerged following two unexpected events: the peasant rebellion in Chiapas and the assassination of the ruling party's presidential candidate. The government also appeared to relax monetary and fiscal discipline in the run-up to the presidential election. Foreign capital inflows began to dry up, and there was a rapid decline in foreign exchange reserves. A critical point was reached when the government found itself unable to roll over the Tesobonos, dollar-denominated short-term debt.

Faced with this external pressure, Mexico decided shortly after the election to devalue the peso. However, the devaluation was botched in several respects. First, the size of the devaluation, at 15 percent, was widely regarded as inadequate; thus the government had sacrificed the credibility of its commitment to a fixed rate without satisfying markets that the devaluation was behind it. Second, by consulting business leaders about the plan, the government in effect gave Mexican insiders the opportunity to make profits at the expense of uninformed foreign investors, helping to discredit the policy. Finally, Mexican officials managed to convey a sense of both arrogance and incompetence to foreign investors in the days immediately following the devaluation.

Perhaps for these reasons, the initial small devaluation was followed by a near complete loss of confidence in Mexican policies and prospects. The peso quickly fell to half its precrisis value; the resulting spike in import prices caused inflation, which had previously fallen to low single-digit levels, to soar. In order to stabilize the peso and the inflation rate, the government was obliged to raise domestic interest rates to very high levels, peaking at above 80 percent. The high rates in turn led to a sharp contraction in domestic demand, and real GDP fell by 7 percent in the year following the crisis.

Fears that the crisis would undermine Mexico's political stability led the United States to engineer a massive international loan to the Mexican government, hoping to buy a breathing space while confidence was restored. This effort was successful: during 1996 economic growth resumed, and Mexico regained normal access to international capital markets, repaying the emergency loan ahead of schedule.

Argentina had initially hoped that its very different currency regime—a currency board system, with the peso rigidly linked to the dollar at a one-for-one parity, and with every peso in the monetary base backed by a dollar of reserves—would protect it from any spillover from the Mexican crisis. In effect, Argentina had ensured that it was not vulnerable to the kind of crisis envisaged by the canonical crisis model. Argentina might also have expected that the absence of any strong trade linkage with Mexico would prevent any contagion. However, speculators attacked the currency nonetheless, presumably suspecting that Argentina might abandon the currency board in order to reduce the unemployment rate. (We might call this the revenge of the second-generation model.)

Under the currency board system, the capital outflows led to a rapid decline in the monetary base. This, in turn, created a crisis in the banking system, which contributed to a downturn milder than Mexico's but still extremely severe. International official loans, albeit on a smaller scale than Mexico's, were needed to prop up the banking system.

In contrast to Mexico, Argentina chose to hang tough on its exchange rate regime, betting that the financial markets would eventually realize that its commitment was absolute and that the pressure would ease. And in 1996 Argentina also resumed economic growth.

The Latin crises thus share some common features with the European experience but also show some strong differences. The most striking commonality was the apparent failure of financial markets to anticipate the crises, or even give any weight to the possibility of a crisis, until very late in the game—in spite of widely circulated warnings by economists that such crises might be brewing. The most striking difference was in the aftermath of crisis. Suppose that one thinks of Britain and France as representing one matched pair—a country that gave in to the pressure and one that did not—while Mexico and Argentina are another. In the first case the devaluing country actually did very well postdevaluation (leading to some facetious suggestions that a statue of George Soros be erected in Trafalgar Square); the nondevaluing country did less well but did not suffer any dramatic catastrophe. In the second case both countries suffered almost incredibly severe recessions, but the devaluing country was worse hit, at least initially.

8.1.6   Case Study 3: Asian Crises

The Asian situation is still in flux at the time of writing, information is still incomplete, and no careful economic studies are yet available. So this can only be a brief and provisional summary.

During 1995 a number of economists had begun to wonder whether the countries of Southeast Asia might be vulnerable to a Latin-type crisis. The main objective indicator was the emergence of very large current account deficits. Closer examination also revealed that several of the countries had developed worrying financial weaknesses: heavy investment in highly speculative real estate ventures, financed by borrowing either from poorly informed foreign sources or by credit from underregulated domestic financial institutions. It is now known that during 1996 officials from the International Monetary Fund (IMF) and World Bank actually began warning the governments of Thailand, Malaysia, and other countries of the risks posed by their financial situation and urged corrective policies. However, these warnings were brusquely rejected by those governments.

As in the case of the other regional currency crises, financial markets showed little sign of concern until very late in the game. The extraordinary growth record of the region seems to have convinced many that the usual cautions did not apply. (One pension fund manager described to me a briefing on Indonesian prospects by someone from Moody's. Some members of the audience had expressed worry about the reliability of the data and the financial reports they had seen. His response was that you should think of it as being like a Javanese shadow puppet show—you couldn't actually see the puppets, but you could see their shadows, and that told the story.)

The slide toward crisis began with an export slowdown in the region, partly due to the appreciation of the dollar (to which the target currencies were pegged) against the yen, partly to specific developments in key industries, partly to growing competition from China. With export growth flagging, the overbuilding of real estate—especially in Thailand—became all too apparent. In turn, dropping real estate prices pulled down stock prices and placed the solvency of financial institutions in question.

Up to this point, the developments were mainly a domestic financial crisis, similar in general outline to the bursting of Japan's "bubble economy" in the early 1990s. During the first half of 1997, however, speculators finally began to wonder whether the financial distress of Southeast Asian countries, especially Thailand, might provoke them to devalue in the hope of reflating the economy. The growing suspicion that such a move might be in prospect, despite government insistence that it was not, led to widening interest premiums; these in turn increased the pressure, both by adding deflationary impetus and by creating cash flow problems for financially stressed businesses.

On 2 July Thailand gave in to the pressures and floated the baht; as in the other crises, this led to speculation against other regional currencies and was followed shortly by somewhat smaller devaluations in Malaysia, Indonesia, and the Philippines. The wave of devaluations, and the troubled financial picture revealed by the crisis, shook investor confidence; in an effort to regain that confidence, all of the countries involved have imposed new fiscal austerity. Thailand received an emergency loan from the IMF; part of the conditionality was a cleanup of its financial system.

At this point the real consequences of the crisis are still to be revealed. There seems to be general agreement that Thailand, like Mexico, will suffer an initial blow to its growth. Typical estimates are that it will go from the 9 percent average rates of recent years to roughly zero growth over the next year. The impact on neighboring economies is a subject of considerable dispute, with the IMF predicting only a small impact while many private economists predict much more severe slowdowns.

At this point it remains unclear how far the contagion will spread. South Korea is the most interesting case: it has severe internal financial problems and a massive current account deficit, but it has few real linkages to the Southeast Asian economies. At the time of writing there does not seem to have been any pressure on China, even though the giant nation is reported to have massive quantities of bad internal debt.

An interesting counterpoint to the Latin experience is provided by Hong Kong, which like Argentina has a currency board and is pegged to the U.S. dollar (and intends to remain that way, even though it is politically now part of China). After a brief probing, financial markets seem to have decided that the Hong Kong dollar is not at risk, and what is now the Special Administrative Region thus seems to have insulated itself from the crisis.

The most peculiar aspect of the Asian crisis has been the reaction of some of the region's leaders. Malaysia's prime minister, Mahathir bin Mohamed, has taken the lead, blaming the crisis on the conspiratorial activities of George Soros (whom he has described as a "moron"), prompted by U.S. government officials. Unless new evidence surfaces, this claim is even odder than it sounds: as far as market participants are aware, Soros was not even a player in this crisis and indeed seems to have guessed wrong, *buying* Malaysian ringgit. Mahathir temporarily imposed limits on stock trading intended to stop the alleged conspiracy and has made public calls for an end to currency trading that have made financial markets understandably nervous that he might try to impose capital controls.

8.1.7   Macroeconomic Questions

Although the currency crises of the 1990s have inspired a good deal of research, one area remains neglected. What are the macroeconomic impacts of crisis, and why in particular have they differed so much between episodes?

The quick review of the main episodes in the decade to date indicates pretty clearly that crises in the 1990s are best described by second-generation models—that is, the motives for devaluation lie in the perceived need for more expansionary monetary policies rather than in budget deficits and inflation. One might therefore suppose that when a country gives in to temptation it would receive a reward—that whatever the cost in political capital or long-term inflation credibility, there would at least be a payoff in terms of short-run economic expansion. And this was exactly what happened in the European crises; indeed, those countries that abandoned their principles seem to have gone completely unpunished.

In the Latin crisis, however, and at least as far as we can tell in the Asian crises, the decision to devalue seems to have led to serious adverse short-run consequences on all fronts. Instead of permitting reflation, the devaluations seem to have led to even more severe contraction. Why? And why has the experience been so different?

Systematic attempts to answer these questions are still lacking (although papers prepared for the NBER's conference on currency crises may supply some answers). A quick conjecture is that the key difference was how well informed markets were about the policy environment in the respective sets of countries. A British devaluation, while it may have shattered the credibility of the current chancellor of the exchequer, did not shake confidence in British institutions in general; markets still had full confidence that the government of the United Kingdom would continue to allow free markets to function, that it would honor its debts, that the Bank of England would continue to worry about inflation, and so on. Thus, once the pound had depreciated substantially, markets were prepared to believe that investment in Britain was actually a good bet.

In Mexico, by contrast, the devaluation made markets question the whole premise that the country was now run by reliable, reformist technocrats. As the crisis deepened, so did concerns that a backlash against the reformers would lead to a return to dirigiste policies—and these concerns, by promoting further capital flight, deepened the crisis. One might summarize Mexico's situation in 1995 as one in which the country had to offer very high interest rates to offset the nervousness of investors about the country's *political* future—and in which that nervousness was largely the result of concern about the political damage inflicted by high interest rates. The rescue package organized by the United States may be seen as an attempt to break this vicious circle.

The Asian crisis, like that in Latin America, seems to have shaken basic confidence in the countries much more than the crisis in Europe. Investors are now emphasizing weaknesses in the political and institutional environment— lax bank regulation, widespread corruption, grandiose policies—that were obvious even to casual observers before this year but that were brushed off as minor blemishes on the Asian miracle until that miracle hit a speed bump.

At this point, however, this is merely loose speculation. More careful analyses are badly needed.

8.1.8 Can Currency Crises Be Prevented?

A world in which major currency crises occur at an average rate of one every nineteen months is not a very comfortable one for economic policymakers. What, if anything, can be done to prevent them, or at least to keep them from happening so often?

One possibility would be to return to the world of the early 1960s, an era in which extensive capital controls prevented the massive flows of hot money that now drive crises. Something like this seems to be what Mahathir is proposing, but nothing along these lines seems likely in the near future.

Another possibility would simply be for countries to follow sound and consistent policies, so that they are not attacked by speculators. There is a lot to be said for this; many crises do seem to be the result of obvious inconsistencies between the domestic policies of a country and its exchange regime. However, the main point of second-generation models may be stated this way: the real cause of currency crises is not so much what you are actually doing, as what the financial markets suspect you might *want* to do. Britain's monetary policy as a member of the ERM was impeccably correct; but Soros and others correctly suspected that when push came to shove the government would choose employment over the exchange rate. In order to have prevented such an attack, the British government would have had to change not its policies but its preferences.

This point also explains why institutional arrangements like currency boards do not offer secure protection against speculative attack. A currency fully backed by reserves means that one cannot be mechanically forced to devalue; but it does nothing to prevent you from choosing to devalue, even if you have insisted that you will not and have up until now pursued policies consistent with a fixed rate.

Incidentally, these considerations have considerable bearing on European prospects. It now appears very likely that a core group of European countries will formally enter European Economic and Monetary Union (EMU) at the beginning of 1999, and they may well lock the parities as early as May 1998. However, actual euro notes will not replace national currencies for several years. As a growing number of commentators have noticed, this means that it will still be technically quite possible for a country to drop out of EMU during this interim period—which means that currency crises are quite possible *after* EMU supposedly has gone into effect.

How can a country ensure that it will not give in to speculative attack? It can attempt to raise the stakes, by placing the prestige of the government on the line; it can sign solemn treaties; and so on. The only surefire way not to have one's currency speculated against, however, is not to have an independent currency. True monetary union is one answer to the problem of currency crisis.

The other answer is simply not to offer speculators an easy target, by refusing to defend any particular exchange rate in the first place. Once a country has a floating exchange rate, any speculative concerns about its future policies will already be reflected in the exchange rate. Thus anyone betting against the currency will face a real risk, rather than the one-way option in speculating against a fixed rate.

Reasoning along these lines has convinced a number of economists working on currency crises that the ultimate lesson of the crisis-ridden 1990s is that countries should avoid halfway houses. They should either float their currencies or join currency unions. It remains to be seen whether this stark recommendation will survive closer scrutiny.

References

Chari, V. V., and P. Kehoe. 1996. Hot money. Minneapolis: University of Minnesota and Federal Reserve Bank of Minneapolis.

Dornbusch, R. 1994. Mexico: Stabilization, reform, and no growth. *Brookings Papers on Economic Activity,* no. 1:253–97.

Drazen, A. 1997. Contagious currency crises. Mimeograph.

Drucker, P. 1997. The global economy and the nation-state. *Foreign Affairs* 76 (5): 159–71.

Eichengreen, B., A. Rose, and C. Wyplosz. 1995. Exchange market mayhem: The antecedents and aftermath of speculative attacks. *Economic Policy* 21:249–312.

Flood, R., and P. Garber. 1984. Collapsing exchange rate regimes: Some linear examples. *Journal of International Economics* 17:1–13.

Krugman, P. 1979. A model of balance of payments crises. *Journal of Money, Credit and Banking* 11:311–25.

———. 1996. Are currency crises self-fulfilling? In *NBER Macroeconomics Annual 1996,* ed. B. S. Bernanke and J. J. Rotemberg. Cambridge, Mass.: MIT Press.

Obstfeld, M. 1994. The logic of currency crises. *Cahiers Economiques et Monetaires* 43:189–213.

Rose, A., and L. Svensson. 1994. European exchange rate credibility before the fall. *European Economic Review* 38:1185–1216.

Salant, S., and D. Henderson. 1978. Market anticipation of government policy and the price of gold. *Journal of Political Economy* 86:627–48.

Schelling, T. C. 1984. Self-command in practice, in policy, and in a theory of rational choice. *American Economic Review* 74, no. 2 (May): 1–11.

Shiller, R. 1989. *Market volatility.* Cambridge, Mass.: MIT Press.

2. *Kenneth Rogoff*

Perspectives on Exchange Rate Volatility

8.2.1   Introduction

Will the introduction of the euro mark the beginning of the end of the modern floating exchange rate era? After nearly a quarter-century of volatile major-currency exchange rates, do we think we now understand exchange rate fluctuations and know how to deal with them? This paper offers a rather sober view of what economists know—and do not know—about the causes and consequences of exchange market volatility.

8.2.2   The Nagging Persistence of Exchange Rate Volatility

During the macroeconomic chaos of the 1970s, the popular perception among economists was that if governments could only manage to whip inflation, calm in foreign exchange markets would surely follow. In the meantime, the only advice economists could give for dealing with exchange rate volatility was to run for cover. The 1970s view laid the blame for unstable exchange rates squarely at the doorstep of the monetary authorities. If officials' plans for monetary policy were hard to predict—and during the 1970s, they *were* hard to predict—then there was no way of ruling out sustained large divergences in countries' price levels.[1] Even a very loose interpretation of the doctrine of "purchasing power parity" suggests that price level instability is incompatible with exchange rate stability.

The theoretical case against the hapless monetary authorities was greatly strengthened by Rudiger Dornbusch's (1976) celebrated "overshooting" model. By introducing forward-looking "rational" expectations into the canonical Keynesian model of open economy macroeconomics (due to Mundell and Fleming), Dornbusch showed that monetary policy shifts can easily lead to disproportionately large movements in exchange rates. Under certain plausible assumptions, the sluggishness of wages and prices means that the exchange rate must bear a disproportionate burden of the adjustment to monetary shocks, at least in the short run. Ergo, a little monetary instability can lead to a lot of exchange rate instability; a lot of monetary instability can lead to near chaos— pretty much the situation in the 1970s, at least in comparison with the 1950s and 1960s.

The theory seemed to fit the facts, and it was intrinsically very elegant to boot (a big selling point in any science). Unfortunately today, as inflation con-

---

1. Obviously, money demand instability also became much more severe in the 1970s, though in principle such instability can be offset by adjustments in the money supply.

tinues to subside, it is becoming increasingly clear that monetary instability is at most a piece of the exchange rate volatility puzzle. It certainly cannot carry the full burden—or the blame—attributed to it by monetary models of the 1970s (or 1980s, for that matter). Consumer price index (CPI) inflation across Europe, the United States, and Japan has fallen drastically over the past twenty years, converging toward the 1 to 2 percent range. (Taking into account the much-ballyhooed upward bias in the CPI, "true" cost-of-living inflation is probably only 0 to 1 percent.) Moreover, market concern over the possibility of a relapse into high inflation continues to recede as improvements in monetary institutions—especially greater de jure and de facto central bank independence—strengthen the hand of anti-inflation conservative elements within governments.

Yet despite the drop in inflation, exchange rates across the big three currencies (the dollar, the euro, and the yen) are still remarkably volatile. Can concern over long-run divergences in inflation rates possibly explain why, between the spring of 1995 and May 1997, the dollar appreciated by roughly 60 percent against the yen and 30 percent against the mark? Indeed by comparison with some of the larger monthly swings in the major currency cross-rates, the mid-August 1997 devaluations in Asia (ranging from 17 to 34 percent cumulated through mid-September) do not seem quite so horrific. One may well ask, has the conquest of inflation brought any drop at all in major-currency exchange rate volatility?

Figure 8.1 asks just this question for the yen-dollar, mark-dollar, and trade-weighted dollar exchange rates. The figure divides the floating rate period 1975–98 into three-year intervals and looks the volatility of month-to-month changes in the exchange rate within each period.[2] Interestingly, the standard deviation of month-to-month changes in the trade-weighted dollar (*filled diamonds*) has indeed been steadily dropping since the late 1980s, from a high of 2.7 percent per month during 1987–89 to 1.6 percent over the most recent period.

The bilateral dollar rates against the deutsche mark and yen are generally much more volatile, each averaging 3.3 percent per month over the entire period versus 2.1 percent for the trade-weighted dollar. As the graph shows, volatility of the mark-dollar (now euro-dollar) rate has been falling, though not as dramatically as for the trade-weighted dollar. The volatility of the yen-dollar rate has barely fallen at all, remaining almost 3.0 percent per month.

Figure 8.2 also provides a different perspective, comparing the evolution in volatility of the trade-weighted dollar with that of the trade-weighted yen and deutsche mark. Not surprisingly, the volatility of the trade-weighted mark is far lower than that of the dollar, with the standard deviation averaging only 1.2

---

2. The standard deviations in figs. 8.1 and 8.2 are calculated as $[\Sigma \, (\Delta e_t)^2/n]^{1/2}$, where Δe_t is the month-to-month change in the log exchange rate and n is the number of observations. Note that we are implicitly assuming that the exchange rate follows a random walk. As we discuss below, this seems to be a very reasonable approximation.

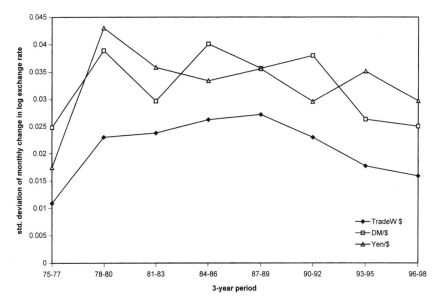

Fig. 8.1   Standard deviation (zero centered) of month-to-month changes in log exchange rate, by three-year intervals, 1975–98

Source: IMF, *International Financial Statistics* (Washington, D.C., 1998), CD-ROM.

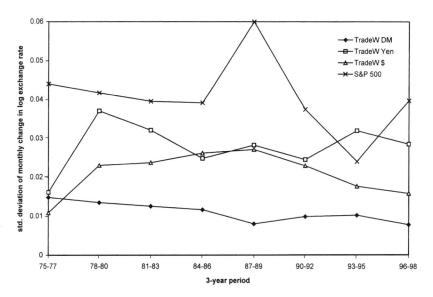

Fig. 8.2   Standard deviation (zero centered) of month-to-month changes in log trade-weighted dollar, deutsche mark, and yen, by three-year intervals, 1975–98

Source: IMF, *International Financial Statistics* (Washington, D.C., 1998), CD-ROM.

percent over the entire period, dropping to 0.8 percent in the 1996–98 subperiod. The low volatility of the trade-weighted mark is not surprising; a large part of Germany's trade is with other countries in the former European Monetary System (EMS). Even counting occasional realignments, cross-country EMS exchange rates were relatively stable even before the advent of the euro.

The trade-weighted yen has been much more unstable in recent years than the dollar or the deutsche mark (euro), and its volatility has even risen slightly since the mid-1980s. Partly this is due to the fact that many of Japan's Asian trading partners peg to the dollar rather than the yen; the fact that Japan's economic growth has been out of synch with the United States and Europe is probably also a factor.

Finally, to put the exchange rate numbers in perspective, figure 8.2 includes a measure of the volatility of the S&P 500 stock index. As one can see, stock price changes, with a standard deviation of 4.1 percent over the entire period, are generally even more volatile than exchange rates (including even the bilateral rates in fig. 8.1).[3]

Thus, overall, exchange rate volatility has indeed fallen somewhat in recent years. Whether one can attribute this decline to the general fall in inflation, or to the switch in central bank operating procedures toward greater emphasis on smoothing fluctuations in very short-term interest rates, is unclear. But what is clear is that despite great successes in the battle against inflation, exchange rate volatility across the major currencies is still quite significant.

8.2.3   Explaining Exchange Rate Fluctuations (or Not)

In retrospect, economists should have realized that the elegant theories of the 1970s overstated the important of monetary factors—and ergo the role of central banks—in causing exchange rate volatility. Ever since the early 1980s, well before low inflation had settled in, a steady stream of negative empirical results began to cast doubt on monetary instability and overshooting as the key elements of exchange rate volatility. Researchers have long been finding that standard monetary models, even when they appear to fit the data well within a given sample period, tend to perform poorly in out-of-sample testing.[4]

The extent to which monetary models (or, indeed, *any* existing structural models of exchange rates) fail to explain even medium-term volatility is difficult to overstate. The out-of-sample forecasting performance of the models is so mediocre that at horizons of one month to two years they fail to outperform a naive random walk model (which says that the best forecast of any future exchange rate is today's rate). Almost incredibly, this result holds *even* when the model forecasts are based on actual realized values of the explanatory variables.

<hr />

3. Obstfeld and Rogoff (1996, chap. 9) also made this point.

4. This result was demonstrated for various major currency exchange rates in Meese and Rogoff (1983a, 1983b) and has since survived extensive empirical testing. For an excellent survey of the literature, see Frankel and Rose (1995).

What does this mean, exactly? Examples of explanatory variables in structural exchange rate equations are countries' relative output growth, interest rates, and money supplies. Obviously, if these variables are extremely hard to predict (say because one or both countries have highly erratic monetary policy), then of course it will be difficult to predict exchange rates one year hence. Prediction will be difficult no matter how well a model can explain exchange rate changes after the fact. But the inability of models to forecast exchange rates runs deeper than that. It turns out that even if one gives models the (seemingly prohibitive) advantage of forecasting with actual realized (one year hence) values of outputs, interest rates, and the like, they *still* fail to outperform the naive random walk model. True, this extreme result breaks down at very long horizons, over two years (see Meese and Rogoff 1983b; Mark 1995), but again even this success relies on using out-of-sample information about the explanatory variables. Therefore, it is by no means established that monetary models can forecast exchange rates in any meaningful way.

The skeptical reader might react to the negative forecasting results we have been discussing by saying to himself or herself: "Well, surely a market-based variable such as the forward exchange consistently outpredicts the naive random walk model." Nothing could be farther from the truth. Indeed, as Lewis (1995) noted, hundreds of studies have consistently found that, if anything, forward exchange rates tend to point in the wrong direction! More precisely, in regressions of the actual realized change in the spot rate on the "forward premium" (the difference between today's forward rate and today's spot rate), one tends to find a negative correlation! A literal interpretation of this result says one *can* use the three-month forward rate to predict the spot rate three months hence. But (ignoring risk), the money-making strategy involves betting *against* the forward rate. The results in table 8.1 for the dollar-yen and dollar-mark thirty-day forward rates are representative of the kind of results one finds in this literature.

If the forward rate were truly an unbiased predictor of the future spot rate, one would expect to find coefficient β_1 on the forward premium near one (on average if the forward rate is 4 percent above today's spot rate, the realized exchange rate will be 4 percent above as well.) Instead, the coefficient β_1 is

Table 8.1   **Forward Premium Puzzle**

Exchange Rate	β_0	β_1
Dollar-yen	.005	−2.62
	(.004)	(1.01)
Dollar-mark	−.001	−.64
	(.003)	(1.15)

Data Source: Datastream International.

Note: Representative regressions for the dollar-yen and dollar-mark exchange rates; nonoverlapping monthly data, 1989:2–97:9. Equation is $e_{t+1} - e_t = \beta_0 + \beta_1(f_t - e_t) + \varepsilon_{t+1}$, where e_t is the log of the time t spot rate and f_t is the log of the thirty-day forward rate. Numbers in parentheses are standard errors.

actually negative. (Here it is not significantly less than zero for the dollar-mark rate, but in larger samples, it often is.)

Of course, there is no theoretical quandary here, since the forward rate incorporates a risk premium, and it is perfectly possible that on average, the risk premium tends to outweigh the trend change in exchange rates (and tends to be negatively correlated with it). It is also quite likely that there is a "peso problem" in the data—the floating rate period is still very young, and markets incorporate expectations of unlikely events (say a significant global conflagration) that (happily) have not been witnessed in the sample (see Rogoff 1980; Lewis 1992). These expectations appear to impart a bias in the forward rate that would disappear in a sufficiently large sample. Overall, though, a reasonable interpretation of results is that there is simply no evidence that the forward rate outperforms the random walk model.

Lest we leave the reader with an image of total darkness in the realm of exchange rate forecasting, one should mention a couple of bright spots. First, there is an increasing consensus across a broad number of studies that purchasing power parity (PPP) considerations do matter for long-run exchange rate determination (see Froot and Rogoff 1995; Rogoff 1996). (The most widely tested form of PPP test posits that over long periods, changes in exchange rates reflect cumulative inflation differentials.) The half-life of PPP deviations, however, appears to be extremely long, on the order of three to four years. That is, if a 10 percent appreciation of the nominal yen-dollar rate leads to a corresponding change in the real (CPI-adjusted) yen-dollar rate, then, on average, roughly 5 percent of the shock will have dissipated after four years. This, of course, does not tell us what happens to the nominal exchange rate because part or all of the adjustment can take place through relative price movements rather than the exchange rate. But at least it is evidence that there is some anchor out there for exchange rates.

Second, newer theoretical models emphasizing nonmonetary factors have increasingly come to supplant the classic Keynesian framework of Mundell, Fleming, and Dornbusch. These "new open economy macroeconomics" models emphasize other factors in addition to money, including government spending and productivity shocks. Whereas it is extremely unlikely that even these newer models will be able to explain very short term fluctuations in exchange rates, early evidence suggests that the other factors they emphasize may be at least as important as monetary factors in medium- to long-run exchange rate determination (see Obstfeld and Rogoff 1996, chaps. 4 and 10).

Overall, the empirical evidence on exchange rates overwhelmingly supports the view that simply making monetary policy more stable and predictable can only go part way toward quelling exchange rate volatility. The steady deregulation of global capital markets since the 1960s and the stunning pace of innovation in global finance make stabilizing exchange rates a much more complex problem that it was in the halcyon days of the Bretton Woods system of fixed exchange rates.

8.2.4   What Are the Costs of Exchange Rate Volatility?

Though simply bringing down inflation is not enough, it *is* possible in principle to stabilize the yen-dollar and mark-dollar exchange rates should global monetary authorities attach a sufficiently high weight to that objective. For example, the United States and Japan could in principle slavishly peg their currencies to the euro. Other mechanisms for fixing exchange rates might allocate the right to steer global monetary policy more evenly, but as the European experience has shown us, the coordination problems involved in such a system can be quite severe, absent political integration. I will return to these issues in the final section of this paper.

Here I want to tackle a different question. How serious are the costs of exchange rate volatility, and how great would the gains be to removing it? At a casual level, it would seem that the costs of exchange rate volatility are rather obvious. Exchange rate volatility presents significant problems for exporters and importers, not to mention any company considering building a plant abroad. At a mundane level, the estimated cost of a two-week trip to Europe can easily rise or fall 10 percent between the time one embarks and the time one returns. But if society is to devote significant resources to squeezing major-currency exchange rate volatility out of the system, it would be nice to have a more quantitative feel for the benefits, rather than simply relying on casual empiricism. Is it a wrench in the works of global trade (a perspective one often hears from Europe), or is it merely a relatively minor irritant?

An obvious point to make is that the ability of firms and individuals to hedge against exchange rate risk places an upper bound on the size of the costs. Hedging may be expensive, but not infinitely so, especially as international capital markets deepen and opportunities for portfolio diversification multiply. Even without hedging exchange risk through financial instruments, a company may still be able to mitigate the effects of exchange rate volatility by simply shifting its purchases and sales in response to price signals. The same is true at the individual level; when the costs of German cars rise due to an appreciation of the euro, Americans can shift demand toward domestic and Japanese models. Demand for international travel is similarly quite price elastic. There is no question that more Europeans come to visit New York when the dollar is weak. Thus the ability of individuals and companies to shift demand across time and goods tempers the costs of volatility.

However, there is an important sense in which the above discussion misses a fundamental point. Even with perfect forward markets—in all things, not just exchange rates—there is no way for the world as a whole to hedge against global risks. For this reason, much of literature on risk premiums in forward exchange markets—or in stocks and bonds, for that matter—neglects the inconveniences of the trading of individual risk and focuses on the equilibrium costs of global risks. Generally speaking, though, this line of reasoning leads to the conclusion that the costs of insuring against global risks should not be all that large, since global output is simply not all that volatile. For example, the standard deviation of postwar U.S. consumption has averaged under 3 percent per year. Even if this risk cannot be diversified away, it is not easy to construct models where the welfare effects are large.[5] (This same logic underlies the so-called equity premium puzzle. How can stocks offer such a consistently high rate of return relative to bonds if the risks to aggregate output are so low?)

Thus the benefits of eliminating exchange rate volatility must lie elsewhere, since the benefits of reducing consumption volatility (and consumption is presumably the ultimate welfare objective) are not likely to be very large even if exchange rates truly are a major cause. Of course, all of this discussion is predicated on the assumption that markets are very complete and global volatility is what matters. This view is too extreme, even if it is true that global capital market innovation is constantly reducing the costs of diversification. Still, these kinds of considerations should cause one to question just how great an evil exchange rate volatility can be.

Empirical evidence comparisons on the volatility of output and trade under fixed versus flexible exchange rates tend to underscore the difficulty of detecting the real effects of exchange rate volatility. It is true that if one looks across a broad spectrum of postwar experiences with fixed and flexible exchange rates, real rates are far more volatile under floating.[6] The reason is that domestic CPIs tend to fluctuate far less than nominal exchange rates. Thus if the nominal exchange rate is fixed, fluctuations in the real exchange rate are inevitably going to be much less. One can try to explain away this fact by arguing that flexible rates tend to be adopted precisely in situations where real shocks are more volatile (indeed, this is precisely the prescription of the classic Mundell-Fleming model). But a careful look at the historical circumstances under which shifts between fixed and floating rates have taken place shows that this argument is quite weak. Real exchange volatility tends to rise precipitously within weeks, if not hours, of when a country shifts to flexible rates. Whereas it is possible that there has been reverse causality in some circumstances, the finding that real exchange rates become more volatile after floating is universal. Surely, the relative rigidity of price levels is the main explanation, not the endogeneity of exchange rate regimes. (The relative inflexibility of prices compared to exchange rates remains even when one looks at very disaggregated price data, and even when one looks at goods that one would typically regard as highly traded.)[7]

So floating indeed makes real exchange rates more volatile. The open question, however, is whether real exchange rate volatility has an effect on any

---

5. This point was first raised by Lucas (1988); for a discussion, see Obstfeld and Rogoff (1996, chap. 5).

6. This point is made very forcefully by Mussa (1986).

7. Again, for a survey, see Rogoff (1996).

other macroeconomic variables. Are trade flows greater under fixed rates than flexible rates? Is output, consumption, or investment more volatile? The small number of studies that have looked at this question tend to find that the exchange rate regime has little or no influence on volatility of macroaggregates (see Baxter and Stockman 1989; Flood and Rose 1995). Admittedly, the evidence is far less conclusive or systematic than the evidence on real exchange rate variability. But at the very least, it appears that differences do not (or at least have not yet) jumped out of the data.

A third reason why exchange rate volatility may not be all that problematic comes out of recent efforts to provide microfoundations for the classic exchange rate theories of the 1970s (see Obstfeld and Rogoff 1996, chap. 10). This new research suggests that while exchange rate volatility may have adverse effects, they are not necessarily first order. If the major distortions in the economy include factors such as labor market distortions, tax distortions, and monopoly distortions, then the welfare effects of exchange rate movements depend to a large extent on whether they exacerbate or ameliorate these distortions. At the moment, the empirics of this question are not resolved.

In sum, the costs of exchange rate volatility are not firmly established, and the weight of recent research points to the possibility that they are distinctly smaller than one might have thought previously. We have already seen that stock markets are more volatile than exchange rates. But should one consider stock market volatility a profound macroeconomic problem? Certainly, some regional economies are dramatically affected by big swings in the S&P 500. Wall Street plays a big role in New York City's economy, and the earnings due to the stock market boom are an important factor in the city's recent rising fortunes (just as the bust of the late 1980s made it temporarily much easier to find New York taxicabs in the rain). Overall, though, squelching stock market volatility is not seen as a pressing national priority that should dominate all macroeconomic decisions (as Europe has chosen to make the goal of achieving intra-EMS exchange rate stability).

8.2.5   What Can Be Done about Yen-Dollar-Euro Exchange Rate Volatility?

One can put a different spin on the embarrassing difficulty researchers have in showing that macroeconomic performance is significantly affected by the exchange rate regime. Flood and Rose (1995) have argued that if there is no obvious macroeconomic cost in shifting to fixed rates, and if there might be gains at the microeconomic level (albeit hard to measure), then why not prefer fixed rates? One answer, of course, is that a sustained exchange rate peg may not even be feasible. Over the past decade, speculators have targeted and overrun one fixed rate regime after another, so that today, by any measure, there are very few long-standing (more than ten years) fixed rate regimes. According to

Table 8.2   **Foreign Exchange Reserves and the Monetary Base, September 1994**

Country	Monetary Base (% of GDP)	Reserves (% of GDP)	Reserves/Base (%)
Belgium	6.7	12.1	180
Denmark	8.6	8.1	94
Finland	11.2	10.4	93
France	4.6	4.6	100
Germany	9.9	6.2	63
Ireland	9.1	16.1	177
Italy	11.9	5.6	48
Mexico	3.9	4.7	120
Netherlands	10.0	13.6	136
Norway	6.3	18.7	297
Portugal	25.0	28.0	112
Spain	12.6	9.6	76
Sweden	13.0	12.1	93
United Kingdom	3.7	4.3	116

Sources: IMF, *International Financial Statistics* (Washington, D.C., 1996), CD-ROM; Obstfeld and Rogoff (1996, 566).

the Bank for International Settlements, the daily flow through foreign exchange markets is $1.2 trillion per day (Ito and Folkerts-Landau 1996), far in excess of the combined reserve holdings (including gold) of any central bank.[8] If speculators are determined to attack an individual country's currency, what chance can it have to defend?

Actually, from a technical perspective, most countries have more than adequate reserves (even without borrowing) to defend their currencies against attack, should they be determined to do so. Table 8.2, for example, shows that all of the European countries whose exchange rates fell to attacks in 1992–93 had sufficient reserves to buy back most if not all their outstanding currency supplies.[9]

But the reason exchange rate attacks can still succeed, even where the central bank has more than adequate reserves, is that governments are often extremely reluctant to raise interest rates to the extent necessary to fend off a major sustained attack. In practice, central banks tend to rely on massive sterilized intervention rather than sharp reductions in the monetary base to fend off exchange rate attacks. The idea is to placate speculators by altering the cur-

8. The exchange market flows certainly include some double counting, but on the other hand, so too do gross measures of global foreign exchange reserves (since Japanese holdings of U.S. Treasury bills are obviously a debt for the United States).

9. Table 8.2 does not include central bank forward positions, which if large can complicate the analysis of reserve adequacy. Though forward contracts do not involve any capital outlay, capital gains and losses suffered on forward contracts lower effective reserves. (The Bank of England is rumored to have lost more than $7 billion dollars this way within a matter of a few hours during the attack on the pound in 1992.)

rency denomination of bond supplies held by the public, an operation that has very little effect on interest rates. While such intervention may or may not be effective at influencing exchange rates during "normal times" (see chap. 3.2 by Kathryn Dominguez), during crises, the effects tend to be far too small to fend off speculators.

What of the example of Europe, which by any measure has achieved a significant level of stability in intra-European rates? Can the EMS serve as a blueprint for the United States, Europe, and Japan? Not in the near term. Even with the high degree of political harmonization in Europe, it is not clear that EMS exchange rates would have stabilized in the mid-1990s if officials had not continued taking dramatic steps toward the ultimate goal of a single currency. It seems highly unlikely that such stubbornly independent regions as Europe, the United States, and Japan would presently be capable of agreeing on a world monetary policy, or that any two or three would be willing to adopt the monetary policy of the third. Of course, if all three regions were willing to permanently relinquish their right to engage in countercyclical monetary policy, and all agreed on targeting zero inflation, the difficulties in coordination would be much less. But even if the (developed) world is an optimal currency area in the sense of Mundell (1961), this does not mean that these countries have the political desire to place nearly as much emphasis on exchange rate stability as the countries of Europe have. The European experience clearly demonstrates that political will is at least as important as any other factor.

What about capital levies on exchange market transactions? Could such taxes, if universally implemented, put "sand in the wheels" of exchange markets as Tobin (1978) advocated? Perhaps, and some recent writers have advocated taking this idea seriously (see, e.g., Eichengreen and Wyplosz 1993). But there are reasons to be profoundly skeptical. First of all, as Kenen (1996) convincingly showed, the practical problems in implementing a Tobin tax are enormous, and problems of evasion would be rampant. And Kenen did not even consider how such laws would create an attractive opportunity for organized crime. The potential costs in terms of microeconomic inefficiency are likely to be considerable, even if difficult to measure. Deep, liquid markets have been essential to many of the financial innovations witnessed by the United States in recent years. These financial innovations have had many spillovers, from making mortgage markets for individuals more liquid to facilitating the corporate restructuring that took place in the United States during the 1980s. Capital market levies would greatly reduce market liquidity and slow the rate of financial innovation throughout the world. It is possible that some smaller economies might benefit from market-based capital levies to help mitigate the notorious "capital inflows" problem. But even this is highly debatable. For the United States, Japan, and Europe, it seems likely that the costs of capital market levies would exceed any potential benefits, even if as a practical matter they did succeed in reducing exchange rate volatility.

8.2.6 Conclusions

Central banks have been remarkably successful in subduing inflation in recent years, but the level of exchange rate volatility among the big three currencies (dollar, euro, and yen) has subsided only slightly. Aside from having some vague idea that financial market shifts are the major culprit behind exchange rate volatility, economists' understanding of the empirical sources of short-term exchange rate volatility is still quite limited. The old idea of purchasing power parity has some force, but only over very long horizons.

At the same time economists are having trouble explaining exchange rate volatility, they are also having difficulty in explaining exactly why it should have profound effects on welfare. Macroeconomic performance is not conspicuously different under fixed versus flexible rates. Nor is it obvious that eliminating exchange rate volatility would have much effect on the volatility of aggregate consumption. So our main conclusion is that exchange market volatility is clearly a nuisance but not necessarily one worth making the focus of international macroeconomic policy.

The view expressed here clearly contrasts with that of mainstream Europe, in which fixed exchange rates have taken on a near religious significance and are thought to be able to cure all evils from unemployment to arthritis. I would argue that European integration has likely been a success in spite of the move to one money, rather than because of it.

References

Baxter, Marianne, and Alan Stockman. 1989. Business cycles and the exchange rate regime: Some international evidence. *Journal of Monetary Economics* 23 (May): 377–400.

Dornbusch, Rudiger. 1976. Expectations and exchange rate dynamics. *Journal of Political Economy* 84 (December): 1161–76.

Eichengreen, Barry, and Charles Wyplosz. 1993. The unstable EMS. *Brookings Papers on Economic Activity,* no. 1:51–143.

Flood, Robert, and Andrew Rose. 1995. Fixing exchange rates: A virtual quest for fundamentals. *Journal of Monetary Economics* 36 (August): 3–37.

Frankel, Jeffrey, and Andrew Rose. 1995. Empirical research on nominal exchange rates. In *Handbook of international economics,* ed. Gene Grossman and Ken Rogoff, 1689–1729. Amsterdam: Elsevier.

Froot, Kenneth, and Kenneth Rogoff. 1995. Perspectives on PPP and long-run real exchange rates. In *Handbook of international economics,* ed. Gene Grossman and Ken Rogoff, 1647–88. Amsterdam: Elsevier.

Ito, Takatoshi, and David Folkerts-Landau. 1996. *International capital markets: Developments, prospects and policy issues.* Washington, D.C.: International Monetary Fund, September.

Kenen, Peter. 1996. The feasibility of taxing foreign exchange transactions. In *The*

Tobin tax: Coping with financial volatility, ed. Mahbub ul Haq, Inge Kaul, and Isabelle Grunberg. New York and Oxford: Oxford University Press.

Lewis, Karen. 1992. The peso problem. In *The new Palgrave dictionary of money and finance,* ed. Peter Newman, Murray Milgate, and John Eatwell. London: Stockton.

———. 1995. Puzzles in international financial markets. In *Handbook of international economics,* ed. Gene Grossman and Ken Rogoff, 1913–71. Amsterdam: Elsevier.

Lucas, Robert. 1988. *Models of business cycles.* Oxford: Blackwell.

Mark, Nelson. 1995. Exchange rates and fundamentals: Evidence on long-horizon predictability. *American Economic Review* 85 (March): 201–18.

Meese, Richard, and Kenneth Rogoff. 1983a. Empirical exchange rate models of the seventies: Do they fit out of sample? *Journal of International Economics* 14 (February): 3–24.

———. 1983b. The out-of-sample failure of empirical exchange rate models: Sampling error or misspecification? In *Exchange rates and international macroeconomics,* ed. Jacob Frenkel, 67–105. Chicago: University of Chicago Press.

Mundell, Robert. 1961. A theory of optimum currency areas. *American Economic Review* 51 (September): 657–65.

Mussa, Michael. 1986. Nominal exchange rate regimes and the behavior of real exchange rates: Evidence and implications. *Carnegie-Rochester Conference Series on Public Policy* 25 (autumn): 117–214.

Obstfeld, Maurice, and Kenneth Rogoff. 1996. *Foundations of international macroeconomics.* Cambridge, Mass.: MIT Press, September.

Rogoff, Kenneth. 1980. *Essays on expectations and exchange rate volatility.* Ph.D. diss., Massachusetts Institute of Technology, Cambridge.

———. 1996. The purchasing power parity puzzle. *Journal of Economic Literature* 34 (June): 647–68.

Tobin, James. 1978. A proposal for international monetary reform. *Eastern Economic Journal* 4:153–59.

3. Stanley Fischer

It is a pleasure to have the opportunity to try to think through some of the issues with which the Asian crisis has confronted us. I had prepared a systematic presentation, which would have been similar to Andrew Crockett's (chap. 7.3), though no doubt not as persuasive. However, rather than repeat much of what Crockett said, I will comment on a series of topics that have come up during the conference.

Crises That Don't Happen

The natural tendency to focus on crises that have happened may lead to certain biases. Almost by definition, these are outliers, outcomes that are worse

---

These remarks have not been updated to reflect developments since the conference. The author's views on exchange rate systems have evolved since then. Opinions expressed are those of the author, not necessarily those of the International Monetary Fund.

than anticipated. We should also think for a minute about crises that don't happen.

First, crises don't happen in most countries, most of the time. Second, in some cases, they don't happen because countries have taken action to avoid crises that were coming. For example, Hungary in 1995 was heading for a serious foreign exchange crisis, a debt crisis. They took decisive action and averted the crisis. Arminio Fraga has said that Brazil has been keeping ahead of the curve, rather than falling behind. They have been, though more decisive fiscal action would be useful. Another example is Israel in 1996, and this year: they could have been heading for a crisis with a very large current account deficit but took both fiscal and exchange rate action that has removed the risk of a crisis in the next few years. Third, there are crises that are expected but don't happen. I must confess that there are a couple of crises I've seen coming for two years that haven't happened yet, and I can't tell you what they are or why I expected them—and still expect some of them. In thinking about crises, we will need to figure out how and why the markets keep financing these countries, possibly long enough for them to avoid a crisis.

Should the Official Sector Speak Out?

We keep being asked whether we shouldn't go public with our concerns when we have them. The Thai case is interesting, in part because this crisis was foreseen. We warned Thai officials of the difficulties they were likely to face, starting in 1996, and with greater force in 1997.

They didn't accept our advice. Why? Because they had a weak government that was not capable of taking action short of a crisis. Possibly, also, they did not believe us. Perhaps we have a tendency to cry wolf more often than is essential. In any case, until the crisis happens, once you've sent more than one warning the recipient is always entitled to say, "Well, you told us two months ago that it would happen, and it hasn't."

Now, should we have spoken out? Well, we did, a bit, in two ways. First, I spoke to the Institute of International Finance, which is a bankers' association, in April 1997. They had just issued a very upbeat report on capital flows to developing countries. We were concerned about some countries, including Thailand, but didn't want to be too alarmist, so I included a statement to the effect that we really agreed with their overall favorable assessment, but we were sure that they had taken into account the special circumstances of countries that had particular problems, like very large current account deficits and weak financial systems, and left it at that. Since it was quite likely they would not pay a whole lot of attention, it's possible that all I was doing was salving my conscience rather than issuing a warning to those who were prepared to listen carefully. Perhaps if we are to issue warnings, we should do so clearly and loudly.

The second time we spoke out on Thailand was when we received requests from some neighboring governments to persuade Thailand to get into an IMF program. In response we did speak out, saying in public that Thailand needed a stabilization program. We said it didn't have to be an IMF program, but the government did need to take action, because the economy was heading for trouble. We were told later that the statement had an impact on the debate inside the Thai government. That worked out as hoped, but it's clear we will not ever be comfortable doing this. This is an issue with which we will continue to wrestle, and perhaps, when the problem is exceptionally clear-cut, we will have to speak out again.

Exchange Rate Systems

We often announce that to prevent crises countries need to have sound macroeconomic policies and a sound financial system. What about the exchange rate system? We generally say that if you have good macroeconomic policies, you'll have a stable exchange rate. Really? Did Japan and the United States run unstable macroeconomic policies between 1995 and 1996? Is that why the exchange rate moved 50 percent in that period?

The position that exchange rates will be stable provided policies are virtuous is not well supported by the evidence. But we're not sure what system to recommend. I am skeptical about the notion of free-floating rates, particularly for developing countries, and believe that a country that is trying to develop through integration into the global economy makes the task that much more difficult if it does not seek in some way to stabilize the exchange rate. In an extreme storm, there are probably benefits to being able to let the rate move, but the rate still has to be defended.

No doubt there is more to be said; but it is surprising that there is still so much uncertainty about this essential issue.

Capital Controls

There are differences among types of capital control. In the first instance there is a need for prudential controls on the foreign exchange exposure of banks and possibly other institutions. We need more work to study the effectiveness of different types of prudential control and also to consider whether anything can or needs to be done to limit the exposures of nonfinancial corporations.

The capital inflows problem of a country that is trying to stabilize, needing high domestic interest rates, is a familiar and difficult one. Not many countries have dealt with it successfully. Chile has. Maybe the controls have nothing whatever to do with Chile's success, as some have argued, but that's a hard case to make. Chile's controls are market based, requiring a reserve deposit to be placed in the central bank. Such market-based measures are preferable to administrative controls with a large measure of discretion.

Let me also discuss the proposal to amend the Articles of Agreement of the IMF to make liberalization of capital flows a purpose of the IMF. At present we have as one of our purposes the promotion of current account convertibility, but not capital account convertibility—though we are allowed to require countries to impose capital controls in certain circumstances. The proposal to amend the articles in this direction has aroused a great deal of concern in many developing countries, though not, I believe, warranted concern. Capital account liberalization is something that in the long run is going to happen to almost every country, as current account liberalization has happened to almost every country. And in the long run, as financial structures strengthen, it will be a good thing. The purpose of this amendment is to bring some coherence to the process of capital account liberalization, allowing us and the profession to develop theories and best practices about how to go about it, to answer such questions as: Which controls should be removed first? Which—including prudential controls—are essential to keep until the very end, perhaps forever? Which controls are more efficient, which are less efficient? We have answers to these questions for the current account. We know that quotas are by and large worse than tariffs, despite the reverse occasionally being true in very specific circumstances. We know something about liberalizing by cutting tariffs proportionally, and so forth. We don't have similar answers on the capital account—and we should try to develop them.

We would have for the capital account, as we have for the current account, two statuses in the IMF. For the current account we have Article XIV and Article VIII status. If a country is in Article XIV status, it has restrictions on current account transactions that have been in place since it joined the IMF, and which should not have intensified; the country would generally be liberalizing these restrictions more or less gradually. Then, at some point when current account liberalization is complete, the country accepts the obligations of Article VIII, not to impose restrictions on the current account. Most IMF members used to be in Article XIV status. We now have 140 countries out of 192 that have accepted Article VIII. For the capital account, a process that is similar, gradual, and possibly quite slow would be likely if this amendment is accepted.

Multiple Equilibria and Contagion

In dealing with a crisis, one has to ask how anyone knows how far the exchange rate ought to move. At the start of the Mexican crisis, the Mexican government prepared a program that had a presumed current account deficit of about 3 percent of GDP and some budgetary contraction and a tightening of monetary policy. I don't think today that that program was inherently impossible, but it was impossible given the markets' complete loss of confidence in Mexico.

As an arithmetic matter, the initial Mexican program held together. Does that mean the Mexican outcome was one of possible multiple equilibria? I'm not sure ex post. The reason I have great difficulty deciding this question is because of a saying of Milton Friedman's—that man may not be rational, but he's a great rationalizer. There is no situation that you cannot explain ex post as having been the only thing that could possibly have happened. We can now explain very convincingly why Mexico had to have a decline in GDP of 7 percent in 1995. If it had been 3 percent, we could explain that as well, and how they managed to get by with that with all the help they got from their friends, and the strong show of support by the international community, and the excellent progress and structural reform that had been made in earlier years, and the determination of the new president to continue it. You could write that scenario perfectly, and it would be just as persuasive as the description of what actually happened.

So I have great difficulty knowing how we know whether the market is doing right, whether there isn't another equilibrium, and what exactly is driving these situations. But if that's what you start believing, then you have to ask whether in a crisis or otherwise, countries shouldn't at least tentatively take a view on where the exchange rate should be. Of course, they can't in these circumstances use reserves extensively to defend a particular rate, but they may try to use the interest rate to keep the rate from moving too far.

Contagion

Contagion exists if, given the objective circumstances, a country is more likely to have a crisis if some other country is also having a crisis. The data show, for instance in a paper by Eichengreen, Rose, and Wyplosz (1996), that contagion exists, a result that is easy to believe given the European crisis, the Latin American crisis, and the Southeast Asian crisis.

Some of the contagion is understandable. Thailand's devaluation affected the equilibrium value of Indonesia's exchange rate, and so Indonesia's rate should have depreciated. But it is very hard to see why Indonesia's exchange rate was driven so far—this looks very much like an overreaction. The official sector, and those in the private sector who had examined the situation closely, believed that Indonesia's macroeconomic fundamentals were initially quite strong. If so, there was a strong case for official intervention. This takes us to the next point, namely: should the IMF be lending in these circumstances and does that create too much moral hazard?

Moral Hazard

Article I of the IMF's Articles of Agreement, which sets out the purposes of the Fund, includes the following: "To give confidence to members by making the general resources of the Fund temporarily available to them under appropriate safeguards, thus providing them with opportunity to correct maladjustments in their balance of payments without resorting to measures destructive of national or international prosperity." We were set up in part to lend to countries in crisis and are thus not going to tell a member that we cannot lend to it because of the moral hazard. Nonetheless, the issue is an important and difficult one.

There is moral hazard in every single insurance arrangement. We all know the analysis that seatbelts increase the speed at which people drive, and increase the intensity of accidents, and could even increase the number of accidents. Nonetheless, we have not decided to reduce the number of seatbelts, nor, as Lawrence Summers puts it, do we insert a dagger into the steering wheel, pointing upward, to make people drive more slowly. We accept that there are trade-offs among speed, the number of accidents, and the number of fatalities.

That is also the case with the moral hazard of lending by the official sector in circumstances in which a country is in severe trouble, and there seems to be nothing else that will help it avoid taking measures destructive of national prosperity, which means having a very, very deep recession. Mexico's 1995 recession was very deep. It is hard to believe it would have been better for Mexico to have output decline by 12 percent instead of the 7 percent that actually took place—and the larger decline would have been quite possible had Mexico not received financial assistance. A similar argument applies in the Thai case.

But we do need to look for measures that will reduce this moral hazard, by finding ways of ensuring that the costs of dealing with a problem like this are shared by private sector lenders.

Reference

Eichengreen, Barry, Andrew Rose, and Charles Wyplosz. 1996. Contagious currency crises. NBER Working Paper no. 5681. Cambridge, Mass.: National Bureau of Economic Research.

4. William J. McDonough

I'd like to begin by applauding Paul Krugman's paper, which is so catholic that I can applaud it without anybody being absolutely sure how I interpret it; and thus Krugman's reputation is not endangered by being endorsed by the president of the Federal Reserve Bank of New York.

By far the best way of dealing with a foreign exchange crisis is not to have one. How does one avoid a foreign exchange crisis? A variety of things have been suggested and can be thought of, but one starts with good macroeconomic policy. Moreover, good macroeconomic policy has to be accompanied by labor market flexibility, so that the economy can respond to changes without high levels of unemployment. I think that this is increasingly important because it is not going to be possible for elected politicians to follow a sensible, stable macroeconomic policy with very high unemployment rates. Very high unemployment rates over a period of time affect a stable economy politically and socially and therefore have to spill over into economic policy.

A robust foreign exchange regime is required. There is no perfect foreign exchange regime. I prefer a floating rate regime for the same reason Churchill preferred democracy: it's less bad than any of the other systems. But a perfect floating exchange rate regime doesn't work perfectly well, and therefore, some modifications to it, especially to avoid an overvalued exchange rate, are appropriate.

It is very important for a country to develop two-way capital markets, both in equity and in debt and debt-related instruments. It is very helpful to have both a high level of foreign exchange reserves and the skill to use them. Using foreign exchange reserves skillfully is hardly a no-brainer. It takes some expertise in dealing in the markets, especially the expertise to make it clear to market participants that risk is two way, and that the central bank has the skill and the guts to intervene in a two-way market.

It's also very important to have a strong banking system because if the banking system is weak, it is virtually impossible for the monetary authorities to use the interest rate tool for any period of time to support a transitory, and fundamentally unjustified, weakness in the exchange rate.

We all know that, even with the best macroeconomic policy, things can go awry and the fundamentals can get out of whack, forcing adjustments in the existing exchange rate, exchange rate regime, or both. Making those adjustments takes courage. We like to think of Domingo Carvalho as resisting all the pressures against the Argentine peso, courageously standing up against the world markets and winning, and he deserves a great deal of praise; and those who supported him, especially a very well done IMF program, should share in that praise. But there are other times when it takes at least as much courage to say that change must take place. It is important that financial officials not get confused between attitude and intelligence in judgment.

If one is going to make a change, the descriptions that were made in Krugman's paper and in our discussions certainly suggest that there is plenty of time. Markets respond to fundamental disequilibria quite slowly. And who knows better than the authorities of the country that they really aren't going to make it?

The reason making changes takes courage is that, as the finance minister, with a term in office that will eventually end, you may have incentives not to tough it out, to let your successor or the next administration worry about it. If one does that consciously, it is a serious disservice to one's country, and not something that should have our admiration.

Using that as a bit of background, I'd like to make a few comments based on my personal involvement in this decade's foreign exchange crises. Let's start with Europe in 1992. I think there are two interesting questions.

Why did the United Kingdom get attacked successfully, while France got attacked and held? What were the differences? I think there were three factors in the British case. First, they entered the ERM at the wrong exchange rate. We all know that, and certainly the British discovered that very quickly after doing it. They were operating with at least one, if not two, hands tied behind their back from day one. Second, the interest rate regime in Great Britain ties mortgage interest rates very closely to short-term interest rates. There is very little that one can imagine as sensitive to the electorate as their mortgage payments. Therefore, this peculiarity in the British financial system made the high interest rate tool unusable for any length of time.

Third, different from the French, British monetary authority officials are very pragmatic. So one could say that if it were perfectly clear they were going to get their brains beat out, they probably wouldn't be likely to continue their current course. On the other side of the English Channel we have the legend of Napoleon's imperial guard: the guard dies, it does not surrender—which was said at Waterloo, and then most of them got blown up to show their great courage. That is an attitude, but it's an attitude that's particularly prone to exploitation if you happen to enjoy the benefit of the entire postwar European history being based on the Franco-German connection. So market participants knew, however much the Bundesbank might detest having to do it, that they were going to back France all the way. They had no choice.

In addition to that, a result of the French characteristic of not being happy to surrender on any battlefield on any day is that a good many market participants normally regarded as being very tough were chatting with the French officials: If someone's attacking your currency, *ce n'est pas moi*. I'm your supporter, I'm in there. And the French authorities, if that reassuring phone call didn't come in, were sort of reminding people that they had very long memories and a dirigiste economy; they could make your life very unpleasant if you wanted to do business in France. That combination is a partial explanation of the difference in what happened in those two countries.

The tequila crisis certainly was a classic situation of the fundamentals getting out of whack, and quite obviously so. Then came the horrible political blows of the two assassinations in 1994. Though one could have argued, and certainly the Mexican officials did, that they were going to be able to tough it out, get into the new administration, and come up with a good macroeconomic policy that would work. It didn't. Probably the single biggest contributor was the political problem from the two assassinations, and there certainly were some spillover effects into Mexico from the doubling of the Fed funds rate between February 1994 and February 1995.

Most of us, and all the officials on the American side, hoped, indeed thought, that the Mexican crisis could be confined to Mexico. We began our approach to the issue with that assumption. In the period between Christmas and New Year's, specifically on 27 December 1994, it became clear that it wasn't working. Contagion, a word used among economists but not much among market practitioners, was taking place. The key country telling us that was Argentina. Argentina was being hit, not because its fundamentals were that much like Mexico's, but rather because, I think, in very thin markets, emerging market fund managers were making the mistake of assuming that the little guy would get scared to death by Mexico and bail out.

As a matter of fact, the little guy didn't bail out, so one could argue that the emerging market fund managers created a problem that didn't need to happen. But at any rate it happened. What was our approach going to be? Our approach had to be that we couldn't solve all the problems cropping up around the world. The main thing to do was to get Mexico fixed as fast as possible. That lent itself to a massive response by the government of the United States and the International Monetary Fund.

You will recall that critics of both the Fund and the U.S. government, mainly from Europe, argued that if we saved the *malditos* Tesobono holders from the consequences of their own poor judgment, everybody everywhere would have to be bailed out in perpetuity. There was a good deal of validity to that argument. I cannot tell you how much effort went into thinking about how we could save Mexico and stick it to the Tesobono holders. Nobody could figure out how to do it. So the Tesobono holders got saved simply because that was a price we had to pay in order to achieve the greater good, which was to help Mexico and, hopefully, avoid the contagion effect. I think it worked reasonably well.

A very brief remark on Hong Kong. An interesting question is: why is Hong Kong holding up so well, even though its stock market has been hit hard? Except for some days, the exchange rate is holding up pretty well. What are some characteristics of Hong Kong that are making that happen?

Hong Kong's fundamentals are good, even if you can argue that the Hong Kong dollar is overvalued after the devaluations of its competitor currencies. If you look at the manufacturing area, most of the things counted as manufactured exports of Hong Kong aren't actually manufactured in Hong Kong. They're manufactured in South China. The front end, the design, and the back end, the marketing and selling, are done in Hong Kong. But the manufacturing, which is where the exchange rate effect would be important, is done in South China, where the exchange rate is just fine. Clearly, the exchange rate will hurt Hong Kong in the invisible areas and is hurting them on tourism. How long that will continue I'm not altogether sure.

Another very important characteristic of the Hong Kong economy is its very robust banking system. And going back to some comments that Arminio Fraga and others have made about Mexico, how do you short the Hong Kong dollar? Even if you use derivatives, somebody in the chain has to be borrowing Hong Kong dollars in order to short the currency. If you're going to borrow a currency, you have to find somebody who has it. There are only three banks in Hong Kong that normally have large, long Hong Kong dollar positions: the Hong Kong Shanghai Bank, the Standard and Charter Bank, and the Bank of China. Do you think any of those three is going to get caught going short in Hong Kong? Not on your life. Therefore, the technical position of Hong Kong is really very powerful, even in these days of derivatives.

Now, once the crisis comes along, how does one manage it? I think, perhaps, and I can say it even more strongly than Stanley Fischer chose to, the IMF absolutely has to be the key player because conditionality must be imposed internationally. The amount of money needed to solve a crisis usually is not terribly large. The resources available to the IMF usually are large enough if the policy package accompanying the IMF program is good enough. Money isn't the problem. If you have the fundamentals fixed, the market begins to turn. The Fragas of this world are looking for a trend they can ride. You can get the market working with you; you don't need vast amounts of money.

What about conditionality? Why does the IMF have to do it? The United States has an immense amount of experience in its own hemisphere with the reasons it doesn't work for the sovereign government of a powerful country to be telling a smaller, weaker country what to do. It's almost impossible for the political leaders of that smaller country to allow the United States to tell them what to do. They don't want to bow, and be seen to bow, to their more powerful neighbor. Therefore, the IMF has to provide the conditionality.

Of course, critics of the government will say that the IMF and U.S. government are the same thing, but in the real world that's not so. Believe me, we have very little ability to tell the IMF how to manage its business. Stanley Fischer would say, "Hell, no," and Michel Camdessus would say something in French that would probably not be quotable.

One can argue that it works pretty well in Europe, doesn't it? With the European Union, everybody works together. I think the reason it works fairly well is that there is not a dominant power. Even though Germany is stronger, especially after unification, and a bit tougher and heavier than everybody else, it doesn't behave that way. And because of the very important Franco-German union, you don't have one power pushing everybody else around. It's much more a community decision. Therefore I think it works better.

In Asia, you have two candidates for the superpower of the area. It's almost certain that any borrowing countries where conditionality has to be tough, as it always has to be, are not going to take such conditionality easily. They would either decide that they didn't like it because the Japanese were behind it, or they didn't like it because China was trying to use this gimmick to take over Asia—which, they would immediately assert, China has been trying to do for the past 2,000 years. I don't think it works but for different reasons than in the Western hemisphere, with the United States being as powerful as it is.

Discussion Summary

Paul Krugman noted that the economics profession is sharply divided about exchange rate regimes. One side heralds the use of currency boards and sees little benefit from floating exchange rates. The opposing side suggests that foreign exchange markets get prices right and should be followed without any fixing of rates. Krugman suggested that both views are wrong and that evidence suggests that no one size fits all. He also noted that while some dimensions of uncertainty have been incorporated into economic models, a fundamental uncertainty may exist about how agents believe the world works. This emphasis on worldviews may explain contagion. Disparate cases, such as the Mexican and Argentinian cases, are tied together by the common worldview of U.S.-trained economists in Latin America. Similarly, an Asian contagion may be explained by a crisis of confidence in the system of Asian values. In a related vein, this distinction between worldviews may explain the distinct outcomes for France and the United Kingdom in 1992. The French worldview couldn't imagine dropping out of the ERM while this was always a possibility for the United Kingdom.

Martin Feldstein suggested that, nonetheless, the French have paid an enormous price over the past fifteen years as a result of their adherence to the goal of monetary union. *Krugman* countered that they may not recognize it as such given their distinctive worldview.

William McDonough suggested that the cases of France in 1992 and Hong Kong now are related. In both cases, borrowing the underlying currency for shorting was extremely difficult given the dominance of a few banks. As such, these restrictions on access to credit amounted to informal capital controls. McDonough also stressed the importance of the support of the Bundesbank in its willingness to ease monetary policy to maintain the level of the franc in 1992.

Mervyn King expressed skepticism about the importance of the Bundesbank in determining the different outcomes for France and the United Kingdom in the European crisis. Instead, he suggested that Germany, France, and the United Kingdom had been at different stages in their business cycles and, consequently, had different thresholds for acceptable interest rates. The two striking outcomes of the European crisis, King noted, were that France was reattacked in 1993 and that the two countries who dropped out in 1992, the United Kingdom and Italy, have had considerable success since dropping out in meeting the Maastricht Treaty convergence criteria. In fact, King noted the irony that the United Kingdom was closer than France or Germany to meeting the criteria with one notable exception—ERM membership—and had better unemployment performance.

Arminio Fraga commented that the centrality of Bundesbank policy was reflected by the importance of a speech by the Bundesbank president in the week prior to the crisis. According to Fraga, this speech was interpreted by speculators as providing a green light for moving against the pound. *Andrew Crockett* noted that the reference was expunged from the official record, and *King* suggested that the source was a wire service leak prior to the actual speech.

Sebastian Edwards suggested that the experience of Mexico after the crisis supports the use of floating exchange rates. Similarly, he suggested that Peru was another situation where a crisis may have been averted through the use of a semifloating exchange rate. While Peru may not be out of the woods, Edwards noted, its accomplishments over the past several years have been notable.

Francisco Gil Diaz also suggested that fixed exchange rates with bands tend to be inherently unstable, resulting in excess reserves or dramatic losses in reserves. As such, freely floating regimes have fewer discontinuities, recommending them over fixed regimes with bands. Gil Diaz suggested that the New Zealand and Canadian experiences serve to exemplify the virtues of cleanly floating regimes. *Robert Feenstra* added that the global sourcing procedures described by Carl Hahn may serve to reduce the sensitivity of firms to floating exchange rates. *Krugman* disagreed and suggested that sensitivity to floating exchange rates could also increase.

Stanley Fischer responded that in the Mexican case, there had been significant variability in the real exchange rate during the floating period. More generally, he suggested that the question is really whether monetary policy should react to changes in external accounts. Fischer argued that monetary policy must react to these changes and that looking only at domestic inflation is not a viable strategy. Indeed, the monetary conditions index used as a monetary policy indicator in both New Zealand and Canada attempts to capture external account conditions as an integral part of the monetary policy decision-making process.

McDonough noted that a recent report of the Bank of Mexico demonstrated a willingness to make monetary policy a flexible tool in response to external account conditions. This statement by an outgoing governor indicated the importance of taking difficult political positions in order to promote sound macroeconomic policy. In a related vein, he suggested that the prevailing practice in the United States, where only one person speaks about the level of the exchange rate and always says the same thing, is extremely valuable in providing a consistent message.

King inquired if Fischer thought that early warnings of crises by oversight agencies hold out the possibility of reduced social costs. *Kathryn Dominguez* added that evidence from foreign exchange markets in the United States and Japan suggest that both speaking out and a credible threat of speaking out can play an influential role in markets. Given that the IMF has never spoken out, it would need to do so in order to establish this threat as credible. *Roberto Mendoza* noted that any release of private information in this context would represent a breach of confidentiality and severely affect the IMF's future access to such information. *Mendoza* and *David Mullins* noted that the reference to Thailand included in Fischer's speech was quite vague.

Fischer responded that while the comment regarding Thailand had been veiled, he considered it sufficiently clear. Moreover, Fischer cautioned that many potential crises do not happen and, accordingly, speaking out can precipitate or magnify social costs rather than alleviate them.

Biographies

W. Michael Blumenthal is former U.S. secretary of the treasury and retired chairman and chief executive officer of Unisys Corporation.

Bankim Chadha is deputy division chief of the Emerging Markets Division in the Research Department of the International Monetary Fund.

Andrew Crockett is general manager of the Bank for International Settlements, Basel, Switzerland.

Kathryn M. Dominguez is associate professor of public policy at the University of Michigan and a faculty research fellow of the National Bureau of Economic Research.

Sebastian Edwards is the Henry Ford II Professor at the Anderson Graduate School of Business, University of California, Los Angeles, and a research associate of the National Bureau of Economic Research.

Robert C. Feenstra is professor of economics at the University of California, Davis, and a visiting professor at the Haas School of Business, University of California, Berkeley. He is the editor of the *Journal of International Economics,* and also the director of the International Trade and Investment program at the National Bureau of Economic Research.

Martin Feldstein is the George F. Baker Professor of Economics at Harvard University and the president of the National Bureau of Economic Research.

Stanley Fischer is first deputy managing director of the International Monetary Fund.

David Folkerts-Landau is managing director and head of global research at Deutsche Bank.

Arminio Fraga is governor of the Central Bank of Brazil. At the time of the conference he was managing director at Soros Fund Management in New York and adjunct professor at Columbia University.

Stephen Friedman is a former chairman of Goldman, Sachs & Co. and is currently a senior principal of Marsh & McLennan Capital, Inc., and a director of the National Bureau of Economic Research.

Peter M. Garber is professor of economics at Brown University and a research associate of the National Bureau of Economic Research.

Francisco Gil Diaz is the chief executive officer of Avantel, a Mexican long-distance phone company. He was involved in central banking and taxation and continues his interest in teaching and economic research.

Carl H Hahn is chairman emeritus of Volkswagen, serves on various boards in North America and Europe, and is a consultant to the prime minister of Kyrgyzstan.

George N. Hatsopoulos is founder, chairman, and chief executive officer of Thermo Electron Corporation and an executive committee member of the National Bureau of Economic Research.

Benjamin E. Hermalin is the Harold Furst Associate Professor of Management Philosophy and Values and chair of economic analysis and policy at the Haas School of Business and associate professor of economics, both at the University of California, Berkeley.

Takatoshi Ito is professor of economics at the Institute of Economic Research, Hitotsubashi University, and a research associate of the National Bureau of Economic Research.

Mervyn King is deputy governor of the Bank of England.

Paul Krugman is the Ford International Professor of Economics at the Massachusetts Institute of Technology and a research associate of the National Bureau of Economic Research.

Hans Peter Lankes is director of transition strategy at the European Bank for Reconstruction and Development.

Robert E. Lipsey is professor of economics emeritus at Queens College and The Graduate Center, City University of New York, and a research associate of the National Bureau of Economic Research.

William J. McDonough is president and chief executive officer of the Federal Reserve Bank of New York and chairman of the Basle Committee on Banking Supervision.

Roberto G. Mendoza is vice-chairman of J. P. Morgan & Co. Incorporated.

David W. Mullins, Jr., was formerly vice-chairman of the Board of Governors of the Federal Reserve System.

Moeen Qureshi is chairman of Emerging Markets Partnership, an asset management company based in Washington, D.C., that he cofounded in 1992. He was formerly senior vice-president and chief of operations at the World Bank and chief operating officer of the International Finance Corporation. He also served as prime minister of Pakistan for an interim period in 1993.

Kenneth Rogoff is the Charles and Marie Robertson Professor of International Affairs at Princeton University and a research associate of the National Bureau of Economic Research.

Andrew K. Rose is the B. T. Rocca Jr. Professor of International Trade, Economic Analysis, and Policy at the Haas School of Business, University of California, Berkeley; acting director of the International Finance and Macroeconomics program at the National Bureau of Economic Research; and a research fellow of the Centre for Economic Policy Research, London.

Nicholas Stern is chief economist and special counselor to the president of the European Bank for Reconstruction and Development and a visiting professor at the London School of Economics.

René M. Stulz holds the Reese Chair in Banking and Monetary Economics at Ohio State University and is a research associate of the National Bureau of Economic Research.

Linda L. Tesar is associate professor of economics at the University of Michigan and a faculty research fellow of the National Bureau of Economic Research.

Jiří Weigl is an adviser to the Speaker of the Parliament of the Czech Republic and to former prime minister Václav Klaus.

Masaru Yoshitomi is dean of the Asian Development Bank Institute.

Zhang Shengman is managing director and corporate secretary of the World Bank Group.

Contributors

W. Michael Blumenthal
227 Ridgeview Road
Princeton, NJ 08540

Bankim Chadha
International Monetary Fund
Room IS12-1300
700 19th Street, NW
Washington, DC 20431

Andrew Crockett
Bank for International Settlements
Centralbahnplatz 2
CH-4002 Basle, Switzerland

Kathryn M. Dominguez
School of Public Policy
University of Michigan
440 Lorch Hall
611 Tappan Street
Ann Arbor, MI 48109

Sebastian Edwards
Anderson Graduate School of Business
University of California, Los Angeles
110 Westwood Plaza, Suite C508
Box 951481
Los Angeles, CA 90095

Robert C. Feenstra
Department of Economics
University of California
Davis, CA 95616

Martin Feldstein
National Bureau of Economic Research
1050 Massachusetts Avenue
Cambridge, MA 02138

Stanley Fischer
International Monetary Fund
Room 12-300F
700 19th Street NW
Washington, DC 20431

David Folkerts-Landau
Deutsche Morgan Grenfell
133 Houndsditch
London EC3A 7DX, England

Arminio Fraga
Banco Central de Brasil
SBS Quadra 3 Bloco B–Ed. Sede
08670-CEP 70074-900 Brasilia (DF),
    Brazil

Stephen Friedman
Marsh and McLennan Capital, Inc.
44th Floor
1166 Avenue of the Americas
New York, NY 10036

Peter M. Garber
Department of Economics
Brown University
Providence, RI 02912

Francisco Gil Diaz
Avantel
Paseo de la Reforma 265
Colonia Cuahutémoc
México D.F. 06500, Mexico

Carl H Hahn
Volkswagen
Porschestrasse 53
38440 Wolfsburg, Germany

George N. Hatsopoulos
Thermo Electron Corporation
81 Wyman Street
Waltham, MA 02451

Benjamin E. Hermalin
Haas School of Business
University of California, Berkeley
545 Student Services Building, #1900
Berkeley, CA 94720

Takatoshi Ito
Institute of Economic Research
Hitotsubashi University
Naka 2-1, Kunitachi
186–8603 Tokyo, Japan

Mervyn King
Bank of England
Threadneedle Street
London EC2R 8AH, England

Paul Krugman
Department of Economics, E52-383a
Massachusetts Institute of Technology
Cambridge, MA 02139

Hans Peter Lankes
European Bank for Reconstruction and
    Development
One Exchange Square
London EC2A 2JN, England

Robert E. Lipsey
National Bureau of Economic Research
50 East 42d Street, 17th Floor
New York, NY 10017

William J. McDonough
Federal Reserve Bank of New York
33 Liberty Street
New York, NY 10045

Roberto G. Mendoza
J. P. Morgan & Co., Inc.
60 Wall Street
New York, NY 10260

David W. Mullins, Jr.
Long Term Capital Management, L.P.
1 East Weaver Street
Greenwich, CT 06831

Moeen Qureshi
Emerging Markets Partnership
Suite 110
2001 Pennsylvania Avenue NW
Washington, DC 20036

Kenneth Rogoff
Woodrow Wilson School
Robertson Hall
Princeton University
Princeton, NJ 08544

Andrew K. Rose
Haas School of Business Administration
University of California
Berkeley, CA 94720

Nicholas Stern
European Bank for Reconstruction and
    Development
1 Exchange Square
London EC2A 2JN, England

René M. Stulz
Max M. Fisher College of Business
Ohio State University
806A Fisher Hall
2100 Neil Avenue
Columbus, OH 43210

Linda L. Tesar
Department of Economics
University of Michigan
Ann Arbor, MI 48109

Jiří Weigl
Investiční a Poštovní banka, a.s.
Prague, Czech Republic

Masaru Yoshitomi
Asian Development Bank Institute
Kasumigaseki Building 8F
3-2-5 Kasumigaseki
Chiyoda-ku
Tokyo 100-6008, Japan

Zhang Shengman
World Bank
1818 H Street NW
Washington, DC 20433

Name Index

Aghion, Philippe, 366n8, 369n12
Aitken, Brian, 345n9
Akerlof, George, 367
Alterman, William, 150t

Bagehot, Walter, 223, 226
Bailey, W., 279, 280
Bank for International Settlements (BIS), 121t, 141t, 142t, 144, 146, 157t, 159t, 212n12, 215n16, 216t, 217, 388–89
Bank of Japan, 161t
Barrel, Ray, 346
Barreras, Felipe, 32
Baxter, Marianne, 252, 449
Bekaert, G., 264t, 268, 272, 287
Berko, E., 286
Bhagwati, Jagdish, 260–61, 269, 345
Bilson, J., 148n9
Bisignano, Joseph, 205n7
Black, S., 136, 150t
Blonigen, Bruce, 344, 346
Bloomfield, Arthur, 312
Bohn, Henning, 250, 253, 254, 283
Bonser-Neal, C., 251
Bordo, Michael, 257
Borio, Claudio E. V., 205n7
Brady, Nicholas, 10
Brecher, Richard, 344
Brennan, M. J., 283
Bruno, Michael, 6n2
Budnevich, Carlos, 31t, 32
Bulow, Jeremy, 380n34

Calvo, Guillermo, 6n2, 12, 18, 23, 25, 34, 48, 254, 275, 276n10, 278, 403
Campbell, J. Y., 284
Campollo-Palmer, C., 264t
Cao, H. H., 283
Cardenas, Mauricio, 32
Chan, K. C., 270, 279, 280
Chari, V. V., 429
Choe, Y., 283, 288
Chuhan, Punam, 18
Chumacero, Romulo, 19, 32
Chung, Y. P., 279, 280
Claessens, Stijn, 18, 251, 286, 287
Clark, J., 286
Cochrane, James L., 245
Cohen, B. J., 136
Cole, Harold, 403
Cooper, Ian A., 252, 263n3

Davis, Kevin T., 199n2
De Long, J. B., 274n9
DeSantis, G., 266, 272
Diaz-Alejandro, Carlos, 344
Dinopoulos, Elias, 345
Dobkin, Eric, 294n3
Dominguez, Kathryn M., 156
Dooley, M., 126, 286, 287
Dornbusch, Rudiger, 6n2, 8n3, 25n7, 281, 283, 434, 441
Drazen, A., 430
Drucker, P., 424
Dunning, John, 312

Subject Index